# Praise for *Edge City*

"To look around at the convulsing of American cities is to wonder WHAT'S GOING ON? Joel Garreau has the answer, and a warm, vicious wit."
—Stewart Brand

"Fascinating . . . entertaining and informative."
—*The Economist*

"An exuberant, witty book."
—*Business Week*

"Lively, thorough reporting."
—*Boston Phoenix Literary Section*

"[A] provocative work that brings to popular attention a major restructuring that is . . . all around us but largely ignored by professional architects and planners."
—*Kirkus Reviews*

"Fascinating and meticulous . . . anyone who wants to understand America, better understand this phenomenon."
—Bill McKibben, author of *The End of Nature*

"Eminently readable, thought-provoking."
—*Publishers Weekly*

> "But I reckon I got to light out
> for the Territory."
> —*Huckleberry Finn*

Welcome to Edge City.

We Americans are going through the most radical change in a century in how we build our world, and most of us don't even know it. From coast to coast, every metropolis that is growing is doing so by sprouting strange new kinds of places: Edge Cities. Not since we took Paul Revere's Boston and Benjamin Franklin's Philadelphia and exploded them into nineteenth-century industrial behemoths have we made such dramatic changes in how we live, work, and play.

Most of us now spend our entire lives in and around these Edge Cities, yet we barely recognize them for what they are. That's because they look nothing like the old downtowns; they meet none of our preconceptions of what constitutes a city. Our new Edge Cities are tied together not by locomotives and subways, but by freeways, jetways, and jogging paths. Their characteristic monument is not a horse-mounted hero in the square, but an atrium shielding trees perpetually in leaf at the cores of our corporate headquarters, fitness centers, and shopping plazas. Our new urban centers are marked not by the penthouses of the old urban rich, or the tenements of the old urban poor, but by the celebrated single-family home with grass all around. For the rise of the Edge City reflects us moving our jobs—our means of creating wealth, the very essence of our urbanism—out to where we've been living and shopping for two generations. The wonder is that these places, these curious new urban cores, were villages or corn stubble just thirty years ago.

Joel Garreau has spent four years exploring America's Edge Cities. From the Washington area (which alone encompasses sixteen Edge Cities) to Los Angeles, Atlanta, New York, Phoenix, Detroit, San Francisco, Boston, Houston, and Dallas, Garreau explains how these Edge Cities are changing our lives in countless ways, many of them elemental and profound. He examines everything, from the kinds of jobs Edge Cities generate to whether they will ever be good places in which to fall in love or hold a Fourth of July parade. For our new civilization, built on the

shoulders of these Edge Cities, reflects once again our perpetually unfinished American business of reinventing ourselves, redefining ourselves,
announcing that our centuries-old revolution—our search for the future
inside ourselves—still beats strong. Thus, by looking at what we have
done, we can more clearly see who we are, how we got that way, where
we're headed, and what we value.

Tysons Corner, Virginia, 1988

Tysons Corner, Virginia, circa World War II

# EDGE CITY

*Also by Joel Garreau*
THE NINE NATIONS OF NORTH AMERICA

# EDGE CITY

## Life on the New Frontier

## JOEL GARREAU

ANCHOR BOOKS
DOUBLEDAY
NEW YORK LONDON TORONTO SYDNEY AUCKLAND

AN ANCHOR BOOK
PUBLISHED BY DOUBLEDAY
a division of Bantam Doubleday Dell Publishing Group, Inc.
666 Fifth Avenue, New York, New York 10103

ANCHOR BOOKS, DOUBLEDAY, and the portrayal of an anchor
are trademarks of Doubleday, a division of Bantam Doubleday Dell
Publishing Group, Inc.

*Edge City* was originally published in hardcover by Doubleday
in 1991. The Anchor Books edition is
published by arrangement with Doubleday.

Maps by Dave Cook

Photograph—Tysons Corner, Virginia, 1988. Photo by Craig Herndon;
copyright © 1988, *The Washington Post*.

Photograph—Tysons Corner, Virginia, circa World War II. Courtesy of
Fairfax County Public Library Archive.

Excerpts from Christopher Alexander's unpublished manuscript *The Nature of Order*
reprinted by permission of the author.

"Manassas, There's No Need for You to Die,"
words and music by David W. Lowe,
© 1988, reprinted with permission.

Library of Congress Cataloging-in-Publication Data

Garreau, Joel.
Edge city : life on the new frontier/Joel Garreau.
—Anchor Books ed.
p.  cm.
Originally published: New York: Doubleday, 1991.
1. Metropolitan areas—United States. 2. Real estate development—
United States. 3. Land use, Urban—United States. 4. Sociology,
Urban—United States. I. Title.
[HT334.U5G37  1992]
307.76′0973—dc20  92-12159
CIP

# Contents

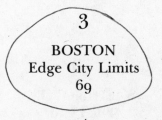
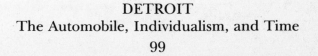

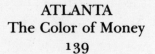

# INTRODUCTION

## Pioneers, Frontiers, and the Twenty-first Century

THE CONTROVERSIAL ASSUMPTION undergirding this book is that Americans basically are pretty smart cookies who generally know what they're doing.

Lord knows, we have sorely tested that premise over the last four centuries. But it is further assumed that this good sense is especially evident when Americans cussedly march off in precisely the opposite directions from those toward which our elders and betters have been aiming us. At such times of apparently rampant perversity, this thinking goes, the correct response is not to throw up one's hands and decry Americans as fools. It is to echo Gandhi when he said, "There go my people; I must rush to catch up with them, for I am their leader."

It is just such a period that is the subject of this book. Individual Americans today are once again inventing a brand-new future—the biggest change in a hundred years in how we build the cities that are the cornerstones, capstones, and, sometimes, millstones of our civilization. As usual, it's all ad hoc: we're making this up as we go along.

That is the importance of engaging in a little anticipatory archeology—figuring out what, exactly, we are doing, and why. For the one thing Americans demonstrably have done better than any other culture in history—for centuries—is handle chaos and change, and invent the future. Americans are part of a wildly individualistic, determined culture that may or may not know how to resolve dilemmas, but that does attack obstacles—compulsively and reflexively. Americans believe, endearingly and in spite of all evidence, that for every problem, there is a solution. Responding to a challenge by doing nothing is not our long suit. There is little more foreign to an American ear than evil accepted. "What will be, will be" is no more from our language than the phrase "It is God's will." Fatalism is outside our repertoire. Once Americans have chosen a future, it is open to being molded and shaped, but anyone merely standing in its way is inviting a trampling.

Sooner or later Americans usually clean up their new order and get it something quite close to right—no matter how terrifying it appears at the beginning. But as a participant in the creation of one Edge City put it, "Go a little easy on these guys. When they started, they didn't know that what they were doing was possible."

In all cases, it's quite a show.

Although this book is entitled *Edge City*, it is only marginally about asphalt and steel. Its central concern is a fraction of a lifetime still in progress. During this historical blink of an eye, we Americans decided to change just about all our routines of working, playing, and living. We created vast new urban job centers in places that only thirty years before had been residential suburbs or even corn stubble. By capturing Americans making the most literally concrete decisions possible, I hope we can achieve a critical understanding of what our real values are—who we are, how we got that way, and where we're headed.

This book is the product of thousands of interviews and hundreds of thousands of miles logged over the last decade. It started with *The Nine Nations of North America,* my previous exercise in trying to figure out how America works, really. During the reporting that led up to that book, and in its aftermath, I became acquainted with large chunks of our very diverse continent. In the early 1980s, then, when I began to see high-rise buildings erupt near my home in outlying Virginia far from the old downtown of the District of Columbia, I knew instantly what I was looking at. This basically was Houston.

Less clear to me was why or how this could be. Or should be. For my first reaction to the phenomenon I would later dub Edge City was to feel threatened. I had always believed that there were only two sensible ways to live—in a yeasty urban neighborhood reminiscent of a Dickens-style nineteenth-century city, or a remote, leafy glade that recalled Thoreau's nineteenth-century Walden Pond. If that made me a nineteenth-century man, so be it. I never could understand why anybody would want anything in between.

This new world being built along the Washington Beltway, however, was not only "in between." It was "in between" triumphant. It seemed insane to me. It was a challenge to everything that I had been taught: that what this world needed was More Planning; that cars were inherently Evil and our attachment to them Inexplicable; that suburbia was morally wrong—primarily a product of White Flight; and that if Americans perversely continued to live the way they have for generation after generation, it couldn't be because they liked it; it must be because They Had No Choice. I even thought that cities were built by Master Architects.

Ah, yes. Live and learn.

Every man is a product of his environment, and mine was the newsroom of the *Washington Post.* Thus, when I decided to "get to the bottom of this," in the back of my mind was the notion that if I could find out who was "doing this to us," it might be possible to get the SOBs indicted. Were not, after all, Edge Cities a clear and present danger to Western civilization?

What I found when I dug into the story was a tale far more rich and complex. It was by turns inspiring, discouraging, heartwarming, and frustrating. It was, of course, summed up in the wisdom of Pogo. I have met the enemy. And he is us.

That is why there is so much "edge" in Edge City. It is a

psychological location—a state of mind—even more than a physical place:

- This new world is the cutting edge—of how cities are being created worldwide.
- This upheaval is occurring physically on the edge—of the urban landscape.
- The rules that govern its creation involve a search for edge—for advantage.
- And right now, at least, Edge City puts people on edge. It can give them the creeps.

*Edge City* is hardly a theoretical work. I am a reporter, not a critic. The characters in this book are real. And characters they are. They genuinely are the sons of the pioneers—endowed with the unfettered human spirit, with all that is both uplifting and despair-causing in that. The thirsts they slake are those of Everyman; their hungers universal. That is the global importance of grasping Edge City—why those who do not will lose power, money, and influence. American traits and American landscapes have been imitated by other nations not so much because they are American but because so much of modern history arrives in the United States first. Americans, after all, are still those humans most commonly in possession of that rare, potent, and dangerous combination: the power, money, and opportunity to do *whatever they think best*.

This is why I take these Edge Cities seriously. It is also why you will find that this book metamorphoses as it moves. The first half is devoted to what make Edge Cities tick. In the beginning chapters you will find me exploring how these places operate, on their own terms. In so doing, I marvel at how ingenious Edge Cities are, and at how successfully they manage to deliver just about anything quantifiable—like jobs and wealth. In so doing, I pay tribute to the infinitely fecund imaginations of the people who created them.

Progressively, however, chapter by chapter, I systematically try to cast my net ever more wide. As the book advances, you will continue to find yourself meeting Americans creating a brand-new world. But the farther toward the back of the book you are, the more you will find them grappling with ever more wonderful and profound questions—about identity, and community, and civilization, and soul, and all the other attributes of the good life for which we yearn. For that is the most interesting and challenging task—of really penetrating our latest attempt at Utopia. And of trying to gauge how far along we are.

At the end of my travels, I remained guardedly optimistic, but by no means tranquil. For it is an enormous challenge we have handed ourselves, to find the future in our deepest desires, and to achieve that future through wisdom.

That, ultimately, is why the book ends with the chapter about the land. That, in more ways than one, is where I found bedrock. That, I came to think, is the real limit beyond which we cannot go. If the rise of Edge Cities is genuinely a turning point in our history—one at least as dramatic as the upheaval of 150 years ago that ushered in the age of the Machine—then the place for us to seize the opportunity is with our relationship to the land.

Only, I came to believe, if we come to see it all as sacred—the land on which we build as sacred as the land we leave untouched—will we break through to higher ground and reunite our fragmented universe. That is precisely how and where we can help save our world.

# 1

## THE SEARCH FOR THE FUTURE INSIDE OURSELVES

### Life on the New Frontier

But I reckon I got to light out for the Territory.

—*Huckleberry Finn, at the close of Mark Twain's novel, 1885*

AMERICANS are creating the biggest change in a hundred years in how we build cities. Every single American city that *is* growing, is growing in the fashion of Los Angeles, with multiple urban cores.

These new hearths of our civilization—in which the majority of metropolitan Americans now work and around which we live —look not at all like our old downtowns. Buildings rarely rise shoulder to shoulder, as in Chicago's Loop. Instead, their broad, low outlines dot the landscape like mushrooms, separated by greensward and parking lots. Their office towers, frequently guarded by trees, gaze at one another from respectful distances through bands of glass that mirror the sun in blue or silver or green or gold, like antique drawings of "the city of the future."

The hallmarks of these new urban centers are not the sidewalks of New York of song and fable, for usually there are few sidewalks. There are jogging trails around the hills and ponds of their characteristic corporate campuses. But if an American finds himself tripping the light fantastic today on concrete, social scientists know where to look for him. He will be amid the crabapples blossoming under glassed-in skies where America retails its wares. We have quaintly if accurately named these places after that fashionable tree-lined promenade created in the late 1600s—the Mall in London's St. James's Park. Back then, its denizens even had a name for the hour when the throng of promenaders "giggling with their sparks" was at its height. They called it High Mall. Pity we've not picked up that usage. We have certainly picked up the practice, because malls usually function as the village squares of these new urbs.

Our new city centers are tied together not by locomotives and subways, but by jetways, freeways, and rooftop satellite dishes thirty feet across. Their characteristic monument is not a horse-mounted hero, but the atria reaching for the sun and shielding trees perpetually in leaf at the cores of corporate headquarters, fitness centers, and shopping plazas. These new urban areas are marked not by the penthouses of the old urban rich or the tenements of the old urban poor. Instead, their landmark structure is the celebrated single-family detached dwelling, the suburban home with grass all around that made America the best-housed civilization the world has ever known.

I have come to call these new urban centers Edge Cities. Cities, because they contain all the functions a city ever has, albeit in a spread-out form that few have come to recognize for what it is. Edge, because they are a vigorous world of pioneers and immigrants, rising far from the old downtowns, where little save villages or farmland lay only thirty years before.

Edge Cities represent the third wave of our lives pushing into new frontiers in this half century. First, we moved our homes out past the traditional idea of what constituted a city. This was the suburbanization of America, especially after World War II.

Then we wearied of returning downtown for the necessities of life, so we moved our marketplaces out to where we lived. This was the malling of America, especially in the 1960s and 1970s.

Today, we have moved our means of creating wealth, the essence of urbanism—our jobs—out to where most of us have lived and shopped for two generations. That has led to the rise of Edge City.

Not since more than a century ago, when we took Benjamin Franklin's picturesque mercantile city of Philadelphia and exploded it into a nineteenth-century industrial behemoth, have we made such profound changes in the ways we live, work, and play.

Good examples of our more than two hundred new Edge Cities are:

• The area around Route 128 and the Massachusetts Turnpike in the Boston region that was the birthplace of applied high technology;

• The Schaumburg area west of O'Hare Airport, near which Sears moved its corporate headquarters from the 110-story Sears Tower in downtown Chicago;

• The Perimeter Center area, at the northern tip of Atlanta's Beltway, that is larger than downtown Atlanta;

• Irvine, in Orange County, south of Los Angeles.*

By any functional urban standard—tall buildings, bright lights, office space that represents white-collar jobs, shopping, entertainment, prestigious hotels, corporate headquarters, hospitals with CAT scans, even population—each Edge City is larger than downtown Portland, Oregon, or Portland, Maine, or Tampa, or Tucson. Already, two thirds of all American office facilities are in Edge Cities, and 80 percent of them have materialized in only the last two decades. By the mid-1980s, there was far more office space in Edge Cities around America's largest metropolis, New York, than there was at its heart—midtown Manhattan. Even before Wall Street faltered in the late 1980s there was less office space there, in New York's downtown, than there was in the Edge Cities of New Jersey alone.

Even the old-fashioned Ozzie and Harriet commute from a conventional suburb to downtown is now very much a minority pattern, U.S. Census figures show. Most of the trips metropolitan Americans take in a day completely skirt the old centers. Their journeys to work, especially, are to Edge Cities. So much of our shopping is done in Edge Cities that a casual glance at most Yellow Pages shows it increasingly difficult in an old downtown to buy such a commodity item as a television set.

These new urban agglomerations are such mavericks that everyone who wrestles them to the ground tries to brand them. Their list of titles by now has become marvelous, rich, diverse, and sometimes unpronounceable. The litany includes: urban villages, technoburbs, suburban downtowns, suburban activity centers, major diversified centers, urban cores, galactic city, pepperoni-pizza cities, a city of realms, superburbia, disurb,

---

* For quick information on sources, calculations, and methods, see "The List," "The Words," "The Laws," and the Notes at the back of this book.

service cities, perimeter cities, and even peripheral centers. Sometimes it is not clear that everybody is talking about the same thing. My heart particularly goes out to the San Francisco reporter who just started calling whatever was seething out there, past the sidewalks, Tomorrowland.

The reasons these places are tricky to define is that they rarely have a mayor or a city council, and just about never match boundaries on a map. We're still in the process of giving each Edge City its name—a project, incidentally, that could use more flair. In New Jersey, for example, there is one with only the laconic designation "287 and 78." The reason there are no "Welcome to" signs at Edge City is that it is a judgment call where it begins and ends.

Take the traditional measure of urban size—population. The out-counties where Edge Cities now rise are almost by definition larger than the cores they surround. After all, these places we thought of until recently as suburbs are where the majority of Americans have been living for decades. Fairfax County, Virginia, is more populous than either Washington, D.C., or San Francisco. Ninety-two percent of the people in the New York metropolitan area do not live in Manhattan.

A more narrow, and I think more accurate, comparison is to take Edge City—that acreage where the huge growth in jobs and other truly urban functions is centered—and compare it with the old central business district, the old downtown. Even by that tight measure, Edge City is almost always more populous. How many people in America, after all, live right in the old downtown? Fewer than live within sight of that Edge City landmark— the office monument so huge it would have been unthinkable to build one anywhere but downtown only thirty years ago.

That is why I have adopted the following five-part definition of Edge City that is above all else meant to be functional.

Edge City is any place that:

• *Has five million square feet or more of leasable office space—the workplace of the Information Age.* Five million square feet is more than downtown Memphis. The Edge City called the Galleria area west of downtown Houston—crowned by the sixty-four-story Transco Tower, the tallest building in the world outside an old downtown—is bigger than downtown Minneapolis.

• *Has 600,000 square feet or more of leasable retail space.* That is the equivalent of a fair-sized mall. That mall, remember, probably has at least three nationally famous department stores, and eighty to a hundred shops and boutiques full of merchandise that used to be available only on the finest boulevards of Europe. Even in their heyday, there were not many downtowns with that boast.

• *Has more jobs than bedrooms.* When the workday starts, people head toward this place, not away from it. Like all urban places, the population increases at 9 A.M.

• *Is perceived by the population as one place.* It is a regional end destination for mixed use—not a starting point—that "has it all," from jobs, to shopping, to entertainment.

• *Was nothing like "city" as recently as thirty years ago.* Then, it was just bedrooms, if not cow pastures. This incarnation is brand new.

An example of the authentic, California-like experience of encountering such an Edge City is peeling off a high thruway, like the Pennsylvania Turnpike, onto an arterial, like 202 at King of Prussia, northwest of downtown Philadelphia. Descending into traffic that is bumper to bumper in *both* directions, one swirls through mosaics of lawn and parking, punctuated by office slabs whose designers have taken the curious vow of never placing windows in anything other than horizontal reflective strips. Detours mark the yellow dust of heavy construction that seems a permanent feature of the landscape.

Tasteful signs mark corporations apparently named after Klingon warriors. Who put Captain Kirk in charge of calling companies Imtrex, Avantor, and Synovus? Before that question can settle, you encounter the spoor of—the mother ship. On King of Prussia's Route 202, the mark of that mind-boggling enormity reads MALL NEXT FOUR LEFTS.

For the stranger who is a connoisseur of such places, this Dante-esque vision brings a physical shiver to the spine and a not entirely ironic murmur of recognition to the lips: "Ah! Home!" For that is precisely the significance of Edge Cities. They are the culmination of a generation of individual American value decisions about the best ways to live, work, and play—about how to create "home." That stuff "out there" is where

America is being built. That "stuff" is the delicate balance between unlimited opportunity and rippling chaos that works for us so well. We build more of it every chance we get.

If Edge Cities are still a little ragged at the fringes, well, that just places them in the finest traditions of Walt Whitman's "barbaric yawp over the rooftops of the world"—what the social critic Tom Wolfe calls, affectionately, the "hog-stomping Baroque exuberance of American civilization." Edge Cities, after all, are still works in progress.

They have already proven astoundingly efficient, though, by any urban standard that can be quantified. As places to make one's fame and fortune, their corporate offices generate unprecedentedly low unemployment. In fact, their emblem is the hand-lettered sign taped to plate glass begging people to come to work. As real estate markets, they have made an entire generation of homeowners and speculators rich. As bazaars, they are anchored by some of the most luxurious shopping in the world. Edge City acculturates immigrants, provides child care, and offers safety. It is, on average, an *improvement* in per capita fuel efficiency over the old suburbia-downtown arrangement, since it moves everything closer to the homes of the middle class.

That is why Edge City is the crucible of America's urban future. Having become the place in which the majority of Americans now live, learn, work, shop, play, pray, and die, Edge City will be the forge of the fabled American way of life well into the twenty-first century.

There are those who find this idea appalling. For some who recognize the future when they see it, but always rather hoped it might look like Paris in the 1920s, the sprawl and apparent chaos of Edge City makes it seem a wild, raw, and alien place. For my sins I once spent a fair chunk of a Christmas season in Tysons Corner, Virginia, stopping people as they hurried about their holiday tasks, asking them what they thought of their brave new world. The words I recorded were searing. They described the area as plastic, a hodgepodge, Disneyland (used as a pejorative), and sterile. They said it lacked livability, civilization, community, neighborhood, and even a soul.

These responses are frightening, if Edge City is the laboratory of how civilized and livable urban American will be well into the next century. Right now, it is vertigo-inducing. It may have all the complexity, diversity, and size of a downtown. But it can cover dozens of square miles, and juxtapose schools and freeways and atria and shimmering parking lots with corporate lawns and Day-Glo-orange helicopter wind socks. Its logic takes a while to decode.

Will we ever be proud of this place? Will we ever drag our visiting relatives out to show off our Edge City, our shining city on the hill? Will we ever feel—for this generation and the ones that follow—that it's a good place to be young? To be old? To fall in love? To have a Fourth of July parade? Will it ever be the place we want to call home?

Robert Fishman, a Rutgers historian who is one of the few academics successfully to examine Edge City, thinks he knows the answer. "All new city forms appear in their early stages to be chaotic," he reports. He quotes Charles Dickens on London in 1848: "There were a hundred thousand shapes and substances of incompleteness, wildly mingled out of their places, upside down, burrowing in the earth, aspiring in the earth, moldering in the water, and unintelligible as in any dream."

That is also the best one-sentence description of Edge City extant.

Edge City's problem is history. It has none. If Edge City were a forest, then at maturity it might turn out to be quite splendid, in triple canopy. But who is to know if we are seeing only the first, scraggly growth? I once heard an academic with a French accent ask Fishman, seriously, what the *ideal* of an Edge City was. What a wonderfully French question! Who *knows* what these things look like when they grow up? These critters are likely only in their nymphal, if not larval, forms. We've probably never *seen* an adult one.

If Edge City still gives some people the creeps, it is partially because it confounds expectations. Traditional-downtown urbanites recoil because a place blown out to automobile scale is not what they think of as "city." They find the swirl of functions intimidating, confusing, maddening. Why are these tall office buildings so far apart? Why are they juxtaposed, apparently higgledy-piggledy, among the malls and strip shopping centers and fast-food joints and self-service gas stations? Both literally and metaphorically, these urbanites always get lost.

At the same time, Edge City often does not meet the expectations of traditional suburbanites, either. Few who bought into the idea of quarter-acre tranquillity ever expected to take a winding turn and suddenly be confronted with a 150-foot colossus looming over the trees, red aircraft-warning beacons flashing, its towering glass reflecting not the moon, but the sodium vapor of the parking lot's lights.

The question is whether this disorienting expectation gap is permanent or simply a phase, a function of how fast we've transformed our world. I discussed this with scholars who had examined the history of Venice. Venice today is venerated by American urban planners as a shrine to livability. What was Venice like when it was new?

"People forget that Venice was built by hook or by crook," replied Dennis Romano, a social historian of the early Renaissance. "Venice was just as mercantilist as Tysons. It was full of land speculators and developers. The merchants' primary concern was the flow of goods, of traffic. Those who now romanticize Venice collapse a thousand years of history. Venice is a monument to a dynamic process, not to great urban planning. It's hard for us to imagine, but the architectural harmony of the Piazza San Marco was an accident. It was built over centuries by people who were constantly worried about whether they had enough money."

In his plan for the urban future that he christened Broadacre City, that most relentlessly American of urban visionaries, Frank Lloyd Wright anticipated with stunning accuracy many of the features of Edge City.

"Nonsense is talked by our big skyscraperites in the blind alley they have set up, defending urban congestion by obscuring the simple facts of the issue," he trumpeted in the 1950s in *The Living City*. "Their skyscraper-by-skyscraper is . . . the gravestone of . . . centralization."

Wright viewed as interchangeable the concepts of individualism, freedom, and democracy. He saw them as fundamentally in opposition to the despised, exploitative "monarchy" of the old downtowns. He yearned for a system in which all men fled the evils of big capital, big authorities, big cities—troglodytes of every stripe—for a connection with nature, the earth, the ground. He thought an acre per person was about right. He saw individuals newly freed coming back together in totally modern agglomerations, on new terms, stronger, growing together "in adequate space." He saw the automobile and aircraft as the glorious agents of that dispersion and reintegration, and he knew exactly what would happen when, inexorably, we blew Edge City out to their scale:

"After all is said and done, *he*—the citizen—is really the city. The city is going where he goes. He is learning to go where he enjoys all the city ever gave him, plus freedom, security, and beauty of his birthright, the good ground."

How *about* that. We've done it! Just as he said. But are we in our new Edge Cities ever going to reap the benefits of what he knew we'd sow?

"Try to live . . . deep *in* nature," he exhorted us. "Be native as trees to the wood, as grass to the floor of the valley. Only then can the democratic spirit of man, individual, rise out of the confusion of communal life in the city to a creative civilization of the ground."

Edge City has quite clearly released us from the shackles of the nineteenth-century city—out into that valley and wood, just as Wright foresaw. It is common for a first-generation Edge City to arise ten miles from an old downtown, and a next-generation, one twenty miles beyond that, only to attract workers from distances forty-five minutes beyond that. At this rate, it is easy to see how a field of Edge Cities can easily cover more than ten thousand square miles. This is why the San Francisco area now statistically is measured as halfway across California, pulling commuters out of Stockton, in the Central Valley, into its Edge Cities east of Silicon Valley.

Whether that spatial liberation leads to Wright's "creative civilization of the ground," however, came to be my main concern, for it is central to the battles being fought in America today over such amorphous essentials as "growth" and "quality of life."

The forces of change whose emblem is the bulldozer, and the forces of preservation whose totem is the tree, are everywhere at war in this country. The raging debate over what we have lost and what we have gained, as we flee the old urban patterns of the nineteenth century for the new ones of the twenty-first, is constant. Are we satisfying our deepest yearnings for the good life with Edge City? Or are we poisoning everything across which we sprawl?

Getting to the bottom of those questions leads directly to issues of national character, of what we value. They come down to who we are, how we got that way, and where we're headed. It is why, when the reeling feeling caused by Edge City finally subsides, I think it is possible to examine the place as the expression of some fundamental values. Nowhere in the American national character, as it turns out, is there as deep a divide as that between our reverence for "unspoiled" nature and our enduring devotion to "progress."

In *The Machine in the Garden,* the cultural historian Leo Marx writes about our complicated attitudes toward utilitarian versus pastoral landscapes. For Americans, he observes,

regenerative power is located in the natural terrain: access to undefiled, bountiful, sublime Nature is what accounts for the virtue and special good fortune of Americans. It enables them to design a community in the image of a garden, an ideal fusion of nature with art. The landscape thus becomes the symbolic repository of value of all kinds— economic, political, aesthetic, religious . . .

A strong urge to believe in the rural myth along with an awareness of industrialization as counterforce to the myth—since 1844, this motif appears everywhere in American writing . . . It is a complex distinctively American form.

One springtime, over lunch near his MIT office, Marx observed that Edge City represents "an escape from the negative aspects of civilization. Too much restraint, oppression, hierarchy—you justify building out there in order to start again and have another Garden. You want the best of both worlds. This would be Thomas Jefferson's Virginia; he very explicitly wanted a land that is midway between too much and too little civilization."

In fact, says Marx, the whole thing goes back to the very dawn of our civilization. Captain Arthur Barlowe, captain of a bark dispatched by Sir Walter Raleigh, described Virginia in 1584 in what became a cardinal image of America: an immense garden of incredible abundance. Virginia is a land of plenty; the soil is "the most plentifull, sweete, fruitfull, and wholsome of all the worlde"; the virgin forest is not at all like the "barren and fruitles" woods of Europe. We "found shole water," Barlowe wrote, "wher we smelt so sweet and so strong a smel, as if we had bene in the midst of some delicate garden abounding with all kinde of odoriferous flowers . . ."

What Barlowe was describing, of course, was Eden. That image inflamed the popular imagination as the first English settlement succeeded in America, in Jamestown, Virginia, 1607. It drove Shakespeare when, three years later, he wrote *The Tempest.*

What is so striking about these reports depicting Virginia as Paradise Regained—tapping a deep and persistent human desire to return to a natural idyll—is how sharply they conflict with the views of the second set of Englishmen to show up in America to stay. Those were the Pilgrims of the Massachusetts Bay. When the *Mayflower* hove to off Cape Cod in November 1620, what William Bradford saw shocked him. He described it as a "hidious and desolate wilderness, full of wild beasts and willd men." Between the Pilgrims and their new home, he saw only "deangerous shoulds and roring breakers."

This wasn't heaven. Quite the opposite.

"Which way soever they turnd their eys (save upward to the heavens) they could have litle solace or content . . . The whole countrie, full of woods and thickets, represented a wild and savage heiw."

His people, said Bradford, had "no freinds to wellcome them, nor inns to entertaine or refresh their weatherbeaten bodys, no houses or much less townes to repaire too, to seeke for succoure."

There was, in short, no civilization. Bradford found this void horrifying, hellish.

Here, then, is established the enduring divide in the way Americans have related to their land ever since. The hideous wilderness appears at one end of the spectrum, and the Garden at the other. These are such antithetical ways for man to understand his relation to his environment that Leo Marx calls them "ecological images. Each is a kind of root metaphor, a quite distinct notion of America's destiny." These vastly different systems of value, noted Ralph Waldo Emerson, would "determine all their institutions."

It comes to this. One vision of the American natural landscape was that it had inherent value and should be treasured for what it already was and had always been. The other saw in the land nothing but satanic wastes; there could be placed on it no value until it was bent to man's will—until civilization was forced into bloom.

The history of America is an endless repetition of this battle. We are fighting it to this day, nowhere more so than in our current frontier, Edge City. In the unsettled, unsettling environment of Edge City, great wealth may be acquired, but without a sense that the place has community, or even a center, much less a soul. And the resolution of these issues goes far beyond architecture and landscape. It goes to the philosophical ground on which we are building our Information Age society. It's possible that Edge City is the most purposeful attempt Americans have made since the days of the Founding Fathers to try to create something like a new Eden.

Edge City may be the result of Americans striving once again for a new, restorative synthesis. Perhaps Edge City represents Americans taking the functions of the city (the machine) and bringing them out to the physical edge of the landscape (the frontier). There, we try once again to merge the two in a new-found union of nature and art (the garden), albeit one in which the treeline is punctuated incongruously by office towers.

If that is true, Edge City represents Americans once again trying to create a new and better world—lighting out for the Territory, in the words of Huckleberry Finn. If that new world happens to be an unknown and uncharted frontier, well, that's where we've headed every chance we've had—for four hundred years. Frank Lloyd Wright genuinely believed that Americans continued to be the sons and daughters of the pioneers. He called us "the sons of the sons of American Democracy." Wright saw us as heading out of our old cities, freed from old verities, creating a new spiritual integrity in community. The enduring, exhilarating, and frightening themes to be examined in Edge Cities are if, whether, and how we are pulling that Utopian vision off.

This goes to the ultimate significance of Edge City. The battles we fight today over our futures do not have echoes only back to 1956, when Dwight D. Eisenhower changed America forever with the creation of the interstate highway program. Nor does it go back only to the New Deal of the 1930s, during which Frank-

lin Delano Roosevelt shaped America into a society of homeowners. It goes to the core of what makes America America,
right back to the beginning, with the Pilgrims in 1620 and the
Virginia Cavaliers of 1607.

It addresses profound questions, the answers to which will
reverberate forever. It addresses the search for Utopia at the
center of the American Dream. It reflects our perpetually unfinished American business of reinventing ourselves, redefining
ourselves, restoring ourselves, announcing that our centuries-
old perpetual revolution—our search for the future inside ourselves—still beats strong.

It suggests that the world of the immigrants and pioneers is
not dead in America; it has just moved out to Edge City, where
gambles are being lost and won for high stakes. It adds another
level of history to places already filled with ghosts. That is why
one day Edge City, too, may be seen as historic. It is the creation
of a new world, being shaped by the free in a constantly
reinvented land.

# 2

# NEW JERSEY

## Tomorrowland

For these are not as they might seem to be, the ruins of our civilization, but are the temporary encampments and outposts of the civilization that we—you and I—shall build.

—*John Cheever, 1978*

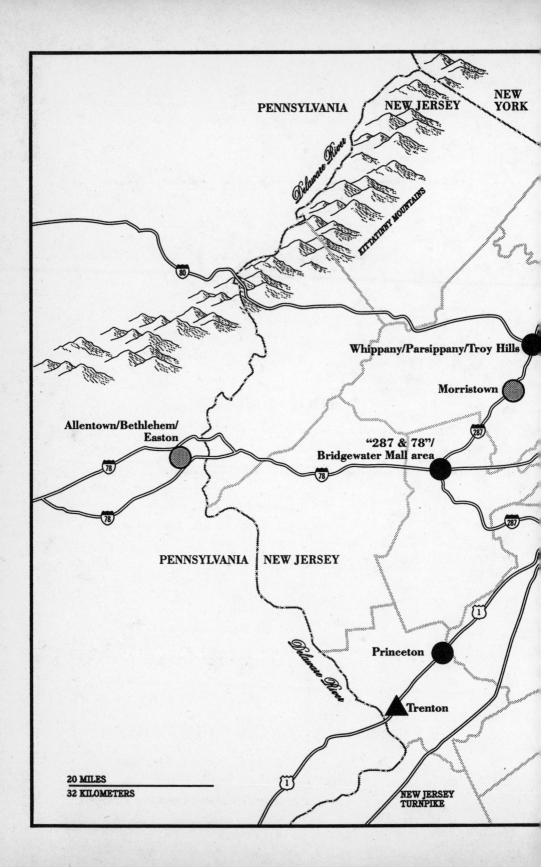

PENNSYLVANIA    NEW JERSEY    NEW YORK

Delaware River

KITTATINNY MOUNTAINS

80

Whippany/Parsippany/Troy Hills

Morristown

Allentown/Bethlehem/
Easton

"287 & 78"/
Bridgewater Mall area

287

78

78

78

287

PENNSYLVANIA    NEW JERSEY

Delaware River

1

Princeton

Trenton

20 MILES
32 KILOMETERS

1

NEW JERSEY
TURNPIKE

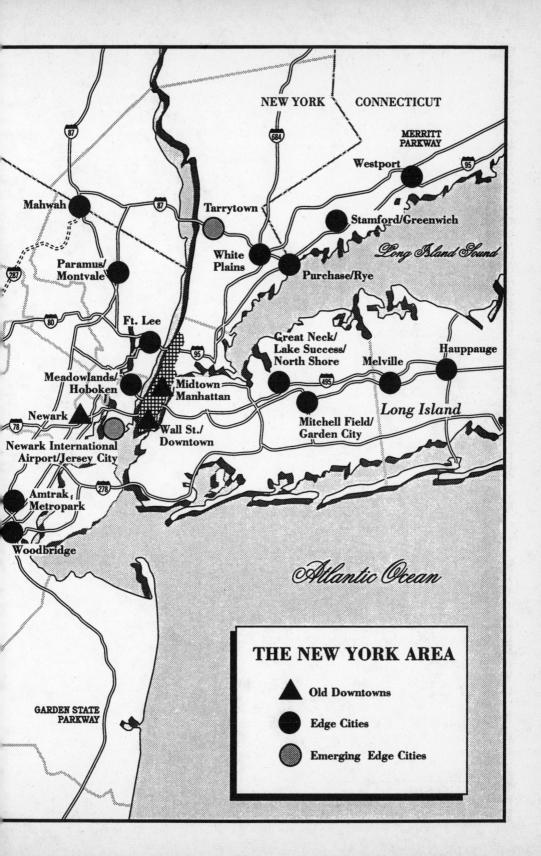

NEW YORK    CONNECTICUT

MERRITT
PARKWAY

Westport

Mahwah

Tarrytown

Stamford/Greenwich

*Long Island Sound*

Paramus/
Montvale

White
Plains

Purchase/Rye

Ft. Lee

Great Neck/
Lake Success/
North Shore

Melville

Hauppauge

Meadowlands/
Hoboken

Midtown
Manhattan

*Long Island*

Newark

Mitchell Field/
Garden City

Wall St./
Downtown

Newark International
Airport/Jersey City

Amtrak
Metropark

*Atlantic Ocean*

Woodbridge

GARDEN STATE
PARKWAY

## THE NEW YORK AREA

▲ Old Downtowns

● Edge Cities

● Emerging Edge Cities

THE SEAFOOD COUNTER alone is world class. Even in the New York area, an emporium grabs one's attention when, for eighty linear feet, it spreads out not only six *different* kinds of sliced octopus—fresh—but snow crab legs next to broiled eel near Chilean abalone next to geoduck sashimi, adjacent to a display of spiny sea urchins with golden, creamy, sensuous interiors intended to be eaten raw.

The fashion plaza, too, is dazzling. Amid cascades of gold and stacks of high couture, a mannequin sports a sexy red jogging suit with this precise mystery across its chest: "Don't Take It Easy: To Be Frank With You I'm Afraid of You at First But, Now Become Changed We Are Great Member."

The electronics mart sprawls under the name Saiko, which connotes "fantastic" in Japanese, and it is. Amid the televisions with vast screens and camcorders that fit in a palm, there are household appliances so unusual that, like the Zojirushi electric airpot, its very function is unfamiliar. Not distant, there is a display of $149.95 Sony Repeat Learning Systems, designed to teach English to Japanese. Sample sentences: "There's something about him that rubs me the wrong way," and "I'm under a lot of pressure."

But the real show-stopper of this sophisticated megamart is actually out in the Hudson River. It stands on piers, with a panoramic view of the skyline. It is the Chinzan-So restaurant, built in the gracefully curved pyramidical image of Rokuon-ji, a fifteenth-century temple. Amid pools of quiet, reflective water is —inside—a two-story, ten-ton pile of volcanic boulders freighted from the side of Mount Fuji. Its Kaiseki cuisine, developed through the centuries by great masters of the tea ceremony, is the height of Japanese culinary creativity. The Aoi entrée is $100. For one.

This strange, fascinating, and wondrous display is the Yaohan Plaza–New York. It is one of the largest such all-Japanese hypermarkets in the world. It features everything from a Japanese bookstore to the Pony Toy Go Around toy store, to a Super Health drugstore that offers cotton gauze masks to people with colds who might be riding the subway, to a bakery producing breads shaped like alligators. Tokyo Gardens sells bonsai junipers. The Promotion liquor mart flaunts an astounding variety of sake. The produce market features everything from ohba leaves to pears flown in from Japan in mesh plastic nests. The UCC Cafe Plaza window displays uncannily realistic plastic models of its offerings. One is labeled HAM SANDWICH.

The Yaohan Plaza–New York organization runs twenty-three such malls worldwide, from Brazil to Hong Kong, and ninety in Japan. This extravaganza, which opened in 1988, is exactly the same as would be found in Tokyo, say its founders. Except, of course, it has more variety. After all, it is almost five times bigger than average. The typical sale in the grocery areas alone is over $100. This should come as no surprise. Yaohan Plaza–New York is serving one of the most cosmopolitan metropolitan areas on the globe, right? Why shouldn't it be the height of sophistication?

This leaves, perhaps, only one question.

Why is it in New Jersey?

Why put such an exotic creation a full $50 cab ride from the presumed worldliness of midtown Manhattan? In the Edge City of Fort Lee? On the far side of Harlem?

Hiroaki Kawai, Yaohan Plaza's spokesman, seems a little perplexed by the question. The answer is perfectly obvious to him. Forty percent of Yaohan Plaza's business comes from the sixty thousand Japanese working for their global companies in the New York area, he patiently explained. Few of them live in Manhattan. He is startled that anyone would think otherwise. Why would a Japanese come to America to live in a cramped apartment?

They live around here, in Fort Lee, he says, where they can have houses and cars and get around. Or in nearby Westchester

County, New York, around the Edge City of White Plains, proximate to the world headquarters of IBM.

Another thing, he says: Look at the size of Yaohan Plaza. It would not be possible to build something like this in Manhattan. Where would you park the cars? A place this large and sophisticated needs support from people all over the region. Even here, the major problem is that there are only four hundred parking spaces, and they are so full now on weekends, what with chartered buses arriving from as far away as Philadelphia and Washington, people sometimes have to wait thirty minutes for a spot to open up. What is really needed is at least eight hundred slots, he says, plus more space on which to build. His consortium covetously eyes the riverfront land next door occupied by the looming Hills Brothers coffee plant, which fills the salt air of Yaohan Plaza's parking lot with the fresh aroma of roasted brew. Knock that flat and you could build a brand-new world out here, with attractions that dazzle the mind, Kawai explains matter-of-factly. A Japanese culture center, a Japanese hotel, amusement facilities, all nice and safe, marked by abundant free parking.

His English is quite fluent, but Kawai nonetheless occasionally stops to ask his listener if he is using the right words to get his points across. He seems to find it curious that anybody would find the Yaohan Plaza's location curious. Oh yes, he says, we've already opened several such hypermarts in North America, and have plans to open ten more in the next ten years. He starts ticking off the locations. Costa Mesa—an Edge City in Orange County, south of Los Angeles. San Jose—an Edge City in Silicon Valley. Arlington Heights, near Schaumburg—an Edge City of Chicago. "In old downtowns it is very difficult to find enough space for us," he says. "So we go out to new towns, where there is plenty of space." Kawai is so engrossed with his Edge City locations around North America that I finally ask, "Who did your site location research for you? Did somebody coach you on this, or did you figure it out all by yourself?"

We figured it out all by ourselves, he says. Japanese people who were familiar with the States because they had gone to school here were a big help. But to him the logic of locating in an Edge City rather than an old center like Manhattan is patent. If you look at the way people live in this country, the land of opportunity is New Jersey.

Joel Kotkin is the California co-author, with Yoriko Kishimoto, of *The Third Century: America's Resurgence in the Asian Era.* Kotkin is bullish on America's future because of its ability to be flexible and innovative and because it is capable of assimilating waves of immigrants who supply immense entrepreneurial energy—especially, in this era, Asians. But even he guffaws when told that the Yaohan Plaza–New York is actually in Edgewater, New Jersey. "When I was growing up," says the transplanted New Yorker, "being from New Jersey was a social disease."

But it is no surprise that Hiroaki Kawai feels at home in New Jersey. New Jersey is, in many respects, America's urban future. It is the first state in the Union to be more densely populated than Japan. It is also the first state in the Union to be more urban.

And in countless ways, if this is America's urban future, the future is bright. Not only is New Jersey headquarters to dozens of Fortune 500 companies, as well as thousands of entrepreneurial start-ups; it is a place of immense diversity, from the Institute for Advanced Study at Princeton, which cradled Albert Einstein, to ethnic neighborhoods like Trenton's Chambersburg, with memorable restaurants on every corner. New Jersey is a kind of California of the East Coast. It gave birth to fiber optics, the transistor, the solar cell, sound movies, the communications satellite, evidentiary proof of the Big Bang hypothesis of the origin of the universe, and Bruce Springsteen. It has 127 miles of beaches. It is the home of the NFL's Giants, the NBA's Nets, and the NHL's Devils. It is lavishly blessed with jealously guarded natural beauty, from the backpacking country of the Delaware Water Gap and Ramapo Mountains in the Appalachian Highlands to the pristine and solitary Atlantic shores of Cape May. New Jersey is not called the Garden State for nothing. Its truck farms supply local supermarket chains with 35 percent of their produce in season. It is laden with extravagant rolling estates. More than 40 percent of the entire state is still in forest. At one million acres, the spooky and beautiful Pinelands, with peat-stained water the color of tea, is by far the largest such horizon-to-horizon wild area north of the Everglades and east of the Mississippi.

Yet all this variety, beauty, economic prowess, density, and urbanity has been achieved without New Jersey's having within its boundaries what most people would consider even one major city. Whatever their virtues, Newark and Elizabeth are rarely described as big time. All this proves, however, is that most Americans' idea of what makes up a city no longer matches reality, because it doesn't encompass the central reality of New Jersey: Edge Cities.

An old-fashioned downtown—sporting tall concrete-and-steel buildings with walls that touch each other, laid out on a rectangular grid, accented by sidewalks, surrounded by political boundaries, and lorded over by a mayor—is only one way to think of a city. In fact, it is only the nineteenth-century version. These sorts of cities, epitomized in the United States by Manhattan and San Francisco, are proud places that will always be cherished. But they are relics of a time past. They are the aberrations. We built cities that way for less than a century. Those years, from perhaps 1840 to 1920, were by no means unimportant. They encompassed both the Industrial Revolution and the era of America's Manifest Destiny. Thriving old downtowns that have bright futures because they continue to be rejuvenated still bear their stamp, from Chicago to Seattle.

This does not begin to exhaust the idea of city. From ancient times, what made a city a city was how it functioned, not how it looked. And this is especially true today, for we have not built a single old-style downtown from raw dirt in seventy-five years.

The Edge Cities of New Jersey, instead, represent our new standard. If New Jersey was described by Benjamin Franklin as "a barrel tapped at both ends"—Philadelphia and New York—suddenly New Jersey is the *right* side of the rivers. In the late 1980s, New Jersey's Edge Cities grew more rapidly and generated more jobs than the entire state of New York. These Edge Cities now rise as their own commonwealths, from the one in the Route 1–Princeton area to the office tower forest emerging along Interstates 80 and 287 near Whippany and Parsippany. New Jersey's Edge Cities exemplify the new mix of urbanity, demonstrating what people want, can afford, and can stand. These Edge Cities, in fact, are the fruit of our attempt to strike a delicate balance between the advantages and disadvantages of 19th-century cities and the opportunities and challenges of the coming age. As such, they are being copied all over the world.

Making sense of an Edge City requires the following leap of

faith: any place that is a trade, employment, and entertainment center of vast magnitude is functionally a city. That is true no matter how sprawling and strange it looks physically, and no matter how anarchic or convoluted it seems politically. If it is sufficiently diverse, vibrant, and specialized—which mainly is to say huge—it is a city. Conversely, any place that isn't, doesn't qualify: Fort Peck City in Montana is not urban no matter what it is called by its six hundred proud denizens.

Libraries have been written about why humans ever built cities in the first place, but most historians agree that, for the last eight thousand years, cities have been shaped by seven purposes:

- industry,
- governance,
- commerce,
- safety,
- culture,
- companionship,
- religion.*

Edge Cities function along exactly these lines, although the emphasis has shifted provocatively over the centuries. Take the New Jersey Edge City an hour west of Wall Street, around the intersection of Interstates 287 and 78, in the area from Bridgewater to Basking Ridge and from Warren to Bedminster. Tracing the effect of these seven historical forces on the shaping of this Edge City helps reveal what it is this civilization values.

Industry, for example—the creation of jobs and wealth—is the very point of Edge Cities. AT&T's world headquarters is in this "287 and 78" world. It is universally referred to as the Pagoda because it is vaguely Oriental in a Frank Lloyd Wright kind of way. Its tiled, cascading tiers of heavy-lidded roofs and hanging gardens are massive and lavish enough to be the envy of any Chinese emperor.

The Pagoda opened in 1976 in the 287 and 78 neighborhood of Basking Ridge because AT&T thought that was the best place to grow and make money. Although AT&T was founded in Manhattan in 1885 and still uses that as its corporate address, not a

---

* For quick reference, see the Notes and other sections at the back of this book.

single top executive is permanently located there. In the 1930s, Bell Labs—AT&T's renowned research and development arm— custom-designed for itself an elaborate 1.7-million-square-foot, high-rise headquarters employing fifty-six hundred people on less than four acres of Manhattan. The plans were shucked in 1939. Corporate archives show that even fifty years ago old downtowns were thought to have competitive problems. "High costs of land in Manhattan," "high living costs," and "the urban noise and dirt," as well as the inefficiencies of skyscrapers and the commuting woes on the ferries and tubes, were already major issues, according to corporate documents.

*Ex.* *BAd* *Things*

So in the opening days of World War II, Bell Labs moved out to a grandly christened "campus" in Murray Hill, near what is now Interstate 78. AT&T never looked back. In 1977, the Long Lines division—the long-distance operation that is now the bulk of the company's franchise—pulled its headquarters from the bowels of lower Manhattan. It, too, moved to 287 and 78—in Bedminster, near the Far Hills fox-hunt estates of boxer Mike Tyson, the late Malcolm Forbes, and the king of Morocco.

This is no small deal. The two-story Strangelovian "video-wall" control center for AT&T's network linking 146 countries is in the foothills there today. If the future belongs to whoever controls the glass-fiber networks of the multibillion-dollar infor-mation marketplace, 287 and 78 someday may erupt like a his-toric boomtown—Chicago in the heyday of railroads or Detroit when the automobile was new or Houston when oil approached $40 a barrel.

*Ex*

Meanwhile, more than fifty years after Bell Labs made its move—which was back when high technology was a phone you didn't have to crank—New Jersey's Edge Cities have proven sufficiently useful that AT&T has 225 facilities in them. They include the headquarters of each major division. AT&T located enough facilities in the New Jersey Edge Cities in the mid-1970s alone to overflow one of the World Trade Center's 110-story towers. AT&T now occupies twenty-two million square feet of space there. That is more than exists in downtown Seattle. More than fifty-one thousand people are employed by AT&T in New Jersey's Edge Cities.

This is increasingly common. Edge Cities are headquarters to such diverse giants as Motorola (Schaumburg, Illinois), K mart

(Troy, Michigan), Black & Decker (Hunt Valley, Maryland), and —the Greatest Show on Earth—the Ringling Bros. and Barnum & Bailey Circus (Tysons Corner, Virginia).* Sears, Roebuck and Company recently pulled its headquarters out of that symbol of old downtowns, the world's tallest building, the 110-story Sears Tower on Chicago's Wacker Drive. After a nationwide search, it located in the Hoffman Estates neighborhood of the Edge City *Ex.* centered on Schaumburg, thirty miles to the northwest. Sears' move illustrated what these corporations are trying to do: heighten competitiveness by consolidating entire operations, save a few bucks, and, it is hoped, enhance the quality of the work force and the living and working environment.

That is why these Edge Cities are hardly one-company towns. A lot of outfits have the same idea. The 287 and 78 area flies the corporate banners of TRW, NYNEX, Chubb, Allstate, Prudential, Beneficial, Bristol-Myers, Hoechst Celanese, Johnson & Johnson, Chase Manhattan, and Dun & Bradstreet. It contains more than sixteen million leasable square feet of office space full of white-collar jobs. That's larger than downtown New Orleans. This Edge City not only has a corporate-jet airfield fifteen minutes away in Morristown; it has achieved such stature that its heavy hitters recently started to feel put upon. It seems that when they returned from Europe and Asia, the federal government had the annoying habit of forcing their private jets to first land at Teterboro, forty miles east. That was the nearest strip with a customs facility. Only after that stop could they fire up the turbines for the five-minute hop to 287 and 78. So the high rollers bought themselves their own customs office for Morristown. This is an airport with no regularly scheduled commercial flights, but it is now in effect Morristown International. They pay for this customs shed, they use it, it's theirs.

(In fact, the rise nationwide of satellite airports with surprisingly high levels of full-blown commercial service is a direct result of Edge Cities. In the orbit of New York's Edge Cities, for example, there are now six airports with serious, scheduled, national-airline jet service. That is because a lot of people in Edge Cities don't want to fight their way into La Guardia, Newark, or JFK. The newly important outer airports include MacAr-

* For a list of Edge Cities, see Chapter 11.

thur in Islip, halfway out on Long Island; Westchester; and Stewart International, in Newburgh, New York, seventy-five miles up the Hudson from Manhattan.)

Although nationally known corporations get a lot of press when they relocate to Edge City, they are not the quoin of capitalism there. It is the young, fast-growing entrepreneurial start-up—especially in high technology—that is the mark of Edge City. *Inc.* ("The Magazine for Growing Companies") in 1989 specifically made the connection. "One lure may lie in the basically unsettled nature of life on the edge," *Inc.* reported. "The people who like the status quo stay downtown where the old elites are. People who are out there redefining themselves, like entrepreneurs, are attracted to places that are new, where things are more flexible."

The creation of enterprise and jobs, and thus cities, has not changed much through history. It's always required a great deal of raw material drawn to one location, to which is added people to shape the material into something different and useful. The result is then shipped back out to an eager world. Today, that location is Edge City.

That's because the raw material has changed. Now that stock is made up of problems. There are so many of them that they come to places like 287 and 78 via huge satellite dishes—the heavy haulers, the railroads of the future. In Edge City, the offices are the factories of the Information Age. That is where problems are accumulated and the information of which they are made is mined for valuable nuggets. There it is digested and decided on by the work force, transformed, and repackaged.

The finished product shipped back out, essentially, is cleverness. It includes everything from decisions to buy and sell, to designs and redesigns, to software, to reports, to legal opinions, to television advertising. The worth of this cleverness can be thought of as independent of the physical object in which it may be embedded. Take the price of a telephone, for example. No one buying one cares about the cost per pound of this lump of plastic and silicon. The value of the phone is in how ingenious it is—how many features it has, how portable it is, how reliable it is. It is measured by how much cleverness it represents.

This shift to Information Age cities is as basic a revolution as the one we went through a century and a half ago at the dawn of the Industrial Revolution. In 1850, for example, 85 percent of the U.S. population was rural. Cities, such as they were, were small and mercantile. Their landmarks were the counting houses down by the wharves. There, the riches of the hinterlands were swapped for the complexities of Europe and Asia. By the turn of the century, that had all changed. Mighty cities like Pittsburgh were built not so much on their relationship to farm and woodlands as on the relation of their factories to iron ore, coal, and sweating labor.

Before the Industrial Revolution, a world like today's would have been utterly unimaginable—in which only 3 percent of all Americans farm and more than three quarters are metropolitan slickers. Edge City represents as radical a shift. This is not because America's manufacturing prowess has rusted. Ignore the gloom-and-doom-sayers. The United States is now so technically advanced that it makes a ton of steel with fewer work hours than any nation on earth. From basic metals to chemicals to pharmaceuticals, American industry is strong. The American worker is by far the most productive in the world. Manufacturing jobs in America are actually increasing in absolute numbers.

But the way the world measures success in manufacturing today is by how quickly the number of blue-collar workers per object created can *decline*. That means increased productivity— more output per person—which means competitiveness with the rest of the world. Thus, it is possible to imagine an America with as strong a manufacturing base as there is now an agricultural base, in which the share of people actually turning widgets is astonishingly low. It is already no more than 18 percent of the work force—and it sank below 50 percent for the first time only in 1953.

That leads to the key work location being the office. That *is* industry in the late twentieth century. Instead of actually making airplanes, people more typically are figuring out how to make stronger, lighter composites to translate less fuel into more passengers in airplanes. Or they are supporting the people who do—either directly as researchers or word processors, or indirectly, by delivering their meals, fixing their Xerox machines, or nurturing their children.

That is why five million square feet of leasable office space is the point of critical mass for Edge City. The developer's rule of thumb is: *One office worker equals 250 square feet.* That's the size of a fair-sized living room, and counts not just the worker's desk area, but her share of reception rooms, file rooms, stockrooms, and Xerox rooms.

Why do Edge Cities seem to hit critical mass at five million square feet of leasable office space? No one knows exactly, at a theoretical level. But the figure does work like crazy as a predictor. When one drives out to see a place so measured, one always finds the same tall buildings, bright lights, and a hustle and bustle that is distinctly urban, albeit a little raw and cracked.

Five million square feet of office is a point of spontaneous combustion. It turns out to be exactly enough to support the building of a luxury hotel. It causes secondary explosions; businesses begin to flock to the location to serve the businesses already there. Five million square feet is a huge number; more than a hundred acres. That much space dwarfs the sizable downtown of Dayton, Richmond, Wilmington, or Spokane. It represents dozens of office buildings that would cover blocks and blocks in an old downtown. The number instantly and decisively rules out our using "city" for any suburban office strip of dentists and cut-rate tax-return accountants. The number represents a reality that is so quantitatively different as to be qualitatively different.

This measure of Edge City is especially useful because it is easily gathered. Edge City is a creature of the marketplace, and commercial real estate agents are its most devoted acolytes. Their mental maps of what constitutes a single commercial real estate "submarket" is usually an exquisite description of the functional outlines of Edge City. If you wish to know whether a place near you is a full-blown Edge City, simply ask a commercial real estate agent to total up the leasable square footage numbers in his computer by submarket.

Interestingly, it has to be office space. Industrial and warehouse space does not create anything urbane. No dense centers ever evolve. Factories usually figure one worker for every forty-five hundred square feet. This is eighteen times less dense than office space. Warehouse space has even fewer workers than that. Only one story high, a warehouse sprawls over the landscape much more than does Edge City. North Carolina is the tenth most populous state in the Union. It has 35 percent of its work force in manufacturing—the highest level in the nation. Yet it has no large downtowns at all, and not much in the way of an Edge City outside the white-collar confines of the Research Triangle: Raleigh–Durham–Chapel Hill. City of Industry, California, aptly named, has a staggering hundred million square feet of factory and warehouse space—almost four square miles under roof. But precious little of that Southern California site passes for civilization. Industrial and warehouse workers rarely demand specialty retail, high-end services, cloth-napkin restaurants, hotels, and bookstores.

With the workplace now centered on offices, cities are transformed. For one thing, "cleverness" is not heavy; it is not measured in tons, like steel or corn or petroleum. Thus, it does not have to be, like an old downtown, near water or rail—the preferred movers of "heavy." Edge Cities, in fact, typically rise at the interchange of freeways. This should come as no surprise. "Whatever its shape, its architecture, or the civilization that illuminates it, the town creates roads and is created by them," Fernand Braudel wrote of the Middle Ages. "We should imagine the great trade route to the East [of the 1500s] as something like today's *autostrada*."

Cities are always created around whatever the state-of-the-art transportation device is at the time. If the state of the art is sandal leather and donkeys, you get Jerusalem. Even when wheeled vehicles replaced pack animals as the freight technology of choice fifteen centuries after Jesus, Jerusalem remained shaped by its transportation origins.

When the state of the art is carriages and oceangoing sail, you get the compact, water-dominated East Coast cities of Paul Revere's Boston and George Washington's Alexandria. Or Amsterdam and Antwerp.

Canal barge and steamship give you Boss Tweed's New York. Intraurban (the El) and transcontinental rail (the stockyards) yield Bugsy Moran's Chicago. The automobile results in Raymond Chandler's Los Angeles.

When, in 1958, you threw in the jet passenger plane, you got more Los Angeles in strange places—Atlanta, Denver, Houston, Dallas, and Phoenix.

The combination of the present is the automobile, the jet plane, and the computer. The result is Edge City. The proof is the half-million-square-foot corporate headquarters of Beneficial Corporation, formerly Beneficial Finance. Incongruously located off a two-lane country road one exit north of the interchange of Interstates 287 and 78, Beneficial's headquarters is a complex of low, brooding brick linked by cobblestone courtyards and crowned by an eighty-foot clock tower that management is pleased to refer to as "the campanile." This headquarters looms like a baronial castle over the swale in which the perfect white spire of the Reformed Church marks the picturesque village of Peapack. The effect is supposed to be campuslike. It did indeed overpower one would-be Beneficial executive. At his hiring interview, having seen the place for the first time, he looked out over one quadrangle and couldn't help himself. Out he blurted, "So how's the football team doing?"

The Beneficial site is achingly bucolic. The "guest house" is Hamilton Farm, the former estate of the Brady dynasty, from which sprang Nicholas Brady, secretary of the treasury under George Bush. The sixty-four-room manse is profusely hung with oil portraits of horses with names like Exterminator and Twenty Grand. Out back, the carefully rolled lawn sports a wind sock. For the helicopters. When I mentioned I'd almost clobbered four deer in the driveway, the chairman and chief executive officer, Finn M. W. Caspersen, replied idly, "Only four?" There are usually more, he said, showing only the mildest interest in the fact that there were all these large wild animals bounding around his Edge City.

The deer, after all, are not the stars of the show in these parts. The horses are. The long-time headquarters of the U.S. Olympic Equestrian Team is at Hamilton Farm. The stables, when they were built in 1916, were described as the largest and most lavish in the United States. They have forty ornate carriage rooms, harness rooms, and human bedrooms featuring tile walls, terrazzo floors, and brass fittings. The floors of the fifty-four twelve-foot-square box stalls are made of bricks of cork.

As it happens, Caspersen is a competitor in an event called the "four in hand." That involves making four horses pulling a carriage perform like gymnasts. It is an exotic sport by the standards of fox hunting. When Caspersen beat Prince Philip at it in England to take the world championship, the glass trophy came home next to him in the seat he'd bought for it on the Concorde.

Nonetheless, Caspersen protests it was not he who insisted that the Beneficial headquarters be built next to the headquarters of the U.S. Olympic Equestrian Team. It was just a happy coincidence. The serendipity of corporate decision making.

Caspersen's version of the logic that brought the diversity, complexity, size, and function of a major corporation out to Edge City—of how his Machine of many parts was brought out to the Garden—goes like this:

Env.

"We came to the conclusion in the 1970s that the rest of the century was going to put a premium on employees in our business—financial services. And many employees were going to want a life style more than just money—a helpful environment and a pleasant environment.

"We also came to the conclusion that women were becoming more and more of a factor in our business. And when a woman has to combine raising a family and working, there's a very strong argument for being out near where people live.

"And personally, I am not a proponent of skyscrapers. I think there's an impersonal feeling about a skyscraper that makes it very difficult to have any kind of corporate culture. The only time you see people is in the elevator.

What
we
Expected

"So with that combination, what we were looking for was 80 percent of our people being able to live within twenty miles. That location had to be within three or four miles of a major interstate and it had to have room for expansion. An hour from a major airport—Newark is now thirty-five minutes away. We also wanted to have a railroad nearby. We weren't quite sure what role that was going to play—it turns out not too much.

"And we decided it was time to build a very pleasant workplace, and make it as personalized as possible. A lot of small buildings—that in practice are all connected, underground. A little more square footage than usual per person. But emphasize the outside. Eat outside, set up tables. There's two ball fields. Obviously you have tennis courts. We have a cafeteria here, we have a gymnasium, we have a company store if people need a new razor and wrapping paper or something. We have a barber shop. We have a gas station.

"As a result we've been able to recruit, even at lower salaries, against—certainly against anybody in New York unless you get a dedicated New Yorkerphile—but against most people even out here. And trying to make quality of life an issue does reduce turnover. Any personnel people will tell you the longer you can keep an able person, the better you are."

The result is over a thousand people working at a corporate headquarters that not only would never have been seen outside an old downtown until recently, but is now located in a part of New Jersey in which the deer are a nuisance and Canada geese on corporate lawns a cliché. The night before I talked to Caspersen, I ended up chatting with a man from Beneficial's Utah offices.

"I like this," he said. "I like this a lot." He couldn't get over the verdant country lanes and all the trees. He knew it was unspeakably craven for a Westerner even to think what he was thinking, but what the hell. He stuck his chin out. "This is enough for me to re-examine my prejudices about the East."

Caspersen, nonetheless, is already looking to move farther out. The corporate goal of having 80 percent of the employees able to live within twenty miles of the office is already a bust. He thinks the number is now no more than 60 percent. The area had so many advantages that even in a sagging Northeast real estate market half a million dollars per house was not unusual. And automobile traffic is a concern. "That may be a fatal defect —the roads. Though what's the alternative? There are the same problems with center city. You have to get there. Mass transit is not a very pleasant circumstance. People don't like it. It's no more pleasant than driving. Things work if there's transportation. They don't if there isn't," says Caspersen, echoing the sentiment of city builders throughout the millennia.

But then he starts talking about Beneficial's computers in a way that reveals how Edge Cities are the creation of a new way of handling ancient transportation concerns. Beneficial's computers allow Caspersen to uncouple the pieces of his corporation and move them around in ways that ground transportation never could.

"Let me explain to you one of our projects," he says. It is called Rapid Refund. "It's a joint venture with H & R Block. For an extra $25, H & R Block will offer to send your tax return into the IRS electronically. You say, 'Why should I do that?' Well, you'll probably get your refund quicker. Then they say, 'By the way, we've got another program. For an extra thirty-five bucks we'll get you your money tomorrow.' "

Here's how it works. The distant office of H & R Block, where the taxpayer is, zaps the return to the H & R Block central computer in Columbus, Ohio. The Columbus computer then zaps the return to an IRS computer in Ogden, Utah; Cincinnati, Ohio; or Andover, Massachusetts; depending on the region in which it originated. If the IRS computer decides it looks like a good return—no liens against the taxpayer, for example—it relays the message back to Columbus. That computer then sends information from the return up to Beneficial's computer at 287 and 78, which decides if it meets their standards for a quickie loan. If so, the Peapack computer instructs the Columbus computer to tell the branch office computer to cut a check. (At the same time, the Peapack computer is taking care of bookkeeping with the Beneficial computer in Wilmington, Delaware, where Beneficial's bank is located.) The taxpayer comes back the next day to the H & R Block office in West Nowhere, Idaho, and picks up his check. "All happens in twenty-four hours. Yes. Just like that," says Caspersen. "And you can do it anywhere. Sure you can. It's all their computers, our computers, and the IRS's computers."

That is why Caspersen is thinking of moving his programmers out of 287 and 78. Theirs, he says, is a highly skilled business. "We're talking average salary, $45,000. They are college educated and have skills that you and I don't. And these are highly transferrable skills, so you really want to keep them happy. If they have a long commute that they don't like, find a place with a comparative advantage."

He thinks the answer may be to locate them nearer the more affordable housing in the Edge City emerging down I-78, across the Delaware River in the Lehigh Valley of Pennsylvania's Allentown-Bethlehem-Easton area. Or, for that matter, in Dallas, Texas. Lot of cheap housing and office space there. "You can set up your programmers really anyplace," he said.

If that's true, I ask him, why bother to have any agglomerations at all? Why bother to have a headquarters? Why build a city of any kind, even an Edge City?

"You know, that's the question of the future. Why don't people all stay at home and work? We've got over a thousand people here and at least 10 percent of them work through our systems at home. Particularly women when they're on maternity leave will do much of their work at home and use their terminals for that. But there's a line beyond which it really doesn't work. It's different for different people. But you lose that team spirit, the ability to work together, if you don't get the touchy-feely, the face-to-face. You can use it part time, you can use it at night, and you can use it on the weekend. But they still have to come in or you lose that synergy between people, you lose the corporate culture. And the corporate culture is very important."

This turns out to be big news. For all of its attenuation, the bulletin is this: Edge City means density is back. "Maybe the wonder," said the urbanologist Jane Jacobs in an interview, "is how *thin* things got."

Humans still put an overwhelming premium on face-to-face contact. Telephones, fax machines, electronic mail, and video conferencing share a problem: they do not produce intense human relationships. They do not create interactions that end with either a fistfight or an embrace. "Trust" is tough to build over a wire. Edge Cities prove that a market thrives for bringing people together physically. Humans are still gregarious animals.

*Problems w.z Technology.*

Edge City is not really a rejection of the nineteenth-century city of Dickens. Nor does it reject the nineteenth-century vision of nature of Thoreau. Instead, perhaps, it strives for a new equipoise, a new but stable urban energy level. Forget our alleged isolation in "automotive cocoons" and "sterile subdivisions." The final value of Edge Cities is—social.

That is why there are more than twenty Edge Cities emerging in the New York area. There are that many huge markets out beyond the old core for this new balance. Ten are in northern New Jersey, two in central New Jersey, one on the border in Pennsylvania, and nine more in nearby New York State and Connecticut. Each of them is or will soon be bigger than Memphis.

Edge Cities are most frequently located where beltway-like bypasses around an old downtown are crossed at right angles by freeways that lead out from the old center like spokes on a wheel. New Jersey can be thought of as having three such beltways that circumvent Manhattan. One is Interstate 95, the East Coast's main drag. In this part of the world, it is called the

New Jersey Turnpike, and it shunts traffic headed south toward Washington or north toward Boston around Manhattan via the George Washington Bridge over the Hudson. The second bypass, which is popular for through traffic because of the congestion of I-95 near Manhattan, is the Garden State Parkway. The third, Interstate 287, the northern leg of which is scheduled to be completed in the early 1990s, is the most obviously beltway-like because it broadly loops halfway around the state, never getting much within an hour of Manhattan.

There are three spokes on the wheel heading west from Manhattan across the Hudson—one bridge and two tunnels. At the New Jersey end of each of these, an Edge City is growing. The northernmost is where Interstate 95 lifts off toward Harlem and the Bronx. That is the high-palisades, high-rise Fort Lee area of Yaohan Plaza fame. The next, opposite midtown via the Lincoln Tunnel, is the Meadowlands, the center of which is the intersection of Route 3 and Interstate 95 at the home of the "New York" Giants and "New York" Jets, as well as the Jersey Nets and Devils. Office plazas are rising all up and down Route 3. Hoboken, which is that part of the Meadowlands Edge City that has the best view of Manhattan because it is right on the Hudson, actually became trendy in the 1980s.

The Edge City opposite Wall Street via the Holland Tunnel is the Newark International Airport area, strategically located at the intersections of Interstates 95 and 78. The civic boosters of the Hudson shore areas of Jersey City are now pleased to call that the Gold Coast. What it really is, is that portion of the Newark International Airport Edge City that has the nicest view of Wall Street, as well as direct PATH train connections to the World Trade Center. That's why some very high-rent residential development, featuring high security and water taxis, was built on the grim industrial waterfront facing Wall Street during its go-go merger-and-acquisition years. When that boom ended in the late 1980s, of course, so did a lot of Wall Street salaries, and it was hello Chapter 11. But, oh well. This place still has a lot of advantages. I bought a sweatshirt there that read "Proud to Be an American. Statue of Liberty State Park. It's in New *Jersey*."

On the second bypass road, the Garden State Parkway, there are three more Edge Cities. From south to north, the first is the Woodbridge Mall area. This is the place just above New Brunswick where you turn off the cruise control and shut up the kids. That is where all the major north-south highways on the East Coast merge, scramble, and peel off. Menlo Park is here, where Thomas Edison invented the twentieth century. Even the *New York Times* has figured out this place enough to stake a turnpike claim on a massive building.

The second Edge City on the Garden State is just north at a curious place called Metropark. This has been described as the first Edge City in the world to grow from a parking lot. That may be true, but this parking lot had a lot of advantages. Metropark is still one of the fastest, safest, and cheapest places to change modes of ground transportation in the Northeast. Leave your car there at Iselin and pick up either good short-haul train connections into Manhattan or Amtrak long-haul. To as distant a destination as Washington, the high-speed Metroliner competes successfully with shuttle jets.

There is another city north of this, which goes by the venerable old name of Newark. Newark has enough office space to be considered moderate-sized by Edge City standards. It even has a new twenty-two-story office tower, anchored by the Seton Hall University School of Law. But it has been around for so long and its growth is so conditional that it should not really be counted as Edge.

Therefore, the third Garden State Parkway Edge City comes after you pass through all those blue-collar neighborhoods on the parkway that look like the opening credits of *All in the Family.* Fifteen miles north, this is the Paramus-Montvale area of Bergen County. It is a relatively mature part of New Jersey, but was originally suburbanized by people looking for sylvan environs who were used to Manhattan-level salaries. It was then urbanized when they brought their jobs with them. Richard Milhous Nixon lives and writes his books in these parts.

Of the Interstate 287 Edge Cities, we've already mentioned one—the Woodbridge area way to the south where 287 is crossed by all those north-south arteries. Then, following around clockwise, there is 287 and 78, the Edge City we've been examining, centered on Bridgewater. That intersection is important because of where Interstate 78 goes. East, it leads right into the international flights at Newark Airport and the Edge City there, and then on into Wall Street via the Holland Tunnel.

West, just over the Delaware River, it dumps into the emerging
Edge City of Pennsylvania's Lehigh Valley.

Out of date are the impressions of this area shaped by the
1982 Billy Joel song that goes "Well we're living here in Allentown / And they're closing all the factories down; / Out in
Bethlehem they're killing time / Filling out forms, standing in
line." Today, the Lehigh Valley is booming—its unemployment
rate fell from 11 percent to 4 right after Joel's song came out.
Because of its abundant skilled labor, pleasant environment,
and bargain housing opportunities compared with New Jersey,
an Edge City of an Edge City is rising there. It is not in the orbit
of New York. It is in the orbit of 287 and 78. That is why
Beneficial is thinking about setting up its backshop of computer
programmers there.

North of 287 and 78, there is old Morristown. Its freeway
approach is memorable: GEORGE WASHINGTON'S HEADQUARTERS,
EXIT, ONE MILE. And people say Edge Cities have no history. Red
Coats—right lane only?

The Morristown area has an arts community, two universities
nearby—Drew and Fairleigh Dickinson—and a thriving downtown. It has not yet hit critical mass as a job center, and probably
won't until Route 24 is extended, so it does not qualify as an
Edge City; it is headed in that direction. Now, though, it is still
serving a residential community; many of the members work in
287 and 78 and in 287 and 80, the next Edge City north around
Parsippany–Troy Hills.

That latter Edge City, 287 and 80, which includes the I-280
spur, is already formidable, and is expected to gain more advantage during this decade with the completion—through environmentally fragile wetlands, after enormous controversy—of Interstate 287 all the way to the New York State border. For that
matter, the area near Mahwah at Route 17—the "Quickway" to
the Catskills—at the other end of 287's so-called missing link
should also profit. If it grows, it will spill over into New York
State's Rockland County.

Those are the Edge Cities of northern New Jersey, but the 287
beltway's influence does not end there. The Tappen Zee Bridge
is the next river crossing up from Harlem, where it takes 287
into Westchester County, New York. There, three more Edge
Cities arise. The biggest is in the center of the county, at White

Plains, where the region's Edge City phenomenon got an early boost in 1954 when General Foods moved its headquarters there from Manhattan. The one emerging to the west is in the Tarrytown area. The one to the east is in Purchase-Rye, the headquarters of Pepsico—one of the world's largest consumer-goods providers. It is located where 287 finally picks up Interstate 95 again as it heads north toward Connecticut—and New England.

There are two more Interstate 95 Edge Cities in southwestern Connecticut's Fairfield County. One is the Stamford area, relatively near Manhattan. The other is the Westport and Fairfield area farther out on 95, in which is the headquarters of General Electric, the corporation that in the 1990s began to challenge IBM as the largest corporation in America.

Long Island was the first place in America to be declared urban by the U.S. Census without having a single significant nineteenth-century-style city. It was also the first such territory to spawn a national-quality newspaper—*Newsday*—which is now challenging the downtown papers on their own turf with a New York City edition. Long Island is even more prototypically Edge City than New Jersey. Suffolk County is that half of the island most distant from the mainland. (It is, in fact, a very long island.) As long ago as the 1980 Census, only 14 percent of the people in Suffolk County commuted to New York. For that matter, only 16 percent of them commuted to neighboring, more built-up Nassau County, to the west. Fully two-thirds worked right there on the eastern end of Long Island. Even in Nassau County, which, like Suffolk, is comparable to Manhattan in population and is separated from it only by Queens, 62 percent never leave the island to go to work.

From west to east, the Long Island Edge Cities are the Great Neck–Lake Success area and the Mitchell Field–Garden City area in Nassau County. In Suffolk, there is Route 110–Melville, just east of the county line, and Hauppauge, ten miles farther east on the Long Island Expressway.

There are yet two more Edge Cities in the region. They are so far into central New Jersey that it is debatable whether they are in the orbit of New York, Philadelphia, north Jersey, or are free-standing. One is the Princeton–Route 1 corridor, which in the 1980s was the fastest growing in New Jersey and among the most traffic-choked. The other is Cherry Hill, the home of the first Rouse-Corporation mall, right there between Camden and the James Fenimore Cooper Rest Area.

━━━━━━
━━━━━━

*unit purpose*

If the ultimate value of Edge Cities is social—if their whole point is a balance between individualism and face-to-face contact—then the uniting of diverse people into federations, that is, politics or governance, remains a historic city shaper. In few places is that made more clear than in 287 and 78. It was the first place in America whose inhabitants were so hungry for a center to their Edge City that they waged a grass-roots struggle for two decades to get it.

The people of Bridgewater Township, at the heart of 287 and 78, decided in the late 1960s that what they wanted was a kind of twentieth-century village green. They envisioned a place that teenagers would instantly recognize as a fine location to promenade before the opposite sex, akin to the Mexican village square. They hoped that the old would come there to exercise early in the morning, as in a Chinese city park. What they wanted was a market meeting place reminiscent of the Greek agora. They could see a place that was warm in the winter and cool in the summer, and festooned with plants in every season. It would provide for every earthly need, exactly like "the heart of Constantinople, its 'bazestan' [bazaar], with its four gates, its great brick arches, its everyday foods and its precious merchandise," as Braudel described that ancient realm. Around it, the people of Bridgewater figured, they would cluster all their public sites—from their courts of law to their courts of basketball. It would be a city center as described by the urban theorist and architect Louis Kahn: "the place of the assembled institutions."

So that is exactly what they got. After a fashion. Their plans collided with the Law of Unintended Consequences: *No matter what you think you're up to, the outcome will always be a surprise.* And they came to recognize the truth of that ancient wisdom: Be careful what you pray for; you just might get it. Nonetheless, a bronze historical marker may someday be affixed to their answer. For their village square is thriving. Their center finally opened in 1988 after half a generation of struggle, and it is known far and wide as Bridgewater Commons.

What it turned out to be, of course, was a 900,000-square-foot mall.

Susan Gruel grins broadly when asked if there was an epiphany in the late 1960s, a moment of truth when the people of Bridgewater rose as one and marched on the town council, carrying torches that flickered on their faces as they swayed in the moonlight, chanting, "Mall! Mall! Mall!"

Well . . . Gruel was chairman of the local redevelopment agency in the mid-1980s, when the final contract for the mall was signed. She now smiles. No, it was not like that. But, she cheerfully admits, the whole thing did seem "peculiar" at times, even to her. Peculiar or not, the people of 287 and 78 went from dreaming about Boston Common to building Bridgewater Commons. The process by which this came about demonstrates how, in this country, we constantly reinvent ourselves by the choices that we make.

Political authorities have called cities of governance into being—Washington and Ottawa, for example—for centuries. Granada and Madrid were primarily governmental cities, as were Paris and London. Bridgewater Commons is in the same tradition as Brasilia.

Bridgewater Commons was also a reaction to the mistakes of the past. It was created by people who had seen the land around them burned in ways they vowed would never be repeated.

The first mistake they rued was in the earliest days of suburbanization. The land in the middle of the township was carved up for country getaways into lots so tiny as to be almost unbuildable. Over the generations, these phantom streets and weed-filled lots became legally choked on ownership mysteries. So the site slept despite becoming a Golden Triangle location in the eyes of the real estate industry: it was served, not to mention landlocked, by three major roads—Routes 22, 202–206, and I-287.

It was the late 1960s when a new horror loomed. A developer scraped together just enough land on the Route 22 side to demand the right to build the one thing the locals loathed even more than the weeds—a strip shopping center. "We just did not want another strip development nightmare, what we had seen

east of us," remembers Al Griffith, who was mayor in the mid-
1970s when the winning proposal for Bridgewater Commons
was picked. "It was ugly. And we didn't want this to be a honky-
tonk town. We even had an ordinance that you could not have
flashing lights on stores."

So to allow something serious to be created, the citizens of
Bridgewater up and condemned all the land, as if it were an
inner-city slum, taking ownership onto their government. They
created the first area in New Jersey with no history of being
urban—or even much occupied—to be declared legally
blighted. They then advertised in the *Wall Street Journal,* seeking
large-scale proposals from redevelopers. They got thirty-seven.

Another reaction to the evils of the day that created Bridgewater Commons was that Bridgewater Township was less a township by any practical standard than a centerless thirty-three-
square-mile legal fiction of disconnected neighborhoods. Mayor
Griffith had to battle personally for Bridgewater Township to
get its own Zip Code. But Bridgewater did not want a traditional
downtown either. Although everybody realized that "a town
center has a retail component," says Griffith, "the downtowns
were not in the best of health. Sure it was a consideration—all
the problems. Plus lack of parking, lack of coordination. If you
allowed people to put up individual stores, we wouldn't have
been able to get them to put forth the money to do the absolutely essential road improvements."

Traffic lights were the reason road improvements were essential. Traffic lights were abhorred. If this town center was going to
have one thing, it was going to have overpasses. "We realized
that there was a tremendous cost involved, even without the
Commons. The state did not have the resources to do the job.
So we realized that you would have to get the funds from a
developer. To make it attractive for a developer, it had to be one
piece. You would never be able to get it from individuals if you
sold it off in pieces"—like an old downtown.

At the same time, by the mid-1970s a strong environmental
movement had grown up in Bridgewater. Again, that was a reaction. Developers building residential subdivisions on the sides
of the Watchung Mountains had caused serious erosion and
drainage damage at tremendous costs to both homeowners and
the township. In fact, Griffith originally got into politics to fight

the flooding of his neighborhood's homes. Ultimately the politics of Bridgewater turned on which candidate could out-environment the other. The result was a demand for greenery in the new town center—for trees, for parks, for berms to hide the traffic and the buildings. The Rouse Corporation, which has a reputation for being a class act, had a plan for the Golden Triangle that, whatever its virtues, was deemed to cover the area with too much asphalt. It was rejected. "People running our town were very sensitive to keeping the town a quality town, which meant a lot of greenspace, environmental sensitivity," said Griffith.

But there was one thing worse than parking lots—and that was anything that smacked of traditional urbanism. The Taubman Company, another quality developer, came up with a plan to maximize the greenery in the Golden Triangle by concentrating a hotel, conference, and retail center into an enormous structure fourteen or fifteen stories high. That too was rejected. "We were not happy with tall buildings," Griffith recalls. "It reminded us of cities."

So, by a process of elimination that took more than a decade of dickering and contract renegotiations and lawsuits and elections, what resulted was the Bridgewater Commons that rises today—a mall with a Sheraton and two huge office towers surrounded by $23 million worth of roadwork paid for by the developer.

The mall's a doozy. The first floor (The Commons Collection) caters to the affluent with Brooks Brothers, Laura Ashley, Godiva, and major-league indoor trees. The third floor, by contrast (Campus), is neon "under-twenty-five" heaven. It has an enormous Sam Goody's record store, a store that sells nothing but sunglasses, a store that sells nothing but artifacts from cartoons, a seven-screen theater open until 1 A.M., and a sixteen-restaurant food court called Picnic on the Green. (You want village green? You got it. Squint a little. This is what it looks like in the late twentieth century.) I made the mistake of wanting to use the pay phones on this floor. Forget it. They are tied up by teenagers. For the rest of time.

In the great—appropriately enough—middle of this three-level mall is the "home and family" floor (the Promenade), which includes two quiet, grown-up, sit-down restaurants, one with a liquor license. They even attract a business-lunch crowd. Thanks to the people of Bridgewater, who cared about things like this a lot, the restaurants actually have windows and the windows offer a view: the county's Watchung Mountains.

Around this complex, in classic Edge City fashion, more hotels and office complexes are growing. But what is far more unusual, the people of Bridgewater have clustered their political and public institutions here, too. Their City Hall is across the road, as are their playing fields, lighted for night games, their housing for the elderly, their library, their low-cost housing, their vocational education center, their mental health facility, their Martin Luther King, Jr., social center for the disadvantaged, their schools, their courts, their highway maintenance yards, their animal shelter, their state police, their local police. The community rooms, where the Boy Scouts meet, are in the mall, facing the parking deck. And yes, there is greenery. A stream still flows through the middle of the property. It is called Mac's Brook. Nobody remembers who Mac was. And it is indeed a brook, not a mighty torrent. But it flows with the blood of citizens who fought to make sure it was not covered by parking lot. Says Griffith, "I am not a big mall person. I go out there four or five times a year." But his daughter loves it, so "my daughter and I have a tradition—she's a sophomore in college now—where we go out there at Christmas. To buy something for my wife. The development has gone better than I thought it would. I feel very good about it."

At that, Griffith has really put his finger on something. Even the former elected official recognizes that whatever the public and political functions of 287 and 78, they are at best ancillary to the identity of the place. For all its groundbreaking politics, 287 and 78 still has no overall leader, no political boundaries that define the place. It is governed only by a patchwork of zoning boards and planning boards and county boards and township boards like Bridgewater's, swirling like gnats—not any elected ruling structure.

Of course, this has not always been bad for cities. For thousands of years, Babylonia was ruled by a Council of the Gods—what Americans would call an Establishment. Perhaps as Edge Cities age and mellow, they will push for formal incorporation to gain powers and perks and titles like Lord High Mayor.

But right now, as Griffith's new Christmas tradition with his daughter indicates, what really shapes the Edge City of 287 and 78 is the historical force of commerce more than governance. After all, Bridgewater Commons *is* a mall. Not that that is any disgrace. Venice, Milan, and Marseille all originally were monuments far more to commerce than to industry. No less an authority than Jane Jacobs, in her landmark work, *The Death and Life of Great American Cities,* notes how commerce is the measure of urbanity: "Diversity is natural to big cities. Classified telephone directories tell us the greatest single fact about cities: the great number of parts."

In fact, if you have any doubts that commerce is a definer of "city," I commend to your attention the retail establishments in the next several hundred miles west of 287 and 78. "There really is no fashion whatsoever from here to Pittsburgh," says David Richmond, Bridgewater Commons' general manager. "I'm not kidding. Lord & Taylor basically has a free swing. People drive tremendous distances. We pull from three states." Nor is this attraction the only source of diversity. The carts set up at the center of the mall are the incubators of the shops of the future, Richmond hopes. Local one-of-a-kind operators sell clever toy blocks in fantastic shapes or hand-made fashions crafted from old tapestry. If they succeed, these entrepreneurs will graduate to renting serious boutique space, Richmond figures. If they go national someday, he knew them when.

For that matter, the most discussed harbinger of civilization when I was in 287 and 78 was the expansion of the King's supermarket chain. If you faxed in your order, the groceries would be waiting for you when you arrived. Its fresh prepared foods were so oriented to the two-career couple that one working woman said with a sigh, "I live there." Most important, the gourmet delicatessen and bakery spread was shockingly close to ethnic-neighborhood quality. (The bagels and lox were "as good as New York—as good as Zabar's," claimed one devotee, not entirely hyperbolically.) One February at a King's at the foot of the ramps to 287 and 78 I encountered soft, fragrant strawberries near a substantial display of crème frâiche. You don't see a lot of crème frâiche in Harrisburg or Altoona. Or, for that matter, in Pittsburgh.

More interesting than the actual commerce that occurs in Edge City is the way its institutions shape our lives. Take the city-shaping category "safety."

For all its newness, Edge City is in some ways more faithful to city traditions than the old downtown. Believe it or not, one of the founding premises of cities—from the beginning of fixed settlements eight thousand years ago—was that you were safer inside one than out. First, people clustered around leaders with a successful track record against wolves, alligators, and big cats. "The archetypal chieftain in Sumerian legend is Gilgamesh: the heroic hunter, the strong protector, not least significantly, the builder of the wall around Uruk," writes Lewis Mumford in *The City in History*. Those evolved into the medieval walls of Vienna, raised against the Turks, as well as walled cities from Avignon to Fez. Walled cities with gates that closed at night existed in China in this century. In America, the walled city was immortalized by frontier stockades like Fort Laramie, Wyoming.

Edge City functions very similarly. "The bedrock attribute of a successful city district is that a person must feel personally safe and secure on the street among all these strangers," writes Jane Jacobs, stressing the importance of safety in her very first chapter. For better or for worse, there is not an endless number of such places today in America. Two that come to mind are our sports stadiums and Edge City's village square—the enclosed shopping mall.

Actually, William Jackson is not so sure about the sports stadiums. "Only when they're winning," he says, thinking of the last time he was at a Giants game at the Meadowlands. "And only when you're in the stadium." Jackson is the senior project manager of 287 and 78's Bridgewater Commons, the man who oversaw its design and construction. "I've walked from the parking lot to the stadium and not felt safe at all. When you walk across the turnpike, there's a very narrow crossover bridge. It's like when you get off the subway in New York and all of a sudden everybody's on the staircase. You don't know who's behind you and who's beside you and what he's going to pull out of your pocket and what he's going to pull out of his pocket. You just kind of go with the flow and hope that nothing happens."

Jackson's professional analysis is germane because state-of-the-art Edge City design pays overwhelming homage to one principle: making women—specifically women—feel safe. In fact, that concern has evolved beyond "safe" and into the art and science of "comfortable," and how people can be made to feel that.

That it works at a place like Bridgewater Commons is unquestionable. Women don't wear their purses in the cross-chest, football-carry, urban-guerrilla mode unless they're doing it for fashion reasons. That's downtown behavior. One crowded Sunday afternoon, toddlers could be seen straggling from their parents much farther than would be comfortable even outdoors in a park, much less a supermarket.

This is not for lack of crime. Shoplifting is always an issue, and some of the mall rats without question deal drugs. One mother recently reported a pair of people at Bridgewater Commons attempting, unsuccessfully, to snatch her stroller with her child and her purse still in it. However, this foiled attempt was viewed as sufficiently unusual to merit major newspaper attention. In such places, there is generally not much violence. Nine million people a year come through the doors of Bridgewater Commons. In the first two years of its existence, the number of assaults reported to the police was two.

This is because Edge Cities have privatized the domains in which large numbers of strangers come together. Edge Cities grew up in the midst of what originally had been residential suburbia. No matter how heterogeneous the population is becoming, the values of the territory's settlers survive. Sociologists who lamented the flight to suburbia claimed the middle class had abandoned the concept of city. They were wrong. The middle class simply built a new kind of city that functions in a Spanish style. It brought its quasi-public spaces in behind high walls, into the atria, open to the sun streaming through the skylights of the courtyards. There, patrol and control can operate at a high level.

"It's pretty hard to walk on my property without seeing some sort of highly visible security," says Jackson. Guards wear uniforms that look like those of the Marines. "I don't want them to be shy and subtle. I want them to be very overt." The gumball-machine lights on the patrol trucks go on at the drop of a lug nut. Even if these paladins are only helping somebody change a flat tire, they do it with stark orange flashers. A local Explorer Scout unit occasionally scans the place from the roof with binoculars. At Christmas, the mall is patrolled on horseback. That's good community relations: the horse is a former member of the Philadelphia Police Department owned by the local animal-control officer who likes to keep his mount's skills sharp by working him amid people and cars. It's also beautiful public relations: children want to pet the horse. The horse patrol has tremendous visibility: the officer sits up so high that he can see and be seen for great distances. The pair can cruise real slow if that seems right. And they are intimidating—it's a big horse.

"You're in a toughie situation," say Jackson. "We're not police and we'll never usurp the police power." But Jackson gladly does everything he can to blur the line. He wants the township's police to have "a knowledge of the center that is very intimate." The chief of police is encouraged to lunch in the food court. The patrol officers are encouraged to park their cruisers in the deck, get out, and walk around. Even the normally desk-bound dispatchers are wooed with awards plaques and private tours. "There's definitely a symbiotic relationship. The police have a substation here. In the mall, sure. I'm trying to encourage that coordination to the $n$th degree. We have a police liaison who just happens to be the juvenile officer for the high schools and the township. Most high school kids, they're very good and well behaved. You will only have a small segment with problems. We recognize them by sight and we ban them. We are private property. Arrest them for trespass and ban them.

"Kids on average will have in their pockets $25 apiece when they walk in the door. We know that. When they leave they are much better than their parents because they leave almost to the penny with nothing. When you stop and think about it, that is very strong economics. You don't want to just arbitrarily throw them out. But being private property, that does give me a lot of rights. High-spirited youth can be escorted off. Quietly, subtly, but out of the picture."

"Sharper Image controls who they let in their store," Richmond picks up. "They have somebody watching who's coming in. Sometimes they have a greeter at the door say 'There's a limit. You can't go in until somebody leaves because there's too many people in there.' Kids get bored and leave. It's their sales philosophy—they want their salespeople to be able to meet, greet, and sell. And they're looking for shoplifters."

Yet no matter how insidious and sophisticated are the methods by which issues of safety are addressed, Richmond and Jackson see it as only part of a much larger issue—what it takes to make people feel comfortable.

They play that game at a very high level. "See that marble floor there?" Richmond asks. "We used to give it a very high, very bright gloss, but we've toned it down." Why, I ask; did women think they were going to slip? Not that, he says. "We found that it brought out feelings of inadequacy. We brought it down to the level of shine on their own floors."

Richmond had earlier given me a serious market segmentation by mall floor. On the floor for the affluent, he said, prime customers on weekdays were wives of those senior executives who were in their late fifties. On Saturday and Sunday, it became the territory of women who were thirty-eight, had 2.3 kids, and were working. I thought he was pulling my leg with data that precise and started to josh him. He cut me off. "I've got my marketing staff if you'd like to talk to them," he said stiffly. They do *not* kid about anything that offers them control.

They take equally seriously the goal of "comfortable." The range of custom-crafted lighting systems for the mall, for example, can be manipulated to create an enormous range of moods, varying according to the time of day, the season, and the crowds. That task is so important that it is handled on a daily basis by Richmond, the manager, himself, not by some flunky. And this devotion to "comfort levels" is not peculiar to Bridgewater Commons or even to malls. In Edge City hotels, offices, and commercial areas, glass elevators and glass stairwells are rarely there for the view out. They are there for the view in. Rape is unlikely in a glass elevator.

Another effort at comfort: the hot trend is to have parking decks with roofs at expensive, "wasted," warehouselike heights, with light levels appropriate to night baseball. Again, the highest goal is to make women feel safe. The older, more "logical" design, with roofs just tall enough for a car antenna, and lights only bright enough to show car keys, has Alfred Hitchcock overtones.

Similarly, the lawn designs of Edge City office campuses also broadcast their values. One can see a stranger approaching for a quarter of a mile. The inside of a soaring glass office lobby is about as public a place as is ever built in Edge City.

Designers who wish to make Edge City more humane frequently advocate that public parks and public places be added to match the great piazzas of the cities of old. That sounds great. But George Sternlieb of the Center for Urban Policy at Rutgers, points out the reason that there's no equivalent of the old urban parks in Edge City. "They don't want the strangers. If it is a choice between parks and strangers, the people there would sooner do without the parks." In Edge City, about the closest thing you find to a public space—where just about anybody can go—is the parking lot. In Edge City, no commercial center could survive if it had as poor a reputation for safety as do the streets of most downtowns. In Edge City, there are no dark alleys.

In the course of my travels, I never did find any sound, practical, financial, technical, physical, or legal reasons why we could not build more nineteenth-century-style downtowns out at 287 and 78 or anywhere else—if we chose. Yet we do not. Edge City is frequently accused of being the result of no planning. Yet a close examination demonstrates that quite the opposite is the case. The controls exercised in the name of "safety" and "comfort" in Edge City are the result of vast amounts of planning. Also design, money, thought, premeditation, listening to people, and giving them exactly what they say they want.

There are homeless people in Edge City, for example. But they are not found sleeping outside the centers of commerce and industry. Our planning, design, and control of public spaces that are really private property make sure of that. Every Christmas there is a national flap over whether malls will allow the Salvation Army into their domains. But it isn't just a question of charity. It's a question of how much we value safety and comfort. In Edge City there is very little truly "public" space. On purpose.

Can Edge City ever be translated into something as fragile as "identity"? Or as selfless as "community"? We enter the amorphous realms of the last three major city shapers: culture, companionship, and religion. Is Edge City a barren, sterile wasteland of the spirit? Is it merely a "slurb," as decried by the architecture critic Ada Louise Huxtable? Does it do nothing but embody "cliché conformity as far as the eye can see?" Does Edge City even deserve to be described by that very word we have inherited from the word "city," the word we use in the English language to describe refinement, learning, and the restraint of base cravings: "civilization"?

A close examination of the everyday lives of a couple like Ron and Nancy Murray is instructive. A careful analysis of how people like the Murrays function in such realms is a significant test of Edge City's claim to urbanity.

The Murrays are worldly people. Nancy Murray has a master's degree in psychology and an M.B.A. She researches what consumers think about AT&T and its products. Her commute from their home in Morristown to the 287 and 78 area in Basking Ridge is twenty minutes. Ron is a computer software consultant who is helping to create a claims system for Blue Cross that will carry it into the next century. His commute to the 287 and 80 area of Florham Park is eighteen minutes.

The Murrays have had a range of experiences with which to compare the texture, spirit, and opportunities of Edge City. Their eleven-month-old son, Gregory, was conceived while they were on vacation in Bali, an island between the Indian Ocean and the Java Sea about as far from 287 and 78 as is possible on this planet. Nancy went to Vassar. Her previous position was with a Wall Street bank. Ron's previous life was with Mobil on Forty-second Street, across from Grand Central. They've lived in Greenwich Village. Ron has voyaged through places like Venezuela, Peru, Brazil, Argentina, and Uruguay. And they do not hate New York. "New York is exciting," says Ron. "It's a place where you walk down the street and things are happening on every corner. Whether good, bad, or indifferent, they *are* happening."

"I have a sister who lives in Boston, and when she comes here we have to go into Manhattan," says Nancy. "She finds it exciting to go to the Village and see the interesting types of people, and go to high-priced restaurants and see the European jet set that isn't in New Jersey. It has a whole diverse culture. It's a little bit of fantasy. It's like a TV show in real life. You have South American dictators' wives at the cosmetics counter in Henri Bendel's. It's not your everyday experience."

In fact, the Murrays are self-described "certified New Yorkers." Ron grew up in the South Bronx and moved to the East Side. He didn't learn to drive until he was twenty-four. We're talking hard core, here. When Ron first started working in Edge City, he would travel an hour and a half, each way, to Fifty-seventh Street, to get his hair cut for $45. But then he gave some local salons a try, and after careful analysis he came to the studied conclusion: "To tell you the truth, there's not much difference between the $45 haircut in New York and the $17 haircut in Morristown." It was an internal struggle, but city boy or not, he finally decided: "To travel an hour and a half each way to get a twenty-five-minute haircut, it's not worth it."

Nancy is equally a product of her upbringing. She grew up in a Boston neighborhood that she compares to Brooklyn. She lived on the West Side of Manhattan so long that she says she forgot how to drive. When she got pregnant after they had moved to Morristown, she says, "I just assumed I was going to have a doctor in New York City and have the baby in the city." It came to her attention, though, talking to the members of her Lamaze class, that "they had their babies here and they were treated better—nicer." She has since learned that Edge City hospitals can be large and sophisticated, with neonatal facilities and medivac choppers and all the modern conveniences. They sometimes find it easier, she's discovered, to attract first-rate interns and residents than downtown hospitals do. In fact, she says, if she gets pregnant again, she thinks it just might be possible that she could find a baby doctor west of the Hudson.

They admit, however, that for all their devotion to Manhattan's virtues, a whole new world, a whole new life, opened up like a flower when Mobil transferred them in the mid-1980s to Texas.

They moved into a brand-new, 2,200-square-foot North Dallas "beautiful sprawling ranch house with lots of room and a nice big yard for the dogs and it was just a so much more pleasant and comfortable way to live," recalls Nancy fondly. "It was tremendous," said Ron. "I lived in a two-room apartment when I was a kid. To me, this—I didn't know that this existed. I much preferred this to living in a two-room apartment in the South Bronx."

They fought the siren song of the late twentieth century to the bitter end, though. These people are tough. They are New Yorkers. "I was going to business school at SMU," recalls Nancy, "and I used to take the bus into downtown Dallas rather than bother driving, and people just thought that was so bizarre. I always used to walk every place and people would see me and they assumed my car had broken down."

It was when they rotated back to Manhattan that their resolve finally crumbled. They sublet an apartment in the Village that their friends considered quite a find. It was, however, "no bigger than that room right here, yeah, the dining room," interjects Ron. "And in New York, that was considered a nice apartment," adds Nancy.

That's what really broke their will. The usual complaints about the dirt, crime, subway, stress, congestion, cost, and taxes of the big city of course were factors. But the idea of having a brand-new house, in which nothing needed fixing, and space— all the space they could ever use, four fifths of an acre of land, four thousand square feet of house, four bedrooms, a sitting room off the master suite—that's what finally got them looking at Morris County. Then came the clincher. In this new realm, they discovered, challenging work was more plentiful than downtown. And what's more, that work was so close to their home that it was almost a return to a younger world. Nancy could actually come home to see her baby—on her lunch hour.

But what about "companionship," I ask them. Companionship is an issue crucial to the quality of cities—the extent to which it offers a choice of associations.

"The women here are very interesting," reports Nancy of her experience. "It's cosmopolitan. The woman across the street used to be a pharmacist and now has her own advertising firm. One woman I got friendly with at the mothers' group is a documentary film producer. In my exercise class I met a few attorneys. Even the women who don't work right now used to, and they're very intelligent and they always have something to say. They go into the city, they see plays, and whatever. People in the

1960s rebelled against the suburbs as sterile. I wasn't rebelling because I hadn't come from there, so it looked pleasant to me. I never quite understood what they were so upset about. The people who live here aren't country bumpkins. You have all religions and races."

"Let me just go up the neighborhood for you," says Ron. "The guy in the house right here is the medical director of Prudential Life Insurance in Newark. The guy in the next house is the head partner of Price Waterhouse in Short Hills. The next guy up is with The Limited. He's British. The Prudential guy is black. The next guy is from Houston. He travels to the Orient a lot for business."

(Earlier, Finn Caspersen had taken that diversity question and shot back, "There's similarity here, sure, but it's no less a similarity than, say, people living on the East Side of New York City. Manhattan is the most parochial area. You talk about diversity in New York City, you're talking about somebody maybe living in the Village.")

Putting on her psychologist's hat, Nancy ventures, "There are younger single people I work with now—they have much more an upbeat social life. A lot of them are engaged and getting married or they're dating. The women I met in Manhattan—a lot were single people who weren't that happy with the situation at this point in life. I think the old idea that [downtown] is an ideal place for single people—it's one thing to be twenty-one; it's another thing to be thirty or forty or fifty and single. Then they'd find out that it wasn't wonderful to just have one dimension to your life. Their jobs became everything to them. They'd be willing to work till ten or eleven at night because they didn't have anything else that took up their energy. That made for quite an unbalanced type of life style, led to neurotic behavior— people would go flipping through my desk to see who was working on what projects. Just really neurotic behavior."

People in Edge City also have changed relationships with nature. They are by no means all benign. But Edge City is a landscape in which more humans are getting closer to other high-order species than at any time in the past century. Edge City is creating a world in which, for the first time since the Industrial Revolution, the majority of the American people— whether they know it or not or like it or not—may soon be sharing their territory with fairly large wild animals. In fact, the New Jersey State Plan, unquestionably the most sophisticated growth-management scheme ever attempted statewide in this country, specifically envisions a world in which "corporate campuses are designed as refuges for wildlife" and "our homes in new subdivisions are clustered and adjoin protected natural streams and wooded areas."

American bald eagles winter only twenty miles from 287 and 78, and they are on the increase, according to Jim Sciascia, the principal zoologist with the Endangered and Non-Game Species Program of the New Jersey Division of Fish, Game, and Wildlife. There are 150 black bears in the mountains not distant. Some weigh six hundred pounds. Where does a six hundred-pound bear sleep? Not only anywhere it wants. But right around Interstate 287. "Sometimes they get disoriented, or they get harassed, and they go up in a tree and won't come down," reports Sciascia.

More than corporate jobs are multiplying in 287 and 78; so are Eastern coyotes. They are bigger than Western ones, in the small German Shepherd range. Red-tail hawks are a common sight sitting in the trees along Interstate 78, staring at the carefully maintained grassland habitats of the shoulder and median, waiting for rabbits, mice, and rodents to make a break for it.

Edge City changes the ecology in ways that can be unexpected. As with any change that happens quickly, specialized species that do not adapt easily are in big trouble. The vesper sparrow, the upland sandpiper, and other grassland birds are endangered by the decline in pasture in the 287 and 78 area. Wood turtles are endangered by the decline in wetland. The bobolink, savannah sparrow, grasshopper sparrow, and bog turtle are threatened. Neotropical songbirds like the wood thrush, oven bird, and vireo require large tracts of continuous forests for their nests; otherwise, they are raided by more competitive birds.

On the other hand, adaptable species like beaver—not to mention raccoon and skunk—are booming. The result is *not* wilderness. What remains is a far less diverse ecology than what was there before. But if you measure it by the standard of city, it is a far more diverse ecology than anything humans have built in centuries, if not millennia.

There is a great deal of "edge," in the biological sense of the word, in Edge City, Sciascia notes. Edge is the zone where different ecologies meet—between woodlands and grasslands, for example, or the wetlands between deep water and dry land. Diversity of life abounds in "edge." Edge City has a lot of it because of the way it has a surprising amount of small grassland and woodlots which add up to tremendously large acreage by any historical standard of city. This abundance of edge is "good for prey population," says Sciascia. Which is why you find predators there. Including rattlesnakes and copperheads. The Garden State, indeed. Right down to the serpents, Edge City does lay legitimate claim to garden-ness. It is not wild. As in agriculture, it is managed and controlled and selected-for by man. Yet it is an urban civilization in which children are at least as likely to be acquainted with fireflies as they are with cockroaches. A relationship with nature is seen as a key element— second only to safety, in the opinion polls—in what makes it a good place to live. You wonder why 76 percent of all Americans consider themselves environmentalists? Perhaps it is because a lot of them live near Edge City.

Sciascia agrees with the New Jersey State Plan that sprawl "compromises the quality of life in our state." He scorns "people who freak out because they don't want to deal with animals" and call him to get rid of critters holed up in their basement or attic. He acknowledges, though, that vastly more numerous are those who "get off on the wildlife." In fact, he says, they lay out so much supplementary food that they contribute to the population explosion, and their neighborhoods offer sanctuary from hunters. There are 150,000 deer in New Jersey. In the Edge City of Princeton, the Institute for Advanced Study had to name a Wildlife Control Officer to recruit bow hunters after the deer population increased by a factor of six.

Throughout human evolution, most people lived in the countryside; few in the city. Only in the last century was that order reversed, and cities became top-heavy. Maybe Edge City is reversing it again. The Machine in the Garden, indeed. Despite the best work of the bulldozers, the hottest topic among foresters today is that oxymoron the "countrified city." The good news is that people who live amidst small woodlots take meticulous care of them. The bad news is that a forest fire would be awesome.

Again, this is an attempt at a new equilibrium. It does not involve moving to Montana, but it is by no means a total rejection of the old downtown. Take another measure of urbanity: culture. Nancy Murray acknowledges that eleven-month-old Gregory has changed her habits. But typically, she said, "we used to go out on Saturday night to a nice restaurant or something; maybe half the time we'd go into Manhattan and half the time we'd just stay out here. Then Sunday every three weeks or so we'd try to go in. I joined some Off-Broadway theater groups where you get tickets for the season. And when I was pregnant I got a subscription to the ballet."

In fact, close questioning of the Murrays reveals that for them Manhattan is primarily an entertainment center. And they are not alone. Tourism is now the number one industry in New York City—ahead of financial services. It is also the fastest growing. This is good news for many of the old city's most fragile and important institutions, from the theater to the symphony.

Many urban visionaries who have nobly devoted their entire lives to reviving the old downtown see the rise of Edge City as nothing but a threat. Every time a corporate headquarters leaves town for literally greener pastures, they bleed. They make it clear that they believe settlement patterns to be a zero-sum game. They assume that to the extent Edge City gains, their beloved downtown—and, by extension, Western civilization—loses.

The more I looked into this, however, the less evidence I found to support their theory. In the last decade, the downtowns have been going through their most striking revivals of this century. From coast to coast—Boston, Philadelphia, Washington, Chicago, San Francisco, Seattle—downtowns are flourishing. Downtowns that no prudent person would have bet a week's pay on twenty years ago—Los Angeles, Baltimore, even, my God, Trenton—are back. Manhattan went from bankruptcy to, for better or for worse, the Gilded Age of Donald Trump.

These downtowns were reborn at exactly the same time as Edge Cities boomed. Maybe it is only a coincidence. But maybe not. It may be that Edge Cities, by relieving the downtowns of trying to be all things to all people, actually did them a favor. The creation of new industry may be inherently messy and chaotic. Maybe moving it out to Edge Cities is what allowed us to look with fresh eyes at our downtowns. Tear up the old docks, for example, now that freighters no longer tie up there. Return the waterfront to the people. Build a South Street Seaport or a Battery Park City. Transform the old warehouses and lofts into condominiums and shops. It is as if our downtowns have become antiques, in the best sense of that word. Edge Cities may represent the everyday furniture of our lives, but we recognize the downtowns as something to be cosseted and preserved. The *New Yorker* magazine writer Tony Hiss has even suggested that it was misguided for Manhattan to compete with its surrounding Edge Cities for so much new office space in the 1980s. He feels that the old city would have been better served by preserving the sense of place that had been layered up there over the generations. "Tourists don't like to visit office districts," he points out in *The Experience of Place*. "Their interests are in seeing safe, beautiful, interesting places—places that afford vivid and memorable experiences."

Whatever the case, the greatest glory of our old downtowns—their world-class museums and theaters—have been injected with new life. The more Edge Cities boomed, the more different places were created within the metropolitan region in which to locate high-paying work places. To the extent that this provided more opportunities for well-to-do people to make a living in the area, it yielded more patrons overall for downtown institutions of minority high culture like opera. If it were not for the attractions of 287 and 78, the Murrays might not be buying tickets to Off-Broadway. They might still be in Texas, fundraising for a ballet there.

Edge Cities may even be helping with the social problems of the old downtowns. The corporations of elite Princeton-Route 1 are taking an unprecedented, even flabbergasting, interest in the schools of gritty-city Trenton. They now realize that is where their future labor force will come from. Trenton is also a source of affordable housing. Huge old Victorians that, in the mid-1970s, were viewed as worthless dinosaurs, fetching $22,000 apiece, are now valued at more than $220,000. It defies description how enormous a change this is in only fifteen years in this once bombed-out burg. It was started by the scores of people who refused to let the old city die, no matter the personal cost. It was further enabled by a state government that would not abandon the state capital, in which George Washington clobbered the Hessians after crossing the Delaware.

But the renaissance could not have happened without money. And the source of jobs in America today is Edge City. That is why the future of downtown would actually appear to be secured by Edge City. Edge City pushes wealth back into blighted areas of the old downtown as its companies seek less expensive housing and labor. Downtown also offers Edge City visitors the amenities of a place built in an earlier era. This is especially attractive for the young and single and those otherwise without children in need of the kind of stimulation only a full-blown arts district can provide.

You can see this symbiosis starting between the Edge City of Cherry Hill and the mean streets of Camden, as with 287 and 78 and both New Brunswick and Allentown. It is hardly a panacea; jobs and housing should be in better balance. But many inner-city residents have found that making long journeys to jobs in Edge City is better than having no jobs at all.

After all, when it comes to the location of our homes, we Americans have been voting with our feet for some time now. Eighty-eight percent of all Americans live outside what has traditionally been defined as a big city—the political boundaries of a place at least the size of El Paso, with half a million population. (Only 8 percent of all Americans live in politically defined cities with more than a million population, like Los Angeles.)

Thus, it could be that without Edge City underpinning our society, the plight of the old downtowns would have been immeasurably worse. After all, metros like Phoenix have demonstrated that you can have many successful Edge Cities without much of a downtown. But places like St. Louis show that heroic efforts to revive downtown are only marginally successful in the absence of the economics that vigorously produce Edge Cities.

In fact, the relationship of Edge City to the old downtown may be parallel to how most people in this country experience the performing arts. Recordings will never replace live performances. In the late twentieth century, though, we usually meet human needs by commodifying them. Even the most dedicated disciple of Mozart buys more compact discs than performance tickets. If an American today has a yen for the finest acting, she'll most commonly go out and rent some at a video store, like any sensible human being.

This is certainly what the Murrays do. "I like to get one foreign film for the weekend," says Nancy. "*Pelle the Conqueror* was one I had out two weeks ago. This week it's a Chinese film, *Eat a Bowl of Tea.* I used to really like going to the ballet. Now they have some good ballet tapes. Gregory loves it. The music calms him down if he's cranky. I waltz around with him."

This is not to say there are no live performances in Edge City. The local brags include the Shakespeare Festival at Drew, the Metropolitan Opera performing at Waterloo Village, the McCarter Theatre at Princeton, and the Playwrights Theatre in Madison. But even if the commodity you require is to have your soul lifted, the place to go is Bridgewater Commons. Select-a-Ticket inside the main entrance one weekend was offering access to *The Phantom of the Opera* on Broadway, Eric Clapton at the Hartford, Connecticut, Civic Center, Cher at the Sands in Atlantic City, the International Opera Festival at Giants Stadium in the Meadowlands, and Willie Nelson, Waylon Jennings, Kris Kristofferson, and Johnny Cash together at the Nassau Coliseum.

If the arts have any real problem in Edge City, thinks the urban designer Patricia L. Faux, it is simply that the founders of Edge City aren't dead yet. Palaces of the arts usually aren't built until the crusty old buzzards croak and the children give the money away.

Americans today spend more money attending cultural events than they do on spectator sports. That is way up from 1970, when, according to the National Endowment for the Humanities, we spent twice as much on sports. This increase is concurrent with the rise of Edge City, as well as the dispersal of the American population to the South and West. It would seem logical, then, that if there can be a serious dance company called Ballet Oklahoma, which there is, or an Alabama Shakespeare Festival that attracts 150,000 people, it's possible to locate high culture in Edge City.

There are two kinds of cultural activity, Faux points out. Active, when the art is being created. And passive, when it is being shown off. Many medium-sized downtowns, such as Fort Worth and Louisville, are setting up "culture districts" designed to

support artists both as they are working and as they are displaying their art. She sees no reason that the idea won't be worked
into Edge City in the future. It wouldn't surprise her, in fact, if
an Edge City culture district ended up looking like a mall. After
all, Edge City is the creation of people with money. If they want
"culture," they'll doubtless get it. Especially if they're nursing a
nagging inferiority complex, and they think of a palace of
culture, locally applied, as a hot, soft, moist poultice on their
egos.

The glitziest temple of high culture built in California in the
last decade, in fact, is the $73-million, three thousand-seat Per-
forming Arts Center in the Edge City of Costa Mesa, in Orange
County, near Irvine. It was completely privately financed. You
can almost toss a croissant to it from South Coast Plaza—the
most lavish mall in America, which does more retail business in a
day than does all of downtown San Francisco. And that is not a
coincidence, I think. The Orange County Performing Arts Center is across from the first mall in North America in which I
encountered valet parking.

Compared to "culture" and "companionship," the seventh
definer of cities is a less comfortable fit in Edge City. It is "religion"—that binder of people together into congregations.

Lewis Mumford saw the start of cities in the most distant times
in cemeteries. In their wanderings, dawn humans first began to
distinguish themselves from other animals in the ritualistic
burial of their dead and their desire to return to those burial
places. Mumford writes:

In these ancient paleolithic sanctuaries, as in the first grave mounds
and tombs, we have, if anywhere, the first hints of civic life, probably
well before a permanent village settlement can even be suspected.

This was no mere coming together during the mating season, no
famished return to a sure source of water or food, no occasional
interchange, in some convenient tabooed spot, of amber, salt, jade, or
even perhaps tools. Here, in the ceremonial center, is an association
dedicated to a life more abundant: not merely an increase of food, but
an increase of social enjoyment through the fuller use of symbolized
fantasy and art, with a shared vision of a better life, more meaningful as

well as aesthetically enchanting, such a good life in embryo as Aristotle would one day describe in the *Politics:* the first glimpse of Utopia.

In Edge Cities, there is still the occasional cemetery here and there. But if it is ever seen as "the first glimpse of Utopia," it is only a wistful real estate agent heaving a sigh, recalling the day when land was so cheap here, people buried their dead in it.

Churches are the same way. They are not anathema to Edge Cities. One Houston developer approves of the one next to the Galleria as a "noncompeting low-density use." But the closest thing I've seen to a cathedral in Edge City is Buckhead Plaza, north of downtown Atlanta. You don't every day see twenty-story, 400,000-square-foot office buildings like this with flying buttresses, accent-spike gargoyles, and a gabled copper roof. If, in fact, one argues that a city is always a monument to the worship of something, it is clear that Edge City worships a prevailing god not the same as the one celebrated in the design of Jerusalem, Rome, Mecca, Kyoto, and Beijing.

But does this really mark any change in America?

While the Pilgrims came to America in 1620 to worship as they chose—and, even more important, to prevent other people from worshiping as *they* chose—that has rarely been the end-all of other American settlements. Cotton Mather wrote of the Massachusetts minister who urged a congregation on the rocky coast of Maine to "walk in the paths of righteousness and piety so that they would not 'contradict the main end of Planting this Wilderness.' " At which point a prominent resident blurted out, "Sir, you are mistaken. You think you are Preaching to the People at the Bay; our main End was to catch Fish."

Just so, the catching of fish has always been the purpose of cities of North America. Most Americans moved out to the frontier to get rich. It's unusual to an American to think of a city as primarily a focus of religion. Salt Lake City has our only celebrated Temple Square.

Americans are about as religious today as they have ever been. Overwhelmingly, they tell pollsters they believe in God. They still flock to the ministry. To be sure, our elites tend to do neither. But that just results in a relationship between the ruling class and the masses in America that demographers have described as the spiritual equivalent of "a Sweden on top of an India."

Even for those Americans who are religious, however, close proximity to a physical monument to God seems not all that important. It is antique to hear a person describe himself in terms of "parish." A large modern church functions like nothing so much as a spiritual shopping mall. It is surrounded by a very large parking lot located astride a good network of roads. If the traffic patterns yield an affordable location in the midst of Edge City, then so be it—the church becomes part of the city.

Otherwise, and far more typically, there is apparently no reason for any "ceremonial centers" dedicated to a "life more abundant" to be at the core of Edge City.

Those are built in residential areas.

The land is cheaper there.

The thick wooden floor planks resound with a nice thunk as one crosses the covered bridge over Mac's Brook at Bridgewater Commons. Even though spring is only a promise and the Watchung Mountains are a cold gold in the late afternoon sun, the sound of the brook is soothing. It meanders through reeds and prickly snare and cedar and low willow in an unpremeditated way. Trails lead off this way and that, but they are low to the ground, arched and domed by vines. They were clearly shaped by animals no taller than a doe.

Down the path from the bridge and the water there is a good-sized gazebo of pressure-treated wood. At first, still in the thrall of the spirit of the stream, my heart sank at the sight of graffiti. But on closer examination, the marks turned out to be not so much the work of vandals. They were more like that of healthy young primates marking their space. "Lie here and dream," somebody had written over one of the benches that edge the interior of the octagon. I did. The sky was moving. Grasses waved. There was no one else around. It was very peaceful.

For all the messages on the gazebo, surprisingly few were coarse. Many invoked the names of revered bands. Others were wry. First message: "I ♥ Heather—From Larry." Below it: "I ♥ Larry Forever." Third line: "He likes a different Heather."

But most of the writing reflected attempts to grapple with the world we have built for these kids:

"And I wear black on the outside because black is how I feel on the inside, and if I seem a little strange, well that's because I am."

"You love to say you've loved, but in all reality you have no concept of what that means."

Pomposity was punctured: First graffito: "Words of wisdom: Be excellent to each other." Second line: "Other words of wisdom: Don't have sex at this gazebo."

Yet overwhelmingly, the wisdom was that of teens from time immemorial:

"Leslie is childish."

"When all else fails, blame it on Sean."

The covered bridge and gazebo at Bridgewater Commons don't look like much from the food court on the third floor, or from the ring road at thirty miles an hour. From those perspectives they seem so small, so peripheral to the forces of Mammon, as to appear almost forlorn. In fact, as Susan Gruel drove me around, she pointed out the greenspace that had been saved here, and the outdoor plaza that was fought for there, and the way the mall had been turned around so that its main entrance would face not the interstate, but the small road that brings the local people here. She told the story of the little concert pit that was built over to the side of the mall. She first saw one just like it in a vest-pocket park when she was visiting her sister in Oklahoma City. People were sitting all around its steps, playing guitars in an ad lib concert, and she figured that would be great for Bridgewater, so she brought the idea home. The concert pit was empty this day, however. Afraid that, through the eyes of a stranger, it didn't look like much, she got quieter and quieter. Then she said, softly, of the amenities she and so many others had fought for: "I guess it depends on the way you look at it, whether you see it or not. But it was there, at least on the plans."

"Edge City is an adaptable creature," said Pamela Manfre later. She is a Washington consultant on the subject with whom I had been discussing my travels. "It fixes itself. It redefines itself. It's almost as if we're working out equations. We 'solve for' problems. We 'solve for' commutes. And then we 'solve for' sterility. And then we 'solve for' choice."

Manfre's vote of confidence came with a little added weight that day, because, although she had made partner at the age of twenty-eight, running the national capital office of a high-flying coast-to-coast firm, she announced she had just quit. She couldn't totally explain it herself, she said. She was, she insisted, the staunchest of free-enterprise Republicans. It was by no means that she'd become a bleeding heart or anything. But it had finally dawned on her that this affordable housing thing out there in Edge City was going to have to get solved. People had to take responsibility. If people like her didn't do it, nobody else was going to. She thought she could see clearly the path that needed to be taken; she was bubbling over with plans. So what the hell. She was going for it.

"We make a lot of mistakes, but we learn," she concluded. "And in this culture, we let that happen more than in those with governments that try to protect people from their mistakes. We just go out there and do it."

One hopes that's true, and I have to admit that at the end of my visit with Susan Gruel, I found myself almost involuntarily stepping out of the reporter role to buck her up a little, to tell her that I did not think her efforts to honor the spirit of her place had been in vain. For Bridgewater Commons, after all, is a first-generation vision. It is an experimental effort in a national work in progress. Who knows whether it will ever be repeated. Who cares? The important part is that it was put together by individual citizens of no particular authority who were determined to bring life to their world. They didn't know that there might be "experts" out there who thought it was impossible. But then again, they weren't operating at the same scale as the experts. They were simply trying to come up with a better center for the people of their Edge City.

With this in mind, I walked back down Susan Gruel's park-bench-lined courtyard that separated the parking lots as Moses did the Red Sea. And I went back and ran my hand over the fieldstone that the people of Bridgewater had insisted be used to build the footings for the covered bridge. That's a material widely used in the walls of these parts, they had said, stubbornly, and they wanted some in their new place. They didn't much care whether the experts thought it fit into the design of the mall. Any more than they were going to let anyone laugh at Mac's

Brook and say it didn't amount to spit, and it should just be buried in a culvert. Those experts, after all, have come and gone, and Mac's Brook and the people of Bridgewater flow on.

And so do the kids. The kids like that gazebo their elders cared enough to build for them near the mall, and they have made it their own. They have noticed that Mac's Brook has a nice wild feel to it, and surprising solitude, even if you can occasionally pick up the distant smell of french fries. It even looks like a stream by which it would be good to read a book.

In fact, I wouldn't be surprised if one spring day some outcast, some kid who doesn't fit in to the food-court crowd, even discovers Susan Gruel's little concrete music hollow.

He might even bring his guitar.

And sit down and begin to play.

# 3

BOSTON

Edge City Limits

Form ever follows function.
—*Louis Sullivan, 1886*

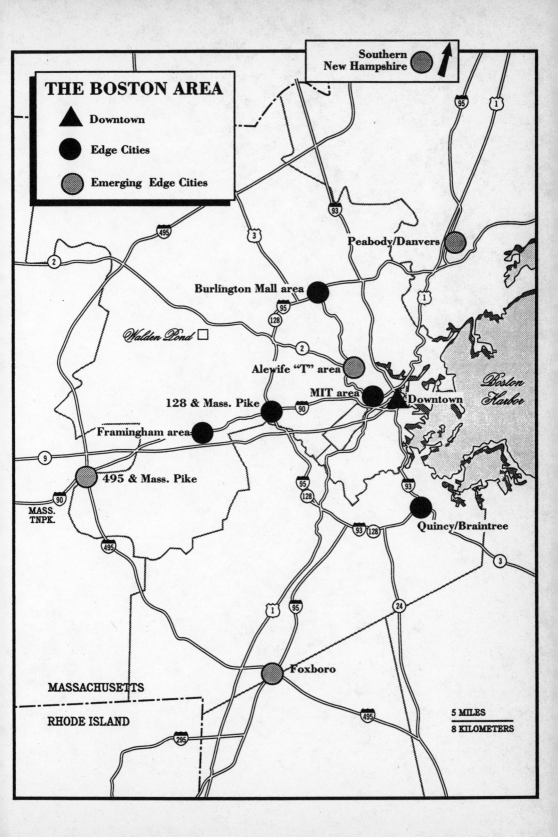

THE BOSTON AREA

▲ Downtown

● Edge Cities

◉ Emerging Edge Cities

Southern New Hampshire

95  1

93

3

495

2

Peabody/Danvers

Burlington Mall area

95

128

Walden Pond

2

Alewife "T" area

128 & Mass. Pike

MIT area

Downtown

Boston Harbor

90

Framingham area

9

495 & Mass. Pike

90

MASS. TNPK.

495

95

128

93

128

Quincy/Braintree

93

3

1  95

24

MASSACHUSETTS

RHODE ISLAND

295

Foxboro

495

5 MILES
8 KILOMETERS

TWICE AS FAR from downtown Boston as Walden Pond, yet close enough to the Massachusetts Turnpike that the road's rumble always sounds like a waterfall, there is a town-house subdivision called Lordvale.

The entrance to Lordvale is distinguished by what its developer is pleased to call an "active water feature." That is a collection of trucked-in rocks, over which water is pumped. The sound of this new waterfall is not as pervasive as that of the Pike, but its size does catch the eye of the highway's drivers as they speed by.

There are perhaps two hundred town houses in Lordvale, arranged in eight-packs. The rhythm of their façades is garage door, front door, front door, garage door—each unit being the mirror image of the one on either side. They are stained in variations of two colors—beige and gray.

Given that Lordvale is forty-two miles into the countryside from Boston Common—a commute of more than one hour each way—it is heartening that the development pays some small homage to Henry David Thoreau's "life in the woods." Several dozen trees still stand on Lordvale's once-forested slope. Boulders have been added to accent the curving drives. There is even an assemblage of oval rocks that has been carefully stacked vertically, then horizontally, for no discernible reason. The residents instantly dubbed it Suburban Stonehenge.

For all that, Lordvale is not at all what most people have come to expect from suburbia. For one thing, there are few lawns. The patches where one might expect grass to grow after the snow melts turn out to be brown year round. They have been covered by wood chips. Wood chips are low maintenance. It is assumed

that the buyers of town houses at Lordvale will be young, struggling, dual-career couples. Where would they find time to mow
lawns?

More disconcerting than the lack of lawns, however, is the
density of this development. Although there is no "town" for
miles, these "town homes" are so crowded together that, as in a
nineteenth-century city, there are few places for an active toddler to play outdoors, other than the street.

People who still come equipped with pre–Edge City expectations of what a suburb is, are amazed by places like Lordvale.
They drive out from the old downtowns into what they think of
as the wide-open spaces of the country, only to find themselves
confronted by town houses jammed together at a distant exit,
miles beyond even the outer beltways. Who would want to live
"like that," these people invariably say, "out here"? Well, Gilbert and Caron Merrill, and their toddler, Wyatt, live "like that,
out here," in Grafton, Massachusetts.

Their Lordvale town house is to the Information Age what the
tenements of Boston were to the Industrial Age: it is worker
housing. As such, it has become one of the distinctive visual
marks of the new order marked by Edge Cities. Housing like the
Merrills' offers exquisite lessons in the forces, worldwide, that
make Edge Cities grow—or die.

In the last quarter of the twentieth century, Boston was a
fascinating place in which to examine the dynamics of growth—
as well as the backlash created by its limits. At more than 350
years, Boston's is the most mature metropolitan area in the
United States. It was also the first area in the East to calve Edge
Cities the way glaciers do icebergs. From the dawn of the computer age, the Edge Cities along Route 128 became synonymous
with the romance of high technology. Companies that made
history clustered around the verdant interstates—Digital, Lotus,
Wang. The Edge City-driven Massachusetts Miracle of the 1980s
in one decade lifted New England from the poorest region in
America to its richest. In 1988, New Hampshire posted the
lowest state unemployment rate ever recorded: 2.0 percent. Vermont was second in the nation, with 2.5 percent. Connecticut
tied for third at 3.0. Rhode Island, at 3.1, was tied for fourth.
Massachusetts, at 3.4, was sixth. Some business names that
cropped up in Bangor, Maine—of all places—were Advanced

Data Systems, Systems Management Services, Professional Financial Consultants of New England. In 1986, grim Worcester got a fashion magazine. Yes, Worcester. It was called *Prelude.*

This kind of extraordinary growth also resulted in the Boston area being among the first to discover the limits to Edge City in the twenty-first century. Despite—and because of—the velocity of this economic boom, Boston's growth imploded as the 1990s began. Growth was stagnant. The actual number of jobs shrank. How could such a brainy, high-technology boom collapse? A central reason is that the region from northern Rhode Island to southern New Hampshire simply ran out of capacity. There were few terrific places left to put new jobs and expanding companies.

Edge Cities are living, growing things. They are ecologies. By examining the first metropolitan area that, for better or for worse, really began to choke off the supply of what they require, it is possible to determine what Edge Cities' most important life mechanisms are. This, in turn, makes it possible to discern how Edge Cities can be shaped by individual and government decisions, both inadvertent and purposeful.

To understand these limits, says David L. Birch, you have to understand growth. And for that, he claims, first you have to understand entrepreneurs. Birch is director of MIT"s Program on Corporate Change and Job Creation. He is also president of Cognetics, Incorporated, a consulting company that tracks growth nationwide.

Cognetics' headquarters, as it happens, is located in the Edge City growing up around the Alewife T (for Transit) station in Cambridge northwest of Harvard and MIT. Its office building has an atrium, indoor trees, blond wood, and hanging vines; the men's rooms have built-in blow-dryers. This is the part of Cambridge's uptown where a rail line connects with the Concord Turnpike—Route 2—which leads out to the high-rent suburbs near Walden Pond.

When a person growing a company starts looking around for places to put his people and his jobs, says Birch, he invokes the Rubber Band Principle of Edge City Location.

Imagine you've got a pegboard, says Birch, on which has been drawn the map of your region. Wherever on that map there exists something that is important for your business—an airport, for example—drive a peg. If affordable housing for your workers is important, drive a peg to the north, where you can find that. Easy access to your most important clients? Drive pegs to the west, where they are located. Access to universities? Drive pegs to the east. Fenway Park? Cape Cod? A mansion for the chief executive officer? More pegs.

Now, imagine you have a metal ring. Imagine that knotted around it are rubber bands of varying strengths.

Here's the trick.

Hook a rubber band around each peg that you've driven into the board. The more important the factor (peg) is to you and the closer you want to be to it, the more heavy-duty should be the rubber band that you attach to that peg.

Now, with all the rubber bands stretched out and hooked over all the pegs, let the ring go. When everything stops quivering, examine where the metal ring stabilizes. It will be over the point that is the best place for you to put your company. That place is the best compromise; the one that puts you as close as possible to everything you say you value.

This ingenious metaphor explains a great deal about why Edge Cities are located where they are. If, in the 1980s, you wanted relatively low land costs, attractive housing, good roads, and proximity to O'Hare International Airport, the metal ring would have settled for you in the Chicago metropolitan area somewhere around Schaumburg or Oakbrook, well west of downtown Chicago. That's why those areas became huge Edge Cities.

If you wanted to be near the most prestigious residential areas of Houston plus the medical research centers plus the towers of its downtown, the ring would have settled for you over the Galleria area.

Tysons Corner, Virginia, is not only in the midst of highly valued housing and roads; it is halfway between Dulles Airport and the Pentagon.

In the Boston area, however—and in other metropolitan areas where the problems of growth became crises in the late 1980s—the Rubber Band Method began to collapse. Therefore, so did growth. No matter how you configured your metaphorical pegs, and no matter how far you stretched your rubber bands, there were few places left for the metal ring to stabilize that did not prove to have fatal flaws. Growth simply had to move elsewhere, or not take place.

To be sure, forces other than geography were at work in the resultant Massachusetts Massacre. Edge Cities do not *create* wealth and jobs. They enable them. Edge Cities are dedicated attempts to clear away obstacles from the path of growth. For growth to exist, however, the world has to desire whatever it is you are producing. And in the Boston area, firms like Wang and Data General, which had bet their futures on pricy midsized computers, found their market in the 1990s cannibalized by powerful and flexible personal computers. Outfits like Raytheon and General Dynamics, which rose with the Reagan military budget, also hurt when it contracted. Politicians like erstwhile presidential aspirant Michael Dukakis, who did not control spending when times were good, were clobbered by budget deficits when the boom years inevitably slowed.

Nonetheless, there are other quite comparable metropolitan areas in America that did not go the way of Boston. In other places, the natural cycle continued. Older companies faded, but they were replaced by new start-ups or concerns that moved in from elsewhere. In the Boston area, however, existing companies found it difficult to grow—the fastest growing high-technology companies in America in the late 1980s were typified by Microsoft, which thrived in Seattle, not the Bay State, and Compaq, which boomed not on 128, but in Houston. And moving a new company to the area from another region was a nightmare. The cost of everything from power to sewers to car insurance became prohibitive. "In almost every category we're first or second highest in the country," noted Anthony J. Ferrera, chief of the Boston office of the Bureau of Labor Statistics. The Boston area essentially declared itself full. The bust, therefore, came. And once again, Boston became a fascinating laboratory —this time, in which to watch Edge City Limits.

Overbuilding is as old as the Pyramids. The historian Frederick Lewis Allen wrote about Manhattan in the 1920s: "The confidence had been excessive. Skyscrapers had been overproduced. In the spring of 1931, it was reliably stated that some 17 percent of the space in the big office buildings of the Grand Central district, and some 40 percent uptown, was not bringing in a return; financiers were shaking their heads."

Just so, since as much as 80 percent of the growth that was financed during the roaring real estate years of the 1980s occurred in Edge City, one might expect to find most of the empty buildings there today. But that is not generally the case. In Boston in 1989, for example, the downtown area had an average vacancy rate, compared with its Edge City competitors. Some of the more far out and hence more speculative locations were worse off than downtown. But the most prestigious and convenient Edge City locations were healthier than downtown. This was typical of most markets. High vacancy rates were not a function of whether a location was in Edge City or downtown. Vacancies were highest wherever the speculation had been greatest—and thus where it had been most easy for developers to overshoot the market. Manhattan's downtown—the Wall Street area—was a victim of speculative excess, as were the Edge Cities of Phoenix. The truly healthy places were those which had grown at only a moderate, boring pace during the boom—the Interstate 494 Edge City outside Minneapolis, for example. At the same time, the Chicago market became so comparatively healthy that in 1991 it passed midtown Manhattan in having the highest rents in the nation.

This is why the lessons of the growth years are the keys to Edge City limits. Consider the distribution of Edge Cities in the Boston area. There are five of them, not counting downtown. Five more are in the embryonic stage.

The map of the Boston area makes the hearts of planning academics go pittypat. It is as close to their theoretical ideal as exists in the real world. At its center is a thriving downtown. As long ago as 1858, the homage accorded that core was so overheated that Oliver Wendell Holmes noted, "Boston State-House is the hub of the solar system. You couldn't pry that out of a Boston man if you had the tire of all creation straightened out for a crowbar." Bostonians, naturally, completely missed Holmes's irony and blithely nicknamed Boston "the Hub."

No matter. Boston's quality of life is justifiably renowned, with beaches and mountains close, neighborhoods on a human scale, universities and cultural attractions of the first order, and, of course, the existential pleasures of the Red Sox. In the 1980s, downtown showed all the marks of prosperity. It was ripped up for tall buildings from Quincy Market to the Back Bay. But its future, too, was to be controlled by exactly the same limits as its Edge Cities.

Around this hub, in an arc with a ten-mile radius, the Boston area has one of the first beltways built in America—Route 128. About twenty miles beyond 128, there is a second beltway— I-495. That one describes a half circle from almost–Rhode Island to almost–New Hampshire. This outer beltway is highly unusual in American urban areas: it is not just on the drawing boards; it is actually built.

The two beltways are regularly intersected by almost a dozen roads that lead like spokes from downtown into the heartland.

It is at each of the intersections of circulating beltways and spokes that, in principle, an Edge City should have sprung up. That is because each such meeting of two high-capacity freeways can be reached by an astounding number of people. The developer's rule of thumb is this: a mall should have 250,000 people within a fifteen-minute drive of it. The quarter of a million people the developers want within a ten-mile radius is more than live in Las Vegas or Des Moines. That's a lot of people in a fairly small place. It should come as no surprise that such intersections have attracted urbanization. It worked the same way when St. Louis rose at the intersection of the Missouri River and the Mississippi.

David Birch of Cognetics thinks that the first big corporations that moved out to Edge City environs did so primarily for the advantage of being near the interchange that allowed people to get there from home, and from there to the world. They did not care about being near other companies. Their relationship to one another was distinctly secondary. The AT&Ts and the IBMs of this world didn't *have* to be near any other company—they brought all their support troops with them, in-house. They didn't require proximity to outside lawyers or accountants or computer experts, of which the downtowns were full. It was just a pleasant coincidence, Birch believes, that these corporations ended up being near one another. They grouped around locations to which it was most easy for people to get. The seeds of Edge City were accidentally sown.

It was the small and medium firms, Birch says, that created true Edge Cities at these intersections. Outfits too small to support a company cafeteria, for example, were the ones that stimulated an appetite for nearby restaurants. They were the outfits that fostered the need for yet other small new entrepreneurial companies, from office-supply houses to helicopter services. They were the shops that gave rise to Edge Cities.

One might expect, then, that Edge Cities would grow up wherever there was a high-capacity interchange. That, however, is precisely what never happens. Ten major roads cross 128, but only four Edge Cities have grown on that inner beltway.

They include the considerable skyline of Quincy-Braintree. It is a backshop Edge City, meaning that it is full primarily of people performing routine functions on computers. With the rise of the chip it is no longer crucial for, say, reservations agents to occupy the same expensive headquarters office space as high executives. So corporations have begun to uncouple themselves. In this case, accounting and filing departments have floated away from downtown, down the T line to where the Southeast Expressway meets 128, closer to southern Massachusetts, where housing is less prestigious and more affordable. Since that means fewer drivers on the suicidal approach to downtown and Logan International Airport from the south that is I-93, everybody's happy.

To the west, there is 128 and the Mass Pike, the largest Edge City in the Boston area and one of the oldest in the country, dating back thirty years. This is the one that really made 128 "America's Technology Road," as the highway signs read. It sprawls around some of the oldest suburbs in the world. Bostonians commuted by rail in 1850. There were three railroads into Boston before the first locomotive pulled into London. Brookline in 1873 became the first place in America to reject annexation by a major city, thereby creating the concept of suburb. Those who view suburbs as not progressive may take heart in learning that George McGovern got more votes in one election there than Ronald Reagan got in two. A vote was recently taken in Brookline on whether the annual town meeting should be opened with the pledge of allegiance to the flag. The flag lost.

Just a few miles up the beltway, in the northwest, is an Edge City in the area where 128 is met by Routes 3 and I-93 north. It is among the most dense of any Edge City in the Boston region. It is centered on the Burlington Mall and the famed Lahey Medical Center.

Then there is the Peabody-Danvers area in the northeast quadrant of 128, where America's East Coast freeway, I-95, resumes its path straight up the coast toward Maine.

Beyond 128, there are two Edge Cities emerging, and they are both on the same spokelike road: the Massachusetts Turnpike heading west toward the Berkshires and Albany. One is located where that highway crosses the outer beltway, at 495 and the Pike, sometimes also known by the name of the nearby town of Westborough. Data General is headquartered there. The other emerging Mass Pike Edge City is between the first and second beltways, near Framingham.

Two other Edge Cities are inside the beltways, in Cambridge. These, growing on top of a pre-existing settlement in the orbit of an old downtown, are comparable to Washington's Bethesda–Chevy Chase or Atlanta's Buckhead. One is near MIT and Kendall Square, right across the Charles River from downtown. The other is at the far end of Cambridge, around that Alewife T.*

Some apparently great locations for Edge Cities, though, have not panned out—in central Cambridge near Harvard, for example, or where I-95 meets 128 to the south. Others, meanwhile, are still in their embryonic stage—I-495 at southern I-95 near Foxboro, or the Golden Triangle area of southern New Hampshire by Manchester, Nashua, and Portsmouth.

For the spread of Edge Cities is hardly random. Nor is it infinite. The critics of Edge Cities who describe them as a cancer on the land are wrong. Cancer is life without laws. Edge City is more rational. It has not only patterns and rules but limits to its growth.

The five Edge City limits are:

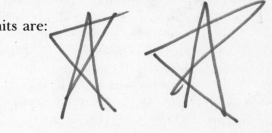

- Insurmountability,
- Affordability,
- Mobility,
- Accessibility, and
- Nice.

In Boston, the first limit you have to contend with is Insurmountability.

---

* For a more detailed explanation of the various kinds of Edge Cities see Chapter 4.

Boston's beltways would work a lot better if they had an eastern half. But they don't. And they won't. Because east of downtown Boston is a whole lot of deep Insurmountability—Boston Harbor. Other places have similar fixes, simply less well understood.

It is no news that Los Angeles has the Pacific to the west and rugged mountains in almost every other direction. They don't call it the Los Angeles Basin for nothing; it's built like a sink. That's why it captures smog as well as it does. But less widely comprehended, until John McPhee memorably explained it in *The Control of Nature,* is that in Los Angeles, the mountains are not standing still, waiting to be built on. The ten thousand-foot San Gabriels are the steepest and highest mountain range abutting any major metropolitan area in the world, *and they're getting taller every day.* The tectonic plates are still pushing them up. That's why Los Angeles has earthquakes.

Mountains that fight back are a prime example of planetary Insurmountability. They really do limit your options. So do excessive snows in the industrial Northeast, or floodplains in the Gulf of Mexico, or lack of water in the intermountain West. Miami has dolphins on one side and alligators on the other. That's a problem. In the Chesapeake Bay area, one novel piece of Insurmountability is jellyfish. There is considerable development on the shores of that beautiful and fragile estuary. But it would have been far greater and doubtless more high-rise had not the region's most popular resorts ended up three hours farther east, all the way to the Atlantic Coast. That's because people won't swim in waters where they get stung.

Planetary Insurmountability is not an absolute barrier. Civil engineers fight Insurmountability with bridges and tunnels and dams and bulldozers. Enterprising capitalists, if they can get away with it, will cantilever their developments out over oceans. Condominiums built on jetties, offices built on piers, and houseboats tied up to docks are all just extensions of the local real estate market into shallow water. Big pleasure boats tied up to marinas are simply the vacation-home industry flourishing in the absence of dry land. The story is oft told of the Florida speculator newly informed that his land was under water. Came this thoughtful reply: "How deep?"

The filling in of wetlands is a classic example of developers shading Insurmountability. The Back Bay neighborhood of Boston used to be a bay in the back of town—until it was filled in. But wetlands are also an acute example of how Insurmountability can be created by citizen action. It is technically possible to build an Edge City in a marsh. But fertile, precious, and threatened ecologies have become such a cause that George Bush promised in 1989 there would be no net loss of them in his administration. This caused no little consternation among oil drillers, road builders, and developers.

Societal Insurmountability obviously surrounds such places as the Cape Cod National Seashore. No matter how much money is tendered, that sand will never be developed. One presumes. Other societal Insurmountabilities surround reservoirs, wildlife refuges, and parks. Especially in an area like Boston's, where Paul Revere rode and the Minutemen farmed and Emerson strolled with Hawthorne, Insurmountability surrounds historical sites.

These add up. It is now not uncommon to have more than 50 percent of a metropolitan area off limits to Edge City development because of Insurmountable obstacles that no amount of money will be allowed to overcome. It has been calculated that as much as 88 percent of the land in the San Francisco area is untouchable. This gets us back to the Rubber Band Principle. If your hypothetical metal ring stabilizes right on top of the Buzzards Bay Light or Harvard Yard, forget it. Start over again. Your allegedly ideal location is unavailable.

This issue of planetary, emotional, and class-based Insurmountability shades into the second Edge City limit: Affordability.

Edge City cannot grow unless and until it creates jobs. And it is pointless to create jobs if there are no workers to fill them. Therefore, Edge City rarely leads. Homes generally have to exist first. People have to be able to find a place to live at a price they can afford—given what they are going to be paid—if you want them to fill a job.

As the boom expanded in Boston, this became not possible. In most sane markets the rule of thumb is that people can afford to buy a house whose price is three times greater than their gross annual wage; if the household made $30,000, it could afford a $90,000 place. The typical single-family home in 1987 in the Boston area cost 7.7 times the average annual wage.

The result, predictably enough, was a labor shortage.

"The reasons for the slowdown are clear enough," the *Wall Street Journal* wrote. "The median single-family home price in the Boston area rocketed to $167,800 in early 1986—the highest level in the country at the time—from $89,400 in early 1984. Meanwhile, household incomes weren't rising nearly as fast, despite the region's healthy economy. By mid-1988, the median family income was $38,652 and the median home price $183,800. In Minneapolis—to take just one contrasting example —the median family income was $40,171, and the median home price was $86,000."

"The Boston area is possibly the most dramatic example of how a surging economy can boost housing prices to the point where they begin to dampen economic growth," an alarmed *Harvard Business Review* wrote. "During the 1970s' oil boom, thousands of families moved to Texas . . . Today, however, people simply cannot afford to move to Boston. Even Boston's prestigious teaching hospitals can't attract enough residents, interns, and nurses."

Traditionally, in America, the solution to the problem of Affordability has been Farther Out. Find a more distant, thus cheaper, cow pasture, subdivide it into quarter-acre lots, and build a remote but more economical subdivision.

The slightly cheaper cow pasture was crucial. That is because of the North Star of economic certitudes of residential developers. Stated as the Law of Four, it goes: *The house that makes a profit for its builder is one that sells for whatever the cost of the land under it is, multiplied by four.*

That is to say, if the lot costs $50,000, you must put enough house on it for the whole package to sell for $200,000, or you court bankruptcy.*

Here is where the Edge Cities of Boston had the distinction of being the first but by no means the last to hit the wall. No matter how far out you go, the dollars-per-hour of the jobs available within a reasonable commute go down quickly. But the dollars-per-quarter-acre do not.

* For a further discussion of this logic, see Chapter 13, "The Laws."

Developers love to blame this condition on "no growthers"—people devoted to their country homes who value the landscape as it exists. And, indeed, the people of New England have been marvelously inventive in finding means to slow growth. In Hollis, New Hampshire, just west of Nashua, owners of a hundred or more lots can obtain no more than four building permits a year. Other towns have found that just running up a year's backlog on processing requests is a very effective means of curbing development.

But there is plenty of land equally unavailable because it is held by speculators waiting for the price to go up even further. Or its ownership is chopped up into tracts that big developers view as too small to offer the advantages of scale they seek. Or it is problematic to build on because of terrain or soil composition. Or it is environmentally or historically sensitive and protected.

As a result, only ten thousand home-building permits per year were issued in the Boston area at the height of the boom—the proverbial drop in the bucket in an exploding population area. And much of that was astoundingly high-end. Of the ensuing developer bankruptcies when the bubble collapsed and home prices headed south, one analyst noted brightly, "Guess we found out what the choke point was for $300,000 condos on the waterfront in Lynn." There are any number of reasons cheaper housing wasn't built. But one that researchers at Salomon Brothers in New York point to was psychological. Builders looking at a boom in high tech thought of high-paid software designers. Nonetheless, there are always far more families headed by heating and air-conditioning technicians and copying-machine salespeople than there are those headed by chief financial officers.

These limits to growth were not an aberration of the Boston area. They were common in New York, San Francisco, Los Angeles, and Washington. But note well that the key here is "available" land. Consider the low population density of the swanky suburb of Wellesley, outside Route 128. Life there is hardly that of the huddled masses yearning to breathe free. The typical house is in the $300,000–$400,000 range. High-end homes are called "estates." Lord knows the area has its share of land Insurmountably off limits to development. Does that sound like a place with sufficient elbow room to be attractive? Okay, suppose we decided to encourage the use of land such that everybody in the metropolitan area could be housed at that low a density. If we did, half of metropolitan Boston would *still* be left as complete and utter wilderness, as pristine as the day the Pilgrims landed. Even at that low density, every single one of the Boston area's four million people could fit into only half the area's land.

For that matter, if we were to figure out a way for all the people of the Boston area to live at the moderate density of the renowned, bucolic, prosperous, job-laden, planned Edge City of Reston, Virginia, *four fifths* of the metropolitan area's land could be left as wilderness. The entire population of the Boston area could be housed on 20 percent of the land.

Instead, of course, from the preservationists to the speculators, we collectively have ended up conspiring either to keep most of our land from being built on densely—or built on at all. The result is urban sprawl challenging yet more distant vistas while not really solving Affordability. This is how strange places like Lordvale get built. Density is accomplished, but in what is invariably described as "the middle of nowhere." Which gets us back to Gilbert and Caron Merrill.

The Merrills are each in their early thirties. He is a Boston-educated attorney. She, until the baby came, was a market analyst for Prime Computer. While Gilbert was in school, they rented a cramped apartment in Watertown, an unfashionable but solid working-class neighborhood within three miles of downtown Boston.

After he passed the bar and they decided they deserved a home of their own, the Merrills discovered the Boston facts of life. They found nothing within forty miles of downtown that they could imagine living in. A small, two-bedroom, 1950s-standard bungalow that needed major work was as close as they came. It was going for $175,000.

The Merrills are quite a few notches up from typical, but even they began rethinking their position. Caron's job at Prime was in the Edge City of Framingham, more than twenty miles outside downtown straight out the Mass Pike, about halfway to Worcester. So the Merrills began to look for a place not just beyond Boston's first beltway, but nine miles beyond its second beltway.

There they finally found a $139,000 town house with brand-new construction and appliances.

It was "only" half an hour away from Caron's job at Prime. But it was an insane commute downtown for Gilbert. Therefore, in classic Edge City fashion, shortly after they moved, Gilbert switched jobs. In order to accommodate his opportunities for housing, he left his Boston practice and joined a firm in Worcester—the old industrial city fifty miles west of downtown that Bostonians have always thought of as halfway to Montana.

And voilà. The Merrills, by using their personal version of the Rubber Band method, successfully organized their lives to live near, and between, their respective downtown-quality jobs. There they sat, waited for son Wyatt to arrive, living "like that, out there" in their late-twentieth-century version of tenement housing for yuppies—Lordvale.

The Merrills are less than thrilled that anybody would want to describe their $139,000 town house as a tenement. But consider the similarities. Tenements were tightly packed three- and four-story buildings in which each family occupied one floor. They were thrown up in a hurry to accommodate the legions of workers who flocked to the dazzlingly high wages of the mills of the industrial Northeast in the nineteenth century. These tenements were the cheapest and most efficient way of getting the highest number of people reasonably close to their jobs.

Brand-new town-house developments at distant locations are Edge Cities trying to do exactly the same thing, a hundred years later. They are worker housing thrown up in a hurry for the mills and factories of the Information Age—Edge City office buildings. These town houses are designed for people like the Merrills, who, just as in the nineteenth-century boomtowns, are making an amazing amount of money by the standards of their parents at the same age. The Merrills are surrounded by amenities the previous generation never dreamed of, from microwaves to VCRs to central air conditioning (in Massachusetts!) to dishwashers to clothes dryers to multiple automobiles.

The price the Merrills have had to pay, however, is measured in land. If the Merrills and their peers did not want to compromise on the size and amenities of their homes, they had to put up with less land. This meant living at relatively high densities, with as many homes as possible put up on every expensive acre.

These densities, in turn, became almost impossible in affluent, close-in suburban Boston areas because of what Miriam
Maxian calls "snob zoning."

Maxian wrote her MIT graduate thesis on affordable housing,
which to her means housing for people who make under
$100,000 a year. She points out that the older a suburban neigh-
borhood is, the more likely the land in it is zoned only for
traditional suburban homes. This means that if a developer
wants to develop town houses, much less an apartment building,
he must go in for a zoning variance. And this, predictably, brings
out all the "abutters," as Maxian refers to the people living
nearby. The overwhelming majority virulently argue that such
densities will lower their property values, Maxian says. "There's
a stigma attached to it. It connotes the projects."

This is why America now finds itself with town houses far from
the old downtowns. The land is cheaper there, and the density is
politically more palatable in an area where a town house selling
for $139,000 is seen as improving the neighborhood.

To complete the analogy to tenements, consider how these
town houses are configured. If you look at them closely, you
realize that what they are, architecturally, is tenements flipped
over on their sides. Instead of stacking single flats one on top of
another, now we rotate our worker housing 90 degrees and pack
it side by side by side.

Turns out there are a lot of advantages to that. First of all, in
such a town-house development everybody gets to enter her
home directly from her garage. Ground-level access is a real
plus when your arms are laden with babies and groceries. What's
more, out back every one of these town houses has a tiny patio
or deck. Good for a little barbecuing. The homeowners' association would have a fit if you tried to hang a clothesline out there
and dry your underwear in the breeze. But the coziness makes it
possible to gossip with your neighbors over the pressure-treated
wood railings. How different is this from the porches, fire es-
capes, and social structures that used to grace each floor of a
tenement?

Meanwhile, when the neighbors are separated from you by
town-house walls—instead of tenement ceilings—living at these
densities is inherently more bearable. It is easier to soundproof
walls than floors. And think about it. In the old days if you could

hear a baby crying in the upstairs apartment, that was maddening. In a town house, being able to hear a baby crying in an upstairs bedroom is a plus.

After all, it is your baby.

The third limit to Edge City is Mobility—the ease with which you can get around within an Edge City area.

Mobility is primarily a measure of commutability. All over metropolitan America the average speed on freeways is going down, and news reports focus on how grim the commuting experience has become. Boston is no exception. Massachusetts has always been famous for its insane drivers. But Route 128 is the only place where I've ever been passed, on the right, by two school buses, each marked as carrying handicapped kids, traveling bumper to bumper, at sixty miles an hour, in the *breakdown* lane.

Scholars have demonstrated that for thousands of years, no matter what the transportation technology, the maximum desirable commute has been forty-five minutes. When state-of-the-art transportation was shoe leather, a city like Istanbul in the sixteenth century was never more than six miles across: it took forty-five minutes to walk three miles from the edge of town to the center.

This is why the goal in Edge City today is finding the magic combination of home and work that is at most a forty-five-minute trip for each person in the family.

But Mobility is also a measure of getting around once the workday has started—to make deliveries, sales calls, and the like. Mobility is so bad in the old downtowns that afternoon newspapers are extinct. You can't move the delivery trucks around sufficiently to give evening commuters a paper that includes closing stock prices. Big Edge Cities are beginning to rival downtowns in those problems.

One might think there would be a simple solution. Why don't Boston employers leapfrog their problems of Affordability and Mobility by moving even more jobs out to southern New Hampshire? For that matter, why stop there? Why not head out into the Berkshires or toward the Canadian border?

It turns out that Edge Cities have limits that control that, too. They are Accessibility and Nice.

If Mobility is the measure of how hard it is to get around

within an area, Accessibility is the measure of how hard it is to get into it from outside.

Nobody that I'm aware of has ever mathematically proven any Law of Accessibility. But there was a good one being thrown around as a strong hunch by people shepherding a lot of Edge City real estate. It went: *Your boss's boss will never approve a remote Edge City location unless he can personally imagine traveling there for a meeting without having to stay overnight.*

*That choke point is one and a half hours by car, one way. Or three hours by plane, nonstop.*

The thinking behind this is that no matter what advantages the boonies offer, sooner or later there will occur out there a memorable, first-rate screw-up. When that happens, somebody from headquarters will have to come out to fix it. When that highly wound and highly paid executive has to go out to clear up the problem, she will be unhappy.

The Law of Accessibility states that if you think that, in matters involving white-collar jobs, she will put up with Wyoming or the Philippines under these circumstances, you are out of your mind.

Who knows whether this Law of Accessibility is absolutely correct? Maybe it's four hours by plane or two hours by car. (The Law of Accessibility simply assumes, by the way, that any potential remote location is electronically Accessible. No location is ever even discussed that is not served by high-quality, high-speed digital phone service. In a place with only rotary-dial service, Touchtone beeps are worthless. You can't even make your answering machine talk to you, much less access the home office's computer. Forget it.) The Law of Accessibility, nonetheless, is the best explanation anybody offered me as to why southern New Hampshire, despite its growth and its apparent advantages, did not in the early 1990s even approach the Edge City pivot point of five million square feet of leasable office space.

"Southern New Hampshire is just too far from Logan," explains David Shulman, director of research at Salomon Brothers in New York, and a pioneering Edge City analyst.

Boston only has one major airport, Logan International, built on landfill out into Boston Harbor. It is separated from New England by water and downtown. It has little room to expand, and is less and less Accessible. Two multibillion-dollar roads, which will be in the works for the next decade, are supposed to address this problem. One will be a third tunnel under Boston Harbor to the airport, and the other, known officially as the Depressed Central Artery, locally referred to as the Big Dig, will try to offer a bypass through downtown. As of this writing, both projects have done little save offer more cruel Dukakis jokes, poor man. Example: "We figured Dukakis could give the road a speech and depress it all by himself."

The only other serious commercial airports in the Boston area are Worcester, which is small and built on top of a hill, which limits expansion, and Providence, which is picking up a lot of traffic, but is more than halfway to Connecticut, which also is a problem. The number one topic among regional growth advocates is where to put a new superairport. Air Force bases are being eyed covetously. But in the absence of such a facility, the Law of Accessibility rules. "For all our reputation for liberal politics," says Glenn R. Miller, a professor of urban geography at Bridgewater State College, "we in Massachusetts are pretty conservative and hide-bound. New Hampshire is just too far away to put anything important."

A spectacular demonstration of the lengths to which people have gone to overcome the limit of Accessibility is the experience of Digital Equipment Corporation. Digital is the second-largest computer maker in America. It is also the largest private employer in both New Hampshire and Massachusetts. As a result, it has had to create its own "Air Force."

"I hear you want to know about the Air Force," says Nikki Richardson, of Digital's public information. "Yeah, that's what everybody calls it. The Air Force. Okay, we have one eight-passenger helicopter up here, and five four-passenger helicopters . . .

Whoa. Background.

"Digital is not really a 128 company," spokesman Mark Fredrickson had explained earlier. "It is a 495 company." Digital's headquarters, which employs three thousand people, is in an old woolen mill in Maynard, forty miles from downtown, with its marketing, sales, and administrative unit in Marlborough, ten miles south of that. Engineering and software are headquartered at Merrimack and Nashua, to the north. Virtually all its keyboards for its worldwide markets are made in an inner-city location in Roxbury.

As a result, Fredrickson said, Digital, being a way-out-there, second-beltway company, had relatively few problems with Mobility or Affordability. But when it came to Accessibility, he audibly sucked on his teeth. Somebody would get back to me with the facts and figures, he said. Enter Ms. Richardson.

Slow down, I said. One eight-passenger chopper and five fours. Okay, what else?

"We have one eight-passenger turboprop, and we have one twin-engine five-passenger job. The three jets are for going to the West Coast, the Orient, and Australia. Then there's the turboprop in Atlanta, the fixed-wing unit in Europe, and the helicopter in Puerto Rico."

Wait a minute. Back up. The six choppers, the turboprop, the twin engine—are they all for local transportation, to get from one Digital installation in the Boston area to another?

"Oh, yeah," she said. "I mean, define local transportation. But those are pretty much for around here. I mean, they're all based at Hanscom Field in Bedford," she explained, patiently.

"It's impossible to get to Logan."

This gets us to the fifth and most intriguing limit to Edge City —Nice.

Nice is the truly double-edged sword for Edge City. Nothing cuts both for and against the growth of Edge City like Nice.

It has no clear definition. Like the Supreme Court and pornography, the rule is "We know it when we see it." But at bottom, Nice is where the big boss will live. Not-Nice is where he will not live. And there is probably no more important law of Edge City location than this: *Whenever a company moves its headquarters, the commute of the chief executive officer always becomes shorter.*

In fact, a standing not-really-joke in the real estate industry is that a corporate headquarters move is always determined by the following methods:

First, a blue-ribbon panel of respected corporate thinkers with long and deep understanding of the corporation's culture is named.

Second, they inventory all of the company's needs and goals.

Third, they conduct a nationwide search of all the best possible locations for the company, comparing economic, demographic, tax, labor, and other competitive issues.

Fourth, they issue a three-inch-thick report, carefully analyzing the pros and cons of each location.

Fifth, the report is thrown away, and the headquarters is put as close to the home of chief executive officer as is physically possible without actually lowering his personal property values.

Little else is more important than Nice. Nice is more important than money. Some people think that Edge Cities rise primarily in locations that are cheap. Wrong. Cost is only one factor. If "cheap" was the only thing important, there would be strong development opportunities available near cheap, bombed-out, inner-city neighborhoods. Or cheap, blue-collar, white ethnic neighborhoods. Or older, cheaper, small-house suburbs.

Forget it. William H. Whyte, in his book *City,* has a great map showing that of thirty-eight companies that moved out of New York City in one period "to better meet the quality-of-life needs of their employees," thirty-one moved to the Edge City around Greenwich and Stamford, Connecticut. On Whyte's map, black circles show where the chief executive officer lived at the time the move was planned; white circles show where the new headquarters was subsequently located. Average distance from the CEO's home: eight miles. The bull's-eye, Whyte reported, was "a circle about four miles in diameter, bounded on the east by the Burning Tree Country Club and on the west by the Fairfield Country Club." The lesson? The thickest rubber band in the Rubber Band Principle of Edge City Location is attached to the peg driven into the place where you can imagine putting "executive housing." The final limit to Edge City growth is the quality that high executives—and, even more important, their spouses —absolutely will not do without: Nice.

What is included in Nice? Schools with astonishingly high average SAT scores. Cultural events. ("That's another thing about New Hampshire," says Professor Miller. "There's just not much to do.") Country clubs. Athletic clubs. Waterfronts. Scenic vistas. Large lots. Abundant parks. Horses.

There is precious little that drives up the price of land like horses. In New Jersey near Far Hills where the U.S. Olympic Equestrian Team rides, or Virginia around Middleburg where

Jackie Onassis rides, or California around Santa Barbara where Ronald Reagan rides, horse country causes real estate agents to roll their eyes.

In fact, horses demonstrate why competition over Nice is the main battleground on which the issues of growth are fought. Nice is the biggest attracter of Edge City there is, because of its appeal to the families of monied executives. At the same time, resistance to the spoiling of Nice is the greatest deterrent to Edge City. This is especially true if the people who are doing the resisting are of at least the same financial, legal, rhetorical, and educational class as the forces of growth—as is always the case in horse country.

It is this conflict—over what we shall do with our most Nice parts of the planet—that decides the fate of Edge City.

James C. Rosenfeld is the poor guy in charge of trying to build a 148,000-square-foot office building across from Walden Pond.

"Yeah, it's my baby," he says, with a sigh, of the proposed Concord Office Park, which, if built, would feature a 518-car parking lot seven hundred yards from Walden's shore.

Asked when the battle started for permission to build, the senior vice president of Boston Properties flips through his notes and groans. "God, has it been that long?" Five years and counting is the answer. At the time.

"I really didn't expect a response of this nature," Jim Rosenfeld says. "You sound incredulous, but it's true. There's nothing particularly special about the site." Rosenfeld works for Mortimer B. Zuckerman, the wealthy Boston developer who has used his profits to buy *The Atlantic,* in the pages of which, ironically, Henry David Thoreau first gained a national reputation.

Jim Rosenfeld sounds like a truly wounded man. He goes on at great length about how his project offers setbacks-this and buffers-that; he's done Environmental Impact Reports until he's numb. Fifty percent of the eighteen-acre site, he says, would be left untouched. The Concord Office Park, he says, would make a great corporate headquarters.

He obviously believes that.

No, he says, no. "I didn't sit down and read the whole thing."

Rosenfeld was referring to *Walden, or Life in the Woods,* the full title of the 1854 book by Thoreau that recounts how he lived for two years and two months, walking this land, reflecting on where, exactly, material wealth and civilization intersected. Yes, Rosenfeld says. He has a copy. The Thoreau Country Conservation Alliance sent every executive in the company a copy.

"I read parts of it," Rosenfeld mutters.

In a burst of passion, he explodes, "They think the ground is sacred! They really do! They think his spirit is there! They think it's hallowed ground! They literally worship him as a god!"

Rosenfeld genuinely doesn't get it. The only thing he can figure is that it can't really be half the citizenry of Massachusetts that has lined up against him, the way it sometimes seems. It is just this band of fanatics who do not believe that even Route 2 should be there. Look at Lincoln, the next town down the road, he says. "It looks like the Berkshires."

These people forget the source of the economy that supports them, Rosenfeld says. Business is conducted in buildings like the one he wants to build. Just wait for the economic downturn, he prophesies, if people keep blocking projects like his. If people suddenly have to start worrying about their jobs, start worrying about a roof over their heads, about not having as much discretionary income, they won't have time or resources to do all this protesting, he grumps. Then they'll be talking out of the other side of their mouth. Lose some of their cushy jobs. That will change their minds.

You really think that's true? Rosenfeld is asked. That an economic downturn will change their minds?

Well, he says, no. Maybe not. But if they were busy looking for a job, maybe they wouldn't have as much time to protest.

It is Jack Borden's turn to sigh. He is a trustee of the Thoreau Country Conservation Alliance. Says Borden, "Thoreau once wrote, 'As the skies appear to a man, so is his mind; some see only clouds there.' By the same token, as the land developers look at land, all they see is office parks and condominiums. Then they build philosophies of progress around that bullshit to justify their greed. Thoreau is part of the nation's psyche, its ideals —self-sacrifice, individualism, hard work, working with your hands, kinship with the American land. Can't we keep something sacred?"

The kind of clash at Walden Pond over the Concord Office Park is the clash that is occurring again and again across the country, between two profoundly different sets of values.

Rosenfeld is doubtless not aware that he is playing the role of the Massachusetts Pilgrim, trying to bring what he views as civilization to this piece of howling wilderness, about which he says he sees "nothing particularly special." But he might have saved himself a lot of time and money had he, in fact, read a little of Thoreau before putting himself into the battle of his lifetime, the battle that goes back four hundred years and forward into our futures, the battle over who we are, how we got that way, where we're headed, and what we value.

The developers of the town-house subdivision of Lordvale, for that matter, might also have found it food for thought.

For in *Walden,* Thoreau wrote:

The mass of men lead lives of quiet desperation . . .
I went to the woods because I wished to live deliberately, to front only the essential facts of life, and see if I could not learn what it had to teach, and not, when I came to die, discover that I had not lived . . .
At a certain season of our life we are accustomed to consider every spot as the possible site of a house. I have thus surveyed the country on every side within a dozen miles . . . In imagination I have bought all the farms in succession . . . I walked over every farmer's premises, tasted his wild apples, discoursed on husbandry with him . . . and withdrew when I had enjoyed it long enough, leaving him to carry it on.
This experience entitled me to be regarded as a sort of real-estate broker by my friends . . . The future inhabitants of this region, wherever they may place their houses, may be sure that they have been anticipated. An afternoon sufficed to lay out the land into orchard, wood-lot, and pasture, and to decide what fine oaks or pines should be left to stand before the door . . . and then I let it lie . . . for a man is rich in proportion to the number of things which he can afford to let alone . . .
I found thus that I had been a rich man without any damage to my poverty . . . I retained the landscape, and I have since annually carried off what it yielded without a wheel-barrow. With respect to landscapes,—'I am the monarch of all I survey, my right there is none to dispute . . .'
None can be an impartial or wise observer of human life but from the vantage ground of what we should call voluntary poverty . . .

I do not speak to those who are well employed, in whatever circumstances, and they know whether they are well employed or not—but mainly to the mass of men who are discontented, and idly complaining of the hardness of their lot or of the times, when they might improve them . . . I also have in my mind that seemingly wealthy, but most terribly impoverished class of all, who have accumulated dross, but know not how to use it, or get rid of it, and thus have forged their own golden or silver fetters . . .

Love your life, poor as it is. You may perhaps have some pleasant, thrilling, glorious hours, even in a poorhouse. The setting sun is reflected from the windows of the almshouse as brightly as from the rich man's abode . . .

Why should we be in such desperate haste to succeed, and in such desperate enterprises? If a man does not keep pace with his companions, perhaps it is because he hears a different drummer. Let him step to the music which he hears, however measured or far away.

There is a replica of Thoreau's ten-by-fifteen-foot handcrafted house on the shores of Walden Pond today, rebuilt by the Massachusetts Department of Environmental Management. It seems as snug and handy as his place must have been 150 years ago, when he refused the gift of a doormat—preferring to wipe his feet on the grass rather than disturb the simplicity of his life by taking in an object he would only have to shake out.

"In the long chronicle of our American distrust of the city, two names stand out above the rest: Jefferson and Thoreau," wrote J. B. Jackson.

Ralph Waldo Emerson wrote of his friend who built that tight, warm, one-room abode, out beyond what is now Route 128, "No truer American existed than Thoreau."

And to this day, Americans harken to his distant drum; there are still some things, it seems, they value far more than the building of cities.

# 4

# DETROIT

## The Automobile, Individualism, and Time

Americans are in the habit of never walking if they can ride.
—*Louis Philippe, Duc d'Orléans, 1798*

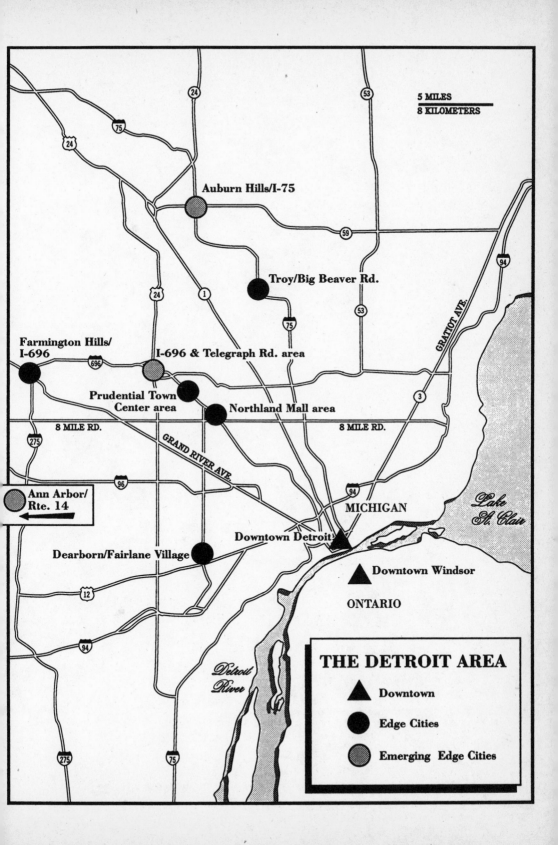

5 MILES
8 KILOMETERS

Auburn Hills/I-75

Troy/Big Beaver Rd.

Farmington Hills/
I-696

I-696 & Telegraph Rd. area

Prudential Town
Center area

Northland Mall area

8 MILE RD.

8 MILE RD.

GRAND RIVER AVE.

Ann Arbor/
Rte. 14

GRATIOT AVE.

MICHIGAN

Lake
St. Clair

Downtown Detroit

Dearborn/Fairlane Village

Downtown Windsor

ONTARIO

Detroit
River

THE DETROIT AREA

▲ Downtown

● Edge Cities

● Emerging Edge Cities

WEST OF DETROIT, just off Interstate 94, stands the classic clock tower and lofty steeple of Independence Hall.

Those who always thought the sanctuary of the Liberty Bell was located six hundred miles east, in Philadelphia, might find startling this apparition on the Michigan plain. But it does have its own compelling logic. For this replica of the building in which the Declaration of Independence was approved on July 4, 1776, was erected in Dearborn by Henry Ford. It serves as the main entrance to the massive Henry Ford Museum, near Ford's old private estate. Ford meant the museum to be a monument to the American genius for invention and change. He regarded the signers of the Declaration to be no less brilliant in this regard than his friend Thomas Edison—or future Americans, for that matter.

The very first exhibit in this vast museum, with twelve acres under roof, makes this point in the most forceful way. There sit two vehicles, side by side. One is the Quadricycle, Ford's first experimental 1896 automobile. The other is a Lunar Roving Vehicle, the first of which was driven on the moon July 31, 1971; three of them are parked up there still.

The two flivvers are stunningly similar. Each is a bare platform, at the four corners of which are wheels. You can see right through the wheels of each, the Quadricycle having spokes, and the Rover having tires made of screenlike mesh to save weight. Each seats two, the moon vehicle with an affair of webs, and the Quadricycle an upholstered love seat. The Rover, six feet wide and a little over ten feet long, is not much bigger than its antique counterpart. The Ford vehicle has on its right front bumper a beautiful brass lamp. The moon vehicle has at exactly the same location a television camera covered in foil of radiation-deflecting gold. It is tied to an uplink transmission dish. The two technologies—worlds apart—are separated by only seventy-five years.

It is fitting that these two monuments to American ingenuity are approached through a replica of Independence Hall, for they are testimonials to a society that has put a boundless value on freedom and individuality for centuries. Those values, embodied in these forms of individual transportation, have in turn resulted in our new Edge Cities.

When the millionth Model T rolled out of Highland Park in 1915, it changed the world. The product of Ford's invention of the moving assembly line in 1913, it heralded the most luxuriant flowering of the Industrial Age. As a result of the breakthroughs in mass production and mobility it represented, all manner of other miracles—the refrigerator, the telephone, the air conditioner, the television—became so inexpensive as to enter the lives of every working person. At the same time, those years brought to surge tide the wave of humans leaving woods and fields for the urban areas where the factory jobs were. These jobs paid so well that when Henry Ford announced in 1914 that he would pay his employees $5.00 a day, there were riots in the streets of Detroit among the thousands who had traveled from as far as Chicago, Dayton, Indianapolis, and Cleveland to claw at one another for the work. That kind of pay, at a time when highly skilled labor secured thirty cents an hour, drew migrations from as far as Eastern Europe, Palestine, and the American Deep South. Detroit in 1915 was a boomtown more raucous even than Houston in the 1970s. In fact, contemporary writers, casting about for something to equal it, settled on the Oklahoma land rush. The Motor City quadrupled its population in only twenty years, from 285,000 at the turn of the century to well over a million by 1921.

Ironically, this massive wave of urbanization, culminating in a high-rise skyline, brought to an end the evolution of the downtown-dominated nineteenth-century-style city in America. We have not built an old downtown from raw ground in seventy-five years—not since that millionth Model T in 1915. True, even today some people have a mental image of the gritty centers of the Industrial Age—Chicago, Cleveland, Pittsburgh, New York —as the standard form of American city. But these old downtowns were highly aberrational. We built those huge, acutely concentrated centers for fewer than a hundred years.

We started building them only in the mid-1800s. The key ingredient for a high-rise city—Bessemer steel—was not poured commercially in America until 1864. Before that, in the decades following the American Revolution, when Americans thought of a city, they thought of places like Paul Revere's Boston or Benjamin Franklin's Philadelphia. Those cozy, compact, European-style centers were the standard form of American city for far longer than any other kind; they were finishing their second century by the time the steam engine was perfected. These early cities of the 1600s, 1700s, and early 1800s were entrepôts— coast-hugging trade centers. Their point was the exchange of the raw wealth from the endless North American interior for the luxuries and finished goods of Europe. They were marked by countinghouses down by the wharves and, up on the hills, magisterial courts, churches, government houses, and mansions. A very small percentage of Americans lived in these antique cities. Most people lived in the countryside.

In the latter 1800s we blew these sleepy old hubs wide open and out—into industrialized cities on a scale far more vast. By the turn of the twentieth century, those Revolutionary-era cities were almost unrecognizable for what they once had been. That transformation was the previous great American revolution in how we built our cities. It was comparable to the tsunami we are undergoing today in Edge City.

The upheaval of a century ago was also technology-driven. We replaced the cities the Founding Fathers knew with the metropolis of the railroad, the factory, and the steam engine. Immigrants flocked to the tenements, apartment blocks, and boardinghouses of these new places, packing themselves together in neighborhoods huddled as close as possible to places of work. The reason for this density was simple: people didn't have a lot of choice. There were only two technologies available for getting to work: walking directly to the job site, or walking to the nearest station to hop some sort of railroad—a subway or a streetcar—and *then* walking to the job site. Either mode put a premium on high densities, because, even then, Americans did not much like to walk.

The beginning of the end of that arrangement was the transportation revolution of 1915. The downtowns of Detroit and Los Angeles—two urban areas famous for their early understanding of the automobile—were among the last nineteenth-century-style centers of their kind.

Americans never much liked living at the densities typical of those old downtowns, either. They were not swell places. Diphtheria and typhoid were common. We lived that way only for as long as it was necessary to get jobs. As soon as we had a choice—the moment the Industrial Age produced a machine that would allow us to live a respectable distance from the poisonous environs we associated with our toil—we jumped at the opportunity. We have been driving our automobiles to work ever since. In some ways, the main astonishment is that it has taken us this long to accommodate the logic of our lives and—seventy-five years after the millionth Model T—reach the point where Edge City has become our new standard American urban form.

All cities, throughout history, have been shaped by the state-of-the-art transportation device of the time. In the early 1800s, Detroit was but a wide place in the wilderness, beloved by few save some French-Canadian trappers. Often as not, you got there by canoe, and in French *détroit* means "the straits"—as in those where the land comes close together between the broad expanses of Lake St. Clair and Lake Erie, where settlement began. It was prohibitive to try to ship export goods like salted fish or flour to the East; it took two months to get to the coast from what was then the frontier. In 1825, however, all that changed. The Erie Canal was finished, linking the Great Lakes to the port of New York. Travel time and freight costs dropped to a tenth of what they'd been. The cities at both ends of the trade, New York and Detroit, boomed. Detroit became the staging area for the settlement of what was then the great Northwest. In 1848, a railroad cut the travel time between Detroit and Chicago by two-thirds. By midcentury, Detroit was closer in time to Liverpool than it had been in 1800 to Cincinnati.

Two things accumulated in Detroit as a result: money and skilled labor. The first belonged especially to the Michigan timber barons of the late 1800s, who were casting about for productive new investments as the state's pine forests dwindled. The second belonged to those mechanically inclined yeoman who had flocked to Detroit as it became a wood-forming and metal-bashing center of the stove and carriage industries. All this entrepreneurial money and those clever hands were the critical ingredients that made Detroit fertile ground for some curious tinkerers when they started experimenting, at the turn of the twentieth century, with something called the automobile.

As we trace the impact of this transportation revolution—the car—on our newest urban form—Edge City—two themes emerge. First, the upheaval illuminates our values; it tells us about our lives and casts into sharp relief those aspects of our world for which we are willing to sacrifice much. Second, it explains why Edge City looks and functions the way it does, and what we can do to shape it to meet our goals.

The most important aspect of the automobile is that it shifted the balance of power from centralized modes of organization toward the individual.

Before the automobile, mass transit was about the only serious transit there was. There were three go-anywhere land transportation technologies: the foot, the horse, and the bicycle. Each was a seriously limited means of moving large quantities of people and goods around and between cities. Therefore, the heavy hauling of passengers and freight in the 1800s went to the railroad companies and the steamship lines—those robber baron institutions which moved people where, when, with what frequency, and at what price the corporations chose.

The automobile changed that. Not for nothing is that most American hymn to individual freedom, Jack Kerouac's magnum opus, entitled *On the Road.* Not for nothing did we build transcontinental railroads for only thirty-five years. We drove the golden spike for the first one in 1869. The last one ever to be built—the Milwaukee Road, from Chicago to Seattle—was finished in 1904. Those railroads were soon eclipsed by the only individual form of motorized go-anywhere transportation until the helicopter—the automobile.

It turns out that if each person in America wants to "have it all," the most efficient way to organize her affairs is in a spiderweb. The home is at the center, and everything else—work, play, shopping, school—surrounds her in dozens of directions. If we multiply the number of combinations this may entail by a quarter of a billion Americans, then at the very least what is required technologically is a system of individual transportation to offer the maximum choices, with the least waste of time.

The system of individual transportation we Americans have devised, of course, is the finest method of moving the most people and freight in the most directions at the most times ever devised by the mind of man. At its center is the automobile and the hard-surfaced, all-weather road.

Place these dreams in a market system that is responsive to what people feel is rational to trade off in time and money, and what you get is Edge City.

This was foreseen by H. G. Wells as long ago as 1900, when the old downtowns were still headed for the peak of their glory. Wells is so well known for his futurist fiction, such as *The War of the Worlds,* that many people do not know he was a historian. What he vividly grasped in his essay "The Probable Diffusion of Great Cities," however, was the social significance of the amazing new networks of electricity, telephones, and transportation.

Wells saw that "the electrical system gave every point in a region the same access to power as any other; the advantage of a central location was accordingly diminished," reports the historian Robert Fishman in *Bourgeois Utopias.*

"In an analogous way, the telephone provided instant communication from any point," says Fishman. "Not only could industry produce its goods more cheaply and more efficiently away from the core; but businessmen would invariably choose to live in quiet country towns."

With astounding prescience Wells wrote, "Indeed, it is not too much to say that the London citizen of the year 2000 A.D. may have a choice of all England and Wales south of Nottingham and east of Exeter."

He was dead on. The metropolitan area of London today— the most America-like urban center in Europe—sprawls more than a hundred miles across. Now the size of the Los Angeles Basin, it has leapfrogged its greenbelts. It is spawning Edge Cities more than thirty miles from the center. As it burgeoned in the nineteenth century from an area of 860,000 people to one of five million, greater London was nothing but a "smeared mass of humanity," noted Richard Sennett, the social historian, with "no neat demographic, administrative, or social borders." But as new Edge Cities form around it, London has taken a familiar shape. The London area today functions a great deal more like Los Angeles than sentimentalists care to acknowledge.

All it took to fulfill Wells's vision, finally, was a transportation network that met people's needs as freely and individually as electricity and telephones moved power and messages.

That network was provided by the system whose virtues we so take for granted that we give them short shrift, rarely stopping to enumerate just how many they are. As a result, we grossly underestimate exactly how difficult they would be to match by other means. It is the mechanization of man's most primitive activity, walking on his hind legs. It is that marvelously effective compressor of time and distance, that self-driven, self-owned, self-maintained bubble of familiar, personal space—the aptly named "auto-mobile."

Just as with the power and phone systems, the internal logic of individualized transportation led to high-capacity transmission devices—eventually, the freeway. This new transportation system was soon knit into a grid, just like electricity and communications. Predictably enough, the powerhouses and switching systems of our economies—the market and job centers—ended up at the most frequented intersections, to which the most people could easily gain access.

At exactly those points rose our Edge Cities.

This new system of dispersing wealth and labor was vastly more efficient than the centralized model of the nineteenth-century city. It soon became obvious that the old idea of pumping gigantic numbers of workers into downtown in the morning, only to see them gush out at night, was grossly unsustainable.

The story of Detroit is instructive in this regard. The first American ruler of the newly organized Michigan territory, Judge Augustus Woodward, in 1805 had a plan surveyed for "the Paris of the West" that was strongly influenced by Pierre L'Enfant's design for the city of Washington. Roads so wide that today they accommodate nine lanes of traffic were laid out to radiate from the hub like spokes. In addition, Detroit wound up with two ring roads that functioned as prototypes for beltways. The inner one, built in 1884, is Grand Boulevard. It once defined the limits of Detroit's urban expansion, and today sweeps around the center like a horseshoe, with its open end facing the Detroit River. The second loop is called, appropriately enough, Outer Drive, although that name seems curious today, since it now traverses an area that has been thoroughly urbanized for half a century. Always keeping a distance of eight to ten miles from downtown, it arcs for forty-two miles from just beyond Dearborn to the west, through parkland and pleasant neighborhoods of middle-class detached homes, until it ends in Grosse Pointe Park to the east.

The intersection of a beltway with a hub-and-spoke lateral road is the pattern that yields the location of so many of today's Edge Cities. What's interesting about Detroit, however, is that this pattern emerged almost the moment that the automobile was mass-produced. In 1919, General Motors started building what was to be the world's largest office building—its new head-quarters. But did this industrial colossus locate its white-collar executive center downtown? Of course not. Only four years after the millionth Ford, GM broke the mold of nineteenth-century thinking about cities. GM distanced its headquarters from downtown in a place grandly called New Center. It was near the intersection of the first beltway, Grand Boulevard, and the premiere radial road, Woodward Avenue. It was accessible to downtown—by car. But it was also close to GM's factories—some of which were purposely located outside the city and its taxing power. It was very close to swanky neighborhoods like the Boston-Edison area where the executives lived. And it offered far more land than the old downtown both for expansion—and parking. Right there in New Center, immediately after World War I, Edge City was probably born. Henry Ford's company followed suit. When he switched production from the Model T to the Model A in 1928, he also switched his factory location from Highland Park, a community within the boundaries of Detroit, to the plains of Dearborn. Dearborn was his home town and the location of his Fairlane estate, just inside the Outer Drive today. It was also where he had built his enormous River Rouge plant in 1917 and where he finally moved his corporate headquarters. Today, not surprisingly, the area around the Ford world headquarters, Ford's old mansion, and the Henry Ford Museum is a burgeoning Edge City. It has more office spires than downtown Indianapolis. Two thousand, three hundred, and sixty acres of that land are being developed by the Ford Motor Land Development Corporation. This Edge City contains massive hotels, a Jack Nicklaus–designed golf course, and over a thousand homes, as well as high-rise offices. Unsurprisingly, it is centered on one of the largest malls in Michigan. That mall has taken the name of Henry Ford's estate. It is called Fairlane Town Center.

The places that first understood the automobile underscore the key element that both personal transportation and Edge City are designed to conserve. That is the most precious element any human has, the very measure of his individuality—*time.* Both the automobile and Edge City are time machines.

Everything we value, from love to lucre, takes time. Time is the measure of the conflicting demands put upon us, and as such is the measure of our very selves. It is the one commodity that turns out, for each individual, irrevocably, to be finite. It is the one thing for which we will readily trade just about anything—especially money. The evidence of this surrounds us, in everything we've built.

Developers don't always use the word "time" to describe the central concern of our lives and their work. They usually use the word "convenience." Interesting word, "convenience." In everyday use it lacks punch. It sounds optional, frivolous. It connotes something we could easily do without. It has no sense of urgency, no aura of importance. "Convenience" especially does not suggest a power to shape worlds.

But that is exactly what it has done. Edge Cities are not created in units of distance, but in units of time. For example, Edge Cities doubtless would not exist the way they do were it not for one of the truly great employment and demographic shifts in American history: the empowerment of women.

By the 1950s suburbanization had exploded, but it was still not common for families to have more than one car. At that time, the stereotypical female role of wife and mother was not only home-based, but home-shackled. William H. Whyte, in *The Organization Man,* referred in 1956 to the world of cul-de-sacs as "sororities with kids." Even if employment and social opportunities had been open to women, those opportunities were scattered, and the family's only car was typically transporting the breadwinning man. Many women did not even know how to drive. For every woman who drove her husband to the train—hence the "station" wagon—far more took the bus downtown to shop. The husband had the car.

It is no coincidence that Edge Cities began to flourish nation-wide in the 1970s, simultaneous with the rise of women's libera-tion. When I started asking developers when, exactly, they first thought it plausible to build quarter-of-a-million-square-foot of-fice monoliths out in some cow pasture, far from the old down-towns, I found it eerie how often the year 1978 came up. In casting about to discover what else happened in 1978 that could explain that, I did not find a whole lot. In computers, it was a big year only in the sense that the first Apple went on sale. The IBM PC was not launched until 1981. Economically and automo-tively, it was merely the year that the economy most staggered toward a recovery from the first oil shock of 1973, before being clobbered by the second one in 1979.

The only thing I've discovered that begins to account for that nationwide pattern is that 1978 was the peak year in all of Ameri-can history for women entering the work force. In the second half of the 1970s, unprecedentedly, more than eight million hitherto non-wage-earning women went out and found jobs. The spike year was 1978.

That same year, a multitude of developers independently de-cided to start putting up big office buildings out beyond the traditional male-dominated downtown. Land was more abun-dant and more automobile-accessible in the residential suburbs that had once been condescendingly referred to as "the realm of women." And the new advantage was proximity to the emerging work force. These Edge City work centers were *convenient* for women. It saved them time. This discovery was potent. A decade later, developers viewed it as a truism that office buildings had an indisputable advantage if they were located near the best-educated, most conscientious, most stable workers—underem-ployed females living in middle-class communities on the fringes of the old urban areas.

Through all of history, revolutions are made of upheavals much smaller than that.

The further evidence that Edge Cities would never have flour-ished the way they have, had it not been for women entering the work force, is that from 1970 to 1987 the number of cars in

America more than doubled. Population growth in America at exactly the same time was not great—a trifle over 1 percent per year. That's a growth rate for cars more than five times the growth rate for population. Most of the automotive surge came from women who were entering the work force. Liberation, indeed. Women were asserting their right to have the same unlimited choices as men. As a result, Edge Cities—convenient to their homes and far more convenient to their chosen form of individual transportation—boomed. In this fashion did the conservation of time and individualism form Edge Cities. Automobile technology, like telephone, electrical, and personal computer technology, empowers the busy individual.

The pivotal role of individual transportation in turn drives the way Edge Cities take various shapes. The three most important are:

- Uptowns,
- Boomers, and
- Greenfields.

Uptowns are Edge Cities built on top of pre-automobile settlements. An example is the former arts colony of Pasadena, California. Its old shopping district survived the 1960s and 1970s without being utterly "urban renewed" or "malled" to oblivion. Now Pasadena is becoming an Edge City office center. A similar example of a former bedroom community turned Uptown Edge City is Stamford, Connecticut. Other Uptowns have been superimposed on crossroads dating to the 1800s, like Buckhead in the Atlanta region. The form has even been adapted to a Colonial port village of the 1700s such as Alexandria, Virginia, in the Washington area. What they all have in common is vestiges of an older settlement built when the most common way of getting around was walking. Because foot traffic was primary at the time these places were laid out, and climate control had not yet been invented, the sidewalks were in the open air, next to the streets. Shops faced outward to display their wares to people passing as they walked, which made them visually interesting. Ownership of the land was usually highly fragmented, because nobody needed much space for their small-scale uses.

These historical usages yield architectural diversity that is

often worth preserving. They also afford an opportunity to locate charming boutiques, craftsmen's shops, eateries, and entrepreneurial immigrants in these small spaces—especially
those shops which are too idiosyncratic or insufficiently profitable to find a location in a mall. There is frequently a grid layout,
which means that buildings are forced to have a relationship to
one another; they often have walls in common. And the people
who live around this kind of Edge City have a close historical
relationship to the old power centers downtown. This means
that there are definite limits to what can be done to these Edge
Cities in the course of blowing them out to deal with the automobile and the gigantic office complex. They are always surrounded by entrenched neighborhoods whose well-heeled residents share vociferous and educated opinions about the future.
If and when new transit systems are built, they come to Uptowns
first. That is both because of their traditional density and because of their history; they've been around long enough as centers that planners are conscious of their existence. What's more,
the residential constituency of an Uptown with a hearty distrust
of change often transfers its anger to support of trains, even
though most of the workers who come to the office buildings
laid on these Uptowns do so by automobile, anyway.

These "limitations," of course, are a blessing. Because of
them, developers must, to some degree, adapt their product to
the Uptown, rather than the other way around. The very fact that
they *have* a history gives Uptowns a leg up on the issues of
"livability," "civilization," and "soul" over newer forms of Edge
City. It means that they have layers of development; they don't
look all the same.

Boomers, by contrast, are the classic kind of Edge City; just
about all the ones in the Detroit region fit into this category.
Filled with cantilevers, ziggurats, soaring columns, and fields of
glass, they are usually located at the intersection of the freeways,
and are almost always centered on a mall. Few buildings are
designed to relate to each other, because Boomers began to
break for glory long before their builders looked around and
realized that the sum of their efforts *was* an Edge City. A Boomer
is like poison ivy. If you have reason to wonder whether that's
what you're in the middle of, chances are that's what it is. The
classic tip-off: a car dealership being bulldozed to be replaced by

an office building taller than the trees. That represents such an extravagant increase in the value of the land that somebody is no longer thinking of it in acres but in square *feet*.

Boomers have grown so lavishly that the academically fastidious have even noted that there are three subcategories:

- the Strip,
- the Node, and
- the Pig in the Python.

The Strip, of course, is that esteemed urban form which goes on forever, miles long and only hundreds of yards wide, on either side of a freeway. The classic ones include the Route 1 corridor near Princeton, Route 128 near the Mass Pike outside Boston, and the I-270, in Montgomery County, Maryland, in the Washington region. It is striking how often the Strip in its most pure form occurs in those areas in which it is the biggest political embarrassment. It is difficult to mass enough density in a Strip to yield the benefits of civilization, and its attenuation guarantees traffic congestion. Yet the three instances above are places where highly educated people thought they had invested hugely and learnedly in public planning. These places ended up the way they did because thoughtful public planners genuinely believed they had a good idea at the time. Ah, well. Not for nothing is the theme of Edge Cities the Law of Unintended Consequences.

Compared to a Strip, a Node is relatively dense and contained. The Galleria area in the Houston region and Tysons Corner in Virginia are two examples. There is enough of a center to them that it is possible to imagine someday adding Disney-style rail transit to these Nodes, simply because it is possible to imagine drawing a circle around each.

The Pig in the Python is a cross between the two. It is a Strip that has begun to develop one or several Nodes along it; for example, the Lodge Freeway in Southfield, northwest of downtown Detroit, which now has three Pig-like Edge City Nodes in its Strip-like Python. Or it is a Node that has begun to grow a tail like a comet as it Strips down one or more of *its* approaching highways. King of Prussia, Pennsylvania, is an example of that.

The final major form of Edge City, and the most ambitious, is the Greenfield. It is increasingly the state of the art, in response to the perceived chaos of the Boomer. It is also the most awe-

some. A Greenfield occurs at the intersection of several thousand acres of farmland and one developer's monumental ego. It
embraces amazingly grand master-planned visions of human
nature and rigid control of vast areas by private corporations. A
Greenfield is what happens when a builder who decides he wants
to "do it right" finds himself in possession of an enormous
amount of acreage that he invariably calls "a blank slate."
Greenfields are meant to show nothing less than that all of man's
needs and desires can be met by the glories of the marketplace if
one developer is willing to aim sufficiently high. Examples are
Las Colinas, near the Dallas–Fort Worth airport; Irvine, on the
southern fringe of the Los Angeles Basin, the Bishop Ranch,
east of San Francisco, and, predictably, a Disney entry near
Orlando beyond Epcot Center. What is remarkable about these
Greenfields is not that there are very many of them. (Because
they require so much land, they are more common in the West.)
What is astounding is how many are on the drawing boards, and
at what projected cost.

Speaking of "doing it right," this is probably as good a place
as any to bring up another issue. For all the moaning about the
plight of the cities, there is really only one major American
downtown that has gone to hell in a handbasket, and that is
Detroit. In the 1980s, most American downtowns did as well or
better than they ever had in any decade of the twentieth century.
This was true from Boston to Seattle to San Francisco to Los
Angeles to Atlanta to Washington to Philadelphia. The squalor
of core Detroit was far and away the exception, not the rule.
*American Demographics* magazine demonstrated in 1990 that there
were basically only two states that faced both slow growth and
high crime in the late 1980s—Michigan and New York. In general, it is places that have been destabilized by high growth, like
Florida, Texas, and Arizona, where one finds a striking increase
in crime. Similarly, places that have seen little change, such as
West Virginia, North Dakota, and Pennsylvania, as a rule also
saw low crime rates in the 1980s. Focusing on downtown Detroit
as an abyss, moreover, was less than fair to the rest of the Detroit
region. In 1990 the Population Crisis Center (PCC), a Washington think tank that advocates family planning, ranked urban
regions worldwide in terms of livability. They were examining
the relationship between rapid urbanization and population

growth and the quality of life. Urban regions were defined as comprising not just the old downtown but the surrounding jurisdictions of the metropolitan areas. By this standard, the Detroit-Windsor area came in sixth highest in quality of life out of a hundred metros examined. It ranked just behind Essen-Dortmund-Duisburg in Germany, and ahead of places like Sydney, Toronto, San Francisco–Oakland–San Jose, and Washington. The Detroit region scored especially well in housing standards, large amounts of living space per person, low infant mortality rates, low high school dropout rates, low cost of food compared to the local wage, and the lack of traffic jams. "The main point to keep in mind is that we looked at the entire metro area, not just the city of Detroit," says Dr. Joseph Speidel, president of the PCC. "Detroit downtown may be in trouble, but it's a much rosier picture when you look at the whole area."

If most of civilization's amenities are located in Detroit's Edge Cities, and one of them, Southfield, is bigger than downtown, one still may be left wondering: Why do these Edge Cities look so unlike anything we are used to? How did they end up transformed into Boomers and Greenfields?

The developers know quite a bit about the answers. Developers gossip. Their code is an almost impenetrable thicket of abbreviations and numbers: FARs, DUs, dollars. But gossips they are, for they are trying to discover the Laws of Human Behavior. Developers are religious devotees of these laws. They don't much care how humans *should* operate; their concerns are not that ethereal. All they want to know is how they *will* operate so that they can respond to those clues to make money.

Here are two of these laws. They both govern physical space, and together they control what an Edge City ends up looking like, how it functions, and what will or will not be there—from subway stations to parks to used-book stores to five-star restaurants.

The developer's first law, to which he adheres tenaciously—for the excellent reason that there appears to be no reason to think it is not true—is:

*An American Will Not Walk More than Six Hundred Feet Before Getting into Her Car.*

Two football fields. If whatever this American desires is farther away than that, she will, if she possibly can, get into her car and drive the distance rather than walk it. She really will.

The developer's second law is even more world-shaping than the first. It is:

*To Park an Automobile Takes Four Hundred Square Feet.*

That's the actual parking spot, per car, plus its share of the required driveways.*

To be sure, there are exceptions to these laws. But they tend to prove the rule. For example, there are a few places where Americans will walk more than six hundred feet:

• *Inside a big airport.* There is no choice. Everybody hates that.
• *Inside an old downtown.* Not much choice. Automobiles are a chore to use at those densities. William H. Whyte, in *City,* grieves over but does not dispute the Six Hundred Foot Law. He thinks, however, that in an old downtown, it is sometimes possible to get the number up to eight hundred, perhaps even a thousand feet. Especially if the weather is nice, and the walk is full of interesting shop windows and faces. Not coincidentally, the distances he's talking about are usually those between anchor stores in a mall.
• *Inside a mall.* There, a person has plenty of choices. In fact, designers are positive that if it were clear to people just how big a regional mall really is, shoppers would go out to their cars and *drive* to the other end of the complex before they'd walk it. Actually, that is the merchants' nightmare. It's not that they are particularly bothered by the idea of people driving the short distance. It's the thought that once the customers got into their cars, half of them might decide to leave the mall entirely. *That* is viewed as a catastrophe. So designers of Edge City malls fight with everything they've got to deflect our urge to dive for the drive. They make the environment inside as interesting and comfortable and entertaining for pedestrians as possible. They stack the stores two and three and even four levels high to make them easier to walk to. They make the exits to the parking lot extremely difficult to find. But most important, they break the

* These and other Laws of Human Behavior as perceived by developers are codified in Chapter 13.

shoppers' lines of sight. They make Herculean efforts never, ever, to let us see just exactly how far away the next anchor store is.

These two laws of space explain just about everything in the physical arrangement of Edge City. The developer's rule of thumb is that in Edge City, there must be one parking space per every worker. Because one employee uses about 250 square feet of work space and each car requires four hundred square feet to be parked, there has to be about one and a half times as much space to park the cars as there is to nurture their drivers.

If the developer does not provide that much parking, he will have grave difficulty getting bank financing. His project will not be judged commercially viable. In fact, in many Edge City jurisdictions, the developer is required by *law* to provide that much parking. The lawmakers don't want people to park on streets and lawns, either. Their experience, too, has led them to believe that one worker will equal one car will equal one parking space.

Parking has been a key determinant of human life since at least the seventh century B.C. That's when the Assyrian king Sennacherib decreed that anyone parking a chariot so as to obstruct the royal road "should be put to death with his head impaled on a pole in front of his house."

Twenty-seven hundred years later, the pivot of urbanity and civilization at the approach of the twenty-first century is still, as it turns out, parking.

It seems curious, of course. But the reason there is a relationship between civilization and parking is that there are only three ways to park cars. Each, compared with its predecessor, is more dense, more esthetically attractive, and vastly more expensive:

• The first way is your basic asphalt parking lot—what developers call "surface" or "on-grade" parking. That costs about $2000 per space to build, not counting the price of the land. (If you find that figure surprisingly high, it's because there is more to building a durable parking lot that drains rainwater well, and is maneuverable in ice and snow, than most people think.)

• Next is aboveground, multilevel parking garages. Those cost about $5000 per space to build, again not counting the cost of the land.

• Then there is underground parking. That costs about

$20,000 per space to build—ten times the cost of surface parking.

These facts of life, in turn, control what gets built where in Edge City, and, hence, how civilized it will be.

A developer's decision on what kind of office building he is going to construct is driven by three factors:

- The cost of the land.
- What he calculates to be the most profitable "footprint" for his building—the size and shape of the floor plan, given the land cost.
- What he calculates is the most profitable number of stories he can build, given the footprint.

Now remember. The developer needs one and a half times as much space for the cars as he does for the humans.*

Given that, the cheapest option a developer has is this. Build a one-story building. Let it cover 40 percent of the ground. That leaves 60 percent of the land to be covered with a simple parking lot. No grass or trees or sidewalks. But the right ratios at the least expense. Which explains why an awful lot of cheap development looks the way it does.

This kind of construction guarantees that all buildings and people will be about as far away from each other as physically possible, surrounded by fields of asphalt. This in turn guarantees that the area so built will be an esthetic and functional sump.

However. That level of development is only the cheapest kind, not necessarily the most profitable. Buildings laid out like that do not command much rent. If the land in that Edge City is expensive, and the developer puts a small, cheap building on it, he will go bankrupt.

So he may decide he needs to bring in more revenue. To do that, he would want to build more office space on the land. This would require him to make his building wider or taller or both.

This sounds easy, but it presents a serious problem. More building kicks all his cost calculations into a new orbit. He needs more parking to match the increased amount of office space. But

* For further information, see Chapters 12, "The Words," and 13, "The Laws."

he has run out of land. Therefore, he must build a multilevel parking "structure." That will cost more than twice as much per parking space as his initial calculations. That levitates his costs, which requires that he build his building larger still—in order to break even. This, in turn, requires more parking, and so the spiral goes.

The developers have one of their totemic phrases for this. They chant: "The world moves at point-four FAR."

FAR, pronounced *eff-eh-are,* is short for Floor-to-Area Ratio. It is the developer's fundamental calculation of urban density, hence traffic, hence parking, hence human behavior, hence civilization. It is the ratio of the amount of building on a piece of property relative to the amount of land. If you've got 100,000 square feet of office space on 100,000 square feet of land, you've got an FAR of 1.0—a one-to-one relationship. If you've got an FAR of 0.4, as in the mantra above, then you've got a ratio of, let us say, 40,000 square feet of office space to 100,000 square feet of land. That configuration succeeds in devoting one and a half times as much land to the parking of cars as you have space to put people to work. But that's the highest building density you're going to get with a flat parking lot. If you want more building than that on a given piece of land, you have to go to more expensive parking garages to accommodate it. That is why the earth moves. You find yourself in a position where you are forced by economics to build an expensive, dense, but potentially more urbane and civilized, Edge City.

In principle, this need for more building requiring more expensive means of parking—which might require more building—would end when a developer has covered all the land he owns with his office building. At that point, the only place to put the parking is underground.

If other developers in the same area came to the same conclusions about the cost-profit equations, and built to similar densities, what you would get, in principle, is an old downtown, with tall buildings shoulder to shoulder.

But as a practical matter, in Edge City that would never happen. At some point—no one knows exactly where, but the numbers twenty to thirty million square feet of office space have been suggested, which is a range on the order of from downtown Minneapolis to downtown Dallas—the hassles of congestion start outweighing the virtues of urbanity. Remember, Edge Cities are competitive with one another. At some point, a newer Edge City that is easier to get around will start stealing market share from a more congested one. That is the time at which the older Edge City has started to become as dense as it is likely to get.

The maximum density thus reached is self-evidently less than the crowding of an old downtown. If we thought downtown levels of density were functional, we'd build more downtowns, and we haven't and we don't and presumably we won't. At those densities, it's hard to use a car.

Nonetheless, long before issues like that come up, civilization can begin to flower in an Edge City. If the location becomes viewed as attractive enough, it starts making economic sense to put up enough structured parking to get the tall buildings within the magic six hundred feet of each other.

When that occurs, a largely unintended consequence comes about—the buildings, no longer separated by impassable moats of parking lot, are miraculously perceived by the people inside them as being within walking distance of one another! And when that happens, all sorts of secondary explosions occur. Real, cloth-napkin restaurants start augmenting those tacky little sandwich shops in the lobby of individual buildings. Bars with character and personality and idiosyncrasy start complementing the fern-strewn pickup joints. An art gallery or a bookstore might even sprout up amid the dry cleaners, branch banks, and travel agencies in the strip shopping centers. Soon—be still my heart—a deadly serious deli devoted to home-made corned beef and face-puckering pickles may arrive. In short, it becomes economically possible for highly specialized places to survive. They may be of interest only to a small portion of the population, but they are of passionate concern to those who are their devotees. They now work because the density of the Edge City surroundings is sufficiently high. There are enough total people within easy access of these places to allow them to survive even with only a small percentage of the market. The result of this density is the diversity, the complexity, that is the singular distinction of both the urban and the urbane. It is a bellwether of livability, of civilization.

If the buildings finally get really close together because of the economics of parking, parking itself becomes less important. Remember, in a thinly built Edge City, the only way to get around is by car, so you have to find yet another parking space every time you move from your office to the shopping center to the restaurant. In a well-developed Edge City—one that is so successful as to justify dense parking—it is possible to create large oases that are both easy to get to by car and easy to get around in once you get out of the car. At the far end of this evolution, the economics of public transit—including Disney-style people-movers and light rail—become less frustrating. It is then feasible to take the pressure off highways and parking needs by employing transportation demand-management techniques. Walking around outdoors can even be attractive if shops are clustered. Cars are shunted to the edges. The result is a place that can deal with both automobiles and humans, even though the first is about twenty-five times more massive than the second. And life is made more pleasant because people are given lots of choices of means to get around.

The lesson of this recitation may seem a little perverse to people sitting in an Edge City traffic jam, fuming at the sea of humanity and exhaust gases around them, thinking that the developers—having totally lost their minds to greed—have built far more than can sensibly be dealt with.

But the moral, nonetheless, is not that Edge Cities are too big. It is that they are not dense *enough*. Done right, the more dense they get, the better they work, because people have more choices, which equals more convenience, which saves time. With a little more density, people are not utterly at the mercy of their cars, because they can get around by foot or people-mover. This actually lessens automobile congestion, because short-haul car trips are fewer. At the same time, with enough people close by, the small amenities of civilization can flourish, such as bistros of exotic ethnicity. You can support diversity.

Mature Edge City realms prove this. "The urbanized portion of Los Angeles County is actually the second most densely settled area of the country, ahead of places like Chicago, Philadelphia, and Detroit," writes Robert Cervero, a professor of city and regional planning at the University of California at Berkeley.

Ironically, he points out, the automobile, like so many other technologies that formed Edge City, simultaneously yields apparently opposite results. Of course it allows the city to spread out. But it also *helps* achieve overall density, compared with other transportation technologies. It allows density to filter into every nook and cranny of the region. In a railroad-era city you got density only within walking distance of the tracks. That is how Philadelphia's Main Line got to be the way it is. With the automobile, though, you get density both near the freeways and in every place that a road or alley can reach.

Moderately high density, in fact, is more typical of maturing Edge Cities than most people think. The twelve fastest growing metro areas in America with populations of over a million—most of which are in the South and West—typically have growth rates in their Edge City environs five times higher than in their old downtowns, Cervero calculates.

At the same time, these urban areas typically have densities *higher* than those in the North and East. This gives them better potential for developing urbanity. Because Edge Cities are almost always economically healthy—that *is* their major reason for existence—they feature few bombed-out areas compared with the old downtowns. Because they usually have a young population, they have large average households. Because they can be expensive to live in, a lot more people live in apartments than is commonly perceived—especially the young, without children, and the elderly. Yet because those apartments are scattered, and frequently low-rise, they do not overwhelm the landscape.

And, of course, there is one more thing to keep in mind about the two laws of physical space that created this new world: it is not that Americans won't walk more than six hundred feet because they are lazy. After all, they will drive a quarter of a mile from their office to a health club for the opportunity to run ten miles. What these laws really do once again is translate distance into our most treasured commodity—time.

The developers who are erecting our new Edge Cities know time's precise measure in dollars and square feet. They look at you strangely if you question them about it. They can't believe any thinking person isn't already aware of this, or might somehow doubt it. The measure of time, individualism, and civilization, they repeat, is *parking*.

All this talk about how Edge City is shaped poses the riddle: Is there any future to individual transportation? Is the automobile not facing attacks from all quarters—from those who revile traffic jams, to those who threaten its oil supply, to those who fear the destruction of the atmosphere of the planet? And if so, don't these threats to the automobile sound the death knell of Edge City?

The answer involves breaking out two completely different issues:

• One is the gasoline-fired internal-combustion engine.
• The other is the actual automobile itself, that privately owned shell of individual transportation in which the main passenger is also the driver. That shell—the actual car—can be pushed around by lots of fuels besides gasoline.

People who view the automobile as a pathology usually take comfort in the view that American and world society somehow "can't" go on as it has. Unfortunately, despite the obvious case to be made that Americans "shouldn't" go on like this, there is little evidence that we "can't."

Put aside the holes in the ozone and craziness in the Middle East for one moment, for the sake of argument. For better or for worse, there are no geological reasons that plenty of oil should not be available throughout the twenty-first century. There is no petrochemical analyst around who thinks there is any supply-and-demand reason—other than war—that the price of oil should go higher than $30 a barrel in constant dollars in this generation. That is, of course, less than the unsustainable $40 peak that accompanied the second oil shock, of 1979. It is also less than the $41 peak hit after Saddam Hussein's invasion of Kuwait doubled the usual market price of about $18.

Even after that invasion, David E. Cole, director of the Office for the Study of Automotive Transportation at the Transportation Research Institute of the University of Michigan, was making the following case:

The decade's most significant change in oil equations was not Saddam Hussein. It was the collapse of Soviet communism. Cole's reasoning: the Soviet Union is the world's largest producer of oil—greater than Saudi Arabia. The major limit on that exploitation is lack of sophisticated Western technology. Therefore, the easiest way for the Soviets to gain hard currency quickly is to allow Western wildcatters to enhance the efficiency of Siberian oil fields.

There really are few shortages of petrochemicals on the horizon throughout the twenty-first century and even into the twenty-second—if we are ready to pay the price. If we choose to accept the political and environmental and military and economic consequences, we can find enough oil on this planet.

Of course, there are good reasons not to do that. Gasoline helps cause the air in places like Southern California to be characterized as "unhealthful" 232 days a year. This is the basis of an important idea: that the liberation the automobile offers is a false one; that it sows the seeds of its own destruction. Individual transportation, in this view, is the Machine that will destroy the Garden.

There's a challenge inherent in that observation. Plenty of more environmentally benign fuels could move our automobiles —natural gas, alcohol from renewable plant life, solar-generated hydrogen, solar-generated electricity. They are not as cheap as gasoline. They might cost the equivalent of as much as $4.00 a gallon, which was the price of gasoline in 1990 in Milan, Stockholm, Paris, and Dublin.

But here's the point. Suppose we as a society decide to turn against gasoline for environmental and political reasons, the way we appear to have turned against nuclear power. There is still little if any reason to think that it would lead to the demise of individual transportation—the car.

Fans of the nineteenth-century cities have a tough argument to make if they think they can ignore the challenge of Edge City, hoping that OPEC or California's South Coast Air Quality Management District will bring about the end of the automobile. They value highly what they perceive as the ancillary benefits: the end of low-density suburbs, the re-emergence of the railroad as the primary mode of transportation, the return of middle-class homes to the old downtowns, and a newly found pleasure in the walk to work.

There is no reason, however, to think that the end to the gasoline engine would produce these results. Many alternatives would become more attractive, and $4.00-a-gallon fuel would doubtless lead to more efficient automobiles. But it would not change this verity: in an affluent America, the dominant mode of transportation for generations is likely to be something with four tires and a steering wheel. In the Depression, the last thing to go was the car. It's simply a question of what we value.

This, then, brings us to the other big problem of cars, their bodies. They are so physically big, and must be spread so far apart when they move fast, that it is impossible to get hundreds of thousands of them into one location at one time without spreading our built world all over the landscape and/or creating traffic jams.

Now *that* is a genuinely limiting factor. Traffic jams are a horrifying waste of that vital commodity, time. Americans tell pollsters that traffic congestion is among the most maddening problems they face.

However, there are reasons to believe that the demographic underpinnings of our newest traffic jams are cresting. And fixes do exist to improve traffic flow somewhat.

The best news for the future of traffic in America is that it is not humanly possible to increase the number of cars on the road at the same rate as in the past. Their number is approaching the saturation point. There are already 19 percent more legally registered motor vehicles in this country than there are licensed drivers. The boom in new drivers has also peaked. The Census is expected to find only four states in the Union—each in the Southwest—with more people eighteen to twenty-four-years old than a decade before. There are not many more women who can work, who want to work, who do not already work.

Typical commutes are becoming shorter, insists Alan Pisarski, author of *Commuting in America.* To be sure, contradictory forces are at work. There are "supercommuters," who travel more than a hundred miles round trip in search of low housing prices or country spreads. But fewer than 4 percent of all work trips are more than thirty miles. Most commonly, they are under ten miles. People typically took 21.7 minutes to get to work in 1980. The new Census number will probably be closer to twenty minutes, Pisarski believes. That is because of Edge City. Commutes to Edge City are two-thirds the typical commute to the old downtown; jobs in Edge City are closer to the homes of the middle class than at any time since World War II.

If these statistics seem hard to believe, it is because the *stress* of driving is going up. In the past twenty years, highway travel has risen 69 percent and capital spending on bridges and highways has fallen 38 percent. There is a huge supply of urban activists, environmentalists, planners, and not-in-my-back-yard subdivision residents who have enforced this trend. They have the quaint notion that it is more important to create neighborhoods that are attractive for people to stay in and enjoy than it is to pave them so that people can rapidly go somewhere else. We once built highways the way the pharaohs built Pyramids. Now we have stopped. This is a genuine threat to the future of the automobile, the undermining of its advantage in terms of choice and time. And there is no absolute solution to this problem. In a popular location, any improvement in traffic flow is probably temporary. The more capacity you add, the more likely you are to make the place more popular, attracting more development, thereby attracting more business, and creating more traffic.

But there are ways of ameliorating this situation some. Each is part of a simple combination: squeeze a little more capacity out of existing roads; decrease demand. None is overwhelmingly important in itself, but together they can amount to a fair improvement. These methods include: creating special car-pool lanes; transforming highway shoulders into travel lanes; squeezing an extra lane into the travel path by reducing the width of every lane from twelve feet to eleven; metering on-ramps to spread out and speed up the flow; creating transportation management authorities to coordinate ride sharing and the shifting of corporate work hours, allowing flextime arrangements that let people go to and from work earlier or later than normal; and legalizing jitneys to allow a kind of private-enterprise minibus to deliver multiple passengers door to door. Anthony Downs of the Brookings Institution, who has long studied Edge Cities, thinks the answer is to buy a good car stereo and commute with someone you love. The Japanese are showing the prototypes of single-passenger cars that are half as wide as normal cars, meaning that you can get twice as many of them in a lane. Then there are the high-tech solutions. Build intelligent freeways that let drivers know where traffic tie-ups are and how to avoid them. On-board navigation computers have been sold in Japan and Europe for several years. A project in California proposes equipping cars with radar and computerizing the highways so that vehicles could zip along at sixty miles per hour, three feet apart. The problem? If something ever went wrong, the liability lawyers would devour every single individual and government unfortunate enough to survive the pile-up.

But the best bet is probably the one we are engaged in right now: building Edge City. It is a world that does not deny the automobile, but at the same time increases density, putting everything a person desires as close as possible to his house while reducing the number of different places he has to park in order to go about his affairs.

Three quarters of all car trips are *not* commutes to work. They involve tending to the effluvia of life. The proof of all this is Los Angeles, the great-granddaddy of Edge Cities. Californians now actually consume less gasoline per person than the national average. They also require fewer cars per capita than people in other big states like Texas and Florida. And their typical commute is under ten miles—the same as the national average.

Just about everybody who looks seriously at the problem of traffic ends up thinking that the answer is to raise the cost of driving. Ray Watson, the first planner of Irvine, California, the largest Edge City created by one corporation, points out that if we merely increased the occupancy of the average car from today's 1.23 people to 1.77 people, we would have more road capacity than we would ever need. He believes that a serious tax on gasoline is necessary and inescapable. He thinks a few presidents of the United States may lose re-election before we come to accept that. But he believes it inevitable. He further insists that when it happens, it is important *not* to shield the poor from the effect of that tax. It is they who are the most likely candidates to switch to car pools and mass transit, he reasons, so in the war against traffic, the first casualty must be egalitarianism.

Cervero of Berkeley also thinks that the biggest problem of the automobile is not the car itself but the lack of appropriate price clues. We think that roads are free, and we use them with abandon. He sees the solution as pricing the automobile "realistically."

That may involve putting tolls on the most congested roads in order to let the market allocate that scarce resource, especially at rush hour. Put a sticker on every bumper. Let it resemble the parallel bars of the Universal Product Code on every cereal box. Station a laser reader on the roadside. Every time it reads the presence of my bumper, let my Visa card be charged. Let those who most use and most value these public road spaces be charged the most amount of money. Transfer the proceeds to whichever additional transit schemes the electorate thinks best: freeways, railroads, buses.

Of course, the problem with other transit systems is that no matter how much we subsidize them, they remain *mass* transit. The cheapest and most flexible form is buses in special high-occupancy-vehicle lanes. But there is something about buses we hate. "Show me a man over thirty who regularly takes the bus, and I will show you a life failure," said one senior mass transit official who obviously wished to remain anonymous. Buses feature the fewest cubic feet of elbow room per passenger of any transportation mode in this century, with the possible exception of the New York–to–Washington air shuttle. Because they have to make so many stops, and frequently have roundabout routes, they are often slower even than bumper-to-bumper traffic. Their ambiance is that of a public washroom. Buses are those contrivances onto which affluent people would like to force everybody else—in order to make it easier for them to drive.

Trains, by contrast, can be charming. They can offer the leg room of a limousine. They can include sleeping cars and restaurants with fine china, if we choose. But the economics of commuter trains are maddening. There is not thought to be a single commuter rail system in the United States that manages even to meet its expenses out of the farebox. They need subsidies just to move, no less to lay track. A new rail car costs a million dollars. If you could attract a hundred passengers into it each rush hour, it would still cost $10,000 per person for the rolling stock—the price of a decent automobile. And that's before you go to General Electric or General Motors and pay up to $4 million for a locomotive. Nor does it count the cost of the track, or the land under the track, or the power guides over the track, or the electrified third rails in the middle of the track, or the building of stations, or maintenance, or fuel, or the cost of a driver for the train, or of conductors and guards. One train set is lucky to make two trips in the right direction per rush hour. These trains carry a heavy load four hours a day, five days a week. Not much time to make up your costs. Nor is the system adaptive. If the driver goes on strike, the system dies. If key equipment fails, so does the system. Because you have to wait at the platform for the train to come, and then sit through all its interminable stops, on a door-to-door basis, commuter rail generally has an average speed lower than that of automobiles in rush hour. Then you get to your office and are stuck without the flexibility of a car. If you need to drop the kids off at the day-care center, or pick up some groceries on the way home, or make a sales call during the day, or go to a meeting some distance away, you have a problem. That is not trivial. There is now usually a third rush hour in Edge City—lunch. Nor is it easy to run trains in the spiderweb pattern of Edge City. Nor is it easy to relay track when development patterns change. No wonder forecasts for recent light-rail projects turned out to be wildly off the mark. They overestimated ridership and underestimated cost by a combined factor of from 200 to 400 percent. An Edge City is thought to need a stunning thirty million square feet of office space—equivalent to downtown Dallas—to justify a new rapid transit train system. None of them is that big yet. A merely huge fifteen million square feet—the size of downtown New Orleans—is thought to be required to make new light rail cost effective.* This is why commuter rail is so frustratingly difficult to justify as a transportation solution. The alternatives have to be pretty wretched to make the calculations work. The air quality has to be utterly desolate, and automobile traffic impossibly congested, and the cost of land for additional lanes of freeway prohibitively expensive, or rail comes a cropper.

Even traditional arguments for the train are facing new competition. Remember the idea that people waste less time on trains, because they can read or work or sleep? Books on tape, concert-quality car stereos, car phones, portable fax machines, and lap-top computers all are making car time more productive. Refrigerators and beds have been in vans for decades. Now there is serious talk of cars with microwaves so that you can start thawing dinner.

But this all focuses on trains as transportation devices. There may be a stronger argument for them than that. Maybe they should be subsidized because they bring civilization. The logic goes like this. A train station invariably results in a knot of dense

* For more such rules of thumb on trains and transportation, see Chapter 13, "The Laws."

development. That is because every builder wants to be able to charge high rents by saying his property is within walking distance of that station. Now, as a matter of fact, the vast majority of all people will continue to arrive at such a rail-served Edge City by car. Even in a building directly over the tracks, 90 percent of all office workers will demand parking. But so what? By building the train station, you *have* convinced people to build unusually high and walkable densities. This density, in turn, serves the purposes of creating civilization in the form of restaurants and bookstores and the like. This civilization, in turn, gives that particular Edge City a blessed competitive advantage. This increases property values. Therefore, a strong fairness case can be made that some of the money should be kicked back to the train.

But these are not major twists. The fact is, the technologies for moving humans have pretty much hit a dead end. Rocket-planes may someday allow the wealthy to get from New York to Tokyo in short order. Magnetic levitation may allow trains to move as fast as a DC-3. But these incremental improvements are not likely to change most people's lives. Would they even be as much of a rumble as the creation of Federal Express? Few seers seem to think so.

No, the final frontier, as Captain Kirk used to say, would appear to be—the "dematerializing technologies." These are emerging technologies so revolutionary we still don't usually understand them for what they really are—which is a new kind of transportation method.

There is no one who is truly suggesting that humans will be turned into Star Trek–like ions, to boldly go to some location where no man has gone before. At least not in the reasonably foreseeable future.

But still . . . But still . . .

Consider the lowly facsimile machine. You stick a piece of paper into it in Detroit. The machine subtracts the paper. It moves everything important about that paper across a wire. At the other end—Stuttgart, perhaps—it adds the paper back. It functionally rematerializes the original dematerialized document.

Have you not, for practical purposes, just transported this piece of paper? You have certainly replaced a whole bunch of motorcycle messengers, mail trucks, and overnight cargo airplanes. That is the essence of the dematerializing technologies. They are what we used to think of as communications devices. But they have become so advanced that they are now backing out the physical movement of objects; hence, they have become a transportation breakthrough.

Since cities are formed by the state-of-the-art transportation device of the time, the dematerializing technologies would appear to be the next shaper of our cities.

When you start looking around, you realize that a lot of things are routinely being dematerialized these days. A newspaper published by the *Detroit Free Press* or the *Detroit News,* for example, makes the first twenty-two miles of its trip to a distant subscriber dematerialized. A page made up at the papers' headquarters is scanned by laser and transformed into computer code that is then transmitted to Sterling Heights over regular telephone lines. There it drives a machine that burns a negative that is transformed into plates that are slapped onto the presses. The transmission takes less than two minutes. In effect, that Sterling Heights plant is where the paper is materializing.

You can dematerialize a door. Suppose you want a fancy one— special height, width, glass, carvings. Right now, a distant manufacturer with special capabilities is probably your source. After meeting your peculiar specifications, he puts the door on a truck to ship it a thousand miles. But it doesn't have to be that way. Say the manufacturer is using computer-driven machine tools. If a shop close to you is similarly equipped, it could easily make the same door—if it knew how. The answer might be to pay the fancy specialty-door maker to transmit the information that sets up the local shop's computerized tools. Then let the local shop make the door. Presto. No long truck trip.

You can dematerialize humans, after a fashion. The more people do their work in front of computer screens, the more corporations realize that they do not need to transport all their employees to expensive central locations. They can let the humans labor near where they live, and electronically transport their work, instead.

Take the Ford Parts and Service Division. It is headquartered in an Edge City in Dearborn. But Ford wanted to locate some jobs in the old downtown, at least partially to demonstrate its civic commitment. So Parts and Services in 1990 moved its Customer Assistance Center to a remote location—the high-rise, riverfront, downtown Renaissance Center. That detachment is linked to the rest of the company by PROFS, Ford's worldwide computer network. For those people who work there and also live in Detroit, the relocating of their jobs to Renaissance Center has effectively caused them to be dematerialized. They do not have to commute to Dearborn. Their work is shipped on a wire, and they are removed from the freeway.

The implications of these dematerializing technologies are staggering. Their very purpose is to make distance irrelevant. When you start thinking of the potential of these technologies, you begin to wonder why we build any kind of cities at all, Edge or otherwise. The key determinants in real estate have always been location, location, and location. But the point of these machines is to make location meaningless. We used to say that somebody lived an hour away from us. Now we say he lives an hour ahead of us. With enough computers and telephone lines, should it not be possible to remove ourselves each to our own mountaintop, never to come together again except electronically?

The answer, mercifully, is no. Too lonely. To the extent that dematerializing technologies make distance irrelevant, they allow other values to come to the fore. As a result, an ancient one now looms newly large in a way that is heart-warming and reassuring. Humans, as it turns out, really are social animals. They like to be with other humans. In the last few decades it was ballyhooed that everybody would soon live and work in electronic cottages, linked only by computer bulletin boards and fax machines. Hasn't happened. Computer industry analysts now think that no more than 3 to 5 percent of all workers will ever be permanently home-based. People may use their home offices to work on nights or weekends, or to start up businesses on the side. Women who are pregnant or families with young children will continue to find home offices a godsend—allowing them to keep in touch with work without losing touch with the kids. But it turns out there's a real problem with working at home all the time. It is just as Finn Caspersen of Beneficial Corporation at New Jersey's 287 and 78 maintained: electronics do not provide the kind of connectedness with other people we get from face-to-face contact.

In fact, it seems that the more cleverness-based and computerized our world becomes, the more we require face-to-face contact. For the most valuable kind of information may be inherently uncomputerizable—because it is ambiguous. Take the question "Can I trust this guy?" Very difficult to establish that over a telephone or a computer.

Or take the creative cross-fertilization that routinely occurs in those wildly undervalued sessions known as "schmoozing" or "B.S.-ing around the water cooler." In those encounters, one person says to a second, "What are you working on?"; a third adds, "Did you know Sarah was doing something on that?"; a fourth says, "Did you think of trying it this way?"; and a fifth says, "I know somebody you've got to talk to; I'll call you with the number."

The entire exchange takes two minutes, yet it may be the most productive encounter of the entire day for everybody involved. What's more, the smaller your enterprise, the less likely you are to gain this sort of unplanned, unplannable, serendipitous cross-fertilization in the halls of your own office. This was pointed out by Edwin S. Mills of Northwestern University in a ground-breaking analysis of ambiguous information.

Such a need to get out and pollinate your thinking is the significance of such powerful urban social institutions as lunch. Lunch, in turn, is a function of cities, Edge or otherwise. This is why bright people will continue to need physical proximity to one another and to Edge City.

———————

The clearest proof that there is substantial life left in the idea of cities comes, ironically, from Dr. Thomas A. Furness and Dr. Robert Jacobson of the University of Washington, in Seattle.

Furness and Jacobson run the Human Interface Technology Laboratory. The Human Interface Lab is regarded by many as the hottest computer lab in the world. Its specialty: inventing virtual reality.

Virtual reality is the *ne plus ultra* dematerializing technology. It is the generating of a computer-created apparition or simulacrum, long distance, that is so startlingly similar to what a human would normally perceive as everyday, concrete, physical reality as to be almost indistinguishable from it.

I reasoned that if dematerializing technologies would be shaping cities in the future, and their limit was our need for face-to-face contact, then virtual reality might be the key to the future of our cities.

Little did I know.

Furness and Jacobson view it as certain that, within ten years, a human being will be able to generate a three-dimensional representation of himself. That simulacrum will be able to sit at a conference table in a distant city and participate in a meeting. The instant the real, remote human moves, speaks, or rubs his eye, this apparition could faithfully transmit the gesture and inflection. In other words, the lab leaders believe, it would go a long way toward transmitting ambiguous information.

One limit to this now is the vast amount of computer firepower required. Another is devising the machines that convincingly deliver the illusion directly to your eye. But equally important is how much transmission capability would be required to make the apparition seem real. Not until regular telephone wires are widely replaced by fiber optics will that kind of virtual reality become real.

Furness and Jacobson—who are serious middle-aged academics—do not see that as a limit. They see the day when people will combine their simulacra with other virtual realities. Two architects might be collaborating, one in Detroit, the other in Seattle. The computers would create not only their personal simulacra in virtual reality, but the unbuilt building they are working on. Their simulacra could then walk through the hypothetical building, experience it in virtual reality, and relay the experience back to the actual humans. If the architects decided they didn't like a wall, their simulacra could point at it with a finger. And it would fly away.

As much as this sounds like science fiction, virtual reality is a research field heavily funded both by the U.S. Defense Advanced Research Projects Agency (DARPA) and Japanese industrial consortia. The National Aeronautics and Space Administration now has a virtual reality generator in its Silicon Valley Ames Research Center; it translates Viking orbiter probes into an experience that makes users feel they are immersing themselves in the Valles Marineris of Mars.

Nor is that all. The Human Interface Lab's researchers look forward to adding the sense of touch. They can imagine a distant human wearing a sensing device, some sort of glove, perhaps. When he reaches out his hand, his simulacrum will be able to pat someone on the shoulder and say well done, and both the real human present and the remote human operating through his simulacrum would feel the warmth.

Not a trivial piece of technology, Furness reports. Not easy to create equipment that realistically reacts to distant pressure and temperature signals and relays those instantly in a way that can be humanly sensed. Again, one of the major headaches is transmission. A good personal computer today transmits 2400 bits of information per second. It is referred to as having a 2400-baud modem. Touch would require tens of thousands of times that. Quite a feat.

As Furness and Jacobson soberly made predictions of one mind-blowing miracle after another—this one in ten years, that one in twenty years—I sat, dazzled. As they spoke, I racked my brain. Surely, I thought, there must be some aspect of human life that will be the one challenge their technologies will never be able to handle.

And that is how we wound up with Dr. Furness breaking the following bulletin: *Satisfactory sex—transmitted long distance, via computer—will require a 3,000,000,000-baud modem.*

Furness had already given the question some thought, it turned out. Not only had he considered what "satisfactory" might amount to; he'd sat down and done the arithmetic. He'd figured out how many polygons of information would be required to re-create the tactile sensations and the visual images and the aroma and so forth, and multiplied how many bits of information that would represent, and calculated how many times per second that information would have to be refreshed in order for the experience to seem realistic. He had then calculated, in effect, what diameter the electronic pipe would have to be to carry that much information.

Three billion baud, he thinks.

More than a million times greater than today's personal computers.

It's going to take a while before such technology is available, he believes. Maybe the year 2050 or so. But he was not kidding. This was his best estimate of the future of his revolutionary research.

Who knows if he is right? But after talking to him, I felt I could confidently make a prediction: I knew at least one good reason why cities won't be obsolete for at least another half century. And is this a great country or *what*—that there are people out there worrying about these things.

But more to the point, perhaps, I was left with a certain ambiguous, unquantifiable feeling.

Why did I have this fleeting thought that Dr. Furness' calculations of a revolution next century just might underestimate the complexity and usefulness of both sex—and cities?

# 5

## ATLANTA

### The Color of Money

I have a dream that my four little children will one day live in a nation where they will not be judged by the color of their skin but by the content of their character.

—*Dr. Martin Luther King, Jr., August 28, 1963*

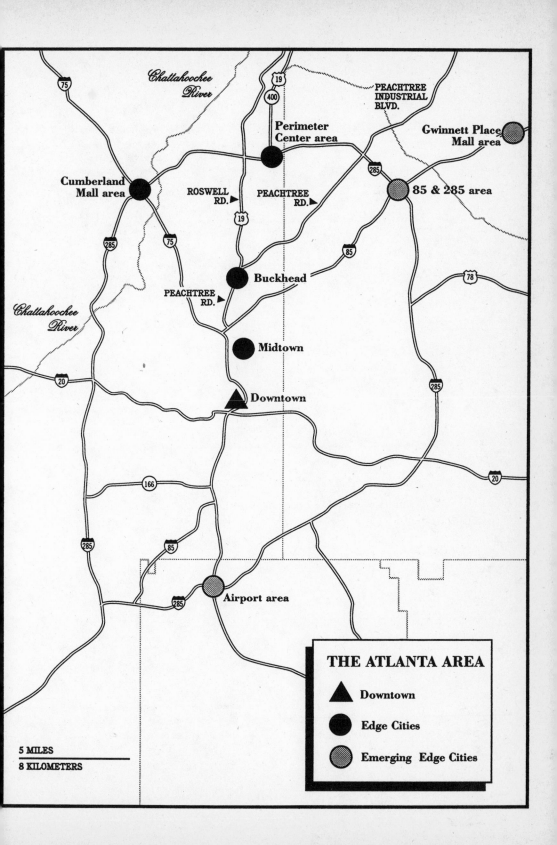

Chattahoochee River

75

PEACHTREE INDUSTRIAL BLVD.

19

400

Perimeter Center area

Gwinnett Place Mall area

285

Cumberland Mall area

ROSWELL RD. ▶

PEACHTREE RD. ▶

85 & 285 area

19

285

75

85

78

PEACHTREE RD. ▶

Buckhead

Chattahoochee River

Midtown

Downtown

285

20

166

20

285

85

285

Airport area

THE ATLANTA AREA

▲ Downtown

● Edge Cities

● Emerging Edge Cities

5 MILES

8 KILOMETERS

IN A CLEARING surrounded by dogwood and pine north of Atlanta's Perimeter beltway, George and Patricia Lottier have carved out a classic little American success story.

A few years ago, George left his job with a Fortune 500 corporation to launch his own company selling durable souvenir drinking cups—like those with the team's emblem which you take home from a Hawks game. His enterprise, Plastic Impressions, is based in an office-condo tastefully clad in stucco and gray clapboard offset by dark green canopies and doors. It grosses about $12 million a year. He believes it will be doing $30 million to $40 million worth of business in three years. He drives a two-year-old Lincoln.

Patricia Lottier, meanwhile, is publisher of *The Atlanta Tribune,* a monthly that focuses on affluent, entrepreneurial business people. The *Tribune*'s offices, adjacent to George's, are marked by blond furniture housing the IBM PS 80 computer driving the makeup screen, the NEC Silent Writer 890 laser printer that sets the type, and a light table. Camera-ready ads from Coors, Benson and Hedges, First Atlanta, and Warner Books are temporarily pasted on the walls.

George Lottier is an avid golfer. He shoots in the low eighties. The Lottiers live in a home that boasts a Jacuzzi next to a built-in gas barbecue, and a lighted sports court for tennis and basketball. It backs up to a fragrant forest in a subdivision built around the Willow Springs Country Club. George said that when they moved, getting a house with a golf course attached to it was not a high priority for him. It was the first priority, "and there was no two, three, or four."

The Lottiers' two sons are Christopher and Shawn. The elder is already in college; the younger recently was trying to choose between the University of Virginia or Georgetown.

The Lottiers' story is so typical of Atlanta today that in their office foyer is a painting of the fabled Fox Theater that actually has *Gone With the Wind* on the marquee. In fact, the Lottiers' story would be utterly unremarkable in America—right down to the fact that it is occurring off Georgia Route 400, north of the booming Atlanta Edge City of Perimeter Center. Except possibly for one thing: the Lottiers are black.

So is everybody profiled in *The Atlanta Tribune.*

For the Lottiers and people like them are part of one of the biggest changes in black affairs in American history. The Lottiers are not some kind of superachievers. They are part of a new black middle class without precedent in size and accomplishment in the more than four hundred years blacks have been in the New World. This black middle class is succeeding by the standards of the majority white culture in mainstream American careers. What's more, this new black middle class is burgeoning in the suburbs surrounding Edge Cities.

The rise of Edge Cities contained a nightmare possibility for America: that because so many jobs were moving out to the fringe, frequently into what had been lily-white suburbs, an entire race would be left behind, trapped, in the inner city, jobless, beyond reach of the means of creating wealth.

Such fears, however, have not been confirmed, despite the plight of the black underclass. A black suburban middle class is booming, statistics show. And it is emerging at the same time and in the same places as Edge Cities.

In fact, by the second decade of the next century, this new American black middle class could be as large in percentage terms for blacks as the white middle class will be for whites, predicts Bart Landry, the University of Maryland sociologist who wrote *The New Black Middle Class.*

Already, in the Atlanta area, of the 19 percent of all families that are black:

• Almost a third make more money than the typical white family in America.

• Forty percent are suburbanites.

• A third live in predominantly white areas. Psychological barriers long thought to separate Atlanta into the "white" Northside and the "black" Southside—such as Ponce de Leon Avenue—are not as impregnable as myth credits them with being.

• Middle-class black families living in middle-class neighborhoods have virtually the same income as their white neighbors.*

Nor is Atlanta an aberration. In the Oakland area, 36 percent of all black families are more prosperous than the typical white family in America. On Long Island, it's 49 percent. In the Chicago area, it's 30 percent. In the Miami area, it's 24 percent. In the Los Angeles area, 33 percent. In the Detroit area, 31 percent. In the Washington area, it's 46 percent. This means blacks are now significantly represented in some of the most expensive neighborhoods in America. To the extent that income is a measure of class, those numbers reflect the size of the black middle class in America.

"There is a story there to be told. And it is a story of the success of the revolution of the last twenty years," acknowledges Milton D. Morris. Morris is the director of research at the Joint Center for Political Studies in Washington. The Joint Center is America's pre-eminent black think tank.

"It's almost as if we would rather not focus on that side of the picture, because, after all, the glass is half empty. Many people still perceive the results as very, very tenuous. It's like 'Yes, there are these things, but we really don't believe it's for real; we can't take it too seriously because it could disappear any minute.' But those successes, they're there. They're real. They ought to inspire us."

None of this is to suggest that the problems of race and poverty in America are solved: the problems of poor black people both in the inner cities and in rural areas are daunting. Some of the highest birth rates in America are recorded in neighborhoods where a third of the population is unemployed half the year. The virulence and toxicity of new drugs such as crack are awesome in their effects. The murder rate in inner-city neighborhoods exceeds one a day. During the sharp recession of the

* For quick reference to the demographic undergirdings of this and other chapters, see the Notes.

early 1980s, the size of the black middle class shrank. Black college enrollment for males has declined from the 1970s. One in four young black males in America is in jail, on probation, or dead before the age of thirty. There is only one black-owned corporation in the Black Enterprise 100 that would compare with any corporation in the Fortune 500. Many people, both black and white, firmly believe there is a resurgent white racism. The Reagan and Bush administrations' civil rights and affirmative action record is hardly viewed as benign. And even the growth of the new black middle class does not necessarily yield racial integration; it sometimes means the rise of affluent suburban enclaves that are still almost all black.

What can be said with a fair amount of confidence, however, is that the rise of Edge City has not had an evil effect on the aspirations of all black people. It has been at least matched by the rise of a large, churchgoing, home-owning, childrearing, back-yard-barbecuing, traffic-jam-cursing black middle class remarkable only for the very ordinariness with which its members go about their classically American suburban affairs.

"Successful blacks are the most forgotten group of Americans there are, and the most interesting," says George Sternlieb of Rutgers. "The focus has been so much on the losers that the very people who have been able to come through have been ignored."*

Broadly sketched, there have been three black elites in American history, and to understand the previous two is to grasp just how different in scale is the new one.

The first black elite emerged after the Civil War. Among blacks of that era, status was determined largely by proximity to whites. Those who had once been "house" slaves enjoyed a higher status among their liberated brethren than did those who had once been "field" slaves. A black barber could be regarded in the black community as having relatively high status if he had a large number of prominent white businessmen as clients. The inarguable demonstration of proximity to whites, of course, was to have relatively light skin. That is where the equation got started among blacks—which persists to this day—that the

---

* In fact, the National Association of Black Journalists awarded its Frederick Douglass Prize to the author in 1988 for his previous reporting on the black suburban middle class, which culminated in this chapter.

darker one's skin, the lower one's status, according to historians and sociologists such as E. Franklin Frazier, author of *Black Bourgeoisie,* the 1957 study universally regarded as a benchmark.

The second black middle class appeared around the turn of the century. This was the preachers-and-teachers middle class, the pinnacle of segregated society. Its core was black professionals serving a black clientele—a small band of doctors, lawyers, restaurateurs, and undertakers, for example. It was particularly well represented in Atlanta because of the clustering there of the five black colleges and universities that now come under the umbrella of the Atlanta University Center, the nation's largest private black institution of higher learning, crowned by Morehouse College, "the black Harvard," and its sister school, Spelman.

The legacy of this second middle class can still be seen in the markers put up by the U.S. Park Service in front of the Victorian and Queen Anne–style homes on Auburn Avenue, near Ebenezer Baptist Church. This is the neighborhood where Martin Luther King, Jr., grew up; it is now a National Historic Site and Preservation District.

In front of 522 Auburn, used as National Park offices, is a sign labeling it the "Bryant-Graves Home, circa 1894." It reads: "In its prime, the 'Sweet Auburn' neighborhood of King's boyhood housed a diverse mixture of people—some poor, some wealthy, some obscure, some prominent. This house reflects the life style of two community leaders. Reverend Peter James Bryant, Associate Editor, *Voice of the Negro,* and a leader of the fight against the 1908 Negro disenfranchisement law, resided here from 1912 to 1925. Later, Antoine Graves, a highly successful Black realtor and contractor, occupied the home through the 1940s."

Members of the second black middle class still did not necessarily equate status with money. Status was measured more in the manner of the British elite, by refinement of manner and education. Being "in trade" was considered déclassé, even though this black middle class owed its position to a captive market. Thus, as integration opened whole new worlds in the 1960s, this middle class declined in influence. But it had always been tiny. In 1950, less than 1 percent of all black people had a median income equal to that of white people with white-collar jobs. Right after World War II, an income of $5000 a year was upper middle class for whites. Perhaps seventy-five thousand black people in the whole country made that kind of money then, out of a total black population of fifteen million. That seventy-five thousand is not much larger than the circulation of the Lottiers' publication aimed at black enterprise in one urban area today. In fact, as recently as twenty-five years ago, it was almost specious to make class distinctions among black people. For the overwhelming reality was—to be black was to be poor.

That is no longer the case. This era's third black middle class is the one that rose with the legal end of American apartheid in the mid-1960s. The Civil Rights Act of 1964 opened up access to public accommodations and most workplaces. The Voting Rights Act of 1965 guaranteed blacks the ballot in the South and attacked the system of terrorism that had been set up to keep them from gaining power at the polls.

This new black middle class was the first to find its circumstances approximating that which white people took for granted for themselves. Not too surprisingly, this middle class promptly became the first to measure status primarily the way most whites do—by the amount of money it could command from society. It was the first middle class to include a serious share of all blacks. And it is a middle class that is still relatively young. If you were eighteen in 1964, in 1990 you were just entering your peak earning years, at the age of forty-four. For that baby boom generation of black people it really is a different world from the one their parents come from.

Both "middle class" and "suburban" can be tricky to define. University of Maryland sociologist Landry is especially leery of describing the black middle class solely in dollar terms. He points out that the combined incomes of a working-class family —a security guard, a domestic, and a teenager working a Mc-Donald's counter, for example—can easily match the income of, say, a single-earner family headed by a civil engineer. But, he would argue, that does not make the three-earner family middle class. Its chances are about maxed out. The civil engineer, by contrast, has far greater access to such economic opportunities as a mortgage, a line of credit, and continuing advanced education.

Suppose then that a middle-class job is defined as one primarily demanding intelligence and judgment. That basically means a white-collar job. Suppose further that a middle-class family is defined as one marked by that kind of work, plus the realistic expectation of college for the kids, plus an above-average income.

Meanwhile, "suburban" is usually defined for statistical purposes as any place in a metropolitan area outside the central city. That definition is less than ideal in both directions. There are beautiful, affluent, quiet, black and white neighborhoods within the political boundaries of the city of Atlanta that feature trees, lawns, and single-family detached homes. For all practical purposes, they look and function like suburbs even though they are usually counted as urban. Similarly, there are downtrodden neighborhoods in outlying "suburban" jurisdictions that are nothing but extensions of either urban or rural poverty. Suppose, therefore, a neighborhood is functionally suburban, regardless of its location within a metro area, if it is predominantly residential, well off, and marked by single-family homes.

By those standards, at least a quarter, if not a third, of the black families in Atlanta are suburban middle class, according to extensive computer runs performed specifically for this chapter by the national marketing demographic firm Claritas. These complex runs were in turn cross-checked for consistency against federal, state, and local statistics, reviewed by demographers at the Atlanta Regional Commission and geographers at Georgia State University, and verified by interviews on the ground.

And this suburban middle class is not peculiar to Atlanta, the research shows. Other cities with vastly different histories are producing suburban middle-class black families just as reliably. In the North, Detroit had the largest proportion of skilled black craftsmen of any city with major black population in 1940. Today in the Detroit suburbs, the children of auto workers are flourishing as engineers and executives. In the West, there was a historic absence of a hard-core legal system of segregation. "I grew up in California, and I never knew about Jim Crow," explains Roscoe Dellums, wife of U.S. Representative Ron Dellums of Northern California. "Our parents didn't talk about such things in front of us. They felt they were preparing the generation that would break through, and we never got the message that we were inferior." Today Los Angeles, America's most dynamic urban area, with a population that is less than 15 percent black, has a black mayor. Nationwide, since 1970, the number of black-owned businesses has more than doubled, the number of black managers and administrators has nearly tripled, and the number of black lawyers has increased more than sixfold.

The result is that the black population in America today is divided roughly into thirds. One-third is the largely suburban middle class. (The way Bart Landry defines middle class, the proportion is 46 percent.)

Roughly a third—30 percent of black families—continues to be in poverty. However, only about a third of that third—perhaps 10 percent of the total black population—is swept up in those profoundly depressing problems clustered under the rubric "underclass," according to most calculations. Estimates by researchers at the Urban Institute indicate that "underclass neighborhoods"—areas where high school dropouts, unemployed men, welfare recipients, and female-headed families are especially numerous—contained a total of 2.5 million people in 1980. That is a dreadful number, but even if that population were all black, which it is not, it would work out to only 9.4 percent of the total black population in America.

Then there is a working class between the two. This class benefited from the sustained tight labor markets of the 1980s. In a report for the National Bureau of Economic Research, the Harvard economist Richard Freeman showed that when the unemployment rate dropped below 4 percent in the cities he studied, the key employment rate for young black men with a high school degree or less improved by a third. To put it another way, in 1983 the unemployment rate in those cities for the members of that group was 41 percent. In 1987, it was 7 percent. Future years in which growth occurs probably will be similar. Fewer young people will be entering the work force in the 1990s than there were during the baby boom.

What's more, assuming they get an even chance—which is admittedly a large "if"—the children of that in-between black working class are in a better position to move into the middle class today than any minority group that preceded them, Landry maintains. That is because the economy is producing more middle-class white-collar jobs than any other kind.

"If you came in in the 1950s and had an equal chance, you

should have middle-class children now," Landry says. "If they went to school, boom, the jobs available to them should all be middle class. At the turn of the century, or during the Depression, a very small percentage of anybody was middle class."

The makeup of these classes is not static. Individuals move up and down within them. People who stay in school make it out of housing projects and up the socioeconomic ladder all the time. By the same token, people of any race who have not accumulated wealth are only four or five paychecks away from slipping several notches.

But the idea that in the 1990s most blacks are somehow behind all whites in achievement is just plain wrong. Since the 1960s, black educational attainment has seen one of the steepest growth curves of any population group in American history— including the Chinese, the Japanese, and the Jews. Only 38 percent of young adult blacks had a high school education in 1960. That figure had soared to 55 percent by 1970, 75 percent by 1980, and had reached 83 percent by 1986. The high school dropout rate plummeted.

Between 1984 and 1989, the number of black students taking college Advanced Placement exams almost tripled. Those who received grades high enough to qualify for college credits more than doubled. Of all black kids who had graduated from high school in 1988, 27.1 percent were in college. To put that another way, a higher percentage of young black Americans are in college than there are young Swiss or English people in college. "Perhaps the most untold story of American education in the past few years is the achievement of black students; the hard data are encouraging," says Gregory R. Anrig, president of the Educational Testing Service in Princeton, which administers the National Assessment of Educational Progress, the Advanced Placement tests, and the Scholastic Aptitude Test.

And this is largely a function of the rise of the black middle class. Among those black kids who took the SATs, the percentage of their parents who had at least an undergraduate degree increased from 17 percent to 25 percent between 1980 and 1989. The percentage of those parents who did not have a high school diploma dropped from 31 percent to 15 percent. Anrig describes the black students who did better on the SATs in the 1980s as "the children of the kids who started to get a better

break in the 1960s." Margaret Simms, an education analyst with
the Joint Center, ascribed the higher scores to "increased access
to integrated, non-ghetto schools" among black students who
have moved into suburban and racially mixed areas or transferred to schools there.

The members of this black middle class are obvious to anyone
glancing around himself in a suburban school, a shopping mall,
a traffic jam, or a bank queue. (Bank lines are particularly fascinating to watch. They tend to be full of people with money.) The
skin of the middle class is coming in a lot of hitherto unusual
hues—brown and yellow as well as black.

In fact, the best evidence that the rise of Edge Cities is primarily a function of class—not race—is simple. Edge Cities are
rising in every North American metropolitan area that is growing—without regard to how many blacks live in that region. The
Minneapolis, Denver, Seattle, and Toronto regions all have
healthy downtowns and tiny black populations. Yet they are
forming Edge Cities just as reliably as are the New York, Atlanta,
Washington, and Chicago regions, all of which have highly
evolved downtowns and large black populations.

The reason some of these distinctions have gone largely un-
noticed is the way statistics are usually reported in the press.
The pivot is: "Compared with what?"

In the Atlanta area, accomplishments usually are measured
against the pinnacles of economic, educational, and social
achievement of the whites who live in the most affluent suburbs
of east Cobb, north Fulton, or north De Kalb counties. Which is
okay, except that if you compare everything to peaks in which
$300,000 houses are "normal," then by definition everything
else—black and white—is going to look like a valley. And it is not
uncommon for the black middle class in many, though not all,
neighborhoods to lag behind the white middle class in several
indices. This new middle class, after all, is young, both historically and in age.

That does not mean that most black people are uneducated or
poor or living in slums. And that becomes clear when you measure the success of black people in Edge Cities nationwide
against a different standard—the levels of income, education,
and housing achieved by most whites nationwide. By the standard of the median white families in America—recognizable in

such places as Milwaukee, Wisconsin; Norman, Oklahoma; Heflin, Alabama; and Pawtucket, Rhode Island—the change is striking.

This suburban black middle class demonstrates that averages are not fully representative of the black experience in America anymore, because those averages are lowered by that third of the black population still suffering extreme tribulation. Yet the third of black America that is fairly described as suburban middle class is becoming indistinguishable statistically from whites of the same class—not only in income and education, but in consumer behavior and attitudes toward government.

This has major national political implications. "As the black middle class shares the same frustrations, problems, and desires as the white middle class, party barriers will break down," says Roger J. Stone, a Republican political consultant who was a senior adviser to the 1988 Jack Kemp presidential campaign. "The party or candidate that offers solutions to jobs, education, traffic, growth, and health care as well as civil rights will be able to attract that vote. Some Republicans already have. Tom Kean in New Jersey, in the [1985] governor's race, won 62 percent of the black vote. That was both suburban and urban."

This also has national economic implications. "If black household and income profiles converged to those of all Americans, there would be a near $100 billion increase in personal incomes, about a 3 percent increase in gross national product (roughly equivalent in scale to the total GNP of Switzerland, Belgium, or Sweden), and a consumer market target that stirs the imagination," reports Rutger's Sternlieb and his colleague James W. Hughes.

And that is clear even in Dixie—Georgia.

To this day, the layout of Atlanta is shaped by race. "On the Southside, the streets had one name, and on the Northside the continuing streets had another, because white folks didn't want to live on the same name street as the black folks," says Stephen Suitts, director of the Southern Regional Council.

As recently as 1962, at the height of white flight, municipal barricades were erected at the Peyton Road Bridge to prevent blacks from even driving through white neighborhoods, much less moving into them. Nonetheless, as whites dumped their houses at fire-sale prices to flee school desegregation, black people were happy enough to buy up some of the most convenient and attractive neighborhoods in Atlanta. To this day, if you take that historic Ponce de Leon–Route 78 divide and extend it east and west out into the suburbs, you still get almost all the predominantly black neighborhoods over on the Southside. And the Edge Cities have all risen on the Northside.

Meanwhile, the booming Edge City counties of Cobb and Gwinnett have refused to allow MARTA rapid rail lines to be built into their jurisdictions, a decision widely viewed as racially motivated.

What has changed, though, in the last twenty-five years is the way middle-class blacks now arrive in the Atlanta suburbs. Today, people—both black and white—with strong commitments to the old downtowns who have lived there all their lives don't think much about moving out. Instead, the black people fueling Atlanta's Edge City growth are, like their white neighbors, moving in from outside the region. Under those circumstances, as predicted by William Julius Wilson in his landmark 1978 work, *The Declining Significance of Race,* class has become a more important predictor of behavior. Black middle-class settlement patterns have changed not just in Atlanta, but all over America, nowhere more dramatically than in the South.

Throughout the middle of this century, millions of blacks with get-up-and-go got up and left Dixie entirely. This became known as the Great Migration—the largest internal population shift in American history, with the exception of the pioneers heading west. In the 1950s alone, one of six Southern blacks left for the greater opportunities of the industrialized North and West. The total black migration from the South was 1.6 million in the 1940s and 1.5 million in the 1950s. In 1900, nine tenths of all blacks lived in the South. Today it is half that.

This was especially a movement of young people. With little save their best clothes and a picnic lunch packed by their families, entire generations boarded buses and trains they nicknamed the "Chicken-Bone Express" from Mississippi to Chicago, or from Alabama to Detroit, or from the Carolinas to Washington, or from Georgia to New York.

This was not a movement just from South to North. It was a

movement out of feudalism into the Industrial Revolution. And most important, it was a migration out of rural subsistence into the big cities. It was this tie to the declining old downtowns that worried a lot of people.

But if anything is proved by the numbers above, it is that American blacks have been extraordinarily mobile in the pursuit of a better life. And their efforts have paid off. It was not only the black population that was liberated in 1964. The American economic system was, too. That system has a well-earned reputation as rough-and-tumble. But it also has a stunning track record of transforming illiterate serfs from every mountain and desert on the globe into middle-class suburbanites in three generations or less. And in the 1960s, that system was freed to work on blacks. This unleashed a pent-up, high-velocity gush of black ambition and frustration and drive, featuring countless tales of individual grit, into the heart of an economy that, as it happens, simultaneously was being transformed into one producing mostly white-collar, middle-class jobs.

And now, the news is that young black people, the sons and granddaughters of those who left for the industrial cities of the North, are on the move again. They're coming back—to Dixie. During the 1980s, the U.S. Census found, the percentage of all African-Americans who live in the South increased for the first time in the twentieth century. And this substantial increase was fueled by better-educated men and women under forty. Noted Larry Long of the Census Bureau, "That's a profile of people who migrate for job opportunities."

By contrast, a generation ago, when segregation blocked access to white colleges, in Atlanta the overwhelming magnet for the middle class was the elite black schools on the Westside. This produced a settlement pattern not unlike that of Cambridge, Massachusetts, or any other major college town, only more pronounced. People who originally came for an education stayed because they found it unimaginable to exist in a place less "civilized." In the wake of civil rights, the black population in southwest Atlanta boomed. Most of the second-, third-, and fourth-generation black "society" families in Atlanta live there to this day. Lillian Lewis, wife of U.S. Representative John Lewis, told me she just didn't know "anybody" who lived on the Northside.

Actually, she said, she had met Pat Lottier, but she expressed amazement that the Lottiers lived in, and the black *Tribune* was published on, the Northside.

Yet this synthesis should be no more—or less—astonishing than the move of this generation back to the South. After all, this new generation—the offspring of immigrants, if you will—is coming back to the South today primarily for the white-collar jobs of high technology and the Fortune 500. These corporations, of course, tend to be headquartered in Edge City.

There are four full-blown Edge Cities in the Atlanta area, with three more in the embryonic state. One is the Cumberland Mall–Galleria area. That is where the Perimeter beltway road, Interstate 285, is intersected by Interstate 75, the northwest spoke coming out of the downtown hub. A second is north of downtown around Perimeter Center at 285 and Georgia Route 400, the landmark of which is the skeletal white dome of the tallest building on the Perimeter, at thirty-one stories, locally called the Birdcage Building. Each of these two is bigger than downtown at Five Points. The third is in the Buckhead–Lenox Square Mall area, the most chic of Atlanta's Edge Cities, with over 150 yuppie restaurants and singles joints, a bookstore that has been built into the circular showroom of a defunct automobile dealership, and a mysterious and intense concentration of Persian rug merchants. The fourth is the midtown area, which boasts most of the region's arts centers, including the one named after Coca-Cola king Robert W. Woodruff. The three Edge Cities that are emerging are a backshop location around Gwinnett Mall to the northeast, the area around I-85 where that northeast radial crosses the Perimeter, and the area around Atlanta International Airport to the south.

When young black people come into the region from the outside for their new corporate jobs, they are not necessarily much more aware of every detail of Atlanta's history than any other recent arrivals. Not being familiar with all the taboos of previous generations about where they "should" or "shouldn't" live, many make the classic suburban calculations. They look for how much house they can afford, at a commute from their job they find acceptable, in an area with good housing resale values and good schools. Frequently they are helped in this search by the relocation services retained by their national employers, like IBM—which enjoys a particularly high profile among the Atlanta black suburban middle class. The assumption underlying their calculation is that one expensive suburban subdivision is pretty much like another in its racial attitudes, an assumption that generally proves correct.

And that is precisely the revolution. Those are calculations in which issues of class outweigh issues of race. The result is the rise of the substantial new black middle class in neighborhoods like Smyrna in Cobb County. Cobb County as recently as twenty years ago was serious Klan country. It accommodated the likes of Lester Maddox and convicted church bomber J. B. Stoner.

And again, this is not just Atlanta. "The latest Census reports reiterated that return migration has not been to the central city. It has been to the outer rim," notes the Southern Regional Council's Suitts of the Dixiewide pattern.

These middle-class locations beat the alternatives. Pat Lottier makes no apologies about this at all. She has vivid memories of what she and her husband left, and a steely determination that her family will never go back to it, ever. "My husband and I have been married twenty-two years. We've always lived in what you call Edge Cities. You probably want to know why. We felt the need from the very beginning to live away from the inner city. We wanted to move away from everything the inner city has. We wanted our kids to have the very best, and the best was outside of any major city. Safety. Amenities. The best shopping centers. A house with an acre or more. The freedom to leave your house and check on one door and not all the doors and not all the windows. The best schools—being able to go into the school and say I need to see the teacher and someone saying, 'Yes, Mrs. Lottier, sit down.' Inner city doesn't give you that. And unfortunately I don't think it ever will. That's a shame to say. It really is a class issue."

The story of the Lottiers' rise to the Edge City middle class is a classic one. It faithfully portrays many of the striking changes that have swept through America in the last twenty-five years.

Patricia Lottier was born in 1948, in Kentucky. "A town called Ashland. It's a little twenty thousand-population place, and that may include a few cows and chickens. My father—eighth-grade education, day work, hourly work, cleaned houses, unskilled labor. Died when I was twelve. My mother, one year college but still not enough to get anything in Ashland, so she was an hourly worker, a cook, worked for the white man."

Patricia grew up literally on the wrong side of the tracks. Her family's address was 3160 Railroad Street. The schools did desegregate quietly in that largely white Ohio River town near the West Virginia line. "The powers-that-be decided how they would handle integration. The few blacks in that town said, 'Yessir, that's fine.' Not a large black population. Probably 5 percent, and I'm guessing, because I doubt if they even counted us except on Election Day, when everybody got two dollars for voting. We were part of that mentality back then. I remember the two dollars. I remember the little men who had the two dollars in their pockets. And I wondered why they were handing out two dollars. My mother explained.

"Your choices back then, you either were a schoolteacher or a nurse if you wanted to do something with your life. I didn't want to be a schoolteacher." Pat Lottier was graduating from high school in 1966. It was right there that the changes in the big world outside Ashland would reach in and change her life. Pat Lottier was not going to get just any run-of-the-mill nursing education. "Johns Hopkins needed more blacks at their nursing school, and they recruited me. Full scholarship. I was a good student. I'd done no traveling before then—you don't travel if you don't have any money, do you. But I knew about Johns Hopkins. Hopkins was the leader in heart surgery. I would watch them on TV, some public station, working on someone's heart. I said, Boy, that's exciting. I shall be a nurse." As an aside, she adds of that time, "I can't be a doctor because that's just not heard of."

It was there in Baltimore she met her husband, George, at a football game at Morgan State, the traditionally black school he attended. George's great-grandfather in 1894 founded one of America's historic black newspapers, the *Baltimore Afro-American*. "So they had prestige," Pat recalls of George's family. "They didn't have money, but they had prestige."

Pat and George were married in 1968. Pat received her nursing certificate in 1969. George, who was born in 1944 and had not had a stellar relationship with academe, enlisted in the Army in 1963, and got out in 1966. He spent his hitch in Germany, in the 504th Aviation Battalion, ending up a sergeant running the aircraft-engine motor pool. He remembers the Army as a worthwhile experience. He says the most important thing it taught him was that "the system can work, and you can have an impact on the system"—that the system, if challenged, can respond. George has a curious dyslexia. As he's telling a white person stories of the worst times he's ever had, he automatically, reflexively, and apparently unconsciously *smiles.* He obviously learned a long time ago how to deal with other peoples' tension.

George chooses to describe the revelation that you can make the Army change as an "interesting situation." So after George got out of the service, he became a salesman. "I thought it was a way of finding out what's going on, how the game is played." And it was. He soon ended up with Dixie-Marathon, the maker of Dixie Cups, where he worked his way up the ladder to district sales manager, then product manager. The way the corporation worked, if you succeeded at one sales job, you were rewarded with a more lucrative district. That made the Lottiers corporate gypsies. They did indeed end up living in one area after another that today is Edge City territory: Framingham, out on the Massachusetts Turnpike between the Boston area's two beltways; Lancaster, Pennsylvania, "Amish country," now in the orbit of King of Prussia; back to Massachusetts, Northborough, at the outer 495 beltway; then to Danbury, Connecticut, working at headquarters in Greenwich, then to north Atlanta, where the corporation had its offices in the Edge City at Perimeter Center.

George's memory of all these predominantly white neighborhoods was that, being transients, "we didn't look at the area and say who lives there. We looked at the area to see how does it look in terms of appearance, what's the resale value of the house? Is it safe for Pat, because I had to travel? It really was a class issue. I want to resell my house and get a higher value, and if I go to an all-black neighborhood, then it means that we're limited to who's going to buy it."

The boys came in 1971 and 1972. Meanwhile, Pat observed that she didn't like changing bedpans. So she decided to go for a degree in public health administration, to get into management.

This led to a master's from Emory, which led to her becoming southeastern operations manager of the home-care division of Baxter International, a national provider of hospital and health supplies.

But in the 1980s, as the Lottiers approached their forties in Atlanta, they became restive in their respective corporations. A promotion for Pat would have involved yet another relocation— to Chicago or Boston. And neither wanted that. The boys were entering their teens, and Pat saw the Atlanta area as "Utopia— beautiful weather, friendly people, Southern hospitality, good food."

So in 1985 George launched his own business. He took his extensive experience with Dixie Cup ("You learn from the masters," observes his wife) to launch his promotional cup corporation. ("Hardee's promotes the Moose Cup. Have you seen the Moose Cup?" asks Pat. "That was his design.")

Then, more or less coincidentally, the Lottiers ended up lending money to a person who had started up *The Atlanta Tribune,* aimed at the black entrepreneurial community. "He had the paper located in the inner city," Pat explains. "And I thought that was crazy. The paper was trying to reach the upscale black consumer. The market that I felt he needed to attract was all over the metro area." So in 1988 the Lottiers bought out the founder. Patricia quit her job to run the *Tribune* out of the Lottiers' Edge City offices just fifteen minutes from their Roswell home and country club membership. Patricia owns 51 percent, George, 49. In two years, Pat has tripled the number of advertising pages. Her demographic study shows the *Tribune*'s typical reader is thirty-six, a business owner or decision maker with an outfit like AT&T or Xerox, has 2.5 children either in college or soon to go, an American Express card, an upscale car, and a vacation home or higher-than-average travel. Window stickers for the paper read "Sold here: *The Atlanta Tribune,* the Right Paper at the Right Time." Pat has allowed herself to think about other cities. *The New Orleans Tribune* has a nice ring to it, she thinks.

Yet when I sat down with Stephen Suitts, his reaction to all these Adam Smith market-economics figures was almost wistful.

Suitts, forty, who is white, has been on the side of the angels in the racial struggles of the South since Selma. His office is in a part of downtown Atlanta to which economic revival has not yet come. He softly jokes about being an old-fashioned liberal—his Southern Regional Council is the oldest interracial organization in the South, dating back to 1919.

For him, the movement was a moral crusade. It was not about just changing laws or reordering macroeconomics. It was to be measured in the openness of hearts. Martin Luther King, Jr., coined the phrase "the Beloved Community" to describe the original ideal. The standard was not how many riding lawn tractors a black suburbanite might own, but how many minds might be cleared. So for Suitts, all these data about the suburban black middle class were bittersweet. While they obviously represented enormous change at levels that could be quantified and measured in dollars, they did not offer him much of a geography of the soul—evidence of the success of ideas in which he had invested his life. "Brotherhood," for example.

On August 28, 1963, at the Lincoln Memorial in Washington, Martin Luther King, Jr., gave his most famous speech. In it, he said: "I say to you today, my friends, so even though we face the difficulties of today and tomorrow, I still have a dream. It is a dream deeply rooted in the American Dream . . . I have a dream that my four little children will one day live in a nation where they will not be judged by the color of their skin but by the content of their character."

More than a dozen times during our conversation Suitts picked up the maps of the Atlanta region that I'd brought, marked by brightly colored Census tracts showing affluent black people and where they lived. He'd stare at the numbers, put the maps down, and then, almost involuntarily, pick the maps up and stare at them some more.

Finally, he said, "Well, it does not surprise me. I have no stake in the past." Suitts picked up the maps again. Put them down. "The opportunity for somebody to be able to go anywhere, put themselves into a suburban house, and buy themselves riding lawn mowers, cut that grass, and have as much neighborly approval as any white is part of what we wanted integration to mean.

"But it wasn't all. It clearly wasn't all. And essentially the question is whether or not one views the efforts, the civil rights movement, as an attempt to try to establish a new moral ground. I think what we have achieved is where people are not judged by the color of their skins, but by the color of their money. And I'm not sure that's quite as far as we want to go."

Suitts was not the only one less than enthralled by these numbers. Michael Lomax, forty-two, is California-born and -raised, and black. He is a literature professor at Spelman College. He also has a considerable reputation as one of the most thoughtful and articulate lights on the formidable Atlanta black political scene, which embraces Andrew Young, Maynard Jackson, and Julian Bond.

Lomax is Fulton County commission chairman. Fulton County, which includes most of Atlanta proper and the poverty therein, also embraces the fanciest black neighborhoods in the region in Cascade Heights, plus some of the most expensive neighborhoods anywhere in Georgia on the Northside, around Perimeter Center.

His reaction to the recitation of the numbers of black people moving into Edge City territory is:

"How does that play to me? That they are not really intimately a part of the social, political, and even economic fabric of the African-American community that is Atlanta. The center of the African-American community in Atlanta is the colleges, the university, the black churches, which are basically in the center of the city.

"People can live in Alpharetta [north of Perimeter Center] and have no connection with the African-American community at all. I don't know whether it's good or bad. It's reality. For many of them, living in a predominantly white suburban area is the essence of the American Dream.

"I think it typically leads to isolation. I don't think you are socially integrated into those communities. If you were, you would be a member of the country club, you would dine socially with these people, you are members of their church. They are the first and second circles around your life. And I don't think in most cases that is what happens. What happens is that you are tolerated, maybe even, to some lesser extent, accepted. But I don't believe very often that's your community."

I mention to Lomax that what I'm trying to get at is the extent to which class is now becoming as large a definer of people as race. He does not buy the premise—at all.

"Believe me, race is the defining issue. Class is a distinguishing and differentiating issue within the race. But race is the issue."

I ask him why he thinks that. Lomax reacts with an expression of such incredulity that it says, If you don't know, there is so much reading you need to do that maybe we should resume this interview in another lifetime. I say, Humor me. Please tell me why you, personally, think race is the defining issue, more than class.

"Because I believe that race is the most powerful defining characteristic in this society. I think more than gender, more than religion, for Western civilization the color of one's skin is the primary defining issue."

If we do have a huge emerging black population in the white suburbs, I ask, how does that square?

"Well, you can reside there. The laws tolerate that. I'm not sure *you* can have a conversation, but if *I* have a conversation with most black people who work in white corporations—they feel tolerated at best, alienated at worst. They may have economic attachments, but they don't feel they are part of the company. They don't hold out the illusion at this stage that they're going to wind up chairman of the board. There may be economic reasons for them to remain attached. They don't feel they can have the same material existence if they were to shift into some business enterprise supported only by the African-American community. But I don't think they feel the same sense of ownership.

"One thing that is happening that reduces the sense of alienation is that there are large numbers like them who then form another group. One of my roommates from college has lived in Reston, Virginia, for twenty-five years. When he got out there he was the only one. Or one of two. Now there is a larger percentage of African-Americans who live there. So I think what you are seeing is that rather than black and white upper-income people being more closely associated, you are really getting black upper-middle-income people in sufficient numbers selecting at what levels they will interact with the traditional black community. They get their sense of community on Sundays. They come into the inner city to go to church.

"Race is an inherently ambiguous and pervasive issue in this country, and there is nothing clear about it except that it has a lot of meaning and it resonates throughout people's lives. In terms of my own mind: I figure if I were to live outside and work outside of the black community, worship outside the black community, have social interactions outside the community, send my kids to school outside the black community—I would feel completely adrift. For me and for my family—which has the choice of doing anything it wants to do—we choose to have anchors in a traditionally black middle-class community. My daughter goes to a predominantly black public school. She intends to go to a black college—Spelman. She wants that. She was in a white private school; she didn't like that. She felt socially isolated. She said, I want to go where I am not a minority."

If there are now some substantial numbers of black people not making that choice, I ask Lomax, are they kidding themselves?

"Who am I to say whether they are kidding themselves? The pendulum swings. When I was ready to choose where to go to college, having gone to a good integrated public school in L.A., I was the only person in my class to go south to Morehouse. Today, twenty-five years later, California is probably the third largest feeder of students into Morehouse and Spelman colleges. Why? Because these kids who grew up in privilege, affluence, now want a racial experience. They want a sense of connection. The allure of integration is not proving substantive. Increasingly I think you are going to see African-Americans choosing to live in racially homogeneous environments. That is emotionally and socially a more satisfying experience for them than always going against the grain or being in some other environment. What also happens is when we get there the whites run away anyway. So you're going to opt for that or you're going to by default wind up there."

What do words like integration and segregation mean in the late twentieth century? I ask Lomax. When I look at affluent suburbs like Hunter's Hill that are virtually all black, is that segregation?

"No. Segregation means that there is an imposed restriction —it's not a choice. When I moved sixteen years ago to the Cascade Road area, it didn't even dawn on me to think of moving into a white area. I don't know why. It wasn't for lack of exposure. I had become a Southerner, I guess. I was a graduate student finishing my Ph.D. It also just happened to be a very nice area, and a lot of my friends were moving there.

It has not had all the amenities. You still can't get decent commercial and retail. But I don't have to walk out of the house and worry about somebody asking me when am I going to pick up the garbage, as if I am a service employee. Life is difficult enough. I don't want to go through that. If I were to move, the likelihood is that I'd either move into another African-American area with a bigger house, maybe. Or I might move into a more urban setting like downtown. But moving into the northern part of the city, which is predominantly white—I've never really felt that was good."

When I was talking to blacks on the Northside, I tell him, I began to get the attitude that Karl Marx was right—that issues of class are what control.

"We all make our choices. If all the black people who could move away did move away, what we left behind would be pretty bad. I think that you cannot run away. I get angry very often when I drive through my community and I see some deterioration, I see the social problems. But at least I have to see them every day. 'To whom much is given, from them much is expected.' You can't run away from that. You shouldn't run away from that.

"My tendency is to feel that for those of my brothers and sisters who choose to live their lives in Alpharetta—they're selling their birthright for a mess of pottage. They are not getting much in return. They're getting middle America. Maybe upper-middle America. They're getting homogeneous affluence. They're getting a kind of nondisturbing terrain. But that's not reality. I hear my own people speak with disdain about the homeless and the unattractive qualities of urban America. They really believe that if they can spend a half million for a home, nothing should intrude upon them that is unattractive. I don't think that's the way the world is.

"I think one of the things you might ask a lot of those people who tell you that class means everything—ask them how long they've had class. Many of them are first generation out! I think that they are running away from something and not just running to something more like them."

They *really* hate what they left, I acknowledge.

"It shows you how painful and violent the scars of race remain in this country."

Lomax's responses are important because they represent the orthodox thinking of many of the middle-class black people I talked to. And many of Lomax's points are dead on. A striking number of the next generation of black kids who could go to college anywhere, for example, are now seeking the black university experience.

Chris Lottier, Pat and George's older son, chose to enroll as a freshman at Howard University in Washington. That is the first historically black school to have a full complement of professional graduate schools. When I sought him out there and asked why he selected a black school after living his entire life in white towns in Massachusetts, Connecticut, Pennsylvania, and Georgia, he said, "I wanted to find out what it was like to be like the blond kid sitting next to me in high school—I wanted to find out what it was like to be in the majority."

Yet, he was thinking about transferring after two years to join his younger brother at the University of Virginia. It was not that he felt he would get a better education there, but he matter-of-factly said he thought that white employers would probably be more impressed with a UVA degree than one from Howard. And making money was important to him.

Gregory T. Baranco, who is black, owns a chain of Atlanta automobile dealerships. One of them is in the working-to-middle-class environs of Gwinnett County, northeast of Atlanta. Gwinnett is among the whitest urban counties in America. Baranco owns the dealership that sells them Lincolns. When, for some reason, I found that amusing, he grinned and said, "All you need is a level playing field."

Baranco, who has also helped start a black bank, and his wife, Juanita, who is a lawyer, have built an entire subdivision off Panola Road in south De Kalb County, where the houses range from $334,000 to $600,000 and the owners are black. The

Barancos were building a spectacular home for themselves there with banks of curved windows and an indoor swimming pool. Such homes are not uncommon in north Fulton. Why, then, did the Barancos choose south De Kalb, where they had to build a whole subdivision to get the house they wanted? Because you are buying not just a lot but community, said Harold Buckley, the other partner in the development, to the *Atlanta Constitution.* "If you are buying a home, you look for places where your family can establish long-time friendships," explained Buckley, whose new home will be next door to the Barancos'.

The Barancos' daughter Evelyn, meanwhile, has had the same impulse as Chris Lottier. She was choosing to spend a year away from prestigious Wellesley, where she was originally enrolled, to attend Spelman. Lomax's crucial point may well be that what matters in this society is the freedom and ability and wherewithal to choose—including the choice of when and how to congregate.

Apart from that, it is exactly as Lomax said: race *is* an inherently ambiguous and pervasive issue in this country. It does echo throughout people's lives. Because for so long it was the same thing to be black and to be poor, some first-generation middle-class black people are having trouble sorting out what it even means to be "authentically" black in the absence of privation. When I was doing my interviews, the trendy label being used by young black Atlantans for affluent people who were not thought to be acting sufficiently black was "pseudos."

At the same time, points out Juan Williams, who wrote *Eyes on the Prize,* the book that accompanied the PBS documentary series on the civil rights revolution, "Lots of white people live up to their asses in debt and don't think that much about it. Middle-class black people are much more paranoid, sensing the wolf at the door. Poverty to them is much more real. They're more likely to have family or friends who've been through an experience like eviction, where their clothes and furniture are put out on the street in an embarrassing display. In truth, the primary fear is of falling into some economic mishap that would take away our dignity, of reducing us merely to another poor black face. Just another 'nigger.' "

The impact on race of our new Edge Cities is similarly ambiguous. The argument that racism thrives is simple: racial patterns of residence are still very strong. Bart Landry claims that even Zip Codes that appear integrated statistically are not so when you get down to the block level. What you find is small enclaves of fifty black homes, not a general distribution, he believes.

But even more telling are perceptions. They can vary tremendously, depending on whether you are black or white—irrefutable evidence of how much race still matters. I once debriefed a young black *Washington Post* colleague from a suburban background after she completed a three-month Edge City assignment. Her articles had given no hint of her private perceptions of Edge Cities. It turned out they were scorching. No matter how many black people may have been there, Edge City reminded her of South Africa. "The people there are so consumed with themselves and their ideas of success that it is to the exclusion of anyone else. In trying to reject failures of any sort, they have lost compassion. The glass buildings are narcissistic. They reflect like the inside of a spa. It's all people admiring their own muscle. They have no soul." She said she had not met a single person during her assignment whom she found herself personally liking.

But again, there are more powerful arguments against the idea of racism being crucial to the rise of Edge Cities. They include Seattle, Denver, Minneapolis, Milwaukee, Toronto, London, and Paris. As for perceptions, take Chet Fuller, a senior editor of the *Atlanta Journal and Constitution,* who is black. He talks about Atlanta, with its overwhelming complement of Edge Cities, as a "place of big dreams. It says, 'We've tried a lot of things and we're not finished yet.' It's sold all these wolf tickets— it's bragged on itself so hard—that it has had to go out and back it up. There's a confidence in the air [among black people]—the way people carry themselves. They look people in the eyes— they don't look down. The word you hear is that anybody with skills and talents can make it here. It's a place of opportunities. There's lots of support. There are networks in place, a good political climate in place, and corporations with black people in decision-making positions. We in the South deal very publicly with our racial problems. On the network news, sometimes. Doesn't keep us from doing business."

These contradictions, this squishiness, is why, talking to Lomax, I couldn't let go of this bone I had in my teeth about class as an explanation of affairs. I couldn't help wondering whether there were any class origins to his elegant college professor–politician's construct. So as I was walking out the door, I asked him a few final questions about his own life:

What did your father do?

"He was an attorney and a businessman in Los Angeles. We've had black businesses for three generations now."

Where did you go to school in L.A.?

"Predominantly white Los Angeles High—[affluent] West L.A."

Your siblings? Where did they end up?

"One's in China, teaching in a university. I have a sister who's an attorney in West L.A. in the Wilshire area. She lives up in the Hollywood Hills. I have a brother who works for the court system and he lives in West L.A., but in a predominantly white area. Another sister who's a dancer and who lives in West Hollywood. My mother lives in Pasadena."

Then, being an intellectually honest man, he saw where this was going. "None of them lives in a black community."

In the early 1990s, the new frontier for Atlanta-area developers was semirural land well outside downtown, and also south of those invisible lines which divide the posh Northside from the Southside.

Urban areas have been divided according to class for as long as there have been cities. Sam Bass Warner, Jr., in *The Urban Wilderness,* demonstrates that in Chicago the residential patterns by class were fully set up by 1894, long before race became an issue.

Around Atlanta, there are a lot of historical reasons, other than race, that Southside traditionally has been full of lower-income people, both black and white. Wealthy neighborhoods in every city on earth are generally upwind, uphill, and upriver from the center—to be cooler and to avoid noxious fumes. Southside has always had the problem of being at the wrong end of the Chattahoochee River. The wisdom of the ancients genuinely is enshrined in the motto—excrement flows downhill.

Nonetheless, the conventional wisdom at this time was that the Southside had become ripe for development. Air conditioning was as available there as anywhere else. If anything, it had less congested roads and more untapped sewer capacity than the booming Northside. (In the late 1980s, there were more cars and trucks in Gwinnett County, to the northeast, than people.)

Best of all, it had Atlanta's Hartsfield Airport, with more nonstop flights to more American cities than any other airfield. The noise was a serious drawback. But if you could get out from under the actual flight path, the Southside should be prime Edge City territory, all the real estate interests believed. The land cost a third of what it did on the Northside.

The issue then became: Would affluent whites live there? Among affluent suburban blacks? Or among semirural whites whom everybody stigmatized as "rednecks"?

To put it another way: What exactly was the home price that would do the trick? If the commutes were equal, how much extra would people pay to live on the Northside, when the same subdivision house was available on the Southside for $10,000 or $20,000 or $30,000 less? What exactly was the price people were willing to put on racism, classism, and its long-time effects —such as the shopping on the Southside being substantially less than good, as were the available jobs?

When I was there, Peter Calabro was betting millions on an 850-acre planned community, Bridgport, in south Fulton County. It was on Camp Creek Parkway, a short, straight shot to the airport. Calabro was planning the development, which surrounded the deep waters of 146-acre Lake Cowart, to include a golf course, a country club, a conference center, shopping, and offices. The single-family detached homes would range from $150,000 to $350,000. We're talking doors of beveled glass, here, in front of a two-story "lawyer foyer," with a mailbox out front embedded in a massive pillar of stonework.

These were ambitious plans. So although he raved about the "picturesque beauty" of the site, and the "skin-contact" quality of the lake's water, Calabro was not banking on the place selling itself. He had used "focus groups" extensively. That's the research technique in which you first analyze the market statistically. Then you go out and find human beings to match the statistics. Then you sit them down in small groups and grill them about their likes, dislikes, and behavior, videotaping the results for extensive analysis. In such fashion do you hope to divine the future.

Calabro had kept class constant, but divided his focus groups racially. In the black focus group, this is what he found:

There were significant concentrations of black people who could afford the homes he wanted to build. That was not much of a surprise. In newly constructed subdivisions nationwide, when blacks arrive, the education and income numbers tend to *rise*. The level of class goes up with the arrival of blacks, over the rural white population that may have preceded the subdivision.

The members of this black focus group said they liked the product he proposed building. They were willing to live in a mixed neighborhood—that is, with whites. But these black suburbanites expressed skepticism about how mixed the development would end up being. If there were a lot of blacks—if they made up as much as half, say—they doubted that there would be large numbers of whites of the same class willing to live there, too.

Calabro would not release to me the results of the white focus group research; he thought it was badly flawed. He said he believes it did not reflect the attitudes of the white portion of his market. (It doesn't take a lot of imagination to guess what these whites had said.)

But Calabro was undeterred. I asked him whether he was kidding himself about white people being willing to live next to black people of the same class. He thought not. There are two kinds of white people, he said: those who had experience with blacks as peers, and those who had not.

Those who had not passed the threshold of sharing any portion of their lives with affluent, educated black people, he said, based their focus group reactions on stereotypes and fears. They would never buy a house near blacks.

Those, by contrast, who had gone past "hello" with a black person, who had routinely dealt with blacks at least as accomplished as they, would rapidly make far more critical decisions, he believed. They would want to know about more class-based issues: how the schools were, what the price of the house was, what the commute was. He was banking on the idea that race was not an issue that was ambiguous—that it just was an issue that was complex. And the complexities were ones that white people would be able to dissect with sophistication, given the opportunity.

Calabro, who is white, was betting his professional life on that belief. It will be interesting to see whether he is right or wrong.

———————

The First Law of Demographics is: *You cannot count on people to change. You can, however, count on them to die.*

That means that members of one generation should not try to predict the future based on their experience. As they die off, they will be replaced by a generation with different life experiences that have produced different attitudes. Not necessarily better, but certainly different. And in this fashion, questions that obsessed one generation sometimes never really get answered; they just end up sounding more and more archaic.

It is only a truism, then, to say that the future of race issues is in the hands of the generation that has recently entered adulthood. After all, this is the first generation to go to integrated schools, the first to operate routinely at a variety of levels with people of other races. So who knows whether it is significant, but it turns out that the hottest disco in Atlanta is Dominique's. It is smack in the middle of the Edge City growing up around the Cumberland Mall and the Galleria.

The Cumberland Mall–Galleria area is a classic of the Edge City genre. The Galleria itself—the mall-hotel-office complex— has a helicopter landing pad. It is directly opposite the Kinder-Care day-care facility, and near the Embassy Suites for business-men who want a little extra space because they plan to live out of their hotel room for a long time. The landscaping is very, very high—the purple wisteria of spring is everywhere, as is the white dogwood, pink dogwood, red tulips, and masses of pansies and azaleas. Near where Sherman took the last high ground before marching on Atlanta, yuppies now spend the weekend rafting. This is probably the only Edge City in America that encompasses a National Recreational Area—the Chattahoochee River

—with its Smokey the Bear park ranger signs. Not for nothing does the real estate profession call this the Platinum Triangle.

And there, right in the middle of it, is Dominique's. Named after Dominique Wilkins, number 21 of the Atlanta Hawks, it has the most heavy-duty sound system I have ever experienced. The bass line from the JBL speakers the size of refrigerators that hang from the ceiling is so serious, it does not merely enter your chest. It moves your shirt while you are standing still. Tumbling neon light displays, shifting from green to pink and blue, reflect off banks of video screens simultaneously showing the same weird cop movie as the beat thunders on.

The Saturday night I was there, I could barely move. It was business suits and ties everywhere—hundreds, if not thousands, of young professional people. The crowd—at ground zero of this majority white Edge City in the middle of Georgia—was 90 percent black. No one seemed uncomfortable with this arrangement.

When I got back to my car, what I saw on top of the hill across the way was a big slab of Edge City office building. It had a sign at the top that seemed a metaphor for what I had just been part of.

In bright blue light, from the top of that hill overlooking Dominique's, it proclaimed: CORPORATE SPECTRUM.

---

John Lewis has had a singular perspective on the American Dream for the last thirty years. When he arrived in Washington in 1986 as a congressman, he was already an important figure in American history. The *National Journal* noted that it's not your typical freshman congressman who is sought out by his senior colleagues wanting to hear the stories he's got to tell.

In 1959 and 1960, John Lewis, then only nineteen, helped organize the first lunch-counter sit-ins in America. They established the right of all Americans to be served whatever they had the money to buy—a meal, in this case.

In 1961, he was one of the leaders of the Freedom Rides. The issue again was whether all Americans could equally use the nation's public facilities—this time, interstate Greyhound bus terminals. For this he was beaten viciously in Rock Hill, South Carolina, and in Montgomery, Alabama.

Lewis was a keynote speaker at the 1963 March on Washington where King gave his "I have a dream" speech. In 1964, he helped coordinate the Mississippi Freedom Project. In 1965, in Selma, Alabama, he helped lead 525 marchers across the Edmund Pettus Bridge. They were attacked by Alabama state troopers using clubs, whips, and tear gas. His cause that time was whether all Americans had the right to vote. The result was the passage of the Voting Rights Act of 1965.

Today, still straightforward and guileless, John Lewis is the U.S. Representative from the Fifth Congressional District of Georgia, whose state flag is still three-quarters filled with the Stars and Bars. Seventy-five years before John Lewis was born, Sherman burned Atlanta flat. Fifty years after Lewis was born, he was a second-term member of the House representing that town. In between, the world into which Lewis was born—a family of sharecroppers in Troy, Alabama—was so antique, so feudal, that Lewis cannot remember even *seeing* a white person until he was eight.

Historians use examples like this to address the matter of scale—the notion that, depending on which lens you use to look at something like change, thirty years can be an excruciatingly long time or a strikingly short one.

There is no question that John Lewis is pretty much astounded by what he's seen in his life so far. "Pockets of south De Kalb, Hunter Hill, Cascade Road, Guilford Forest, Loch Lomond, Stone Mountain—it's wealth. Nothing but wealth. Lots of blacks doing extraordinarily well. And it's all happened in the last twenty-five years.

"It's altogether a different world. If you had told me twenty-seven years ago, when I first moved here, that I would be able to go into a neighborhood and knock on the door and say, 'I'm John Lewis. I need your help. I need your support. Will you vote for me?' I'd've told you you were crazy. You were out of your mind. It would have been very dangerous for me to go some places. I wouldn't have gone to some neighborhoods that are now in my district. I just wouldn't have done it."

He means it. Although these are neighborhoods he won with

90 percent of the white vote in his last seriously contested election.

This has, of course, not been without a price. He recalls a day not long ago when he had a nodding acquaintance with virtually everyone in Atlanta in the black middle class. Now, "I go to places, I go campaigning, I go to a church, a restaurant—I feel I should know that person. And I don't. We are dispersed. We had a greater feel of solidarity in the days of segregation. Twenty-five or thirty years later, we have choices, and we're taking them. People don't want their children to come in contact with the undesirable elements. Fear of crime, fear of violence. So they move away. You can even see it in the churches. We are paying a price.

"The revolution is not complete. But in so many ways we have witnessed a quiet, nonviolent revolution. Could I imagine it when I was growing up? No, no. Those days of the marches? No, no."

Lewis points out the window of his district offices in a downtown high-rise near Five Points, just beyond an American flag behind his desk. He says, "Right in that building there, where the drugstore is—I was arrested in that building in 1964."

When I chatted with him there was a controversy going on. Affluent black parents in suburban De Kalb County wanted the local public schools upgraded. Yet, as Lewis noted, "you hear black parents say, 'I don't want my children bused.' For the first time in my life, in thirty years in the Movement, 'I don't want my children bused.' Strange to hear that. 'We want our school, this school, in this neighborhood, upgraded to a first-class school.' "

So much for "separate but equal."

I had just come from Lenox Square Mall, the most chic in Atlanta and, arguably, the South. It is well patronized by black people, as is Cumberland Mall, where more people shop in a month than live in Atlanta proper. It occurred to me to have the temerity to ask Lewis what he thought Martin Luther King, Jr., would have made of these Edge City malls.

That gave Lewis pause. "Dr. King was born and raised here in Atlanta. For the most part he knew the old Fourth Ward [the Sweet Auburn neighborhood]. There was a sense you could not go any farther. It was unthinkable, living beyond North Avenue." Lewis' voice turns into a reverie as he goes on. "This friend of mine has built this unbe*liev*able house near Stone Mountain. Swimming pool. *Heated* swimming pool." Pause. "That covers itself," he continues, so softly that he is almost talking to himself. "I've been living here since 1963. I think I've been to Stone Mountain maybe twice. I heard of Stone Mountain [back then], I heard of the Klan. At least once a year there would be a fiery cross on Stone Mountain. Now there's a black guy with a swimming pool."

Lewis is in his fifties, which almost makes him too old to be statistically part of the new generation of the black middle class, and he recognizes that. "The young black professionals know much more than I do about what has happened all around this place," he says. And Lewis, now a congressman, has layers of aides. That insulates a person from life's grottiness. Hence, there are lots of thoughtful people who differ with Lewis. They look at America's promises to itself and see the glass as, at best, half empty. So I ask Lewis, Is this what the Beloved Community looks like?

"Atlanta's not the Promised Land," Lewis reflects. "It is not the Beloved Community. But it is in the process of becoming. It's like democracy. It is ever becoming."

When the interview seemed to be over, I thanked Lewis for his time, and started packing up my gear. Somehow, we got talking about what had been Lewis' favorite pastime—collecting antiquarian books by and about black people. Recently, he said, he had pretty much lost the desire to pursue his hobby because he'd completely run out of space. "My wife accuses me of being a pack rat," he said. I joked with him that what he needed was to move out to one of those semi-Tara tract mansions out in some Edge City, out in Cobb County, in Marietta.

No, Lewis said, I have to stay close to the airport, really.

Then he added, "I will show you a house that I would love to have." It seems a couple of his supporters held a grand fundraiser for him once. And "across from them is this old, old house." Lewis has discovered that it's not up for sale yet because the ancient lady who lives in it has established a lifetime trust. But it is on eighteen acres within the city limits, on Cascade Road, the most affluent black suburban neighborhood in Atlanta.

"It's beautiful," said Lewis. "For a politician it would be an ideal place. Have a barbecue or something for all of the people in the district. It's an old house, a great house. They had a dairy. In the back you will see the old windmill, and what you put the corn in, the silo. And this is near to the city.

"I would love to have a little place I could raise chickens. There's enough room. Eighteen acres. I would love to be able to raise some chickens there. They are such innocent creatures. That was life growing up. It was fine—made me responsible. Made me a better person. No question about it. A sense of responsibility, in the sense of caring for something. I owe a great deal to my early life, and to the chickens."

We joshed. So all you need is eighteen acres on Cascade Road and a few chickens. "And a few chickens," he replied, laughing. And you'd be a happy man! I teased. "That would be. Al*most.* The Beloved Community," he replied. We laughed. "I'm kidding," he insisted. "Just kidding."

His voice trailed off. Earlier, he had dismissed his longing for this place. Think what eighteen acres in suburban Atlanta costs. But as he continued, I thought, This is not entirely a joke.

"Beautiful sight," he added, so softly as to be almost inaudible. "I have never seen the inside of the house," said he, sounding surprised at his own revelation. "But I would buy it without seeing the inside. It reminds me of growing up on the farm. Just the outdoors, the trees, the oak trees. And that's the thing about Atlanta. If you're flying over this city, it's a city of trees. You can be living in the city, but you're *out there,* in the grass, the trees, the flowers. Beautiful dogwoods. All in a line. As they get older, they just get shadier."

That's when it finally occurred to me. John Lewis has a dream.

He has a dream that's a very familiar American one. That one day, he might have a *big* old house. Surrounded by the most expansive lawn in creation. In a fashionable neighborhood. Among his peers. Three minutes from the beltway. Fourteen minutes from the Edge City of Cumberland Mall–Galleria. Closer to that Edge City than to downtown. With extraordinary access to the airport. In the most vibrant metropolitan area of the Deep South.

It's what generations have sacrificed and strived for. It's the way a lot of people have reassured themselves that they do, in fact, live in some kind of a meritocracy—in a system that, for all its grievous flaws, sometimes approximates fairness. It is the residential portion of the dream that made Edge City inevitable.

In other words, maybe John Lewis has an image of the Beloved Community that some people might dismiss out of hand as a silly, irrelevant, middle-class suburban caricature of the American Dream.

But I, for one, ended up seriously hoping that John Lewis gets that house. For all that he has gone through—in the service of his country—on mature reflection it seemed to me *he has earned it.*

# 6

## PHOENIX

### Shadow Government

Democracy is the theory that the common people know what they want . . . and deserve to get it, good and bad.

—*H. L. Mencken*

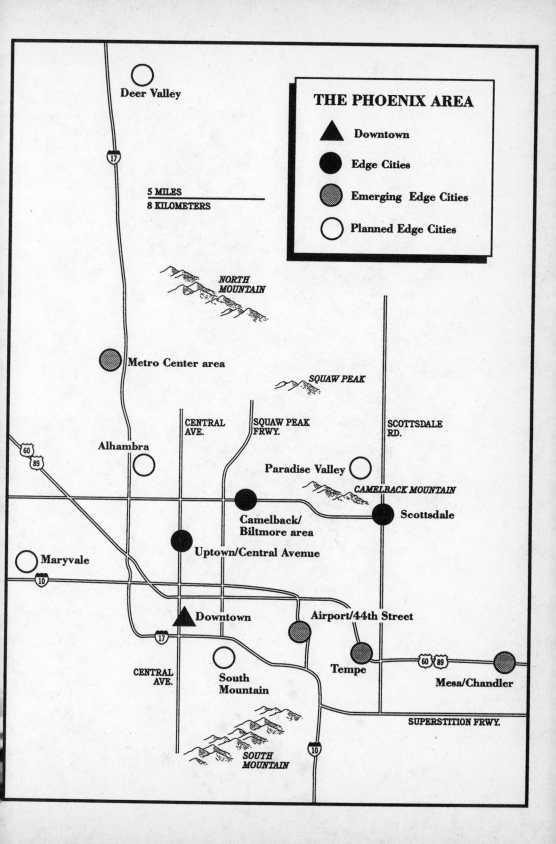

THE PHOENIX AREA

▲ Downtown

● Edge Cities

◔ Emerging Edge Cities

○ Planned Edge Cities

Deer Valley

5 MILES
8 KILOMETERS

NORTH MOUNTAIN

Metro Center area

SQUAW PEAK

CENTRAL AVE.

SQUAW PEAK FRWY.

SCOTTSDALE RD.

Alhambra

Paradise Valley

CAMELBACK MOUNTAIN

Camelback/ Biltmore area

Scottsdale

Uptown/Central Avenue

Maryvale

▲ Downtown

Airport/44th Street

CENTRAL AVE.

South Mountain

Tempe

Mesa/Chandler

SUPERSTITION FRWY.

SOUTH MOUNTAIN

DOROTHY KRUEGER, sixty-one, stood squarely amid the rust-golden grit of the Sonoran desert. She wore orange-red lipstick, bright yellow earrings, blue sweat pants, new white Reeboks, two gold chains, and a matte black semiautomatic Glock 17. There were seventeen bullets in the grip of the pistol. On the webbed black belt around Krueger's waist hung two more clips —for a total of fifty-one rounds—inside the tooled leather cases that matched her holster.

Krueger fired at a human silhouette target first with her strong hand, then her weak hand, then with both hands. She shot quickly, three rounds in four seconds, timed with a stop watch. From three yards, seven yards, fifteen yards, twenty-two, she blazed professionally. Five points for a chest shot. Only two for the head. On order, she reloaded from the belt. "You *never* want to holster an empty weapon" came the fierce scold of the instructor over the loudspeaker. Up and down the line, the thirteen senior citizens—most of them noticeably older than Krueger—quickly complied.

Jack Goodrich and Dick Schiefelbein wore the brown shirts of their uniforms crisply creased; their badges shone brightly in the Arizona sun. They watched Krueger, a candidate for promotion, critically. These two commanding officers of the Sun City Posse, seventy-one and fifty-eight respectively, had always preferred the .357 Magnums hanging on their belts. But as the cacophony of firepower erupted and slugs volleyed in bursts of dust into the backstop of a flood-control canal, they could see why Krueger liked her Glock. With plastic parts, it was lighter and easier to draw and aim than their enormous six-guns. It was also much quicker to reload. No wonder the "bad guys," as they put it, had come to favor that handgun—causing many police forces to switch to the new 9mm standard. And no way was the Posse going to be behind the times.

After all, the Posse had an image to uphold. The uniforms of its members—which included everyone on the Posse-owned firing range—were virtually identical with those of the county's deputy sheriffs, right down to the handcuffs and the Mace. The Posse's full-sized Chevrolets, with the flashing lights on the roof and the star painted on the doors, were also practically indistinguishable from the real police. The Posse's equipment, of course, tended to be newer than that of the police. And their headquarters featuring a color portrait of John Wayne was bigger than the nearby substation. Their big brown beaver Stetsons were more beautiful. For that matter, their shooting range was nicer.

But then again, there were 183 members of the Sun City Posse —far more than there were police officers in the area. That was why this partnership between the privately funded, privately organized Posse and the Maricopa County Sheriff's Department was formed, Goodrich explained.

"In the days of the Wild West, the sheriff would go into a bar and pick out four or five people and deputize them and go out and catch the bad guy," Commander Goodrich said. "Now bring it up to modern status, why, we are on a continuing posse status. They don't let us go when the job is done. We just keep doing it. We're a permanent crime-control posse."

Sun City, Arizona, on the west side of metropolitan Phoenix, bills itself as the largest "adult" community in the world. It has ten shopping centers and forty-six thousand residents. It is a privately owned development that has fervently resisted incorporation into any municipality in order to avoid a new level of taxation. But, though private, it has taken on many trappings of a city. It runs everything from libraries to parks to swimming pools to an art museum to a crisis-counseling hotline to a fire department to a symphony orchestra. The squad cars of its legally franchised, armed, unpaid private posse routinely patrol the public streets. Its innocuously named Recreation Association, meanwhile, has the power to assess fees that are functionally indistinguishable from taxes. If a homeowner does not pay the fees, the association has the legal right—so far unexercised —to slap a lien on that person's house and sell it at auction.

Sun City is by no means an aberration. It represents several forms of private-enterprise governments—shadow governments, if you will—of which there are more than 150,000 in the United States. These shadow governments have become the most numerous, ubiquitous, and largest form of local government in America today, studies show. In their various guises shadow governments levy taxes, adjudicate disputes, provide police protection, run fire departments, provide health care, channel development, plan regionally, enforce esthetic standards, run buses, run railroads, run airports, build roads, fill potholes, publish newspapers, pump water, generate electricity, clean streets, landscape grounds, pick up garbage, cut grass, rake leaves, remove snow, offer recreation, and provide the hottest social service in the United States today: day care. They are central to the Edge City society we are building, in which office parks are in the childrearing business, parking-lot officials run police forces, private enterprise builds public freeways, and subdivisions have a say in who lives where.

These shadow governments have powers far beyond those ever granted rulers in this country before. Not only can they prohibit the organization of everything from a synagogue to a Boy Scout troop; they can regulate the color of a person's living room curtains. Nonetheless, the general public almost never gets the opportunity to vote its leaders out of office, and rarely is protected from them by the United States Constitution.

"The privatization of government in America is the most important thing that's happening, but we're not focused on it. We haven't thought of it as government yet," notes Gerald Frug, professor of local government law at Harvard.

These governments are highly original, locally invented attempts to bring some kind of order to Edge Cities in the absence of more conventional institutions. Edge Cities, after all, seldom match political boundaries. Sometimes they do not even appear on road maps. Few have mayors or city councils. They beg the question of who's in charge. Are these places exercises in anarchy? Or are they governed by other means?

The answer is—government by other means. Nowhere was that more clear than in Phoenix in the early 1990s.

Objectively, metropolitan Phoenix should have been writhing in anarchy by 1991. It seemed as if the entire leadership class had been decapitated. Arizona had been functionally without a governor since the mid-1980s, when the former Pontiac dealer Evan Mecham squeaked into office with a minority of the vote and then disgraced himself so badly that the ensuing impeachment proceedings were launched by his fellow Republicans. The relentlessly pro-growth old-boy elite called the Phoenix Forty had lost control of events when Terry Goddard, a political outsider who championed neighborhood power, became mayor. Then Goddard quit the mayor's job to run for governor—an election he lost. In Phoenix, his void was filled by a new mayor who meant well, but he was a thirty-one-year-old contractor who hadn't finished college.

Meanwhile, the majority and minority leadership of the state legislature had almost completely turned over. High-rolling developers who had overbuilt Phoenix's commercial real estate market by 30 percent dropped like citrus after a heavy frost. The region's most prominent bankers disappeared as their institutions were gobbled up by Los Angeles and New York giants like Security Pacific and Citibank. The area's savings and loans were devastated by the federal clean-up of the industry. The very symbol of that scandal nationwide became Charles H. Keating, Jr., once the most visible man in Phoenix. Keating's campaign contributions and influence peddling tarnished most of the state's congressional delegation, not to mention senators from California, Michigan, and Ohio.

Paradoxically, in the middle of all this the number of jobs in Phoenix continued to grow. So did the number of immigrants. Phoenix even became recognized as a national model for ways to bring life and civilization and esthetic appeal to downtown and Edge Cities.

How could this be?

At least partially, the answer was shadow governments. While highly visible institutions took a beating, thousands of low-profile, small—and sometimes not so small—regimes filled the vacuum, taking on power and the responsibility for running daily life. To the extent that means for getting things done became highly dispersed, localized, and privatized, they were shielded from the damage to public institutions.

Edge Cities nationwide display an ingenious array of such shadow governments. These shadow governments are usually organized like corporations and given names that do not begin to hint at their power. But they can be broadly grouped into three categories:

• Shadow governments that are privately owned and operated, such as homeowners' associations that can rigidly control immense residential areas. Typical of those in the Phoenix area are the Arrowhead Ranch Homeowners Association in Glendale and Leisure World in Mesa.
• Shadow governments that are quasi-public institutions but have accrued power and influence far beyond their original charter. Typical of those in the Phoenix area is the Salt River Project.
• Shadow governments that occupy a murky area between these private and public sectors. They are often referred to as public-private partnerships. Typical is the Downtown Management Partnership of the Phoenix Community Alliance.

What makes these outfits like governments, scholars say, is the extent to which they have the following three attributes:

• They can assess mandatory fees to support themselves: the power to tax.
• They can create rules and regulations: the power to legislate.
• They have the power to coerce, to force people to change their behavior: the police power.

All governments have these powers. What sets shadow governments apart is that they have three additional attributes:

• The leaders of shadow governments are rarely if ever directly accountable to all the people in a general election.
• When and if these leaders are picked in a private election, the vote is rarely counted in the manner of Jeffersonian democracy, with each citizen having a voice. Instead, it is usually one dollar, one vote.
• These leaders are frequently not subject to the constraints on power that the Constitution imposes on conventional governments.

Take Don Smith, for example. In the press, he has been labeled The Enforcer. He rather fancies that designation.

Smith was an FBI agent for twenty-five years. But now he is the "field supervisor" of Arrowhead Ranch, not far from Metro Center, the emerging Edge City in northwest Phoenix. Arrowhead Ranch is a subdivision of almost two thousand homes run by a homeowners' association. That shadow government reaches farther into the lives of its more than three thousand members than any ordinary government has ever been allowed to in America.

The Arrowhead Ranch homeowners' association, for example, passed a law that dictates what residents in its subdivision may or may not park in their own driveway—on their own land. This shadow government does not like the looks of campers, commercial vehicles, motorboats, motorcycles, buses, travel trailers, and motor homes. In fact, it will not put up with an unstacked pile of firewood. And what the Arrowhead Ranch homeowners' association says, goes.

Recently, Smith relates, a homeowner at Arrowhead Ranch parked a Winnebago-like motor home on his private property, beside his house. The shadow government sicced Smith on the perpetrator, and Smith sent the homeowner what he calls a "gig letter," pointing out the offense. When the homeowner did not shape up, the association responded with lawyers. They filed suit in Maricopa County Superior Court—"the same court where you try a homicide case," Smith observes pointedly—demanding a permanent injunction against the offender. When the homeowner resisted, the judge not only backed the association, but demanded that the Winnebago owner pay almost $2000 in the association's attorneys fees, in addition to his own. There is no reason to think the homeowner has not learned his lesson. But if he ever parks that Winnebago next to his house again, it could mean jail. Contempt of court. "You bought yourself a definitive ruling," the judge told him from the bench. In other words, this Maricopa County court may plop a citizen in a public jail if he fails to obey a privately owned and operated shadow government.

Another homeowners' association Smith works for is that of Pinnacle Peak Estates in swanky Scottsdale, the Edge City to the northeast. There, the average home is worth perhaps $400,000.

Yet the shadow government has decided it will not permit anyone to grow a lawn on his own property. In fact, it has "plant police," who control what homeowners are allowed to grow in their ground, because this shadow government has decided that the only horticulture it chooses to allow is that native to the desert. One man with the silly idea that his home was his castle planted a hedgerow of eucalyptus trees in his back yard without the approval of the architectural committee. It ended up costing him over $20,000, Smith estimates. That would be the cost of the trees, plus the lawyers he had to hire to defend himself against the shadow government, plus—when he lost—the court costs of the shadow government's lawyers. Then, of course, he incurred the cost of cutting down the trees.

These are hardly isolated cases. "If you want a new home, it is increasingly difficult to get one that doesn't come with a home-owners' association," said Douglas Kleine, a consultant and former research director for the Community Associations Institute (CAI), the national trade group for private-enterprise shadow governments that includes condominium, co-op, and townhouse associations as well as planned urban developments. The CAI estimates there are at least 130,000 of these shadow governments nationwide.

The powers of the shadow governments derive from the idea that subjecting oneself to them is a voluntary act. When a family chooses to buy a particular home, it is legally presumed that they fully understand what such an association really means to their lives.

However, once that house is chosen, membership in the community association is not voluntary. Neither is compliance with the association's rules. Embedded in the deed are "covenants, conditions, and restrictions"—invariably pronounced *cee-cee-en-ares*—that make obedience mandatory. And the enforcement powers are awesome. "Your peers, the community association, have the power to take your house away from you," Kleine explains. "They also have the power to go into small claims court and have the sheriff go after the TV set. And they have the power, usually, to suspend certain privileges—or rights, depending on your definition—including the right to vote. It's like the old poll tax. If you didn't pay your tax, you can't vote."

They can regulate how many pets you may have, what size

those pets can be, and where you may walk them. They can regulate whether or not you may live with your children. Charles Keating buried C C & Rs in the deeds of one of his most ambitious Phoenix developments, Estrella, that banned "pornographic" films, books, magazines, and devices from a homeowner's bedroom.

In Mesa, where another Edge City is growing southeast of central Phoenix, John Lafferty once found himself facing two problems. Lafferty is the administrator of the community association of Leisure World, a walled development with almost five thousand residents. He is a paid professional who reports to a board of directors elected by homeowners grouped in districts; he is in effect the city manager of a shadow government with a budget of over $5 million.

The first problem was an illegal immigrant—a physician, forty-two. The doctor had had a nervous breakdown and become incapable of working or taking care of himself, so his parents had brought him into their home.

The problem was that Leisure World has a law that no one may live there who is under forty-five. If the parents wished to continue to care for their broken son, they had to move. They were very understanding, Lafferty said. They were going quietly. But they *were* going. They were leaving their home. They understood the association would enforce its rules if it had to. There was no doubt about that.

The second problem Lafferty faced was the newspaper. It seems that the developer of Leisure World, Western Savings and Loan, had long published one that was circulated for free, available for the taking from racks placed in the common areas. Western also made the paper widely available outside the walls, since a publication trumpeting all of Leisure World's activities was thought to boost real estate sales. Every supermarket and drugstore within sight of the Superstition Mountains carried copies, and *Leisure World News* became quite an institution, with a full-time editor and a circulation of fifteen thousand. Because it delivered an affluent market, it attracted a healthy ad base, which swelled the size of the paper to as many as ninety-six pages.

Then Western was taken over by the wrathful *federales* of the Resolution Trust Corporation, who could not imagine why they should be in the newspaper business. So they stopped paying for the publication. This created a void for the management of Leisure World, which had always used the publication as its house organ. It also created a void for Doris Mathews, the paper's editor, who was going to be without a job. Mathews, like a good Arizona capitalist, decided to take over the paper and keep it going as an independent voice.

But here was the hitch: the First Amendment does not force shadow governments to allow freedom of the press.

Less than eager to encourage a Leisure World newspaper over which he had no control, Lafferty prohibited the distribution of Mathews' paper from its traditional racks in the common areas. Mathews retaliated by getting friends to distribute the paper. But Lafferty was holding the aces.

Lafferty's shadow government is a private corporation. The common grounds of Leisure World are private property that the shadow government controls. Therefore, Lafferty can start up his own newspaper and, with rare effectiveness, suppress competing voices. A conventional government would never be allowed to force all of a newspaper's vending machines off the public sidewalks. But Lafferty legally may pull the distribution boxes of any newspaper he doesn't like—even the *Arizona Republic,* the state's foremost daily—if he chooses. If his action squelches Mathews' paper—if she finds it prohibitively expensive to distribute her newspaper by mail, or if she loses advertisers because of her distribution problems and is run out of business—those are the breaks.

Mathews—who describes herself, accurately, as looking like Aunt Bee in *The Andy Griffith Show*—acknowledges Lafferty is completely within his rights. The Constitution says only that regular, aboveground governments "shall make no law . . . abridging the freedom of speech, or of the press; or the right of the people peaceably to assemble."

But that is the key distinction about a shadow government. It is not a regular government, even if the association does hold elections for its board of directors. Private corporations have broad powers over private property.

"They are setting up internal courts," Kleine points out. "Due process may be desirable, but it is not required. The Fourteenth Amendment does not apply." The Fourteenth Amendment guarantees equal protection for all. "The application of the

Fourteenth Amendment would cause all kinds of things. It would subject the board of directors to the Voting Rights Act. If you're elected by district, and you wanted to redraw those lines, you'd have to go to the Justice Department. You couldn't have one dollar, one vote, or one house, one vote.

"The First Amendment? The association newspaper is a house organ. It's just like a company newsletter. It's there for us to communicate with you, not for you to communicate with each other." That is why the Leisure World paper—on purpose— never had a letters-to-the-editor page.

Defenders point out that homeowners readily obey and encourage shadow governments. And indeed, such units are very successful at what they do. They control nuisances and unpleasantness and keep the community swimming pool clean. Thus, property values rise. These disciples further observe that if the larger society finds the actions of these private governments objectionable, it is not without recourse. The power of homeowners' associations is based on the covenants written into the deeds. In decades past, offensive covenants—such as those prohibiting house sales to blacks and Jews—have been thrown out when challenged in court.

These supporters also point out that shadow governments devise new solutions to the new problems that Edge City faces every day. If conventional governments had been doing such a great job, people would not have felt obliged to invent new forms, taking governance into their own hands, this argument goes. Perhaps. But such opportunities as arise, these shadow governments certainly seize. Take the quasi-public shadow government called the Salt River Project.

The land around Phoenix is martini-dry. The only reason a city exists there at all is that as long ago as the time of Christ, humans of the Hohokam tribe recognized that by the standards of the Sonoran desert, the Valley of the Sun can be made water rich. These native Americans built a 250-mile canal system that permitted an advanced civilization to support twenty thousand people. For reasons that remain a mystery, the Hohokam disappeared from the valley just before Columbus sailed. A century and a half later, the Spanish showed up and gave the name Rio Salado—Salt River—to the broad gravel bed from which the canals radiated. A miner, scout, and Confederate cavalry veteran named Jack Swilling reintroduced canal building to the area in the late 1800s. Then, in 1902, President Teddy Roosevelt championed the National Reclamation Act, which provided government loans to "reclaim" Western lands with irrigation projects. Metropolitan Phoenix rose around the bed of the Salt River because, in 1903, the shadow government called the Salt River Project was born.

Jack Pfister (pronounced Feester) is the general manager of the Salt River Project. His chaste reaction to my initial questions was "I would not describe the Salt River Project as a form of regional government—because of our limited functions, basically only delivering water, with the power business being supplementary to that."

Nonetheless, this shadow government has vastly more influence over the lives of the people of Phoenix than do most conventional governments.

In the dry Southwest, water is the linchpin of the universe. With water you can create charming cities, fields of agricultural plenty, thriving industry, or wild rivers that charge the spirit. But there's not enough water to have all four. Who gets what is determined in a highly expensive, complex, and politicized fashion. And in central Arizona, that means the Salt River Project. An entity like the Salt River Project, which determines the price and availability of electricity, has the power of life and death. In Arizona in the summer, people without air conditioning die, just as surely as do people in Montana without winter heat. When the Salt River Project decides to encourage water conservation—or, conversely, subsidizes water use by making it artificially cheap— or decides to share the cost of a nuclear reactor forty miles upwind of Phoenix or builds a coal-fired generator whose pollution is accused of obscuring the Grand Canyon, it exercises more control over the Arizona environment than virtually any other player.

With powers like that, it seems but the tiniest and most inconsequential leap for a quasi-public shadow government like the Salt River Project to get involved with such social services as day care. Or with transforming central Arizona into a boating and fishing center by offering recreation on its reservoirs. Or with determining the quality of Edge City life by controlling development along urban canals in a fashion that might transform metropolitan Phoenix into a series of River Walks echoing the one in San Antonio.

Nor are such quasi-public shadow governments with vast influence unusual in America. They range from airport authorities to regional transportation commands to water conservation districts. One reason they have been so eagerly seized on as the means to run Edge Cities is their abundant history. One such shadow government, the Los Angeles Department of Water and Power, had a movie made about it. It was called *Chinatown.* The potential of these quasi-public shadow governments was dramatized by Robert A. Caro in *The Power Broker,* his biography of Robert Moses.

Moses "had glimpsed in the institution called 'public authority' a potential for power . . . that was exciting and frightening and immense . . . adding a whole new layer to urban government in America," Caro wrote. Through the use of public authorities, Moses tore down vast swatches of old city to build bridges, roads, parks, and public housing, making him a person whose "influence on the cities of America was greater than that of any other person." Indeed, Moses changed the physical shape —the actual outline—of Manhattan Island.

No one I interviewed suggested that either the Salt River Project or its general manager, Jack Pfister, suffered from that kind of megalomania. In fact, Pfister's rule was so benevolent that as he approached retirement, even Phoenix's "alternative" tabloid, *New Times,* eulogized him. It is startling in what used to be called the underground press to find a headline about an Establishment figure that asks: IF THE HEAD OF THE SALT RIVER PROJECT DOESN'T KEEP PHOENIX SAFE FROM THE STORM, WHO WILL?

Such power is typically grounded in how elusive a shadow government's authority can be. The Salt River Project presents itself to the public in any of four different guises, depending on what purpose suits the board of directors. Over the years it has taken on the rights and privileges of a private, for-profit, dividend-paying, stockholder-owned corporation; an unregulated investor-owned utility; an agent of the federal government; and a municipality-like political subdivision of the state—which is where it gets its right to issue tax-free bonds. It mixes, matches, and retains all these identities to its own ends. The closest it comes to public oversight is an election in which voting power goes to owners of irrigated land in a one-acre, one-vote fashion. Thus, the owner of a two-square-mile cotton operation has exactly 5120 times as many votes as someone with a home on a quarter-acre lot. As a result, although this shadow government is highly urban, with tremendous powers to shape Edge Cities, it is still run by a board of directors on which you see a lot of bolo ties.

As Pfister got talking, he acknowledged that he and his organization had more of an impact on metropolitan Phoenix than he initially had been willing to admit.

Yes, he did discourage people from having lawns in their own front yards. He did encourage desert landscaping called xeriscaping. Yes, he does have a tree specialist on his staff for that.

Yes, he does have five thousand employees and a financial intake of $1 billion a year, and a double-A bond rating, tax free, and a governmental-affairs staff of thirteen people (read lobbyists) with their own political action committee handing out campaign contributions. Yes, his real estate does spread out over hundreds of miles. Yes, he did first begin to get his shadow government involved in public affairs in 1979 when he discovered, during massive floods, that regular governments had no idea what they were doing. It was at that point he discovered, as he put it, that the Salt River Project had "resources and expertise they could contribute to water and environmental management. These are public resources. And we will contribute them."

This is how it always works. Edge City is a place where the game is not yet set up. Shadow governments "move into vacuums," one long-time observer says. "They get into one issue and they've got a professional here and a technician there. And then they'll give you an opinion on what you're ordering for lunch. And before you know it, they've named two of your children. They eat up power, like the science-fiction movies. They eat living things, derive power from what they've ingested, and develop an independent power base."

Pfister acknowledges that "because of the expertise of Salt River Project people, we have an impact disproportionate to other organizations." Indeed, before he finished his term, he or his outfit had helped shape the legal framework for groundwater management in Arizona, helped determine whether state projects should be required to make environmental impact statements, pushed for rail links to Phoenix's Edge Cities, and encouraged building at increased densities in those Edge Cities. Not only do dense nodes have social benefits, Pfister points out. But they are more efficiently supplied electricity.

"I'm a believer in filling vacuums," he admits. "Vacuums don't work well. That's a theory that I understand well. I look for vacuums to fill. Hopefully not in a mercurial way, but one that supports the overall community good. People would debate about that, I'm sure."

One well-connected local attorney says, "It *is* amazing that a lawyer-engineer as uncharismatic as Jack has risen to something of a cultural institution in Phoenix." Because of his role as head of the Salt River Project, Pfister was asked to help create a strategic plan for state economic development. He acknowledges that when water policies and energy policies are formed statewide, "we are always at the table." His outfit has taken an active role in dam safety, Indian affairs, regional planning, and strip-mining regulation. The SRP has its own security division. Because of his prominence with the Salt River Project, Pfister was asked to facilitate a business group charged with reforming the school system. He became chairman of the state board of regents just in time to defend the state college and university system against attacks from the governor. He helped raise $4 million for disadvantaged students in the Maricopa community college system. He chaired the Arizona Humanities Council. When asked whether he was ranging a little far afield, Pfister replied, "I have a belief that the arts and cultural amenities really add to the vitality of a community, so it is in the best interests of the Salt River Project to support the arts."

It was not enough that, because of the Salt River Project, Phoenix probably has the most carefully managed watershed in the world. Pfister decided that to "restore economic competitiveness," he had to start thinking about providing day care. "Without doubt that is in the cards for the future." Then he got involved with repackaging benefits to deal with "untraditional family environments." I asked him whether this meant medical care for gay couples and he said, "Again, it's only a matter of time. Ten years ago I probably did not know any for-sure gay people. Now I know a great number of gay people. That's just part of what's happening in Phoenix and we will have to adjust to that. The Hopi culture had a clan whose job it was literally to go out and meet with the outsiders, the conquistadors or whoever it was coming through, to try to understand what they were all about and try to bring that message back to the people to kind of alert them to what was going to happen. And essentially, I have tried to view my responsibilities as general manager to fill that role."

Pfister has been characterized as sounding like a New Age philosopher. I found him buttoned up a little tighter than that— but I understood the point. And thanked the stars. This is, after all, a man who ended up helping shape new industry safety standards after the Three Mile Island near-meltdown, and helped shape the electric industry's response to acid rain.

His successor will presumably have at least as much impact on Phoenix, the state of Arizona, and the United States. One hopes he is equally enlightened. After all, remember who will pick him: a corporate board of directors elected on the basis of who owns how many acres of irrigated land.

In addition to the way they fill vacuums, what's fascinating about these shadow governments is the way they operate in the gray. They take on all manner of public responsibilities, but they retain their private prerogatives to do largely as they please. Take the form of shadow government called the public-private partnership.

Phoenix is the first municipality in America to recognize formally, for planning purposes, that it is made up of a constellation of Edge Cities, locally referred to as "urban villages." It is logical that Phoenix came to this conclusion early. The urban village referred to as "downtown" historically never amounted to much. As recently as World War II, it was the trade and government center for a rural area that did not add up to more than 185,000 people. Even as the Phoenix area erupted to an urban population of two million, downtown did not become grand. Two other cores with better parking and fewer derelicts grew larger. One was the area north, along Central Avenue, called "uptown." The other was the posh area along Camelback Avenue near the Frank Lloyd Wright–styled Arizona Biltmore. In fact, compared with older, Eastern metros, there is no sharp distinction between downtown Phoenix and those other centers. They all look and function like Edge Cities. Downtown sealed that when it formed a shadow government to help it compete with the other urban villages.

The Phoenix Community Alliance was started by a group of developers and bankers to promote the development of the downtown area and, hence, their properties. Soon the Alliance members realized their private, voluntary organization didn't have the powers they needed. They couldn't tax, they couldn't run a police force, they couldn't keep the streets clean, they couldn't control the looks of the streets to make them attractive to pedestrians. So they cast about for a way to gain some real leverage in their Edge City. What they came up with was a public-private shadow government they modestly named The Management District.

The organization of The Management District is a prototypically hazy hybrid. It is a private, nonprofit corporation, but it levies its fees through the public sector. Its operating money comes from a special surcharge on the property tax collected by the municipality, yet the surcharge is made only on owners within the boundaries of the Edge City area. The money would appear, then, to come from the owners of private property. But since the municipality of Phoenix owns much land downtown, half of that money is actually public. The Management District has a board on which the mayor and the city manager are represented, as are ethnic minorities and the arts community. But the majority of the board members come from the private business side—the Alliance. The result is a thorough blurring of distinctions between public and private.

This private organization writes checks to the city to make sure that on public land the palm trees get trimmed, and the leaves raked, and the streets swept far more frequently than is the case in other parts of the city. It also writes checks to the police department to make sure that it gets more officers on the beat than in other parts of the city. These are genuine Phoenix policemen, deployed from headquarters, working their regular shifts, fully armed, and capable of making arrests, as usual. Hardly mall guards. But if the private Management District wants them to appear more tourist-friendly by wearing shorts or blazers or by patrolling on bicycles or horses rather than in their squad cars, something can be worked out. After all, the Management District is paying the freight. For that matter, if they wish an additional dozen cops, all they need do is write a bigger check. The shadow government also runs the wonderfully lurid purple-and-orange downtown shuttle bus system. It even has a marketing role, convincing the private sector to buy or lease property in its area. It is, in short, an institution that formalizes and justifies an ambiguous zone in which the public sector gets the private sector to pay for keeping a business area safe, clean, mobile, and prosperous. And the private sector gains unprecedented leverage over the public sector, especially for services not available to the mortal taxpayer. The power of the state, meanwhile, is brought to bear to enforce the will of businessmen.

There are many advantages to this kind of cooperation. One is markedly higher levels of efficiency. "There's no question that they're faster and cheaper. The incentives for prompt performance are stronger in the private sector," points out Robert C. Ellickson, a professor of law at Yale who has studied shadow governments. "People can coordinate with one another to their mutual advantage more than is generally recognized. Take the English language. The people living on the island of Great Britain came together and just created a language. Nobody was put in charge. People are now coordinating in a sophisticated way. I think it's terrific that property owners pay. This is not a calamity. This is a terrific thing."

Indeed, in Phoenix this form of shadow government has worked sufficiently well that the Edge City competing most directly with downtown, Phoenix's Central Avenue uptown, has created a similar but less ambitious body for itself. It is called The Improvement District. Ellickson views as a positive sign that there are many different kinds of shadow governments. This, he avers, reflects the wide and healthy range of choices people have. Shadow governments are solutions clever people have voluntarily cooked up, Ellickson argues. They will be onerous only if they become unavoidable. When he asked me if I lived in a place ruled by a shadow government, and I responded, "Hell, no," Ellickson offered that as triumphant evidence that liberty and choice were alive in the land.

He has a point. A very sensitive gauge of what people view as their biggest problem is whatever issue causes them to create a shadow government. Among the hottest such concerns today is traffic. And sure enough, a common form of shadow government is the transportation management authority. Initially, such a power draws movers and shakers together to get roads built, traffic lights synchronized, parking rationalized, and car pools organized. Then it is typical for such an organization to branch out, in the absence of any other appropriate authority, to grapple with problems from day care to garbage collection.

But this leaves the question of whether shadow governments are of, by, and for the people. Their rights and obligations are almost always defined by property and ownership and money. They bow less to the notion that all men are created equal than to that equally venerable American aphorism, "Them that has, gits."

These shadow governments are democratic to a point. But they rarely have much use for the principle of one citizen, one vote. If you rent your home in a place with a community association, it is generally your landlord who gets the vote, not you. If you are a spouse or a son or a daughter whose name is not on the deed, you usually do not vote. In condominiums, the property principle can be fine-tuned to five digits to the right of the decimal place. In one such place, the owner of a one-bedroom apartment got 0.06883 of a vote, and the owner of a two-bedroom with den got 0.12350 of a vote.

This one-dollar, one-vote democracy harks back to the earliest days of the Colonies, when the vote was reserved for white male owners of property because they were viewed as having the biggest stake in how the society was run. Scholars who examine these shadow governments repeatedly note how strikingly similar shadow governments are to legal and governmental structures that date back before Thomas Jefferson. Historical comparisons are as easy to make to the feudalism of Renaissance Italy or the authoritarian efficiencies of Napoleonic France as they are to the dreams of a Lincoln, Wilson, or Roosevelt.

At the very least, says Gerald Frug, "it's a return to the nineteenth century, when there was no legal distinction between a city and a private corporation. All had the same powers and restrictions. Railroads could take your land and pay you for it without your consent. You could do anything privately that you could do publicly."

Because these shadow governments usually gain their authority from property rights instead of through the powers granted to the people by the Constitution, they are acutely class-conscious.

"If you go back and look at suburbs built in the 1940s and 1950s," says Douglas Kleine, "there are dog kennels and chain-link fences and four or five trucks, two of which are up on blocks. People want to be protected from the class below them. There's very much an anti-blue-collar bias in all the truck restrictions, and how many dogs and fences. That's the first restriction people put in—no chain-link fences at all. You might be able to put a little split rail in. Two rails high. But the front yards are supposed to remain this Victorian green pasture that you can afford not to put cows on."

"These are governments by the wealthy, for the wealthy," says Frug. "It is plutocracy, not democracy." Bruce McDowell of the U.S. Advisory Commission on Intergovernmental Affairs points out that in times of tight public budgets, governments lose their independence. Transportation work is not necessarily done where the public most needs it. It is done where monied interests can have their priorities moved to the front of the line by putting up cash. With enough private money behind it, an interchange can be built not where it would best move traffic for the citizenry, but where it would best funnel potential customers into a development.

Ellickson of Yale counters that shadow governments are not anywhere near as oppressive as conventional governments. Shadow governments, he points out, rarely if ever shoulder the heaviest of burdens: the attempt to redistribute people's incomes. Somehow, however, that is probably more comforting to those with incomes than to those without.

That is why I ended up questioning Thomas Espinoza closely on how he felt about the new Phoenix Management District.

I suppose it should not be cause for note that Espinoza is now president of the Phoenix Community Alliance. After all, Arizona became a state in 1912, and Espinoza's grandparents became Americans before that. They helped settle the territory not long after America settled the border through the Sonoran desert between the United States and their native Mexico. Espinoza, a third-generation Arizonan, is now the head of his own development corporation. He took me for breakfast to Café la Tasca, an extraordinary Mexican place downtown that made its own tamales, fresh. His native dialect, however, turned out not to be Spanish, but that hybrid of dollars-per-square-foot arithmetic and the jargon of the Deal peculiar to American commercial English. It was with considerable relish that he explained the power plays that went into the creation of The Management District.

But the fact of the matter is that Mexican-Americans are still not what you'd call common in the halls of power in Phoenix, so I had to ask him: Won't this district work great at keeping out "undesirables"?

"I don't think anybody would admit this," he acknowledges. "But what first started driving the Management District was people basically saying, 'City, you are not doing your job right. Therefore we are going to pay more money to do it the way we want it done.' And some of that has been the homeless issue. The private sector saying, Gee, we ought to make sure these areas are safe, secure, clean, da, da da, da da. Nobody's ever told me that. But my political instincts say that some of that is there."

Suppose, I ask, they decided they don't like people downtown with brown skin like yours?

"No, that doesn't concern me," replies Espinoza in a studied analysis of realpolitik. "The shit would hit the fan. We're too much of a power base. Now if it had been fifteen years ago? That would be the agenda. And I say that without any hesitation. But not anymore. We're part of the fabric of this power structure now. Within the next fifty years, we will *be* the power structure. I don't mean that in an arrogant manner. But in my lifetime, I will see our power base shift to the other direction. I will see the day where Anglos and blacks are complaining about Mexicans being discriminatory. I will. In my lifetime I will see that."

Is this a great country or what? I ask. We laugh.

"And I've got to tell you this one thing. When I came on, the Alliance had pissed off a lot of poor folks and community groups and neighborhoods in Phoenix. Luckily the board became sensitive after I told them a number of times: 'If you keep building high-rises and don't worry about surrounding neighborhoods, eventually those people are going to turn on you. The day will come when those neighborhoods will have a political power base, and they are going to come after the city council and the mayor's office and we are going to have some major problems here if the business community does not start addressing the homeless issue, neighborhood revitalization, and those kinds of things.' So we are putting together a Local Initiative Support Corporation—a pot of funds that will lend money to neighborhood groups to revitalize neighborhoods.

"I don't buy into the theory that we'll just have more police force and we'll just keep them out. I have been part of the receiving end of the Chicano community. I am part of that generation, forty to forty-six—when the airport needed to expand? They bulldozed down all the Chicano neighborhoods. And we're saying that ain't gonna happen again. You may have done that one time, but you ain't gonna do it again."

Espinoza clearly feels he is helping forge new ways of uniting disparate people for the creation of a common good. He feels he is breaking down barriers to bring together business interests and the community, the public sector and the private. There is plenty of reason to applaud people seeking new avenues for cooperation, to be sure. Confrontation certainly doesn't have that great a track record.

Yet there is tremendous reason historically to think that the cooperation inherent in shadow governments is akin to foxes telling chickens they should unite to pursue common goals. Not for nothing was the Constitution written to protect the isolated and the helpless from the authorities and even the majority. After all, these shadow governments are making open and clear-cut distinctions between the weak and the strong, between people with property and people without. To this day nobody has refuted Karl Marx's observation that the revolutionary basis of the great divide in power among humans is class. It is no small irony that as democracy flourishes in formerly communist worlds, in the United States it seems far less popular than corporatism.

It is hard to know, listening to Espinoza, whether he is a

stirring example of the American Dream gone right, or a massively delusional pawn of monied interests. Nor is this a small matter. The central issue in the phenomenal rise of shadow governments is whether they are on an enlightened track. If such institutions become powerful and efficient enough to solve our abundant problems, will they also become strong enough to ignore our desires?

To be sure, if shadow governments are attempts to form a more perfect Union, there is a case to be made for that. "Two forms of government—democracy and socialism—grew directly from city life," James E. Vance, Jr., notes in *This Scene of Man.* "Democracy was devised while the tolerance of strangers, innovation, and change was greatly increased over the levels characteristic of the rural clan era. It was in the cities in the industrial districts of Britain, the United States, and northwestern Europe that socialism—the acceptance of the view that society had rights along with individuals and that social objectives stood above economic ones—was nurtured."

So perhaps it is only natural that our revolution in creating Edge Cities is also causing an upheaval in our forms of governance. Like all other collective works of man, Edge Cities can be seen as living organisms, fighting disorganization, willing order out of chaos. Traditional means of distributing power—from organizing labor to voting for president—are declining in popularity. Perhaps this depreciation should be viewed as sensible people telling us old ways are no longer working and new ones need to be born.

After all, this argument goes, this is not the 1960s, much less the 1930s. Nobody is naïve anymore. Lots of people are educated enough to read zoning codes for themselves. Even the poor have access to organizing powers and the media, and a complex understanding of where the levers of power really are. In the last thirty years, United States citizens of Mexican ancestry have never voted in percentages anywhere near their representation in the population. Yet they have a track record of organizing in sufficient numbers in front of television cameras to get plenty of attention from powerful interests. So why shouldn't we applaud individuals coming together to create shadow governments? In this cosmology, if people feel they can

defend their rights themselves, and at the same time view elect-
ing their representatives as a distasteful sideshow, what's the
harm? Alexis de Tocqueville remarked, in *Democracy in America* in
the 1830s, that we are an extravagantly creative people, we
Americans, in the way we generate new social forms. When we
push our homes and jobs out past our old-fashioned sense of
what a city and its government should be, perhaps it is only
natural that we not get hung up on the problems that causes. We
go out there and we solve our new problems, filling power
vacuums with whatever seems to do the job. Which, of course,
always causes new problems, not that that stops us. If even the
homeless now have a voice, this argument goes, it is not the
death of liberty and the road to tyranny. It simply means we are
replacing the old New Deal–era reliance on big government with
a new "informed pragmatic idealism."

So this argument goes.

Linda Nadolski casts the idea differently. Nadolski originally
was the proverbial housewife turned grass-roots activist. She
parlayed her opposition to developers running roughshod over
established neighborhoods into a regular election victory that
gave her a seat on the Phoenix City Council. She now represents
the district that includes the Edge City in the Camelback–Arizona Biltmore area. But she is still a partisan of grass-roots
involvement and participatory democracy. As a result, she cham-
pions the village planning committees. These were purposefully
created by Phoenix's aboveground government as a kind of
mini–town council in each urban village. Appointed by elected
officials, the committees are charged with clarifying at the most
local possible level the merits of proposed changes affecting the
quality of life in each Edge City. They are an embryonic form of
genuine, constitutional Edge City government. But even more
important, they attempt to give some real level of control to that
nebulous notion, the community.

Councilwoman and activist Nadolski has given considerable
thought to where the concepts of "government" and "community" meet.

"Communities," Nadolski feels, "are exercises in doing the
things that are important to people. Like getting in touch with
each other. Where are you going to leave your kids when you go

to work? Who's the person I can actually call to find out if my son went out drinking last night? Who do you talk to if your grandmother is getting older and you've got to find a place for her? The stuff that really counts. Let the government do the other stuff. These things don't sound important. But the whole sense of how you find the real information that counts is what drives the sense of community. Who do you invite around your table so that you're *safe*.

"Safety. Today, that's the operative word. You like to feel safe. I used the word 'control' for a while. I decided that control was the thing that everybody was looking for. But I've left that word behind. I decided that the reason they wanted or felt like they had control was so they could feel safe. As long as they felt safe, they would have been willing to give up their control.

"People feel abused. They feel raped. That's the kind of intensity they feel in terms of 'out of control' and 'violated.' By government, yeah—because those are the guys who are in the paper, those are the guys who are supposed to be in charge. But it comes down to economics, too. People's ability to protect their future. Economic power to provide safety. People are sensing that they are out of control—the stock market's in trouble, Charlie Keating, the S & Ls, and we're pretending it isn't happening. They're afraid we're going to run out of money. Our children will never have what we have.

"When people get backed against the wall, they get angry, and anger is not rational. They look around after their anger happens to figure out what excited it. And that's how you get those homeowners' groups that dictate where they will allow your dog to poop. The reason they feel anger in the first place is that they feel attacked—out of control—not safe. They translate their anger into control. They try to create their world so they can feel they are in control so they can feel safe. They go home to their back yard and they fence it in and they feel safe. And when you violate that, you're in trouble."

This gets her back to the Edge City protogovernments, the neighborhood advisory committees. One of their charges is to encourage density in the middle of their urban village so that the Edge City will be walkable and urbane and easily serviced by mass transit and all these other wonderful things that planners drool over. As a practical matter, though, Nadolski has found, the real communities in her district hate a lot of this stuff. They hate the idea of high-rises invading their space.

"It's instinctual. We don't have a tree that we can hug, and we don't see a river. The only thing we see day after day that reminds us that God and nature exist is the sky. We go everywhere and we do this," she says, saluting the spirit of the place by raising her arm in a sweep toward the cloud-flecked, Christmastime-warm, desert-blue heavens. "Every once in a while we see this short little stump we call a mountain and we think it's wonderful, because its against *our sky*. And *those things* [the office and hotel towers] intrude on our sky. They penetrate our sky. Even when I say it my blood boils. In theory, they are better, because they provide all this open space down here and all that other stuff. All that great theory. Right. Yeah.

"No. This is our world. These people in their back yards came here from somewhere else. We are creatures of our back yard. It's an extension of our living room. We've got the highest per capita number of swimming pools in the world. And then when this high-rise comes here and looks down in our back yard and pool and barbecue and takes away our piece of that, it's, it's—'If I wanted to live in New York, I wouldn't have *left.*'

" 'How *dare* you take this away from me. Again. And P.S., you can take your light-rail system and shove it.'

"Yeah!"

In short, the community deep in its guts knows what's important to the people in the neighborhoods.

So, increasingly, the committee that represents their values in the Edge City scheme of things is not parading in lock step with the city's elders and betters and the planners and the development interests. Instead, it is questioning density and height and mass transit. It is willing to hear from the individual. It is giving voice to the inarticulate, the amateur, the cranky, even the ill-informed. It is giving a focus and a sense of identity to its Edge City. And it is doing so out in the open, not in the gray, not surrounded by shadows.

In fact, this committee is ornery and recalcitrant. It is unpredictable, inefficient, time-consuming, and frustrating. It is stubborn and perverse—marching to the beat of its own drummer.

It is, in short, displaying every full-blown, time-honored, and fought-for safeguard of that standard of justice, domestic tranquillity, common defense, general welfare, and the blessings of liberty that we shaped in Philadelphia in 1788 and sealed with the words "We the people . . ."

It looks as if it might be becoming a democracy.

# 7

## TEXAS

### Civilization

*What happened to you living in England—what exactly did you see?*

I saw how much more in tune I am with a forceful society like our own, fueled by immigration, where the ambition is naked and the animus is undisguised and the energy is relentless and expended openly, without embarrassment or apology. I'm speaking of intellectual and literary intensity no less than the intensity behind all the American trash, the intensity that's generated by the American historical drama of movement and massive displacement, of class overspreading class, region overtaking region, minority encroaching on minority, and the media cannibalizing the works. Try to imagine England inviting, on the scale that the U.S. does, the cultural and political clash.

*—Philip Roth, 1988*

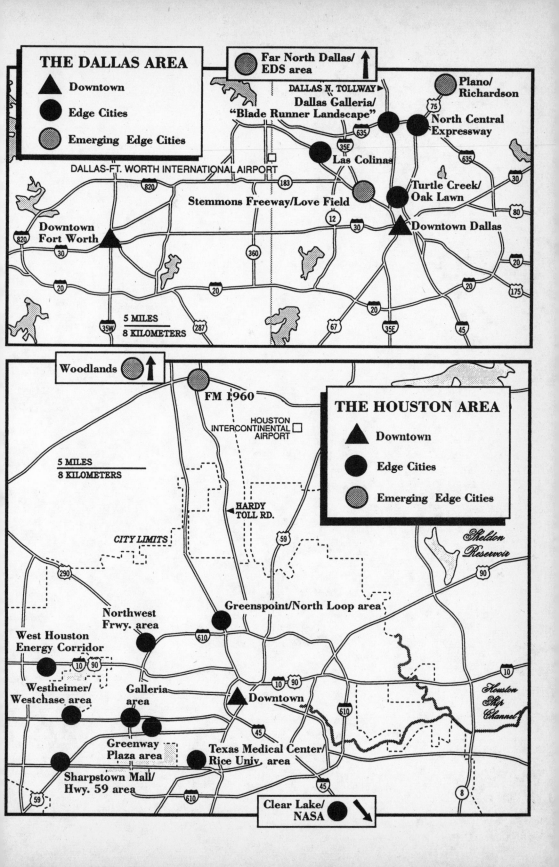

## THE DALLAS AREA

▲ Downtown

● Edge Cities

⬤ Emerging Edge Cities

⬤ Far North Dallas/ EDS area ↑

DALLAS N. TOLLWAY ▶

Dallas Galleria/ "Blade Runner Landscape"

⬤ Plano/ Richardson

75

Las Colinas

North Central Expressway

635

635

DALLAS-FT. WORTH INTERNATIONAL AIRPORT

820

183

30

Stemmons Freeway/Love Field

Turtle Creek/ Oak Lawn

80

12

30

▲ Downtown Dallas

Downtown Fort Worth

820

30

360

20

20

20

175

20

35E

45

5 MILES
8 KILOMETERS

35W

287

67

## THE HOUSTON AREA

Woodlands ⬤ ↑

FM 1960

HOUSTON INTERCONTINENTAL AIRPORT

▲ Downtown

● Edge Cities

⬤ Emerging Edge Cities

5 MILES
8 KILOMETERS

HARDY TOLL RD. ◀

Sheldon Reservoir

CITY LIMITS

59

290

90

Greenspoint/North Loop area

Northwest Frwy. area

610

10

West Houston Energy Corridor

10  90

10  90

Houston Ship Channel

Westheimer/ Westchase area

Galleria area

▲ Downtown

610

Greenway Plaza area

45

Texas Medical Center/ Rice Univ. area

Sharpstown Mall/ Hwy. 59 area

59

610

45

8

Clear Lake/ NASA ● ↘

THE HOTEL CLOCK read 7:34 A.M. Headlights were glaring through the room's windows. This is no small deal, a half-awake brain reported; we're on the twelfth floor.

The guest wrapped a towel around himself, gingerly parted the drapes, and peered out the floor-to-ceiling glass. The searing high beams were just hanging there, slung beneath the belly of a yellow-and-white helicopter, floating at eye level across the way. The chopper had loomed out of a gray morning, bringing a commuter in to a pad on top of a ten-story parking deck. On closer examination, it turned out the parking structure onto which the helicopter was settling sported concrete accent spikes, like castle battlements. It also flew two orange wind socks, like knights' standards.

This was before the guest's first cup of coffee.

But the rest of the vista was no less extraordinary. Just below, outdoors, on what was the fifth level relative to the ground, twelve canopies the shape of mushrooms, boldly striped in red and white and yellow and green, spanned spa tables. They clustered in pods around a heated pool giving off wisps of white steam. A man sat down and stripped to his bathing trunks for a dip. He took off one of his cowboy boots. Then he took off one of his legs. He plunged in and smoothly started the breast stroke. Sure enough. One of his flippers ended at the knee.

Just beyond the primary blue water through which he knifed was an alfalfa-green padded track. On it jogged a solitary blond, in black-and-fuchsia aerobic tights and gold jewelry. The track circled a faceted smoked-onyx barrel vault. The skylight was over an ice rink. Four levels below. Which turned out to be actually in the middle of a mall.

Up on this roof, an unadorned tan cube behind the green jogging track housed ten air-conditioned University Club tennis courts. The tennis courts were on the same level as the sixth tier of that parking structure with the helicopter still on it, its blades turning languidly. To the left, soaring out of sight, was the handsome black glass of the sixty-four-story Transco Tower, the tallest building in the world outside a traditional downtown.

New noise interrupted the guest's reverie, noise from behind, to the north. A second helicopter, with red and white blades, burst into sound straight overhead. Skids up, it lighted next to the first, directly opposite this twelfth-floor room. A crowd gathered around it. The guest's dazzled stare was broken.

How did it get to be 8:04?

Room service, please? Coffee. Lots of coffee.

The stunning juxtapositions of this panorama are all part of a place called the Houston Galleria. It is a megastructure surrounded by one of the largest Edge Cities in the country—now, appropriately enough, simply known as the Galleria area—west of Houston's downtown. But more important, the Galleria raises questions that will resound across America well into the twenty-first century.

If Edge City is our new standard form of American metropolis —if Edge City is the agglomeration of all we feel we want and need—will these places ever be diverse, urbane, and livable? Will our Edge Cities ever be full of agreeable surprises? Will they ever come together gracefully?

Will they ever be sociable places found by struggling students to be spirited? Will they ever yield memories treasured forever by the traveled? Will they ever be delightful places about which love songs are written?

If the future is Out There, will we ever get good at it?

The answers to these questions are of no small moment, for as we push our lives into the uncharted territory of Edge Cities, places like them are becoming the laboratories for how civilized urban America will be for the rest of our lifetime. Therefore, the battles that swirl to form these places are battles being waged over all our futures.

Texas is a wonderful place to ponder where the ancient concept of civilization intersects with that of Edge City, because so much of Texas is utterly new: history is being made there every day.

It's a wonder the Texas Historical Commission can keep up. But it does. In the middle of one Edge City in burgeoning North Dallas one can find a formal bronze historical marker dedicated in 1988. It reads, in part, "Jack St. Clair Kilby, an engineer at Texas Instruments (TI) . . . on September 12, 1958, demonstrated the first working integrated circuit to TI personnel in the semiconductor building on this site. This conceptual breakthrough . . . led to the development of the microchip."

If the very world that we now view as standard, tied together by wafers of silicon, was invented in an Edge City—in Texas—there's no reason there shouldn't be more bronze plaques waiting to be laid out there in the future. Perhaps the new ones will mark breakthrough efforts to create an innovative, humane, livable, and brand-new kind of city. Perhaps someday there will be a historic marker out in front of the Houston Galleria. Here, future chroniclers may say, a social revolution was pioneered in high-density mixed use. The Galleria, which started to evolve in the late 1960s, was the first place to bolt hotels to the sides of a mall, the first place to have office towers rise from the middle of a mall, the first place to put a darkly wooded prestigious club on top of a mall. And this was in addition to the skating rink at the bottom of the mall. These hotels and pools and skyscrapers and courts and shopping areas and promenades and multilevel parking and helicopter pads connect intricately, in dense combinations never before achieved in America outside a downtown. Ages and occupations mix in a fashion approaching that Holy Grail for urban planners: the twenty-four-hour city. Sleepy-eyed skaters arrive for their before-work lessons at 5:30 A.M. As youngsters twirl and glide in colorful tights on the ice at midday, people on three levels stop to watch. "It's a human mobile," one observer notes. At night, from the rooftop bar with the hot jazz-rock band that attracts a suit-and-tie crowd that is 70 percent black, you can watch a gigantic spotlight revolve on top of the Transco Tower. It's a scene straight out of *Batman*. All this, of course, in addition to a view from a hotel room that can compel a visitor to stare out the window for half an hour, transfixed by the variety and drama of the human enterprise.

How many urban areas are there in the world that can claim all that?

The truth, however, is that the Galleria is uncommon. When it comes to hopes for civilization evolving in Edge City, there are many reasons for deep caution. At least one of these caveats is our definition of words like "urbane." The dictionary is not of much help, referring to areas that possess civilities, courtesies, and amenities. But what does "amenities" mean? Edge Cities are terrific at delivering amenities—when amenities can be measured numerically and flowed to the bottom line. Safety. Jogging trails. Day care. Fountains.

The difficulty arises when this civilization produces a landscape that purports to "have it all"—and there's still something obviously and desperately missing. When it comes to "urbanity," I think of the mark of this something-else as "urban mine canaries."

Small songbirds used to be carried down into nineteenth-century coal mines as safety devices. These canaries were very sensitive to poisonous gases. If one died, you knew quickly that there was something wrong with the atmosphere of the place.

Just so, civilization has mine canaries in all the best urban places. They are small in themselves. But they test for something far larger. Everybody has his or her own list. Mine includes secondhand bookstores; cobbler shops with craftsmen who know how to take apart and carefully fix good boots; fine, cheap, authentic restaurants of exotic ethnicity, like Ethiopian; and bistros where you can nurse a glass, people-watch, and read all afternoon if you choose. None of these places makes any real money; none will ever become a mall cliché, like Victoria's Secret or Banana Republic. They are so fragile, their existence so precarious, that if they fail to thrive, that tells you something ominous about the quality of an Edge City environment.

This something-else quality, in turn, helps determine whether Edge City will ever join the ranks of history's renowned and beloved urban places. Whether Edge City will ever be the place we take visitors to show off our shining new city on the hill. Whether Edge City will ever be inspiring. Whether it will be a place we cherish.

To arrive at a short-hand for this something-else, I offered historians and designers this query: If Edge City is the future, will it ever turn out as well as Venice?

Venice is venerated by American urban planners as a shrine to livability. But my question, as it happens, is not as outlandish as it may sound. The uproariousness of today's Edge City is nothing new; wildness is pretty much standard for a metropolis in its early stages. All American cities looked like amorphous boomtowns at the beginning, reported the historian Siegfried Giedion. He described Chicago, "America's boldest testing ground of the 1880s," as "looking like a gold-rush town."

Nor is the apparent chaos of so many of our Edge Cities peculiar to our time and place.

"Oh, yeah, Venice was bizarre. In more ways than one," said Larry Gerkins, Ohio State professor of the history of city planning.

"Out sitting in its lagoon. Highly unusual. There was no overall plan for Venice. There was nobody sitting down, saying this is the way it'll be. It happened over hundreds of years. People were driven off their farms and found themselves on tidal flats, and had to live with it. At the time, the concept was that ownership of land equaled political power. Depending on what land you controlled, you had producing farms and serfs. In time of war, suddenly a group of people found themselves sitting out on the middle of a sand spit. Ain't no land. Ain't no serfs. So they were going to have to develop mercantile power. It changed Western Europe. Banking. Trading. They couldn't be dependent on land. It opened the door into the Renaissance.

"They built the firmaments one at a time. They were respecting the deep spots—that's how the Grand Canal came about. That's where the channel was deep enough. It just kind of grew with time. Delightful thing.

"They were 100 percent mercantile, just as in Edge Cities. Had the only really sizable marine force when the Crusades started. Made a hell of a lot of money shipping people over to the East. The Piazza San Marco was not planned by anyone. It evolved over hundreds of years. Each doge made an addition that respected the one that came before. That is the essence of good urban design—respect for what came before. Over the years, you build something that you couldn't build all at once.

"But remember, it was dry landers forced out into a lagoon,

looking for a place they could defend. They were forced to build a city unlike anything that had ever been built before."

Full disclosure: no matter how hard I tried to be fair, more than once, traveling around the country, I found myself in deep despair that the Edge Cities I was looking at would ever amount to anything physically uplifting or beautiful. But when that happened, there always seemed to be some thoughtful people around who would, in effect, repeat to me Gerkins' advice: Calm down. Take deep breaths. These Edge Cities are only ten or twenty years old. It took Venice five hundred years to become what it is today. Our new Edge Cities are works in progress. It's just beginning to dawn on us that they *are* cities. The reason you think places like London and Paris are so wonderful is that you don't see all the mistakes. That's because the people who built those places have had time to tear down all the miscalculations. Time is of the essence in city building. Give Edge Cities time before you lose your composure.

In Texas, however, it is easy to see how one might arrive at an acute ambivalence punctuated by active anxiety attacks. David Dillon, the art historian who writes on architecture for the *Dallas Morning News,* recalls driving the dean of Harvard's Graduate School of Design out to one Edge City rising due north of downtown Dallas.* Dillon finds the area fascinating.

He calls it the Blade Runner Landscape.

*Blade Runner* is a cult-classic film in which the idea of what Los Angeles might be in the year 2019 collided with that cinematic genre best described as swirling hypercolored lovingly cybernetic punk. And, indeed, Dillon named well this North Dallas Blade Runner world. There is so much to it that the best way to absorb everything that's going on is in a convertible with a completely unobstructed, wraparound, sixty-mile-per-hour view. At its heart, just above the LBJ Freeway, the North Dallas Tollway is quite high off the ground—three or four stories or more. It undulates sensuously—and then the barrage on the senses begins.

California Spanish-tile-covered Asian postmodernist buildings. Pink bronze reflective glass. Unintended intimacies: town houses built right up next to the elevated speedway. A vaguely

* For the complete list of Edge Cities in the Dallas and Houston areas, see Chapter 11.

British office castle with an enormous archway cut right through the middle of it—a portcullis eight stories, count them, eight stories high. Blue reflective glass. The Marriott. Unfinished cement walls. A Mercedes symbol four stories high, right next to a place that calls itself Leather Land. Women in expensive silk shirts whipping by in jacked-up Ford Ranger 4 × 4 pickups. A starkly green field full of alfalfa. It's all so close, so immediate, so reeling. The North Dallas Athletic Club with the American flag, the Texas flag, and the American flag again. Billboard: VANTAGE BEATS MARLBORO. A sign that says LAST FREE EXIT. It points to a flyover that is uplifted by highway sculptures in cruciform. They are so huge, they would be worshiped by the Toltecs. The toll plazas, by contrast, try to be cozy. They are made of wood and have shake roofs. Corporate America: Digital. The Hilton. An office building with both crinkled multiple corner offices *and* curved glass, with the word on the top—OXY— right up against the highway as it dips and churns. The Galleria with its Westin Hotel, featuring barrel tops centered on circular windows, and Marshall Field's. And Macy's. And parking garages matching the curve of a ramp as it swirls around like the frozen contrail of a jet fighter on the attack. Dark male brown marble façades, meant to connote not just wealth, but old European wealth. Stop and Go Fax Send and Receive Service. More homes right up against the elevated highway. Gold-bronze-pink windows. Something called the Grand Kempinski. With the Grand Kempi's nightclub. Crystal Wood Town Center, Neiman Marcus, Lord & Taylor, J. C. Penney. Taiwan!—"A Chinese Restaurant in Dallas." A roll of curved horizontal glass off an office slab in a series of waves exactly repeated by a roll of water falling beneath it. Atria. Steel pylons carrying the power, ah yes, the power. A billboard: MAKE YOUR NEXT DATE A TWO-BAGGER. Two people pictured, each with potato chip bag over head. Billboard: SO MANY MESSAGES, SUCH LITTLE TIME, METRO CELL CELLULAR. Billboard: PICK UP THE PHONE INSTEAD OF THE PIECES. FIRST STEP CRISIS PREVENTION CENTER.

After a few miles, the landscape begins to recede. A man finds himself exhausted, having drunk deeply from the cup of astonishment, gasping for words beyond a simple bellow of "¡Yo, arriba!" The word "surreal" has no juice left to it. It no longer has the power to punch up the workings of the unconscious mind as manifested in dreams: irrational, noncontextual arrangements. I want to put a bag over my head and pick up a cellular phone to call the 800 number that beckoned so seductively in that ten-foot-high script, to talk intensely to whoever answers—about crisis.

Dillon, nonetheless, seemed surprised to report that the Harvard dean, whom he described as "probably an eight or nine in terms of enlightenment," did not join him in the spirit of inquiry and the rolling back of intellectual frontiers when confronted by the Blade Runner Landscape. Instead, the dean went into the intellectual equivalent of the fetal position. And he apparently did not emerge from brainlock until he was taken off the plane back East.

The dean's reaction is instructive. It explains a lot about how our Edge Cities have ended up the way they have.

When I started reporting on Edge Cities, one of my first genuine surprises was to discover just how little architects usually have to do with the appearance of these places. The height, shape, size, density, orientation, and materials of most buildings are largely determined by the formulaic economics of the Deal. It was stunning how completely it was the developers who turned out to be our master city builders. The developers were the ones who envisioned the projects, acquired the land, exercised the planning, got the money, hired the architects if there were any, lined up the builders, and managed the project to completion. Often, it was the developers who continued to manage and maintain the buildings afterward. The works of the design professions were very much ancillary. Even officials of the American Institute of Architects ruefully conceded the point. Architects were lucky if they got to choose the skin of the building.

Oddly enough, this turn of events seemed to suit a lot of designers and planners just fine. Their hearts were not in Edge City. They were elsewhere—usually in elegant projects to rejuvenate the old downtowns to aristocratic days that were so long ago that the designers could only have read about them in books. One of the reasons that the benefits of their design prowess were so frequently missing in Edge City, I discovered, was that an astounding number of these design professionals, especially the older ones, were themselves missing from Edge City.

They not only regarded the suburbs as sprawl gone morally wrong. They considered these places and the people in them so banal as to be utterly remote from their experience and interests. They viewed themselves as having a higher calling—trying to find someone to pay them to define space in ways that relate man to his environment with fresh insight and artistic vision, perhaps. It was not so much that these designers had been banished from playing a role in the major decisions about Edge City. As often as not, they had exiled themselves.

In the midst of reporting this chapter I was asked to address the American Institute of Architects, which was holding its convention in Houston. After the talk, one architect came up and basically said, Okay, fine. I want to examine an Edge City; how do I get there. Well, I said, you get into your car and head straight out Westheimer until you see more big buildings than in downtown Copenhagen, at which point you start cruising around. And he got this stricken look on his face. Car? he asked. Car? My God, he said. Can you get a cab in this town?

Now I do not mean to derogate this man's sincerity in any way. But a *building* designer who comes to *Houston* for a convention and does not rent a car is not part of the solution; he is part of the problem. In a culture like America's, in which more households have a car than have a water heater, he is not being morally pure. He is being willfully and aggressively ignorant of the stone-cold realities of the late twentieth century. Going to Houston and not renting a car is like going to Venice and not hiring a boat. It is missing the point.

Nonetheless, this man is not alone among his peers. In the late 1980s, when I wanted to find out what was going on in Edge City, I could rarely turn to architects and planners for insight. They often were not even curious about the place. Instead, I had to turn to the people who were actually bulldozing the landscape to get any straight answers.

Why did you think this project was a good idea? I'd ask the banker. Why did you put that building there and there and there? I'd ask the developer. Why didn't we build a railroad over there? I'd ask the engineer. Excuse me, sir, would you explain just what, exactly, you thought you were doing?

Their answers were startling; they seldom had anything to do with lofty urbanologists' theories about the ways people "should" live, and cities "should" be arranged. But this was not because they had no answers. Quite the contrary. Edge City, as it turned out, had an exquisitely fine-tuned logic. Indeed, as soon as one saw Edge City the way the people who were building it did, a magnificent panoply emerged. The developers had spent lifetimes laboring to uncover what they regarded as the verifiable, nontheoretical realities that govern human behavior. They had then gone out and built an entire world around their understanding of what Americans demonstrably and reliably valued. Their unshakable observation was this: if they gave the people what they wanted, the people would give them money. The crazy quilt of Edge City made perfect sense if you understood the place as the manifest pattern of millions of individual American desires over seventy-five years.

The developers viewed Edge City the same way they viewed America itself: as problem-driven, not ideology-driven. In this way, their perspective was quite the opposite of the designers'. The planners seemed to think that human behavior was malleable, and that nobody was better equipped by dint of intelligence and education than they to do the malleting. They believed that the physical environment they wanted to shape could and would shape society. The places they would like to plan would lead, they believed, to fundamental, welcome, and long-overdue changes in human mores and human attitudes.

The developers saw it just the other way. They saw Edge City as very much the *product* of society. They viewed themselves as utterly egalitarian observers, giving people what they repeatedly demonstrated they desired, as measured by that most reliable of gauges: their willingness to pay for it.

Edge City, of course, is that land of such apparently contradictory postmodernist future visions that both realities are probably accurate. After all, Winston Churchill once wrote, "We shape our houses, then they shape us."

But of the two camps, it is clear that the developers with the common touch, who thought they were merely responding to the people's will, are the ones who have had far and away more influence on the world that now surrounds us than have the theoreticians and designers. For this they all may take both the credit and the blame.

Forget commodity, firmness, and delight. Those are the three

qualities that were thought to embody excellence in city building according to Vitruvius, the Roman architect of the early
imperial period who wrote the only text on architecture to survive from Greece or Rome.

Forget zoning. "There is no zoning, only deals," Sam Lefrak
once said. He ought to know. Lefrak was such a savvy developer
that he got the University of Maryland geography building
named after him.

Those are sideshows. Edge City is built the way cities always
have been built. It is shaped by the most powerful forces unleashed at the time. If the Pope shaped Rome and the doge
Venice and Baron Haussmann the *grands boulevards* of the
Champs-Élysées, the *marketplace* rules Edge City. Its most devoted acolytes are the developers. "They are the Medici of the
twentieth century," agreed one Houston planner.

Well, then, who are these guys? Again, I found the answer
surprising. Development is very much a participatory sport in
this country. Giant national firms like Trammell Crow are the
exception. The typical story of a developer is that he—it is
almost always a he—was something else first: a lawyer, a broker,
an engineer, a contractor. The more developers this person
dealt with, the more he realized that there was nothing that they
were doing that he couldn't do, too. Except that they were
making far more money. So he joined the party.

The most important thing to understand about developers is
this: these guys are not rocket scientists. If you devote a lot of
energy to conspiracy theories about them, you may be missing
the point. It's not that they aren't into greed. The stuff developers do all day, like talking to bankers, is debilitating and degrading; it would make no sense unless there were abundant money
in it. It's not that they can't be devious. Some have proven
capable of felonious quantities of guile. And it's not as if they are
self-effacing. Everybody in the building trades, including the
architects and planners, is an egotist. They aspire, after all, to
change the world.

Still, developers are the kind of people who carry around
brochures of their projects as if they were baby pictures. They
*love* the places they build. The first thing they do when they start
talking about their efforts is to start chopping the space in front
of them with their arms, building castles in the air. By and large,

this is not an introspective collection of people. A very few in this brotherhood are genuinely brilliant. But a gathering of the clan—including their cohorts the bankers, builders, and brokers —resembles nothing so much as a fraternity fervently committed to varsity athletics.

The more I talked to these people, the more I became convinced that there are not that many legal, technical, or practical reasons that almost anyone with the brains to read this far into a thick book couldn't get into a partnership and go out and build a quarter-of-a-million-square-foot office building tomorrow, if he was willing to devote his life to that. It is not as challenging as subatomic physics.

The ease with which the development game is entered does not by any means suggest that it is trivial to *succeed* as a developer. The number of ways that our hypothetical quarter-of-a-million-square-foot building could erupt into fiasco are limited only by imagination. One hotshot, musing about three people he knew who were big-time developers before the economic downturn of the 1970s, swore this was true: one of them is selling newly manufactured Brazilian "antiques" to Europeans; another is pushing Vietnam-era airplanes to developing countries; and a third is peddling Malaysian oil futures.

People who are consistently successful as developers, by contrast, surviving both boom and bust, have special gifts of character. Not the least of these is their ability routinely to roll the dice with millions of dollars on the table and then sleep at night.

But by and large, developers as a breed have only one specialized skill not generally available in the population: they have the ability to do fairly high-level arithmetic, in their heads, while talking about a completely different topic. What developers do, fundamentally, is run the numbers. And the most impressive number they run is the one in which they manage to divide extremely large dollar figures by 43,560, which is the number of square feet in an acre. By so doing they can and do reduce much of human experience—quite accurately, as it turns out—to the Deal.

I'll never forget David Hunter, one of the first developers I ever interviewed back in Virginia. He was bulldozing hundreds of acres of forest around a lovely stream called Little Rocky Run for a subdivision. I had found the forest delightful in its erect state, so I was keenly interested in his reasoning. Especially because he was touting his massive subdivision as a "planned community."

How was it "planned"? I asked him.

I still find Hunter's answer memorable because it so thoroughly blew away any liberal-arts preconceptions I may have had about how things get built in our world. Hunter basically said: Planners? Architects? Say what? Here's what happened. And he started running the numbers. It was like a mantra. Like a Gregorian chant:

"Anybody knowledgeable about the sewer system knew that there was only one place growth could go, and that was west, and there were only two roads heading west, Route 50 and Interstate 66. There was this triangle of roads that the county plan said was supposed to be a mall, but there was a zoning battle between DeBartolo and Taubman, and Taubman won, and so the mall went two exits east. The area could not support both. That's when I saw the possibilities for this watershed. There were four thousand acres in the shed, okay, and there were eight or ten major owners holding twenty-two hundred acres. They had held the land for ten or fifteen years.

"That land at the time was investor land. Not farmland. Just investor land. It's in that holding period where it's too expensive to farm and not yet matured to the point where it's developable. It was all wooded, yeah. All of it was wooded.

"The first obstacle to overcome was the sewering of the watershed, which took some $3 million in funding from the consortium of eight owners, especially from one guy who had four or five syndicates that owned probably 30 percent of the land. So I came in and bought about four or five hundred acres from him at $10,000 or $12,000 an acre with no sewer.

"These areas are already zoned, but 75 to 80 percent of the density was all within one half of the watershed. So if you took this four thousand acres, the density here is one to two on two thousand acres and down here it's like probably four to five. Dwelling units per acre, yeah. Okay. This P.S. is a pumping station. The county gave us that approval. The second line of approval was a matter of formality.

"Now up here was where the county was having problems. This is where the court suit was; this is where the septic fields were failing. A long ways from here to here, two or three miles. The county had budgeted like $800,000 with some kind of an escalator in it and later on the amount of it was like a million-four. And they were going to avoid sewering all this area and do a forced main here and go over into a sewage treatment plant over here. And then let's say a million dollars of expenditure would serve this little area right here. Well, they got a little bit of flak on that.

"Then the Housing Authority got involved and over here was a little underprivileged area called the Louis-Lincoln-Vannoy area. So they got the Redevelopment Housing Authority in there with some matching federal funds, they came up with a dynamite program. Two million-eight, okay, and they bought eighty acres over here and this was a spray system. And they were going to go down here and spend this $2.8 million to serve forty-six houses, which meant that it was somewhere in the area of $40,000 to $50,000 a house and they were worth about $20,000, okay. So they had a fight on that.

"Well, I proved to them that I didn't have to go there and there was a gap, but I also knew they had this million-four, okay. So with the million-four I did a civic duty here of simply at cost I extended the line from here to here which was virtually no benefit to me and I fumbled around with getting reimbursed for $850,000. Okay.

"That was done on the basis that this would be reimbursed by the county, coupled with these two people right here agreeing to run the line from here over to here, and the Housing Authority to go from here down to here and then to give back or do whatever they wanted with about $2.3 million in money, okay, because it only cost them $500,000 so they had all that money left and they still owned eighty acres down there.

"So that's really how the whole thing came about."

I was breathless. I scarcely knew where to start.

"The controlling thing was sewers?" I cautiously generalized about his "planned community."

"Yeah. Not traffic, no, no. This was, let's say it started in 1979 and was in operation 1983 over a four-year period. And I started buying the land in 1978. Really what I had was eleven hundred units, and Little Rocky Run now is about twenty-five hundred units. So I had purchased eleven hundred units and of those, seven hundred were town houses. What it's zoned for, yes."

I was still struggling to catch up. "You don't think in terms of acres; you think in terms of units?"

"Yes. Zoned units. There was a couple of hundred acres and this equated to X number of units. So Little Rocky Run started out as eleven hundred units of housing, seven hundred town houses, three hundred single family. And, you know, a couple of curious things started occurring. These people who had participated in bringing in the sewer did not want to be in a development mode whereas it would change their tax situation. They kept saying, 'Won't you buy the property? Won't you buy the property?' Finally what happens I end up taking them over. Then a lady owned this and then I bought that and then a Mr. Jenkin owned this and I bought that, okay, so it just kept going right on down."

I was reeling. As it happened, a contractor had ruptured a transcontinental natural-gas transmission pipeline nearby only the previous week.

"Thank God it wasn't your bulldozer that hit the pipeline," I said fervently.

"That's exactly right. That's right," agreed Hunter. "That pipeline runs right through here and right over here is where it was hit. Right there. I don't think it's even a thousand yards, I think we're talking a thousand feet. I'll tell you what, it's awful close. That is Sunset Ridge that they evacuated. Here's the elementary school over here."

Weak-kneed, I responded, "I see."

Years later, David Hunter's recitation of the facts of life remains a classic vignette of the way our world is shaped, really.

It also shows why the Law of Unintended Consequences governs our built world. Both the developers and the planners are plagued by the same problem: they repeatedly face disconnects between their actions and their consequences. Edge Cities that are devoted to automobility end up traffic-choked. Places that tout their "amenities" and "quality of life" end up so contrived that the mine canaries of urbanity struggle to survive.

The big problem with the developers is that they follow the numbers. Yet there are few market mechanisms that make the connection between what they build and all the social consequences. The game is not set up that way. The developers tend to their own projects and hope that Adam Smith's "invisible hand" will clean up the consequences, rewarding good and bankrupting evil. If the net result of all their actions is perceived as chaotic, the response is, well, any market in full-blown operation—whether it be a souk in North Africa or a real estate play in east Texas—can be mistaken for anarchy.

And they are not wrong. Historian Robert Fishman claims that all urban forms when new—whether they are the streetcar suburbs of a hundred years ago or the Levittowns of forty years ago or the Edge Cities of today—evolve this way:

• First, planners of genius comprehend what makes them tick.

• Then, speculative builders of less candlepower get the general idea and try, approximately, to replicate it, slowly and incompletely.

• Finally, individual property owners continually upgrade their places. They look around at what other people are doing, decide what is good or bad, eliminate discordant elements, and bring their community closer to what is perceived to be the ideal. "We might hope that a similar process is now at work in the postsuburban outer city," Fishman writes.

Yet the time scale of developers is unnerving.

"Developer" is an interesting word for these people. The dictionary says it means one who causes something to become fuller, who causes it to unfold or evolve, who makes it stronger or more effective, who causes it to progress. Yet developers are rarely rewarded for taking the long view and looking at the big picture. They all know the histories of the "new towns" of the 1960s and 1970s: they almost all went broke. Some, like Reston, Virginia, ran through several corporate owners. The one in the Houston area, The Woodlands, signals to developers only a perverse lesson. For all its charms, they say, the only reason planning on that scale did not go bankrupt is that The Woodlands was backed by an oil company, an outfit with deep enough pockets to wait ten or twenty years for a payout.

It is this short horizon that is at the root of that frequently heard call: what Edge Cities really need is more planning. But the role that planners have played in the development of these places is, if anything, even more disturbing than that of the developers. At least the developers' claims for their social worth are modest. At bottom, they attempt only to create wealth. The planners, by contrast and by definition, proclaim much more. After all, they call themselves planners. This suggests at least some larger vision of human affairs. That is why people hire them. It also suggests that their plans will reliably produce social good; that there will be a general relationship between their intentions and the cold, hard results.

An examination of the real world, however, suggests that the facts are far more troubling. Precisely because planners believe their goals are lofty, when their crystal ball shatters, the crash can be heard for decades. The world moved on July 15, 1972, for example. That was the day the city fathers of St. Louis blew up with dynamite the Pruitt-Igoe housing projects. The design, which followed the foremost architectural theories of its day and had won an award from the American Institute of Architects, was so utterly unlivable, even by the standards of the wretched of the earth, that Class A explosives were the only solution.

Take for a more grand example Las Colinas, west of downtown Dallas. It is one of the most planned, long-horizon Edge Cities in the world. It will be half a century before this place is built out.

In the central plaza of Las Colinas, there are nine bronze mustangs, forever wild and free. Each seems to be balanced on, at most, one foot, in water calculatedly splashed by jets to appear, for the rest of time, as if cast up by the ponies at a dead run. A plaque nearby, entitled "The Mustangs of Las Colinas," memorializes them. In part, it reads:

These horses bore Spanish explorers across two continents. They brought to the plains indians the age of horse culture. Texas cowboys rode them to extend the ranching occupation clear to the plains of Alberta. Spanish horse, Texas cowpony, and mustang were all one in those times, when as sayings went, a man was no better than his horse, and a man on foot was no man at all.

Like the longhorn, the mustang has been virtually bred out of existence, but mustang horses will always symbolize Western frontier, long trails of longhorn herds, seas of pristine grass, and men riding free on a free land.

These sculptures—they have tremendously ridged veins and a nice deep hollow ring to them when rapped—are huge. Each is one and a half times life size. The most endearing are the two colts, one of which appears to be leaping into the water as if off a tall bank.

And they are much loved. One warm Mother's Day, a daddy could be seen standing his daughter on his shoulders so that the child could pet a big bronze nose eight feet off the ground. The number two colt has a mane that seems to be turning colors. All the other animals have a patina of dark green. This pony, which is just short enough for its top to be easily reached by human hands, has been rubbed so often, affectionately, that its mane has turned to gold.

But behind the mustangs, the high-rise office towers of Williams Square loom. The surfaces are hard and cold. The plain across which the horses seem to gallop is made of corporate marble. Not a sliver of grass is to be seen.

This is far and away the most inviting landscape in Las Colinas. Yet it is full of ironies. For in Las Colinas, the freedom and individualism the mustangs represent appear as extinct as the horses themselves.

In few urban landscapes in America has planning been so lavishly funded. "What they did, planners in old cities look at trying to do and despair," one academic critic observed. "It's rare to see something executed at that scale with that degree of meticulousness and expense. Nothing was done on the cheap out there."

Yet the dominant feature of this place, in which twenty thousand of the affluent live and sixty thousand work, is walls. The walls separate the people on the inside from the people on the outside. They separate people within Las Colinas who can afford a $500,000 home from those within Las Colinas who can afford only a $200,000 home. Chain-link fences topped by two stretches of triple-strand barbed wire, meeting in a V, separate children from the waterways around which they might think to hunt for frogs.

Las Colinas is a landscape in which spontaneity has been utterly tamed. Every master-planned one of its twelve thousand acres seems to gleam, in an eerie sort of way. Its not just the office towers, although they are featured in the opening credits of *Dallas*. The golf courses gleam. The endless gold fixtures in the bathrooms gleam. The robot monorails gleam. So does the polished mahogany of the Venetian water taxis, the geometry of the BMWs and the Mercedeses, the uniform trim on the shoulders of the Mexican fishing minute cigarette specks out of the water features, and the heavily carved cathedral–weight doors that false-front the parking garages. They all gleam. This is not so much a community as a simulation of a community. When a raucous grackle starts chattering in a tree, you look up in honest wonder to see whether it is really a bird, or whether they've wired the trees with speakers and are running a tape. In front of the Four Seasons hotel, there is a jogger whose hair will be bouncy and moussed, forever. Her earphone headset keeps her entranced, permanently. She is the ideal athlete; she never sweats. She is a statue. In every detail, right down to the trademark on her Nikes, she is absolutely perfect. Because what has been subtracted is life. Gary Cartwright, in *Texas Monthly,* wrote of Las Colinas:

"There is no hint of the tawdry, the profane, no residue of grit or squalor or sweating masses. It is Disney World for the affluent. In fact, when executives from Disney World visited the development a few years ago, one of them commented that it was a shame ol' Walt couldn't have lived to see the real thing."

Indeed, in its determination to conquer the unexpected, Las Colinas is as deliberate and premeditated as an interstate interchange. Its vistas resemble nothing so much as its neighbor, the Dallas–Fort Worth Regional Airport.

This is not urbanity. Molly Ivins, the *Dallas Times Herald*'s premier Texas observer, noted of this monument to planning, "There is something inorganic about Las Colinas, something utterly unspontaneous. I get the feeling there is nowhere you can get a bowl of banana pudding." It no more matched her vision of civilization than did the Blade Runner Landscape match the standards of humanity of the Harvard dean.

How did this happen? How did urbanity fall between *these* cracks—between chaos and the control junkies? How did we end up missing most of the benefits of design?

The marketplace is the place to start rounding up the usual suspects, since that is where the developers worship. There is no question that in an Edge City, the introduction of any institution that might be equated with civilization is totally and at root dependent on the Deal.

The issue, then, that is central to Edge City is whether the market is an efficient way for people to communicate what they really want, or whether it is a debased and degrading caricature of humanity that leaves out everything that is valuable about the human condition.

This is a stimulating subject for debate. But here is what I found striking about so many planners, architects, and other design professionals. They were not much interested in the question. They did not much understand the marketplace. Nor did they care to. Often they dismissed it as wearisome. I found this curious. Someday, someone will write an intellectual history explaining why so many highly educated building professionals ever thought it was a good idea to neglect the landscapes in which the vast majority of Americans lived, worked, and played. Especially at a time when that's where most of the construction was being done. But it is undeniable that its effect has been perverse. This shunning by the designers has not caused Americans to change their habits, nor has it imbued the world with charm, nor has it gained these professions much in the way of lucrative work. If the mine canaries of civilization were having a rough time in Edge City, I couldn't help wondering to what extent that was a function of anything inherent in Edge City, and to what extent it had something to do with the intellectual absence of so many people I had always viewed as the guardians of our built environment.

Jack Linville helped put it in perspective.

"What the architects and the planners, the trained professionals, all believe is that Edge City is wrong. It all goes back to the *Costs of Sprawl* report. The whole concept is—the suburbs growing is the wrong way to develop. That what you really want to do is protect the vitality of downtown. So everything you do is aimed at bringing people back to the CBD [central business district]. Get them back downtown. Get them back into the vibrant areas. Things happening after dark in the downtown. Make sure they have that wonderful city vibrancy.

"The forces at work in our society are much stronger than that. So the planners and architects got way out in left field trying to fight against a surge that is just overwhelming."

Linville once headed the research foundation of the American Planning Association. He is now president and chief executive officer of a Houston-based design outfit called The Office of

Pierce Goodwin Alexander and Linville. (When I talked to Linville, his company was performing the sorely needed redesign of Washington National Airport.)

Linville's manner is chronically open, sunny, aw shucks, and down home, as befits his firm's roots. The experience and opinions of Texans when it comes to civilization nonetheless are of considerable significance. Since most urban areas west of Kansas City are a function of history after 1915 and the emergence of the millionth Model T, these people have been thinking much longer than people in the East about life as we will know it in the twenty-first century.

"I came here, I was running this research program at Rice Center, teaching at Rice in the School of Architecture," Linville said. "One of the things we did was this study for a group of developers out on—the Katy Prairie, it was called. It was the one that was probably the fastest created anywhere." (This means Linville was a founding father of one of the quintessential Boomer Edge Cities: the West Houston Energy Corridor.)

"The other study was the study of the South Main Center area, which was an in-town area, Rice University, the Texas Medical Center. It was old; it had big trees. It was saving and revitalizing an in-town area." (That is, it was an Uptown Edge City.)

"It was the same group of people—the same young architecture students, graduate students, early professional people working on both studies. And the perception in the architectural community was that what we did in South Main was really good. And what we were doing in West Houston was selling out. To the suburbs. Because you are so indoctrinated to believe that cities are the old downtown areas. You go to London, you go to Paris, they're all tight, they're close, you're in. There's a lot of vitality there. A lot of vibrancy. There are also a lot of problems. Far greater problems than we're going to have to deal with in our new American cities. Like poverty, crime, sanitation, sewer systems falling apart.

"It is a totally different way of living. In Paris, you've got roughly six million people living on maybe a hundred square miles, an area that would fit inside Loop 610 here [the inner beltway]. We have about 200,000 living inside that area. We've got three million people on three thousand square miles. The people in the United States are not going to live the way the people in Paris live. They will not live in a thousand-square-foot apartment and raise a family and go out and get the loaf of bread and the jug of wine and walk down the street and live their whole lives within one square mile. That is not the way Americans live. They have a different level of freedom, a different level of expectations. There's still a lot of Daniel Boone left in America.

"I don't know what the people in Paris want. But what they have is a very very small amount of space that is theirs, and a lot of public amenities. What we have is a huge amount of space that is ours and that we control, and very little in public amenities. We have much more individual life styles. We have our own excellent interior spaces. We have our *own* park. It's right out back. The yard.

"The architects and planners—the design community—has a lot of disdain for the kind of things that middle Americans want that lead to the development of our Edge Cities. You don't create a Paris with them. You can't even create a London this way. Just not going to happen. Not going to be."

This is the trap that leads some designers to dismiss the value of the marketplace. The intellectual ambush works like this. Okay, say these architects and planners, let us assume for a moment that Americans are not fools. Nevertheless, they live in ways that fly in the face of everything we cherish—like the re-creation of a traditional Paris or London.

How can this contradiction possibly be resolved? It must be that the reason the American people have followed this path is that they have been *forced* to live in such a terrible style. It can't be that they like it. It must be that capitalism enslaves them, and the developers give them no choice.

The problem with this surmise, of course, is the evidence that there is no such thing as a mass market anymore in America. If anything, the economy's entire thrust over the past four decades has been to offer paralyzing levels of choice. Ever more highly specialized, even individualized niche markets are the rule. This is especially true in housing. People with money can live in this country in just about any fashion imaginable—including, if they so choose, in yeasty, artsy, diverse, walkable, renovated neighborhoods in the center city.

Even more telling is the evidence that it is by no means merely

American capitalism that is producing Edge City. You get the same result from Chinese communism.

Immensely different political, economic, and cultural systems —with vastly different attitudes toward government planning, home ownership, tax deductions, and freeways—are producing startlingly similar results. In the late twentieth century, urban areas worldwide are growing Edge Cities.

Canada is a particularly interesting place to watch Edge Cities flourish, because it is, in many ways, the control experiment for America. Despite draconian government controls that American planners only dream of, despite an emphasis on mass transit and a relative lack of freeways, despite vibrant and bustling and safe urban centers, despite a relative lack of racial problems, and despite there being no suburb-enhancing tax deductions for home mortgages, downtown Toronto has only 46 percent of its area's market. Almost a dozen Edge Cities are growing up around it.

Paris has that awesome concept, an Edge City designed by de Gaulle–era French bureaucrats. It is called La Défense, and has been described as so inhuman as to be the only stop on the Paris Métro system where it is more inviting to stay underground. Still, it, more than downtown, is the corporate and economic capital of France. It bristles with more than forty office towers occupied by the likes of Elf, British Petroleum, IBM Europe, IBM France, NEC, Colgate Palmolive, Hitachi Metals, Fiat, Peugeot, Crédit Lyonnais, and *Le Figaro*.

In addition, the Paris area has five Greenfield Edge City sites on its fringes: Cergy Pontoise, Saint Quentin-en-Yvelines, Evry, Melun-Senart, and Marne-la-Vallée. Only the first two have gone much of anywhere, and, just as in America, they are west of downtown, where the rich people live. The French have figured out what it takes, though. They are building the La Francilienne outer beltway (Route A87) to assist Edge City development. And in the master stroke, thirty-two kilometers from downtown, just east of Marne-la-Vallée they have located—Euro Disneyland! Sure. If it worked for Orlando, no reason it shouldn't work for *Les Grenouilles*.

Sydney, Australia, even without a beltway, is seeing Edge Cities emerge. The largest is North Sydney, the fourth-largest office market in Australia, marked by Amdahl, Arthur Andersen,

Mobil Australia, and Qantas. It is across the Harbour Bridge from downtown.

Land-ownership patterns in London are influenced by the legacies of both feudalism and socialism in ways that are unimaginable to Americans. London's physical plan dates back more than two thousand years. Its environmentally protected Green Belt, which runs from twelve to twenty miles wide, was specifically created by planners to limit the dispersion of urban functions. The London area has a well-developed, fully integrated rail system. The Underground is the oldest subway system in the world.

But it also has the M25 beltway, and thus Edge Cities have leapfrogged the Green Belt to rise twenty and thirty miles from the center of London along the M4 motorway heading west, with good access to Heathrow Airport and tony residential areas, the M11 heading toward the technology magnet of Cambridge University, and the M1. The M20 is coming on strong because it is the main road link to the Eurotunnel entrance in Kent. As a result, the greater London area is now more than a hundred miles across, reaching out toward Bristol and Dover. It sprawls across as much land as does greater Los Angeles. London's outer Edge Cities, meanwhile, have the same share of their market as do Chicago's.

The Canary Wharf area on the Isle of Dogs in the Docklands has demonstrated once again that Europeans can produce new urban environments that are every bit as hard, sterile, and contrived as Americans'. Not only that, but they do it in a place where they don't even *try* to move cars! Quite an accomplishment.

In fact, there is that group of perverse American design professionals who have labored in the Edge City vineyards. They are watching the evolution of European urban areas with small smirks. They, of course, have been lectured at their entire lives about how great European cities are. But they have a sneaking suspicion that these European sites are living off the leftovers of their soul—the stockpile of ambiance they built up before the twentieth century. They note with interest that when Europeans build new, *they* don't build more charming places reminiscent of old Paris, old Rome, old London. Their modern stuff is frequently worse than our urban landscapes. Check out the mainland side of Venice. Many of the high-rise apartments ringing Paris and London have all the Stalinist charm of the Cross Bronx Expressway. In Amsterdam, in 1989, they were still holding symposia at which one of the key questions was: "Should architects take consumer preference into consideration in the design of housing?"

Edge Cities are a function of growth, these Americans point out. It is their conjecture that the major "advantage" European urban planners have had up to now is a relative absence of it. What happens to these places, they wonder, when it becomes clear that computers and telecommunications mean heavy cables and heavy heating, ventilation, and air conditioning? In North America, which has always had a harsher climate than almost all of Europe, this was not a big adjustment. In old European buildings, in which central heating was until recently considered optional, this is a challenge.

What happens when it becomes clear that would-be world financial centers need office floorplates of at least twenty thousand square feet? A full-service trading floor needs at least that much space to produce the all-important eye-to-eye contact. That space is standard in American Edge Cities. There is no such space in old European downtowns.

What happens when it becomes clear that there is a connection between more affluent populations and a desire for more individual transportation, despite every imaginable disincentive? say the designers.

Oh. Not had much luck handling those problems in your old city before?

Pity.

These professionals basically believe that if American urban areas have problems, one of the foremost is that they have had the dubious privilege of wrestling with the future first. Their sneaking suspicion is that Americans are doing as well as anybody when it comes to struggling with these forces.

Actually, what they deep down believe is that they are doing orders of magnitude *better.* For when they look around, they see that it's not just European urban areas that are displaying these patterns. Bangkok is throwing the classic Edge City motif east of downtown in the Pathoylotah Road area. The Central Plaza Edge City on the expressway that runs northward to the airport is going tech—home to Toshiba and Hitachi. The hotel? The Hyatt Central Plaza. Djakarta is seeing the same sort of thing out the long straight arterial to Menteng called Tamarind, as well as to the east in an area called Tibet. Even in desperately poor Karachi, the action is between downtown and the airport. In Mexico, on the west side of Guadalajara, in the Plaza Del Sol, the first mall in Latin America, you hear people say they never go downtown anymore. In Puebla, east of Mexico City, and Morelia, to the west, you see white-collar office towers around malls equipped with fast food so that you don't have to go home for lunch. Seoul is trying to force Edge Cities at two locations: Bundang, about twenty-five miles south of downtown, and Ilsan, about twenty-five miles northwest. Even in China, in Tianjin, Beijing's port, all the development is moving out to the ring road. "I see a lot of similarities in terms of physical development between Asia and the United States," reports David Dowall of the University of California at Berkeley. "There's a lot of copying going on in terms of architecture and land use. Incomes are going up so fast, auto ownership is increasing at breakneck speed even though they have these punishing tariffs. In Bangkok a stripped-down BMW may cost you $50,000. People still buy."

Nevertheless, there is tremendous resistance among design professionals. Few appear interested in seeing whether there may be something intriguing to be made of this new pattern.

"An Edge City, as I see it, doesn't have enough people of diverse interests and variety and sufficient concentration of talent to make a particular civilization sparkle, to produce great centers of excellence like the Manhattans or Parises or Londons, Romes or Moscows or whatever," Jonathan Smulian insisted. "Sad, sad."

Smulian is British both by birth and manner. He is an architect and urban planner who has practiced from Bogotá to Lahore to Cairo. He is now where the action's at, in the belly of the Beast, the Houston Galleria area. Yet he is hardly a convert to the place.

"Most people do not appreciate the compactness and the high densities of cities," Smulian admitted. "I do buy that. Yes. I can tell you that every Frenchman would like to have his little villa outside Paris. Every Londoner I can think of would be only too delighted to have his little house out in the countryside. It's not an American characteristic by any means. It's a people characteristic.

"People went to cities for one reason only. Survival. Survival in terms of opportunity to find work. Survival in terms of opportunity to get better education and health care and because they perceived that in farming, manpower is becoming less and less important.

"The move to the cities wasn't because of greater diversity and interest and fascination with urban life. To this day the people in the slums of these cities—however poor and miserable you may think them—have a better chance at survival than somebody living out in a rural area farming his own little patch. That's why they're there in the city. Not because of any other reason. Even those people would *rather* be out in the countryside."

Okay, I said, since you understand that, then what would you do for Houston if you were handed a magic wand? You have just been named God. Go for it. What do you do to create a great place, a civilized place?

"Well, straight off the top," he replied, "I would increase dramatically the real residential population, the people who are dependent on that area if not for their employment then certainly for their everyday social and recreational activities. There would have to be sufficient demand for smaller, less individual residences. But give me 100,000 people and I'll make your Edge City into a place that's worth being in. And not 100,000 suburban dwellers living within a mile or two miles. I want them living right here. I'd raise the gasoline tax by 300 percent. I'd raise the price of automobiles enormously. I mean I would just limit movement. I'd limit movement completely and there would be a massive rush to live near your work, your social or commercial activity. And then I would put enormous costs on parking. I think just take transportation alone, you could change these places dramatically."

Fascinating. What Smulian would do, given vast powers, is force Americans to live in a world that few now seem to value. His prescriptions may or may not have merit. But meanwhile, there have been some developments in the marketplace that may be related. From 1978 to 1985, enrollment in college planning programs dropped 20 percent. Doctors and lawyers enjoy near monopolies in their professions; architects control a mere 30 percent of their market—the market for the design and execution of buildings. Contractors and engineers are viewed as far more sane.

Why is that? I ask Donald R. (Chip) Levy. He is the senior director for professional development of the American Institute of Architects. Why is it that architects and planners cling so tenaciously to their traditional solutions, no matter how often they get their teeth kicked in?

He says, You want me to go into that on the record? Are you out of your mind?

After negotiation, he says, "Well, I just want it to be really clear that I'm speaking about a very ancient and noble profession, that architects are well intentioned and, in large part, beleaguered keepers of the flame. Some of the holes in the feet of the profession have been put there by the hands of architects, but most of them have not."

Okay, Chip. So where did we go astray?

"We are finally admitting that the era of the architect as large-scale functional sculptor may no longer be a viable career path.

That was the ideal?

"Yes. That was the ideal. You expand a city to be an exhibit of sculptures, if you will. A crown made of many jewels. The strain between the academic community and the architectural practitioners runs to the effect that practitioners say, I don't know what you're doing but these kids can't architect to save their necks. They can't design buildings that can be built. They don't want to spend lots of time on the boards doing the drudgery of architecture—window details. They have no field experience. They don't know how to boss around construction crews and perform site inspections and lots of the real honest-to-God workaday stuff that architects do. They know the economics only in the most cursory and academic kind of way. They got into the business to design the big beautiful buildings and to solve social ills. Solving social ills is still very much part of the game, yes. They see social planning, city planning, building planning, all being one large kind of integrated process. It's 'architect as visionary.'

"They end up with a bias against Edge City because it's a community in spite of planning, not because of planning. They see the subservience to the automobile. They rail against it rather than try to plan around it. The bottom-line reduction of that argument is that cities are not about cars; cities are about people. Cars and hence Edge Cities are just not 'healthy for humans and other living things,' or so the argument goes.

"When they do go out to look at it, they'll look at each building as an isolated artifact rather than see the entire Edge City as a cohesive architectural whole. Because they don't see a whole there. It's city ad hoc rather than the intentional, beautifully planned fabric that is Washington, D.C., for example. One of the things that may be operating here is that because Edge City is such a recently evolved reality, architects don't know how to think about it. In no one place or in no consistent stream throughout that process are you taught about finances and business and the development process and how to work with the bank. That's very much an along-the-way kind of thing. Development ethic or even theory is not a real part of the program.

"The academics, meanwhile, say, 'It's not our job to produce sawn-off baby architects.' The academics say that it's their job to produce people with the great foundations of the big ideas and the technical skills. See, there's a lot of ego in the artistic process, and architects consider themselves artists. We tend to value the art more than the technology. Sneering, I think, is a little overdone. Condescend? Yes. I mean, in your industry the people who write the big novels or the definitive biographies are different than the people who crank out the obits and the want ads."

Okay, so why did they try to run John Portman out of the fraternity?

Levy rolls his eyes.

John C. Portman, Jr., is the godfather of Edge City design. He changed forever the way American cities work and look. He is the architect who, in 1967, developed the first of those classic Hyatt Regency Hotels with the rooms all around the edge and the enormous thirty-story atria in the middle, with their hanging gardens and crystal elevators and their ziggurats. But even before that, he celebrated the enclosure of ever larger and more lavish megastructure environments, such as Atlanta's Peachtree Center. His efforts like the Embarcadero in San Francisco and the Renaissance Center in Detroit have been major hits with the public and widely copied by other builders, lending credence to his claim to be "the people's architect." But he is viewed in many architectural circles as the Dark Side of the Force—as guilty of apostasy.

His first sin was that his exuberant American design yawps turn life inward toward the air conditioning and away from the beastly streets. But on top of that, he went on actually to build his own buildings. He stopped waiting around to find a client to put up the buildings he wanted to build and started putting them up himself. As recently as the 1980s, AIA chroniclers explain, it was considered a gross breach of ethics for an architect to have an equity interest in the buildings of his own design. It was thought that an ownership interest would encourage the cutting of corners. The public's interest would not be kept foremost. It was cause for formal censure. Portman broke through all that. He became—gasp!—a developer. His conduct eventually inspired other architects to adopt a more hands-on attitude toward city building, but not before he was summoned to a high inquisition before the AIA priesthood.

Explains Levy: "Architecture had for years been seen as a gentleman's profession. It's an interesting avocation and a wonderful combination of art and science. It's very easy to get so involved in making the beautiful building come true that you can go out of business. To this day, I know architects who'll do a couple of development projects to make enough money, and they'll practice architecture until their money runs out and then they'll do another couple of development projects to make some more cash.

"The people who could practice over the long haul were able to ignore the vagaries of commerce—they were gentlemen. If it took five thousand hours to do a building that had been budgeted for only four thousand hours, they could afford to spend a thousand hours for free because they didn't have to make a living. They had independent incomes.

"I mean somebody like Jefferson, who is held to be the first American architect—he spent the latter part of his life building and rebuilding and unbuilding and overbuilding Monticello. It was only because he had money and education and prestige and had traveled to Europe to see Palladian buildings—only because of his gentlemanly status that he could exercise his architecture.

Had he been a cobbler, he probably couldn't have been an architect.

"The marketplace? I think we're a lot better at it than we used to be. I think it's a kind of benign myopia. It's been said that architects are business people who lose a little on each project and try to make it up in volume.

"Capitalism is a wonderful system and it's given us the ability to have these little toys and to eat good lunches. But in this culture you can justify nearly anything—nearly anything—if you can make a buck at it. Therefore, decisions that are based on business precepts rather than esthetic precepts will have primacy. And they can be countervailing forces, yes. Business *can* get in the way of art. People are drawn to architecture for the art of building beautiful spaces that house well the human enterprise.

"I think there is a real difference between art and business. Traditional architecture is on the side of art, not on the side of business."

Fine, responds art historian Dillon. No argument, none at all. But even if you revere art, what sense does it make that "all of our models for urbanity and cities and what they mean are all nineteenth-century models? Even though if you look around Dallas and Houston, you have a hell of a hard time figuring out exactly how those would fit.

"If you pick up all of the current literature on cities, every one of them has the model with one downtown. Where all the tall buildings were. Where people lived close to work and where there was this street life and it's Hudson Street or something. Most of the discussion about cities is still very much imbued or infected or infested with that kind of thinking. Therefore it's very difficult to come to terms with the reality of a place like Dallas. Our parent is Los Angeles; it's not Boston or San Francisco. Our next of kin are Albuquerque and Phoenix and Atlanta.

"I'm interested in this part of the country because it attempts to come to terms with certain realities like the car and the garage and the freeway. I can make a case for a downtown as essentially a tourist, entertainment, and business center. It's not what we would all have as the best of all possible worlds. But it's more realistic—the notion of a downtown as one of five or six specialized districts. Sort of picking out this part of the urban pie—maybe no housing or very little housing; maybe very little shopping. Maybe all of the other stuff will go out somewhere else. Houston's already that way, you know.

"But when I say things like that, it's oh, no, the worst possible thing. It's kind of a blindness. I spend a fair amount of time in architectural schools around the country. You look at what students are drawing and what they're being taught, and you see the house for the collector or an art museum. A big one a few years ago was some project for the Berlin Wall. Students need a passport to see the sites that they're designing for.

"In the meantime this other stuff is all around them, and nobody's addressing it, because it's too difficult. It's not a traditional design problem. It's not about buildings necessarily; it's about spaces and landscapes."

Indeed, I came to wonder about parking lots. They're the most ubiquitous built form in Edge City. Why are they so ugly? Could there conceivably be something inherent in Edge City parking lots that requires them to be that way? Or is it simply that most designers have not considered them worthy of study? Gas stations from the 1930s, after all, are now thought of as neat, and worth preservation. I wonder what will happen when certain strip shopping centers get old enough and unfashionable enough to not be worth bulldozing. (In Texas, developers say, a building "don't wear out; it uglies out.") Will they end up being renovated by artists who suddenly realize what a wonderful big, cheap space an old K mart is? After all, somebody had to be the first to have the brainstorm of turning an old brick warehouse or textile mill into condominiums. I wonder what these new places will look like.

In Houston, in recycled neighborhoods such as Montrose, and the Village, near Rice University, gas stations are becoming florist shops, and old theaters are becoming bookstores. But not a lot of that has happened yet nationwide. "It's just outside the pale of the traditional nineteenth-century image of urban—which is about street, block, and square," says Dillon. "I mean, that's the kind of architecture that is history. Yes, it's history.

"Suburbs are all just dismissed as seas of anonymity. That's scary to me, because you can't define the problem. Design professionals want to have nothing to do with these places; they have almost no interest in them.

"Sort of like a 1950s' way of thinking, as though nothing ever happens out there."

"I don't think we were social revolutionaries," Gerald D. Hines demurs. "Developers are not leaders of the trend. People who are point men get killed. You want to be out in front of the market a little bit. One step. But you're not out there five steps ahead. You hope. You better not be. Survival is the most important thing for a developer."

Disclaimers aside, Hines conceptualized at a higher level than most of his clan. He attempted to reconcile the automobile with the requirements of urban amenities. He invented the Houston Galleria.

This is how he figured:

Americans are individualists. The automobile is the finest expression of transportation-individualism ever devised. Edge Cities never succeed financially without accommodating the automobile. However, parking lots spread buildings apart. The farther apart buildings are, the less willing people are to walk between them. The fewer people there are within walking distance of any one place, the less able that place is to support civilization as measured by the existence of restaurants and bookstores. Therefore, individualism in the form of the automobile, fights the formation of society and community and civilization.

Hines, by examining the apparent chaos of Edge City and building the Galleria, found a way to address the problem.

To be sure, this part of Texas is never going to be confused with the Left Bank of Paris. When pairs of battle choppers start slowly sweeping the sky over the Galleria area in muscular, deliberate arcs, the locals glance up at the Cobras with their weapons platforms akimbo and say, "Guess George is coming home." This area is home to enough unabashed mercantilism to make a Renaissance Venetian blush. The Houstonian complex, where President Bush maintains his Texas voting address, is a five-minute drive away.

Nonetheless, the Galleria area is evolving. The best restaurants in the Houston region are there, not downtown. A newspaper poll revealed that the most beloved place in the whole urban area was the six-story, Philip Johnson–designed water-wall sculpture and park right next to the Transco Tower. And society has rewarded Gerald Hines for his insights into the human condition. To get to Hobby Airport, where he parks his white Cessna Citation III jet, Hines drives a chocolate Ferrari Pinin Farina 400i with a speedometer that winds out to 180 miles per hour. His offices in the Transco Tower look down not just on the Galleria, but on traffic helicopters.

The Houston Galleria area is larger than downtown Amsterdam, or Cologne, or Denver. Twenty-five years ago, the land on which it stands was only a prairie with a one-room schoolhouse on it. By any rational assessment of attempts to create a whole new urban world from scratch, what is there today is not all that ragged. How did this come to be?

"I don't think anyone could honestly say they knew at the time about the effects of density," says Louis S. Sklar, the Galleria's overseer for Gerald D. Hines Interests. "The equation was a very simple one: the driving force was a refined version of greed."

The land cost so much that most of it had to be covered with leasable buildings if the project was to be economically feasible. That meant that parking had to be multilevel rather than surface, which drove up the cost even more. It was so high, in fact, that the Galleria was forced for economic reasons into a conceptual breakthrough: diversity.

Hotels and office buildings were incorporated because the different kinds of people they attract were needed for the package to make money. And the parking arrangement worked, Sklar says, because it is "all weather-controlled, it's pleasant, there's activity, it's safe, there's no third-party violence, no potholes, no curbs to step off, no cars to splash you, there's plenty of parking, it's free, it's clean, it's well lighted, and you don't have a choice.

"That should come first. You don't have a choice."

To students of human behavior like Hines, what is going on in Edge City is no great mystery.

"We felt we were just following a trend of making people more efficient. That's why we were the pioneers of mixed use. If you have everything in one place, you minimize your travel time. That's why high-rise apartments will really never succeed. People are creatures of convenience. They want to park next to their house. They don't want to go into a garage and walk up into a high-rise. Can't bring my groceries into my back door. I have to jog on the asphalt, the concrete jungle. Give me a choice, and I'm going to go out to suburbia. They's why Edge Cities are developing. People say, 'I can have both. I can work and live in my twenty-minute span.' "

Hines and Sklar say that the real trick to the 45-acre, 3.9-million-square-foot, 11,263-parking-space Galleria is that it has gone through an aging process similar to the old downtowns. Buildings of various eras and visions are adjacent to each other, offering layers and textures. "The Galleria will never be finished," says Sklar.

Notes Sklar, "We weren't just doing architectural fantasies, nor were we backed up with a family fortune that would allow us to develop thirty or forty acres and see whether anybody came or not. Everything we did had to meet the test of the market. It's good. It causes compromises. The difference between success and failure—soul or no soul—has a lot to do with both our incremental approach and whether or not you stay on top of the market."

Some architects and planners have come up with exciting visions of how to bring civilization to Edge Cities.

One idea getting a lot of attention is that of Peter Calthorpe of San Francisco. He proposes that "pedestrian pockets" be built. These would be dense, walkable centers, a quarter of a mile in radius, with mixed use: residential, jobs, shopping. Citylets, if you will. They would be dotted throughout the otherwise thinly developed suburban landscape, and linked together by light rail until they formed a web.

There is, unfortunately, not yet anything like them built. So it's tough to imagine all the Unintended Consequences that may ensue. The plan, for example, would require significant government involvement, both in setting the site of the "pockets" and in paying for the light-rail lines to connect them. That would be a challenge. But the idea of alternating high, walkable densities with low, car-oriented ones does sound promising. In principle, it would be like the Galleria, only open-air, and with housing.

Then there was the urban village idea as practiced by Scott Toombs in his Princeton Forrestal Center. On the north end of the New Jersey Edge City of U.S. Route 1, he developed a dense, walkable, outdoors-oriented place that was meant to be a magic small town of the twenty-first century. Offices were located above shops, and there were restaurants and a hotel, and people could walk everywhere, but there was still plenty of parking on the streets and in the decks at the exterior of the village. There were flags and bands and it was really neat. It was not unlike New Canaan, Connecticut, in fact, where Toombs had his main office. Only it was built from scratch.

There were a few unresolved problems. One was that there was a real village not far away. It had the benefit of having taken centuries to evolve. It was called—Princeton. It was a more inviting place to be. Another problem was that Toombs's village had no people actually living in it. There was no residential development. Another was that the priests of the market—the bankers—were not all of the same church. It is a given that those who understand office real estate deals rarely understand retail deals, and those rarely understand hotel deals. This is a problem that also afflicts Galleria-style solutions. Toombs, unfortunately, ended up with a consortium of eleven lenders, all of whom had to agree in order for him to correct any flaws that might crop up in his scheme. That turned out to be a recipe for rigidity. This division of expertise among financiers is a genuine problem for mixed-use places. It is not easily fixed. It makes some people wonder whether mixed-use developments have any future at all.

But another, more serious, problem is that other attempts at creating "urban villages" have been put together by designers who are so addicted to planning and control that they make anarchy look inviting. They validate Robert Venturi's command: "Messy vitality over obvious unity." Their places never seem to come alive, for there is no easy way for them to evolve. In South Hadley, Massachusetts, Graham Gund designed a place across from the campus of Mount Holyoke College called the Village Commons. It is sort of an idealization of what New England would have been like if the original settlers had had air conditioning and Evian water. The Village Commons, like Forrestal Center, has been hailed in all the right design magazines. But this "first postmodern New England village" is the kind of place where a battle went on for months over what kind of sign the hairdresser could have outside his shop. It seems that the hairdresser saw the interior of his place as sleek and hip and full of shiny surfaces and loud music. He wanted to continue this kicky motif on a stylized white, gray, and scarlet logo outside. The protracted fight was literally measured in inches over how far outside his door he could carry his design into the exterior controlled by Graham Gund. The question is, Is this any way to create life? Did villages really evolve under strictures like this any place other than in *The Scarlet Letter?*

Another innovation in the Village Commons is that it includes homes over the shops. But it turns out that mixed use does have its limits. Not everybody, as it happens, considers it swell to be paying premium rents to live over an emporium that attracts drunken undergraduates.

Meanwhile, Paolo Soleri is still out there in the desert in Arizona building Arcosanti, last anybody checked. A disciple of Frank Lloyd Wright, he has for decades been putting together a megastructure meant to be an environmentally benign architectural blueprint for the future. But he keeps talking about things like eschatology, the branch of theology concerned with the final events in the history of mankind, and nobody can understand a bloody thing he says, so he has had little practical influence.

The ideas of Andres Duany and Elizabeth Plater-Zyberk of Miami have achieved the greatest publicity. They lead a movement that claims the answer for twenty-first-century cities is— surprise!—a radical return to the nineteenth century. Their version, though, is more sophisticated and plausible than most. They are banking on the idea that Americans' nostalgia for white-picket-fence small towns can be manipulated. They think if you give Americans a product that reminds them of what communities used to be, as opposed to cul-de-sac suburbia, you can slip into these places all sorts of things that planners view as highly desirable, like streets laid out on a grid, and walkable environments, and—most important—relatively high densities.

The real contribution of Duany and Plater-Zyberk, however,

may be that they recognize and manipulate market mechanisms. First, they studied small towns in the South built before the 1940s. They concluded that a community of genuine variety and authentic character could not be generated by a single designer. Therefore, if they wanted to produce something that was not just another subdivision, the key was in writing *and* administering a master plan and a zoning code, as often as not at the behest of a developer.

Their conclusion is that they should control the overall patterns: the size of the lots, the narrowness of the streets, the relationship of houses to the street, the relationship of houses to one another, how and where the cars will be parked, the alignment of streets, the creation of a downtown-like center. If they get all this under control, they feel, imaginative people can be trusted to take care of producing the rest of the community themselves.

Dozens of Duany–Plater-Zyberk projects are in the works, but so far only one of their places has a substantial number of buildings up—Seaside, Florida, which is an eighty-acre development on twenty-three hundred linear feet of the Gulf of Mexico due south of Alabama. It took Duany and Plater-Zyberk two years to write the code for that place. It mandates arcades and porches and walkways and alleys and, yes, white picket fences, all to encourage a lively street life. It invites skinny widow's-watch towers so that everybody will have a view of the water. Outbuildings are favored on the back of the building lots, so that rentals will ensure a mix of ages and incomes. There is a premium put on how lively and innovative building plans can be while staying within the code.

The ideas of Duany and Plater-Zyberk all sound marvelous and promising, especially when Seaside is compared with most of the Florida strip wilderness that surrounds it. But their concepts are tough to evaluate at this stage other than theoretically, since Seaside is possibly anomalous. It is a resort community that does not require much parking.

The aspects of their ideas, however, that offer the most hope are, first, they understand why people like to live the way they do in suburbs. Second, they have codified a generic version of their new-old-town ideas into something they call the Traditional Neighborhood Development, or TND. It is packaged so that a jurisdiction can easily vote the whole thing into law as a pattern that mandates mixed-use developments designed as small towns. And third, their ideas encourage flexibility; they attempt to strike a balance in which only the truly important things come under rigid control.

In the days of the past century, when it was thought that the universe was a vast piece of clockwork, chaos was feared because it was the exact opposite of the machine, notes the urban designer Patricia L. Faux. Those were the days in which urban planning as we know it was born. It was expressed in the perfect street grids of the nineteenth-century downtowns.

As we approach the twenty-first century, however, physicists view the world through the prism of relativity and quantum mechanics, and "chaos" is the name of a new paradigm. The workings of a babbling brook or a column of cigarette smoke or the weather cannot be expressed in mechanistic linear equations; the apparent chaos of these complex structures is actually expressive of a higher order, the kind of order from which springs that most nonlinear of all phenomena—life itself.

Our methods of planning, however, are still in the old, mechanistic mode, in which people try to leave nothing to chance. Especially if they have to face bankers. "The world of Disney is the ultimate example of this sort," Faux notes. "It is a vision of total safety, where every need is met. It is an egomaniac's version of what a community would do to itself if it had the time. It's spooky. It's false. It is predictable, not real. It is not what a community builds. There are no little mom-and-pop stores. Parks are used as buffers. Their function has been changed. They are not places for people to congregate; they are places to keep people at bay."

In short, in this kind of planning, spontaneity is choked off at exactly the point in our lives when, in civilized places, looseness and flexibility seem to be the key. Edge Cities, after all, are places that can metamorphose so fast as to be almost unrecognizable from one year to the next. They are nothing if not monuments to change. And in this way they are reflective of the society that produced them. We live in a world in which people

have difficulty forecasting wisely enough to park their retirement funds competently for two years. Pity the poor planner,
then, when he figures that a rail line should go from here to
there and by the time it is built his decision looks ludicrous;
development has followed a wholly different pattern. "The very
dynamism of our society produces these disjunctions and screw-
ups, which are practically unavoidable," muses Anthony Downs
of the Brookings Institution. Some planners have questioned
whether it is possible to do urban planning in a society that
reveres market forces. Others have asked, seriously, whether it is
possible to do urban planning in a society that reveres the individual.

But they go too far. Planning clearly has value. During the oil
crash of the mid-1980s, the housing markets in Houston that
prospered were those which were master-planned. In addition
to The Woodlands, there are four primarily residential developments that are huge—each totaling thousands of acres, and each
roughly twenty-five miles from downtown Houston. These five
had 11 percent of the market for new homes in the early 1980s,
and a 45 percent share by 1990. "In periods of uncertainty,
there is a flight to quality," noted Roger L. Galatas, president of
The Woodlands Corporation. "Neighborhoods that are fraught
with foreclosures don't look too good. People want to see that
the places were well planned. They look for a more manicured
landscape, a more formal landscape. They want to see an existing presence in the marketplace, not signs saying 'Coming in
the Future.' "

Cultures do evolve, as the AIA's Chip Levy points out.
"Thomas Jefferson said that we might as well expect a man to
wear the coat that fit him as a child as to remain ever under the
regimen of his barbarous ancestors. If cultures do not progress,
they will die. And therefore, by extrapolation, the plan that is
put in place which serves you well today may not be germane in
the mid or distant future. And we ought not to expect it to."

It's not as if turmoil is going away. Louis Sklar, the Galleria
overseer, points out that retailing is up for grabs: chains are
going bankrupt or are being acquired at a dizzying pace. Retail is
a major ingredient in Edge City, yet it's "hard to know who the
players are anymore. Are we going to end up with only a few

major department store companies that are both competent and solvent going into the latter part of this decade?"

Sklar sees the turmoil in the oil markets, and what that does to global stability, and thinks that "sooner or later, after all the political trading is done and some presidents don't get re-elected, we're going to end up with a program that lessens dependence on foreign oil. People are still going to have their cars. Even if they are powered by ozone or who knows. But it's going to cause some major changes."

Then—as an object lesson in never projecting the present into the future in a straight line—there are some people, like planner Jack Linville, who think that we may have built all the Edge Cities we are going to for a while.

He looks at the building binge we've been on and sees little unmet demand for a whole lot more of anything—office space, industrial space, even homes. The baby boom, with its unprecedented creation of new households, after all, has crested. He thinks that our future may involve taking a pause, and a deep breath, and figuring out what we've gone and done. At that point the task would be to start filling it in and tinkering with it and making it work.

That would be a blessing. As Sklar points out, one of the main reasons older cities may be more pleasing than our new ones is that in the older places "we don't see any of those failed experiments. Because they're gone. In any reasonably affluent society, as time has passed, all the eyesores have been spruced up, fixed up. The raw cut through the mountain is landscaped. The bare concrete wall gets a brick facing or vines. The billboards eventually come down."

Houston itself is a monument to that. "Houston is much funkier than people think," says John Ashby Wilburn, editor of the *Houston Press,* the arts and entertainment weekly. "When I first came here, I just felt like I'd stepped off the edge of the world, that I'd made a horrible mistake. In New York, everything is so above the surface, you see so many things because everything is so squeezed together. It took me a year to realize that (a), there were interesting people here, and (b), I could find them. You do bump into them, but it takes longer, because they're farther apart."

Jennifer Womack can testify to that. One spring morning in

the Galleria, at all three levels of the rails above the ice rink, people were stopped, gazing at this arresting brunette in a loose orange Reese's Pieces T-shirt and black Spandex tights. She would start at one end of the ice, dig in, and, at midpoint, she would achieve escape velocity and leap, spin, twirl, and then leap, and leap again, to spin to a stop in a bursting shower of ice flakes.

Phew, you could hear spectators exhale, explosively.

She would intently glide back to her precise starting point, eyes down, a study in concentration, and go through the same routine. Again and again. Two dark-skinned middle-aged gentlemen were among the spectators. They appeared to speak little English. They made hand gestures at the only other figure on the ice, a man who obviously was finding it all he could do simply to keep his rented skates under him. They twirled their index fingers as if mixing a drink. Go ahead, try a spin like that, they mimed. That gave everybody on the rails a good laugh.

Jennifer Womack, it turns out, once skated with the Ice Follies. Then she fell in love with a man in the "awl bidness"—the Texas oil business—and followed him to Houston. There she found herself in culture shock. She emphasizes the word "shock" with her light hazel eyes open wide. Home to her was the cool, laid-back land just north of San Francisco across the Golden Gate, in Marin County. In Houston she was utterly lost. The different pace of life. How loud people spoke. The flat coastal plain. The Gulf heat. She is still able to recall in considerable detail sitting home for months, experimenting with air-conditioner settings.

That has changed, though. She has begun to feel comfortable in Texas. "Did you know that armadillos can jump?" she asked. But she doesn't think she could have made it if she hadn't stumbled on the Galleria and its rink.

She made friends there, on the ice. She found people with whom she had much in common.

"I owe this place my sanity," she says. "I found community here."

Trolling around within sight of the Galleria area's office towers, seeking out civilization—hunting for mine canaries, if you will—you discover that the 1980s' oil bust had interesting side effects on Houston. There was an explosion of intriguing ethnic neighborhoods—Vietnamese, Hong Kong Chinese, Salvadoran, Honduran, Iranian, subcontinent Indian. Houston was a bargain for immigrants in the 1980s. Cheap place to buy a house, buy an office building, start a business. Now that the place has bottomed out and is turning around, you find a plethora of diverse shops. Peel off the Southwest Freeway at Hillcroft, outside Loop 610, and there's a discount warehouse sari emporium.

Didn't used to always be this way in Texas.

Some things never change, though. The *Texas Monthly* crowd is especially high on a restaurant called the Bombay Grill, so that is where the crowd ends up for dinner. Those who know absolutely nothing about Indian cuisine let those who do order lamb shahi korma, chicken tikka masala, peas pullao, and a sauce called raita.

Mickey Kapoor, the owner of the place, then asks if the table would like "bray-yad." Eager to learn as much as possible about the exotic customs of colorful lands, the stranger in the crowd goes up for the bait like a marlin.

Certainly. Great idea. Now what, exactly, is "bray-yad"?

You know. Bray-yad. The stuff on either side of the meat in a sandwich? Slices of bray-yad? Pronounced in Texas the same as in southern India?

The next evening, somewhat more seriously, Kapoor talks about the countries he has lived in, and the cultures he has encountered, and what led a nice Hindu boy like him to try to bring civilization to an Edge City in Texas.

Bringing cosmopolitan, authentic, high-end Indian cuisine to Houston has provided him with more than his share of adventures, he acknowledges. There were all the people who wanted to know what kind of Indian restaurant his was. Navajo? Comanche? Then, when he was running the place called the Taj Mahal, there were the people who wanted to talk to Mr. Mahal, the short guy with the glasses. All the waiters learned to say, Oh yeah, you mean Taj, and sent Kapoor out front.

For reasons that are inexplicable even now, the location of his first place was on the southeast side of Houston, on the way to the Edge City of Clear Lake–NASA, three miles from a saloon and dance hall called Gilley's. Remember the movie *Urban Cow-*

*boy?* Remember the mechanical bull? Remember the pickups and the shotgun racks? That was Gilley's. Real "Bubba and Skeeter country," Kapoor recalls, in his clipped Empire sing-song.

Yeah, I've really done my bit for civilizing this market, he deadpans. There was this redneck who sauntered up to Kapoor once as he was shopping for a car. Jabbing a middle finger in Kapoor's chest, he bellowed that he believed he'd located a "stupid Iranian." That indictment was a real hazard to your health in Texas at the time. No, sir, Kapoor explained, sir. "I am a stupid Indian, sir." Reincarnation or no, passing for a Persian was the last way Kapoor figured he needed to die.

But getting more serious, Kapoor notes there is a difference between a beautiful city and a beautiful society. Kapoor really hoped that this strip-shopping-center world he found himself in at the Bombay Grill was a transitory phase for Houston and for America. That it was part of an evolution toward a finer structure. "Things do happen by accident, but they do evolve to a higher form of perfection, which lends credence to the concept of God," he notes. "Because, you know, whatever we do, we are propelled forward by some natural forces beyond our comprehension and our immediate senses."

As far as he could tell, though, "we haven't changed much from the village concept except that these Edge Cities are self-contained little villages intertwined and interconnected and compacted into a larger thing called the metropolis. Eventually, in my mind, a perfect form of this would be that in a particular neighborhood everything should be so accessible that a final form will develop; even, I think, where you won't have to drive that much. You will work closer to home; you will have shopping closer to home; and it is only in cases of extreme necessity that you will do the traveling and commuting. The ecology, the air—taking all this in consideration, the sooner we go with this into areas where people work where they reside, or reside where they work, people can stay closer to home; it eventually will resolve some of the more troubling issues."

Right now, Kapoor feels, the reason his restaurant's neighborhood is interesting is that it is on a border between the fancy environs of the Galleria area and "the large and very sizable Indian community that lives within a five-mile radius. There are

Indian grocery stores, Indian clothing stores, Indian appliance stores."

Indeed, you talk about cosmopolitan climes. No more than two miles from the Galleria there is something called the Fiesta Market. The simplest way to describe it is as a kind of Third World village market run by a sophisticated, knowledgeable, sympathetic, and sensitive American outfit with an organizational firepower reminiscent of Safeway.

The sign over the entrance to the Fiesta says WELCOME, then BIENVENUDO, and then goes on in five more languages in which not even the script, much less the alphabet, is familiar. This place is so international, so sophisticated, so diverse, that all the *important* signs are in English. Just English. The multilingual possibilities and combinations are just too hard. Nobody has enough else in common. Makes your head hurt.

Yet the prices are right, the selection stunning; and Fiesta has become a chain that is carving up market share left and right in Houston, even in Anglo neighborhoods.

Why is the Indian community out here? I ask Kapoor. Out past the Loop? Out past 610? Not in the older, denser areas? I thought Indians were accustomed to density.

"Density is something they would like to get away from," says Kapoor, who is Rajasthani. He is from that tan, desert area between Gujarat and the Punjab, up against the border with Pakistan—not much farther from either China or Afghanistan than Houston is from Dallas.

"Yeah, sure. It's like privacy. In India you don't get a thing like privacy. There's no such thing. Because you live in a house with thirty other members of the family. But here, you get your first taste of privacy. It becomes very precious all of a sudden. Oh, yes."

The previous day I had chatted with Stephen Fox, who teaches at Rice, and who had just written the *Houston Architectural Guide.* We had been talking about what was wrong with Houston, and what had to be made right. And he, quite independently, mentioned that he had students from around the world, and the first thing he asked them to do was write a paper describing the architectural history of their home places.

He said he had been struck especially by the Malaysians, who described their place in terms that to him seemed idyllic. Tightly knit. Dense. Walkable. Surrounded by community that was generations thick and centuries deep. But it was they especially, he reported, who seemed most to love Houston. They were singularly articulate about the limits of where they came from. The stifling rigidity. The paternalism. Yes, Houston is nuts. But it's so much fun. There is such individualism. You have so much freedom.

"I take that for granted," Fox noted sheepishly.

I tell all this to Kapoor, who says, "The thing is that Americans—native-born Americans—I don't know whether they understand it, but they probably undervalue the elbow room they have. That is commonly known as freedom.

"The liberty that we have over here. It's not comparable with anything anywhere in the world. You cannot compare, not even Canada. Not England, not Germany. Not even close. The enjoyable thing over here is that you can express yourself. You can just be yourself. You can be left alone if you want to be left alone. Not so in even the more advanced or self-professed civilized countries of the world. And I have lived in ten or eleven of them.

"When I say Americans don't understand it, people ask what I mean. The basic things are taken for granted over here because they are just given to you at birth, like a kid given a Cadillac on his sixteenth birthday. You know, simple things like ten people can get together and start a political party if you want to. You can deride anyone you want to. You can write a letter to the newspaper if you want to. You can just assemble on the street and start talking.

"You can start a business if you want to. You can quit a job if you want to and get another one if you want to. To an American these are everyday things. You can turn on the telly, turn on the radio, listen to any station you want to, read any newspaper you want to, adhere to any belief you want to. To Americans these are like, so what is the big deal?

"Well, the big deal is that you cannot do this in any other place in the world. In England you cannot just go and start a business. I could never have a restaurant this big. First of all the hindrance would be getting a lease. They would want references. Money in the bank. Need everything cash up front. You have to belong to a certain class of people over there.

"In New York, Houston, you can sell an idea and fructify the idea into something solid. Very, very different to do it any other place in the world.

"Civilization is not just physical attributes or the structure of buildings. It is the quality of life, the psychological impact. The evolution, I think, cannot be on the level of just the structure. It must be the people who live in the structure, too. How are we going to be thinking?

"What I think we must think now, about Edge City, is that this is screwed up. If this is evolution, then I'm happy. But if it is closer to the final product, then it is very scary.

"I am not saying that everything that is haphazard has to be controlled. It's not what you do, it's a state of the mind—being urbane. An urbane person, to me, is someone who, in a fire, can stand in line and wait to get out. Know which way things are going. Not just dress up and at the critical moment go bonkers. That is not very civil.

"Houston is already there. The one thing that impressed me about Houston when I came here twelve years ago was the basic friendliness. That 'howdy' attitude they had. That they still do. Even if they think my first name is Taj. If it comes from the goodness of their hearts, that is quite acceptable to me.

"It is a sense of community. You have to create the conditions. Create the environment, for someone to evolve to that final product.

"What are you wanting, eventually? A pretty structure? Or a pretty society?"

# 8

## SOUTHERN CALIFORNIA

### Community

Man is returning to the descendants of the wandering tribe—the adventurers, I hope.

—*Frank Lloyd Wright, 1958*

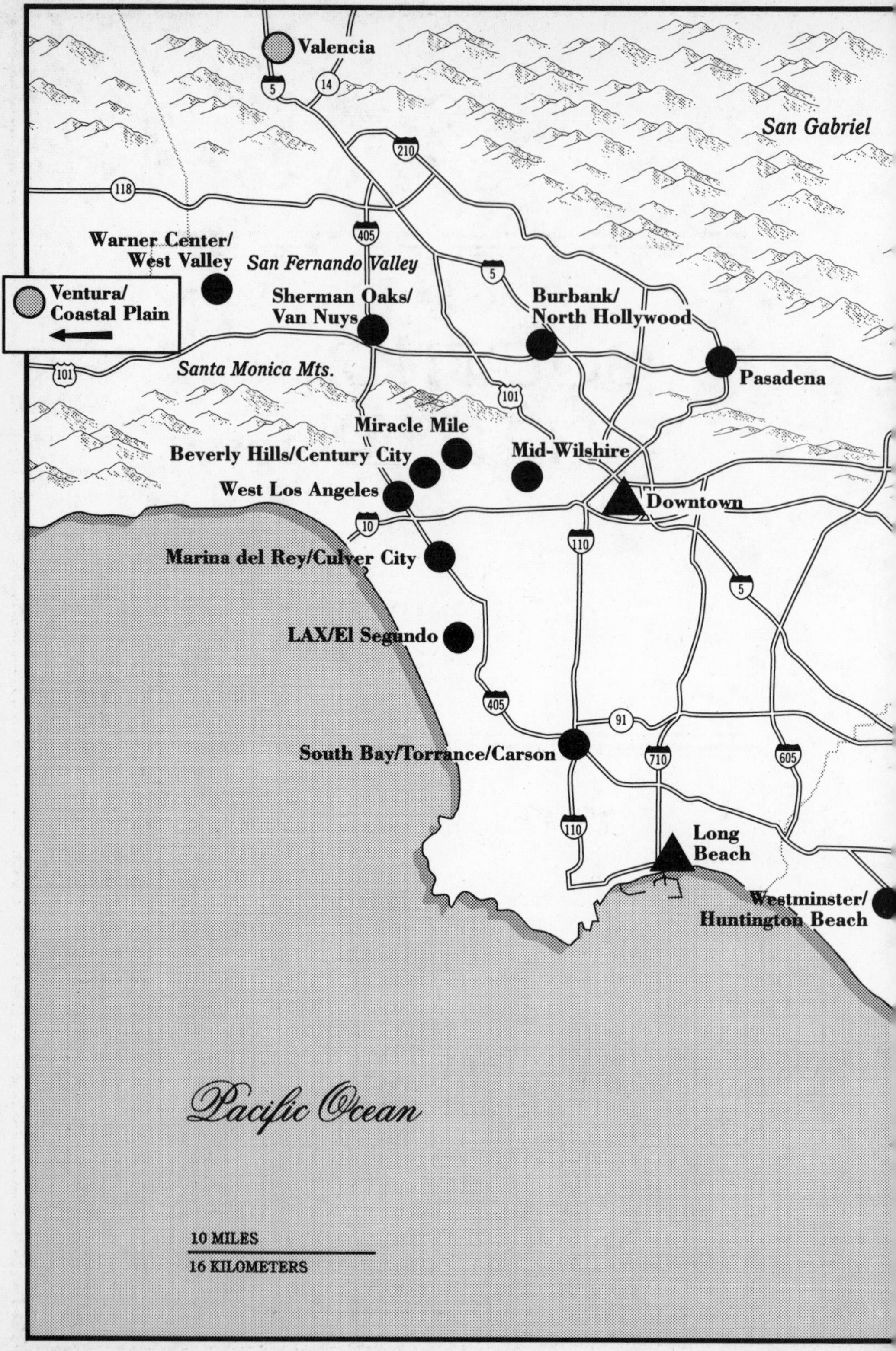

Valencia

San Gabriel

5  14

210

118

405

Warner Center/
West Valley

San Fernando Valley

5

Ventura/
Coastal Plain

Sherman Oaks/
Van Nuys

Burbank/
North Hollywood

101

Santa Monica Mts.

101

Pasadena

Miracle Mile

Beverly Hills/Century City

Mid-Wilshire

West Los Angeles

Downtown

10

110

5

Marina del Rey/Culver City

LAX/El Segundo

405

91

South Bay/Torrance/Carson

710

605

110

Long
Beach

Westminster/
Huntington Beach

Pacific Ocean

10 MILES

16 KILOMETERS

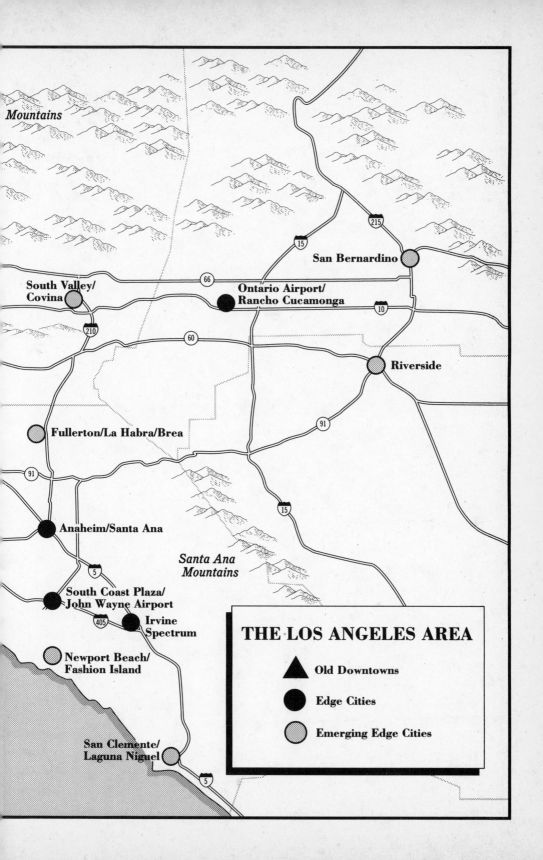

Mountains

215

15

San Bernardino

66

South Valley/
Covina

Ontario Airport/
Rancho Cucamonga

10

210

60

Riverside

91

Fullerton/La Habra/Brea

91

15

Anaheim/Santa Ana

Santa Ana
Mountains

5

South Coast Plaza/
John Wayne Airport

405

Irvine
Spectrum

Newport Beach/
Fashion Island

## THE LOS ANGELES AREA

▲ Old Downtowns

● Edge Cities

● Emerging Edge Cities

San Clemente/
Laguna Niguel

5

"MY BROTHER PETER has a wife and three children and he lives in a group of identical houses and I used to think it was very eerie. But then I remember going over there on Halloween," says John Nielsen.

Nielsen, thirty-four, is talking about community and identity in the new American world built by developers like his father. The elder Nielsen, Tom, is a leading light behind a place in Southern California called Irvine. It is by far the largest Edge City landscape ever developed by a single company.

"Every place I've lived since I got out of college, Halloween is known as the nightmare movie. It's not known as a holiday. Except here. Here were all these people who had just moved into this suburb at the same time, brand new. And no one knew what was going to happen—whether there was going to be a tradition in this place.

"Here were my nieces Emily and Sara; one was dressed up as a crayon. They kind of poked their heads out the door. It was just at dusk and here comes a crayon looking out this door. They gathered in their cul-de-sac, this herd of kids, and they had a herd of parents behind them. It was the first time I realized that everybody was the same age and there was that kind of community, I guess. They came out not knowing what's going to happen and they turned the corner and there was this army of children. They all just went back and forth, door to door, and I thought, That's neat. That's a tradition that has died elsewhere that's being sustained here. I remember my mother following me with a staple gun because I was a mummy. I would unravel, she'd come up and snip me back together while I was collecting Sugar Babies. There is something historical about that.

"Then Emily and Sara came home. I was helping one trade with her sister for the right kind of treats. You want the Milk Duds, and you want the red Life Savers. You don't want the green ones.

"I just felt I was passing on some sort of higher knowledge."

John Nielsen grew up in a family where the food was put on the table by his father's converting thousands of acres of orange groves and pastureland into the Southern California that exists today. John wound up an environmental writer for National Public Radio. He is the kind of person who, no matter in what region he finds himself, lives in the most Dickensian neighborhood available. He has thus spent much of his life considering where his world intersects with that of his father's, and where both connect to personality and character.

"People ask me where I'm from and I don't know what to say. 'I'm from the suburbs,' is what I usually say. And they say, 'Oh, me too.' It doesn't matter where they're from, we'll exchange some stories about *Gilligan's Island* and then we're friends." He pounded on his chest: "Tarzan of the 'Burbs. Raised by developers." He gave a soft, ironic version of a jungle yell: "Aiiieyaeyaeyaea."

Flashing back twenty years, he recalls, "Me and my brother, we had this Allan Sherman record: 'My Son the Nut.' Ever hear that record?" John sings:

> Here's to the crabgrass
> Here's to the mortgage,
> And here's to sah-BURR-bee-yah.
> Lay down your briefcase,
> Far from the rat race,
> For nothing can dis-TURR-bee yah.

"My brother and I had that memorized. They'd bring us out and we'd sing it."

Nielsen loves neighborhoods that "seethe." He loves places where you can walk to work and if you regularly stop at a little joint on the way to pick up a carton of coffee, soon everybody in the neighborhood knows you. He likes to talk to people in different strata of society. He likes urban areas that are full of surprises. He thinks the whole point of cities is to bring diverse people together.

That is why it troubles him that he feels personally excluded from Edge Cities like the one built by his father, vice chairman of the Irvine Company. His dilemma is sharpened because each such development emphasizes the idea of community. As in "master-planned community."

"I feel locked out in the financial sense," says Nielsen of the Irvine that has been such a market success that the median home prices in its region are the third highest in America.

"But I don't mean to imply that if I had enough money that is where I'd go. The things I am interested in are not part of a place like Irvine. There's that whole notion: We're going to build this thing that is perfect for you. We haven't met you but we know what you're like and we know you're going to like it here. That is a repulsive idea, and I wouldn't trust the person who tried to tell me that. You're in the artist's conception. You wake up and you're one of those lanky people walking around evenly spaced. I can't see that. My experience has been that in places like that you have a lot of people who think they have it figured out. You just have the coffee-bean machine here and . . ." Nielsen's voice descends to a whisper. He is almost talking to himself. Then he hurtles back.

"That kind of ordered circumstance is scary to me. Maybe the world is divided into people who love to hum 'Is that all there is?' and take random walks and people who don't. It's a hard thing for me."

What Nielsen is struggling with is the extent to which Edge Cities weave or unravel the American social fabric. For this reason, his conflicts are historic. Ever since the rise of what used to be called "bedroom communities"—that is, classic residential suburbs—scholars have been trying to define where these places fit into a larger social scheme. Especially in the 1950s, when the floodtide of homes moved out past our old conception of city, the outpouring of journalism, fiction, and sociology on these issues was prodigious. It had a distinct tone. Herbert J. Gans, in his landmark 1967 work, *The Levittowners,* pungently described the shots that were taken. If you believed the critics, he wrote, the "myth of suburbia" would have you surmise:

"The suburbs were breeding a new set of Americans, as mass-produced as the houses they lived in . . . incapable of real friendships; they were bored and lonely, alienated, atomized, and depersonalized . . .

"In unison," Gans wrote of that time, "the authors chanted that individualism was dying, suburbanites were miserable, and the fault lay with the homogeneous suburban landscape and its population." Gans described John Keats, author of *The Crack in the Picture Window,* as "perhaps the most hysterical of the mythmakers."

Keats's book began: *"For literally nothing down . . .* you too can find a box of your own in one of the fresh-air slums we're building around the edges of American cities . . . inhabited by people whose age, income, number of children, problems, habits, conversation, dress, possessions, and perhaps even blood type are also precisely like yours." They were, Keats claimed, "developments conceived in error, nurtured by greed, corroding everything they touch. They . . . actually drive mad myriads of housewives shut up in them."

Subsequently, Gans observed, "literary and social critics chimed in . . . Suburbia was intellectually debilitating, culturally oppressive, and politically dangerous, breeding bland mass men without respect for the arts or democracy."

Gans bought a house and *lived* in New Jersey's Levittown for two years to study what processes turned a group of strangers into a true community in the waning days of the Eisenhower era. Of course, the sociologist and city planner could uncover little evidence that there was much change in people when they moved to the suburbs, or that the change that took place could be traced to the new environment: "If suburban life was as undesirable and unhealthy as the critics charged, the suburbanites themselves were blissfully unaware of it. They were happy in their new homes and communities, much happier than they had been in the city."

This has not, however, prevented Edge City from giving people the creeps. When I first started reporting on these places, an art critic of my acquaintance pulled up a chair, pushed his face toward mine closer than was really comfortable, and proceeded to get agitated about my project. "Those are not cities!" he exploded.

When I systematically questioned him as to why he felt this way, given all the job numbers and market numbers and population numbers, what I found was intriguing. His real beef was that he refused to believe these places brought people together in any larger social sense. He was saying these were not "cities," but what he really meant was that he could not believe they were "communities." It was very specific. To him, Edge Cities were hollow because, among other things, there were not, as in the neighborhoods he loved, front stoops for people to sit on to watch the human drama.

Here we were, more than thirty years after David Riesman's *The Lonely Crowd*, William H. Whyte's *The Organization Man*, Sloan Wilson's *The Man in the Gray Flannel Suit*, and the stories of John Cheever. And he was still proclaiming the landscape out past the old downtowns as having no ties that bind, no sense of identity, no way of making people believe they were part of something larger than themselves. He felt people had no personal stake in these places. Nobody cared about them. Therefore, these places could not be regarded as cities.

I had come to believe that it was not particularly useful to insist that a place was not urban merely because it contained few front stoops or political boundaries. But that didn't mean my friend the art critic had it all wrong. After all, for a place to have an identity, people really must feel they are stakeholders in it. They must feel that it is, at gut level, theirs; that they are willing to fight over it and for it. They must see it as having an importance relative to their personal interests. They must see it, at some level, as community.

Yet the forces that bring about Edge City pull strongly in different directions. Edge City arose as a result of individuals seeking out the best combinations of how and where to live, work, and play. Maybe Edge City isn't the puddle of atomization and anomie that 1950s critics of American society wished to believe. But it is less than clear where it connects with ideas like community—the hunger for human contact and the yearning to belong to a larger whole.

This is why Irvine is interesting. It is part of the Los Angeles Basin, the birthplace of the American landscapes and life styles that are the models for Edge Cities worldwide. Moreover, Irvine, thirty-five miles southeast of downtown Los Angeles, is at the center of a development of staggering proportions. Originally a Spanish land-grant ranch, the hundred-square-mile holdings of the Irvine Company span Orange County, that vast jurisdiction between San Diego and Los Angeles that in the 1980s was the fastest-growing part of Southern California. The Irvine Company controls sixty-four thousand acres of land, much of which stretches past the incorporated city of Irvine. Some of those acres sell for $1 million apiece. Irvine is not just another Levittown, a suburb from which people can find work only by commuting somewhere else. The stages of Edge City growth that took two generations elsewhere was collapsed into a third of a lifetime here. The Irvine area is now so big that it can be described as encompassing all or part of three job-rich Edge Cities.

The two middle-sized ones are known as Irvine Spectrum and Newport Center–Fashion Island. But the third, the size of downtown Seattle, is named after—it had to happen—John Wayne. Actually, the area's continental-connection airport is named after John Wayne. And the Edge City, which includes the Costa Mesa–South Coast Plaza complex, has become known after the name of the airport. But it was only a matter of time before it came to something like this. Orange County, the birthplace of Richard Nixon, has such a reputation for conservatism that a politician once only half kidded about joining the John Birch Society in order to capture the middle-of-the-road vote. The Irvine area's rapidly growing population, meanwhile, already approaches 200,000, with a high-technology job base of 150,000. The Irvine Company's spread is so big—stretching from the Pacific Ocean to as much as twenty miles inland—that its tentacles ensnare an entire University of California campus and two Marine bases.

Irvine, moreover, is the latest version of the Southern California dream. This makes it a prototype of great importance. Irvine is only ten miles from Disneyland in Anaheim. Disney produced such resonant dreams that people carry them around in their heads all over the globe. His Main Street is a more real crystallization of idealized community for more people than any actual nineteenth-century small American town. And Irvine is deep kin to this ideal. It is full of newcomers who are still reaching out to find why they came, what they lost, and who they are.

In fact, a travel guide called *The Californias,* published by the California Office of Tourism, describes Orange County this way:

It's a theme park—a seven hundred and eighty-six square mile theme park—and the theme is "you can have anything you want."

It's the most California-looking of all the Californias: the most like the movies, the most like the stories, the most like the dream.

Orange County is Tomorrowland and Frontierland, merged and inseparable . . .

The temperature today will be in the low 80s. There is a slight offshore breeze. Another just-like-yesterday day in paradise.

Come to Orange County. It's no place like home.

The danger of a dream, however, is that a place that reminds people of Eden can also taunt them. People's fears and anxieties may be heightened when the dream does not turn out to be as boundless as it first seems; when it quickly hits limits. In fact, Irvine has been compared with the Stepford Wives—perfect, in a horrifying sort of way. The development's newest residential section, Westpark, is an unbroken field of identical Mediterranean red-clay roof tile, covering homes of indistinguishable earth-tone stucco. Homes in Irvine are far more repetitive than those in the old Levittowns. The old Levittowns are now interesting to look at; people have made additions to their houses and planted their grounds with variety and imagination. Unlike these older subdivisions, Irvine has deed restrictions that forbid people from customizing their places with so much as a skylight. This is a place that is enforced, not just planned. Owners of expensive homes in Irvine commonly volunteer stories of not realizing that they had pulled into the driveway of the wrong house until their garage-door opener failed to work. Driving around, what one mainly sees is high blank walls. The shopping center near the University of California at Irvine struggled for years, unsuccessfully, to support a bookstore. And this is the place that bills itself as America's premiere master-planned community. It underlines the "community" symbolism with a ten-minute sound-and-light show called *Roots and Wings.*

*Roots and Wings* is a singular production. It is a twenty-thousand-slide, sixteen-projector extravaganza housed in its own little theater, and it culminates with the rotation of a hydraulically controlled model of some 150 square miles of the area. The model weighs half a ton. It is so exactly detailed, with 385,000 separate structures, that people living in Irvine can identify their own houses. This show is so lavish that the Irvine Company refuses to divulge its cost.

Intriguingly, this hymn to community is not used to sell homes. People who are in the market merely for quarter-million-dollar residences never get the red-carpet treatment that includes *Roots and Wings*. The people who see this pageant are those thinking of moving their companies to Irvine. *Roots and Wings* is reserved for customers looking for massive amounts of Edge City research-and-development or office space. Yet in this pitch, the customers never hear a word about dollars per square foot. The Irvine Company believes that the following approach is what sells commercial real estate in their Edge City.

The lights go down, the sea gulls start flashing on the screens, the music comes up, and the deep male voiceover booms from multiple concealed speakers:

"How long since you watched the new day lean down upon the shore? No one about but you and your thoughts. And time, sliding by on its spiral glide.

"Here, along the sea, far from the crowds, one can see how perfectly Nature casts her characters and places them upon her stage. Each living thing is drawn to that habitat most ideally suited to the development of its full potential. It is a law of Nature. Instinct, we are told.

"But, we wonder, what of that wandering species called man? Called woman? Called child? Are we not also embraced by Nature's laws? Shaped by our habitat, just as the sea bird's flight is shaped by the wind for that special place on earth to hold and nourish our lives?

"It is said there are only two lasting things we can give our children; one is roots, the other is wings. This then is the dream. To find a place where we can put down roots; to find a place where our lives can take wing."

The Irvine show proceeds to extol the development's "beauty," "work style," "life style," and its "critical mass of finance, knowledge, and resource to rival any major city in America." But then it swings right back and starts hammering at that community theme some more:

"If the human community is to work, there must be a lively

interplay between the commerce and the arts, between nature and technology, between work and leisure, between private interest and the public good. In a sense it's like planning and creating a living mosaic . . . The design of this living mosaic is especially refreshing because of the rare relationship between where one works and where one lives, in communities where planning brings the workplace closer. It is a gift of time. More time to enjoy another gift. The gift of family . . ."

Then the wind-up:

"Here is a place where life is lived with a grand and glorious sense of quality and style. Here is a place providing opportunities for the full range of human experience . . . Here is a place where individuals are free to shape their own future, as a sculptor shapes clay."

A daddy is shown lifting his child. Freeze frame. He lifts the child higher. Freeze frame. The child is lifted all the way up. Freeze frame.

Then the pitch:

"We have the dream. We have the plan. We have the people. We have the patterns of a vision firmly in our minds and in our hearts."

The child's image melds into that of a sea gull, which, in multiple-image long-lens slow-mo, explodes into flight.

"We have the place where we can put down roots.

"And our lives can take wing."

Music swells, image fades, screen lifts, gauze curtain rises, dramatic lights flare, and the half-ton model of Irvine, turning on its gimbles, rotates into view, beckoning.

One is left in awe, speechless.

Heavy freight being loaded here. Loaded on ideas and values that are elemental: Roots. Wings. Community. This is the place that Tom Nielsen built, that John Nielsen can't handle. Irvine thus demands that these words—and what they mean to us in the late twentieth century—be probed.

The meaning to developers of the word "community" has evolved over the last half century. In the case of the New Jersey Levittown in the 1950s, for example, it was not enough that there were three basic house types costing from \$11,500 to \$14,500. A collection of such houses would have been merely a "subdivision." What made it a "community" was that for each cluster of twelve hundred units or so, there was an elementary school, a playground, and a swimming pool. Not only that, but a complex of ten or twelve such "neighborhoods" was complemented by a large shopping center, some smaller ones, high schools, a library, and parks, some of which were provided by the builder himself. This was considered real breakthrough stuff. It was no less than an attempt to create from scratch what the builder honestly and open-mindedly thought was the entire range of local institutions and facilities found in the old communities people were enthusiastically leaving.

The venerable Gans—who was one hopping sociologist in the late 1950s—came to his Levittown project still whirling from having spent two years living in that part of Boston outsiders regarded as your basic Italian slum. In his book *The Urban Villagers,* he established that the West End was not a slum at all. What it was, he found, was an archetype of the even-then rapidly disappearing working-class ethnic "traditional" community. Marked by exotic shops and fragrant restaurants and narrow streets and high densities, it was exactly the kind of place that developers are now using as models when they try to breathe life into their new places today.

To be sure, the West End did not look like any architect's rendering of community. It had garbage in the alleys, rubble in the vacant lots, tenements with poorly maintained exteriors and rudimentary heating arrangements. So, soon after Gans studied the place, the West End was bulldozed. In the name of progress and on the order of the best and the brightest planners of the day, urban renewal rolled through. The population of the community was scattered.

The West End's influence lives on, though. The very phrase "urban village" is now used as it is in Phoenix, a hopeful synonym for Edge City. Developers still strive to create places that also "have it all." In Irvine, that includes not only executive-level housing and stupendously high-end malls, but transcontinental airport connections and, most important, the high-flying white-collar jobs that lift this place out of bedroom suburbia and into Edge City.

But some things do not change. Edge City is similar to what Gans found to be community in the West End three decades ago.

Sociologists in the 1950s were still working with the classic definition of "community": "an aggregate of people who occupy a common and bounded territory within which they establish and participate in common institutions."

What Gans found, however, was that community and neighborhood were not the same thing. "The West End as a neighborhood was not important to West Enders," he discovered. "I expected emotional statements about their attachment to the area. I was always surprised when they talked merely about its convenience to work and to downtown shopping. After I had lived in the area a few weeks, one of my neighbors remarked that I knew a lot more about the West End than they did."

Gans discovered that "life for the West Ender was defined in terms of his relationship to the group," not geography. What West Enders meant by the "group" was divided into three levels: the peer group, those local institutions which supported the peer group, and "the outside world." The "outside world" covered all other aspects of Boston, New England, and America that "impinge on life—often unhappily, to the West Ender's way of thinking."

An awful lot of people in Edge City organize their lives the same way today. In America the main idea behind community now is voluntary association, not geography. And the people of Southern California have sophisticated technology to cast wide their search for that bond with others we call community.

Take Evan and Ann Maxwell of Laguna Niguel. They moved to the hills just above the Pacific Coast past Irvine in 1970. The place was then mostly rural. They paid $39,000, with a $212-a-month mortgage and a less-than-$600-a-year tax burden. The location was considered breathtaking for two reasons: its natural beauty and its long commute to downtown Los Angeles.

Times changed, and so did the Maxwells. They are co-authors of the *Fiddler* series of mysteries set in Orange County. These and other books they produced were so successful that the Maxwells ended up relying less and less on Evan's Los Angeles paycheck. It was the half-yearly royalty statements from their publishers in New York that would shape their lives—and loosen their ties to the area.

In 1984, the Maxwells "cut the umbilical cord to corporate socialism," as Evan puts it. His final assignment for the *L.A. Times* was one he views as the ultimate for a "cops-and-robbers reporter." He covered security for the Olympics. "I figured, it doesn't get better than this. I'd done as much as I could in daily journalism. So I left." He does not regret it. He and his wife "have elements of freedom you cannot purchase, my friend," he said.

But, he observes keenly, the price was giving up an aching amount of community. "The newsroom fills up your life. Twelve or fourteen hours of your day. It is just as consuming and controlling as the small town in Minnesota where I'm from. When I left, I found myself absolutely liberated—and adrift. The paper gives you a sense of who you are. The first time I tried to sneak into a courtroom past a guard and I didn't have a press card of the *L.A. Times,* it was like I didn't have a last name."

Like any small, close community, "the social setting of the newsroom is supporting and constipating. I never realized how much my mindset would change. I have a close friend with whom I can't talk about the newspaper anymore. He takes it absolutely seriously. We can't kid about it the way we did when I worked there. I am an outsider now."

Soon, the Maxwells began to note that they had lost more than the community where Evan worked. They'd lost any sense of community where they lived.

"The last five years, all hell has broken loose. The last two years especially, there has been astonishing development. Runaway growth with remarkable similarity. The Alpha Beta, the Lucky supermarkets, all surrounded by video outlets, and an Italian or Japanese restaurant with carry-out, and a bagel and doughnut shop."

Evan does not believe that he is reflexively against this growth. He has noticed, for example, the seeds of civilization being planted first in the dry-cleaning establishments. "That is where diversity begins. Places that were first run by former USC athletes and then by South Americans were replaced. In came the Asian families, and they remember your name. The others couldn't remember your name after ten years. The new people are eager to do business, and the stuff is always there when they say they'll have it. You can't fault that."

He expects this pattern to expand. "It takes time to do diversity. The Chinese restaurant must fail and be replaced by an aggressive soft-taco place that is part of a local chain of three or four." There is now a secondhand bookstore called Mr. Goodbooks, in Mission Viejo, onto which, Evan reports, he has just unloaded a portion of his library. He views this retail development as a hopeful sign.

Nevertheless, the Maxwells are leaving Orange County. Leaving the place that has been their roots for twenty years, the place where their two kids were raised, the place that was the inspiration for the books that have given them the independence to take wing.

"We are no longer comfortable here physically. There is too much traffic. Our community is not our neighbors here. We don't interact with Roz across the street except once a year, when her dog gets loose. Our community is really much broader."

They put their four-bedroom Laguna Niguel home on the market because they believe that, for them, community is voluntary and hence portable. They hoped to get $370,000 for their place on an eighty-by-hundred-foot lot. That would pay for a "fifth-wheel"—a big, articulated pickup truck–mobile home combination—plus a large home on 260 acres of southwestern Colorado. The Maxwells would spend part of their year on the road, visiting friends. The rest would be spent in their Colorado retreat four or five hours over the mountains from the nearest interstate, seven to nine hours from an international airport. "We can live out there in Colorado without being a part of the local economy," Evan figures. "Money to us is the basis of our freedom."

Their community includes writers in Seattle and Indiana, agents and editors in New York, a computer junk man in the Silicon Valley who buys and sells overstock equipment, and a refugee from the Massachusetts Route 128 computer realm who now reconditions covered wagons. "We're in touch with them on a weekly basis by telephone, by fax, by UPS.

"Our daughter, Heather, loves to travel. Her role model is a friend of ours who works in the Canadian embassy in London. She met her husband here when he was working for the Border Patrol and she was working with Asian refugees. We speak to them regularly and visit [in England] once a year. The world is now a place where it is possible to achieve a sense of community that would have seemed idealistic or idiotic only ten years ago."

In fact, a semiretired Seattle physician who raises big draft Paso Fino horses is the friend who brought to their attention the Four Corners region of Colorado, where they are planning to move. There, Evan says, "the West still lives. Real Louis L'Amour country. We like open landscape, an outdoor life. Looking at the San Juan and La Plata Mountains."

In the old days in Laguna Niguel, "the hills were absolutely glowing. They were green in spring, turning to gold in summer. The prettiest landscape in the coastal West. There were red-tail hawks and golden eagles. We became particularly fond of raptors. This *was* the best place in the world to watch raptors conduct their daily lives. They are now living off the freeway margins, but it's not the same." The Maxwells expect soon that their neighborhood will hold 150,000 to 200,000 humans, instead.

There are considerable ironies to all this. The Maxwells are thinking about moving to that part of Colorado where old ideas of connections between humans and community still live. The reason they can do so is that their personal sense of community is dependent on microchip connections.

They recognize the incongruity. In fact, they plan to use it as material in their next book. They will be looking at the West as a two-tiered place with the old-line landowners and ranchers and café owners on one level and Third Wave people like them— semiretired doctors from Seattle and writers from California— on another.

To be sure, the Maxwells' portable definition of "community" is more advanced than most. And it is not without its flaws. Evan acknowledges that his son harbors some anger that the place he has always thought of as home is somewhere he will not be able to return. But the Maxwells illuminate a key aspect of any discussion of "community" in Edge City.

"Community" today is different from "government," "shadow government," or "neighborhood." It is entirely voluntary and thus fragile. If you don't like the ties that bind you to others—for even the most ephemeral or transitory or stupid reasons—you can and may leave. You are no longer forced to proclaim your identity as part of any inexorable membership in a larger whole. You must find in yourself the reason to create a bond with other humans. In America, the most highly mobile society in history, people reach out in a myriad of directions for work and play—and now they search in varied directions for society and friendship, even family. It is rare to the point of being bizarre to have the bulk of one's peers living in one neighborhood today. Even if you are "in the neighborhood," you do not just "drop in." You call first.

Peer groups—community—are defined by job, avocation, church, or some other institution, far more than by location. Oddly, government bureaucrats for once have used a word accurately. It may seem silly to see Washington news stories with references to "the intelligence community," or "the arms control community," or even "the journalism community." But these turn out to be real bands of brothers. All the people within them know each other. Often, they went to school together. When they were young and single, they dated the same people, many of whom are now spouses of somebody else in the group. They turn to their tribe for jobs when they're fired. Even when they toil for rival countries, when the chips are down they can be counted on to respond to their community. That's more than you can say for many neighborhood blocks.

This haphazard connection between neighborhood and community reflects how legendary in America are the stifling, deformed, busybody tyrannies of small towns. There's Sinclair Lewis' *Main Street* and Sherwood Anderson's *Winesburg, Ohio*, and the works of William Faulkner, and Peter Bogdanovich's film *The Last Picture Show.* Not for nothing have young people fled the rigid burg for the big city every chance they've had. The city is kinder to the stranger and the free-thinker than the tight-knit community. *Stadtluft macht frei* is a proverb the Germans invented in the Middle Ages; "City air makes men free." It does not choke them with community.

To this day, it is not hard for humans to create physical community. Any peasant in the world knows how it works. Just compromise your liberty. Stay in one house in one village for several generations. The rest follows.

The way we have built our Edge Cities, however, demonstrates once again that we have put an overwhelming value on individual freedom. Richard Louv, author of *Childhood's Future,* points out that the goal of the liberation movements of the last three decades has been to unfetter the individual. Traditionally, the nuclear family was both the fundamental social unit and the fundamental economic unit. No longer. If parents wish to "do their own thing," they may. A couple rarely *has* to stay together or face starvation.

This loosening of ties has had positive effects. But there has been a price to pay. Louv notes the increased sales in homes marketed as "family-oriented." That means a development with afterschool recreational facilities or day-care services. Parents feel guilty about not giving their kids enough time, so they pay tens of thousands more for a home in a subdivision that seems willing to share their childrearing burdens.

Homes have become financial commodities more than emotional entities. This may change in the 1990s. But with the appreciation of the 1970s and 1980s, homes became people's prime savings repository: their retirement nest eggs, kids' inheritance, college savings plan, ticket to a European vacation. Christmas memories in the living room were no longer vital. Nor could doorjambs be treasured for recording the height of children as they grew. Nor could these homes be secure havens for succeeding generations. For what was important was how easily and efficiently these places—these financial instruments—could be turned over when the time came to cash in and move on. Any feelings of community they represented were held hostage to the ever-present need to trade up.

Americans think nothing of moving. Families get larger, they move. Families get smaller, they move. Go to college, get a job, get married, get divorced, get remarried, get promoted, retire— each time, they move. Americans will leave behind houses that were the most emotion-filled places of their lives to move to a "retirement community." When asked why, they tell interviewers it was because they got tired of mowing the lawn.

No wonder Irvine looks the way it does, with the similar layouts and stucco façades that come only in colors that are variations on Caucasian skin tones from sand to tan, rarely broken even by a pastel.

This is real estate that moves.

When new, this real estate moves because it is the cheapest way to create new homes, given the way the market is now organized. Even if you use first-class materials, if you build two hundred of the same thing at a crack, there are considerable economies of scale. The alternative, says Raymond L. Watson, the Irvine Company's vice chairman and first chief planner, is not the beautiful old Victorian house on ten acres near the Condor Refuge. It is the concrete apartment block. Those traditional urban forms, he maintains, with their empty lobbies and door-lined corridors, are even more sterile and dehumanizing than the dwellings he pioneered. Forget factory-built homes. The cheapest and most successful way to build homes under existing rules is to move the assembly line out to the subdivision with prebuilt trusses and prehung doorframes and nail guns, the way it is done now.

Real estate built in such a fashion also moves when Americans do, which is, on average, once every six years. (In hot markets like Phoenix in the mid-1980s, the average turnover was every three years.) In a revealing handbook by Barbara Jane Hall, entitled *101 Easy Ways to Make Your Home Sell Faster,* one of the first tips is: "Avoid eccentricities: Your chances of selling quickly will be greatly improved if you can make your home appeal to a broad spectrum of buyers. It may be tempting to say of your home, 'But this is *me!*' but this is not necessarily a wise home-selling policy . . . In the game of selling, you have to play the odds."

What a wonderful irony! In order to improve your individual choices, the best bet is to have a home with no individuality.

It is in this context that forbidding walls around subdivisions make a kind of sense. In this analysis, it may not be important if those walls don't deter crime. They are social boundaries. They define "community" and give it an entry point, financially and socially: only certain people can get in. The argument is as follows: When you move to a new place, you still want people like you around. You feel more secure knowing the neighbors must have incomes above $100,000 or whatever to live inside these walls. In a world that is in flux, that standard offers certainties about people's values and education. Your fellow homeowners will have kids like yours—kids you could imagine yours marrying, if it came to that. The walls thus become a definer of social strata, a community recognizer.

This analysis pushes back several notches the question: What do we mean by the word "community"? Okay. "Neighborhood" is not the same thing as "community." It has not been for at least half a century. "Mobility," however, is important; we want to be able to join communities as we choose. "Voluntary" is also important; we want to be able to leave. Community should not be stultifying nor should it interfere with our freedoms. It should be a social grouping that is readily available. So where does that leave the relationship between Edge City and community?

Richard Sennett, a culture critic, offers this approach. "A community is more than a set of customs, behaviors, or attitudes about other people. A community is also a collective identity; it is a way of saying who 'we' are."

A city, to Sennett, is "a human settlement in which strangers are likely to meet." It is a "milieu of strangers whose lives touch."

Therefore, he reasons, Edge City must create community in the sense of being a place where strangers—people who used to be "them"—are transformed. They join "us." For Edge City to be a community, it must be a place that creates "us-ness" out of our separate and anonymous lives.

Mark Pisano worries about whether this is in fact happening in Edge City. Pisano is executive director of the Southern California Association of Governments—SCAG, as it is known. SCAG is the nation's largest regional-planning agency.

At one level, it seems astonishing that Pisano has any worries at all. After all, more strangers have been thrown together in the Los Angeles area in the last few decades with more manifest success than anywhere else in the world.

The future of greater Los Angeles would appear radiant. If you were to draw a circle with a sixty-mile radius around Los Angeles, and declare the domain an independent nation, it would be the eleventh richest realm on earth. That Sixty-Mile Circle would be the third richest country in the western hemisphere, after Canada. It would be the third richest in the Pacific Rim, after China. It would be richer than most of the twelve members of the European Economic Community. It would have the second highest gross national product per person in the world—ahead of Japan, ahead of all Europe, ahead of the United States, trailing only the United Arab Emirates. In fact, if the

Sixty-Mile Circle were a state of the Union, it would be the fourth largest in population and total personal income—behind only Texas, New York, and California itself.

As the great-granddaddy of twentieth-century-style urban areas, the Los Angeles Basin sports twenty-six full-blown or rapidly growing Edge Cities in five counties—the largest number of any urban area in the world.* If we count only those trips made by workers to their jobs, its transportation network moves the equivalent of the entire population of Massachusetts daily. Downtown has prospered, having undergone sparkling change in the 1980s, including even a subway. Of course, it still is not the center of very much, accounting for no more than 4 percent of the region's jobs.

The region's jobs, however, belie the image of Tinseltown or La-La Land. Los Angeles is the world capital of nonprint media, from movies to television to music. But it is also one of the most dynamic and diverse manufacturing centers in the world. The Sixty-Mile Circle produces more than 10 percent of the American total of everything from nuts, bolts, rivets, and washers, to pens, games, toys, women's fashions, welding equipment, radio and TV communication equipment, aircraft, space vehicles, and rockets. It rivals Northern California's Silicon Valley in its computer industry. It created 1.5 million jobs in the 1980s alone— double that of the New York area. The world capitals of Pacific Rim import-export and finance are Tokyo, Hong Kong, and the Sixty-Mile Circle. Greater Los Angeles is served by five major commercial airports.

At the same time, within the Sixty-Mile Circle one can find a stunning diversity of environments—ocean surf, rolling hills, canyons, mountains, lakes, deserts, and some of the most productive farmland on earth, as well as 139 colleges and universities and so many wealthy museums and lavishly endowed arts centers as to challenge the primacy of those in the East. The Edge Cities of the Los Angeles Basin contain a vibrant ethnic mix. America is going through the greatest wave of immigration since the turn of the century. It is absorbing more *legal* immigrants than the rest of the world combined. Los Angeles is its premiere entrepôt. The Sixty-Mile Circle is the second largest

* For the complete list, see Chapter 11.

urban economy in the western hemisphere, after the New York area. It is the second largest Mexican city in the world, the second largest Guatemalan city, the second largest Salvadoran city, the second largest Cambodian city, the second largest Laotian city . . . the list seems endless. It has the largest concentration of Koreans in North America, the most Filipinos, the most Vietnamese, the most Iranians, the most Thais . . .

Marc Wilder, an urban planner and former Long Beach City Council member, sees this exotic mix as a geography of hope—a unique opportunity to build a bracing, multiracial, multicultural urban civilization. "We are going to be different from anywhere," he says, "and we are going to do things differently because a Cambodian, a Hispanic, and a Jew share the same space . . . We will see new kinds of institutions made by new kinds of people."

But Mark Pisano of SCAG is worried. "We're grasping for a new community," he says, "and we don't know yet what that new community is. The individual, I feel, is very disenchanted and distanced from his sovereignty, whether that's a country, a state, or a city. It is the most significant challenge facing the United States without exception; after all, there is no more international hydrogen bomb. The historical example is the Tower of Babel. We all have our single interests, and you can't talk to one another, relate to one another. There's no way to develop commonality."

What Pisano dares to worry about is a Blade Runner future. He doesn't mean that in the Dallas architectural sense. He means armed insurrection.

That image is raised even in *LA 2000: The Final Report of the Los Angeles 2000 Committee.* The report is a sweeping survey of the area's possible destinies sponsored by some of its most prestigious elders. In its conclusions, it asks:

"Where will Los Angeles 2000 find its community, its city in common, its civic unity? There is, of course, the Blade Runner scenario: the fusion of individual cultures into a demotic polyglottism ominous with unresolved hostilities. There is also the possible continuation of armed camps occasionally sortieing out in attack or negotiated truce."

The *LA 2000* report proceeds from there to end on an upbeat note, seeing the future as bright—but wait a minute. Wait a minute, I say to Pisano. *"Continuation* of armed camps"? I know about the southcentral and eastern flatlands of the basin. That is an industrial landscape away from the upper-middle-class "nice" areas near the beaches to the south and west and the mountains to the north and east. That East L.A. and southcentral area is full of people who are struggling. Many of them are black and Mexican. I know they have more than their share of drive-by assault-rifle shootings perpetrated by the Crips and Bloods gangs. But I mean, seriously, how bad can this get?

Says Pisano: "Lebanon."

He means it.

"I don't think we know what the limit is. When things that are important for the whole aren't tended to, then you start having deterioration in a society. I think that's where we are. Southern California has just one luxury now. This deterioration is masked by incredible wealth-creating capacity. If that wealth-creating capacity starts deteriorating, I think we're in for one hell of a lulu. The gangs, for all practical purposes, are organizing units for the underworld economy. Hazing grounds for the labor force for the drug industry. That's a pretty well-known fact."

Pisano is not panicked by traditional Edge City problems. Traffic and air quality, he points out, have been a concern for decades. There are solutions, if we have the will. He is not even alarmed about crime as such; that too has been around for a long time. What he is specifically worried about is a breakdown in political stability. He is worried about a rupture in what everyone feels they are a part of; what everyone feels they belong to. He is worried about a breakdown in community between those who have achieved the Southern California dream and those who have not. He is worried about "those who've been disenfranchised; they may just go outside the political process. You have real anger, and you can have real terrorism. Now, I don't want to paint a bleak picture. But you asked me, If you were to push this line of reasoning, where does it go? It could be pretty grim."

When I talked to Pisano, the air was still heavy with the smoke from brushfires that had just destroyed more than six hundred luxurious homes and killed at least one person.

"A good percentage of the fires that we had in the last couple of days were arson," Pisano noted. "In the morning paper, the caption read, 'Angry and Alienated Individuals Characteristic of the Arsonist.' Well, isn't that Lebanon?

"That's why I think there's a real yearning for something—that individuals can no longer be every man for himself. They have to be *responsible* individuals. Until we find a way that special interests can exist with commonality, we'll build some nice individual communities but won't be able to deal with the needs of the full or the broader community."

Pisano's definition of "community" is one of the broadest. When he worries about a lack of community, he's talking about a perceived absence of civic virtue. Pundits have repeatedly measured it in the declining number of people who vote, the declining number of nonprofessional politicians who run for office, the declining number of people who are even willing to answer a Census questionnaire. And Pisano has a right to worry about privilege without responsibility. In Los Angeles, white Anglos are down to 12 percent of the population of the public schools, and Orange County is becoming a bastion of the affluent. The middle class is being pushed out to the inland desert realms of Riverside and San Bernardino counties in search of affordable homes.

But this idea of "community," and the perception of its decline, is intertwined with Pisano's belief in conventional government—especially a regional one.

What Pisano is really worried about, thus, is a loss of the sense of citizenship, what he refers to by the Latin word *civitas*. He yearns for a mayor and a city council. This is precisely the kind of ruling structure Edge Cities rarely have.

The distinction between community and citizenship is not a small one. After all, one of the things Pisano hates is the power of the special-interest groups. Yet who are these groups that so frequently block projects of large social worth? In many cases they are real communities that feel threatened by change. This is why destruction of a wetland or the building of a dump can spark so astoundingly loud a battle. The argument is not about asphalt and concrete; it is about endangered community. You can see it in Irvine when strangers band together to fight the developer's plan for new growth in a beloved canyon or along a special shore.

Developers are first and foremost agents of change. In Edge

City, change is a constant that people can get mighty sick of. Voluntary community takes time; instability is its enemy. Change causes people to feel like strangers in their own place. Community and identity then retaliate. They become the enemy of change—and the growth of Edge City.

And this is true not just in the Anglo sense of community. There is, in addition—especially in a place as diversified as Los Angeles—the vastly powerful ethnic sense. For many first-generation Vietnamese, Afghans, Bolivians, or Ethiopians, the knowledge that they are part of a clan, a band of blood brothers, is still their strongest identity. It is the primary way that they describe who they think they are.

So, exactly to the extent that community brings people together as "us," it also separates people. It creates "them," too. If "them" is Pisano's regional government imposing decisions from above, then the community may easily find itself in opposition to citizenship in his sense. In fact, in a highly pluralistic society, it may be dangerous to bring disparate groups together too closely. A certain distance might be healthy.

The lack of allegiance to *civitas*—the lack of conviction that most conventional government really is of, by, and for the people—is of no small concern. New York City in 1990, for example, was coming so unglued that the majority of residents told pollsters they would rather be someplace else.

But this sense of "us" and "them" is not peculiar to the twentieth century. History's keenest observer of American culture, Alexis de Tocqueville, pointed out in 1840, in *Democracy in America,* that when the common good was faced with narrow but intensely felt interests, there was much to worry about:

"Individualism" is a word recently coined. Our fathers only knew about egoism. Egoism is a passionate and exaggerated love of self which leads a man to think of all things in terms of himself and to prefer himself to all.

Individualism is a calm and considered feeling which disposes each citizen to isolate himself from the mass of his fellows and withdraw into the circle of family and friends; with this little society formed to his taste, he gladly leaves the greater society to look after itself . . . Individualism is of democratic origin.

De Tocqueville, however, did not see this as a fatal problem:

It is difficult to force a man to take an interest in the affairs of the whole state. But if it is a question of taking a road past his property, he sees at once that this small public matter has a bearing on his greatest private interests . . .

What's more, I have often seen Americans make really great sacrifices for the common good. When help was needed, they hardly ever failed to give each other trusty support.

De Tocqueville specifically noted, with his uncanny prescience, that community was rarely the same thing as formal government here.

Americans are forever forming associations. There are not only commercial and industrial associations . . . but religious, moral, serious, futile, very general and very limited, immensely large and very minute. Americans combine to give fêtes, found seminaries, build churches, distribute books, and send missionaries to the Antipodes. Hospitals, prisons, and schools take shape in that way. In every case, where in France you would find the government or in England some territorial magnate, in the United States you are sure to find an association.

I have come across several types of association in America of which, I confess, I had not previously the slightest conception . . . The first time that I heard in America that one hundred thousand men had publicly promised never to drink alcoholic liquor, I thought it more of a joke than a serious matter and for the moment did not see why these very abstemious citizens could not content themselves with drinking water by their own firesides.

In the end I came to understand that these hundred thousand Americans, frightened by the progress of drunkenness around them, wanted to support sobriety by their patronage . . .

Nothing, in my view, more deserves attention than the intellectual and moral associations in America . . . Even if we do notice them, we tend to misunderstand them, hardly ever having seen anything similar before . . . The most democratic country in the world now is that in which men have . . . carried to the highest perfection the art of pursuing in common the objects of common desires.

That is why, to this day, Edge Cities are the places where we invent new institutions to create community, new ways to connect with each other. Community in Edge City is disparate people voluntarily seeking connectedness in a single whole.

Many of these communities are as familiar as the Girl Scouts, the Sierra Club, and the Rotary. But as de Tocqueville predicted, the variety and scope are astounding. Not surprisingly, associations designed quickly to build community in Edge Cities are often created the way Edge Cities themselves are—ad hoc, innovatively, sometimes strangely, and usually starting from nothing.

Bob Kelley is the chief executive officer of an outfit called SO/ CAL/TEN, short for the Southern California Technology Executives Network. Orange County has been a magnet for high-tech firms. It attracted a horde of hard-driving, proud entrepreneurs, who started up their own companies and flourished. But when these individuals had difficulties, they found themselves isolated. It was, indeed, lonely at the top, not least because so many of these aggressive, action-oriented people were worried about exposing weakness. Further, many of these honchos had moved to Southern California from someplace else; they knew nobody.

SO/CAL/TEN became a kind of shelter for them. It is headquartered in Newport Beach, where 180 of these techie executives come together, in groups of eight to twelve, to be, in effect, constructively vulnerable. They acknowledge and describe the problems they have run into with their companies, and find out whether anybody else has dealt with a similar conflict. It is, essentially, safe ground.

The business of comparing notes on the pains of growing companies, meetings with venture capitalists, and other commercial activities at first went well enough. But soon it became more than that. People who worked together started playing sports together. Some who had come together for business reasons stayed together to work on the Orange County Philharmonic, Opera Pacifica, and the Boy Scouts. Members found themselves being invited to one another's weddings.

Then there was the day, Kelley remembered, that a chief executive officer walked in and announced that he had just been diagnosed as having inoperable cancer. Help me, he asked the group. What am I going to do?

That was the day this group really became more than a technical support structure; it became a community. It inspired trust and caring. The man came to the group to get his head together before goig to his wife. Since then, Kelley said, other personal problems have surfaced, with executives reaching out for help with everything from an extramarital affair to a child on drugs.

This is not an easy country to feel alone in. Singles know that. It is why Irvine has a branch of an outfit called Great Expectations.

Great Expectations was originally created by Jeffrey Ullman in the Los Angeles Edge City of Century City. It may be the ultimate high-technology matchmaker. More than a dating service, Great Expectations finds its main market, Ullman explained, among people in their thirties who are professionally secure, earn a decent income, are comfortable with their lives, but single —and not happy with that. The object of the game for this market, Ullman explains, is to *stop* dating. They are sick of people fixing them up with "jerks, airheads, and flakes"; sick of the bar scene's fake sincerity; beyond the kicks of the one-night stand. They are in the market to find somebody with whom to get serious. That means quickly meeting, in a safe and non-threatening environment, people who are reliably (1) single, (2) in the right geographic area, (3) looking for a relationship, (4) of like interests, and (5) reasonably solid professionals. It is not easy in Edge City for these singles to find each other, says Ullman. They work fifty, sixty, and seventy hours a week. In a large urban area, it's risky to approach somebody whose looks you like. "We don't smile at strangers as much. If we make eye contact, we look away, as in 'Oh, I've been caught.' " Many of the time-honored ways to meet other young people are not available. People in the Great Expectations market have already been through school. The church choir isn't doing it for them. Neither is hanging out near the chips and dips at the supermarket, waiting for a party.

"So these people end up very dissatisfied, and for a long time they stay at home. They figure, better you should read a book, or do some work, or go out with same-sex friends, than go through all that," Ullman says.

Or, for a hefty $2000 a year, these singles can avail themselves of Great Expectations. Its routine is complex, involving three levels of screening on each side, which makes everybody feel less vulnerable. Great Expectations leaves medical testing up to the individuals. Nonetheless—and most important—the system saves time. "You should be able to find ten good people in an hour, using Great Expectations. How long would it take you to meet that many people on the outside?" asks Ullman.

As a result, Great Expectations is now the largest dating service in the world. It grosses $45 million a year, has made the Inc. 500 as one of the nation's fastest-growing companies, and has been written up in everything from *Ms.* to *The New Republic.* Its forty-five North American branches are overwhelming in Edge City locations from Nassau-Suffolk, Long Island, to King of Prussia, to Orlando to Houston to Mountain View, in the heart of the Silicon Valley, to Bellevue, near Seattle, and to Edina, outside Minneapolis. The network has thrived by producing serious and stable relationships in brand-new places in the absence of the webs that used to be formed by family and society.

Leaps to create other senses of the word "community" have been made across even more astonishing divides. One of the more mind-bending TV spots for any local political race in the 1980s in America had to be Michael Woo's cable effort. Woo is of Chinese descent, and looks it. He was running for the Los Angeles City Council. The council at the time remained one of the West's more white-bread political institutions. But in the Thirteenth District, where Woo was running, forty languages and dialects were in common use. So to become the first Asian-American elected to this bastion of Anglo power, Woo made an entire commercial in Armenian. He read it phonetically, from cue cards. His message? It was about ties that bind. He explained how some very different ethnic communities—there's that word again—can strongly share important values: a sense of identity, a belief in family and church, a respect for elders.

It worked. In 1985, he was elected.

By far one of the largest new definitions of community in Southern California was created in Irvine by Tim Timmons. Timmons, forty-five, came to Irvine in 1975 as a professional motivational speaker, doing the corporate circuit, pumping up salesmen, renewing their flagging enthusiasm. After five years of that, Timmons realized that Irvine was a place with a far larger market than the one he had tapped. (Timmons is the kind of person who to this day refers to the Irvine area as his "market.")

So he started a church. The South Coast *Community* Church.

Timmons acknowledges up front that he has never been ordained. "I didn't think it was critical. I wanted to be able to deal with people eyeball to eyeball and just read ahead a little bit in the Bible. I wasn't interested in acting like I had it together. It was more critical to be one of them."

It worked. Timmons now has a flock of ten thousand. More than six thousand show up to be ministered to on any given weekend at one of four major services, the first of which is on Saturday night. Most churches in America have fewer than 350 souls. Timmons has a staff of sixty-eight, including twelve pastors. "I realized we would have phenomenal growth and impact, because I saw the church as the vehicle to create community here, where there is a lack of it," he said.

When he was first thinking about starting the church, Timmons recalls, a lawyer friend happened to say, "In the old days in Santa Ana, we had community."

"I said, 'Keep talking.'"

"And he said, 'I see my neighbors and talk to 'em. But we don't have community.'"

"I told him about what I wanted to do. He said, 'That may be one of the few things that could pull off a major community in this area.'

"All of a sudden, that clicked for me. So we started the Bible study in May 1980, and started the church in a gymnasium in Corona del Mar in August of 1980. We've gone from four hundred in that summer to a little over ten thousand in ten years."

Timmons probably will never go down in history as a theological scholar. "Christianity is so filled with man-made garbage and man-made deviations and rules," he says. "I was growing up, I was given ten things I couldn't do if I wanted to get my ticket to Heaven. Well shoot, I looked at these and saw about eight of 'em were my goals in life."

He goes to great lengths to dissociate himself from any whiff of culthood. His brand of Christianity is very laid back; he prefers to think of it as "pragmatic." He likes to keep appointments not in his office, but in the homey confines of the Village Pantry, a nearby coffee shop, where he shows up wearing shorts and a gym shirt and Converse sneakers. He goes way out of his way to avoid being judgmental. His catalogue of $3.00 inspirational tapes runs toward such selections as "Game Plan for Living: A Strategy for Personal Success." He's very observant about money. He reveals his salary to anybody who asks. It's $120,000.

Not chickenfeed, but not out of proportion to the mortgages in these parts. He drives a Jeep with no vanity plates.

In short, Timmons has been careful. As a result, an informal survey of cynical Southern California journalists voted him the big-time local pastor they figured least likely to wind up in front of a grand jury on their watch.

No one, of course, can judge Timmons' relationship to his God. But on a secular plane, he seems to have come up with a pretty good recipe for creating community in a place that desperately wanted some. Sixty percent of his flock did not have a previous connection to a church, he says.

Timmons sponsors parties in the courtyard of the church compound that give kids a place to go after football games on Friday nights. There is free pizza, free bands, free soft drinks, inconspicuous adults, no booze, and no drugs. He attracts two thousand to twenty-five hundred kids at a pop.

He actively seeks out members of Alcoholics Anonymous, and preaches at their funerals. He has a ministry for singles who are thirty and over. He has another one for singles in their twenties. Another for single parents. Another to get kids ready for adolescence. He has a children's ministry, a junior high school group, a high school group, and a college group. He has sent missionary groups to help people in Romania and China. "Who knows if it does the Chinese any good," he says. "Does our people a lot of good."

A competing evangelical nondenominational church that he refers to as "obnoxious Christians" spent the previous election trying to run homosexuals out of Irvine. "We did not do that," Timmons stresses, firmly. His stand on abortion boils down to community social work. "We're saying, look. If you have an unintended pregnancy, if you are considering abortion, please call us. If it's a financial situation, we will pay for the baby, we will pay for your counseling, for your medical care and for the delivery, and we will help you get the baby adopted or whatever you need to do. There's 20 percent of the people who are anti-abortion and 20 percent pro-abortion, okay? I'm going for the 60 percent in the middle who are basically lost. They'll always gravitate to the normal. What I want to show them is that the person of Christ is very, very normal and that that will make you normal as well. And that's the real issue here. We're all abnormal. Our M.O. here is "I'm not okay, you're not okay. But that's okay. See?"

In fact, Timmons is running something of a spiritual shopping mall. You can see it in his physical plant. The anchor is the fan-shaped twenty-five-hundred-seat auditorium with no kneelers but marvelous acoustics; a strong whisper at the focus of the stage echoes easily off the far back wall. Most of the surrounding structures look like low-rise corporate offices but function as spiritual boutiques. They contain meeting rooms of various sizes to which demographically targeted groups go to have their specific needs met. Some Sundays, he has to use satellite parking with shuttle buses. Timmons describes himself as "audience-analysis oriented," but says he's never found a need to advertise. In the basement there is a day-care center. Of the four hundred families enrolled in it, he says, 70 percent are not even part of his church.

What does community mean to him? "I think community is where people feel safe. I think it's where they feel that they're not going through this thing alone. There's something about that ache of loneliness that everybody's got. You've got to make contact somehow.

"We have a time in our service where everybody stands and they greet one another and I usually give 'em something to do. If the Lakers are playing I'll say whisper a prayer for the Lakers. It's the kind of thing where you've got to get people to touch people. I sense that's what they need. All these transplants need a safe environment where they can trust and depend on some-body. They need to know that they're not alone."

Perhaps it is in such fashion that roots are put down in an Edge City the size of Minneapolis that was nothing but a cattle ranch twenty-five years ago.

━━━━━━━
━━━━━━━

Tom Nielsen, vice chairman of the multibillion-dollar Irvine Company, is a calm, solid man. The face of his son, John, got a lot of its best chiseled features from him. Of course, the two look more clearly alike if you discount the senior Nielsen's buttoned-down corporate garb and adjust for windage with John, who has been known to show up for an appointment with long blond hair, peach fuzz on his face, glasses with thin gold rims, and a shirt marked with the logo of a pizzeria.

Tom Nielsen is a thoughtful man. He says ruefully, of the early years of Irvine, "I don't think we thought of ourselves as building cities. There was no vision that we were building a city for tomorrow. We were doing a better job of suburbanizing Southern California and trying to take the conflicts out of traffic patterns." It is he who, unbidden, volunteers that he has a son who is critical of all the works of Irvine. It is he who urges me to speak to John.

Tom Nielsen grew up in Orange County, in Fullerton. He remembers when "it seemed that the three miles from Fullerton to Anaheim was a long distance. You'd actually leave one place and go through some orange groves and arrive at the other one. Yes, I played in the orange groves. Well, now you don't know where Fullerton and Anaheim or any place stops and ends."

That's not the only thing that's changed since he was growing up, he acknowledges. "The way we've built houses—there's nothing that encourages you to get to know anybody next to you. You never see anybody in the back yard. I've lived in houses where all around me I didn't know any of the neighbors. It didn't bother me because I was so busy. We moved from place to place. Maybe I don't have the same need—the sense of this community that they're complaining isn't here. It doesn't resonate to me personally."

When we first spoke, he mentioned, "I've talked about that at length to my son who is a writer. My son? He grew up in a lot of different places. Never really lived in Irvine. I don't think he'd like to live in Irvine. Why? For all the reasons you've cited. We argue about this all the time.

"Have we created a place where you can have roots? I think you can. I admit my dad did stay in the same house for forty-five years. I don't know how my children would feel. We didn't stay in any house more than five years; I don't know where their roots are. I know where John thinks they are. He thinks they're at a place called Piru, where we lived in a huge old Victorian mansion and he was in the midst of a community that was a very special place for him."

Piru is just below the Sespe National Condor Sanctuary in a valley in Ventura County. It is beyond the San Fernando Valley, as far north of Los Angeles as Orange County is south. The Nielsen family was living there because the mansion belonged to scions of the Newhall Land and Farming Company, another legendary and ancient California landholding family, for which the elder Nielsen was working at the time, developing a place called Valencia.

"We moved because of another job. I'm sure my son would be happy to chat with you, because he has more than a passing interest in this subject. He reminds me that when we built this, we destroyed all the places for the nesting owl. That's why there's an owl on Tower Two. That's right. He keeps telling me you've got to worry about the raptors in this part of the country and you can't develop it all. He wrote a story on the condor that appeared in *Sports Illustrated.*"

Wings. The condor, which has a greater wingspan than any creature in North America, is so threatened it no longer exists in the wild. John, who his father acknowledges has a thing about roots, writes about endangered wings.

This was how John ended up in Virginia one balmy spring afternoon; he had come to work in Washington. Sitting over a platter of cold cuts, he talked of the intense conflicts he had had over such communities as Irvine, at the same time that he was going out of his way to be fair. His particular desires and aspirations, he understood, hardly reflected the American statistical norm. He mentioned his brother Peter to make the case. "My brother lives in Irvine, you know, and he just loves it. He works for the National Bank of Canada. He's younger than me. My role in the family—I'm one of those early rockets they launched right after Sputnik; in the old films they blew up. I'm the one that went with the monkey in it."

The first time I talked to John Nielsen, he made an effort to give Irvine an even break.

"I'm trying to be real rational about it, because I have a great amount of respect for my father, if not for everybody in his business. Building a community from scratch is not that old a science."

This day, he notes, "My father's really proud of all these things, you know. He's the kind of person who would not feel uncool saying, 'Every day in every way I'm getting better and better.' He's a very intensely mainstream person. That's why my father's in the business. He likes to shake hands, and his idea of a good time is either let's go to a zoning hearing or let's drive around and see the new project."

He acknowledges that he and his father have had a continuing dialogue about the soul of such places as Irvine.

"We don't have big long talks. It's not like we sit down and have an exchange and debate. It's like, 'John, we bought this house in Palm Springs and want you to come out any time. We want to give you the membership in the tennis club.'

" 'I don't want it.'

" 'Why not?'

" 'I don't know.'

" 'Why don't you want to come out to Palm Springs and golf?'

" 'I don't like to golf.'

" 'What do you mean, you don't like to golf?'

"That kind of conversation. I said, Dad, let's go listen to the blues. Let's paint each other and run naked down the street.

"He's a Horatio Alger. He really believes in that, and I think many more people agree with him than agree with me—BUT THEY'RE WRONG! I notice the principle of exclusion—extreme separations of wealth and a class system. They're not what I was taught these places would be, which is mixed places, attempting to re-create the city environment. These are places that people go to so they don't have to be around whatever they deem undesirable.

"There's something that gnaws at you. I don't know whose fault this is. But I think the idea of killing the birds that land in your lake because they foul the grass—you know, poison—I think there's something bizarre about that. And they say, 'Well what do you mean? Birds are a problem.' "

John is intensely interested in his family's roots. "Hans Peter Nielsen and his brothers came from Denmark and settled in Lexington, Nebraska, and most of 'em moved as a group to Orange County in the late 1920s. H.P. came with his kids Harold and Arthur and Carl and everybody but Einar and Olga. And Harold is my grandfather. He opened Nielsen's Menswear in Fullerton, which was this little island in a sea of orange trees. The clothing store stayed open till the early 1960s, when they introduced credit cards and he thought that was the end of society. My father and his brother lived in the same house essentially their whole life. They had a giant train set in the back, in a second house my grandfather had built. It was a re-creation of Fullerton. It was very exact.

"I guess you can see it coming. My grandfather always seemed in a daze when I would drive home. His wife died in 1969. He lived in this house and he wasn't leaving it. They would gradually widen the road and cut back the front yard. It was one of those L.A. homes that look terrific now. It was low, with a big patio and a shuffleboard court in the back and you have that weird green plastic stuff but it's all been bleached white from a zillion years in the sun. You'd sit out there with a dart board. My grandfather drove me to work once and he hadn't been to downtown Los Angeles for thirty years and he was just shocked. There were so many people everywhere.

"My father comes from that old Orange County world. He feels very much that he's a local boy. He's trusted. Although he has said to me, you know, 'Sometimes I go to these Rotary meetings and I'll talk to 'em—the older guys—and sometimes I feel like they look at me as if to ask, What happened? What happened to our world?' "

John's world was one in which "we were always moving into brand-new houses." The elder Nielsen was correct about where his son's roots lay. "I lived in all these suburbs and for two years of my life I lived in a Victorian mansion surrounded by orange orchards. It is just so radically different. When I come back, I go there. I took a girlfriend out to see it. I go back to Piru and walk into Sanchez Liquor. He says, 'Hey! That's Nielsen!' I haven't been there in twenty years. He says, 'It's Nielsen! Yeah, I caught you shoplifting!' He did! I stole a little red squirt gun. He told me to go tell my mother."

Community.

"I remember the place. I remember the sign that says 'If you ask for your beer in Spanish, you'll get your change in pesos.' It is the only part of Southern California that I know that has not changed."

Roots.

"I think everybody has a little treasured place and if that goes then they're not coming back."

Home.

"My father would always bring my grandfather over, put him

in the room, turn on the football game, and go in the computer room and work on the computer. I'd sit there with my grandfather.

"My grandfather would turn to me and say, 'There he goes. Going to play with that machine again.'

"I'd say, 'Well, that's the way he is.'

"He'd say, 'He was always like that, too.'

"So I'd sit there and talk to old Harold."

The Nielsens, father and son, readily talked into my tape recorder separately for more than two years about the differences in their perspectives. More of a challenge was getting them together. Finally they agreed. They chose the locale: California. Then they chose the place: the dappled pastels of the coffee shop at the Irvine Hilton.

They chose to sit side by side. Sure enough, the conversation soon came around to the subject of that Victorian house in Piru.

What is it that that Victorian has? What does it have that Irvine doesn't? I asked.

JOHN: This house was built to be a Utopia. The guy planted the yard with biblical fruits. It had square nails. It had curved windows. It was ridiculous.

That's not a legitimate alternative to anything—to live in a Victorian mansion in an orange orchard in an abandoned part of a country. I'm not saying I disliked it, either.

I've always thought that that would be profoundly sad, more sad than anything else, when I drive out there and all that stuff's gone. I don't care if they change the onion fields or the walnut trees—which they've done. But when I come and all of a sudden the Newhall Land and Farming Company has converted that whole thing to "Orchardsville"—that will be profoundly depressing. What for? I can't tell you. If you don't know, I can't tell you.

TOM: I see it as almost irrelevant to what we're trying to talk about. I wouldn't feel that way at all if I went out there. If the Newhall Land and Farming Company had found a way to convert the land and provide a place for people to live, I mean that wouldn't bother me. Yes, I'd view it as an improvement, if it ended up being a nice area that people were living in and enjoying and all that. They could even do parts of the San Fernando Valley there, as far as I'm concerned.

JOHN: Oh, Dad. [He looks up at his father in an almost pleading way.] You and Mom lived in the same house your whole lives, and I don't know how many times I've moved. You feel that I've missed out on something that you had. What is it?

TOM: I had the continuity or the association with a group of people over sixteen or seventeen years. What did I get from that? I'm not sure. I mean, I don't know.

JOHN: Well, there you go.

TOM: I know where my roots are. They're right here in Fullerton. Absolutely it has changed. But I don't go up there and say, "Oh isn't it too bad there are no more orange trees." I mean, I don't think we regret that there are no more orange trees left, no. Happy to see a new university and happy to see lots of things that have happened. I'm accepting the fact that we're going to have more people in this part of the world than we do today. If that involves the conversion of land in the Simi Valley to handle 'em adequately, that's okay with me.

*Is that okay with you? I ask John.*

JOHN: No. It might have been ten or twenty years ago. But now the thing that heightens it is, you know, the Simi Valley's all that's left. I mean, that might not be literally true, but look at Orange County. It's just plastered.

TOM: There's land in Ventura County. There's all kinds of land all over. All I'm saying is if we could come to some agreement I'm perfectly willing to say, "Okay, let's preserve the area out along that river." Maybe that's important. But we want to develop this part. Now, John wouldn't even let us do that. John says no to everything.

*Is there anything like sacred ground in the late twentieth century? I ask.*

TOM: Sure there is. There is lots of sacred ground and it's being protected in lots of places by lots of people.

JOHN: You talk and talk and I think you're right, you make it sound all so overwhelming, and this is the way it should be. But still it leaves me cold. You know much more than me and you've got it all figured out. And I still don't want to live there.

The coffee shop of the Irvine Hilton is called Le Café, and it is a pleasant place. The flooring and the glass walls have been calculated so as to blur the distinction between indoors and outdoors, making it air-conditioned cool but vivid. The table at which the Nielsens sit has taupe benches, with accents of yellow, aqua, and pink. On the walls there is a sixteen-unit enamel-on-aluminum piece of modern art. It shows palms, water, highrises. Next to it there is a little plaque. *Irvine Landscape 1985,* it is called.

The conversation with the Nielsens goes on through most of the afternoon. But it doesn't go much of anywhere else. Both are calm. Both are rational. Each is polite to the other. Neither changes the other's mind.

That outcome is probably telegraphed in the early part of their conversation. Maybe it is when I ask the elder Nielsen the same question I've asked so many other people in Orange County by then: What does community mean to you, as in "master-planned community"?

What he seems mostly is a little perplexed by the question.

Says Tom Nielsen, "It doesn't mean—anything more than a marketing term."

# 9

# THE SAN FRANCISCO
# BAY AREA

## Soul

Until it has had a poet, a place is not a place.
—*Wallace Stegner,* CROSSING TO SAFETY

5 MILES
8 KILOMETERS

San Pablo Bay

San Rafael

Concord

Pleasant Hill BART area

Walnut Creek

Berkeley

Golden Gate Bridge

Oakland

Downtown

Bay Bridge

Bishop Ranch area

Daly City area

San Francisco Bay

Dublin/ Pleasanton area

Airport/San Mateo area

Redwood City area

Sunnyvale area

San Jose area

## THE SAN FRANCISCO AREA

▲ Downtown

● Edge Cities

● Emerging Edge Cities

THE RESTAURANT looked like a California salad—twenty variations on the color green, with the occasional strip of purple. It was called, inevitably, Chardonnay's.

From a window table, the middle-distance view was of raw, turned ground. It was not, however, as in the old days of Northern California's San Ramon Valley, being readied for new walnut groves. Instead, it would soon be planted with a "town center" —a mall for the 585-acre Bishop Ranch Business Park, which already had more office space than downtown Milwaukee or Tampa or Memphis.

Despite the size of Bishop Ranch, Chardonnay's was its first "gourmet" restaurant, taking reservations and offering cloth napkins. And indeed, it was a sufficiently pleasant lunch place that you almost forgot it was inside a new Marriott designed with all the stolid, Stalinist, blocky masses of a Works Progress Administration municipal building for an industrial city on the decline. The balcony rails looked like bars on a state prison.

That Marriott exterior really frosted Alex Mehran, the thirty-nine-year-old scion of Bishop Ranch, which is at the core of one of the biggest Edge Cities in the San Francisco Bay area, well into the mainland on I-680 in Contra Costa County.

Here he was, trying to bring some civilization into this place, said Mehran, something beyond just office space, and the design was changed; the execution was flawed—

"Oh *yeah*, it pissed me off. No question about it. We've spent millions of dollars out here attempting to create the highest quality environment. It was a big deal. I was very upset."

Alexander R. Mehran is to be taken seriously about what he

views as a quality environment and civilization, for he is an urbane man. Of Persian descent, he was educated at Harvard in government, and then went on to England's Cambridge for law.

"I thought I was going to be a public international lawyer," he said. "Government, yeah. That's what I really wanted to do. As a kid, I always wanted to figure out what can you do to influence the most people to make their lives better."

He ended up at Morgan Guaranty Trust for three years, and he still looks the part. His impeccably tailored double-breasted suit is of a fabric so luxuriantly black as to match his angular jaw, where even the most glistening shave cannot eradicate the shadow of his beard.

But in 1977, he returned to what had been the residential development business of his father, Masud. There Alex became the foremost Edge City builder in Northern California.

Mehran is very much part of the San Francisco scene. He commutes seventy miles round trip across the Bay Bridge to San Ramon each day so that he and his family can live at that pinnacle of San Francisco culture and wealth, Presidio Heights. He is a trustee of the San Francisco Fine Arts Museums, which oversee the Asian Art, De Young, and Legion of Honor museums near the Golden Gate. His wife, Lucinda, is an heiress, the daughter of Tom Watson, who made IBM what it is today. Mehran's fingernails are manicured; his manner is both charming and disarming.

In short, if America were looking to put someone in charge of building its new urban prototypes, it presumably could do a lot worse than to hand the task over to Alex Mehran.

That is, at any rate, what we've done.

For out on the floor of the San Ramon Valley, over which Mount Diablo looms with a Fuji-like presence, four Edge Cities have erupted, and Alex Mehran's is the most premeditated. In 1987, his Bishop Ranch won the Urban Land Institute award as "a model of foresight, planning, and partnership between public and private interests." A previous winner was Disney World.

Indeed, no twig, no blade of grass is out of place. The Mexicans with leaf blowers are everywhere. Mehran has spent a fortune on landscaping.

"Big money," he agrees. "Huge money. Our crews that look after the stuff go through intensive training. How to prune and how to deal with an irrigation system that's very conservative in the use of water. It's very state of the art."

Chevron USA's largest office facility in the world is at Bishop Ranch. Ten of the top fifty of the Fortune 500 are here. Toyota is here. The seventy-five-hundred-employee administrative head-quarters of Pacific Bell at Bishop Ranch is so large, it features a fourteen-acre lake. There are master plans. There are enforce-able covenants. There is a three-pad heliport.

Mehran is very pleased with Bishop Ranch 8, his latest devel-opment; he is eager to show it off to a visitor. Out front, thirty-eight jets of water dance, in a Rockettes-straight line. They are surrounded by miniature pansies this October day.

Bishop Ranch 8 is three, identical, 200,000-square-foot, five-story buildings. Each has black granite accent stripes. Each has curtains of smoke-gray reflective glass. Each is crowned by triple barrel-vault skylights. Each has a five-story atrium at its core.

The catwalks at each level, inside, are railed by smoke-gray transparent glass. Each walkway has a half-moon balcony. The edges of the balconies are equipped with an irrigation system from Sweden to allow ivy to cascade in proper Hanging Gardens fashion toward the sculpture and trees below.

The central sculptures in each building are made of metal and moving water. In the first building, silvery brushed sheets have been rolled into a curve. That curve matches exactly the one made by the sheet of silvery water ejected from the front of the sculpture, completing a half circle. Neat trick. In Bishop Ranch's brochures, such sculptures are referred to as "quality state-ments."

The indoor trees are not in tubs. They appear to grow right out of the floor.

"Why trees?" I ask Mehran.

"Quality of life. What I'm really trying to say more than any-thing else is, this is *nice*. When I drive you up and take you into the building, what I hope you'll say is 'This is nice. I could work here.' We have a lot of significant art that's around. Those are all important elements of this place."

"Would you want to live here?" I ask him.

No, he haltingly concedes. No.

"Would your wife want to live out here?"

"Well, again, that presumes that the . . . We are city people.

Both my wife and I prefer to be closer to those cultural attractions of San Francisco," Mehran admits.

This is no small issue. Here is a worldly man who believes in the benefits of civilization as it is enshrined in San Francisco, which prides itself on being the most civilized city in America. Here is a man with education, taste, money, and know-how. If anybody should be able to build civilization into our Edge Cities, it is he.

But what he is building is Bishop Ranch. That, according to the Urban Land Institute, is as good as it gets in America. Yet it is a place so devoid of what Mehran values personally as to be unrecognizable as a center for the soul.

This is the paradox of Edge City. Will it ever have civilization? Will it ever have life? Or will it be a vampire, without a spirit of its own?

And if you can't build a civilized Edge City in the San Francisco area, where can you build it?

San Francisco worships the notion of urbanity. It revels in comparisons to cosmopolitan European climes. The weather is Mediterranean, rarely burning or freezing, and so are the views. San Francisco, like Rome, is built on seven hills, and the vistas from their garden-cascaded spines are of the sailboat-dotted, ever-changing Bay.

Preservation and renewal of pre-automobile downtowns—not only San Francisco's, but even Oakland's—are unquestioned issues of civic patriotism. The Old World charms of residential neighborhoods, from the intricately painted Victorians of Russian Hill to the donkey-climb roads of the Berkeley Hills, are cherished. San Francisco is so dedicated to "quality of life" that this town, which rose on the muscular commercial shoulders of gold miners, China traders, financiers, and stevedores, now finds its number one industry to be tourism.

Yet in the San Francisco Bay Area the majority of new jobs and wealth are being created in Edge Cities that have been pushed as far as physically possible from the undeniable charms of the old urban core. Half a dozen logical, closer-in Edge City locations have been leapfrogged.

This conflict between life and growth is crucial. To understand it requires some grasp of San Francisco's enduring schizophrenia.

At the same time that it trumpets its worldliness, San Francisco is a relentlessly introspective, parochial, and not very large place. Fewer than 750,000 people actually live in that political jurisdiction, out of a Bay Area population of six million. More people live in San Jose, to the south, and far more live in Alameda County, on the East Bay, than live in San Francisco. The docks have moved to Oakland. The melting pot to Los Angeles. The financial muscle to Tokyo. And new wealth and jobs to the Edge Cities of the Santa Clara (Silicon) and San Ramon valleys. The financial district of San Francisco, of postcard skyline fame, has only a third of the Bay Area's white-collar jobs.

Nonetheless, the *San Francisco Examiner* delights in referring to San Francisco as, capitalized, The City. There is something about old downtowns on small areas of land almost surrounded by water that fosters an islandlike mentality. (Downtown Boston is the same way.) San Franciscans are convinced there is little save barely explored unpleasantness beyond the Tiburon Ferry. Silicon Valley is regarded as a weird, separate, sprawling world. It is as though, inexplicably, a chunk of Los Angeles has floated up into the back yard. It is viewed as certainly alien and probably evil. Similarly, the wine country of Sonoma and Napa, an hour to the north, is distinct. These valleys may be great places to eat, drink, and show visitors, but with inland afternoons a panting 20 degrees hotter than Nob Hill, they certainly are not part of the *Bay*. Oakland's existence is grudgingly acknowledged only because the A's are such a vastly superior baseball team to the Giants.

At least San Franciscans concede these places exist. That is not true for the land beyond the Berkeley and Oakland Hills. Abandon hope, all ye who venture beyond San Pablo Ridge. At the other end of the Caldecott Tunnel the world ends. That is the edge of urbanity, of hope for one's esthetic soul. "No one" lives beyond Tilden Park. To move beyond the sight of the TransAmerica Tower is to renounce civilization. One restaurant critic who did so—for the sensible reason that he could no longer afford the prices of the Bay—felt compelled to justify his defection by insisting, desperately, that he could "still get the *New York Times* delivered daily" to his Contra Costa address.

And in fact, over that ridge—the Contra Costa County line—and through that tunnel, one does enter into the economy and mindset of a different world. If, as the political demographer Michael Barone notes, the coasts of California belong to liberal Democrats, and the inland ground to conservative Republicans, San Pablo Ridge is the cultural divide. Contra Costa's Walnut Creek is not merely twenty minutes from Berkeley. It is separated by world views and values and assumptions about humanity.

Right there, inland, paralleling those north-south hills, is the valley-floor artery of Contra Costa, Interstate 680. That is exactly where four of the Bay Area's most voluptuous Edge Cities bloomed in the 1980s: around Concord, Walnut Creek, Bishop Ranch, and the Hacienda Business Center near Pleasanton. And that is where some people think the center of gravity of wealth and jobs in the Bay Area may someday be.

There are seven Edge Cities in the Bay Area with more than five million square feet of office space, not counting downtown San Francisco or Oakland. The four mentioned above are east; two are south in Silicon Valley—the area around Sunnyvale and the one around San Jose; and one is on the Peninsula, surrounding the airport.

Depending on whose growth estimates you believe, between two and five more Edge Cities are surfacing. One more is out on that Contra Costa strip, around the Pleasant Hill Bay Area Rapid Transit (BART) station. Two more may clot in San Mateo County on the Pacific Coast Peninsula, of which San Francisco is at the tip. One would be to the north, in the Daly City area near the San Francisco line, the other to the south, in the Redwood City area near Palo Alto and Stanford University. One may conceivably mature someday in Marin County, around San Rafael. And there's always the unlikely possibility that the Berkeley-Emeryville area may grow up.

But this distribution of wealth and jobs is not the way anybody really wanted it or planned it, neither the developers nor the preservationists. It is a function of the Law of Unintended Consequences.

Given the patterns in other regions of the country, in principle the most likely places for Edge Cities to arise in the Bay Area would have been around the intersections of whatever road functioned as a beltway and the spoke roads that radiated from downtown. Especially favored would be the areas of Nice, where chief executive officers would want to live.

Near San Francisco, most of those options were blocked. That is what made Contra Costa inevitable.

The San Francisco area is surrounded by wall-to-wall In-surmountability. Most of the 88 percent of the land in the Bay Area that is undeveloped is *undevelopable,* according to Richard LeGates of the Public Research Institute of San Francisco State University. Everywhere you look, there are wetlands, or flood-plains, or mountains, or ridges, or seismic or geologic problems, or dedicated permanent open space, or land that is *verboten* for reasons of public safety or the protection of natural resources. Even after a third of the Bay was covered with landfill—which now, in an earthquake, shakes like an overweight jogger—there remained a very limited amount of firm, flat land on which to build cities.

To that has been added a great deal of political In-surmountability. Petaluma, a small town north of San Francisco in the Sonoma Valley, became nationally famous when, in 1972, it radically departed from traditional community planning by shutting growth down to five hundred building permits per year. Until then, communities in the United States had viewed growth as desirable or at least inevitable, and focused on means to accommodate it in an orderly fashion, even to court it.

Given that the opposition to growth it pioneered is now ubiq-uitous, it's hard to believe that it was only twenty years ago that Petaluma's call for a stop was new. But in the late 1960s, the quality-of-life and environmental movements were young, and in Petaluma, the widening of a freeway attracted hordes of com-muters seeking inexpensive housing, large lots, and good schools. This, of course, led to congestion, strain on city ser-vices, heedless exploitation of beautiful and sensitive portions of the environment, skyrocketing taxes, and long-time residents vilifying newcomers for destroying Petaluma's small-town char-acter.

The result was the sparking of the American limits-to-growth movement. Petaluma's stance has been copied, with results both good and ill, in hundreds of communities. In few places, how-ever, were the lessons heeded so thoroughly as in the areas near San Francisco.

Marin County is marked by mammillary hills, magnificent beaches, coastal wetlands, baylands with spectacular views, rural pastures, and narrow wooded valleys between untouched ridge-lines. The range of breathtaking juxtapositions may be unmatched in such small compass anywhere in the United States. Add the easy commute to San Francisco, and you get an extremely desirable jurisdiction that is the most rabid in the Bay Area about retaining open space and protecting the environment. Not surprisingly, the limits to growth have driven up housing prices. The people who live there are well-off, educated, and environmentally aware. Forget about an Edge City achieving escape velocity there anytime soon. San Rafael would have to more than double in size.

The other direction from downtown San Francisco, south, has similar constraints. The Peninsula is marked by places like elegant, manicured Hillsborough and Atherton. They sport stone-wall-lined lanes and the highest median home prices in the Bay market, a market that is hyperventilated by the standards of New York or Los Angeles. The old-money, "right" families made it to the Peninsula long before the Golden Gate made Marin accessible in 1938. This still counts in San Francisco.

Downtown San Francisco itself has put unprecedented limits on high-rise office growth, fearing the growth that has occurred already threatens the human scale of the place. In essence, only two new buildings, totaling a million square feet, may be built per year.

Due east is the town still referred to, by both its admirers and detractors, as the People's Republic of Berkeley. It was recently looking to put rent control on *commercial* space, to protect marginal home-grown retailers from the threats of more popular and profitable chains. Capitalism, most especially as it is practiced by real estate developers, is a whole lot less than welcome in Berkeley, practically and philosophically. Berkeley, like Palo Alto, has residents and shops that are impeccably urbane, but both places are accurately referred to as college towns, not large cities.

Thus, within the bowl defined by sharp edges of land sloping down to the Bay's flat bottom, there is not much left on which to build Edge Cities save the flatlands of the East and South Bay. Logically, the freeways around the Bay shore should have functioned as a beltway, with Route 101 on the west mirrored by Routes 80 and 880 on the east. Given the constraints to the west, it would not have been a surprise if an Edge City had grown up at every eastern point where this circulating highway was intersected by a Bay bridge—one to the north at the end of the Richmond–San Rafael Bridge, one to the south at the end of the San Mateo Bridge, and one in the center, at the end of the San Francisco–Oakland Bay Bridge.

That didn't happen, either. When Edge Cities began to take off in the 1970s, those flats either were covered with seriously unattractive industry, such as oil refineries, shipyards, warehouses, and containerized freight docks, or were packed with the homes of people who were blue collar to lower class to underclass. Many were black. A large number were unionized. This labor force did not have the education, skills, or attitudes that Edge City developers had in mind. These places represented too many headaches even to bulldoze.

It was at this point that developers took a deep breath and started casting covetous glances beyond the hills, away from the Bay, toward the far suburbs that had once been the arid farm country of central Contra Costa County. Walnut Creek was the emotional center of this area. It had been the market and financial center of the region from the 1920s, when it was, in fact, the walnut-growing capital of America. By the late 1970s, central Contra Costa was marked by big homes in bosky glens. These homes would have been viewed as breathtakingly expensive in most markets, but they were reasonable by the standards of the Bay. More important, they were physically and psychologically far enough from San Francisco that people already were beginning to look less and less toward the old city for their needs. When Edge Cities began to erupt in the early 1980s, then, all the ingredients were in place: an educated, affluent, underemployed work force of women; a great deal of relatively cheap land for expansion; high-end housing for executives; and business-oriented governments that saw in growth increased opportunities for tax money.

The result was office *Platz* up and down I-680. That road in effect became the outer, outer beltway of the San Francisco area. Where the spoke road from downtown and the Bay Bridge crossed I-680 at Walnut Creek, there grew the hottest job and retail center in the East Bay—larger than Oakland in white-collar jobs and more fashion-conscious than Berkeley. Concord, a few miles north, where the tracks for Bay Area Rapid Transit end, also boomed. Twenty miles south you got two more Edge Cities. That is where another spoke road crosses I-680—the road from the bridge crossing the Bay at San Mateo, leading to the international airport. One of these Edge Cities was centered on the Hacienda Business Park near Pleasanton, Livermore, and Dublin, almost forty miles southeast of downtown. Another was built in the vicinity of the Bishop Ranch near San Ramon, with the illustrious Chardonnay's. These southern Edge Cities are oriented toward San Jose and the Silicon Valley as well as San Francisco and Walnut Creek.

In fact, these last Edge Cities are sufficiently far from the old city of San Francisco that way on the other side of the Altamont Pass, smack in the middle of the San Joaquin Valley, the inland agricultural terminus of Stockton is now part of their commuter shed. Some people working in Silicon Valley endure sixty-five-mile commutes one way, starting at 4 A.M., in order to be financially eligible for a traditional suburban home and yard in such San Joaquin County towns as Tracy. No wonder the San Francisco metropolitan area now statistically includes Davis, eighty-five miles from downtown, almost halfway to Nevada.

Yet here is the antagonism between life and growth.

The preservation of nature, especially when it is as spectacular as that found in Northern California, is seen as a good. In fact, such nature is so valued that people will pay great amounts to live in its midst, as in Marin. But such homes are not seen as compatible with nature. They are said to "spoil" the serenity and peace and one-ness with the universe that people came to the area for in the first place. As does the traffic these homes bring.

Meanwhile, the yeasty cosmopolitan flavor of a diverse and complex metropolis such as downtown San Francisco is seen as a good. The most romantic and expensive neighborhoods of the old metropolises are in the "old town" neighborhoods, like Telegraph Hill, that boast three- and four-story walk-ups and very high residential densities—as many as sixty families to an acre of land. These, in turn, support all manner of good things in places like North Beach—from sidewalk cafés, to bookstores, to imaginative and idiosyncratic shops.

However, the most virulent and thankless zoning battles fought today are over any attempt to build new housing at such densities. Most people don't think they will be charming. They think they will be concrete towers or ill-named cinder-block "garden" apartments. They hate the very idea of living packed together, cheek by jowl, in such constructions. They view them as antihuman and antihumane. They don't even like the idea of living *next* to such structures. Under no circumstances is crowding like that associated with integration into nature. And yet without such densities, land-eating sprawl is a certainty.

Still, the creation of new enterprises—increasing jobs and wealth—is viewed as a good. Such activities take place, by definition, in commercial buildings. And most people put a premium on living close to their jobs. But if a residential neighborhood does become established as having life and spirit and a center and a wholeness, its partisans view the building of a modern office center close by as the end of the world. And Heaven forfend somebody should suggest a mall.

Thus, the contradictions between life and growth. Residential development is seen as incompatible with the preservation of nature; the residential neighborhoods that are associated in a magical way with the idea of civilization, like the Hyde Park–Kensington area of London or the Montmartre area of Paris, are seen as threatened by the twentieth-century structures that accommodate the creation of prosperity and abundance that pay for those homes. All this, while design professionals worship at the altar of mixed use, the notion that a "good" place is one that has jobs and homes and shops, as was common in Benjamin Franklin's Philadelphia.

This, in a nutshell, is the dilemma of the San Francisco Bay Area, the place that has always prided itself on livability and civilization. San Francisco has demonstrated that it has few if any acceptable mechanisms to bring new people and new jobs into its existing structure, other than by trying to crush the opposition. Instead, it forces growth out into the desert, into the area's most nether regions. There, in what businessmen love to refer to as "the real world," economic forces are more readily dealt with. But the price is high. Any sense of civilization or soul—the very commodity that distinguished San Francisco from old East Berlin—is scant.

Is this any way to build cities? Are home and nature and work forever cloven in the late twentieth century? Are they antithetical, doomed to remain in conflict, as every zoning board hearing seems to suggest? Does it have to be this way?

The evidence suggests the answer is—probably yes. But there is one man who does not think so. His name is Christopher Alexander.

Depending on whom you listen to, Alexander is the most innovative thinker of the last hundred years on the way we design and build our lives; or he is a dangerous radical who threatens the fabric of the building, banking, real estate, and architecture industries; or he is a delusional flake. Or some combination of the above.

He thinks we can build all of our buildings, all of our Edge Cities, with "life." That is to say, he thinks we can fix our world.

The views of this fifty-three-year-old professor at the University of California at Berkeley are the focus of deep respect and thorough disdain. This is why: Alexander, for the last twenty years, has been laying out a foundation for a new way of thinking about what we build. It is so sweeping, and so at odds with the existing order, that it is important to understand why he thinks its adoption inevitable.

Alexander believes that the way we have been designing buildings and cities, and our very lives, is so screwed up that the whole rickety system is soon going to collapse of its own weight. Even England's Prince Charles has taken up the cudgel. He has denounced Britain's architects as worse than the Nazis: "You have to give this much to the Luftwaffe: when it knocked down our buildings, it didn't replace them with anything more offensive than rubble," Charles said. "We did that."

Even the architects who are designing our world know there's something very wrong, Alexander would argue. Otherwise, why do they desperately tart up their Bauhaus skyscrapers with Postmodern neon lights along the edges, and Chippendale curves along the top? Even that last resort of bad architecture— ivy—is newly popular, cascading in every Edge City direction, shielding office buildings so harsh and disturbing that they are specifically built to be covered with the stuff.

Little wonder Alexander thinks he sees evidence in all directions that our current means of doing things—from the neighborhood-destroying skyscrapers of downtown San Francisco to the sprawling office parks of I-680—cannot hold. The collapse of this structure, Alexander figures, will occur as surely as did the collapse of the Iron Curtain.

When that happens, Alexander wants to be there with a declaration of independence. It starts by holding this truth to be self-evident. When people walk around a village that was built two or three centuries ago—whether that village be in Virginia or France—they feel better than they do on an asphalt strip of gas stations and fast-food outlets. Similarly, there are great cathedrals and mosques in which we feel an awe or a peace that is not present when we stand in the atrium of a new insurance company tower.

"Everyone knows that there is something special there . . . something which does not appear, almost at all, in our own time—something palpable and definite," he writes.

He calls this something "life."

And, he says, the idea that some buildings and neighborhoods have it, and others do not, is a fact.

Not an opinion. A fact. As incontrovertible as the idea that, with a tape measure, you can discover whether a door is wide enough to get a refrigerator through.

If you buy the idea, as a fact, that some places have wholeness and others do not, then, he maintains, you have set yourself up to buy his idea that a lot of twentieth-century architects' and developers' mumbo-jumbo is headed for a fall.

Alexander and his Berkeley associates are attempting, in the most empirical way they can, to discover patterns in the ways some buildings and cities and nooks and crannies in our world have life, and others are sterile and dead—and shunned.

This led, in 1977, to the publication by the Oxford University Press of *A Pattern Language: Towns, Buildings, Construction*. It was the second of what are now six books Oxford has published in Alexander's search for a "timeless way of building."

In *A Pattern Language* are no fewer than 253 rules of thumb that Alexander's team believes capture what it is that environments with life have in common, no matter in what century the environment was built or by which culture. What's more, the book outlines ways in which laymen can build more places of a satisfying nature, despite the burdens of our modern age.

For example, pattern number 159 is "Light on Two Sides of Every Room." As with all the other patterns, it starts by stating a proposition: "When they have a choice, people will always gravitate to those rooms which have light on two sides, and leave the rooms which are lit only from one side unused and empty."

A discussion of the logic of the pattern follows: "Please try these observations yourself. Examine all the buildings you come across in your daily life. We believe that you will find, as we have done, that those rooms you intuitively recognize as pleasant, friendly rooms have the pattern; and those you intuitively reject as unfriendly, unpleasant, are the ones which do not have the pattern."

An explanation is proffered: "Rooms lit on two sides, with natural light, create less glare around people and objects; this lets us see things more intricately; and most important, it allows us to read in detail the minute expressions that flash across people's faces, the motion of their hands . . . and thereby understand, more clearly, the meaning they are after. *The light on two sides allows people to understand each other.*"

The narrative then takes a shot at one of the Great White Gods whose architectural dicta have produced the slabs that make our world what it is today: "A supreme example of the complete neglect of this pattern is Le Corbusier's Marseilles Block apartments."

*A Pattern Language* discusses how to handle the pattern practically. In this case, it suggests that it pays to get as many corners into a building as possible—"wrinkling" the exterior design of the building.

(Digression: The ultimate symbol of a promotion in our culture is that we get moved to "the corner office." That has replaced "getting a key to the executive john." That is, if we do well, we are rewarded with an office that has light on two sides. Not coincidentally, developers have responded by building office centers with as many crinkles and jukes on the outside as possible, thus creating the largest possible number of corner offices, for which they can charge high rent. Remember Bishop Ranch 8? Its brochure brags ten "executive corner" office locations per floor, not four. How? Twenty-eight right-angle exterior corners and wrinkles per building. Whether inadvertent or not, this produces as many offices as possible with "light on two sides.")

The patterns are meant to identify the ideas that underlie pleasing places all over the world. At the same time, the book encourages the expression of this order in as many million different ways as individual imaginations can conjure up.

The patterns progress from the largest scale to the smallest. Number 1 is "Independent Regions." My personal favorite is Pattern 90, "Beer Hall," which asks that screamingly important question, not often addressed in theoretical works, "Where can people sing, and drink, and shout and drink, and let go of their sorrows?"

Being relentlessly practical, the patterns also address such unromantic issues as 213, "How should the spacing of the secondary columns which stiffen the walls, vary with ceiling height, number of stories, and the size of rooms?"

*A Pattern Language* thus shows people how to design and build to great and beautiful effect themselves, demystifying the priesthood of a lot of the professions—none more than those of architects and planners.

Although Alexander's ideas have rattled the teacups in more than one intellectual cupboard, some design professions have come to recognize the book as a benchmark. You can barely pick up a shelter magazine like *Fine Homebuilding* without finding yet another person who has worked out his new house or restoration on the precepts of *A Pattern Language.* The American Institute of Architects published a 1974 survey in which the pattern language ranked number one among methodologies considered essential for architects to know. More than a decade after it was published, as many as ten thousand copies are snapped up each year, at the daunting price of $50 a copy.

Alexander's critics, however, sniff that his output of actual buildings is modest. Even Alexander has expressed reservations about some of those. One project, he said, came out "still a bit more funky than I would have liked." Indeed, Reynar Banham in the *Times Literary Supplement* succinctly stated what can be described as the Establishment position on Alexander: " 'Arts and Crafts' seems an appropriate description of Alexander's activity." This deftly suggested both that Alexander was about as important as macramé and was merely derivative of the nine-teenth-century design movement of that name.

Those who consider him a threat, meanwhile, agree with *Progressive Architecture,* the bible of the trendy in the profession, which wrote, "What really irks many people about Alexander is his rejection of basic precepts of the architectural and building professions involving the allocation of money, timetables, levels of finish and tolerances, etc., that are now deeply engrained in the system." MIT's *Technology Review* observed, "Like Thoreau, Alexander marches to a different drummer with a kind of open-shirted, holy-man persona that can be irritating."

This is because Alexander couldn't let go of the idea that "thousands of people came to the conclusion that the statements in the pattern language are not statements of opinion but *are* in some sense true," as he later wrote. "To these people . . . the patterns represent a triumph of common sense."

This triumph of common sense was not trivial, he perceived. In fact, it attacked the logical foundations of the building of cities as we know it. Indeed, it attacked the Western world's view of science and logic. The key thing to understand about Alexander is just how basic his ideas are. He dates what he views as our current inability to build with common sense to the early twentieth century. But the origins of that, he says, go right back to the 1600s, the foundation of our modern world—the generation, not coincidentally, in which the Cavaliers first landed in Virginia, and the Pilgrims at Plymouth Rock.

It was in those decades that the French philosopher and mathematician René Descartes forged a revolution in the way we in the Western world think. Descartes's idea was essentially that if you want to know how something works, you can find out by pretending that it's a machine.

Suppose, for example, you want to understand how your arm works. The essence of Cartesian thought was to stop worrying about the hocus-pocus of the Middle Ages and to try to imagine the arm as an isolated mechanism. Can you invent in your mind a system of pulleys and levers that does this and this and this, and has certain rules, and will match the behavior of your arm?

If so, you have now got a model of reality with which you can beat back the superstitions of the previous thousand years' long dark night of the human mind. You can break down that model

into its constituent parts and adhere to strict principles of observation. Examine your arm. Does the way it works match your
mental model of it as a machine? If not, you must reject your
model as false. Strive to view your arm more purely as a complex
mechanism; completely remove your self and your emotions
from the equation. Seek a higher, better, and more detailed
understanding of how this thing works when you imagine it as
made up of rubber and steel, not flesh and blood.

This method of Cartesian thought is the foundation of the
Industrial Age. It has power almost beyond belief. It led our
civilization to fragment the atom and stand on the stark, dusty
plains of the moon. It has made us the world we have today.

According to Alexander, there is one hitch:

The crucial thing, which Descartes understood very well but which
we most often forget, is that this process is only a *method*. This business
of isolating things into fragments, and of making little machinelike
pictures (or models) of how things work, is not how reality actually *is*. It
is a convenient mental thing we do to reality in order to understand it.

Descartes himself clearly understood his procedure as a mental trick.
He was a religious person who would have been horrified to find out
that we in the twentieth century have begun to think that reality *itself* is
actually like this. But in the years since Descartes lived . . . after
people had used the idea to find out almost everything mechanical
about the world during the seventeenth to twentieth centuries—then,
some time in the twentieth century, people shifted into a new mental
state that began treating reality as if this mechanical picture really was
the *nature* of things: as if everything really *was* a machine.

This, Alexander feels, has had a devastating impact on our
lives. It limits our discernment of what is true or false to those
aspects of life which can be thought of as like a machine.

Somewhere, Alexander says, we got to the point where any
concern that did not fit into the machine model was tossed aside
as not relevant. If it was not quantifiable in that fashion, it was
not real. Even those who studied human behavior, such as psy-
chologists and sociologists, felt compelled to ape the methods of
physics, attempting to reduce the realities they observed to
equations. Considerations that could not be so rendered came
to be viewed as ephemeral, tangential, unimportant—even embarrassing. At best, they were relegated to the realm of the
"artsy." Let those wild and crazy creative types whom we toler-

ate as adornments to our civilization deal with it. Whether a building has "life" is certainly not of central importance to serious people as they routinely and soberly make important decisions about business and high finance.

Alexander wants nothing less than to bring that world view to its knees.

He thinks it's going to happen.

Alexander thinks that this mechanistic world view is beginning to collapse of its own weight and contradictions. If you really believe, like Louis Sullivan, that "form ever follows function," you can get some splendidly functional shiny new gas-and-go marts. But does anyone find them a comforting addition to the neighborhood, like an old stable? Or even like an old gas station? If you really think, like Le Corbusier, that "a house is a machine for living in," you may be able to mass-produce apartment slabs, but are they even as interesting as the engine block of a V-8?

This mechanistic view of the buildings with which we surround ourselves, Alexander feels, is imploding in a fashion not dissimilar to that of world communism, and for identical reasons. It is just not describing reality very well. It is producing lousy results.

If and when we come to the collapse of this belief—that if it can't be thought of as like a machine, it isn't factual—Alexander intends to be there with a more commonsense, functional model of reality. He intends no less than to define, systematically and empirically, what brings life into buildings, and to develop a how-to system that will integrate those elements into everything from our garages to our office parks. If he were to succeed, it would change how we build everything.

Alexander wants to come up with an empirical system producing replicable results that will allow people to view as a matter of *fact* whether a design is good or bad, true or false.

In the current understanding of the Cartesian method, that idea is preposterous. But that is one of the gravest flaws of the current method, Alexander feels. It goes a long way toward explaining why we have been building cities in the twentieth century that do not feel as good as the ones we left behind.

If facts—notions that can be logically demonstrated to be true or false—are thought to be exclusively mechanistic ones, consider the implications. If you were trying to figure out what kind of a door to put into a room, you could establish the mechanistic fact that a given one was tall enough to walk through. But any ideas about what kind of door would work best in terms of making the room *feel* right—whether it should be wood, or glass, or steel—could be expressed only as an opinion.

Here's the problem with that. If it is sheerly a matter of opinion that one kind of door works better than another in terms of how it makes the room feel, then it is *in principle* impossible to discuss the matter. You've got as much right to your opinion as I to mine. If you think it's one thing, and I think it's another: end of discussion. How do we measure who is closer to the truth?

The corollary is, if you think that a strip shopping center is ugly, and the guy who built it did not, that's your problem. He's got his opinion, you've got yours. How can there be an appeal to higher reason?

Here's what's so potent about the direction Alexander is taking. He thinks it is possible to establish that one kind of place will be a good place, and another a sterile, inhumane one, *as a matter of fact.*

He thinks it is possible to re-establish qualitative comparisons on a basis of yes or no, good or bad, beautiful or ugly—beyond opinion. True or false. What color the door should be can be determined as definitively as how wide it should be.

Like all grand theories, Alexander's can lead to some very strange places. His principle, though, is simple.

He describes different aspects of a place by calling them centers. To pick a tiny example—a doorknob. To discuss how big it should be, of what materials, what shape, what color—that is a discussion of one center.

Alexander then establishes that there are orders of magnitude to centers. If the doorknob is one center, then the door itself is one order greater. The room in which the door is placed, in turn, is one order greater than that.

Thus, the whole of any given place can be described as the sum of many different centers, and they of different magnitudes.

Alexander then says, simply, that every design decision will be valid as long as the following three principles are observed:

• That whatever is picked for each center is that which *feels* most comfortable and whole to you.

• Plus it must help the center that is one order higher feel most comfortable and whole to you.

• Plus it must also be supported by the wholeness of the centers below it.

That is to say, if the doorknob feels right *and* it helps the door feel right, it is right. If the door works *and* it helps the room work right, it is right.

This can be reliably established, he says, by an application of common sense that is so representative of the works of earlier ages as to make one wonder how we ever got into our modern fix.

When you have to make a design decision, he says, for the color of a wall or the size of a parking lot, ask yourself a few simple questions. For that matter, debate it with other people who will be using the space. Of all the possible ways you could handle any given relationship between centers, which feels best? Which of these possibilities contributes the best feeling to the whole of which this center will be a part?

If you phrase it that way, he claims, you'll discover that humans have amazingly more in common than you may think. You'll be struck by the unanimity of responses you get from a broad group of people. What's more, you will have a basis for logical debate. It won't be a matter of one person considering the mechanistic issue of a shade of red and saying, "I like this," and another saying, "Well, I like that." That conversation goes nowhere.

The point is this: you are not debating whether one person or another likes this particular *object*—a door, say. You are debating the relative merits of *relationships:* which choice for the design of one center feels best in the service of another.

You can then tack up models, splash on colors, pace off areas. You can experience how the alternatives feel and, he thinks, convince each other, as a *fact,* which answer works best relative to both the larger and smaller wholes.

This goes back to the overwhelming responses his crew got to *A Pattern Language* from readers buying the notion that they had hit on underlying principles. Alexander writes:

What are we to make of this? Since the prevailing canon of mechanistic science says these statements in the patterns *cannot* be true in any sense, we may consider two possible conclusions:

1. Those people who believe or feel that the material in *A Pattern Language* is true, are deluding themselves. Only the cartesian [sic] idea of what can be true can be correct.

2. There is some other way (not covered by mechanistic thought) in which statements can be true. The cartesian idea of what kind of statement can be true is too limited.

The second of these conclusions is less arrogant than the first. It is also much more useful. It is the main philosophical assumption which underlies [these] arguments.

The revolutionary aspect is that there is no limit to how high this process goes.

In other words, if you get to the point where you've got a whole building on the design boards, but it does not help the Edge City in which it is located feel right, then the design is wrong and must be rejected. Unless the building helps Edge City feel right, it will not have life. People will not feel comfortable in it. They will not like it. They will refer to it as sterile, antiseptic, chaotic.

Which, of course, is exactly the slam made at Edge Cities.

Alexander's focus on feelings is not necessarily as flaky as it sounds. The marketing and advertising industries, for example, are nothing but systems to perceive and alter feelings, yet they are recognized as about as hard-nosed as business gets.

Everyday business language recognizes that instinctual facts exist beyond rigid Cartesian logic: "I feel comfortable with that decision"; "I have a gut feeling about that." "Hunches," "instincts," and a "nose" for opportunities are ineffable but crucial keys to success.

Alexander is not talking some loopy definition of feelings—"like hot tubs in the rain," he says. "It's a more rational process. The actual bedrock is what's real out there. There is a wholeness in the material universe. Feeling happens to be a very accurate indicator of it."

Developers may have less of a problem than designers in dealing with "feelings" as a serious idea. Mall operators—who are rarely burdened with abstract theories of human behavior or political ideologies—deal with feelings all the time. That's why they are constantly sticking skylights and trees and atria all over their buildings—to make people feel like staying longer.

Prince Charles, meanwhile, has independently come to many of the same conclusions as Alexander. (Alexander was pleasantly stunned to get reinforcement from such an unexpected quarter. He was getting tired of people trying to label him a "communist" in zoning hearings because he believes people and designs have to work together.)

In fact, the Prince of Wales, in his 1989 book *A Vision of Britain,* sounds like a bomb-throwing Louisiana populist, compared with Alexander.

Charles writes:

As a result of thirty years of . . . burning all the rule books and purveying the theory that man is a machine, we have ended up with Frankenstein monsters, devoid of character, alien and largely unloved, except by the professors who have been concocting these horrors in their laboratories—and even they find their creations a bit hard to take after a while. The rest of us are constantly obliged to endure the results of their experiments and . . . very few people are pleased with the situation.

Charles rails against the

wanton destruction which has taken place in this country in the name of progress; about the sheer, unadulterated ugliness and mediocrity of public and commercial buildings, not to mention the dreariness and heartlessness of so much urban planning.

I believe that when a man loses contact with the past he loses his soul. Likewise, if we deny the architectural past—and the lessons to be learnt from our ancestors—then our buildings also lose *their* souls.

Deep down in our subconscious an uneasy feeling persists that there is something missing if we sacrifice ourselves on the altar of progress, and live and work in buildings which only reflect the technology of the moment.

One place that began to feel as if it were being sacrificed on the altar of progress in the 1980s was Pasadena, California. That is why it invited Alexander to rewrite its zoning code for multiple-family housing.

Pasadena stands at the foot of the impressive San Gabriel Mountains east of downtown Los Angeles. Originally a haven for the wealthy, and later something of an artists' colony, it has been marked by beautiful plantings and cottage-style architecture since the turn of the century.

Twenty years ago, it began to become an Edge City when downtown Los Angeles corporations started moving their back-shop clerical workers out to Pasadena's less expensive environs. As a result, there was a tremendous demand for apartment buildings to house these workers. Unfortunately, the apartments have often obliterated or disfigured the charming single-family neighborhoods in which they were placed.

That, Alexander said, did not have to be. As is demonstrated in every older village in the world, you can fit hundreds of people together into very small land areas and still have a warm, inviting place. What you can't do, he says, is what had been going on in Pasadena: plunking down outsized, cookie-cutter apartment cubes in a nice neighborhood, hoping the result will have life and feel whole.

Alexander's approach in Pasadena was instructive. In his proposed zoning ordinance, for example, he started by describing the key to Pasadena's grace as its gardens; after all, this *is* the home of the Rose Bowl. He then proposed to write into law the following: any Pasadena apartment builder, when figuring out where on his lot to locate his building, would first have to determine where he was going to put the apartment's garden of such-and-such a specified size. Then his building could take its shape from whatever space was left.

The garden had to come first.

The developers did not know whether to laugh or lose lunch. This man must be mad! He is not in touch with how the world works.

But how far away from common sense was this? A successful garden is a lot harder to site than a building. With enough reinforced concrete, you can locate a building just about anywhere. But a garden has to pay attention to the slope of the land, the direction of the sun, the existence of old-growth trees that can be adapted to use—the dictates of the earth itself. Moreover, when the garden is planned first, the building that is placed on whatever land is left tends to be less boxy. It almost *has* to be more narrow and long. Which automatically floods its interior with sunlight. Which would seem to be a gift.

But that wasn't the end for Alexander. He then said, Okay,

this is your maximum FAR—the floor-to-area ratio, the total amount of building that would be allowed on a given piece of land. That is, you can bring this many units in, with this many square feet, and this many people.

There was much groaning, but since the density was not vastly different from that achieved in current practice, it was not the end of the world.

The end of the world came when Alexander said, There's one more thing. When you are surrounded by beautiful two-story cottages, you are not going to put all that density into depressing three-story monsters, jutting up above the bungalow roofs. Your apartment buildings also must be no more than two stories to preserve the feeling of the landscape.

That was, as Alexander remembers it, the precise moment when the developers "split their gut."

"They said, 'You cretin, we can't build that FAR with that height. It's impossible.' So I said, 'Well, here are some drawings to show exactly how it can be done in a million and six ways.' I swear, to this day, they think that I'm a cretin for having pointed this out. But, I mean, if you're working at two stories in a situation where they would typically have been working with three, same FAR, here's how it goes:

"When you're at three you can place a bunch of identical boxes. You don't have to fuck around with the plan. You just put them in there, box, box, box, box, box. Finish drawing. Take to planning department. End of story.

"In order to do it at two stories, what happens is you end up with one apartment a little bit squeezed, and longer than the others, and thinner. And another one has an odd situation because it's on a corner or it's in the middle. It becomes slightly funkier, right.

"Now to me that's a plus because that of course is what happens when you pay attention to life. That's what always happens. Things tend to get more complex.

"The developers don't want it to be like that. They want it to be like a grid. Here is the plan. Finish operation."

The builders don't want to hear that in order to conserve ground, they might have to construct the apartment building's driveway at something other than interstate standards. Maybe they would not have room for two lanes of asphalt. Perhaps the drive might be one lane, with a cut-out to let another car pass. Or two separately owned apartment buildings might have to share one driveway! (That proposal was the one that had people trying to brand Alexander a communist.)

"I'm talking about the trivial stuff," says Alexander. "You know, the parking aisle has to be twenty-six feet wide. Really and truly, limit yourself to major safety questions. You can certainly make do with twenty-two. You can in fact make do with eighteen. All kinds of stuff like this. It just mounts and mounts and mounts. I mean, if you're going to fuck up hundreds of square miles of land just to deal with that kind of thing, you're well on the road to insanity. It's just silly."

In other words, in order to get life, you, the builder, might have to be careful not to waste space, waste land. You might have to bring more sophistication to your design and manufacturing processes. You might not be able to crank your product out in Soviet tractor-factory bulk.

But it can be done, Alexander claimed, on time and within budget. And, he claims, there is a huge penalty if this condition is not met. If the development does not have life, people will hate it; they will not take care of it; there will be high turnover. It will not help the property values in the neighborhood. It will not best serve the purposes of the investor or the owner. And if you don't do it right, somebody else, someday soon, will, and you will be driven out of business.

Ah, yes.

Well, in Pasadena, Alexander did not prevail.

The developers organized politically. They made the case that Alexander's zoning law would attack their methods of construction, financing, and design so radically as to make it impossible to do business in the fashion to which they were accustomed. The zoning law as adopted has perhaps 60 percent of Alexander's ideas incorporated into it, but in such a legalistic and sterile fashion that he views it as a defeat.

Not the first or the last, Alexander notes. For the one point on which he agrees with the builders is that his ideas, if adopted, would explode their current methods of operating.

That's the point. Alexander is not trying to shore up or tinker with our existing ways of building our cities. Alexander feels that the goal of every building today should be to "heal" the neighborhood in which it is located. And that, he feels, is the revolution.

What would a Bishop Ranch 8–style 200,000-square-foot office center look like if it were built to Alexander's standards?

Well, for one thing, it might not be one building. Alexander believes it is perfectly possible to build a good building that huge. But in this case, he points out, distributing the office space might be less of a headache than trying to figure out how to park the cars around the edges of such an immense cube and still end up with a place that felt human. The structure might also wind up with more or fewer than 200,000 square feet. If the structure ended up with life, a lot of space and money might be saved by not having to tack on atria and indoor trees and ivy. The space and money thus saved might go into making people's actual work space larger—more like the kind of workplace they've always imagined building for themselves someday. Or it could simply mean that the building never had to be so many square feet at all.

Also, is it not possible that some of the 250 square feet per worker is wasted because of the rigid way it is now allocated? The major corporate furniture design firm of Herman Miller, Incorporated, thinks so. It has retained Alexander to design a line of office furniture.

Suppose that line of furniture included as many as fifty components, in many sizes. Suppose those shapes could be configured and reconfigured by the office workers themselves in tens of thousands of different ways. Might be tricky. Might cost a little more up front. But suppose people no longer felt trapped in a slick and image-ridden workplace full of industrial gray and burnt orange. Suppose, instead, that office felt normal—felt as comfortable as home. Suppose that it also avoided wasting a few square feet of office space worth dozens of dollars each. Might that not be worth it?

The building also might not look like it came off a Henry Ford–era assembly line. If you posit that the only way you can create a building cheaply is with identical precast-concrete wall pieces and identical curtain windows and identical steel beams and a building site bulldozed flat . . . Well, then, Alexander points out, you've got a problem. You're going to end up, like the Modernist architects of the early twentieth century, with endless cubes; with things that look and feel like boxes, like machines.

Building a building that feels whole—that relates down to the land on which it sits, and up to the neighborhood in which it resides—requires thousands of individual decisions, Alexander feels. It could be that if you have an assembly-line building technology that cannot adapt to that reality, you will be at a competitive disadvantage.

Alexander does not think this makes him antitechnology. Quite the opposite. The systems he's talking about require considerable innovation. "The answer is not to go back to silly things like brickwork and stonework, which are completely impossible from the point of view of labor costs, but to use highly advanced, more flexible technologies and production."

Of course, the entire trend in world manufacturing today is headed toward increased customization, extremely short product runs, computer-aided design, and quick turnaround. Therefore, if the building trades insist on an inflexibility that even an American automobile manufacturer would no longer put up with, they might be threatening their own survival.

But what about the costs? Won't all this drive up the cost of your design? The cost of construction? Isn't this elitist? Won't you price yourself out of the market?

That line of attack makes Alexander crazy. He is devoted to the idea of budgets. He has no idea how you make rational trade-offs without them. He has built housing in Mexico and Colombia for under $10,000 a unit. He knows from cheap. Beautiful buildings of traditional societies are not all Notre-Dame and Chartres, he points out. They were built by ordinary people, using ordinary tools and ordinary design standards. Architects did not exist as a licensed, certified species until the late nineteenth century. Which, come to think of it, is about the time things started going wrong.

Okay, he says. Suppose that we were to pay more money for constructing walls with interesting nooks and crannies rather than sheer blank planes. Could we not make that up somewhere else? Suppose we make the driveway out of crushed stone. Doesn't take much. A couple of dump trucks with their tailgates cracked open can lay it down in a morning.

Would you have to rake the stones to get them flat? Sure.

Would you have to add more stones every few years as these sank into the ground? Of course. Will that force people to drive more slowly than they might on asphalt? Yes. Will it be cheap? You bet. Will it have a nice crunch that announces cars as they arrive? Yes. Will grass grow up in the crown between the wheels? Yes. Will that look interesting over time? Yes. Is it possible under the zoning laws of most jurisdictions today?

Absolutely not.

Instead, a driveway is required to have so much excavation and concrete that it will not crack under any foreseeable earthquake.

Was that well intentioned?

Perhaps. But, Alexander says, don't tell him he is the one being irrational about costs. Not when zoning requirements force people to spend $30,000 on an impregnable driveway that gets an occasional five-mile-per-hour use.

"We're talking about real life here. We're not talking about some fantasy. Something that's going to be in a magazine. Real life has linoleum. It has cracks. It has diapers. Real life is just different from *Architectural Digest*. If you try to create an environment that's not like real life, you're in deep trouble."

Here is the issue. Here is where the rubber hits the road on Alexander's theories, politically and economically.

Let us suppose, for the sake of argument, that Alexander's foes are correct. Let us say that if developers followed the precepts that Alexander claims are necessary to produce Edge Cities with life, they would have to alter everything they do. Let's say they'd have to rethink how they use land, the technologies they use to build buildings, the zoning methods, the "safety" standards that waste resources, the financing, the priesthood of planning and architecture.

Let's say that's all true.

Here's the key question.

Does this hoot Alexander's commonsense patterns out the door?

Or is this just another example of an apparently impervious twentieth-century system that is heading for a collapse once its contradictions are acknowledged?

All it takes is for a system—no matter how seemingly unassailable—to have flaws that consistently outweigh its benefits.

Stephen Grabow, former director of architecture at the University of Kansas, thinks this raises Alexander's ideas to august company, indeed.

People used to think that the earth was the center of the universe, around which all else revolved, Grabow points out. The logical corollary of this was that man was the most important thing in the universe, the prime thing on God's mind. Then along came Copernicus. His model of reality fit the observable facts better, with the earth revolving around the sun, a not particularly distinguished star on the outer edge of a not terribly important galaxy. And ideas have consequences. People were forced to think about themselves in a more broad way. It affected theology, literature, government.

That kind of wholesale rethinking of who we are, and what kind of world we live in, is referred to by the students of such things as a "paradigm shift." A paradigm is a basic model of how things work. It touches everything. After a shift in world paradigms, it is tough to remember how or why people used to think the way they did.

Another paradigm shift occurred in this century when Einstein's discoveries began to seep into the public consciousness. Realities that we thought to be distinct—matter and energy, space and time—were different aspects of the same thing. We began to realize that everything really is relative.

Grabow thinks we may be on the verge of such a paradigm shift in our cities. In his 1983 book, *Christopher Alexander: The Search for a New Paradigm in Architecture,* he says: "Modern architecture no longer produces buildings that satisfy people's needs . . . Modern buildings are dysfunctional . . . They do not look and feel pleasing to an increasing number of architects themselves."

What heralds a paradigm shift? A period in which "the existing or current paradigm starts to break down in the face of novel events that it cannot explain or deal with," he says.

Could such a paradigm-shifting event be the rise of Edge City, the first urban agglomerations of the values and attitudes of the late twentieth century?

Alexander, Grabow notes, was a scientist (trained in mathematics, physics, and chemistry) as well as an architect, and he approached the dehumanizing qualities of the concrete, steel, and glass boxes of our era with a scientific rationalism not usually associated with architecture.

This is how Alexander ended up examining cities as if they were spiderwebs or snowflakes or humans. They can be beautiful, and never the same twice. But could not each one be the result of some simple, basic rules that are there for the discovery?

Indeed. "Like H. G. Wells, Julian Huxley, or Teilhard de Chardin . . . Alexander is convinced that the deep sense of human purpose and meaning previously provided by religion can be objectively rediscovered," Grabow writes.

This too puts Alexander in august, if disconcerting, company.

Many physicists now seriously believe that in order for quantum mechanics to mesh with general relativity in a "theory of everything," the universe must be thought of as having at least eleven dimensions.

If you do not find that sufficiently unnerving, on the frontier of "chaos theory," other physicists state that only about 1 percent of reality can be described by direct, mechanistic, linear equations. Life itself, they say, is most especially the kind of thing that can not be modeled by Cartesian reduction.

Thus, what should perhaps come as no surprise is the direction that cosmologists are taking as they look at the first trillionth of a trillionth of a second of the birth of the universe. "There appeared a singularity, a dimensionless point containing all there was to be," they write about the moment of quantum fluctuation in which everything was created out of nothing. Sober reviewers read this stuff, shake their heads, and mutter, "This sounds an awful lot like 'And God said, "Let there be Light."'" Cosmologists shrug their shoulders. They do not disagree.

It is into similarly spooky terrain that Alexander has headed as he searches to uncover his rules for what creates "life."

ALEXANDER: One of the things you haven't asked me very much about is God, and spirit and soul.

GARREAU: I knew we had to get to that.

A: The only thing I want to say is we've been talking about

these amiable little things—is death visible in everyday life, is the window painted, et cetera. You might think, well, those are practical matters; now let's talk about spirit and soul. And my statement to you is we *have* been talking about spirit and soul.

What I am saying is, that *is* God and spirit and soul. All of that. All of that. The discussion we've been having for the last hour has been about that. The "life" which really exists in space and in the world is not a separate issue from the issue of God and soul. You've got to take it as seriously as the question of "What is 'life'?" or "What is 'wholeness'?"

It isn't enough to say: Well, yes, the developers are looking for wholeness just because they happen to want to throw a bunch of shops in. That's not wholeness. I mean, that may be an intelligent idea. But it's not wholeness. And just because they want to mix workplace with housing, that's also very intelligent, a good idea.

G: Is the logic that somehow this is an affront to God?

A: You mean in what they do? I think the answer to it is yes, it is. It's a somewhat quaint and old-fashioned way of talking about it, but if I take it at face value, the answer is yes.

G: This is the core of my question. These places lack soul. How then do you get soul into 580 and 680? Your position would be essentially that there does exist a sense of spirituality and Godness? What we are trying to do is no less than create places that are as spiritual and as whole as the old villages and cities of Britain and France that everybody loves when they go there?

A: Right. And churches. In a nutshell.

G: Not trying to re-create those villages per se. But how do we do our vernacular version of that?

A: Exactly. That's the whole thing in a nutshell. Good statement.

G: It's not just that we're talking good architecture or good dollars, but if this works you are aiming at a reconnection between humans and their world and by implication the universe and a Godhead?

A: Yes, and the ultimate stuff the universe is really made of. Yes, it's a godlike stuff, yes. And may *be* God. I'm not sure.

G: You think there are principles out there which you are discovering and stating?

A: Yes. Right. Absolutely. Discovering is the operative word.

Actually, I view myself almost as a physicist. You know, a lot has been written about these so-called paradigm shifts. And the main test is not—does this experiment work or does that experiment work? The main test is—afterward so many more things all make sense. You just gradually abandon the other thing. I think that one of the things people are beginning to say about what I've done is that, apart from appearing to be true in the small, somehow the whole picture just seems incredibly more similar to what we actually believe deep down but haven't had a model for. It conforms to human experience as she is, more.

The curious thing is, you still have stars in your eyes that money is the driving force. That it's backstopping American freedom and freedom of thought and freedom of action and the best of all possible worlds.

G: I have a very healthy regard for greed as a social motivator.

A: Right. I think that's where you and I differ. I believe that motive will not produce what you are looking for. That seems to me a very serious matter. I'm not sure I've faced it ever quite that straightforwardly. I suspect it's fundamentally incompatible.

Let me just tell you the extreme. I don't know that it's correct. But one extreme version is: The only way to produce life is—to be religiously inspired. That's definitely what happened in the Middle Ages for sure. It's what happened in Buddhist constructions in Japan and so on and so forth. We know that. People were trying to make something as a gift to God. One possibility is you can't get life unless that's the only thing you're trying to do.

G: The *only* thing you're trying to do?

A: Well, okay, let's try a couple of versions. That's number one. That's the extreme. And the second one is—you can't get life unless this is what you're *trying* to do. That's the second possibility.

Now the third one is that there's some mixed motive.

G: If you build life into your building, it pays off, therefore you do it?

A: My guess is that that is complete foolishness. That it just simply isn't like that.

G: There is one place in Walnut Creek that's 100 percent full. I plan on going to look at it.

A: Very interesting. Anyway, I'm just telling you that on the one hand you're concerned about spirit and soul; I think it's fair to say in some sense you'd like to see it there. Exactly. I think you believe at the moment that by some minor modification in the Adam Smith thing you're going to get it. Or at least that's the hypothesis that you've been putting to me. If this thing could be quantified and if it pays off, then it's just going to happen, right?

G: If true, the millennium would be at hand.

A: Yes, and what I'm saying to you is that I assume that it is not true. It's not like money plays no role. That is just nonsense. I think money plays a fundamental role in this thing. You have to decide exactly how much to spend on what. You can't be trivial about that. Money plays a fundamental role even in the most extreme version.

G: But your getting a lot of it is not part of it?

A: You understand the difference?

G: Budgets are tremendously important, but that doesn't necessarily mean that you get rich?

A: Exactly. Right. It has never occurred to me that life would quote "pay off" in the way that you're talking about. Honestly, it seems a bit crass to me. The formulation you gave of quantifying life—the Adam Smith version, exactly. That one I don't believe in—just from a practical point of view. I don't think it pays off in monetary terms. It pays off in other terms. It may not translate easily into money.

I know you don't like that.

G: Edge Cities are monuments to maximization of the individual ego and monuments to profit.

A: Right. So anyway my middle ground, which I'm sort of trying to figure out right now, is some kind of mechanics where there is some sort of profit motive for people who want to spend their lives doing development. Whether such a model is possible, I don't know. I mean I don't know that it's humanly possible to have those two things in your mind in such a balance.

G: Are you saying it is as utterly desirable and utterly unlikely as the Greek ideal of the philosopher king?

A: It's like that, yes. It's something like that.

My last evening in Walnut Creek I decided to spend searching for Walnuts or the Creek.

The walnuts were easily dispensed with. Little of their legacy is left. Jim Kennedy, Contra Costa County's redevelopment director, had shown me one small grove that still stood, jutting into Oak Road. It was perhaps four acres, guarded by a wire fence, and obviously threatened. Oak Road had been widened to four lanes as it approached this grove and as it left. So the trees that had once been beside the road were now out of place, intruding into the new road. The little piece of land had been bought for a park, but the trees in the middle of the road's new path were obviously an anomaly, their days numbered. A thousand yards beyond them, tower cranes were busy, erecting the precast concrete of the brand-new Pleasant Hill BART Edge City.

While I was at it I asked Kennedy if there was in fact a hill in Pleasant Hill. Scanning the near horizon, all I saw were bulldozers.

He said there were several hills, actually.

I asked if they were pleasant.

He laughed.

The creek was harder. Studying maps, I found no watercourse. Just two little roads called Creekside Drive and Cross Creek Road. They turned out to be right where I-680 dumps down into Main Street. I got in the car and did in fact discover the Creekside Terrace "garden apartments." But the only thing I found that looked like a creek was this muddy little thing that was basically a channelized ditch. It had been lined with vertical concrete walls laid out straight as an arrow. Flood control. It had a little water at its bottom. But this couldn't be the Walnut Creek creek.

Could it?

The old Southern Pacific line to town was built on one side of this ditch, parallel to it. Main Street was on the other.

I kept driving.

The channel disappeared from view as the parking lots and stores that lined South Main Street came between it and the road. It reappeared suddenly behind the Broadway East Chinese Restaurant. I made a U-turn, came back. Went in, asked the nice young Asian people in the restaurant if they knew where I might be able to find the creek of Walnut Creek. Right up the road, they said, Walnut Creek. No, I said, not the city. The creek. Gee, they said. Sorry. What's that water thing, I asked, ten yards from the back of the restaurant? Everyone was very mystified.

I got back into the car.

As I was coming back into town, the creek disappeared completely. It seemed to vanish beneath a store called Emporium Capwell, near Broadway. I kept driving, past Nordstrom's, Victoria's Secret, and The Nature Company, and came out the other end of the city center. A cop off to the side of Mount Diablo Boulevard was aiming a radar gun at the citizenry. I stopped and asked him if he knew where the creek was. Sorry, he said. I'm new here myself.

I drove back through town and stopped in the parking lot of the Devil Mountain Brewery Restaurant to take another look at the channel. It was maybe twenty feet deep and the same across. A square concrete trough with an open top. "Property of the Central Costa County Sanitary District," said the sign on the mean-looking fence. In case of emergency call 1-415-933-0955.

I retraced my trail, back through town.

Passing a Mexican restaurant called The Cantina, at Broadway and Lincoln, through the car's open windows, I finally heard what I'd been listening for. Rushing water. I stopped.

The evening was fragrant with live oak trees. Abundant bamboo edged a very steep rocky gorge. A pleasant wooden walkway stretched along it, with soft lighting. A hole had been cut in the pathway to spare a big tree. Nearby had been placed heavy bronze silhouettes of a man and a woman and a dog, playing. Abundant water splashed over natural rocks.

The screened-in porch of the Cantina overlooked the edge of the water sound. With the soft autumn lights, and the Mediterranean air, it was, in fact, full of life.

Yes, said The Cantina's manager, dressed in a kelly green sweater, with a mariachi band playing behind him. You have found Walnut Creek.

Prince Charles comes to this conclusion:

It was Edmund Burke who wrote that a healthy civilisation exists with three relationships intact. It has a relationship with the present, a relationship with the future, and a relationship with the past. When the past feeds and sustains the present and the future, you have a civilised society. It was only in this century that we broke that pact with the past and tried to obliterate its meanings and its messages.

So writes the prince at the end of his book.

What is the point, for example, of being the most technologically advanced society if, at the same time, we lose our soul, and forfeit the right to be considered civilised? For this is what we have allowed to happen by deluding ourselves that we are somehow immortal; by losing our faith in eternity; by believing that this Earth was made for our dominion, and by losing that proper sense of humility that enables us to live in gentle harmony with our surroundings and with God's creation. Why else is it that we now find ourselves confronted by such complex and disturbing environmental problems threatening, as they do, the very survival of this planet and *all* of its living inhabitants?

Everything cries out for a reappraisal of our values and attitudes.

Don't be intimidated by those who deride such views. They have had their day.

Look at the soulless mess in which they have left us all!

# 10

# WASHINGTON

## The Land

The past is never dead. It's not even past.
—*William Faulkner*

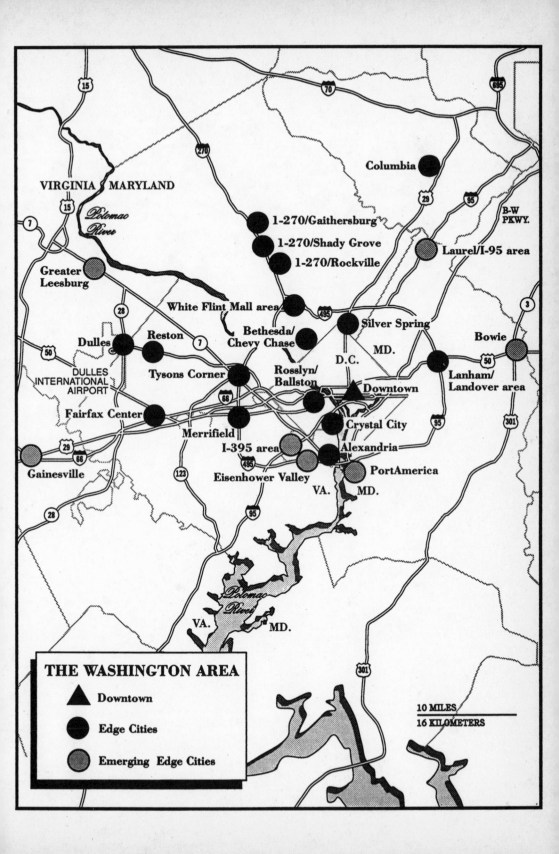

# THE WASHINGTON AREA

VIRGINIA    MARYLAND

*Potomac River*

Columbia

I-270/Gaithersburg
I-270/Shady Grove
I-270/Rockville

Laurel/I-95 area

B-W PKWY.

Greater Leesburg

White Flint Mall area

Silver Spring

Bowie

Dulles    Reston

Bethesda/Chevy Chase

MD.

Lanham/Landover area

DULLES INTERNATIONAL AIRPORT

Tysons Corner

Rosslyn/Ballston

D.C.

Fairfax Center

Downtown

Merrifield

Crystal City

I-395 area

Alexandria

Gainesville

Eisenhower Valley

PortAmerica

VA.    MD.

VA.    MD.

*Potomac River*

▲ Downtown

● Edge Cities

● Emerging Edge Cities

10 MILES
16 KILOMETERS

# I

# Manassas: Long Ago and Far Away

THIRTY MILES west of the U.S. Capitol, out Interstate 66, there is a small Virginia stream, name of Bull Run. Over a century and a quarter ago, in the brutally hot summers of 1861 and 1862, great armies clashed in the swale of this brook, testing no less than whether a nation conceived in liberty could long endure.

In the Second Battle of Manassas, in 1862, Robert E. Lee had his headquarters on Stuart's Hill, overlooking the field of blood. In 1988, 542 acres of this land, including that hill, had come into the hands of an organization headed by one John T. (Til) Hazel. Hazel was by far the most prominent developer in these parts. He had fledged his law career in the 1950s by condemning the land for the road that would come to be known as the Capital Beltway. And for thirty years he had been a key player in the economic and social revolution that culminated with eight Edge Cities blooming in Northern Virginia. One of them, Tysons Corner, drew astounded observers from around the world to its high-rises and intersections; it was bigger than downtown Miami.

Til Hazel, who was born and raised Southern, took no little satisfaction in watching his native land of Northern Virginia approach and then eclipse the economic energy of that Yankee bastion across the Potomac, the District of Columbia. Lee's personal command, after all, was not called the Army of Northern Virginia for nothing.

Thus it was, with a firm faith in the inevitability of progress, that Hazel in the late 1980s turned his attention to the land he had acquired near the exit from Interstate 66 labeled MANASSAS.

For, he came to see, right there next to the Manassas National Battlefield Park—Bull Run to Northerners—was a prime place for a new Edge City. It could contain as much as 4.3 million square feet of nonresidential space—the size of downtown Fort Lauderdale—plus 560 homes. It would do the local economy a lot of good.

The last thing he expected was a fight.

Abraham Lincoln, a century before, on November 19, 1863, had also focused his attention on a bloody battlefield. The address Lincoln gave that date—its opening words were "Four-score and seven years ago"—was in Gettysburg, of course, not Manassas. But his words echoed eerily exactly 125 years later, and eighty miles south, on Til Hazel's development abutting the National Park on which soil Thomas Jonathan Jackson had first been described as standing against the Union "like a stone wall."

"In a larger sense, we cannot dedicate—we cannot consecrate—we cannot hallow—this ground," Lincoln said. "The brave men, living and dead, who struggled here have consecrated it far above our poor power to add or detract . . .

"It is rather for us . . .." said the tall, gaunt man, "that we here highly resolve that these dead shall not have died in vain."

# II
## Present at Creation

---

*In the beginning all the world was America.*

—*John Locke*

---

THE SEPTEMBER AFTERNOON AIR is warm and thick, even at this altitude. Long gray wisps of mist snag on trees and rolling hills to the east, in the direction of Washington. From the walkway near the top of Tycon Tower, Til Hazel can point to just where he farmed, before the earth had moved.

"You know, it's a strange thing. We took very few pictures. One of the great disappointments is that I have no picture at all of our horses. The old team that I used to work and plow and everything," says Hazel.

"But as far as Tysons, let's try to set the stage. Basically, 123 was a narrow two-lane road. There was a big hill over here and 123 snaked around. Oh, yes, it's been leveled. The topo has dramatically changed.

"In 1939, when I first saw it"—Hazel was nine—"Route 7 had a beer joint and it had the feed store. The beer joint—it seems like to me I remember one of those Coca-Cola signs that said 'Tysons Inn.' But around here, you wanted to talk about it, you just said 'the beer joint.'"

Hazel steps over a rope the diameter of his wrist, from which a window washer dangles, a hundred feet below. The brick precipice from which he dispenses history rims a Philip Johnson–designed skyscraper.

"The famous orchard was right over here at the entrance to

the mall. It was just on the other side of the Marriott.'' Pointing, he leans far enough out over the parapet to make his companion queasy. ''Apple orchard.''

''Then you had a ninety-five-acre dairy farm that was fore-closed on during the war. It was on the market for $18,000 in 1945. Owned by a family named Ayers. That was the farm I tried to get my aunt to buy. She said to me—and I remember it vividly —she said, 'Well, tell me, what in the world would I want with a property way out in the country?' ''

From the perimeter Hazel prowls, one can enjoy a vista from the National Cathedral in Washington, ten miles east, to the foothills of the Blue Ridge, twenty-five miles west. What he points to as he walks this day are not those wonders, though. Instead, he is consumed by the hundreds of strange, sprawling, towering shapes below.

The hill with all the tower cranes—that's where old one-eyed Marcus Bles grazed his Angus cattle in the 1950s. ''Bles bought the gravel pit, and his first moneymaker was gravel fifty cents a ton, and you haul it.''

Only from this height is it clear that a hill existed where Hazel pointed. It is not that the rise is inconsiderable. To the contrary, it is the highest natural point in this part of Virginia. It is just that closer to ground level the landscape has been so bulldozed and banked, it is easy to think no contour of the land was left that had been put there by the Creator. On the slopes of that cow pasture and gravel pit of yore now rises the Tysons II Galleria, a $1 billion, fifteen-year office, retail, and hotel project that, all by itself, dwarfs many of America's old downtowns.

From the top of this tower, Til views a landscape that John Rolfe Gardiner referred to in his novel *In the Heart of the Whole World.* To be sure, Gardiner was being irreverent when he barely fictionalized this mall-centered metropolis. But then again, there is something about Tysons—the largest urban agglomera-tion between Washington and Atlanta—that evokes that from people. Over to the west is the megastructure with the curved white six-story entrance that causes everybody to refer to it as the Up Toilet Seat Building. Above Hazel, at the very pinnacle of the JTL Tycon office tower on whose edge he paces, jut two crowning brick arches. It is these arches that led this building to be variously dubbed the World's Tallest Shopping Bag and the World's Tallest McDonald's.

Directly below is the mall in which the arrival of Bloomingdale's—seen in the early 1970s as the epitome of New York fashion, not to mention decadence—caused a sensation. When one pioneering diplomatic contingent from Beijing arrived in Washington, the first thing they wanted was not a tour of the Lincoln Memorial or the Washington Monument. What they wanted was to get out past the legendary eight-lane Beltway that reputedly separates Washington from reality. They wanted to go to Tysons. They wanted to see "Broomie's." They wanted a stiff dose of America.

As Hazel walks and talks this day, he points out what are literally the landmarks of his six decades of life. But he also marks the revolution in America that has crystallized in such Edge Cities.

Hazel should know about this revolution, for he has done more to shape the Washington area than any man since Pierre L'Enfant, the Frenchman who designed the District of Columbia for George Washington. A comparison of Hazel to L'Enfant is by no means idle. Metropolitan Washington today is not only one of the ten largest urban areas in America. In the late 1980s, it was the fastest-growing white-collar office job market in North America and Europe for four years in a row. Its private-enterprise, high-information, high-education, post-Industrial Revolution economy made it a model of what American urban areas would be in the twenty-first century. Its growth, of course, was marked by this strange new Edge City form, not by the old ways of L'Enfant. As a result, it became an archetype for every city worldwide that was growing.

Hazel, by being among the first to comprehend and enthusiastically clear the way for this kind of world, also became an intriguing model of the Edge City creator. Originally a lawyer and then a developer, by the late 1980s he had accumulated a personal fortune estimated at $100 million. The estate on which his family lived, an hour from the White House, spanned a fair-sized valley and four thousand acres of land—a respectable spread by the standards of Montana. To understand him was to understand how a whole new world had been shaped.

John Tilghman Hazel, Jr., has a face you could carve into a

jack-o'-lantern. Angular slabs dominate. They descend outward from his eyes and his nose in parallel diagonals, like corporal's chevrons. His jaw is a meaty block. His crew cut—crew cut!— makes the top of his head as flat and square as its bottom, although less wide. The effect is like looking at the end of a barn with its peak razored off.

Over the decades, Hazel has so successfully, rapidly, and visibly transformed entire Northern Virginia landscapes that his vanquished opponents have been reduced to describing him in satanic terms—no less than the Prince of Darkness and the Father of Lies. He is thought by them to symbolize rapaciousness and hypocrisy and greed. They hiss about the time he bulldozed one tree a day in a pristine wilderness, in protest of a government delay. They scream about the time that he clear-cut twenty-six acres rather than have it spared for a park. They point knowingly to his successful legal defense of a senior official charged with bribery at a time of rampant corruption. They rage about his legal wiles before the state supreme court, his capacity to frustrate and overturn the decisions of any government, any planning board that might dare to oppose growth. They speak in hushed tones about his connections to governors and senators. Why, a U.S. Representative even made a home on Hazel's estate! Hazel is seen as invincible. He is the legendary despoiler of the soil, the destroyer of the planet, the raper of the land. He is vilified for the traffic, for the pollution, for the chaos, for the noise, for the Change. He has been, in short, elevated to the status of a monster.

His friends and allies tell a strikingly different story. They speak of him as being a real gentleman, a man of cordial, even antique manners, a man of his word. They tell glowing stories of his generosity. They talk of how he graduated from Harvard Law and was now chairman of the Harvard College Fund, the university's major fundraising arm; how he helped steer Northern Virginia's George Mason University from its origins in a strip shopping center and an old elementary school to its current glory, when one of its economists has won the Nobel Prize and its performing arts center is making those of the old downtown nervous. They describe him as that rare individual who has a grand vision for the entire region, from its airports to its seaports, from the Blue Ridge to the Chesapeake Bay. If there are problems as a result of all this growth, say they, the fault is not Hazel's. It is the fault of those petty, selfish, and parochial minds, from the bureaucrats to the bleeding-heart ankle-biters, who stood in the way of building everything for which he foresaw the need—especially the roads.

But of all the things said about Hazel, the most startlingly incongruous is about his relationship to the land. For this is what his allies repeatedly volunteer: they say what authentically distinguishes him as a developer and as a seer is his uncanny feel for the land. Yes, the land. The way he understands the land. They insist this is true.

And, indeed, he is devoted to Alaska. He repeatedly returns there, frequently with his wife. On the coffee table in the waiting area of his office, with his name on the address labels, are, in addition to *Harvard Magazine,* such periodicals as *Alaska, Virginia Wildlife, Smithsonian, The Nature Conservancy Magazine, Ducks Unlimited,* and *Antiques.* They appear to have been read.

Compared with his depiction as an arrogant and reprehensible despoiler and exploiter by his legion of detractors, there can be no more profoundly and diametrically opposite a characterization of this force behind the bulldozers. Yet it is true that he never seems more comfortable or animated than when he is recounting the most particular details of the fruits of his farm. He easily remembers on exactly what dates corn was planted in which fields. He takes more pride in his farm having won the state corn championship for highest yields four years in a row than he ever expresses in his stylish office park. He knows what the expected harvest dates are, how much water there is in a given field, how likely it is the tractors can negotiate that, and what the odds are of frost. This day he knows that he has exactly 1020 cows—mostly Angus with a few Hereford crosses—with six hundred calves just weaned, another four hundred to go, and an additional six hundred in the feed lot. He is proud that the calves have come in at 750 pounds.

Hazel is, in short, a man of contradictions, as is the Edge City world he has created. And the contradictions he embodies illuminate a great deal about both the America that will soon be and the America from which he came.

The world into which Til Hazel was born, on October 29, 1930, was later so eradicated by the new one he helped create that today that place is difficult to imagine. Hazel was born not where his family lived, in Virginia, but across the Potomac River in the District of Columbia. That is because, as he is fond of saying, "it was either that or the kitchen table." His Virginia homeland was then so rural and backward that it had no hospital of its own.

Today Arlington County, where Hazel grew up, is one of the more urban places in America. It is more densely populated than Dallas or Denver or Cincinnati. It has one of the largest office buildings in the world—the Pentagon. Its airport, Washington National, is busier than Houston Intercontinental. It has two mirror-finish Edge Cities, each the size of downtown Milwaukee, and 8700 hotel rooms. Its public school students speak more than forty-nine languages, including Arabic, Vietnamese, Farsi, and Urdu. It has ten snazzy subway stops. And, of course, it has half a dozen hospitals.

In 1930, none of that existed. Arlington was a dozen crossroads punctuating fields and forests in which Hazel's relations hunted wild turkey. Segregation that was "very distinct," as the old saying went, was the rule. Most of the roads were dirt. Hazel's father told him vivid tales of the cavalry at local Fort Myer shipping out to fight Pancho Villa. Across the river it was an era when a motorist caught in the rain with his top down could pull under the porte cochère of the White House and be invited in to shake hands with the president. America itself was still a land of unthinkably vast spaces. For a quarter of a century to come, the southwesternmost baseball team would be St. Louis.

In 1930, Herbert Hoover was president, and though the stock market crash was three months old when Hazel was conceived, it was not yet clear that the Depression was at hand. Not until the second half of 1930 did "people feel the ground give way beneath their feet," as a contemporary economist put it. By the time Hazel was two, 24 percent of the work force would be unemployed. Birth rates—that statistic which probes most deeply into people's personal lives—had plummeted.

Thus Hazel's character was shaped in a world far different from the one he ended up building. It had different hopes, different fears, even different referents. "The War," for example, was automatically understood to mean the Civil War. His mother's grandfather was a Confederate soldier. Her family's roots were in nearby Southern Maryland, which even in the 1930s took pride in its Rebel sympathies. The foremost historical site in Arlington, looking out across the Potomac toward the Capitol in the distance, was the mansion of Robert E. Lee.

Hazel's father's father, William Andrew Hazel, wound up in Fort Laramie with the Seventh Cavalry only a few years after its last conflict with Indians at a place called Wounded Knee. When William returned from the West after the turn of the century, he stuck with what he knew, and became the stable manager for the delivery wagons of the Chestnut Farms Dairy. Hazel remembers riding his horse, Honeypot, in the 1930s in the median of that novelty, one of America's first concrete roads.

These were rough-and-ready days. In the 1920s a group including Til Hazel's grandfather decided that an area down by the river had become infested with squatters, riffraff, and various perpetrators of crime. So they got together secretly one night and "blew the place away," as Hazel related it.

It was a considerable departure for a Hazel when Til's father, John T. Sr., decided to become a surgeon. His brothers were lucky if they finished high school. John Sr.'s father opposed his continuing education. It was not trivial in the 1920s that John was making as much money keeping books at Chestnut Farms as was his dad tending horses.

John Sr. paid no small price for being the first to better himself. He was able to complete his medical education only by signing up with the Public Health Service. That outfit moved the twenty-six-year-old father to Boston only weeks after Til, the firstborn, arrived. On John Sr.'s return to Arlington, he had to move his little family into the home of his prosperous father-in-law.

The mid-1930s saw John Hazel, Arlington's only surgeon, making good money by the standards of the South and of the Depression. But all that meant was that he could finally build his family their own house—if he kept his office in it. And John Sr. did not think that things were looking up. When he looked into the future, he saw war. He would talk about it to his wife, Ruth, and Til could hear. John Sr. had vivid memories of hunger from his days growing up. If those meager days were *before* the Depression and now there were breadlines, what would war bring?

He became worried about barest subsistence. He worried that his family would starve. He plotted to meet gravest disaster—to make sure his wife and children could raise their own food.

"Today he's a fairly senile man," Til recounts, "but he remembers having an overcoat and a car when East Boston was full of people with no work and no food. It's a very real thing."

The solution was land. John Hazel bought land from his father-in-law. He started with twenty-nine acres, but his "subsistence" farm in time came to 110 acres—a sixth of a square mile. It was a lot of land for one family by the standards of the East.

This land was even farther out than Arlington. It was in the next county, Fairfax. In distance, the "next county" meant something in Virginia. At the time of first founding, county seats were flung purposefully far so that one would be within a day's horse ride of each settler.

The farm was in an area known as McLean. John Sr. sent away for hundreds of pamphlets from the Department of Agriculture on subsistence farming. The result was bacon for the family from home-butchered hogs, and cottage cheese Til's mother made from their own cows' milk. Gardening was serious. Putting up food for the cold time was an important part of life.

For all his desperate concern, though, John Hazel, Sr., had absolutely no time himself to raise crops. He scarcely had time to raise sons. He was a driven man, working long hours. Church was never very important to the family, Til recalls. "Dad was so involved in medicine that it was like Sunday was the same as any other day for him. That was the day he made rounds. The only difference was he didn't schedule any operations on Sunday. He operated every other day of the week." For two years, just as Hazel became a teenager, his father was gone completely, working at the Mayo Clinic.

That was why Til, even before he reached his teens, became the mainstay of the farm, working alongside a hired man and his aging grandfather, the cavalryman. He started by bicycling or hitchhiking the eight miles from Arlington to the McLean farm. But by the age of twelve, he was getting out of school by noontime and driving an automobile out there himself. Because few tractors were available during the war, he worked behind draft horses and a borrowed pair of mules.

At an early age, Til Hazel repeatedly proved that he could be every bit as driven as his father. The family legend has him reading encyclopedias as he lay recovering from such dreadful maladies as appendicitis and acute poison ivy.

But more significantly, working the farm was the means by which he gained contact with his father—and his approval.

"We used to have kind of a routine session after dinner—if he was home. Before he made his evening rounds. Where we would discuss what had happened at the farm. What the plans were. He got a lot of enjoyment out of that. And I got a lot of enjoyment out of it." His mother called that precious half-hour ritual the Men's Club.

It was not that Til Hazel held any romantic notions about the land. "I figured out it was better to do something at school. Because you sure in hell weren't going to get very far on a farm. That was clear to me from day one."

So when a teacher advised her bright, hard-working, and precocious young ward that he really only had two choices—to go to Iowa State to study agriculture, or to go to Harvard—for Til the decision was easy. Hazel knew nothing about Harvard. His classmates thought the acme of achievement was to attend William and Mary in the Colonial Virginia capital of Williamsburg. But his father had taken a few courses at Harvard while working for the Public Health Service. "My father said, 'That's good. I know Harvard,' " Hazel recalls.

With that ringing endorsement, Til—ever dutiful—went off in the direction he was pointed. He had no sense that anyone thought it a particularly big deal. One influential uncle even doubted Harvard would do a future Virginian much good. Til's mother's concern was that he have a good suit. His personal attitude was that if college was the next thing on the agenda, Cambridge had to be better than Ames.

In 1947, Til Hazel left Northern Virginia for New England. He would remain distant from the affairs of Arlington and Fairfax for ten years, only a sporadic visitor until after completing Harvard Law and his stretch in the service in the Army Judge Advocate's Corps.

Of his final summers on the farm, however, two things stick in his mind. The first was what a pleasure it was finally to have a tractor. Photos of him on top of his McCormick-Deering Farmall International Harvester Model H—with those two tiny wheels snugged together up front—show a satisfied man. Cutting the wheat and barley and oats and rye of McLean by pulling a combine behind a tractor was infinitely better than working with horses and mules. He never sentimentalizes that experience.

The other thing that remains with him was watching, as he was making hay, the building on the horizon of a place called Pimmit Hills. It was the area's first big postwar subdivision—hundreds of three-bedroom, one-and-a-half-bath, single-level, $7950 homes. "I remember looking over there, and they probably had fifty or seventy-five houses all being framed at once. It was a really big deal." Hazel remembers a picture on the cover of *Life* just like it. "It was a general topic of conversation among the farmers. It was, 'Goodness, look at all these new houses and look at how much good it's doing in the area.' It was a fraction of the agenda that you now have out of these things. You know, a very minimal understanding of all that went with it." So minimal, in fact, that one of the things Hazel noticed in streams that watered milk cows were feces that had escaped the subdivision's primitive sewage facility.

But the pollution was by no means what people were talking about. It was the blessing of this new growth, this prosperity. It seemed a miracle. "It was a tremendous new change. I was generally alleged to have been a pretty serious kid and I was interested in what was happening and what it meant for the farms."

Indeed, almost nobody in America expected this. If anything, the lurking fear had been that the war years might end up being the high point of people's lives. There was little reason to think life would be much different after the war from the way it had been before. With all the veterans returning home looking for jobs, most people figured America would return to the Depression. Had not Roosevelt tried everything to pull the nation out of its doldrums? Nothing had worked. Now half the world was in ashes, Roosevelt was in his grave, and his third vice president, a man almost no one knew, was in charge. This was a recipe for prosperity? The most strike-ridden year in American history was 1946. Shortages of meat were widespread. In 1947, America's GNP hit its lowest level since 1942, adjusted for inflation. The pessimists' worst fears seemed confirmed. The reason the Hazel family has no photos of Til with his team of horses is probably simple. There was no reason to think that era would ever end.

The rest—as the saying goes—is history.

Michael Barone in *Our Country* refers to 1947 as "a hinge in American history, a time in which the country changed quite markedly from one thing to another."

Following 1948, America's gross national product, adjusted for inflation, grew at an average rate of 4.0 percent every year, for twenty years. That kind of sustained boom was without precedent in the annals of mankind. America was changed forever.

While Til Hazel was away from his homeland, meanwhile, other things happened that would reverberate in the decades to come, as they influenced his view of the land.

First, as an undergraduate at Harvard College, Hazel majored in American history. He started with the Revolution, wherein it seemed every other hero was a Virginian who had trod the ground he knew so well—from George Washington to Thomas Jefferson to George Mason. That led him backward into European and especially British history from 1500 on, because it related directly to the Revolutionary history with which he was entranced.

Decades later, the fact that he had been an American history major was as dumbfounding to one interlocutor as was Hazel's relationship to the land. What about the Civil War? he was asked. That seemed an important question to ask a man who had thought to build a mall next to Manassas National Battlefield Park. Great sweeps of the Civil War were fought in Virginia, from Manassas to Chancellorsville to the Wilderness to Appomattox. Did you study much history of the Civil War?

No, he says. "The Civil War always struck me as a great waste and a great tragedy and, you know, I don't know whether it was I don't like to lose or not. But I just never got all wound up in the Civil War. I was never particularly intrigued by the Civil War, except as it relates to physical things. Did I identify with the Confederates? Yes, oh yes. You've got to if you're raised in my family. Lots of courageous activity, lots of exciting things, but all for no danged good reason. When you say 'Lost Cause,' you've said it all.

"It just seemed to me a great waste."

A few years after he came to that conclusion, a second thing happened.

His father sold Til's farm.

The farm that was the basis of their relationship, the land on which Til had sweated to build a concrete-block barn for his younger brother, Bill, to milk cows and even live sometimes . . . The place designed to be the family's salvation, where it could go to ground in hard times . . .

His father sold it. To developers.

Hazel claims to this day that the transaction was of no particular concern to him. After all, the farm had been replaced by a new and far grander one two counties west, in Fauquier County. "In those days," says Til, "it never occurred to anybody that you weren't supposed to use the land for whatever purpose it was needed."

But on the warm September day in 1989—the one that started out with Hazel pacing the tower in Tysons—Til ended up concentrating seriously. Back and forth he swung the giant Oldsmobile, trying to get his bearings amid the convoluted swirls of an old subdivision three miles east. He was looking for some particularly huge old trees, much larger than the suburban growths nearby. He wanted to show them to a reporter. They were the last things left from the farm where he had turned himself into a man.

"My father was big on something he called a scarlet oak. He got some and I planted 'em and watered 'em and pruned 'em and picked the caterpillars off until I thought I'd never ever want to see another oak tree. Hey, you know what? There they are over there. Well I'll be damned. See that oak tree? Yeah, I planted that tree in 1940. And there's a couple more. We had a house in the middle of 'em. Those are our trees right there. This was a cornfield. And the creek is right down here. Boy, getting across that creek was a big issue. Now that cinder-block barn was right about there. And this was our garden and the hog pen. We had a little orchard back there. And those are the trees we planted. Those are the famous scarlet oak trees. I'm going to come back in the fall and see what color they turn. Most red oaks just get kinda dirty red. But those get brilliant red. And Dad, who was not much of a nature type, somewhere heard about that, and he insisted we were going to have scarlet oaks."

In fact, Hazel said, the boy and his father had talked about it at length. It was during their ritual evening rendezvous in which they shared a little time, just the two of them. The news that this serious, husky man-child, soon to be eleven, brought home of the progress of the oaks pleased his father a great deal, Hazel said. And that pleased him.

This, of course, all happened—before the earth had moved.

# III

# The Machine, the Garden, and Paradise

Man aint really evil, he jest aint got any sense.

—*William Faulkner*

IF YOU READ America's favorite poets and novelists long enough, you notice that the last time we went through so fundamental a change in how we build cities, something ended up deeply severed in our souls.

The "last time" was especially the 1840s on. That's when America began to end as a place marked primarily by farms and quaint burgs with names like Harlem and Greenwich Village. With the Industrial Revolution came an upheaval in which the majority of people no longer lived in and off the countryside, or on eccentric hamlet lanes. By the turn of the twentieth century they were drawn to those teeming, steaming cities epitomized by New York and Chicago and Pittsburgh. There, wealth and jobs were created with the vast, clanking, astoundingly complex machinery of the textile mills, the steel mills, and the steam locomotives. These cities were built triumphantly on man's new-found abilities to slash the very dirt from the ground—limestone from Ontario to Indiana, iron ore from northern Michigan to Minnesota, and coal from Pennsylvania to West Virginia to Kentucky—and turn it into such miracles of organization and genius as the Model T.

These brawny, brawling, muscular cities, the legacies of which are our old downtowns, became the centers of our civilization. They were the place where the arts and museums were most "sophisticated," the mores most "broad-minded," the politics the most "progressive," the attitudes most "tolerant." They were where the energy levels of enterprise were deemed highest, enlightenment most bright, and where the nation's values were well enough represented that we acculturated our immigrants there; it was where we turned them into Americans.

But in some very deep ways, we hated those cities. American literature is shot through with a sense that this wealth of cities, this sense of progress, this urbanization, came at a horrific price. It came with a pervasive feeling of dislocation, alienation, conflict, anxiety, and loss.

Again and again, our most respected writers make their meaning most clear—we left behind something vitally important when we fled to these cities. You can see it in the works of James Fenimore Cooper, Henry Wadsworth Longfellow, Nathaniel Hawthorne, Ralph Waldo Emerson, Henry David Thoreau, Herman Melville, Walt Whitman, Henry Adams, Washington Irving, Mark Twain, Sherwood Anderson, Willa Cather, Eugene O'Neill, Hart Crane, Theodore Dreiser, John Dos Passos, William Faulkner, Ernest Hemingway, Robert Frost.

What is mourned in hundreds of different ways is the same thing: the severing of our direct ties to nature and to the land. There is in the writings of these Americans a constant yearning for connectedness between society, landscape, and mind. They do not find peace in the noise and hurly-burly of the big city, this land of the Machine. In 1844, Hawthorne sat down in a wood near Concord, Massachusetts, locally known as Sleepy Hollow, to record "such little events as may happen." In the middle of his literary reverie, a steam locomotive—only recently invented —ripped through. With sudden abruptness it disrupted Hawthorne's sense of time, nature, and reality. According to the cultural historian Leo Marx, "The train stands for a more sophisticated, complex style of life than the one represented by Sleepy Hollow; the passengers are 'busy men, citizens from the hot street . . .' The harsh noise evokes an image of intense, overheated, restless striving—a life of 'all unquietness' like that associated with great cities as far back as the story of the Tower of Babel."

Hawthorne's was not an isolated flummox. For Americans, Leo Marx observed, "regenerative power is located in the natural terrain: access to undefiled, bountiful, sublime Nature is what accounts for the virtue and special good fortune of Americans. It enables them to design a community in the image of a garden, an ideal fusion of nature with art. The landscape thus becomes the symbolic repository of value of all kinds—economic, political, aesthetic, religious.

"A strong urge to believe in the rural myth along with an awareness of industrialization as counterforce to the myth—since 1844, this motif appears everywhere in American writing . . . It is a complex, distinctly American form."

We are bound up in this conflict to this day. Our most fashionable foods and fibers are ones that are "natural." The rugged individual at ease with the forces of nature even sells cigarettes, from the Camel man in his ravine-ringed Jeep to the Marlboro man on his backlit bronco. Families that have managed to find a "little place"—ten acres or so—"in the country"—a few hours' drive beyond their homes—"that needs some work"—it'll cost them a fortune—are envied. Others are eager to hear their tales. Seventy-six percent of all Americans describe themselves as environmentalists. There is precious little else about which we so thoroughly agree.

Sigmund Freud was astonished by this yearning for "freedom from the grip of the external landscape . . . How has it come about that so many people have adopted this strange attitude of hostility to civilization?"

But it is hardly an immature romanticism that drives this American idea. In *The Machine in the Garden*, Leo Marx argued that it was basic to the American psyche. In 1844 Wordsworth wrote a sonnet protesting the building of a railroad through the Lake District. Marx noted: "By placing the machine in opposition to the tranquillity and order located in the landscape, he makes it an emblem of the artificial, of the unfeeling . . . It is a token of what he likes to call the 'fever of the world.' "

In America this reinforces two contradictory world views that today are everywhere at war. These are the ones we have traced back to the very beginnings of America. The Virginia Cavaliers, arriving in Jamestown in 1607, looked out over the landscape and in their letters home wrote that this untrammeled nature is no less than a miraculous, bounteous Eden. Thirteen years later, the Pilgrims hove to off the coast of Massachusetts, and what they reported was a vision of unredeemed demonic Hell. This land would have no hope, yield no value, until it had been tamed by the civilizing influence of man.

The dichotomy endures to this day. One sees the untouched land as an object of veneration, a source of spiritual strength. The other sees the land as a commodity to be used and exchanged for money, like any other. This division is crystallized in the reactions people have when they suddenly come upon a bulldozer as it bites into an "unspoiled" landscape. How you feel about the abrupt appearance of this Machine in the Garden is doubtless predicated on your idea of "progress."

Robert Nisbet, in *History of the Idea of Progress,* demonstrated that the basic notion was set up by the Greeks and Romans. The idea of progress originated in the belief that mankind has slowly, gradually, and continuously advanced from an original condition of cultural deprivation, ignorance, and insecurity to higher levels of civilization, and that such advancement will, with only occasional setbacks, continue. The Greeks saw the natural growth in knowledge over time as progress that would yield the natural advance of the human condition. The early Christians believed the spiritual perfection of mankind would culminate in a golden age of happiness on earth, a millennium ruled by the returned Christ. They got this idea in part from the Jews, who believed that history was divinely guided. As early as Augustine's *The City of God,* Nisbet reported, all the essential terms of Utopia were in place: affluence, security, equity, freedom, tranquillity, and justice.

When knowledge of the New World arrived in Europe, the possibilities seemed unlimited. By 1750, progress was not simply an important idea among many; it had become the overwhelming idea. From it were hung yearnings for equality, social justice, and popular democracy under law. These aspirations, attached to progress, were no longer deemed desirable; they were believed inevitable. Soon, freedom and liberty became thought of as necessary to progress. More important, they became seen as the very goal of progress—an ever-ascending realization of freedom, to the most remote future. That was why the opening shot of the American Revolution was the one heard round the world.

By the 1800s, the idea of progress was no longer dependent

on divine guidance. It was attached instead to faith in reason, science, and technology—the works of man himself. Then, as the twentieth century approached, progress was seen in the accumulation of power, especially by the state. For it was thought that the redemption and salvation—and especially the perfection—of man would be possible if his consciousness could just be shaped and elevated by sufficiently powerful means. Thus was the idea of progress ultimately perverted: Lincoln Steffens' famously incorrect report upon his return from Russia in 1919 was: "I have been over into the future, and it works." The Nazis' Final Solution was so called in order that it be viewed as—progress.

The belief in the inevitability of progress, Nisbet believed, took body blows when people representing every conceivable ideology stopped believing one or more of the five premises that were its underpinnings:

- *That the past had value.* Those who stopped believing this argued that ignoring or eradicating the past was an acceptable, even a desirable, aspect of progress.
- *That life itself, in all its manifestations, had unerasable value.* Those who turned away from this idea were willing to accept the notion that loss of life was an acceptable cost for progress.
- *That reason alone, and the scientific knowledge that can be gained from it, was inherently worthy of faith.* Those who stopped believing this no longer accepted that the Cartesian method of logic, in isolation, could reveal all important truth.
- *That economic and technological flowering was unquestionably worthwhile.* People who stopped believing this gave up the faith that if Cartesian logic produced it, and it was turned into a product—for example, mustard gas—it must be good.
- *That Western civilization was noble, even superior to its alternatives.*

The final, resounding disconnect between the advances of the Machine and the idea of progress came with the atomic bomb. That is the point, Siegfried Giedion noted, from which the technological imperative "If possible, then necessary," rang hollow. That is the point at which it became ineluctably clear that what we could do was by no means the same thing as what we should do.

Nisbet, in fact, observed that among the "clerisy"—that marvelous word he used for the priesthood of our self-appointed intelligentsia—the idea of progress is now a dead letter. And there is no question that any serious expression of long-term optimism today is obliged to carry some awful asterisk. Such as: assuming there is no nuclear war, no planetary environmental meltdown, no economic debacle, no universal cataclysm.

But while most people are all too aware of these dire possibilities, it is not clear to me that the *spirit* of progress has been rejected by most Americans. An optimist has been defined as someone who is still engaged in the problem. By that standard, it would appear self-evident that America remains a nation of optimists. We are battling like demons over the most basic ways we should organize our lives. This is not the behavior of people who are resigned to their fate; it is the behavior of people with a touching faith in their enduring ability to change the world—for the better. I think that our most knock-down, drag-out, hair-pulling fights are those over competing visions of the Promised Land. That is why the noise is so loud.

The problem, of course, is the way the armies in this millennial battle fail to recognize its outlines in the arguments of their opposition. Return to that unexpected moment when the bulldozer is spied turning the virgin soil, and how various people may react to that sight.

Those who unquestionably see in such technology the progress of civilization are also likely to believe it obvious beyond challenge that "more" is better, that "growth" is good, and that "change" means progress. Their position is a time-honored one. As now we swim in our sea of technology, it is almost impossible to imagine attitudes before. But in 1776, James Boswell described the moment of epiphany when he first understood the Machine. In Soho he visited a factory where a mighty steam engine was in production in all its vastness and intricacy. He wrote that he would never forget the account of its maker, the "iron chieftain": "I sell here, Sir, what all the world desires to have—POWER."

Boswell found the spectacle exhilarating, and Leo Marx noted that in so doing he anticipated America's response precisely. During the dawn of the Industrial Age here, in the first half of the 1800s, America became the wonder of the world. It doubled and then redoubled its population. Pushing south and west, it quadrupled its territory, settling, annexing, buying, or conquering land claimed by Britain, Spain, France, Mexico, and the Indians. During those fifty years, the gross national product increased sevenfold. No other country could match even one of these boasts. Such growth was seen as intrinsic to the very idea of America; in fact, its Manifest Destiny. It was accepted as an emblem of God's special favor. The Bible itself seemed to demand this view. Did not the first book of Moses, Genesis, enjoin man to "be fruitful, and multiply," to "subdue . . . the earth" and "have dominion . . . over every living thing"?

What other mandate could you conceivably need?

In this view, land untouched by man was "vacant" or "waste," and those words came fully loaded. Vacant meant empty, a vessel useless until filled. Waste was immoral. The creation of wealth and jobs and comfort and leisure was not seen as easy or automatic. Growth was progress—though there was more than a little schizophrenia surrounding that. On the one hand, the mantra of the men of the Machine was "You can't stop progress." On the other hand, they deep-down feared that might not be true. They worried that if people didn't pursue material progress totally, the abyss of want and depression did await.

This vision of progress became especially prevalent in the years after World War II, when more and newer homes for all Americans seemed beyond question a social good. When we had the slightest hope of income beyond our needs for food and warmth, what did we instantly spend it on? Those homes which maybe had a little yard, some place for the kids to play. On a quarter acre or so? A place that could be made into—a Garden? What more primal demonstration does one need?

Thus did we start our push out past the old downtowns, out into the landscape we invented to further our pursuit of happiness: that suburbia which is now culminating in Edge City. We lit out once again, in the words of Huckleberry Finn, for the Territory.

And on that very ground across which we sprawled we have met the other great countervailing American idea in what was good: the belief in the primal restorative power of the undefiled land. In that idea, the land has value in and of itself, with no crass calculations of how it may be "used." It should not all be profaned; it should not all be "spoiled," as people use that interesting word, by the works of man.

It's the battle we fight to this day. The sound of the clash echoes backward and forward for centuries.

Our yearning for a simpler and more natural life can be phrased in the most positive of ways: Americans are looking for a new unity in their lives, a way to bring themselves together, to avoid the fragmentation that they perceive all around them, from drugs, to bad schools, to teenage pregnancy; they seek a connection that brings the American centuries, from the seventeenth to the twenty-first, into some kind of focus.

Yet it seems clear that we are sadly lacking that toward which we so clearly grope—a model that integrates all our apparent contradictions.

The circumstances surrounding the implosion of another nineteenth-century system of thought may be instructive in this regard.

Communism was premised on the belief that the exploitative conditions of industrialism created by early capitalism were hopelessly contradictory—beyond mere reform. But as we look around us in the late twentieth century, we see that, though the social-democratic West may not have achieved nirvana, some forms of capitalism seem attractive to a whole lot of people.

Now comes the question: If industrialism did turn out to be reformable, can we now resolve the contradictions in our new, post-Industrial, Information Age world? Can we now turn to reshaping our new cities?

I think the test of that is going to be how we come to view the land.

There are those in sympathy with Cassandra who I believe are well meant. These are the people who grimly count on a cataclysm that they hope will bring us to our senses before it is too late—a new Great Depression, global warming, the immolation of the Middle East. As prediction—who knows?—betting on calamity may well be the odds-on proposition.

But I have difficulty conjuring up a sequence that *forces* us onto the path of righteousness. I do not see how we are going to be deflected from our current ways simply for lack of naked power, at least in time to do us any good. With the technologies at our command, we can do virtually anything we want, if we're willing to pay the price. The question is not what we can do. The question is whether we will come to any kind of agreement on what we should do—in our everyday world.

If one believes in progress, as I think most Americans do—if one accepts the notion that humanity is redeemable precisely because we do have the capacity to learn from our astoundingly abundant mistakes—one wonders whether there may not be less drastic ways than Armageddon of arriving at resolutions.

I've often thought you can tell a great deal about a civilization by what it protests. You can tell what it believes it has far too much of.

In 1910, five young Italian painters issued a publication that would become known as *The Manifesto of the Futurists.* It was an emotional, political, cultural, and esthetic document regarded as significant because it proclaimed the sensibility that created modern art.

In part, it read:

We will fight with all our might the fanatical, senseless, and snobbish religion of the past, a religion encouraged by the vicious existence of museums. We rebel against that spineless worshipping of old canvases, old statues, and old bric-a-brac, against everything which is filthy and worm-ridden and corroded by time. We consider the habitual contempt for everything which is young, new, and burning with life to be unjust and even criminal.

Comrades, we tell you now that the triumphant progress of science makes profound changes in humanity inevitable, changes which are hacking an abyss between those docile slaves of past tradition and us free moderns, who are confident in the radiant splendor of our future."

It is obvious what the Futurists thought they had too much of. It was the cold dead weight of the past.

It's odd; now it is their words that sound antique. I've often wondered what the Futurists would make of our drive today for historic preservation. I suspect they would think us nuts. Completely out of our minds. But that is the side on which one finds today's passionate young. They lie in front of the bulldozers to keep old buildings, old trees—keep, even, old battlefields.

What are we to make of that? I think the logical conclusion to be drawn from our protests is that what most people now think we have too much of is the new. Change comes at such a rate that we search for refuge from the impermanence of our lives. We are weary of returning to places we care about and finding them changed beyond recognition. We are weary of the complexity and the chaos and the time pressures of our lives. Maybe the problem is that what we are seeking is a higher sense of order, and what we are mourning, when we think of decline, is our lack of anchors.

We know this is not the way we once lived. We resent it. And we lash out, rebelling particularly against those self-proclaimed and self-congratulatory agents of change whose work is the most flamboyant, the least ignorable, those who bring this change at the highest social and emotional cost—the developers.

If that is where our pursuit of progress—in the most genuine sense—is headed, our pursuit of the future inside ourselves, our American pursuit of happiness, then the question is how these contradictions can ever be resolved.

It seems to me that we can start by striving for an understanding, at the most basic level, of how we value something as fundamental as the land.

If we can do that, perhaps we can graduate to working out what some other words mean in our world—words like community, civilization, and soul.

Full disclosure: The lens through which I personally see and report on the world is not all that rare in the late twentieth century, polls show. It is that of the devout agnostic. While it would surprise me not at all if it turned out that there is a larger force in the universe than man, the organized religions I've encountered have served only to unnerve me. I report this only to explain that I am made mightily uncomfortable by any assertions that have words like "reverence" in them.

But Robert Nisbet, the esteemed historian and social theorist, did use such concepts as that of the "sacred" in addressing the outlook for our futures.

"What is the future of the idea of progress in the West?" he asked. "Any answer to that question requires answer to a prior question: what is the future of Judeo-Christianity in the West? For if there is one generalization that can be made confidently about the history of the idea of progress, it is that throughout its history the idea has been closely linked with, has depended upon, religion or upon intellectual constructs derived from religion.''

He based his conclusion on the observation that the single most quoted poem in all of English literature is by William Butler Yeats: "Things fall apart; the centre cannot hold"; "mere anarchy is loosed upon the world"; "the best lack all conviction, while the worst are full of passionate intensity."

If we genuinely believe that, of course, there is no hope.

If we quote those lines as a warning to ourselves, however, of a future we know we can avoid—and I think that is what we do—therein might be our salvation.

That is why, after all the miles spent reporting this book, I found Nisbet's conclusion persuasive; that we are going to resolve our differences and push through to higher ground only if we come to an agreement like this: "Only, it seems evident from the historical record, in the context of a true culture in which the core is a deep and wide-sense of the *sacred* are we likely to regain the vital conditions of progress itself and of faith in progress—past, present, and future."

If in fact we are approaching a turning point in history—a turning point at least as dramatic as the one of 150 years ago that ushered in the Machine Age—perhaps the place to start in redefining ourselves is with our relationship to the land.

If we are to reunite our fragmented worlds, we might see whether there is room for agreement on so basic an idea as what exactly we believe is hallowed ground.

# IV

## Pilgrim's Progress: Boom

---

For we must consider that we shall be a city upon a hill. The eyes of all people are upon us.

—*John Winthrop, on board the* Arbella, *1630.*

---

TIL HAZEL'S PARTNER, the developer Milt Peterson, remembers precisely when the earth really did move in the pastures of Northern Virginia. It came with the erection of Melpar.

"It was real early, even before the Beltway," Peterson recalls. It was 1952. An electronics firm with a name like that of a science-fiction creature, Melpar built its headquarters way, way out into the farmland—past Arlington County, past Falls Church, ten miles out from downtown, all the way to Fairfax County. It was surrounded by fields. The planners and builders and politicians and developers of the day were agog. They had never seen anything like it.

"Melpar sat back about four hundred feet from Route 50," recalls Peterson of the building that was such a departure from those downtown that it stuck in his mind four decades later. "It bought about three times more land than it needed. It had a little pond on the side that had a willow tree. It had its parking in the back and it had a brick front and a flag. There was a big lawn leading up to it. Melpar, like, became a word. You know how a feeling becomes a word? That became what all development should be—Melpar. Everyone said we want Melpar all over here. I mean that's the *only* kind of development we wanted. It became, 'Where can you get more of that Melpar?' "

Melpar was an electronics-warfare contractor, so when it built its headquarters, it took its cue from the Pentagon—in more ways than one. The Pentagon—the actual building—remains the world's archetypal Edge City structure. With a still-astonishing 3.7 million square feet of office space—equivalent to downtown Fort Lauderdale—it attracts twenty-three thousand employees every day. It has four Zip Codes.

Opened in 1942, it gave form to the idea of bringing the most awesome Machine of all time—the American war machine—into a Garden. The Pentagon is surrounded by a lot of lawn. Light colonels fill its myriad jogging trails. It has a yacht basin, trees, and hanging vines. The courtyard in its center is a nice place to catch some lunch-hour sun. Yet the building is fully oriented toward the transportation technologies of the late twentieth century. It is encircled by parking lots, freeways, and helicopter pads. When the Pentagon was built, the nearest major structure was National Airport. Four decades later, an underground Metro rail station was added.

But that was not what brought the Pentagon to the epitome of Edge City. That came in the late 1980s, when another mega-structure was built just across Interstate 395. It was—yes—a mall. Very flashy, very upscale, the development was called the Fashion Centre at Pentagon City. The advertising got more than a little weird around Christmas. Some found it tough to deal with the whole peace-on-earth, goodwill-to-men routine in a place called Pentagon City.

Be that as it may, in the early 1950s Melpar located itself just as the Pentagon had a decade before—out in the fields in campuslike splendor on a big open highway, suspended between two magnets. The customer that it emulated was in one direction, toward town. On the opposite bearing were all those wonderful new suburban houses that John Cheever would glorify, in which one could "shout in anger or joy without having someone pound on the radiator for silence." A whole new world was being born.

Of all the breakthroughs of Melpar, what is remembered as something truly different was the brick. The brick on the façade. What daring! You could work where you could feel the breeze, and be in contact with God's good ground, but not have to work in a tin warehouse or a barn. You could have the sophistication and urbanity of brick just like that of Capitol Hill. Way out here! That the combination was even possible had never occurred to anybody before. It was no less than a vision of a new and better world.

"The demander of space is like a voter," explains Peterson. "Developers, what do they build? They build what they think they can sell. So they're saying, You voter or consumer, what do you want, what would you pay for, okay? The consumer has got the option of going downtown. But the ultimate, okay, is Melpar. Melpar was the flag, the lawn, and set back from the road, but the big thing was to have a brick front. Why was brick a big thing? Because everything else anybody had seen was shitty old aluminum or steel.

"Now you look at a building and if it's brick, you say well now there's a trade association that didn't have enough money to have a building with precast concrete. Precast concrete is a step up from brick, yes. And then you go to marble, okay? But then marble, it's not gutsy enough. Marble has a softer feel—like a library. But then there's granite. It's like the word, *granite*—it's tough. So that is state of the art now.

"But coming back to this, you build with what you think the people want and that then was Melpar. Trying to be the antithesis of the city. Total antithesis. Curvilinear as opposed to rectilinear. See, the whole thing in sales and marketing is making people feel good about themselves. Suburbanites live on country lanes. They picture themselves going home in their Porsche or whatever—it is down a lane with trees on it and they swing along. The other reason you don't do the streets straight is if you line 'em up, cars is all you see. But if you make it go like this"—Peterson undulates his arms—"you can have one tree here and one tree here and one tree here and one tree here and as you drive down here you go along and what do you see? You see this tree and you start around here and you see this tree. So all you need is a little bit of open and you start swinging and you're doing this and you get everything in here."

Peterson, at the time he was recounting this in 1989, was waving his arms toward the newest development he and Hazel had built. It was called Fair Lakes. At build-out, its 657 acres was scheduled to have more than five million square feet of office, retail, and hotel space—comparable to downtown Dayton or

Wilmington. Nonetheless, it was by far among the most green and leafy and parklike of all the Washington area's Edge City locations. Including, as it did, shops and homes, it was the state-of-the-art Machine in the Garden. "This is not the 1960s Melpar," Peterson said. "This is the 1990s Melpar." I asked Peterson why he hadn't built an old downtown out there, a place with grids and blocks and sidewalks.

"We could have made this all straight," he responded, "but hell. You make it *vroooom*—you swing around. You want the mind to not know what to expect next. You want it to be eventful. You want it to be different.

"Everybody when they come to the suburbs they want the trees and bunnies and birds, okay? And that's why we put two swans out there and feed the damn ducks so all the frigging geese and ducks come around and people say, 'Gee, I work out in a place where they have paths and running tracks, ponds, birds. Do you have a running track where you work?'

"It comes back to what does the employee feel that his employer feels about him—he gives them ducks and ponds and paths and workout facilities. Heck, you have workout facilities in all these buildings. They never get used. But people like to say they have one. It's like me. I've got a great big machine—I'm going to frigging work out? I use it to hang my pants on.

"Employers have to go where they think they can attract the best employees they can afford. So they have to locate their facilities in a place and in a setting that'll give them the most chance of having a successful business. All could have gone downtown. Some of 'em have moved out from downtown. The choice is always there. Power to the persons that are making the decisions. So that their overall life—real and perceived—is best.

"We're trying to make a person feel as though he's going to drive in the country and his office just happens to be off in the woods next to the birds and the bunnies. Yes, a city in a garden. Here we had one goal—make the person feel they were with the birds and bunnies, they got residence, they got shopping, they got everything. Trees, ponds, lakes. Good access, right on Interstate 66, but swing in here, you get rid of those ugly, garish signs —now you're going to get an earthy-toned sign. Then you get special permission from the highway department to put trees closer to the road. You're going to take your bridges, see, and make 'em curved and put stone over here so they'll feel as though they're out in the country. If they would've let us, we would have taken the cobblestones on that so when you drove over, your wheels would go *bllllmmmmm bllllmmmmm bllllmmmmm*. Just like going over a bridge, yeah. Tried to get it. They wouldn't let us do it. Those are the kinds of bullshit and baloney stuff you pick up."

Highly evolved indeed. But to hear Til Hazel tell it, all this was inevitable and inexorable.

When Hazel returned to Virginia in 1957, his former Harvard Law classmates felt a small pang. Here they were, moving on to jobs of significance, like Wall Street. He was returning to that jerkwater county, Fairfax. He seemed so bright, too.

Truth be told, his first job didn't sound like much. It was spending endless hours amid dusty deeds to condemn land for a new road. It was not, however, just any road. It was to be built with funds from the brand-new National Defense Interstate Highway System. This road was going to serve as a bypass up the East Coast around both sides of Washington. It would be roughly a circle, sixty-six miles all the way around. It would skirt the city by a goodly distance—more than ten miles—so as to not be severed by an atomic bomb hitting the White House. (This *was* a defense highway.) That distance—beyond even Melpar— went through land that Hazel remembers as being "like Kansas." By that he meant there was nothing there—as far as he could see. Anything—anything—would be a higher use than this void of pasture and forest that had not seen real prosperity since its conquest in the Civil War, nine decades earlier.

The land was considered so vacant, Hazel recalled, that the highway engineers saw no significance in the way the new highway would cut across two little farm-to-market roads, Routes 7 and 123, just east of their corners, named after a nineteenth-century landholder, William Tyson. It didn't register on them that the resultant triangle would instantly become a place easily driven to from any direction in the region. This superhighway was designed to get people from Maine to Florida. Local traffic? What local traffic? No commercial development was even imagined at any interchange. The only reason the triangle got created the way it did, reported Hazel, was that the engineers located their superhighway along the most geometric curve they could lay down to a point five miles distant where the Potomac narrowed. That seemed the best place to build a bridge.

When the die was cast for this prototypical and enormous Edge City, nobody knew the Beltway would become known as Washington's Main Street, or that an international airport, Dulles, would be built a dozen miles west. One of the area's earliest real estate speculators, Frank Kimball, himself started buying up property in 1959 only after he could not convince his employer, the Marriott Corporation, to view the place as a credible location for a hamburger stand. It was too far out.

This was land Til Hazel came to know better than anybody. Decades later, he would still take great pride of craft in his work as a young lawyer. By the time the alignment of the Beltway was in place in 1960, he recounted, his decisions were never appealed, either by the highway department or the owners. His word had come to be viewed as that of authority. When he put a value on a piece of land, it stuck.

No small accomplishment. It was a time when many other values were coming unstuck:

In 1954, General Foods Corporation moved its headquarters out of Manhattan to White Plains, in Westchester County.

In 1955, the first McDonald's restaurant opened in Des Plaines, outside Chicago.

In 1956, Southdale Shopping Center, the world's first climate-controlled shopping mall, opened outside Minneapolis.

In 1965, William Levitt, of Levittown fame, started building houses outside Paris.

In the early 1960s, at the same time as the completion of the Beltway in the Tysons area, Hazel was spotted as a comer by the courthouse crowd. The Byrd machine was still the juggernaut of Virginia political power. Its power lay with large landholders, and its conservatism was so deep that even issuing bonds to build roads was viewed as a newfangled, hence suspect, idea.

The population of Fairfax County by 1960 had tripled in only one decade, to more than a quarter of a million. Subdivisions erupted like mushrooms after a warm rain. The first rezoning of the rural land around Tysons for commercial purposes began in 1962.

In 1966, a federal grand jury gained nationwide attention when it indicted fifteen people under the recently enacted Federal Racketeering Act on charges of conspiracy to exchange bribes for rezonings in Fairfax County. Among those indicted were county supervisors, planning officials, developers, zoning attorneys, and one former state senator so prominent he was referred to in press accounts as a "civic leader."

Hazel, who that year had just started his own full-time law practice, took the defense of the grand old man, Andrew W. Clarke. Clarke was charged with being the kingpin of a scheme to distribute some $52,000 in bribes. Hazel pled him innocent. Next, he got the federal counts dismissed. Any alleged conspiracy ended four days before the passage of the Federal Racketeering Act under which the indictments came, he argued. Thus no federal laws had been violated. Then, to the outrage of the prosecutor, he succeeded in getting Clarke excused from trial on state charges. The grounds were failing health. Clarke had, in fact, suffered three strokes, and died in March 1968. But he did so while vacationing in Florida. Several of his fellow indictees ended up vacationing in Lewisburg Penitentiary. This bottom line escaped the attention of no one. Both Hazel's friends and enemies saw he was going to be a legal force to be reckoned with.

Little did they know. By the time the population of Fairfax had passed half a million, in the early 1970s, Hazel was blamed and credited with being personally responsible for the presence of 100,000 of them. He was the John the Baptist of development, making clear the way. With righteous prowess did he ceaselessly pursue the rezoning of farm and forest into quarter-acre lots attracting more and more people. He had become the pre-eminent force for growth, the legal sledgehammer systematically destroying on the anvil of the Virginia courts all attempts to slow it. Hazel knew the Old Dominion had always been shaped by this moral certitude: a man may not have taken from him the value of his land, save by due process of law.

At the time Hazel was really beginning to roll, however, America, near the end of its second decade of unprecedented growth, was changing profoundly. The Apollo program was sending back photographs that altered people's dreams forever. Our planet, from the perspective of the July 1969 moon landing, looked like a precious little marble, lonely in its vast black void. The idea of Spaceship Earth brought people to understand that

the planet really was a closed and finite system. It did have limits.
The first Earth Day, in April 1970, rallied national attention to
the perils of unrestrained economic development. In 1972,
a report entitled *Only One Earth,* by Barbara Ward and René
Dubos, was presented to the United Nations World Conference
on the Human Environment. It argued that man's foremost
allegiance had to be to his planet.

This all began to fit into people's heads in ways that had
profound consequences. By the late 1960s, wealth might have
flowed like a mighty stream for a generation of Americans. But,
better fed, better housed, and better educated than ever in history, they were nagged by fears that something had gone terribly
wrong. The grammar school nuclear air-raid drills had blunted
the idea that change equaled progress. Rachel Carson had published *Silent Spring* in 1962; it turned out that pollution endangered not only the continent's fertility, but the very song of its
birds. In January 1969, an underwater oil platform ruptured off
Santa Barbara, California; the televisions of America were filled
with the beaches and sea birds of one of America's most beautiful—and richest—communities covered with deadly black goo
and highly articulate outrage. It became the symbol of greed
damaging nature, both wild and human.

As our attitudes shifted rapidly around the value of the patriarchal family and of religion and of authority, important questions were asked about the point of all this growth. In pursuit of
"standard of living," were we sacrificing "quality of life"? Where
did humans fit in the scheme of things?

The answers that penetrated the national consciousness came
from the new studies of biology. They emphasized our interde-
pendence with our soil, our air, our water, our forests, our
farms, and our food. They showed the importance of instinct.
They did so rationally and testably—scientifically. They demonstrated that man's genetic potential included a grammar of behavior as powerful as his sense of language. They resonated with
the words of the emerging computer revolution. They showed
that we were "hard-wired"—unalterably connected—to our nature, the nature that sprang from our evolutionary, planetary
experience.

The ideals of progress thus began to come uncoupled from
the Industrial Revolution's premium on the behavior of the

worker bee. New ideas of human improvement—our most enduring values, those which surrounded the advancement of freedom, liberty, individualism, and progress—became linked with the flowering of human potential. Yes, man could be improved, even perfected, but only in harmony with nature, of which he was a part. The potential of our future, in this view, flowed from our connection to our futures as human animals. What, came the question, was the "carrying capacity" of our habitat?

In 1972, the widely cited Club of Rome report on limited resources fanned Malthusian fears of runaway population growth. In 1973, the first oil shock hit, giving Americans a cram course in the costs—economic and sociologic—of their way of life. Not one American in a thousand in the 1950s knew that the word "ecology" referred to the study of energy flows within a closed system. By the 1970s, ecology had come to express the belief that *change specifically did not mean progress.* Drastic change within a closed system—Earth—or any change that could damage a species was viewed as wrong.

No culture can truly survive which ignores the human spirit and human values, this argument proceeded. Such values and spirit rose from what was natural. Progress, therefore, could not encompass exploiting and polluting our earth. It was not progress to cut down our trees and erect buildings so ugly and wasteful that human beings could not flourish within them.

"Human beings dwell in the same biological systems that contain the other creatures but, to put the thought bluntly, they are not governed by the same laws of evolution . . ." wrote Barry Lopez in his National Book Award volume, *Arctic Dreams.* "Outside of some virulent disease, another ice age, or his own weapons technology, the only thing that promises to stem the continued increase in his population and the expansion of his food base (which now includes oil, exotic minerals, fossil ground water, huge tracts of forest, and so on, and entails the continuing, concomitant loss of species) is human wisdom.

"Walking across the tundra, meeting the stare of a lemming, or coming on the tracks of a wolverine, it would be the frailty of our wisdom that would confound me. The pattern of our exploitation of the Arctic, our increasing utilization of its natural resources, our very desire to 'put it to use,' is clear. What is it that is missing, or tentative, in us, I would wonder? . . . It is restraint."

Enter Til Hazel.

At the height of his Edge City building powers.

Hazel genuinely believed in everything he did. But what made him a legend in his own time was his capacity to drive his opponents mad. As one colleague put it, he had the remarkable knack "to reduce the most complex issues to a single, pungent sentence that rallied his friends and pissed off his neighbors—I mean, enemies."

Hazel once boasted that what he did for a living was "crack open watersheds."

He meant it. In 1970, a ban on sewer hookups for new developments was put in place because three treatment plants were overloaded. Hazel attacked, saying the government had to build more sewer plants. Meanwhile, the hookups resumed.

In 1971, an attempt was made to mandate affordable housing at a time when 40 percent of the county's policemen were forced to live outside the jurisdiction. Hazel attacked, calling the measure an "unlawful, imprudent intrusion into the rights of private business," an attempt to "put off on the private sector the public problem." It was overturned.

In 1972 a new county board took office. Elected on a platform of skepticism toward growth, the members tried to suspend land rezonings to give county planners time to draft a five-year strategy. Hazel attacked. He crushed the moratorium in the courts. Then he rubbed it in. To his foremost antagonist, Audrey Moore, he sneered, "I think your approach is bankrupt—morally, socially, and financially. This county has an obligation to provide for the people."

In 1973, the county attempted to slow growth by not hearing rezoning requests or approving site plans. Hazel attacked, arguing that the government had an obligation to undertake these functions. The result were frenzied proceedings round the clock and well into the morning, night after night, as the county worked off the backlog.

In 1975, Hazel again triumphed. The county had attempted to limit growth to places where public facilities, such as roads and schools, already were in place. Hazel attacked, arguing that not providing such services everywhere was "arbitrary and capricious." It was an exercise in "discriminatory zoning" to restrict new homes to those "costing $100,000 or more." This one went all the way to the U.S. Supreme Court; when the Court failed to back the county, once again Hazel prevailed. Once more he rubbed it in. Said he, demurely, "You'd have thought we were out to rape the county."

He was a buzz saw. During his heyday, he never lost a zoning case in the Virginia Supreme Court. But his real skill was in grinding his opponents' noses in the dirt. He described the county's attempts to limit growth as "pie in the sky." When he blew up a moratorium on new sewer connections in Tysons Corner, he ensured his adversaries would never forget by forcing the county to refund his clients $400,000 in taxes he felt had been unjustly levied while their bulldozers had been stilled.

"We've got a tiger by the tail," he said in the mid-1970s of his struggles. "We're going to hold on till we tame that tiger or it gets the best of us. It's war. How else would you describe it?"

If he brought no little arrogance to his vision, it was because he was creating no less than a new world. He was bringing civilization to the "howling wilderness" into which he had been born. He was bringing it the benefits of modernity, the world of the Machine, so that never again could Yankees sneer, "Beyond the Potomac, it's all Alabama."

It was ironic that he, a Southerner, was now taking the position of the Pilgrims on progress—that civilization should overwhelm the land, in contrast to the Virginia Cavaliers' view of the untouched land as Paradise. But, then, he had not studied at Harvard for nothing.

So, in the pursuit of progress, he plowed his old world under —in the most literal sense.

Hazel was firmly in the tradition of the men who had pushed the railroad across the American frontier, at the cost of the buffalo and the Indians. Or of William Mulholland, who brought water to Los Angeles, at the price of turning the blooming Owens Valley into a desert. Or, in our lifetime, of the builders of the Alyeska oil pipeline across the Brooks Range that allowed the loading of North Slope crude into fragile supertankers—like the *Exxon Valdez*. A close associate of Hazel's was once asked if he thought Til believed in God. "I don't know," came his response. "I don't know. He might not. That would imply a higher Being."

The more Til drove environmentalists out of their minds, the more he was seen as the Machine that would annihilate the Garden. To the extent that he was seen as destroying the very pastoral benefits that had attracted people to Fairfax in the first place, he was stigmatized as a monster, seeking the almighty dollar at the most outrageous, amoral costs to society and the planet.

Yet, objectively, there was not a great deal of evidence that Hazel was motivated primarily by avarice for material goods. Surely the Oldsmobile of several years' vintage was not a display of opulence. Nor were his suits, puckered at the shoulder seams and so antique that when a lapel pin fell off, one could see a tiny circle of a darker hue around which the suit had faded.

Granted, Hazel was the kind of man who, when the air conditioning became too fierce in the Oldsmobile, tabbed down the electric window to let in warm air rather than turn down the chill. But as a greedhead, Hazel hardly fit the Donald Trump mold. This was a man devoted to his children and to his long-time and only wife. There was never any suggestion that he had given or taken bribes. It seemed to him a mystery, in fact, why anyone ever went that route. Beyond the immorality of it, as a practical matter it was lazy and sloppy and stupid. The system could so clearly be made to work on the side of everything that he viewed as righteous that he could not imagine why anybody thought corruption was necessary. In fact, if he indulged any personal vices, attempts to discover what they might be were markedly unsuccessful.

Nonetheless, his enemies took it as an article of faith, as obvious beyond any suggestion of doubt, that he was a liar of proportions beyond the merely monumental. He spoke in evangelical terms of the glories of covering the planet with subdivisions and malls and office parks and asphalt. His opponents, seeing this as an attack on the very underpinnings of the planet and of nature, and of man in nature, assumed that he could not possibly mean what he said. It was alien to their system of belief. The logical conclusion, then, if he was not a monster, was that he was a fool or a liar. And they knew he was no fool.

Not one person in a thousand who opposed him could imagine that he might be principled. Much less did they attempt to imagine what those principles might be. His response was identical. He could not comprehend that they might be serious about finding social worth in leaving the land alone, untouched, without regard to the needs of man.

Their morality, he concluded, must be hideously twisted.

The 1980s, for Hazel, were a voluptuous expression of that old adage "Don't get mad, get even." Fairfax passed Washington, D.C., in population—600,000, 700,000, 800,000—becoming one of the larger local jurisdictions in America, with an annual budget of $2.3 billion and more than ten thousand employees. As one of the nation's five wealthiest counties, Fairfax became a template for America's future: five formidable Edge Cities rose there. Ah, vengeance was sweet. Fairfax was no longer a bedroom satellite. It was the New Dominion, with an economy and a power to make both the rest of the state and the District of Columbia quake.

In this decade Hazel's legal firm became pre-eminent at ensuring that the economic engines of progress could continue to build this new world. With its mortal lock on the state supreme court in Richmond long established, the firm extended its reach to the legislature, becoming the state's most powerful lobbying outfit. Hazel himself was spending little time as an attorney, though. He no longer represented developers. He'd become one. Everything from traditional subdivisions called Franklin Farm to a "new town" called Burke Centre came out of his partnerships. At one point, he had major projects at half the exits on Interstate 66 from the Beltway to the exit in the next county marked MANASSAS.

Hazel seemed even more ubiquitous than that. He contributed hundreds of thousands of dollars to political campaigns, especially those of conservative Republicans. He backed ventures from George Mason University, to the promotion of pari-mutuel race tracks (Virginia *is* horse country), to the Fairfax Symphony, to toll roads, to a football stadium aimed at removing the Washington Redskins from Washington, to the creation of a private academy, to a magazine called *New Dominion,* to a new outer Beltway, to a social club with an abundance of dark wood paneling on top of that singular Tycon Tower.

His brother, William A. Hazel, built his own earthmoving empire of twelve hundred employees. Brother Bill owned more heavy equipment than many African nations. The Hazel clan shared thousands of acres in a valley farther out Interstate 66, in Fauquier County. With their beautiful herds of Angus, the arrangement was about as suggestive of TV's *Dallas* as one finds in the East. The displays of wealth, though, were mercifully not all that vulgar. The sweeping drive to Til's red brick Georgian mansion resembled either an English formal garden or an interstate interchange, depending on your perspective. The house may have been larger than America's first supermarkets, but Til's library—the whole thing, including the floor-to-ceiling columns—was finely sculpted walnut. In the kitchen Hazel had installed a Vermont Castings Resolute wood stove, of which he was particularly fond. Vermont Castings was a totem of self-sufficiency to the environmental crowd. But Til had one too. It was one of the few things about which they could probably agree.

For it seemed that what Hazel was doing in realizing his dreams was burying his past. It was like watching Scarlett O'Hara vow she would never be hungry again. "The problems we have are ones of prosperity!" was the ammunition he shot back relentlessly at his critics. He could not believe that did not end the argument. If any public opprobrium ever got to him, Hazel was far too tough to reveal it. But there was one thing that seemed to mystify him a little. Why were people not more grateful? For all he'd done.

One Fauquier County neighbor of his, to be sure, recalled the blackberries. There was a hedgerow, a bank, that gave her great joy as she walked by it of a summer's dawn. It had three colors of morning glory, and twines thick with goldenrod and blackberries. The berries were there just for the picking. In a nearby field, there were great rosy puffs of the Virginia wildflower called Joe Pye, and wild sunflowers. There was Queen Anne's lace and wild asters and wild rose. The hedgerow was home to bluebirds. It had taken half a century to grow.

Hazel's crews came in and bombed it all with herbicides. Then they strafed it with weed eaters and bush hogs.

The neighbor tried to be rational about all this. It was, she accepted, Hazel's land. And the highly productive pastures that replaced her idyll had their own logic. But why, she asked plaintively, could they not have spared the blackberries and bluebirds at the edges? Were they not symbols of the beauty of Virginia?

She could no more begin to understand Hazel than Hazel could her. For Hazel really did have an intense feel for the land. He did know it, in his way, better than just about anyone: he knew it in the fashion of a Confederate general.

He saw how it could be used.

When Rebel commanders looked out over the land, they saw it as a place to hide divisions and funnel opposing forces for massacre. They saw high ground as a place to marshal artillery, streams as lines of defense, and thickets as snares for foot soldiers.

And so exactly did Til look out on the land. He saw it as no different from coal or oil; it was a natural resource. That was why the most fervent swear word in his vocabulary was "waste." Save an unspoiled 101-acre woodland that he wanted rezoned as an industrial site? He saw that as a waste. Surround houses with ten-acre lots? He also saw that as waste; the land could have supported forty families in affordable, quarter-acre comfort.

When he looked out over the land, he saw it as starkly vacant until the brilliance of the human mind was brought to it, to find its most ingenious use.

He sincerely did not comprehend how people could see things differently. He could understand the value of places that should be kept open for ball fields, or jogging trails, or picnic spots—for human use. But the idea that land should be left untouched, in and for itself, without reference to human use, because of some oddball idea that there should be reverence to an abstract notion of the land—well, it was beyond him. He was the bringer of civilization. Didn't they understand what "howling wilderness" was? His father certainly had. Did they not understand "civilization"? What did they have against the works of man?

The narrow view, he realized, would be to see his opponents as liars and fools, rich people caring only for themselves who wanted to pull up the drawbridge after they had achieved their dream of a nice home, without regard to any higher needs of civilization. But Hazel, especially as he grew older, was not the kind of man to organize his life around such poisonous formula-

tions. He would do what he knew to be good, and let the chips
fall—for those of narrow mind—where they may.

It was with this attitude that he turned to one of his most
ambitious projects. It continued his inexorable march out Interstate 66, cracking open watersheds and converting farmland
into things he knew would be used by thousands—like malls.

It never occurred to him that there might be anything peculiar
lying in wait for him around his newest five hundred acres in
Prince William County. After all, as he would point out in one of
those memorable phrases which made his opponents so crazy,
"It's not a particularly pretty piece of ground. One of the worst
we ever owned."

No way did he expect a confrontation in which Americans
would end up fighting the same battle they had been fighting
since the first settlers arrived, with the same sort of implications
for the globe. No way did he imagine that he would open a gulf
between those who believed in him and those who did not,
which would turn out to be as large as any since the North and
the South had fought on this very land, 125 years earlier, over
issues that were in many ways similar.

Never did he believe that the very bones of those soldiers
might rise up against his bulldozers, or that on land already
filled with thousands of ghosts from over a century before,
Americans would once again engage in a struggle over who they
were, how they got that way, where they were headed, and what
they valued.

It was easy to miss the small sign as the highway crossed a
stream on approach to the land where Hazel's bulldozers began
their great roar.

All the sign said was BULL RUN.

# V

## But What About the Land?

---

Make no little plans; they have no magic to stir men's blood.

*—Attributed to Daniel Hudson Burnham, 1902*

---

IN THE LATE 1500s, what most fascinated Englishmen about the New World "was the absence of anything like European society; here was a landscape untouched by history—nature unmixed with art."

By the early 1900s, H. G. Wells and Le Corbusier and Frank Lloyd Wright were telling us we would soon mix nature with our artifacts to create extraordinary new cities. They would be surrounded by lawn, served by individual transport, crowned by skylights and atria, permeated by indoor trees and light, the climate would be controlled, and the potholes and puddles banished.

And we did it. Just as they said. We built Edge City.

Nagging questions remain. One is whether this world we are building will be a marvelous new synthesis in which all our urban functions will be artfully combined with nature in a *"land in which to live,* a symphonious environment of melody and mystery," as Benton MacKaye, the father of the Appalachian Trail, envisioned it over half a century ago. Or whether nature is about to be smothered by "a wilderness not of an integrated, ordered nature, but of . . . structures whose individual hideousness and collective haphazardness present that unmistakable environment we call the 'slum,' " as MacKaye caustically feared.

Precisely parallel is whether our polarized attitudes toward the price of change and progress will ever find a compromise of profit to all. The question is whether the forces of preservation and the forces of growth can ever somehow be resolved. Can the Garden-like aspects of what we are doing be encouraged while the hellish scourge restrained that despoils the land, crowds the schools, devours open space, jams traffic, and leaves nothing but a fast-food crisis for the soul?

It is no great mystery, of course, why the compromise is desperately needed. The battles of our last four centuries are coming to a head today because one of the most explosive building cycles in our history has been pursued at a time of competing demands on all our land.

There is little slack left in the system. Our dreams conflict. There is less "someplace else" to go. Few landscapes in the Lower Forty-Eight are not in some important sense man-made. Wildernesses continue to flourish, to be sure. But today, even apparently untouched landscapes are usually deliberate human artifacts. These wild vistas exist because one set of people, through purchase or government fiat, stepped in and prevented another set of people from using the land as they thought best. Even setting aside a landscape to remain pristine has become a choice of man, a function of his intelligence, of his benevolence; it is his creation. It becomes a land dedicated to a different kind of harvest. "The crop they raise is serenity, an article hard to come by in Megalopolis," wrote Jean Gottmann thirty years ago.

The noise of this conflict is greater than might seem justified, though. After all, if you housed every household in the United States in that beloved suburban "sprawl" density of a quarter-acre lot each, that would still take only around twenty-three million acres—1.22 percent of all the land in the United States even if you leave out Alaska. If you housed all these people at the moderately dense levels of such a leafy and bucolic planned community as Reston, Virginia, you could bring the amount of land in America covered by housing down under 1 percent of that in the continental states. In fact, right now, 70 percent of all Americans live on 1.5 percent of that land. The U.S. Census says that by the turn of the century, 75 percent of all Americans will live within fifty miles of a coast. It is easy to demonstrate that it is possible to build every single road and office and warehouse and vacation home this country will ever need—even at shockingly low densities, compared with that of the old downtowns—and still have more than 90 percent of everything else left for farm and wilderness.

Why then do all sides in the debate over the land seem so overwhelmed and embattled? Why does it have to be this way?

Because, of course, that is not what anybody perceives as the reality. Those who wish to build anew see themselves facing kamikaze opposition to sewers and roads and landfills and power plants and the works of man in general, opposition that drives their costs to astronomical heights, which they know is a moral outrage, which they know people can't afford. But they feel in a helpless bind, given all the alternatives they have been denied. They feel squeezed on one side by what they know human beings will buy, on a second by the laws of zoning and government regulation, and on a third by their economics and the biases of banks.

Those who wish to protect the land, meanwhile, continue to demonize developers. They cast them as rapacious despoilers, because they see the disappearance of the wetlands and forest and prairie that they treasure. Worse, they are mourning the blight of entire landscapes, for it takes only a little bit of modern development forever to alter a vista.

I conclude from all this noise that the only way we will ever arrive at a new and higher approach to our environment—the man-made environment every bit as much as the natural environment—is if we all somehow achieve a new and higher level of cooperation. "All ethics so far evolved rest upon a single premise: that the individual is a member of a community of interdependent parts," wrote Aldo Leopold in *The Sand County Almanac,* the twentieth century's *Walden.*

Wisdom, of course, is rarely in oversupply in the human condition. But Tony Hiss reported on a heartening amount of it in *The Experience of Place.* He neatly stated the challenge:

The places where we spend our time affect the people we are and can become. These places have an impact on our sense of self, our sense of safety, the kind of work we get done, the ways we interact with other people, even our ability to function as citizens in a democracy.

This means that whatever we experience in a place is both a serious environmental issue and a deeply personal one. Our relationship with the places we know is a close bond, intricate in nature, and not abstract, not remote at all . . . The danger . . . is that whenever we make changes in our surroundings, we can all too easily shortchange ourselves . . .

The way to avoid the danger is to start doing three things at once: Make sure that when we change a place, the change agreed upon nurtures our growth as capable and responsible people, while also protecting the natural environment, and developing jobs and homes enough for all.

But how do we go about doing three things at once when we're still having trouble finding ways to do two things at once—helping the economy prosper while at the same time preventing damage to the environment?

Hiss, intriguingly, went on to spell out a logic with striking similarities to the thinking of Christopher Alexander. He saw a "science of place" arising, based on our built-in ability to experience our environs—and draw valid conclusions from how they make us feel. That, he believed, could yield commonsense approaches to replenishing the latitudes we love. The human animal has habitat needs. Not for nothing are academic and corporate campuses open and leafy. Since the 1850s, a "total environment" has been considered an indispensable aid to learning. In 1984 the journal *Science* reported, "View Through a Window May Influence Recovery From Surgery." Over a nine-year period, it turned out, gallbladder patients who could see a cluster of trees instead of a brick wall "had shorter postoperative stays" and "took fewer moderate or strong" painkillers.

Hiss also reported some practical approaches around the country that were meant to conserve our great good places without denying growth.

First, he made useful distinctions about what is to be conserved. There are three kinds of landscapes, he posited:

• *Natural or primeval landscapes.* Those which are perceived as not significantly altered or interfered with by humans—mountaintops and ocean vistas, for example.
• *Working landscapes.* The feel of these have been shaped by human activities, but in cooperation with nature over a length of time that seems comparable to those of natural processes—for example, Pennsylvania Dutch farmland, a Maryland Eastern Shore fishing village.

• *Manufactured or urban landscapes.* These are our old down-towns, our old suburbia, and our new Edge Cities.

The point of these distinctions is to draw attention to the special qualities of each, to establish that *each* has a highest and best level at which it can and should be maintained, and that humans need ready access to each in order to feel whole. For example, a working landscape—which frequently translates into one devoted to farms—is a place where the "terrain and vegetation are molded, not dominated," noted the landscape historian John Stilgoe, author of *Borderland.* It is a "fragile equilibrium between natural and human force." The biologist René Dubos wrote about the "charm and elegance" and "soft luminosity" of one of his favorite places in the world, the landscape of his childhood, the farm country of the Île-de-France around Paris. Woods were cleared there, to be sure. But that gave rise to "an environmental diversity that provides nourishment for the senses and for the psyche . . . from the mosaics of cultivated fields, pastures, and woodlands, as well as from the alternation of sunlit surfaces and shaded areas." The oldest such working landscapes in America, by virtue of first settlement, are those in the stewardship of New England, the product of ten or eleven generations.

There are three ways that humans feel connected to the land around them that is worthy of preservation, reported Hiss:

• *The sense of kinship with all life;*
• *The sense of partnership with working landscapes;*
• *The sense of companionability that is traditionally fostered by villages and cherished urban neighborhoods.*

These, too, are valuable distinctions.

I personally feel most pained when I see the land that for generations was a farm being ripped up for a subdivision or a shopping center. It usually would not occur to me to feel outraged at seeing fallow ground newly replanted with corn or wheat or cotton. I view that as one working use being replaced by another. Nor in the past has it broken my heart to see a strip shopping center being replaced by a high-rise. What is Mammon's, I felt, was Mammon's.

But in the course of talking to people around the country, I came to realize that my sense of discontinuity was hardly the only kind. I had conversations with serious young people who found it wrenching to see even second-growth forest being leveled to create farmland for big-time operations that they found barely removed—either sociologically or technologically—from corporate chemical plants.

Even more surprising to me, I found people who saw the end of their community—and thus the end of their world—in a transition from one kind of commercial landscape to another. They genuinely mourned the disappearance of what amounted to a 1950s strip shopping center. This place, where the hardware store full of judicious advisers on the mysteries of the mechanical had always been found, and where the luncheonette with its diagonal-to-the-curb parking had thrived for two generations, was their village. When it was replaced by the high-rise office towers and subway stops, they never returned. The soul of their world was gone.

This led me to a meditation on the word "unspoiled." What a ubiquitous word that has become! It is the word used to describe any variety of landscapes, immediately before the bulldozers rip through. Why is that? Why are the newest works of man held in such low regard?

There turn out to be a multiplicity of landscapes over which people are willing to die. Thus, Hiss suggested that the first step in establishing rationality about what we value is making a regional inventory of what we love. After all, we are now at the stage where it's possible to have an Edge City fifty miles or more from the old downtowns, our homes a forty-five-minute commute beyond that, and our "country place" a three- or five-hour drive beyond that. By this arithmetic it is clear there is almost no jurisdiction in America that shouldn't right now tap into its people's hidden expertise in the locale. Ask them: What places are there in the region whose change would cause a deep sense of melancholy? Albert F. Appleton, New York City's Environmental Protection Commissioner, suggested, "The first 5 percent of development in a countryside region generally does 50 percent of the damage, in terms of altering people's mental geography of an area. And the second 5 percent of development enlarges this damage by another 50 percent."

This inventory, however, is not as antigrowth a measure as it may sound. "Conservation," after all, is merely "a state of harmony between men and land," Leopold pointed out. Identifying where the emotional flashpoints are in the population is a surprise-reducing measure for everybody. This is especially useful to businesspeople. They hate surprises. By establishing which places people are willing to die for, they can turn their attention toward those other landscapes—hardly rare in this country—where there is plenty of room for improvement; where change and growth would be a blessing. There *is* a lot of land in this country. The issue is whether we can come to any agreement on what we do with it, where, and in what harmony.

Such an inventory is also useful in that it educates those who compile it. For one thing, it gives them a crash course in a line of reasoning they may not be familiar with: thinking like a developer. Given that the developers have obviously had far more success in shaping the landscape than those who are not students of the marketplace, this exercise is of no small use. How secure are these beloved places? Who is in charge of them? A study of the regional landscape will soon make it clear even to the novice that development is not random or arbitrary or smoothly distributed. It is closely tied to such public investments as roads, sewers, and schools, as well as proximity to the same natural beauty that people wish to preserve.

The inventory also establishes the limits of any assessment that measures the worth of a piece of land only as a commodity; by its monetary exchange value. It establishes the importance of supplementing such a look.

"One basic weakness in a conservation system based wholly on economic motives is that most members of the land community have no economic value," Leopold noted half a century ago. "Wildflower and songbirds are examples . . . When one of those noneconomic categories is threatened, and if we happen to love it, we invent subterfuges to give it economic importance. At the beginning of the century songbirds were supposed to be disappearing. Ornithologists jumped to the rescue with some distinctly shaky evidence to the effect that insects would eat us up if birds failed to control them. The evidence had to be economic in order to be valid."

The good news is that if the region examined is sufficiently large, the inventory will point to the soul-satisfying value not merely of large wild tracks but of the cherished less obvious landscapes, especially those within areas thought to be built up. Hiss used as an example the valley of the Blackstone River, the very first place in North America—in 1790, in Pawtucket, Rhode Island—to get a factory. The falls of the Blackstone powered textile mills for more than a century, and as recently as twenty years ago, the river was a paragon of pollution. Running through such gritty cities as Woonsocket and Central Falls, its waters were a stunning study of iridescent slicks. The skies above were frequently flocked with mysterious foam floating on the breeze.

Now, $150 million later, the river runs so clean that glass-bottomed tour boats ply the waters below Pawtucket's falls; the original factory, the Slater Mill, is a museum; the air smells sweet; it stays cool all summer; many of the river's banks are heavily wooded and feel almost remote. This restoration is an example of the partnership landscape that is possible even in an anciently built-up area. The proximity of such an amenity even encouraged gainful new development in the 1980s.

Finally, if preservationists started looking around at landscapes that they value and tried to figure out how to save them before they became embattled, they would probably discover what the developers have always known: that the most ironclad way to control the future of a piece of land is to own it. There is nothing like having a deed—or, almost as good, conservation covenants embedded in a deed—to ensure that land is used in ways you see fit. A trust like the Nature Conservancy, which operates on the same playing field as developers, is vastly more effective than any kind of regulatory measure such as zoning. The police powers of the state over land use have repeatedly been exposed for the flimsy, legally bendable reeds that they are. Most Edge Cities, no matter how many land-use restrictions and zoning codes have been written, do not look substantially different from Houston. And Houston historically has had no zoning laws at all.

The whole idea is to harness the apparently antithetical forces of the developers and the preservationists. Such a partnership would aim to recognize the human ecology as well as the natural one. The alliance would demonstrate a respect for the people who love the land as it is and the needs of people in the future. If it is easier for builders to find places where the value of their offices and shopping centers and homes are seen to fit, it will be easier to take the development pressure off the land that we wish to preserve.

The odds are high that we will not bother to search for such a peace. We will probably prefer our current course, beating at each other with clubs. There is little reason to expect that to avail; neither side will fold its tent any time soon. But conflict has almost become our ritual.

No small portion of the problem is that a partnership that would reckon with *all* the land would put an express burden on the people who wish to preserve the wild and working territory. Those who want to see such landscapes taken out of the cycle of the manufactured would have a new obligation: they would have to turn their attention back to the land on which man has already built. Holding their nose if they must, they would have to immerse themselves in Edge City, understanding why man built there, and why he built the way he did. That's what it would take to participate in realistic conversations about future building. An inviolate law of the land is this: only if life is perceived as pleasant and affordable by the real human beings living farther in, will there be any hope of relieving pressure on the land farther out.

"The fate of the American landscape, its ponds and hollows, its creeks and forests, its prairies, wet glades, and canyons, cannot be addressed solely in terms of 'wilderness' or be solved by 'wilderness preservation,'" wrote Barry Lopez. "What we face now in North America—and of course, elsewhere—is a crisis in land use, in how we regard the land.

"We need to rethink our relationship to the entire landscape. To have this fundamental problem of land ethics defined, or understood, as mainly 'a fight for the wilderness' hurts us . . . It preserves a misleading and artificial distinction between 'holy' and 'profane' land.

"If we have a decision to ponder now, it is how to (re)incorporate the lands we occupy, after millennia of neglect, into our moral universe. We must incorporate not only our farmsteads and the retreats of the wolverine but the land upon which our houses, our stores, and our buildings stand. Our behavior, from planting a garden to mining iron ore, must begin to reflect the same principles . . .

"Wild landscapes are necessary to our being. We require them as we require air and water. But we need to create a landscape in which wilderness makes deep and eminent sense as part of the whole, a landscape in which wilderness is not an orphan."

This "moral universe" must include the developers. But in this there is hope. For most builders share a distinct moral code: they genuinely believe they are providing a service to mankind. And they have a very quick, firm, and direct feedback mechanism on whether needs are met. If they fail correctly to guess what people want and need, they go bankrupt. Therefore, if those who are most sensitive to the future of the earth can direct some of their attention back toward the portion of it on which we have already built, the outline of a deal may appear.

We may find that this weird and incongruous new Edge City form is working with us as much as against us. For one thing, the landscape it represents is enormously malleable. It frequently changes almost beyond recognition from year to year. There is usually vastly more land tied up in an Edge City landscape than there are pressing uses. The parking lots alone represent a land bank of enormous size, waiting for a higher and smarter and more economic use. The buildings themselves are often regarded as having a life span of no more than twelve to twenty-five years. By then, the original logic of their use, or their electronic, mechanical, energy, ventilation, communications, or internal transport systems have been overrun by events. They are no longer competitive with the rest of the market. At that point, their owners become highly interested in new ways to retrofit or replace them. If at that point they can be convinced that there are cheaper or more effective methods of making their places useful and attractive than the usual routine of refitting a marble façade with a granite façade, there is a golden opportunity for those who wish to offer change.

Remember: Edge City has already done the cause of livability a great service. It has made a direct contribution to the environment in that it has smashed the very idea behind suburbia in ways that the old downtowns never did. Suburbia always was meant to be green, which is hard to argue with. But that was not its most important characteristic. It was originally meant to be a place specifically designed to get away from the environmental and social dislocations—the factories and slums—of the first hundred years of the Industrial Revolution. At least since William Blake first placed the "dark Satanic mills" in opposition to his beloved "green and pleasant land," Americans have been carrying around in their heads the despairing baggage that the price of growth was bad smells, foul water, deteriorated neighborhoods, and debased landscapes. That was why suburbs were invented. They were supposed to be places separate from the world of commerce and manufacture, places to which we could flee as soon as we could afford the move.

Edge City has ended all that. It reflects our passing from the Industrial Age to our current one. By moving the world of work and commerce out near the homes of the middle and upper-middle class, it has knocked the pins out from under suburbia as a place apart. It has started the reintegration of all our functions —including the urban ones of working, marketing, learning, and creating—into those once-suburban landscapes that, after all, are among the most affable we have built this century.

The challenge, then, is to get actively involved in improving Edge City so as to make it contribute once again to the environment, to take development pressure off the natural and working landscapes. "Man takes a positive hand in creation whenever he puts a building upon the earth beneath the sun," Frank Lloyd Wright believed. "If he has birthright at all, it must consist in this: that he, too, is no less a feature of the landscape than the rock, trees, bears, or bees of that nature to which he owes his being."

That Edge City is inherently decentralized may even make an ironic contribution to new partnerships. It may mean that we can forge them without dawdling around, waiting for some mystical "regional solution" to be arrived at by "experts" and executed by vast bureaucracies. It may simply involve, at a local level, highly diverse individuals having the guts to recognize that their lives are of limited duration, and their antagonists will be with them all their days. The next step is to reach out, no matter how hateful that may seem. If these ancient enemies insist on complications, let them hire a mediator. If that doesn't work, they can talk to a younger generation of the opposition. You may not be able to count on people to change, but you can count on them to die, and be replaced by a generation with a different life. By definition that means a distinct view.

Our civilization, in short, may be viewed as halfway home. With help from those who care most deeply about the land, and about quality of life, we may make some real progress toward that Garden. It would put environmentalists in the position of making the built environment in which we live one of their foremost concerns. An effort at cooperation that addressed the universal hunger for a more humane life might also attract the developers. If nothing else, it would offer hope of addressing the growth revolt, our great national stress reaction lashing out at rapid change of all kind, demanding it all be shut down. It may even rescue the developers' personal social standing from its current abysmal low.

That notion is admittedly a rosy one. Even I have difficulty imagining the National Trust for Historic Preservation sitting down with the National Association of Industrial and Office Parks, the Sierra Club sitting down with the Building Owners and Managers Association. Each recoiling from the alien, pathological beings across from them like the barroom scene in *Star Wars*. Rather an entertaining vision, actually.

But that is exactly what I am talking about. And who knows? Maybe we are at a cusp in how mankind builds, a rebirth of that uncommon wisdom called common sense. Human life has not always been like this. Perhaps we should give more credit to the redemption, even the perfectibility, of man. Such a partnership with each other, and with the land, would be one in which conservation and development were no longer antithetical, and dreams could be compared. Above all there would be this guarantee: the places you grow up caring about most will be there for you when you're ready to start a family of your own.

And finally, it may be the foundation for an agreement in which building with "life" would reflexively attempt to help heal the neighborhood and the region. It would gradually turn out to be viewed as simply a social obligation.

The virtue of this deal—as a deal—is that it beats the hell out of the reality we have now.

All we do now is fight, and fight, and fight.

Though, truth to tell, this is not the first time such internal dissension has raged. We are continually drawn to our Armageddon of a century and a quarter ago; it echoes to the days of our lives. We cluster to it in our battle re-enactments. It is our Passion Play, our Iliad, our Agony, our Golgotha.

It is the Civil War.

In it we Americans fought each other over our most basic values—over who we are, how we got that way, and where we were headed.

That is why, when we fought, we fought to the bitter, ugly, final end.

# VI

## The Final Battle

Look! There stands Jackson like a stone wall! Rally behind the Virginians!

—*Brigadier General Barnard Bee, CSA, just before his death, First Battle of Bull Run, July 21, 1861*

IN THE DUST and the swirl of the 1988 battle in which Americans debated the moral worth of Til Hazel and his land, it was difficult, as always in war, to pinpoint exactly when the turn of fortune came.

It may have been the ad with the photo of the churning bulldozer and the words: "Without Your Support, the Soldiers Who Died at Manassas Will Be Turning Over in Their Graves."

The work of volunteer copy writers from an obscure Richmond agency, the advertisement was prepared for a ragtag collection of preservationists and history buffs called the Save the Battlefield Coalition. That ad hit people's hot buttons. The idea of the bones of the Civil War dead rising up from forgotten mass graves before the racking blades of the bulldozers as they pushed dirt for a mall—that really, *really* got to people.

The ad continued: "As you read this plea, bulldozers are razing a sacred place in American history. A place where the blood of over 28,000 men was spilled in two valiant struggles which would determine the fate of the American republic . . .

"Indeed, the slaughter was so great that the bodies were piled into mass graves. Many who died here were not men at all. They were little more than boys doing what they thought was right.

"If developer John T. Hazel has his way, the tranquil 542 acre tract at Manassas Battlefield will be transformed overnight into a snarling traffic jam adjacent to a huge office park and shopping mall . . . This national historical site will no longer pay tribute to the men who paid the ultimate price for their country. Instead, it will pay tribute to plastic watches, fastfood, movie theatres and video stores . . . If Manassas battlefield can be turned into a parking lot, then is any part of our heritage safe from developers? Help us stop the 'progress.' "

Then again, maybe the turning point was the testimony of Princeton's James M. McPherson before a panel of the U.S. Senate.

McPherson's book, *Battle Cry of Freedom,* having been widely reviewed as the best one-volume history of the Civil War, had just rocketed to the national best-seller lists on its way to winning the Pulitzer Prize, contributing to the most unprecedented wave of interest in that conflict since the bloodshed actually stopped.

McPherson called Stuart's Hill—the site that Hazel had bought and rechristened William Center—"one of the most significant Civil War monuments I've ever seen—the Virginia monument to Lee and the Army of Northern Virginia." McPherson told the senators: "The property is equally important in historical significance to Seminary Ridge at Gettysburg, where Longstreet and Lee had their headquarters, from which Pickett's Charge was launched.

"I think this issue is of importance to the United States Congress, but more than that, it is important to all of the American people. This is a significant part of our national heritage. What was at stake in the Civil War and at Second Manassas and in the William Center tract was the very fate of the nation. Whether it would be one country or two, would be a nation with slavery or without slavery. That part of our heritage can best be understood by studying it. And Civil War battles can best be studied by going to the battlefields. Walking them as I've done to this one several times. Bicycling over them as I've tried to do in the midst of the traffic that we've heard about today.

"I would have liked to go to the William Center tract—to go on Stuart's Hill—so that I could see from that height the large part of the battlefield, to go where Longstreet's troops were, and to try to understand why Fitz-John Porter would not attack across there. That has not been my opportunity in the past, but I hope that as a result of congressional action it will be my opportunity in the future."

Maybe it was the cumulative work of the world media. Every outfit with a Washington bureau from *Time* to the Japanese newspapers saw the larger implications of this battle. Their reports, day after day, had their impact, congressional mailbags showed. Especially powerful was the piece on CBS *Sunday Morning,* the host of which is Charles Kuralt, that doyen of the American landscape. That was the one with the chopper shots showing the land laid open like a raw red wound beneath the frenzied earthmovers. Even more wrenching were the clear young voices, backed by two acoustical guitars, singing the battle hymn of the resistance as the camera panned a golden landscape of split-rail fence:

> So I drove out to Manassas
> Stood alone and watched the sunset
> I imagined I could see grandfather fall.
> Behind the place where he was standing
> Just before the bullet took him
> Is where they're gonna build a shopping mall.

When all was said and done, however, the pivotal moment—like Pickett's Charge—probably came watching Annie Snyder cry.

Annie was not the kind of woman you ever expected to see cry. Snyder, the sparkplug and ringleader of the Save the Battlefield Coalition, had a curious face. Its lower half was that of a man. She had a powerful jaw, a broad nose, and cheeks flat as plates. Nonetheless, from the bridge of her nose up, she really was quite a vamp, her eyes flashing brilliantly, even vivaciously, beneath the fashionably short cut of her auburn hair. In fact, she was more sensitive about her good looks than might be thought common in a woman of sixty-seven, even if she did appear fifteen years younger. When a builder's magazine referred to her as a little old lady, she went so crazy as to send the publication a rather fetching photo of herself doing aerobics in tights, which of course they proceeded to print. As she discussed the work of various national reporters who had reported sympathetically on "her" battlefield, it was as if she were reminiscing about old flames.

The contradictions were not all in her face. The more innocent and exposed Annie seemed, the more her incongruities had the capacity to startle. They might include her casual references to her professional prowess as a long-gun marksman. Or her years picking up calves that weighed ninety pounds. Annie weighed 135. Or her devout belief in conservative Republicanism. Or the way she could consciously choose to adorn her lima bean–sized earlobes with large, flat earrings the crimson color of which matched exactly the red of the U.S. Marine Corps emblem on her polo shirt.

Annie's history was as illuminating of the strains on America at midcentury as was Til Hazel's. Anne D. Snyder, née Annie Delp, was born nine years before Til, in 1921. The daughter of a prosperous Pittsburgh attorney, she was as intellectually gifted as Hazel, accelerating through high school to enter college at sixteen. She was also just as bull-headed.

"I'll tell you how I got liberated," she recalled. "I grew up in a neighborhood of boys. There were no girls. We lived next to a farm, and we were allowed to play baseball and football in their pasture. So I grew up with all these boys. I could play football as well as the rest of them. But when I started developing bosoms they decided I was an embarrassment to them and they kicked me off the football team. I've been a women's libber ever since. That made me so *mad.* Yeah! So it was perfectly normal for me to join the Marine Corps."

Which she did. The outbreak of World War II found her enrolled in the law school at the University of Pittsburgh—hardly routine or even welcome at that time. But as the war progressed, she espied a challenge that made any law school malevolence seem ludicrous. "I'm a flag waver. Yeah, really. My brother was a Marine," she said simply, to explain what she did next.

Annie left law school to join the first class of women to graduate Marine Officers Candidate School. Then she became a recruiter, attracting other young women to the world of Leathernecks.

The men hated all of it. The Marines were absolutely the last service to accept women. They capitulated only because of the exigencies of war. " 'Free a man to fight' was our motto," Snyder recalled. Her father was beyond shocked. "The men had the idea all women in uniform were prostitutes." She constantly had to conquer men's worlds, proving her mettle not only to other Marines, but to her own family, as well as the fathers and brothers of the women she was trying to recruit.

"When I graduated from OCS I was a recruiter in New Orleans, and the day I arrived—my first plane trip—the commanding officer said, 'Come on, Lieutenant, you have to give a speech at the St. Charles Hotel in twenty minutes.' I'll never forget it. The St. Charles had these gorgeous, gorgeous staircases, ceilings forty feet high. Very impressive to a twenty-one-year-old. We go careening up these steps and over to this room and I looked in and there were 150 men sitting there. I was just stunned. I backed up; I thought we were in the wrong place. What the hell was I doing talking to men? Well, you didn't have to talk the women into joining. You had to talk their fathers, husbands, sons. My job was to convince them that I wouldn't be selling their daughters into prostitution. The male chauvinist pigs in this country. To somebody living in your era, that might just seem incredible, I know."

When Snyder mustered out of the Marines after the war, it was with some magnificent life stories to tell, and a marriage to Waldon Peter (Pete) Snyder, one of the Marines' earliest Pacific Theater aviators. Pete would soon join a new elite: airline pilots. But Annie would come away with a life foundation singular for young women of that day and time: there were not many challenges she would ever view as daunting. Not compared with what she'd already done. She and Pete ended up buying a 180-acre Angus cattle operation in Prince William County that Annie ran for twenty-eight years. "I think I'm the only woman in the world who annually asked for something for Christmas that I never got. And that was a hay-bale elevator." She and the kids ended up throwing hundreds of tons of hay way up into the loft by hand over the years.

The farm turned out to have a stream running through it called Little Bull Run. It was an accident of geography that would end up changing her life as she fought fight after fight for the battlefield next door, which she came to love.

All those fights. And of course it ended up with Annie squaring off against the most powerful force in the region, Til Hazel.

It's curious, but Hazel's most persistent and successful opponents in life have been women. In fact, throughout America, from California to Texas to Florida, it is striking how often, whenever the partisans in the battle over progress collide, the builders are men, and the preservationists, women. It is by no means a hard-and-fast divide. There is always crossover. But throughout history, there is a pattern. Joseph Campbell discussed it in *The Power of Myth.* "Society is always patriarchal. Nature is always matrilineal. Since her magic is that of giving birth and nourishment, as the earth does, her magic supports the magic of the earth. She is the first planter. The hunter is an individual in a way that no farmer will ever be."

The media would enjoy describing the cataclysm between the forces marshaled by Annie Snyder and those of Til Hazel as the Third Battle of Bull Run. But that clever label was misleading; it suggested that the fight was the only one since the gunfire. That was by no means right. The intense struggles over the use of the land began almost before the Rebel yells—heard for the first time at Manassas—had died away. The land was bought by a real estate speculator only weeks after the battle in 1861. He thought it would make a good tourist attraction.

The fields were haunted by ghosts of battles that always seemed to swirl around Manassas. For it was there, in the First Battle of Bull Run—only three months after Fort Sumter fell—that it first became clear there would be no cheap victory, no quick score.

Annie counted the 1988 struggle as her sixth Third Battle of Manassas. And she got started only in the second half of the twentieth century. One reporter checking the clips back to 1890 counted it as at least the tenth.

Snyder's first battle came in the 1950s, over the interstate. That was an awesome struggle. Deflecting the intentions of freeway engineers in those days was unheard of—even if they did see the shortest distance between two points as straight through the middle of a historic battlefield. In the end, however, deflected they were. The battle is marked on the atlases of America to this day. Just west of Fairfax, for no apparent reason unless you know your modern history, the freeway dips idiosyncratically to the south.

Another of Snyder's several battles of Manassas involved Marriott's plan in 1973 to put a Great America theme park on the land. Seemed like a good idea to put roller coasters and Ferris wheels and water slides and cotton candy next to the battlefield there. That plan too was brought to its knees. And it too served to burnish Annie's legend.

But by the late 1980s, it seemed the battles might have come to an end. For decades, the Prince William County government had tried to encourage commercial development. It was urgently needed to help meet the crushing tax burden of providing schools and services for all the residential subdivisions popping up around one of the fastest growing jurisdictions in the nation. The county had earmarked nearly six hundred acres adjacent to the interstate—and thus, incidentally, next to the National Battlefield Park—as among the most promising sites. In the late 1970s, the county had fought desperately to prevent those woods and fields from being included in the National Park. They wanted jobs there. So in 1986, the Hazel/Peterson Companies came up with a plan. Its centerpiece, the county believed, would be a wooded Edge City corporate park of glass and steel and trees for highly educated, high-tech, white-collar workers. It would be screened from the battlefield. The traffic impact, it was promised, would be minimal. It seemed that the outline of a decent compromise was at hand. Those like Snyder who had fought so much for the battlefield were hardly happy with the idea of having mid-rise offices where Longstreet swept forward to close the vise on the Federals. But if development was inevitable, a relatively classy and low-rise Planned Mixed-Use Development such as the one the Hazel/Peterson Companies were proposing, with 560 new homes and 2.9 million square feet of commercial space—half the size of downtown San Antonio— might be about as good a deal as they were going to get. Hazel/ Peterson ran tours of their office park eight miles down the interstate, at Fair Lakes. It did indeed have trees and lakes and geese. The shopping area was small scale. Politics, after all, is the art of the possible. The special PMD zoning ordinance was passed. And that seemed to be about the end of that. Annie even announced her retirement as an activist. The doctors had read her the riot act. If she didn't slow down, they told her, a combination of ills threatened her life. In the *Washington Post* article intending to bid her farewell and recap her long history of struggle, however, up cropped another of those Annie Snyder incongruities. She was photographed out in one of her lovely fields, attractively dressed. But what she was leaning on was her shotgun. Almost as if she knew.

When the final battle resumed in Manassas on January 28, 1988, it started with a shock like a thunderclap on a sunny day. Without warning, Hazel/Peterson announced a change in plans. The future corporate campus at William Center needed a shot in the arm, they announced. So they were going to switch some uses in their Planned Mixed-Use Development. Almost half the 2.9 million square feet of nonresidential use to which they were entitled was not going to be corporate campus after all. The page one headline in the *Washington Post* the next day said it all: HUGE MALL PLANNED AT MANASSAS. 600-Acre Project to Be Located Near Battlefield

"It excites me in the sense that we're no longer going to stand in the shadow of Fairfax County," said the Prince William supervisor representing the district. "This is going to be nicer than Fair Oaks," he said, referring to the mall of astounding size only eight miles away with 1.4 million square feet and 213 stores.

Once again, the earth moved. But this time the shudder was an emotional and political Richter reading far above anything Manassas had felt in a century.

In the torrent of abuse directed at Til Hazel during the ensuing weeks, "double-crossed," "defrauded," "cheated," and "deceived" were among the more printable words. Hazel swore that when the Edward J. DeBartolo Corporation—the largest shopping center developer in the United States—approached him with the idea of putting one of their five-anchor, 1.2-million-square-foot behemoths next to the battlefield, it was a bolt out of the blue. A mall was the furthest thing from his mind at the time. Although, truth to tell, he'd always felt a little uncomfortable about whether the market was really ready for office parks this far out into the countryside. When the idea came up, he said, he decided that the mall was needed as a "catalytic agent" to attract corporate offices on the remaining acreage at William Center. "That's been the history of malls all over the country," he said. "They bring along offices." And besides, his spokesman pointed out, it was a done deal. There would be no chance to challenge the decision, no public hearings. No additional action by the county supervisors would be required. The head of the National Park Service could write as many letters as he wished saying that the new plan "does not even resemble the good faith agreements we thought had been made." They would be beside the point. The language of the rezoning that the county had gratefully accepted two years before had been very carefully crafted by Hazel's pre-eminent legal arm. There was nothing in there about "corporate parks" or "malls." All it had been written to say was that permission was hereby granted to develop 2.9 million square feet of nonresidential space.

Hazel thought that said it all. Little did he know. He had rumbled a deep sleeping fault in the American psyche, a revolt against everything about growth that Americans had come to despise. If there was any one piece of paper that said it all, it was not the boilerplate in the legal documents. The mark that something different was afoot was the brand-new sticker on the bumper of Charlie Graham's truck. It read:

"Have a Nice Day. Shoot a Developer."

This was no small deal. Charlie made his living as a carpenter.

As it turned out, there were historic dimensions to that tension between Graham's chosen profession and his bumper sticker. Graham was the kind of independent cuss who carried a Civil War–replica .58-caliber black-powder Minié-ball Springfield rifle into battle re-enactments. Even though he was yet another Fauquier County Virginian, he wore the Union uniform of the 116th Pennsylvania. The Harvard historian William R. Taylor described such romantics at the end of his 1957 work *Cavalier and Yankee: The Old South and American National Character*. The Charlie Grahams of the 1980s were those young, mustachioed, skilled small-business entrepreneurs who made so much of America tick. As Taylor described them, they were the direct psychological descendants of the Southern yeomen whom Thomas Jefferson revered and saw as the foundation of the Republic. They were "ardent and impassioned," "strongly partisan to liberty," "vigorous and more natural than the gentleman planter," possessing "a great natural intelligence" and a "chivalric sense of honor." At the same time, they were just plumb ornery—and of precious little comfort to those in positions of authority. In this way, in short, they were the reincarnation of the original Virginia Cavaliers, said Taylor. Those Cavaliers, of course, were the men who saw the land of America in 1607 as the Garden.

Poor Hazel. In hindsight there is a kind of awful inevitability to it all. The women who saw themselves guarding the flame of Western civilization would take him high. They would succeed largely by not playing the game of dollars and numbers he played, by the rules he knew. They would appeal to the truths recognized by the heart, a practice he viewed as underhanded and dastardly, if not immoral. Meanwhile the swashbucklers, the Cavaliers—of whom there were more than a few feisty enough to have become United States senators—would take him any way they could get him.

Hazel, the Pilgrim lawyer, had it all correct, legally. But he had it all wrong in the terms that turned out to matter—those of human emotion and the American *Zeitgeist.* He made the same two errors as the Union at Bull Run a century and a quarter before. First, he gravely underestimated what he was up against. Second, he was blind-sided by the counterattack.

But that is only hindsight. In the early days of the struggle, there seemed to be no possibility that he could lose. When the battle cry of freedom rose once again, it sounded as forlorn as ever in its time. The first day that the plans for the mall were announced, the sound of the opposition seemed hollow. "It would destroy the battlefield," the newspaper quoted a lonely "civic activist"—one Annie D. Snyder—as saying. "We'll fight it with everything we've got."

What *is* it about malls? Is it not in fact curious that it took the idea of constructing a mall—specifically a mall—to elicit such a reaction to the idea of building on hallowed ground? In a way, Hazel had a point when he failed to anticipate the reaction his switch would ignite. Office buildings place just as much steel and concrete on the landscape as malls do. Just as much asphalt is laid to get to them. What's the big deal about shifting the ground to a mall?

Opponents answered the question by trotting out traffic studies. The mall would attract gridlock at different times from office buildings—on weekends, when tourists came to enjoy the serenity of the battlefield, not just nine to five. True. But so what? Since when do dry traffic studies arouse feelings of sacrilege? That explanation hardly seemed to satisfy.

Biblical explanations were offered. Perhaps we Americans are more tolerant of the places where people make money than we are of the places where they spend it. Jesus threw the moneychangers out of the temple, it was observed. He did not throw the fishermen out of the boat. But again, does that explanation satisfy? Since when has shopping been seen as sinful in this country? Some anthropologists view the shopping bag as the most human of archeological artifacts. Other vertebrates, they point out, wouldn't believe the effort humans put into gathering material from all sorts of places to bring it home and share it with others of their species. Most sensible creatures eat it where it lies.

No, it seemed to be something about that symbol, that place— the mall—that was getting to us.

Maybe it worked like this. The force that drove the creation of Edge City was our search deep inside ourselves for a new balance of individualism and freedom. We wanted to build a world in which we could live in one place, work in another, and play in a third, in unlimited combination, as a way to nurture our human potential. This demanded transportation that would allow us to go where we wanted, when we wanted. That enshrined the individual transportation system, the automobile, in our lives. And that led us to build our market meeting places in the fashion of today's malls.

In theory, at least, the malls exemplified our devotion to individualism. The major way analysts distinguish one from another is by how many unusual shops each has. The most upscale malls are those which strive successfully to deliver something different. Something special. They offer goods and experiences not available elsewhere—an impossibly chic boutique, a special art exhibit on the weekend, an expensive antiquarian bookstore. The more downscale malls are those with little individuality, where the goods and chain stores and events are undistinguished and indistinguishable from those available anywhere else. What does that say? That the moment we have a little extra money, the first thing we do—once again—is strive toward expression of our individualism.

Perhaps that is why the malls at the centers of our Edge Cities so frustrate us. The very moment they succeed in finding a way to help us express our individuality, their distributive function denies it—by spreading it nationwide. The crossed tusks of Banana Republic were transformed from a distinctive statement of San Francisco hip to a mall cliché in a period measured in heartbeats.

Long after the battle for William Center was over, Robert C. Kelly, Til Hazel's spokesman, was still groping to explain how he managed to run himself into a buzz saw. Kelly, being a thoughtful man who took pride in his ability to get along with people, finally explained it to himself this way. Developers, he said, are agents of change. That is what they do. That is what they are for. That is their social and economic role. They look for ways to convert land profitably from one use to another.

And, Kelly concluded, that is what the American people at last began to rebel against. The Change.

Fair enough. Kelly was on to something. But perhaps he did not push his logic far enough. He didn't take the next step. What, then, was the problem with the Change?

Maybe it was the way the change was so impersonal, driven only by the relentless logic of the marketplace, which is wildly efficient but incapable of quantifying the human ecology of a place, its sense of home, the intangibles of our culture. Maybe that's why when we see the bulldozers, we cringe. Maybe deep down we see the problem as the Change denying—even attacking—the specialness of our lives. We see it as attacking the very individuality and individualism that we had been building this stuff to achieve in the first place. Each piece of the new world we build caters to our dreams of freedom. But right now, the totality does not make us feel like individuals. It makes us feel like strangers. Strangers in our own land. We look around and recognize nothing. It is all changing so fast, we cannot find our own place in the universe. Not even our old house or favorite hangout. It alienates us. Sometimes we barely recognize ourselves.

Now *that* would be a contradiction in our souls. *That* would explain a lot about our reaction to Manassas. It would also explain why our heart sinks when we see a threat to other landscapes that we love.

We see those places as distinct. As one of a kind. Just like each of us. And to the extent that they are removed from the face of the earth—especially to be replaced by a symbol of homogeneity like a mall—well. It would be the symbol of the mass, of the ubiquitous, of the ordinary, destroying the singular, the irreplaceable. And just to that extent would we see the singular and the irreplaceable in our own lives, in our very selves, diminished.

Maybe that is also why we cling so tenaciously to whatever history we can. Maybe that is why we are rallying to save sad Art Deco movie houses and Main Streets with old Kresge's. This is us, we say; this is our time. Time is the only thing we have. Time is the measure of our lives. These places are our memories of a time when our identities were clear. And you're taking that away.

Perhaps that is why the idea of violating Manassas—the symbol of a place where our ancestors died to define us as Americans, our basic sense of self—made something snap. And if that is true, it would offer a new reason to believe that we may be at a turning point.

Perhaps if we can reach down into ourselves to understand truly what we value, we can hope to move forward. If we understand and involve ourselves in our built environment and the way it reflects our lives, maybe we can break through to higher ground. Then we may find a means of measuring Edge City on a scale in addition to its exchange value, its worth as real estate. We may be able to assess the way it nurtures the individualism and freedom to which it was meant to speak in the first place.

It's a long shot, to be sure. But if we are coming to the point where we can appraise Edge City in terms of how it nourishes our relationship with one another, as well as our relationship to the land, it would mean that the world of the immigrant and the pioneer is not dead in America. It has moved out to Edge City, where gambles are being lost and won for high stakes. Of course Edge City is cracked and raw right now, and subject to a lot of improvement. But if it is really the sum of our hopes, then maybe someday it will be seen as historic. As historic, in its way, as our most revered battlefields. For Edge City, then, would be seen by future generations as the creation of a new frontier.

It would be a new frontier being shaped by the free, in a constantly reinvented land.

The first mass meeting in opposition to the William Center mall, on Friday, February 5, 1988, did not make strong men quake. Yes, an American flag hung upside down in distress from the Groveton Road overpass, and yes, 227 people gathered at the visitors' center of the National Battlefield Park. Yes, they reached deep into their wallets to finance the impending legal battles. But the take? Fifty-six hundred dollars. Heartwarming, but beside the point. There were not many ways to challenge the legalities of the mall. With the news full of budget deficits and draconian spending cuts, the idea of the federal government stepping in to buy the land at a projected cost of $50 million or more seemed ludicrous.

Hazel's machines soon ground at the earth with breakneck speed. Quartz lights turned the night into death-pallor day as crews worked round the clock, double shift, blasting dynamite as late as 1:30 A.M. to tunnel a sewer under Interstate 66. Legions of belly-dumping earthmovers wheeled at speeds akin to tanks on flank attack. An antebellum-style house disappeared one night; all that was left were the surrounding trees. Dust clouds as if from brigades on maneuver rose to the sky. Wetlands were banked. Chain saws roared. If Hazel thought the land was not "particularly pretty" in its original state, when it was planed of all its green it made people sick. Hazel chastely claimed that the delirious attack of the heavy equipment was normal—just meeting contract schedules. Could he help it if that drove the cost of condemning the land higher and higher, to unthinkable peaks?

The frenzied destruction backfired. The national and international media knew a great story when they saw one. The red, raw ground, the bulldozers running roughshod, probably over Confederate bones—it was agonizing. And galvanizing. The National Park Service likened it to "booking a roller derby in the Sistine Chapel." The idea that in a matter of weeks that portion of the battlefield would be completely gone drew high-powered action. Some of the country's leading preservation groups, including the National Trust for Historic Preservation and the National Parks and Conservation Association, took on Manassas as a cause célèbre. Tersh Boasberg, a nationally recognized preservation attorney, was retained. Jody Powell—the high-profile and savvy former presidential press secretary with the politically useful Southern drawl—came on board as a tactician and spokesperson.

It was he who sat by Annie Snyder in the congressional hearing room and delivered the impassioned speech that made the big fat tears run down Annie Snyder's cheeks.

"On that little hill, Mr. Chairman, history is palpable. Today you can see it and feel it . . ." As Powell orated, the network cameras were zooming in tight, filling screens nationwide with Annie's face. Her blue eyes filling to overflowing. Her face scrunched up as she fought unsuccessfully to control her lower lip. "You can see it and feel it, a blood-soaked piece of Virginia countryside." In countless living rooms around the country, viewers discovered that they, too, seemed to have something in their eyes.

Those who knew Annie well knew that she could, in fact, get emotional about the way her husband dealt with dirty dishes. But, as always in human affairs, that was beside the point. What mattered was a woman like Annie puddling up before U.S. congressmen on national television, over a battlefield and a landscape that she clearly loved so deeply. It was not something the citizens of the Republic saw every day. The signatures on petitions from around the country rolled in by the tens of thousands. Events did turn.

In some ways, the war for Manassas and the future of our lives will never end. But Friday, October 7, 1988, will probably be marked by future historians as the decisive battle, even if it didn't seem that way at the time. That is when Senator Dale Bumpers of Arkansas—the kind of Cavalier that *The Almanac of American Politics* described as "challenging" and "the town iconoclast"—got up in the well of the Senate.

Bumpers, the respected chairman of the National Parks and Forests Subcommittee, gave a long, impassioned, and very Southern version of history that night. It was late. The sense of the Senate was that everybody desperately wished to be someplace else—especially home campaigning in the election season that marked the end of the Reagan years. Nonetheless, an astounding number of senators remained on the floor to listen to history.

"[Longstreet] sent out a couple of brigades to see what the strength of the Union was right here." Bumpers pointed to the Civil War maps behind him. "And this occurred on the William Center tract, bear in mind. He found out that the Union was there in strength. He pulled those brigades back and deployed all thirty thousand of his men in woods. Those woods are *still there.* You go down there *right now* and you will see where Longstreet had his men deployed behind all those trees down there . . .

"Sixteen thousand men in about forty-eight hours either lost their lives or were wounded in this battle. It was perhaps the third bloodiest battle of the war. Lee, after he won this, thought France and England would recognize the Confederate States. But they were not quite ready. They said you have not won a battle in Northern soil. So Lee took his troops to Antietam."

The Battle of Antietam began three weeks later, on September 17. It was the most awful battle of our bloodiest war.

"I told you about these hospitals. They are our Confederate troops buried on this property around the hospitals . . . I believe strongly in our heritage and think our children ought to know where these battlefields are and what was involved in them. I do not want to go out there ten years from now with my grandson and tell him about the Second Battle of Manassas. He says, 'Well, Grandpa, wasn't General Lee in control of this war here? Didn't he command the Confederate troops?'

" 'Yes, he did.'

" 'Well, where was he?'

" 'He was up there where that shopping mall is.'

"I can see a big granite monument inside that mall's hallway right now: General Lee stood on this spot.

"If you really cherish our heritage as I do, and you believe that history is very important for our children, you will vote for my amendment. I yield the floor."

James A. McClure, the reserved Idaho Republican who has one of the most conservative voting records in the Senate, got up in opposition to the Bumpers amendment. But he actually added fuel to the greater argument over the land. Said he:

"There is not a single battlefield free from development pressures. We are not just talking about Manassas, we are talking

about what is going to happen to every one of the other elements of the National Park System where battlefields are involved . . . A cable franchise in Frederick, Maryland, proposes
construction of a 160-foot microwave reception and transmission tower on Red Hill, less than one mile from Bloody Lane, the
center of the Antietam Battlefield.

"Does it sound familiar in the context of this debate?

"A 100-foot microwave tower threatens the Bolivar Heights
Battlefield associated with Major General T. J. (Stonewall) Jackson's siege and capture of Harpers Ferry, the site of the largest
surrender of U.S.–led troops. Such a structure, within five feet—
I repeat, five feet—of the park boundary will impair not only the
battlefield but also much of the skyline about historic Harpers
Ferry.

"Sound familiar in the context of this debate?

"Fredericksburg and Spotsylvania National Military Park's
greatest need is to establish a legislated boundary, as land immediately adjacent to the park is scheduled for development."

He went on and on. Cold Harbor, threatened by development
from an expanding Richmond. Kenesaw Mountain National Battlefield Park in Georgia. Vicksburg, Chickamauga-Chattanooga,
and Stones River. "The list," he acknowledged, "is overwhelming." Where will this all end?

In context, he was asking a budgetary question. "This will not
be an acquisition for spare change. By this action we are signal-
ing other landowners at other sites that the way to obtain federal
funds is to destroy, or threaten to destroy, resources which the
federal government has authorized for acquisition but which
have not filtered to the top of the annual appropriations process;
or, as in the case of Manassas, resources which are not even
within the boundaries of an established park."

Of course in the context of our futures, he was asking a more
profound question, perhaps more profound than he knew.
Where, indeed, will this battle over the land all end?

Then again, maybe McClure did have an inkling. In what was
meant to be his clinching argument, he said, "Perhaps the most
significant battle of the entire Manassas Battlefield with respect
to the William Center tract is that being fought now, not the
ones that were fought there 125 years ago."

With that, he sat down, and the Senate came to a roll-call vote.

Adams.

Armstrong.

Baucus.

Boschwitz . . .

It was not at all clear what the result would be.

. . . Thurmond.

Trible.

Warner.

Wirth.

The votes were tallied. The vote was 50 to 25 in the U.S. Senate to save the battlefield.

Senator John Warner of Virginia, the Republican who had tried to find some wiggle room between the two absolute positions of this battle—who had tried to write legislation that amounted to a compromise on the cheap—voted against the bill. But the instant the vote was tallied, he got up to save his soul: "Mr. President, I ask unanimous consent to vitiate [cancel] the roll-call vote."

The acting president pro tempore: "Is there objection? Hearing none, it is so ordered."

That was the passing of the amendment. At that moment on October 7, 1988, the people of the United States of America redeemed their heritage.

On October 12, the Senate passed the tax bill to which the amendment was a rider. A Reagan veto seemed likely. Two days later, the battlefield measure survived conference with the House.

On Friday, October 14, George Bush, in a speech in La Jolla, California, tried to cast himself as a modern-day Teddy Roosevelt, distancing himself from the years of controversy over Ronald Reagan's restrictive environmental policies.

"In George Bush you will have a president committed to conservation," he said. Bush promised to "strengthen and preserve our parks" under a new program called America the Beautiful, and to seek new Clean Air legislation. He vowed to pursue reductions in acid rain pollutants, stop ocean dumping of sludge and medical wastes, enforce the Superfund restrictions, convene an international conference on the environment, back new parkland acquisition in the California locale in which he spoke, "take a very close look" at his earlier opposition to restrictions on offshore drilling in the area, back urban "greenways," propose using oil and gas tax revenue funds to finance new park acquisitions, and create a new National Endowment for the Environment.

The fate of the Manassas bill, however, was still a cliff-hanger. Negotiations between key House and Senate conferees over the tax bill in which it was embedded broke off. It appeared almost certain that a tax compromise could not be worked out before Congress adjourned at the end of the week. By October 21, the headlines read BILL TO BUY MALL SITE NEARS FAILURE.

Nonetheless, at 1 A.M. on the twenty-second, in the legislative equivalent of seconds left to play as both houses rushed to adjourn, the bill did pass. On Wednesday, November 2, it reached the White House.

On Friday, November 11, without fanfare or even comment, Ronald Reagan signed it.

November 11, 1988, was one and a quarter centuries, less eight days, from Lincoln's Gettysburg address.

"The moment the ink from the president's pen was dry," reported John F. Harris in that Saturday's *Washington Post,* "ownership of the property transferred from the developer, Northern Virginia's Hazel/Peterson Cos., to the federal government as an addition to the adjacent 3800-acre Manassas National Battlefield Park.

" 'We're done,' said Robert Kelly, a spokesman for Hazel/ Peterson Cos. 'My understanding is we're supposed to leave the property in an orderly fashion . . . and we'll be doing that.' "

Harris noted that Hazel would make a fortune on the taking. The federal government ultimately paid $81 million for the William Center property. Hazel had bought the land for $11 million two years before.

But it was a wonder nonetheless, and the next morning Annie Snyder led fifty of her resistance fighters into the promised land. They marched onto Stuart's Hill for the first time, the land on which the frenzied workings of the machines had just been stilled. Soon, signs around the perimeter of the once but not now future William Center were posted by park rangers. They encircled three model homes, a stretch of four-lane divided road, water and sewer work, and bulldozed site preparation throughout most of the eastern section of the 542-acre place.

The sledgehammers drove the message home. U.S. PROPERTY, the signs read.

———————

The few early stalwarts of the Save the Battlefield Coalition had long before promised one another—back when they most needed promises to each other, for other promises were so scant —that if they ever won this battle, on the first Saturday afterward they would have a ceremony of thanksgiving. If the bulldozers were ever stilled, to thank the Lord for the miracle—which at times had seemed as improbable as the parting of the Red Sea— they would gather one more time to honor the spirit of the place.

That Saturday, November 19, dawned foul. As they gathered near the site of one of the houses that had been used as a field hospital during the war, the air was dank and chill. The drizzle was steady.

But that did not dampen the spirits of the coalition. They had survived 104 degree heat the previous July when they held a massive rally at the battlefield. It featured a March of the Ghosts, in which specters with astonishing resemblances to Abraham Lincoln, Robert E. Lee, James Longstreet, Stonewall Jackson, and J.E.B. Stuart had prowled the land as drums rolled and bagpipes keened. A little rain and cold would not disturb them. And, they laughed, they finally had few tactical considerations. It's not as if they had to worry anymore about the television cameras shorting out. This was for the faithful.

That is why, as the small crowd of 140 began their hymns and their prayers while the rain continued to fall, they wondered exactly how it had happened. When the engine roar came from the north, they murmured to each other, Where in the name of God will this all end?

If they thought the war was ended, they were wrong.

The roar came from a small, single-engine plane. It passed over them again and again, across the lowering skies, its low-altitude buzz a never-ending pain. It would not go away. It seemed it would always be there. As indeed it would resonate into the future.

The Cessna pulled a banner behind its tail, through the cold mists over the battlefield of centuries. Once again it proclaimed defiance. Endless defiance. It promised that the war was not over among the Americans. The battle would be fought again that had been fought this year, for it was the same battle that we had fought on this very ground twice, a century and a quarter ago. The same battle we've been struggling with since we first landed permanently on these shores, in 1607 and 1620.

It came down to who we are, how we got that way, where we're headed, and what we value. Whether we will ever resolve the difference between what we can do and what we should. Whether the land belongs to us, or we belong to the land.

Behind that little buzzing plane was this reminder: THE TAKING OF PRIVATE LAND IS UNAMERICAN.

# 11

# THE LIST

## Edge Cities,
## Coast to Coast

THE FOLLOWING is a select compilation of Edge Cities in North America.

Although this is one of the more thorough such lists at this writing, the nature of the beast doubtless makes it incomplete. Edge Cities are a function of growth; they change. In a time and place of rapid expansion, as in the Washington region of the late 1980s, the number of Edge Cities swelled from thirteen to sixteen in two years. By the same token, while the area around Atlanta's Hartsfield Airport does not qualify as a mature Edge City in the early 1990s, that is probably not a permanent condition.

The definition of an Edge City is the five-part test described in Chapter 1:

A full-blown Edge City is marked by:
- Five million square feet of leasable office space or more.
- Six hundred thousand square feet of retail space or more.
- A population that increases at 9 A.M. on workdays—marking the location as primarily a work center, not a residential suburb.
- A local perception as a single end destination for mixed use —jobs, shopping, and entertainment.
- A history in which, thirty years ago, the site was by no means urban; it was overwhelmingly residential or rural in character.

This definition requires some judgment calls on the part of the observer. A few Edge Cities listed below are so dispersed across the geography as to challenge the definition—Boston's intersection of Route 128 and the Massachusetts Turnpike, for example. In other places, several Edge Cities are packed together, as along northern Interstate 680 in Contra Costa County and along the San Diego Freeway, in Orange County, California. Where one begins and the other ends is debatable.

Some other centers cry out for consideration because of their history or the overwhelming size of their office population, even though they may not meet all the other elements of the definition. Merrifield, Virginia, site of the world headquarters of Mobil—the second largest oil company and sixth largest industrial corporation in the United States—is some distance from major retail.

This list, then, is meant to be suggestive, not exhaustive. It is intended to spur the reader to go out and look at some of these places, make critical judgments, and arrive at personal conclusions.

While every effort has been made to ensure the accuracy of the list, experience, alas, demonstrates the unlikelihood that perfection has been achieved. Readers who wish to suggest changes may write the author in care of The Edge City® Group, Broad Run, Virginia, 22014-9501.

The symbols in this list match the symbols in the maps. A triangle means the old "central business district"—usually thought of as "downtown." A black circle means an Edge City. A gray circle means an emerging Edge City. A clear circle means an Edge City that is expected to be built, according to local plan.

National sources include Salomon Brothers, New York; Robert Charles Lesser and Company, Los Angeles; The Office Network, Houston; the Urban Land Institute, Washington; academic geographers and demographers noted in the Acknowledgments, and personal observation. Local commercial real estate sources are listed in the Notes. For references to Edge Cities in Europe and Asia, see Chapter 7.

## ATLANTA

▲ Downtown (Five Points)
● Midtown
● Buckhead (The Lenox Square Mall area)
● The Cumberland Mall–Galleria area (at the 285 Perimeter beltway and Interstate 75)

- The Perimeter Center area (at 285 and Georgia 400 in north Fulton County)
- The Gwinnett Place mall area (off Interstate 85 in Gwinnett County)
- The Perimeter and I-85 area
- The Hartsfield-Atlanta International Airport area

## AUSTIN

▲ Downtown
- The Northwest area (centered on Loop 360 at the Mo Pac Expressway and Research Boulevard–Route 183)

## BALTIMORE

▲ Downtown
- Towson
- Hunt Valley
- Columbia

*Demonstrating how independent Edge Cities can be, Columbia, with ties to two metropolitan areas, is also considered part of the Washington region.*

- White Marsh
- Owings Mills
- Security Boulevard
- Baltimore-Washington International Airport

## BOSTON

▲ Downtown
- The Kendall Square–MIT area
- The Alewife T station area (in north Cambridge)
- Quincy-Braintree (at 128 and the Southeast Expressway)
- The Massachusetts Turnpike and 128
- The Burlington Mall area (at 128 and Route 3)
- Peabody-Danvers (I-95 north)
- Southern New Hampshire
- The Mass Pike and 495
- The Framingham area (the Mass Pike between 128 and 495)
- Foxboro (495 and 95 south)

## CHARLOTTE

▲ Uptown
*This, confusingly, is what the old central business district is locally called.*
● Southpark

## CHICAGO

▲ The Loop (and environs)
● The Schaumburg area (including Hoffman Estates and the Woodfield Mall area near the Northwest Tollway)
● The O'Hare Airport area
● "The Illinois Research and Development Corridor," (including the area around Oak Brook, Lisle, Naperville, Aurora, and the East-West Tollway)
● The Lake Shore Corridor area (around the Edens Expressway and the Tri-State Tollway)

## CLEVELAND

▲ Downtown
● The Chagrin Boulevard and Interstate 271 area (east of Shaker Heights)
● The Rockside Road and Interstate 77 area

## DALLAS–FORT WORTH

▲ Downtown Dallas
● Turtle Creek–Oak Lawn (Midtown)
● The North Central Expressway area (from north of Downtown to Beltline Road)
● The Dallas Galleria–LBJ Freeway area
*Also known as the Blade Runner Landscape.*
● Las Colinas
● The Stemmons Freeway–Love Field area
● The far North Dallas–EDS area
● The Richardson–Plano area (the North Central Expressway area beyond the LBJ)
▲ Downtown Fort Worth

## DENVER

▲ Downtown
● The Tech Center area (including the Greenwood Plaza area)
● Cherry Creek

## DETROIT

▲ Downtown Detroit
● The Southfield–Northland Mall area (off I-10 nearest Downtown)
● The Southfield–Prudential Town Center area (I-10 northwest of Northland Mall)
● The Southfield–Telegraph Road area (I-10 at Interstate 696)
● The Troy–Big Beaver Road area (off Interstate 75)
● The Auburn Hills area (off Interstate 75)
● The Farmington Hills area (at Interstate 696)
● The Dearborn–Fairlane Village area
● The Ann Arbor–Route 14 area
▲ Downtown Windsor, Ontario, Canada

## FORT LAUDERDALE

▲ Downtown
● The Cypress Creek area

## HOUSTON

▲ Downtown
● The Galleria area
● The Greenway Plaza area
● The Sharpstown Mall–Highway 59 area
● The Texas Medical Center–Rice University area
● The Westheimer–West Belt–Westchase area
● The Katy Freeway–West Houston Energy Corridor
● The U.S. 290–Northwest area
● The Greenspoint–North Beltway–I-45 area
● The Clear Lake–NASA area
● FM 1960
  *This is not a radio station; it is a reference to an Edge City that is growing up around a highway that fairly recently was a farm-to-*

*market road.*
● The Woodlands

## KANSAS CITY

▲ Downtown
● The College Boulevard–Overland Park area
● The Country Club Plaza area
● The Crown Center area
● The Kansas City International Airport area

## LAS VEGAS

▲ Downtown
● The Strip
*The Strip, while not having much in the way of leasable office space, is so much the center of people's perception of what Las Vegas means that it is something of an Edge City paragon. How many visitors to Las Vegas discover that downtown even exists?*

## LOS ANGELES

*Greater Los Angeles now covers five counties: Los Angeles County at the center, Ventura County up the coast to the northwest, Orange County down the coast to the southeast, and Riverside County and San Bernardino County inland. It includes:*

▲ Downtown Los Angeles
*Then, marching straight west from downtown, toward the ocean, there is:*
● Mid-Wilshire
● Miracle Mile
● Beverly Hills–Century City
● West Los Angeles

*North of this central Los Angeles County corridor, on the other side of the Santa Monica Mountains, is the San Fernando Valley, which includes, from east to west:*
● Burbank–North Hollywood
● Sherman Oaks–Van Nuys
● Warner Center–West Valley

*North of the San Fernando Valley, there is the Santa Clarita Valley, with:*

● Valencia

*West of the San Fernando Valley, toward the ocean, in Ventura County, is:*

● Ventura–the Coastal Plain

*Heading down the coast, to the south, back in Los Angeles County, there is:*

● Marina Del Rey–Culver City
● The Los Angeles International Airport area (LAX/El Segundo)
● The South Bay–Torrance–Carson–San Diego Freeway area
▲ Downtown Long Beach

*Continuing down the coast, crossing into Orange County, there is:*

● North Orange County (Fullerton–La Habra–Brea)
● Central Orange County (Disneyland–Los Angeles Rams Stadium–the Santa Ana I-5 Freeway–Santa Ana–Anaheim–Garden Grove)
● Western Orange County (Westminster–Huntington Beach)
● The John Wayne Airport area (including South Coast Plaza–Costa Mesa as well as the bulk of Irvine)
● Newport Beach–Fashion Island (also largely Irvine)
● Irvine Spectrum
● South Orange County (San Clemente–Laguna Niguel)

*Heading inland from downtown Los Angeles, to the east, up against the San Gabriel Mountains, is the San Gabriel Valley portion of Los Angeles County, with:*

● Pasadena–North Valley
● South Valley–Covina

*The Inland Empire comprises San Bernardino County and, to its south, Riverside County, which includes:*

● Ontario Airport–Rancho Cucamonga
● San Bernardino
● Riverside

## MEMPHIS

▲ Downtown
● The Poplar Corridor–East Memphis
◗ The Airport area

## MIAMI

▲ Downtown Miami (including Brickell Avenue)
● The Airport area (including west toward the Doral Country Club and the Miami Free Zone)
◗ Coral Gables

## MILWAUKEE

▲ Downtown
● Wauwatosa-Mayfair
● Brookfield–Blue Mound Road

## MINNEAPOLIS

▲ Downtown Minneapolis
● Bloomington-Edina (southern I-494 west of the airport)
◗ Minnetonka (western I-494)
▲ Downtown St. Paul

## NEW YORK

### New Jersey
#### Bergen County

● Fort Lee
● Paramus-Montvale
● Mahwah

#### Hudson County

● The Meadowlands/Hoboken area
◗ The Newark International Airport–Jersey City area

#### Essex County

▲ Downtown Newark

#### Morris County

● Whippany–Parsippany–Troy Hills ("287 & 80")
◗ Morristown

### Somerset, Union, and Hunterdon Counties
● The Bridgewater Mall area ("287 & 78")
### Middlesex County
● The Woodbridge area
● The Amtrak Metropark area
### Mercer County
● U.S. 1–Princeton
▲ Downtown Trenton

## NEW YORK STATE
### Manhattan
▲ Midtown Manhattan
▲ Downtown Manhattan (the Wall Street area)
### Westchester County
● The White Plains area
◗ The Tarrytown area
● Purchase-Rye

## LONG ISLAND
### Nassau County
● Great Neck–Lake Success–North Shore
● Mitchell Field–Garden City
### Suffolk County
● Route 110–Melville
● Hauppauge

## CONNECTICUT
### Fairfield County
● The Stamford-Greenwich area
● The Westport and I-95 north area

## PENNSYLVANIA
◗ The Lehigh Valley (Allentown-Bethlehem-Easton)

## ORLANDO

▲ Downtown
● Maitland Center
◗ The Airport area
◗ The University of Central Florida area

## PHILADELPHIA

- ▲ Downtown
- ● King of Prussia
- ● Willow Grove–Warminster (the Pennsylvania Turnpike and 611).
- ● Cherry Hill, New Jersey

## PHOENIX

*Phoenix is the first major American municipality formally to recognize for planning purposes that it is made up of Edge Cities—in local parlance, urban villages. Three within the political boundaries of Phoenix have hit critical mass: Downtown, Uptown, and the Camelback Corridor. Nine are planned within that municipality alone. In this listing, planned Edge Cities that have not really begun to emerge are indicated with a clear circle. Edge Cities are also emerging in such adjacent areas as Scottsdale, Tempe, and Mesa.*

- ▲ Downtown Phoenix
- ● Uptown–the Central Avenue Corridor
- ● The Camelback Corridor
- ● Scottsdale
- ◗ The Metro Center Mall area (North Mountain)
- ◗ The 44th Street–Sky Harbor Airport area
- ◗ Tempe
- ◗ Mesa-Chandler
- ○ Deer Valley
- ○ Alhambra
- ○ Maryvale
- ○ South Mountain
- ○ Paradise Valley

## PITTSBURGH

- ▲ Downtown
- ● The Penn Lincoln Parkway–Airport area
- ◗ The East Side (especially Monroeville)

## PORTLAND, OREGON

▲ Downtown
● Beaverton-Tigard-Tualatin
◐ The Sunset Freeway Corridor

## THE RESEARCH TRIANGLE, NORTH CAROLINA

▲ Downtown Raleigh
▲ Downtown Durham
▲ Downtown Chapel Hill
● The Research Triangle Park area

## SACRAMENTO

▲ Downtown
◐ The Arden Fair Mall–California Expo State Fairgrounds area
◐ The Natomas area (between Downtown and the airport)

## ST. LOUIS

▲ Downtown
● Clayton
● The Westport Plaza area
◐ The Highway 40–Chesterfield Village area (west of I-270)

## ST. PETERSBURG

▲ Downtown
◐ The Gateway–Howard Frankland Bridge area

## SAN ANTONIO

▲ Downtown
● The Airport area
● The South Texas Medical Center Complex area
◐ The Austin Highway area

## SAN DIEGO

▲ Downtown
● Kearney Mesa

- Mission Valley
- North City (including University Town Center, Torrey Pines, Sorrento Center, East Gate Technology Center, and the like)
- The North Coast area (Encinitas to Oceanside along I-5)
- The I-15 North area (Miramar Naval Air Station to Escondido)

## SAN FRANCISCO

▲ Downtown San Francisco
### North
- San Rafael (Marin County)
### East
▲ Downtown Oakland (including Lake Merritt)
- Berkeley (including Emeryville)
### Farther East (the I-680 Corridor)
- Concord
- Contra Costa Centre–Pleasant Hill BART
- Walnut Creek
- Danville–Bishop Ranch–San Ramon
- Dublin–Hacienda–Pleasanton–Livermore
### South
- The Daly City–northern San Mateo County area
- The San Francisco International Airport area
- The Redwood City–southern San Mateo County area
- The Sunnyvale–northern Silicon Valley area
- The San Jose–central Silicon Valley area

*It is a matter of some dispute whether San Jose could genuinely have been considered an urban area thirty years ago, which is why it is listed here as part of an Edge City.*

## SEATTLE

▲ Downtown Seattle
- Bellevue
- "The Technology Corridor"—Interstate 405 north
- The I-90 Corridor (Mercer Island and east)
- South Center–Kent Valley
▲ Downtown Tacoma

## TAMPA

▲ Downtown
● The West Shore–Airport area
● The Tampa Parkway–Interstate 75 area

## TORONTO

▲ Downtown
### North
● Midtown–Yorkville
● North York–North Yonge
### West
● Mississauga
● The Downsview Airport area
● The Etobicoke-427 area
### East
● The Don Valley Parkway–401 area
● The Markham–404 area
● The Eglington–Don Mills area
● Scarborough

## WASHINGTON

### District of Columbia
▲ Downtown

### Maryland
### Montgomery County
● Bethesda–Chevy Chase–Upper Wisconsin Avenue D.C.
● Silver Spring
● The Democracy Boulevard–North Bethesda–White Flint Mall area (I-270 and the Beltway)
● Rockville–I-270
● Shady Grove–I-270
● Gaithersburg–Germantown–I-270
### Howard County
● Columbia
### Prince George's County
● Lanham-Landover-Largo (the Beltway and Route 50 east near the New Carrollton Metro and the Amtrak Metroliner station)

- Laurel–I-95 north
- Bowie New Town
- PortAmerica–southern I-95

### VIRGINIA
### Arlington County

● Rosslyn-Ballston
● Crystal City

### Alexandria

● Old Town
- The I-395 Corridor
- The Eisenhower Valley area

### Fairfax County

● Tysons Corner
● Merrifield (the Beltway and Route 50 west)
● The Fairfax Center–Fair Oaks Mall area (I-66 and Route 50)
● The Reston-Herndon-Dulles Access Road area
● The Dulles International Airport–Route 28 area

### Loudoun County

- The Greater Leesburg–Route 7 area

### Prince William County

- Gainesville

The following numbers were provided by The Office Network in Houston. They compare the relative size of office markets in seventeen metropolitan areas selected by the author. The first number is for the old downtowns—the central business districts. The second is for the area outside those CBDs—i.e., in Edge Cities or emerging Edge Cities. These markets were chosen as roughly representative of the broad middle range—between 20 million and 150 million square feet of office space total. All figures are in millions of square feet. They include buildings under construction. Figures are for the first quarter of 1991. Due to rounding, the two columns may not equal the total. All figures copyright © 1991, The Office Network®. Reprinted with permission.

| Urban Area | CBD | Outside CBD | Total Market |
|---|---|---|---|
| Houston | 37.0 | 101.6 | 138.6 |
| Boston | 37.2 | 94.6 | 131.8 |
| London | 58.3 | 66.0 | 124.3 |
| Dallas | 28.8 | 84.5 | 113.3 |
| Copenhagen | 26.0 | 84.7 | 110.7 |
| Toronto | 45.7 | 51.0 | 96.7 |
| Philadelphia | 35.6 | 37.7 | 73.3 |
| Denver | 23.1 | 46.0 | 69.1 |
| Amsterdam | 21.3 | 45.8 | 67.1 |
| San Diego | 11.6 | 27.3 | 38.9 |
| Pittsburgh | 24.5 | 12.4 | 36.9 |
| St. Louis | 13.6 | 19.0 | 32.6 |
| Baltimore | 12.7 | 19.6 | 32.3 |
| Kansas City | 11.8 | 20.3 | 32.1 |
| Miami | 10.4 | 18.0 | 28.4 |
| Tampa | 6.7 | 21.2 | 28.0 |
| New Orleans | 16.2 | 7.3 | 23.5 |

# 12

## THE WORDS

### Glossary
of a New Frontier

THE BUILDERS of Edge City—the developers and their cohorts—are the biggest gossips since federal prosecutors, and for the same reason: they are constantly trying to figure out what makes human beings tick.

As professional gossips, they have evolved their own code. It includes:

**ACTIVE WATER FEATURE:** Any man-made body of moving water out of which you are not supposed to drink. A waterfall. A fountain. See Passive Water Feature.

**AMENITIES** (also, **AMENITY PACKAGE**): Frills. E.g., trees. An Amenity Package is that collection of all nonessential and not readily justifiable elements in a development which, it is hoped, if sold creatively enough, can be transformed from an obvious drag on earnings into an inducement for a tenant to pay more rent than he might do otherwise. E.g., day-care centers, jogging trails, subsidized restaurants, a concièrge, picnic tables. See Quality of Life.

**AMPLE FREE PARKING:** The touchstone distinction between Edge City and the old downtown.

**ANIMATED SPACE:** A place in which an attempt is made to overcome barrenness and sterility by the addition of anything that suggests life, especially flags. In use: "Jeez, can't you do something to animate that space?" See also Amenities, Quality of Life, and Programmed Space.

**ATTITUDE, AN:** A negative mindset. Thought to be the source of most, and see also, Situations.

**BACK DOOR:** The first thing a smart developer looks for. His

Back Door is his ultimate fall-back position, should the worst possible Situation materialize. No matter how grand a scheme he proposes, a savvy operator has first calculated the minimum he has to do to survive. In use: "We had a Back Door. If all else failed, we could just perc the damn lots and go." The Back Door is most especially what you use when you are faced with, and see also, Five Thousand Mexicans Knocking on the Door of the Alamo.

**BEAUTIFUL BUILDING, A:**    One that is fully leased. Oldest joke in the developer's lexicon. Not really a joke.

**BEAUTY CONTEST:**    An attempt to inject Quality of Life into an Edge City in which government zoning officials offer a developer higher densities—and thereby profits—than would otherwise be politically palatable in exchange for such concessions as, and see also, Amenity Packages, Quality Statements, and Active Water Features.

**BILLBOARD BUILDING:**    A building designed to announce the presence and enhance the image of the corporation whose name appears prominently at its top. Structures like this are especially common in areas with laws that restrict communication via real billboards or other large signs. A Billboard Building can be curious-looking because it is not designed to face the access road by which a person actually reaches the office. It faces out on the freeway, where the maximum number of passersby will receive the message at high speed. Also, Signature Building.

**BLANKS:**    What residential developers call land. A blank is a lot on which a house can be built. As in blank slate. But more important, it is a basic conceptual unit. Land is not a meaningful commodity to a residential builder until it has been reduced to Blanks by a process that includes taking the entire amount of land available, subtracting that on which homes cannot be built (because of provisions for parks, floodplains, roads, shopping centers, and the like), and dividing the remainder by the total number of homes the developer can get zoning for. Not until land has been translated into Blanks can it be entered into the play of a Deal. When residential developers and builders think about land, they do not run the numbers through their heads in acres, as farmers do, or in square feet, as office-space builders do. In fact, if a builder were to bid, say, $30,000 on a Blank, it is of relatively minor importance whether the Blank is 0.5 acres or 5.0 acres, since it represents only one house. The actual size of the Blank is significant only when it is so unusually large or small as to offer major constraints or opportunities. Note: Blank is used especially to refer to "raw" land as opposed to "improved" land. This means that the building lot has been subdivided and zoned, but no Hard Costs have been incurred, such as those for sewers, water, power, phone lines, or roads, nor most Soft Costs, such as, and see also, Carry.

**BLUE WATER:**    The stuff you put into the fountain of your mall to offset the unsightliness of the pennies that people throw in, as well as the grout that washes off. It is this fluid you then discover kids will stick a straw into and drink, as you watch, horrified, having utterly no idea of its level of toxicity. See Situation.

**BRICK-SNIFFERS:**    Renovators and gentrifiers. Also called White Painters. How builders refer to those young couples who, when they rehabilitate an old place, sandblast all the plaster off, right back to the brick, frequently causing structural damage in the process. They then ritualistically stick their noses right up against this brick and inhale deeply, immediately after which they paint everything white except the wood that they varnish.

**BRING TO THE TABLE, TO:**    To demonstrate an intent to be taken seriously as a player in a Deal. In use: "What can he Bring to the Table?" The etymology is that of poker, in which, to belly up to the table, one must show the color of one's money. But in an Edge City Deal, a player may also be regarded as having *gravitas* if, for example, he can Bring to the Table a specialized knowledge of the market, or an unusual facility with legislative or zoning bodies, or an influence on federal funding authorities.

**BUZZ THE NUBS:**    Closely trim the grass.

**CAMPUSLIKE SETTING:**    What every office building in an Edge City is invariably said to have.

**CARRY, THE:**    The cost of a loan. Therefore, the most feared cause of bankruptcy. It is a unit of time as well as money. It's how much money a developer has to come up with out of his pocket periodically, off the top, to keep right with his most important constituent, the bank. It is the prime unit of negative cash flow, and a noun. As in, "The board still hasn't rezoned him, and he's getting killed by the Carry." See also Soft Costs.

**CC&RS:** Pronounced *cee-cee-en-ares,* and short for Covenants, Conditions, and Restrictions, these are the legal ridings embedded in the deeds to homes in most new housing developments. They allow community associations—the most ubiquitous form of shadow government—to do just about anything they want.

**CHALLENGE:** What you call a Situation after careful study reveals no possible way out.

**CHI-CHI FROU-FROU:** Shops inside an office building that cater to a high-end clientele. E.g., a gourmet take-out, a tasteful lingerie boutique. Pronounced *shi-shi fru-fru.* In use: "If you're gonna try to get $24 a foot for this sucker, the lobby's really gonna need some Chi-Chi Frou-Frou." See also Animated Space.

**CLASS A SPACE:** Premiere office space, appropriate for a corporate headquarters. How much of this there is in an Edge City is the key means of determining its market quality. Since it always comes measured precisely in square feet, it would be nice if there were a uniform definition of what it is. Like the Supreme Court and pornography, the definition is—we know it when we see it. Generally, it means the newest buildings, charging the highest rents, but that in turn is determined by and influenced by intangibles. See Amenity Package, the Hanging Gardens of Babylon Parking Garage, One Hundred Percent Corner, Great Big Oak Trees Right up Against the Windows, and Quality of Life.

**CLASS B SPACE:** Office space for the grunts. Places in the medium-price range in an Edge City market where you put the wage slaves and the computer key punchers. Susceptible to the same definitional problem of what means "middle" as Class A is to "top."

**CLASS C SPACE:** The pits.

**CLUSTER:** An attempt to encourage open space in a development—without altering the development's overall density, and hence economics—by allowing or insisting on a dramatic increase in the amount of building on that land which is disturbed.

**COMANCHES COMING OVER THE BRAZOS:**  A Texas formulation of the ultimate Situation. The Comanches were the most savage, brutal, and feared Indians on the Texas frontier. The Brazos River flows just to the west of both Dallas–Fort Worth and Houston. In use: "That Situation was no biggie. It wasn't the Comanches Coming Over the Brazos." Federal regulators shutting down a developer's proprietary S & L, however, is a prime example of the Comanches Coming Over the Brazos. See also Five Thousand Mexicans Knocking On the Door of the Alamo.

**COMMERCIAL:**  Office space. As opposed to Residential and Retail. This is the usage in an urban, Edge City context. In markets with little office space, such as the traditional suburb, Commercial sometimes is used to lump office and shopping space together, as in a strip shopping center. In *Edge City*, Commercial is used to mean office space.

**COMMUNITY:**  What every new residential development is described as being. E.g., a "master-planned, low-maintenance, Campuslike Community." In this usage, it is irrelevant whether anybody in this Community knows or cares about anybody else in it. See Neighborhood.

**CORPORATE CAMPUS:**  A bucolic setting on which are located the office buildings of a number of different corporations. A Corporate Campus location is equivalent to, in residential terms, a "farmette"—more land than is logical to mow but not enough to plow.

**CORPORATE ESTATE:**  A vast sylvan location for a single corporate headquarters. The possible number of Corporate Estates in any Edge City is thought to be identical with the number of available hilltops. The ultimate Corporate Estate is the Two Wind-Sock Model. Two wind socks indicate that the Estate is so large that helicopter pilots fear the weather on one side of headquarters is significantly different from the weather on the other side.

**CORPORATE OFFICE PARK:**  The equivalent of a subdivision.

**COVERAGE:**  The built environment that replaces all life forms susceptible to being removed by a bulldozer. In use: "When you mix it up at .25 gross, look at the coverage you got. The trees and things. That's very low-density office."

**CRAMDOWN, A:**   The bankers' nightmare in which, in a devastated market where property values have dropped below the amount of the mortgage, a bankruptcy court takes pity on the owner and orders that his obligation to the bank be reduced from the original amount borrowed to one that can be covered by the sale of the property. The derivation obviously is based on the relationship of the practice to the bankers' throats.

**DEAL, THE:**   The fundamental Edge City conceptual unit.

**DELICATE DETAIL:**   An expensive architectural flourish meant to distinguish a development from its competition. The structural element that skateboarders invariably discover makes a great ramp.

**DIRT LOAN:**   That which a developer gets to acquire land. As distinct from the construction loan, which allows him to build, or the permanent loan, which secures the property once it is completed.

**DOWNZONE:**   The battle cry of a population sick of growth and its negative attributes. Downzoning is that method by which the amount of development in an area is reduced, by decreasing the legally allowable density. By spreading development farther apart, Downzoning often has ironic effects—such as increasing the need for automobiles, hence creating traffic congestion, which decreases the Quality of Life that Downzoning was originally meant to advance. But for the purposes of the groups advocating this remedy, that is generally beside the point. Since there are few other effective legal methods currently available to fight growth, they go with what they've got. And Downzoning does increase developers' costs—thereby having a genuine effect on growth.

**DU, A:**   A home. Short for Dwelling Unit. Pronounced *dee-you,* but written "du," like a French preposition. Not to be confused with a "dua," which is the fundamental measure of residential density: Dwelling Units per Acre. A standard subdivision of quarter-acre lots, for example, would by its arithmetic have a dua of 4. A town-house development may have a dua of 7 to 10. In the midst of an Edge City, dua's as high as 30 or more may be encouraged. That is because the land is so expensive that such densities are the only ones economically feasible. But also, a large residential component in the midst of an Edge City is thought to increase the possibility of a true sense of community and urbanity being formed.

DUMB GARAGE: And you thought there was no other kind. A Dumb Garage is one that makes no effort to inform the driver where and whether there are any empty parking spaces. As opposed to an Intelligent Garage, which does. A Passive Intelligent Garage is one designed to allow the eye easily and quickly to sweep all parking spaces and rapidly collect information about their availability. An Active Intelligent Garage achieves the same end through electronics; e.g., a sign that reads "500 Spaces on Level 4."

EPAULETS: Horizontal stripes of a contrasting color at the corner, or "shoulder" of a building.

EYEBROWS: Same as Epaulets, only higher.

EXECUTIVE HOUSING: Housing of a high enough quality that a corporation's top officials would consider it desirable. Proximity of it is thought to be essential to the growth of an Edge City, inasmuch as fancy executives will not put up with long commutes. In context, it does not simply mean an expensive house. It means an expensive house with easy access to clubs, health facilities, shopping, excellent schools, and, frequently, horses.

FAR: Short for Floor-to-Area Ratio. Pronounced *eff-eh-are*. The fundamental unit of density, from which all calculations spring—parking, hence profitability, hence human behavior, hence civilization. It is the ratio of the amount of building to the amount of land. If you've got 100,000 square feet of office space on 100,000 square feet of land, you've got an FAR of 1.0 —a one-to-one relationship. Interestingly, from the point of view of predicting how functional an Edge City will be, particularly in terms of transportation, it does not make much difference whether this 100,000 square feet of office space is configured as a ten-story building, each story ten thousand square feet, surrounded by ninety thousand feet of open land; or a two-story building, each story fifty thousand square feet, surrounded by fifty thousand square feet of open space, or a one-story building utterly covering the available land. The amount of building is still 100,000 square feet, the FAR is still

1.0, and that ratio works magically to predict automotive use and traffic crunch, without regard to what the Edge City looks like.

**FAST COMMUTE:**   One that is painless. Of California origin, the idea is that the absolute amount of time or distance involved in a commute is not as important as the level of stress it invokes. Thus, a Fast Commute of twenty miles, on an unclogged freeway, during which a person's mind can freely wander, can be thought of as preferable to a Slow Commute of half that distance or time, if the Slow Commute involves teeth-grinding exposure to stop-and-go traffic.

**FIVE THOUSAND MEXICANS KNOCKING ON THE DOOR OF THE ALAMO:**   A Texas definition of the ultimate Situation. In use: "That was no big deal. That wasn't Five Thousand Mexicans Knocking on the Door of the Alamo." See also Comanches Coming Over the Brazos.

**FLOORPLATE:**   The shape and size of any given floor of a building. The floorplate that touches the ground is called the footprint, after the shape it leaves on the land. An ideal Floorplate size in an Edge City is thought to be roughly half a football field—on the order of twenty thousand square feet—for reasons enumerated in Chapter 13, "The Laws."

**FRICTION FACTOR:**   The path of most resistance. The notion is that the degree of difficulty of getting from one place to another, by whatever means, can be calculated and used to predict the paths people will take. One grocery store may be twice as far as another from a consumer. But if the path to the far store has minimum friction, and the path to the near store involves hassles, the store with the longer but easier path may be the one picked. In a downtown setting, getting a car out of an underground garage has a high enough friction factor that people are inclined to walk moderate distances. In Edge City, however, the Friction Factor in walking from one place to another may be so high that people will choose to drive trivial distances. The significance is that friction can be both good and bad. When a high friction factor discourages long-distance travel, it can contribute to the rise of civilization in Edge City by forcing goods and services to be provided locally. And to the extent that it makes a downtown difficult to get to, or move around in, it can lead to the center's decline. See also

Fast Commute. See also chapter Thirteen, "The Laws," regarding foot traffic.

GOLDEN TRIANGLE, THE:   A place claimed to be especially development-worthy because of its location at the confluence of three roads. At extreme levels, reference is made to the Platinum Triangle. See also One Hundred Percent Location.

GOOD DIRT:   An investment-worthy location. In use: "Even at $115 a foot, that's good dirt."

GREAT BIG OAK TREES RIGHT UP AGAINST THE WINDOWS:   Currently the most ambitious and fashionable stunt in the repertoire of the developers of Class A Office Space, it is the creation of Softscape by the locating of extremely large buildings right in the middle of a forest, without disturbing the trees. No small trick. It involves cutting the hole for the foundation without knocking over the surrounding tall vegetation, stabilizing the hole until the roots heal, and then building the building, again without knocking over the trees. This frequently involves great big equipment to lift everything in that building up and over the six- or seven-story height of the vegetation. But the biggest hassle is the endless threats required to convince the cracker equipment operators—who view trees as weeds—not to "accidentally" knock over a beech with their backswing. Great Big Oak Trees Right Up Against the Windows is the successor stunt to the hitherto most fashionable similar effort, the Hanging Gardens of Babylon Parking Garage.

GROUND COVER:   An automobile dealership, or a ministorage facility, or any other easily bulldozed land-intensive use in Edge City that provides an income stream and keeps the whole place from blowing away while its owners figure out what they want to do with the land, really.

HANGING GARDENS OF BABYLON PARKING GARAGE:   This is Structured Parking, the Hardscape ugliness of which has been struggled with, through the planting of Softscape hanging vines cascading over every edge, in an attempt to make it look like a terraced garden. When built-in irrigation is included all the way around each level, inside the planters, it is thought to be a prime component of Class A Office Space, particularly in quasi-tropical environments epitomized by the Perimeter Center–Georgia 400 Edge City north of downtown Atlanta. Similar efforts are being made on the outside of the actual office buildings, and inside their atria. The ultimate Class A Hanging Gardens Parking Garage is one in which the entire top deck is also covered with dirt and then planted and even decorated with fountains and sculpture, so that denizens of high office suites looking down have a view of gardens, not of parked cars.

HARDSCAPE: A landscape consisting of man-made building materials such as asphalt, precast concrete, and the like, that developers feel customers perceive as forbidding. Hardscape especially refers to objects that are machinelike or machine-made. See Softscape.

HEADACHE BARS: The horizontal pipes over the entrance to parking garages meant to prevent large vehicles from entering.

IDENTITY POINTS: Landmarks. Since knowing where an Edge City begins or ends is problematic, planners and developers encourage Identity Points to announce that you have indeed entered the grounds of your destination.

I'M NOT GOING TO BE NAMED IN A PATERNITY SUIT: Explanation of mall operator as to why his guards break up teenagers who dare use the benches in the atrium to neck.

IMPACT FEE: The increasingly popular method by which governments assign to developers the social costs brought about by their building. The developers are made to pay for some of the new roads, sewers, water taps, and the like that have traditionally been provided by the taxpayers, but that would not be required were it not for the development. This has a fairness benefit in that it does not assign to existing residents the costs of providing new services to future residents. But to the extent that growth is less subsidized, it drives up the cost, which contributes to issues of affordability. See Proffers.

KIT OF PARTS: A limited number of design elements repeated endlessly throughout a development in the hope that such recapitulation will give the project an identity.

LAND BAY: The Edge City equivalent of a city block. It is that portion of a commercial development on which nothing has yet been built, but that has been surrounded by major secondary roads, and thus marked off as one unit. The curious word here is "bay." Possible etymologies: this is the land equivalent of a bay of water, waiting for its ship to come in. Or perhaps it is the equivalent of a loading bay, waiting for something to be dumped.

LANDSCAPE UPGRADE: Bushes. Especially when offered as an option at additional cost in a development that otherwise would not have any.

LEARNING EXPERIENCE: A screw-up of such monumental proportions that its memory has been seared into the brains of the participants for life. In use: "Oh yeah, owning that sucker was a real learning experience."

LEECHES: Journalists, politicians, attorneys, regulators, government planners, environmental lobbyists, bureaucrats, and the perpetrators of all other sniveling, caviling occupations seen as producing nothing of value, at great expense to those who do, i.e., the developers, who coined the word.

LULU: Locally Unacceptable Land Use. E.g., nuclear waste dump, AIDS hospice. Any societally important facility for which it is impossible to find a location because of the massive resistance by property holders near its proposed location. In some areas, even a day-care center is viewed as a LULU. See also NIMBY.

LUMINAIRES: Lights. Especially those thought to be complementary to, and see also, Signage.

MASTER PLANNING: In theory, that enterprise which all design professionals and a great number of citizens believe an Edge City never has enough of. In practice, that attribute of a development in which so many rigid controls are put in place, to defeat every imaginable future problem, that any possibility of life, spontaneity, or flexible response to unanticipated events is eliminated.

MEMORY POINT: An element of a development meant to be regarded as so spectacular as to stick in the client's mind long after he or she has gotten home that night. Lavish use of real gold in the bathroom, for example. Or marble. See Ooh-Ahs.

MOON, TO: To situate a building so that its back side is presented to another building in a distasteful fashion.

NEGATIVE ABSORPTION: That dreaded condition in which more people are moving out of Edge City's offices than are moving in. Not only is the overall market not filling up (new space is not being "absorbed"), but the market is actually shrinking. Especially when additional new space is completed and added

to the market at the same time, this is the Situation immediately prior to, and see also, Restructurings and Workouts.

NEIGHBORHOOD:    Any collection of hitherto unacquainted individuals with physically proximate homes who find themselves
suddenly united in vigorous opposition to unpalatable
change, especially a rezoning, development, or highway. See
also NIMBY, LULU, and Community.

NIMBY:    Not In My Back Yard. Same as, and see also, LULU.

NONCOMPETING LOW-DENSITY USE:    A church. As seen, positively, by
the owner of an adjacent mall.

NONEXEMPT, A:    A working-class person. Specifically, someone
who is not exempt from laws requiring overtime pay for overtime work. In use: "You don't want a mix of shops in your
mall so high that the Nonexempts won't come." One class up
from, and see also, the Transfer-Payment Population.

NORC:    Short for Naturally Occurring Retirement Communities. Golden-age ghettos. Neighborhoods that spontaneously
attract unusually large numbers of the elderly.

OFFICE, TO:    The verb form used to describe where a person
spends his productive hours. In use: "Where is he officing
now?" "He offices over by the Galleria." Parallel in all uses to
the verbs "to live" and "to work."

ONE HUNDRED PERCENT LOCATION:    A prime site; a locale thought to
have all the desirable attributes for development, from image
to accessibility, and none of the negatives. In practice, a
phrase used to describe the geography of all development
schemes for which financing is still up in the air.

ON-GRADE PARKING:    Your basic, flat, parking lot. As opposed to,
and see also, Structured Parking.

ON-TIME-AND-UNDER-BUDGET:    Utterly devoid of imagination. A
slur used by architects. In use: "Oh yeah, him, yeah, he's just
full of On-Time-and-Under-Budget."

OOH-AH:    An unusual Amenity inserted into a development specifically to elicit an animated reaction from a client. No Tract
Mansion is thought to be salable for over $800,000, for exam-
ple, unless it includes a bidet as an Ooh-Ah. This, although
bidets serve in America as nothing but cat waterers. Commercial Ooh-Ahs include built-in hair dryers in the men's rooms.

OVERHANG:    The developer's equivalent of a hangover. After a
binge of building in which vastly more space is erected than

the market can "absorb," the "inventory" left over, vacant, is referred to as the Overhang. It is that which must be worked off before another binge can be contemplated.

PARATRANSIT:   Supplemental forms of transportation, especially those small in scale. While sometimes as prosaic as vans, they also can be as much a form of entertainment as a method of mass transit. E.g., San Francisco's cable cars, and the Disney-style railroads that move people through the Atlanta and Tampa airports. Also, People-movers. Also, Horizontal Elevators.

PASSIVE LEISURE ENVIRONMENT:   A park. Although, more generally, any quasi-public place to sit down and rest, including such a place indoors. See also Unstructured Open-space Environment.

PASSIVE WATER FEATURE:   Any man-made body of still water in which you are not supposed to swim. E.g., a reflecting pool.

PAVEMENT DEFICIENCY:   A pothole.

PEDESTRIAN WALKWAY:   A sidewalk.

PLOP ART:   Abstract sculptures placed about a development for reasons that are an utter mystery. See also Quality Statement.

PRODUCT:   Everything in a development that was put there by the hand of man. Whether it be a parking lot, a curbing, a planting of flowers, or a high-rise, somebody views it as Product, and can go into astounding detail about whether it is good or bad, cheap or expensive.

PROFFERS:   The system of legalized extortion by which governments convince developers "voluntarily" to build such socially desirable facilities as ball fields, day-care centers, schools, and intersections, in exchange for the governmental unit being kind enough to give the developer permission to build at higher density than usual or, sometimes, to give him approval to build at all. Proffers can be in addition to, or instead of, and see also, Impact Fees.

PRO FORMA:   The document meant to demonstrate the financial logic of a development. It is a target, a yardstick, a budget, a bible, a profound hope, and frequently a lie. It is supposed to reveal all a developer's underlying assumptions—his costs, for example, and what he thinks he will be able to get in rents. It is the financial analysis developers take to investors and the bank to justify being given money. No matter how carefully and honestly a Pro Forma is drawn up, reality will rarely match it. Hence the chilling question: "Are you achieving the rents in your Pro Forma?"

**PROGRAMMED SPACE:**   A place where a spontaneous expression of Community is thought to be so unlikely that a consultant has to be paid to hire a street musician to play. Similarly, a place where people have to be paid to march in a Fourth of July parade. Psychologically similar to, and see also, Animated Space.

**PUBLIC-PRIVATE PARTNERSHIP:**   A method by which developers and governments engage in a cooperative rather than confrontational exercise in getting a development built in a fashion that mollifies the neighbors. This is seen by its advocates as the height of developer enlightenment, a Zen in which the builder works "with" the Community, recognizing that he does not really "own" the land he is paying the bank for. It is seen by its detractors as either communist horse pucky or the system by which foxes and chickens are brought together to achieve common goals.

**QUALITY OF LIFE:**   That attribute which a development is said to be sensitive to when attention is being drawn to intangibles that do not directly contribute to the bottom line. See Amenities.

**QUALITY STATEMENT:**   Very large, heavy, expensive, neutral sculpture. Ideally, brushed steel or aluminum. Totally plain geometry a plus. Moving parts, and/or integration into an Active Water Feature, daring. Located at the entrance of an office park or complex, a Quality Statement is supposed to suggest absolutely nothing to the viewer except somewhat understated wealth, to which, it is hoped, a customer's aspirations will be stimulated sufficient unto the rental of office space. Also used to induce government officials to grant higher zoning than otherwise probable. See also Beauty Contest and Plop Art.

**RESTRUCTURING, A:**   The system by which the terms of a loan are renegotiated to decrease the immediate cost to the developer rather than have the loan go into default. The developer's art of sensing when a lender can't afford to let him go under. What a developer does in a down market while he's got a lot of time on his hands since nothing is selling. A particularly vigorous version of Restructuring is known as, and see also, a Workout.

**RETROFIT:** To gut beyond recognition, or bulldoze. That which is done to an Edge City building when, in as short a time as, say, twelve years after original construction, it is viewed as obsolete either because the decor has aged hideously or the mechanical systems—air conditioning or telecommunications—are seen as massively inefficient relative to new technologies. In use: "You want to lease it up, you're gonna hafta Retrofit the hell out of that sucker."

**SIGNAGE:** Signs. Especially those which are products of the expenditure of vastly more money on design review than would seem plausible, given the appearance and function of the result, which is to announce "No Left Turn" and the like. Etymology: The guardians of urban esthetics have for decades decried the proliferation of shopping center beacons that makes each nonlimited-access highway resemble the Las Vegas Strip. Thus, developers of large tracks of land who aspire to the label "megadeveloper" indicate their seriousness of purpose, attention to detail, and desire for social acceptance by hiring designers to create signs of a style that are not merely informative, but are distinct to the development. Hence, Signage—probably a contraction of "signs" and "signature." Note: Signage, being an expression of high taste, *never* radiates light from within, in the fashion of a Gulf or Holiday Inn sign. Its highest expression was once thought to be in the form of sand-blasted, hence three-dimensional, wood. But etched glass and engraved stone have begun to make a strong showing. See Kit of Parts.

**SITUATION:** A problem of unimaginable, much less soluble, proportions. (The worst thing a boss can hear from an underling: "I wonder if I could have a minute to talk to you about a Situation.") Etymology: In a macho business environment, it is utterly unacceptable to say one has a "problem." That implies negative thinking, which at best equals high wussieness, and at worst raises serious questions about one's ability to function competitively. At the very least, it indicates an individual who is pathetically behind in reading the latest best-selling motivational literature. Calling a problem a Situation, by contrast, allows for the possibility that enough analysis may reveal a germ of opportunity.

SOFT COSTS:   The fees charged to obtain the services of architects, government registrars, and the like. The costs of whatever goes into a building that does not represent a tangible object such as a brick. The location where developers have the highest danger of losing their shirts.

SOFTSCAPE:   Plants. Trees. The work of nature, as opposed to the work of man. See Hardscape.

STICKS AND BRICKS:   The materials with which Residential is usually built, as opposed to the steel and concrete of Commercial. Also, Stick-Built.

STREET FURNITURE:   Everything exposed to the weather put there by the hand of man, not counting roads, buildings, and plants. This "everything else" is far more considerable than most people recognize, because it is usually so plain or so ugly —and thus ignored as a feature of the landscape—as to render it virtually invisible. It includes newspaper vending boxes, stoplights, no-parking signs, and those circular iron grills sometimes put around the bases of trees when they are embedded in a sidewalk. Not to mention, of course, furniture. Like benches.

STREETSCAPE:   A road on which sufficient design review has been expended such that the Street Furniture, Signage, and Luminaires all match and/or are festooned with flags.

STRUCTURED PARKING:   An aboveground, multilevel parking garage. Considerably more expensive to build than, and see also, On-Grade Parking. It is economically feasible only if the land under it is very expensive, and thus must be conserved.

SUPERCOMMUTER:   A person whose round trip to work exceeds a hundred miles each day.

TRACT MANSION:   The ultimate subdivision house. A residence of extraordinary size (four thousand square feet and up) and expense (approaching a million dollars or more) built amid homes that are very similar, if not identical. Tract Mansions are distinct from estates in that they are located on relatively tiny plots of land, sometimes as little as a sixth of an acre.

TRANSFER-PAYMENT POPULATION, THE:   Poor people. Especially those who live in ghettos surrounding the old downtowns. The class below, and see also, Nonexempts.

TREE SHIT: Such byproducts of the life cycle of trees as fall to the ground. E.g., leaves, fruit, seed pods, bird excrement. The cleaning up of such detritus is seen as the primary argument, other than cost, for not putting trees in parking lots. In use: If a mulberry tree were to leave a purple stain on a Mercedes, or a roosting jay to leave a white stain on a 300 ZX, the complaint would be "The trees are shitting all over my clients' cars."

UNSTRUCTURED OPEN-SPACE ENVIRONMENTS: Parks. See also Passive Leisure Environments.

VALUE ENGINEERING: The process of designing structures so that they can be built as cheaply as possible, usually by systematically eliminating such frivolities as esthetics.

WORKOUT: Financial aerobics. A developer's last stand before bankruptcy. If a developer cannot repay a loan in the midst of a recession, he may try to construct a Workout with the bank in which the bank does not foreclose but allows him to retain ownership for several more years while paying almost nothing on the loan, on the theory that the arrangement will be more lucrative for all sides than either forcing a bankruptcy that will eat up millions in attorneys' fees, or forcing a sale of assets at the bottom of a market.

# 13

## THE LAWS

### How We Live

THE NORTH STAR of moral certitudes, or at least prayerful assumptions, for developers is that human nature, and hence the marketplace, is rational. Hence, predictable.

Therefore, they believe, all they have to do is figure out what the rules of human behavior are, and they will be rewarded greatly.

There are two things they find most perplexing:

• Government bureaucrats and planners. These people, developers believe—to the extent that they are not familiar with the market principles that yield these Laws—have self-evidently preposterous ideas about how human nature works in the real world.

• Human nature itself. Which, developers acknowledge, has an unsettling habit of appearing rational only in hindsight.

As E. Wayne Angle of Homart Corporation ruefully put it, "The market has laws, although they do not grind as fine as the laws of physics."

The following are some of what developers believe to be the Laws. Note how many of them boil down to one of two tyrannies: (1) time; or (2) because that's the only way anybody could figure out to park the cars.

Note also how many of the Laws are formulaic. They are rules of thumb about human behavior expressed as equations. They have been found to produce reliable results under circumstances that are disparate or that sometimes seem to be utterly alien. In other words, they reveal an underlying order in what appears to the uninitiated to be chaos.

In fact, while some developers may bring unusual insights or instincts to their work, as a breed they usually have only the one skill not typically found in other people, that of doing high-order mental arithmetic while talking about a completely different subject. Sources are in the Notes.

**THE LAW OF UNINTENDED CONSEQUENCES:**   No matter what your plan is, the result will always be a surprise.

**THE FARTHEST DISTANCE AN AMERICAN WILL WILLINGLY WALK BEFORE GETTING INTO A CAR:**   Six hundred feet. The length of two football fields.

**FIRST COROLLARY TO THE SIX-HUNDRED-FOOT LAW:**   In a mall, thou shalt never let a shopper see how far it is to the next anchor store. Thou shalt break her line of sight. If you make her aware of how much walking she is really doing inside a mall, she will leave the building and take her car to the far end rather than walk. And once you've let her out of the building and into her car, there is a significant chance that she will say forget the whole thing and go home.

**SECOND COROLLARY TO THE SIX-HUNDRED-FOOT LAW:**   The most remote parking space in Edge City is rarely more than three hundred feet from its building's entrance.

**THIRD COROLLARY TO THE SIX-HUNDRED-FOOT LAW:**   In either a downtown or an Edge City, if you do everything you can to make casual use of the automobile inconvenient at the same time that you make walking pleasant and attractive, you maybe, just maybe, can up the distance an American will willingly walk to fifteen-hundred feet. A quarter of a mile. And this at the substantial risk of everybody saying forget it and choosing not to patronize your highly contrived environment at all. See also Friction Factor in chapter 12, "The Words."

**WHYTE'S LAW OF THE NUMBER OF BLOCKS AN AMERICAN WILL WALK IN MOST DOWNTOWNS:**   Three, maybe four.

**THE NUMBER OF BLOCKS AN AMERICAN WILL WALK IN NEW YORK CITY:**   Five.

**THE SPEED AN AMERICAN MAN WILL WALK IN A BIG-CITY DOWNTOWN:**   A little under three hundred feet per minute.

**STROLLING SPEED PAST A SHOP WINDOW OR MERCHANDISE DISPLAY:**   Two hundred feet per minute.

**THE NUMBER OF PEDESTRIANS PER HOUR AT MIDDAY REQUIRED TO MAKE AN URBAN CENTER WORK AND BE LIVELY:**    One thousand.

**WHY ELECTED OFFICIALS FEEL THEY MUST ENCOURAGE COMMERCIAL DEVELOPMENT OR DIE:**    For every $1.00 of tax revenue that comes in from a residential subdivision, as much as $1.22 goes out to provide services, especially schools. By contrast, for every $1.00 of tax revenue that comes in from commercial development, at most thirty-two cents is required in expenditures, usually for roads. (By the same calculation, if you really want your jurisdiction to remain solvent, you could leave it as farmland. Agriculture requires almost no expenditures of public funds—a maximum of seven cents for every $1.00 it brings in.)

**THE TRACT MANSION HYPOTHESIS:**    There is some speculation that the one exception to the above law is homes over $350,000. Some calculations seem to demonstrate that they may bring in more in tax revenue than they consume.

**THE FIRST MULTIMILLION-DOLLAR STRUCTURE USUALLY BUILT IN EDGE CITY:**    A mall.

**HOW MANY CUSTOMERS MUST LIVE WITHIN A FIFTEEN-MINUTE DRIVE OF A MALL FOR IT TO BE SUCCESSFUL:**    A quarter of a million. Roughly the population of Las Vegas.

**HOW BIG A MALL MUST BE BEFORE ITS DEVELOPER IS VIEWED BY HIS PEERS AS HAVING HAIR ON HIS CHEST:**    One million square feet (twenty-five acres under roof) and/or three levels.

**WHY ONE-STORY MALLS ARE OBSOLETE IN POPULAR LOCATIONS:**    If the mall had enough shops to meet demand put upon it, it would be viewed by customers as too sprawling to walk. (Also, the land would be too expensive to build on at that low a density.)

**THE AMOUNT OF GROWTH IN AN ESTABLISHED EDGE CITY THAT IS GENERATED BY COMPANIES ALREADY LOCATED THERE:**    Eighty-five percent.

**HOW MANY STORIES UP OR DOWN AN AMERICAN WILL USE THE STAIRS:**    One. Frequently zero.

**FIRST COROLLARY TO THE ONE-STORY-CLIMB LAW:**    In a three-level mall, the main entrance should be at the second level, from which it will only be one story up or down to get to the other levels. Otherwise, people may never go to the farthest level.

**SECOND COROLLARY TO THE ONE-STORY-CLIMB LAW:**    In a three-story town house, the garage entrance, and hence the kitchen, where one unloads the groceries from the car, should be at the second level, for the same reason as in the First Corollary.

**THIRD COROLLARY TO THE ONE-STORY-CLIMB LAW:** In an office environment, even if a building is only two stories tall, it must have an elevator.

**FOURTH COROLLARY TO THE ONE-STORY-CLIMB LAW:** Multiple-family housing—apartments and condominiums—that are three stories or taller must have an elevator.

**FIFTH COROLLARY TO THE ONE-STORY-CLIMB LAW:** Since elevators and escalators demand rigid and heavy support structures, buildings that require them are more easily built of concrete and steel than Sticks and Bricks, thereby substantially increasing the cost, and increasing the likelihood that the structure will be viewed as Hardscape.

**SIXTH COROLLARY TO THE ONE-STORY-CLIMB LAW:** The world moves, in residential construction, at three stories. Residential structures either have to be less than three stories above the main entrance, in order for you to build them without elevators, or they have to be high-rise. Once you start building a residential structure of concrete and steel to accommodate an elevator, your costs kick into so much higher an orbit that you have to build vastly more dwelling units per acre in order to make any money.

**HOW MUCH TOTAL SPACE IS REQUIRED TO MEET THE NEEDS OF AN OFFICE WORKER:** Two hundred and fifty square feet. (Actually, this can vary from 175 to 350 square feet depending on market conditions. But the rule of thumb is four workers per thousand square feet.)

**HOW MUCH TOTAL SPACE IS REQUIRED TO PARK THE CAR OF THE OFFICE WORKER:** Four hundred square feet.

**HOW MUCH SPACE A HUMAN TAKES UP, RELATIVE TO HOW MUCH SPACE HIS CAR TAKES UP:** Five-eighths.

**THE RULE OF THUMB FOR CALCULATING HOW MUCH TRAFFIC EDGE CITY WILL PRODUCE:** Ten million square feet of office and retail space equals forty thousand trips per day.

**THE AVERAGE DISTANCE FROM THE MAIN OFFICE OF A COMPANY IN EDGE CITY TO THE CHIEF EXECUTIVE OFFICER'S HOME:** Eight miles by road.

**HOW TO MAKE A SUBWAY PAY FOR ITSELF FROM THE FAREBOX:** Give its riders only three choices: take the train to work; live under Chinese communism; or swim the South China Sea. (Hong Kong has the only subway system in the world that does not require subsidies.)

**HOW MANY SWITCHES IN TRAVEL MODE A COMMUTER WILL PUT UP WITH:** Usually no more than one. Typically, zero. In other words, it is conceivable that a commuter will walk partway and take a bus partway, switching travel mode once. It is also possible that a commuter will take a car partway, and then switch to a train, switching mode once. But a car-bus-train two-mode-switch will rarely be utilized. Far more typically, once a person is in his car, you will never get him out of it into a different mode, no matter how bad the traffic is.

**THE PROBABLE MAXIMUM NUMBER OF RIDERS YOU CAN HOPE TO SWITCH OUT OF THEIR CARS AND INTO A COMMUTER RAILROAD, SHOULD YOU BUILD ONE:** Twelve percent. In other words, ten million square feet of space may yield forty-eight hundred train trips.

**THE NUMBER OF RIDERS A HEAVY-RAIL SYSTEM NEEDS PER DAY TO BE COST EFFECTIVE:** Fifteen thousand.

**HOW BIG AN EDGE CITY WOULD HAVE TO BE TO GENERATE THAT MANY RIDERS:** More than thirty million square feet of office space.

**NUMBER OF EDGE CITIES THAT BIG AT THIS WRITING:** Zero.

**NUMBER OF RIDERS A LIGHT-RAIL SYSTEM NEEDS PER DAY TO BE COST EFFECTIVE:** Seven thousand.

**HOW BIG AN EDGE CITY WOULD HAVE TO BE TO GENERATE THAT MANY RIDERS:** Fourteen and a half million square feet of office— more than downtown St. Louis or Cincinnati.

**CERVERO'S LAW OF THE VALUE OF TIME WASTED IN TRAFFIC JAMS:** People view the time they waste in a traffic jam as equal, in dollar value, to half of their hourly wage.

Robert Cervero of Berkeley, author of *Suburban Gridlock*, came up with the above calculation, which he believes works as follows:

Suppose somebody makes $10 an hour; $400 a week; $20,000 a year. Cervero thinks that person will pay $5.00 an hour—half of the $10 value of his wage—or $1.25 per quarter hour, to save fifteen minutes of commuting time. Conversely, he or she will eat fifteen minutes of additional commuting time to save $1.25 one way, or $2.50 round trip, or $12.50 a week, or $625 a year.

That is to say, if she saves $625 a year on her mortgage payments, which is to say she saves more than $6000 on the price of her house, she will be willing to eat a fifteen-minute addition to her commute in exchange.

Let's scale that up. A person makes $50,000 a year, or $1000 a week. Which works out to $25 an hour, assuming a forty-hour week. Cervero thinks that person will gladly pay $3.12 cents to save fifteen minutes on his or her commute. Which is $6.25 a day, or $31.25 per week, or $125 a month, or more than $1500 a year.

According to Cervero's analysis, it does not matter a whole lot how that money is spent. If you put in a toll road that saves time over surface roads, they will pay the toll. If you find a way to run a train that is actually faster than a stop-and-go commute, they will pay for it. If you run up the real estate prices— this is how it normally works—so that they can live nearer to their work, they will pay it.

According to his formula, if a person makes $50,000 a year, and is willing to add fifteen minutes to his commute, that should be worth a reduction of about $15,000 in the price of the exact same house closer in. Shortening the commute by a similar amount is probably something for which he will pay $15,000 more.

If he makes $250,000 per year, or $30.00 per fifteen minutes, a limo and driver at $1.00 per minute saved possibly makes sense. If he makes $2,000,000 per year, or $250 per fifteen minutes, it may seem rational to save time by renting a helicopter and pilot at $8.00 a minute, or $480 an hour, which is about the going rate. It's worth it to him.

**THE PRIME LOCATION CONSIDERATION WHEN A COMPANY MOVES:**  The commute of the chief executive officer must always become shorter.

**WHAT A NEW HOUSE MUST SELL FOR IN ORDER FOR A DEVELOPER TO MAKE A PROFIT:**  The price of the land under it times four. If you build too much house on the land, it will not sell because it will be viewed as too expensive for the neighborhood. If you build too little, it will be viewed as substandard, given the price. Actually, examples exist of houses selling nicely for the price of the land times two. Also, for the price of the land times seven. However, those examples reflect unusual market conditions. The standard calculation, from which all exceptions spring, is the price of the land times four.

**WHAT AN OWNER WHO HOLDS HIS MORTGAGE TO TERM WILL ULTIMATELY PAY FOR HIS HOUSE:** The original sales price times three. Two out of every three dollars will go for interest, not lumber and land.

**THE PLATONIC IDEAL OF THE SIZE OF AN OFFICE BUILDING'S FLOORPLATE:** Twenty thousand square feet. ("We decided the way the Law happened was, in 1978, there were six brokers drinking in Clyde's, all from Coldwell Banker," reported Jim Todd, a developer who is active in the Urban Land Institute. "And they all decided that from that point on, twenty thousand square feet would be the size of the office floor and it's always been. And when those six guys get together and change it, it'll change, but in the meantime it's the Law.")

Actually twenty thousand square feet—about half a football field—is the golden mean because an Edge City building is usually a hundred feet wide in order to yield the maximum number of windows and, hence, offices with windows that command high rent, at the lowest total building cost per square foot. The building tends to be two hundred feet long because a hundred feet in any direction is thought to be the maximum distance that can be served by one costly "core." A core is that vertical tunnel in the middle of the building containing all elevator shafts, bathrooms, air conditioning, utility connections, and the like.

Actually, the typical floorplate range is from eighteen thousand to twenty-five thousand square feet. Smaller floorplates carve up better for multitenant use, notes David Shulman of Salomon Brothers. But the largest practical floorplate is thought to be thirty thousand square feet, because that holds the maximum number of employees a manager can effectively walk around and deal with personally in one day.

Although it does increase building costs, it is frequently thought valuable to integrate as many twists and turns and sharp angles as possible into the edge of a floorplate. If the number of corners is increased, the number of corner offices is maximized far beyond the traditional four per floor.

See also Floorplate in Chapter 12, "The Words."

**THE FUNCTION OF GLASS ELEVATORS:**   To make women feel safe. Not to offer a view out. Rapes rarely occur in glass elevators.

**THE POINT OF CRITICAL MASS OF EDGE CITY:**   Five million square feet of leasable office space.

**THE LEVEL OF DENSITY AT WHICH AUTOMOBILE CONGESTION STARTS BECOMING NOTICEABLE IN EDGE CITY:**   When you get as much as twenty-five square feet of office space built on each hundred square feet of land. In developer's parlance, this is a floor-to-area ratio (FAR) of .25. See also FAR in Chapter 12, "The Words."

**THE LEVEL OF DENSITY AT WHICH IT IS NECESSARY TO CONSTRUCT PARKING GARAGES INSTEAD OF PARKING LOTS BECAUSE YOU HAVE RUN OUT OF LAND:**   0.4 FAR.

**THE LEVEL OF DENSITY AT WHICH TRAFFIC JAMS BECOME A MAJOR POLITICAL ISSUE IN EDGE CITY:**   1.0 FAR.

**THE LEVEL OF DENSITY BEYOND WHICH FEW EDGE CITIES EVER GET:**   1.5 FAR.

**THE LEVEL OF DENSITY AT WHICH LIGHT-RAIL TRANSIT STARTS MAKING ECONOMIC SENSE:**   2.0 FAR.

**THE LEVEL OF DENSITY OF A TYPICAL OLD DOWNTOWN:**   5.0 FAR and up.

**THE DENSITY-GAP COROLLARY TO THE LAWS OF DENSITY:**   Edge Cities always develop to the point where they become dense enough to make people crazy with the traffic, but rarely, if ever, do they get dense enough to support the rail alternative to automobile traffic.

**THE MAXIMUM DESIRABLE COMMUTE, THROUGHOUT HUMAN HISTORY, REGARDLESS OF TRANSPORTATION TECHNOLOGY:**   Forty-five minutes.

**THE MAXIMUM DESIRABLE DISTANCE A BACKSHOP LOCATION CAN BE FROM A CORPORATE HEADQUARTERS:**   One and a half hours by car, or three hours, nonstop, by plane.

**THE MOST RATIONAL EXPLANATION OF WHY THE FIRST THING A DEVELOPER USUALLY DOES IS BULLDOZE EVERYTHING FLAT:**   A parking surface may not undulate more than 6 percent, by law. If a car is parked sideways on a grade steeper than that, its door will be very difficult to open on the uphill side, or close on the downhill side. Also, the surface will offer unacceptable liabilities when covered with ice.

**THE MOST PROBABLE EXPLANATION OF WHY THE FIRST THING A DEVELOPER USUALLY DOES IS BULLDOZE EVERYTHING FLAT:** Because architects use T-squares. Therefore, when designing a building, the first thing an architect usually draws is a horizontal base line, which in turn gets incorporated into the final building by the work of a bulldozer.

**THE COST OF BEING CANADIAN:** U.S. plus 25 percent. A Swiss economist, attempting to calculate what Canada's kinder, gentler form of urbanity costs the average Canadian, by factoring in differences in currency value, differences in cost of living, differences in wage levels, differences in taxation, differences in levels of government service provided, and myriad other such factors, came up with that fudge factor.

**THE GENDER THOUGHT DESTINED TO SELL COMMERCIAL REAL ESTATE, BY THOSE WHO SELL COMMERCIAL REAL ESTATE:** Men.

**THE GENDER THOUGHT DESTINED TO SELL RESIDENTIAL REAL ESTATE, BY THOSE WHO SELL COMMERCIAL REAL ESTATE:** Women.

**WHAT PEOPLE WHO HIRE COMMERCIAL REAL ESTATE SALESMEN LOOK FOR IN A RÉSUMÉ:** Background as a jet-fighter pilot. It is an article of faith that the best commercial salesmen are former sky jockeys, although it is the sheerest speculation exactly why that correlation may exist.

**JAKE PAGE'S LAW OF SEVERED CONTINUITY:** "You name a place for what is no longer there as a result of your actions. So one has Foxcrest Farms, for example, where no fox will ever again hunt and no plow ever make a furrow worth the name."

**THE KEITH SEVERIN COROLLARY:** All subdivisions are named after whatever species are first driven out by the construction. E.g., Quail Trail Estates.

**THE THREE LAWS OF BUILDING:** (1) Build. (2) Build at the lowest possible cost. (3) If rule number one and rule number two come into conflict, rule number one takes precedence.

# Acknowledgments

ANY LARGE-SCALE LOOK at America ends up involving a legion of co-conspirators, I've discovered. Hundreds of people all over the country contributed interviews, information, candid advice, incisive readings, and lasting companionship to this effort. It quite simply could not have been done without them. I regret that I cannot either thank each of them here or cite them all adequately in the text. Any errors of fact, emphasis, or interpretation in this volume are entirely my own.

However:

Milton Coleman, the assistant managing editor for the metropolitan report of the *Washington Post*, actually sought the opportunity to ship me out on long patrol. When I returned with tales of "emerging cities," "shadow governments," and "Cluster 31," he did not flinch, much. My line editor, Douglas B. Feaver, voluptuously fulfilled his promise to kick my butt to new heights. Deborah Heard, my number three boss, held my hand.

Benjamin C. Bradlee, the executive editor of the *Washington Post*, Leonard Downie, Jr., its managing editor, and Richard Harwood, former deputy managing editor, gave me the job from which this book sprang, and then the leave of absence to write it. Few were more supportive of my efforts than Don Graham, the *Post*'s publisher.

My wife, Adrienne, was my most trusted editor. She adjusted fairly gracefully to my materializing in her workday. (Although unsolicited analysis of the dialogue in another person's favorite lunchtime soap opera turns out to be more of a threat to a marriage than I would have guessed.) Toward the end she even volunteered that when I was on the road, she found my perpetual presence missed.

Henry Allen—America's foremost practitioner of that oxymoron, a journalism of ideas—was my moderately patient tutor, asking questions to which I did not have answers, and reading books I did not know existed. He also claims he had a 1960s New York crash pad on the wall of which he painted "Welcome to Edge City." Osmotically, I must have gotten even my title from him.

Barbara Blechman Sherbill, my indefatigable researcher, was a bountiful source of wit, cheer, files, books, babies, and bagels. My mother, Gloria Garreau, of Pawtucket and Little Compton, Rhode Island, continued to be exceedingly generous with her time and resources. Rafe Sagalyn, my agent, who never got over selling a book about places like Tysons Corner, was always calm, reassuring, thoughtful, effective, and right. Michael Barone, Jerry Knight, Joel Kotkin, and Barry and Sandy Lopez were sources of expertise and kindred souls. John Loberg's abiding interest in the woods, its critters, and horticulture kept me grounded. Olwen Price transcribed hundreds of tapes, sitting under her headphones making wry Welsh anarchist asides. Dave Cook, cartographic wizard, created the maps. Dennis (Gomer) Pyles kept running a commentary and, more important, my computer. Ken Garrett made my author photo. It only seemed right: for the *National Geographic* he spends half his time in exotic terrain.

In the topsy-turvy world of New York publishing in the late twentieth century, quite a few editors got a chance to improve my manuscript as they passed through Doubleday. Nancy Evans and Nan Talese helped jump-start this project. Patrick Filley was strikingly imaginative in shaping it and getting it off the ground. Steve Wasserman provided critical midcourse corrections. Ann Godoff flitted in solely, it seems, to provide a crucial in-flight refueling, wrestling a key check out of the bureaucracy. David Gernert brought the project in for a landing in style. The legendary copyeditor Frances Apt swept up the debris.

In the middle of all this, God bless him, there was Paul Golob. There is nothing like having your manuscript come under the pencil of a bright twenty-six-year-old who has spent his entire life in Manhattan, except for four years at Harvard, to remind you just how many extraordinary ways there are of looking at this country.

Many colleagues at the *Washington Post* contributed to this work, including, alphabetically, David S. Broder, Ron Browne, Victoria Churchville, Al Crenshaw, the late Herb Denton, Kirstin Downey, Lynda Edwards, Noel Epstein, Patrice Gaines-Carter, Cynthia Gorney, John Harris, Alison Howard, Rob Howe, Gwen Ifill, Robert G. Kaiser, John Lancaster, Jay Mathews, Eric Charles May, Caroline Mayer, Peter Lester Milius, Courtland Milloy, Dan Morgan, William Raspberry, T. R. Reid, Paul Richard, Lynda Richardson, Phyllis Richman, Wendy Ross, Bob Thompson, James M. Thresher, Mary Lou Tousignant, Bob Webb, Linda Wheeler, and Juan Williams.

Christopher B. Leinberger, of Santa Fe, pioneered in the popular press the concept of Edge Cities—which he called "urban villages"—in his October 1986 article in *The Atlantic* with Charles Lockwood called "How Business Is Reshaping America." Ever since he has offered great quotes, good cheer, and sartorial inspiration.

Claritas, L.P., one of America's premiere marketing demographic outfits, burned mainframe computer time lavishly, helping me around statistical time lags caused by so much of Edge City rising after the 1980 U.S. Census, but before the 1990 results dribbled out. I am especially indebted to Mark Capaldini, Robin E. Rice, and Doug Anderson.

As this work progressed, market analyst Pamela Manfre and urban designer Patricia L. Faux became my esteemed cohorts, dedicated to the idea that it is possible to make Edge Cities come out right. Cory Amron is the guardian of the trade and service marks. The manuscript was lawyered by Kathy Trager.

Among those who offered crucial insights into this new world were Boyd Van Ness and his troops at Coldwell Banker Commercial, E. Wayne Angle of Homart Development Company, Wilbur Zelinsky and Peirce Lewis of Penn State, Leo Marx of MIT, Robert Fishman of Rutgers at Camden, E. M. Risse of Synergy Planning, Katherine Gehbauer of The Office Network, Peter O. Muller of the University of Miami, James Rouse of the Enterprise Foundation, Tom Baerwald of the National Science

Foundation, Ron Abler of the Association of American Geographers, Tony Downs of the Brookings Institution, Tom Black of the Urban Land Institute, James Todd, president of the Hazel-Peterson Companies, Josef W. Konvitz of Michigan State, Charles Fenyvesi, author of *When the World Was Whole*, James Burke, author of *Connections*, Larry Harrison, author of *Underdevelopment Is a State of Mind*, Nick Lemann of *The Atlantic*, and Jean Gottmann, author of the book that is godfather to us all, *Megalopolis*.

I shall never forget the eight-lane drift across Georgia Route 41 demanded by Peirce Lewis so that he could pounce on an unsuspecting artifact of the culturally significant landscape.

Others not already mentioned here or in the text who served as compasses, orienting me in my travels, included:

In the New Jersey–New York–Connecticut area, George Sternlieb of Rutgers, William H. Whyte, author of *The Organization Man* and *City*, Scott Toombs of Princeton Forrestal Village, Roger Garreau of A T & T and Lorrie Garreau, Sally Lane of the *Trentonian*, and Richard K. Rein, editor of one of the first newspapers specifically targeting an Edge City. That paper is called, appropriately enough, *U.S. 1*. Most especially, David G. Shulman of Salomon Brothers and his globe-girdling band of young analysts, who produce, in the far-too-modest guise of real estate reports, some of the most insightful cross-cultural examinations of cities, both old and Edge, I know.

In the Philadelphia area, Robert Venturi, Denise Scott Brown, and Steven Izenour, authors of *Learning from Las Vegas;* James Timberlake and Steve Kieran of Kieran, Timberlake & Harris; and Don Cook, my clip service and sounding board.

In the Boston area, Ralph and Barbara Whitehead of the University of Massachusetts at Amherst, Gene Mallove of MIT, David Birch of Cognetics, Tom Grape of Spalding & Slye, Glenn Miller of Bridgewater State, and the incomparable Sheila Murphy of Mount Holyoke.

In the Detroit area, Chris Cook of the *Detroit Free Press* and Kathy Sue Horn, Peter Gavrilovich of the *Free Press*, David Cole and David Lewis of the University of Michigan at Ann Arbor, John L. Wright of the Henry Ford Museum, and Leo Tosto of Trerice Tosto, commercial real estate. In addition, on the subject of how the automobile shaped Edge City, I am indebted to Robert Cervero and William Garrison of the University of California at Berkeley.

In the Atlanta area, Stacy Jolna of Cable News Network, Gregg Logan of Robert Charles Lesser & Company, Carol Edwards, Bart Lewis of the Atlanta Regional Commission, Truman Hartshorn of Georgia State, Dana White of Emory, Marilyn Milloy of *Newsday,* Ron Roach of the offices of U.S. Representative John Lewis, and Bill Dedman and Nathan McCall, now or then of the *Atlanta Journal and Constitution* and the *Washington Post.*

In the Phoenix area, former mayor Terry Goddard, former city planner Rick Counts, Tom Miller, author of *On the Border* and other tales, Jana Bommersbach of *New Times,* Grady Gammage, Jr., Elizabeth Rogers, Larry Landry, Mike Rappoport of the Salt River Project, Don Dyekman of the Community Associations Institute, and Ioanna Morfessis of the Greater Phoenix Economic Council.

In the Dallas area, Ben Carpenter, the founding father of Las Colinas, and David Dillon and Rochelle Riley of the *Dallas Morning News.*

In the Houston area, Gerald Hines and Louis Sklar of Gerald Hines Interests, Incorporated, George Mitchell of The Woodlands, Tom Curtis of *Texas Monthly* and Sandy Sheehy, architectural theoretician Douglas Pegues Harvey, architectural historian Stephen Fox, and Barrio Santos, who has one of the world's keenest understandings of the hidden life of the city and who is probably the world's only Mexican-American cabdriver and locksmith pursuing his master's degree in transportation planning at the University of Houston after gaining a degree in economics from Berkeley and studying at the University of Notre Dame.

In the Los Angeles–Irvine area, Mark Baldaserre of the Program in Social Ecology, University of California at Irvine, Ray Catalano, now of the University of California at Berkeley, Ray Watson, first planner of Irvine, Larry Agran, former mayor of Irvine, Tom Kendrick of the Orange County Performing Arts Center, spiritual consultant Jack W. Sims, Richard Louv, author of *Childhood's Future,* Kathy Louv, and Susan Kelleher of the *Orange County Register.* But most memorably, Edward W. Soja of UCLA, the only avowed Marxist I have ever interviewed about Postmodernism while melting in his Jacuzzi/hot-tub spa.

In the San Francisco Bay area, Brad Inman, John Jacobs, and Kate Macdonald, then or now of the *San Francisco Examiner,* Nora Gallagher, Ernest and Christine Callenbach, David Dowall and Cynthia Kroll of the University of California at Berkeley, and James Kennedy of the Contra Costa planning department. Most unforgettably, Jay Vance of Berkeley, Jean Vance of San Francisco State University, and Bonnie Loyd, editor of *Landscape* magazine. It is with them that I spent that October evening in the Berkeley Hills sipping Louis Martini Special Reserve 1978 by candlelight while we gazed out through the Vances' picture window watching San Francisco burn. There was not a lot else to do that night, in the immediate aftermath of the Great 1989 Earthquake.

In the Washington area, Tysons Corner historian and geographer Shelly Mastran, Roger K. Lewis and Robert D. Mitchell of the University of Maryland, Joseph E. Brown of EDAW, Incorporated, Bob Kelly, April Young, architects Philip A. Esocoff of Keyes Condon Florance, and Michael E. Hickok, the region's premiere demographers George and Eunice Grier, and Alicia Mundy and Duncan Spencer of *Regardie's* magazine.

Finally, while most of the developers I met were congenial and even idealistic people, the two who contributed the most, in their way, were Don White and Sid Jacobson of Gainesville, Virginia. They developed the land around my first Virginia farm, causing me to vainly beat my little fists against their schemes, driving me deep into that study of the limits of the law and the American national character which culminated in this book. For launching me on my journey, I have no choice but to be in their debt. Not coincidentally, as a result of their work, *Edge City* can be read as something in the way of my final report to all the people—all the people—of Fauquier County, Virginia, concerning the grace of the future of our lives.

What a long strange trip it's been.

# Suggested Readings

*Edge City* draws on the efforts of many thoughtful people. It is not possible to list all their works. So this, instead, is a cull of items that I think the general reader may find useful, enjoyable, and even startling. Many of these, in turn, have bibliographies and notes that lead off in yet more directions.

This is a personal list—hardly an attempt at a complete one. Nor is it a list of prime sources. Many of those were interviews, several were computer runs, and more than a few were too boring to inflict casually on other human beings. Readers with specific questions about resources and research opportunities are welcome to contact the author in care of The Edge City™ Group, Broad Run, VA 22014–9501.

## On the Shaping of America

Allen, Frederick Lewis. *The Big Change: America Transforms Itself, 1900–1950.* New York: Harper & Bros., 1952.

Bailyn, Bernard. *Voyagers to the West.* New York: Knopf, 1986.

Barone, Michael. *Our Country: The Shaping of America from Roosevelt to Reagan.* New York: Free Press, 1990.

———, and Grant Ujifusa. *The Almanac of American Politics 1990.* Washington, D.C.: National Journal, 1990.

    The biennial review of who we are, how we got that way, and where we're headed that focuses down to the county level and up to the perspective of centuries. Quite a stunt.

Baudrillard, Jean. *America.* London: Verso, 1989.

    A postmodernist de Tocqueville. More about postmodernism under "The Rise of Edge City."

Bell, Daniel. *The Coming of the Post-Industrial Society: A Venture in Social Forecasting.* New York: Basic Books, 1976.

Boorstin, Daniel. *The Discoverers.* New York: Random House, 1983.

Conzen, Michael P., ed. *The Making of the American Landscape.* Boston: Unwin Hyman, 1990.

Garreau, Joel. *The Nine Nations of North America.* Boston: Houghton Mifflin, 1981.

Gottmann, Jean. *Megalopolis: The Urbanized Northeastern Seaboard of the United States.* New York: Twentieth Century Fund, 1961.

    The work that introduced a new word to the language and changed the way America saw itself.

Herbers, John. *The New Heartland: America's Flight Beyond the Suburbs and How It Is Changing Our Future.* New York: Times Books, 1986.

Kotkin, Joel, and Yoriko Kishimoto. *The Third Century: America's Resurgence in the Asian Era.* New York: Crown, 1988.

Louv, Richard. *America II.* Los Angeles: Jeremy P. Tarcher, 1983.

Marx, Leo. *The Machine in the Garden: Technology and the Pastoral Ideal in America.* London: Oxford University Press, 1964.

Meinig, D. W. *The Shaping of America: A Geographical Perspective on 500 Years of History.* Vol. 1, *Atlantic America, 1492–1800* (New Haven: Yale University Press, 1986).

    The best single volume on how America was shaped in the three centuries leading up to the Revolution. The maps alone—showing how the world was viewed by people dependent on wind and tide —are worth the price.

Mitchell, Robert D., and Paul A. Groves, eds. *North America: The Historical Geography of a Changing Continent.* Totowa, N.J.: Rowman & Littlefield, 1987.

Tocqueville, Alexis de. *Democracy in America,* 2 vols. Edited by J. P. Mayer. Translated by George Lawrence. New York: Anchor/Doubleday, 1975.

Toffler, Alvin. *Future Shock.* New York: Random House, 1970.

———. *The Third Wave.* New York: Morrow, 1980.

Twain, Mark. *The Adventures of Huckleberry Finn.* Edited by Leo Marx. Indianapolis: Bobbs-Merrill, 1967.

Wiebe, Robert H. *The Opening of American Society: From the Adoption of the Constitution to the Eve of Disunion.* New York: Knopf, 1984.

Zelinsky, Wilbur. *The Cultural Geography of the United States.* Englewood Cliffs: Prentice-Hall, 1973.

## On the Art and Science of Seeing One's Surroundings Anew

Clay, Grady. *Close-up: How to Read the American City.* Chicago: University of Chicago Press, 1973.

———. "The Street as Teacher." In *Public Streets for Public Use.* New York: Van Nostrand Reinhold, 1987.

———. *Right Before Your Eyes: Penetrating the Urban Environment.* Chicago: American Planning Association Press, 1988.

Gould, Peter, and Rodney White. *Mental Maps.* Harmondsworth: Penguin Books, 1974.

Jackson, John Brinckerhoff. *Landscapes: Selected Writings of J. B. Jackson.* Edited by Ervin H. Zube. Amherst: University of Massachusetts Press, 1970 .

———. *The Necessity For Ruins.* Amherst: University of Massachusetts Press, 1980.

———. *Discovering the Vernacular Landscape.* New Haven: Yale University Press, 1984.

Lewis, Peirce F. "Axioms for Reading the Landscape, Some Guides to the American Scene." In *The Interpretation of Ordinary Landscapes: Geographical Essays,* edited by D. W. Meinig. New York: Oxford University Press, 1979.

———. "Learning from Looking: Geographic and Other Writing About the American Cultural Landscape." In *Material Culture: A Research Guide,* edited by Thomas Schlereth. Lawrence: University Press of Kansas, 1988.

Liebs, Chester H. *Main Street to Miracle Mile: American Roadside Architecture,* Boston: Bulfinch Press, 1985.

Lynch, Kevin. *Image of the City.* Cambridge: MIT Press, 1960.

———. *What Time Is This Place?* Cambridge: MIT Press, 1972.

Venturi, Robert, Denise Scott Brown, and Steven Izenour. *Learning from Las Vegas.* Cambridge: MIT Press, 1988.

Whyte, William H. "A Guide to Peoplewatching." In *Urban Open Spaces.* New York: Cooper-Hewitt Museum, 1979.

Zelinsky, Wilbur. "Oh Say, Can You See? Nationalistic Emblems in the Landscape." *Winterthur Portfolio* 19, no. 4 (Winter 198 4): 77–86.

———. "A Toponymic Approach to the Geography of American Cemeteries." *Names* 38, no. 3 (1990): 209–21.

And cemeteries? And cemeteries.

Grady Clay, J. B. Jackson, Peirce Lewis, and Wilbur Zelinsky are America's foremost chroniclers of everyday places. Like most cultural geographers, they are also delightful reading companions.

## On the Shaping of Cities

Bacon, Edmund N. *Design of Cities.* New York: Penguin, 1976.

Barnett, Jonathan. *The Elusive City: Five Centuries of Design, Ambition, and Miscalculation.* New York: Harper & Row, 1986.

Braudel, Fernand. *The Mediterranean and the Mediterranean World in the Age of Philip II.* Vols. 1 and 2. 2d rev. ed. New York: Harper & Row, 1972.

Fishman, Robert. *Urban Utopias in the Twentieth Century.* Cambridge: MIT Press, 1988.

Goldberg, Michael A., and John Mercer. *The Myth of the North American City.* Vancouver: University of British Columbia Press, 1986.

Gottmann, Jean, and Robert A. Harper, eds. *Since Megalopolis.* Baltimore: Johns Hopkins University Press, 1990.

Jacobs, Jane. *The Death and Life of Great American Cities.* New York: Random House, 1961.

———. *Cities and the Wealth of Nations: Principles of Economic Life.* New York: Random House, 1984.

Hamer, David. *New Towns in the New World: Images and Perceptions of the Nineteenth-Century Urban Frontier.* New York: Columbia University Press, 1990.

Hartshorn, Truman A. *Interpreting the City: An Urban Geography.* New York: Wiley, 1980.

Konvitz, Josef W. *The Urban Millennium: The City-Building Process from the Early Middle Ages to the Present.* Carbondale: Southern Illinois University Press, 1985.

Le Corbusier. *The City of Tomorrow and Its Planning.* New York: Dover, 1987.

Monkkonen, Eric. *America Becomes Urban.* Berkeley: University of California Press, 1988.

Mumford, Lewis. *The Culture of Cities.* New York: Harcourt Brace, 1938.

———. *The City in History: Its Origins, Its Transformations, and Its Prospects.* New York: Harcourt Brace Jovanovich, 1961.

———. *The Lewis Mumford Reader.* Edited by Donald L. Miller. New York: Pantheon, 1986.

Vance, James E., Jr. *This Scene of Man: The Role and Structure of the City in the Geography of Western Civilization.* New York: Harper & Row, 1977.

> The most useful one-volume work on the rise of cities throughout history that I know. I found myself turning to it more often than to Mumford.

Warner, Sam Bass, Jr. *Streetcar Suburbs: The Process of Growth in Boston, 1870–1900.* Cambridge: Harvard University Press, 1962.

———. *The Private City.* Philadelphia: University of Pennsylvania Press, 1968.

———. *The Urban Wilderness: A History of the American City.* New York: Harper & Row, 1972.
   Wonderful photos.

Whyte, William H. *The Last Landscape.* Garden City, N.Y.: Doubleday, 1968.

———. *City: Rediscovering the Center.* New York: Doubleday, 1988.


### On Suburbia

Fishman, Robert. *Bourgeois Utopias: The Rise and Fall of Suburbia.* New York: Basic Books, 1987.

Jackson, Kenneth. *Crabgrass Frontier: The Suburbanization of the United States.* New York: Oxford University Press, 1985.

Stilgoe, John. *Borderland: Origins of the American Suburb, 1820–1939.* New Haven: Yale University Press, 1988.
   These are the three major modern books on suburbia. I am partial to Fishman's work, for he is the most forward-looking analyst, seeing clearly how the desires that produced suburbia inexorably lead to Edge City.


### On the Rise of Edge City

Baerwald, Thomas. "Emergence of a New Downtown," *Geographical Review* 68 (July 1978).

———. "Major Diversified Centers in Midwestern Metropolises." Paper presented to West Lakes Division of the Association of American Geographers, November 1983.

Birch, David. "From Suburb to Urban Place," *Annals of the American Academy of Political and Social Science* 422 (1975).

Downs, Anthony. *The Need for a New Vision for the Development of Large U.S. Metropolitan Areas.* New York: Salomon Brothers, August 1989.

"Edge Cities." *Landscape Architecture* 78, no. 8 (December 1988).
   With a cover story by Joel Garreau.

Fishman, Robert. "Megalopolis Unbound." *Wilson Quarterly* (Winter 1990).
   The definitive work on Edge City topics to that date.

Forbes, Bryan, director, and Edgar J. Scherick, producer. *Stepford Wives.* Columbia, 1975.
   Be careful what you ask for.

Garreau, Joel. "The Emerging Cities of Washington: From Suburbs,

Cities Are Springing Up in Our Back Yards" *Washington Post,* March 8, 1987.

————. "The Emerging Cities: Civilization and the Suburbs." *Washington Post,* June 19–20, 1988.

Hartshorn, Truman A. "Industrial Parks/Office Parks: A New Look for the City." *Journal of Geography* 62 (March 1973).

————, and Peter O. Muller. *Suburban Business Centers: Employment Implications.* Washington, D.C.: U.S. Department of Commerce, 1986.

*Landscape Magazine* 30, no. 3 (1990). P.O. Box 7107, Berkeley, CA 94707.

> *Landscape Magazine,* which was founded by J. B. Jackson, is always a font of earthly delights, but this issue includes a remarkable compilation of insights on Edge City topics, especially Robert L. Thayer, Jr., "Pragmatism in Paradise: Technology and the American Landscape," p. 1; Richard West Sellars, "Why Take a Trip to Bountiful—Won't Anaheim Do?," p. 14; and Judith A. Martin, "European Models and American Realities: A Perspective on Urban Design," p. 36, in which Martin trashes European models.

Leinberger, Christopher B. "The Six Types of Urban Village Cores." *Urban Land* 47 (May 1988).

————. "Development Trends and Real Estate Opportunities in the 1990's." *Urban Land* (December 1990).

————, and Charles Lockwood. "How Business Is Reshaping America." *Atlantic,* October 1986.

> This was the article that introduced the idea of Edge City in the popular press.

Lewis, Peirce F. "The Unprecedented City." In *The American Land,* New York: Norton, 1979.

————. "The Galactic Metropolis." In *Beyond the Urban Fringe,* edited by Rutherford H. Platt and George Macinko. Minneapolis: University of Minnesota Press, 1983.

————. *The New City.* Lecture delivered at Harvard University Graduate School of Design, conference, Changing Scale: Recent Projects, April 7, 1990.

> Of the people who saw Edge Cities coming early, the ones from whom I learned the most were Robert Fishman, Christopher Leinberger, and Peirce Lewis.

Muller, Peter O. *Contemporary Suburban America.* Englewood Cliffs, New Jersey: Prentice-Hall, 1981.

————. "Transportation and Urban Form: Stages in the Spatial Evolution of the American Metropolis." In *Geography of Urban Transportation,* edited by Susan Hanson. New York: Guilford Press, 1986.

Scott, Ridley, director, and Michael Deeley, producer. *Blade Runner.* Warner Bros., 1982.

Soja, Edward W. *Postmodern Geographies: The Reassertion of Space in Critical Social Theory.* London: Verso, 1989.

> Postmodernism, as I understand it, is that school of thought whose bottom-line observation is that human reality is always more complicated than any structure you can erect to describe it. Hence, it refers to a diverse collection of people who are united less by what they believe than by what they do not believe—i.e., that the giant system-makers of the past like René Descartes, Adam Smith, Karl Marx, and Sigmund Freud have a lock on truth. Postmodernism is especially embraced by those of the left, like Soja, who recognize that today's communism is terminal but who nonetheless can make a convincing case that today's capitalism is a less than pretty description of what makes humans tick. Sadly, the term "postmodern" is also all too often wrapped like a protective cloak around writing that mistakes incomprehensibility for profundity. But the postmodernists, I think, are on to something. In a war today, for example, the ephemeral perceptions of millions of individuals around the globe watching that war live on CNN are far more likely to produce results that lead to tangible change than are the actual physical realities produced by the bombings of the war itself. Those who are groping for a larger explanation of the working of that and the myriad other weirdnesses of our times that appear to defy description—much less sense—are not wasting their time.

Warner, Sam Bass, Jr. "Suburb City Relations: When Suburb Becomes City." Paper presented at the Conference on the Future of the Design of Suburbs in America sponsored by the Smithsonian Institution and Maryland National Capital Park and Planning Commission, Boston University, February 8, 1988.

Welfeld, Irving. *Where We Live: The American Home and the Social, Political, and Economic Landscape, from Slums to Suburbs.* New York: Simon & Schuster, 1988.

> An authoritative dose of reality that dashes much of conventional wisdom. The book is made even more attractive by the fact that the author actually has a sense of humor.

Wells, H. G. "The Probable Diffusion of Great Cities." In *Anticipations and Other Papers,* vol. 4 of *The Works of H. G. Wells.* New York: Scribner's, 1924.

Wood, Joseph S. "Suburbanization of Center City." *Geographical Review* 78 (1988).

Wright, Frank Lloyd. *The Living City.* New York: Horizon Press, 1958.

## On the Automobile and the Future of Mobility

Batten, David F., and Roland Thord, eds. *Transportation for the Future.* Berlin: Springer-Verlag, 1989.

Bruce-Briggs, Barry. *The War Against the Automobile.* New York: Dutton, 1977.

The combative tone of this defense of the automobile can be excessive. Nonetheless, it remains the best single explanation of why our great-grandchildren will probably be conveyed to the maternity ward to have children in an individual transportation device that has four wheels and a steering column.

Cervero, Robert. *Suburban Gridlock.* New Brunswick, N.J.: Center for Urban Policy Research, Rutgers University, 1986.

———. *America's Suburban Centers: A Study of the Land Use/Transportation Link.* Washington, D.C.: U.S. Department of Transportation, 1988 .

———. "Jobs-Housing Balancing and Regional Mobility." *American Planning Association* (Spring 1989).

Downs, Anthony. "The Law of Peak-Hour Expressway Congestion." *Traffic Quarterly* 16, no. 3 (July 1962), updated.

Dunphy, Robert T. "In Search of the Holy Rail." *Urban Land* (May 1990).

Gregor, Harry P. "Alcohol Fuel: The One for the Road," *Washington Post,* July 9, 1989.

Laas, William, ed. *Freedom of the American Road.* Dearborn: Ford Motor Company, 1956.

With a foreword by Henry Ford II and an introduction by the historian Bernard DeVoto, this is a wonderfully antique cultural artifact that presents with pride the virtues of the freeways and makes no bones that first among them is freedom.

Lynch, Michael C. *Oil Prices to 2000: The Economics of the Oil Market.* London: Economist Intelligence Unit, May 1989.

There really is a lot of oil on this planet, if we are willing to pay the political, military, environmental, esthetic, and social price.

"Make them pay." *The Economist,* February 18, 1989 .

A cogent argument that the best way to ration roads whose capacity cannot be increased is to charge a market price for the right to use them.

Miller, Catherine G. *Carscape: A Parking Handbook.* Columbus, Ind.: Washington Street Press, 1988.

*Myths and Facts About Transportation and Growth.* Washington, D.C.: Urban Land Institute, 1989.

*National Transportation Strategic Planning Study.* Washington, D.C.: U.S. Department of Transportation, March 1990.

Noto, Nonna A. "The Economics of Commuting in a Higher Cost World." *Business Review* (September-October 1977).

Orski, C. Kenneth. "Transportation Management Associations: Battling Suburban Traffic Congestion." *Urban Land* (December 1986).

———. "Toward a Policy for Suburban Mobility." In *Urban Traffic Congestion: What Does the Future Hold?* Washington, D.C.: Institute of Transportation Engineers, 1986.

———. "The Problem of Traffic Congestion," *Vital Speeches of the Day,* January 1 , 1990.

Pisarski, Alan E. *Commuting in America: A National Report on Commuting Patterns and Trends.* Westport, Conn.: Eno Foundation for Transportation, 1987.

———. *The External Environment for Public Transit to the Year 2020: A Speculative Assessment.* Prepared for APTA, January 8, 1988.

———. *Issues in Transportation and Growth Management.* A discussion paper prepared for a Joint Conference of the Urban Land Institute Center for Urban and Regional Studies, August 15, 1988 .

> Of the many people writing about how to untangle Edge City surface transportation, the three most useful to me were Robert Cervero, C. Kenneth Orski, and Alan Pisarski.

*A Toolbox for Alleviating Traffic Congestion.* Accompanied by Executive Summary. Washington, D.C.: Institute of Transportation Engineers, 1989.

> A discussion of just about all the tricks available today to reduce traffic congestion and increase mobility.

Witcher, Gregory. "Smart Cars, Smart Highways." *Wall Street Journal,* May 22, 1989.

### On Time, Freedom, Stress, and the Automobile

Abler, Ronald, Donald Janelle, Allen Philbrick, and John Sommer. *Human Geography in a Shrinking World.* Belmont, Cal.: Wadsworth, 1975.

> With an especially fascinating chapter by Ronald Abler on the devices—from the stagecoach to the railroad to air mail to the telephone—that ultimately made time and space interchangeable in Edge City.

Allen, Henry. "Driving Us Crazy: Anatomy of a Traffic Jam." *Washington Post,* October 21, 1990, Style section, F1.

> The cultural history of the automobile's ultimate betrayal—the loss of our time and freedom.

*The Automobile in American Life*. Dearborn, Mich.: Henry Ford Museum and Greenfield Village, 1987.

> The guide to the exhibition by the same name shows how much automobiles have meant to us emotionally. In the portion named "Car as Symbol," for example, the displays are labeled everything from "Freedom" to "Individuality," with a 1931 Bugatti Royale Type 41 thought to epitomize "Style," a 1920s Stutz Bearcat to mean "Youth," the Rolls to embody "Success," and, of course, the 1965 Pontiac GTO to mean "Power."

Baerwald, Thomas J. "Commuter Attitudes Toward Ridesharing." *Environments* (University of Waterloo, Canada) 17, no. 2 (1985): 96–99.

> They hate it.

Kimbrell, Andrew. "Car Culture: Driving Ourselves Crazy." *Washington Post*, September 3, 1989.

Levine, Robert. "Waiting Is a Power Game: Who Waits Up Front, Who Waits in Back, and Who Waits Not at All—Privilege Has Its Power." *Psychology Today*, April 1987.

———. "The Pace of Life: Most Cities Where People Walk, Talk, and Work the Fastest Also Have the Highest Rates of Heart Disease. But What Do the Exceptions Tell Us?" *Psychology Today*, October 1989.

———, and Ellen Wolff. "Social Time: The Heartbeat of Culture." *Psychology Today*, March 1985.

Novaco, Raymond W. "Objective and Subjective Dimensions of Travel Impedance as Determinants of Commuting Stress," *American Journal of Community Psychology*, 18, no. 2 (1990).

———, Daniel Stokols, and Louis Milanese. "Commuting, Stress and Well-Being," *Review* 12, no. 2 (February 1989).

Packard, Vance. *A Nation of Strangers*. New York: McKay, 1972.

Paris, Ellen. "Trading Free Time for Better Housing." *Forbes*, July 23, 1990, 88.

> The world of the supercommuter.

Stokols, Daniel, and Raymond W. Novaco. "Transportation and Well-Being: An Ecological Perspective." In *Transportation and Behavior*. New York: Plenum Press, 1981.

## On the Underpinnings of the Dematerializing Technologies

King, Thomas R. "Working at Home Has Yet to Work Out." *Wall Street Journal*, December 22, 1989.

McLuhan, Marshall. *Understanding Media: The Extensions of Man*. New York: McGraw-Hill, 1964.

Miller, Michael W. "Digital Revolution: Vast Changes Loom as Computers Digest Words, Sound, Images." *Wall Street Journal,* June 7, 1989.

Mills, Edwin S. "Sectoral Clustering and Metropolitan Development." In *Sources of Metropolitan Growth and Development.* New Brunswick, N.J.: Center for Urban Policy Research, Rutgers University, 1991.
  The source of the wonderful idea that all truly important information in life may be ambiguous and thus inherently resistant to computerization.

Schwartz, Tony. *Media: The Second God.* New York: Random House, 1981.

Stewart, Doug. "Through the Looking Glass into an Artificial World—via Computer." *Smithsonian,* January 1991.

### On the New Black Middle Class

Branch, Taylor. *Parting the Waters: America in the King Years 1954–1963.* New York: Simon & Schuster, 1988 .
  With an especially fine depiction of John Lewis.

Farley, Reynolds, and Walter R. Allen. *The Color Line and the Quality of Life in America.* New York: Russell Sage Foundation, 1987.

Frazier, E. Franklin. *Black Bourgeoisie: The Rise of a New Middle Class in the United States.* New York: Free Press, 1957.
  This is the benchmark on the subject.

Freeman, Richard. *The Black Elite.* New York: McGraw-Hill, 1976.

Garreau, Joel. "The Emerging Cities: Blacks—Success in the Suburbs." *Washington Post,* November 29–December 1, 1987.

Green, Constance McLaughlin. *The Secret City.* Princeton: Princeton University Press, 1967.

Jaynes, Gerald D., and Robin M. Williams, Jr., eds. *A Common Destiny: Blacks and American Society.* Washington, D.C.: National Academy Press, 1989.

King, Martin Luther, Jr. "I Have a Dream." In *The Words of Martin Luther King, Jr.,* edited by Coretta Scott King. New York: Newmarket Press, 1987.

Lake, Robert. *The New Suburbanites: Race and Housing in the Suburbs.* New Brunswick, N.J.: Center for Urban Policy Research, Rutgers University, 1981.

Landry, Bart. *The New Black Middle Class.* Berkeley: University of California Press, 1987.
  This generation's Frazier.

McFate, Katherine, ed. *A Statistical Portrait of Blacks and Whites in Urban America.* Washington, D.C.: Joint Center for Political Studies, 1988.

Massey, Douglas S., and Nancy A. Denton, "Hypersegregation in U.S.

Metropolitan Areas: Black and Hispanic Segregation Along Five Dimensions." *Demography* 26, no. 3 (August 1989).

———, and Mitchell L. Eggers. "The Ecology of Inequality: Minorities and the Concentration of Poverty, 1970–1980." *American Journal of Sociology* 95, no. 5 (March 1990).

Murray, Charles, with Deborah Laren. *According to Age: Longitudinal Profiles of AFDC Recipients and the Poor by Age Group.* Washington, D.C.: American Enterprise Institute for Public Policy Research, September 1986.

> The statistical link across gender and racial lines between middle-class attitudes toward education, family structure, and work, and middle-class incomes.

Sowell, Thomas. *Preferential Policies: An International Perspective.* New York: Morrow, 1990.

> Thomas Sowell is the black Hoover Institute economist who analyzes the preferential government policies of various cultures that favor disadvantaged minorities (blacks in the United States, Maoris in New Zealand, untouchables in India, etc.). He argues that minorities worldwide succeed or fail largely without regard to well- or ill-meant social programs. This is his most recent work.

Steele, Shelby. *The Content of Our Character: A New Vision of Race in America.* New York: St. Martin's Press, 1990.

> Shelby Steele is a professor of English at San Jose State University. He has been attempting to resolve issues of race and class in a "new vision of race in America," in which blacks reclaim responsibility for the internal as well as the external condition of their lives.

Wilson, William Julius. *The Declining Significance of Race: Blacks and Changing American Institutions.* Chicago: University of Chicago Press, 1978.

> The works of Frazier, Wilson, and Landry, in that order, can be read as a trilogy. Each builds on the previous one, consciously using similar categories.

Welniak, Edward J. *Money Income of Households, Families, and Persons in the United States: 1987.* Washington, D.C.: U.S. Department of Commerce, Bureau of the Census, 1989.

> The bible on who's got it and who doesn't.

Woodson, Robert L., ed. *On the Road to Economic Freedom.* New York: Kampmann, 1987.

### On Politics and Government

The Mayflower Compact
The Declaration of Independence

The Constitution of the United States
Abraham Lincoln's Gettysburg Address
Franklin Delano Roosevelt's "Four Freedoms" Speech
John F. Kennedy's Inaugural Address
The Civil Rights Act of 1964
> All or parts of these documents, along with many others that are well worth rereading, are made pocket-size in *The Little Red, White, and Blue Book: A Collection of Historic Documents and Chronology of American History*, compiled by the editors of *The World Almanac and Book of Facts* (New York: Scripps Howard, 1987).

Goodgame, Dan, and Richard Hornik, with bureau reports. "Is Government Dead? Unwilling to Lead, Politicians Are Letting America Slip into Paralysis." *Time*, October 23, 1989, cover story.
> "Paralyzed by special interests and shortsightedness, the Government risks slipping into irrelevancy," this report charged.

Lapham, Lewis H. "Democracy in America?: Not Only the Economy Is in Decline." *Harper's*, November 1990.

Taylor, Paul, "Citizenship Fades Among Disconnected Americans." *Washington Post*, May 6, 1990, A1.
> Fewer people are voting or standing up to be counted in the Census or voluntarily paying their taxes.

## On Shadow Governments

Alexander, Gregory S. "Dilemmas of Group Autonomy: Residential Associations and Community." *Cornell Law Review* 75, no. 1 (November 1989): 1.
> Shadow governments as a clear and present danger.

*Articles of Amendment to Articles of Incorporation of Leisure World Community Association*. Phoenix: Leisure World Community Association, 1989.
> The laws of a shadow government.

Ellickson, Robert C. "Cities and Homeowners Associations." *University of Pennsylvania Law Review* 130, no. 6 (June 1982).
> A ringing defense of shadow governments.

Garreau, Joel. "The Shadow Governments: More Than 2000 Unelected Units Rule in New Communities." *Washington Post*, June 14, 1987 , A1.

Hanke, Byron R., Jan Krasnowiecki, William C. Loring, Gene C. Tweraser, and Mary Jo Cornish. *The Homes Association Handbook*. Washington, D.C.: Urban Land Institute, 1964.
> The classic study on the impact of such a shadow government on home values: they go up.

Ingram, Kenneth J. "The Community Association: Mini-Government or Business Entity?" *Common Ground: The Journal of the Community Associations Institute* (Alexandria, Va.), November-December 1986.

What would happen, constitutionally, if we ever decided to force these shadow governments to live up to the standards of conventional governments?

McDowell, Bruce D. *The Privatization of Metropolitan America.* Washington, D.C.: U.S. Advisory Commission on Intergovernmental Affairs, June 1990.

*1991* Revised Preliminary Community Budget. Leisure World Community Association, prepared for the Board of Directors, October 31, 1990.

How a shadow government can collect and spend $4,989,220 a year.

*Residential Community Associations: Private Governments in the Intergovernmental System?* Washington, D.C.: Advisory Commission on Intergovernmental Relations, May 1989.

Washington wakes up to the news that it has competition.

*Residential Community Associations: Questions and Answers for Public Officials.* Washington, D.C.: U.S. Advisory Commission on Intergovernmental Relations, July 1989.

Among the most thorough looks at community association shadow governments to date. It examines them as real governments.

### On Design, Planning, and Architecture

Apocconio, Umbro, ed. *The Documents of 20th Century Art: Futurist Manifestos.* New York: Viking, 1973.

*The Costs of Sprawl.* 2 vols. Washington, D.C.: Government Printing Office, 1974.

Crary, Jonathan, Michel Feher, Hal Foster, and Sanford Kwinter, eds. *Zone: A Serial Publication of Ideas in Contemporary Culture.* New York, Urzone, 1986.

A wonderfully surreal and challenging look at the new city.

Fleming, Ronald Lee, and Renata von Tscharner. *Placemakers: Creating Public Art That Tells You Where You Are.* Boston: Harcourt Brace Jovanovich, 1987 .

Fondersmith, John. "Downtown 2040: Making Cities Fun!" *The Futurist,* March-April 1988.

Giedion, Siegfried. *Space, Time, and Architecture.* Cambridge: Harvard University Press, 1941.

———. *Architecture, You and Me.* Cambridge: Harvard University Press, 1958.

Gruen, Victor. *The Heart of Our Cities*. New York: Simon & Schuster, 1967.

————. *Centers for the Urban Environment*. New York: Van Nostrand Reinhold, 1973.

Hall, Barbara Jane. *101 Easy Ways to Make Your Home Sell Faster*. New York: Ballantine, 1985.

   Another one of those small pieces of reality therapy which America from time to time throws in the face of grand theory.

Harvey, David. *The Condition of Postmodernity: An Enquiry into the Origins of Cultural Change*. Cambridge, Mass.: Basil Blackwell, 1989.

Lennard, Suzanne H. Crowhurst, and Henry L. Lennard. *Livable Cities*. Southampton, N.Y.: Gondolier Press, 1987.

Lewis, Roger. *Shaping the City*. Washington, D.C.: AIA Press, 1987.

Lynch, Kevin. *A Theory of Good City Form*. Cambridge: MIT Press, 1981.

MacKaye, Benton, and Lewis Mumford. "Townless Highways for the Motorist: A Proposal for the Automobile Age." *Harper's*, August 1931.

   In which two of America's foremost defenders of the landscape at that time strongly advocated the virtues of the cul de sac, the bypass, the overpass, and a federal system of superhighways—largely on environmental and esthetic grounds.

Maddex, Diane. *Master Builders: A Guide to Famous American Architects*. Washington, D.C.: Preservation Press, 1985.

   Maddex's work, and Nuttgens', below, are excellent compact guides.

Newman, Oscar. *Defensible Space*. New York: Macmillan, 1972.

Newton, Norman. *Design on the Land: The Development of Landscape Architecture*. Cambridge: Harvard University Press, 1971.

Nuttgens, Patrick. *Simon & Schuster's Pocket Guide to Architecture*. New York: Simon & Schuster, 1980.

Reps, John W. *The Making of Urban America: A History of City Planning in the United States*. Princeton: Princeton University Press, 1965.

Saint, Andrew. *The Image of the Architect*. New Haven: Yale University Press, 1983.

   An eye-opening guide to the wounds architects have suffered—many self-inflicted—which have often resulted in impotence.

Schwartz, Gail Garfield. *Where's Main Street, U.S.A.?* Westport, Conn.: ENO Foundation for Transportation, 1984.

Scully, Vincent. *American Architecture and Urbanism*. New York: Praeger, 1969 .

Stilgoe, John. *Common Landscape of America, 1580–1845*. New Haven: Yale University Press, 1982.

Tafuri, Manfredo. *Architecture and Utopia: Design and Capitalist Development*. Cambridge: MIT Press, 1988.

Venturi, Robert. *Complexity and Contradiction in Architecture*. 2d ed. New York: Museum of Modern Art, 1977.

Vidor, King, director, and Henry Blanke, producer. *The Fountainhead*. Warner Bros., 1949. (Screenplay by Ayn Rand from her novel. New York: Macmillan, 1943.)

> Check out the building that Gary Cooper blows up. Premature postmodernism?

Vitruvius. *The Ten Books on Architecture*. New York: Dover, 1960.

Von Eckardt, Wolf. *Back to the Drawing Board: Planning Livable Cities*. Washington, D.C.: New Republic Press, 1970.

Weightman, Barbara. "Gay Bars as Private Places." *Landscape* 24, no. 1. (1980).

> Let the record show that one of the things cities are for is the exercise of extremely private lives. Note also Denis Wood, below.

Whyte, William H. *The Social Life of Small Urban Spaces*. Washington, D.C.: Conservation Foundation, 1980.

Wolfe, Tom. *From Bauhaus to Our House*. New York: Farrar, Straus & Giroux, 1981.

> A brief history of designers who should have been smothered in their cribs.

Wood, Denis. "In Defense of Indefensible Space." In *Urban Crime and Environmental Criminology*. Beverly Hills: Sage, 1981.

## Designs with Edge City in Mind

Boles, Daralice D. "Reordering the Suburbs." *Progressive Architecture* (May 1989).

Calthorpe, Peter. "Pedestrian Pockets: New Strategies for Suburban Growth." *Whole Earth Review*, Spring 1988.

Derven, Ronald, and Carol Feder, ed. *Mixed-Use Business Parks*. National Association of Industrial and Office Parks, 1988.

> How the developers see our world.

Gillette, Howard, Jr. "The Evolution of the Planned Shopping Center in Suburb and City." *APA Journal* (1985).

Harvey, Douglas Pegues. "Of Malls, Garages, and the Fertility of Freeways." *Texas Architect* (July-August 1985).

Knack, Ruth Eckdish. "Repent, Ye Sinners, Repent: We Can Save the Suburbs, Say Advocates of Neotraditional Town Planning." *American Planning Association Journal* (August 1989).

Lemire, Robert. *Creative Land Development: Bridge to the Future*. Boston: Houghton Mifflin, 1979.

Van Der Ryn, Sim, and Peter Calthorpe. *Sustainable Communities: A New Design Synthesis for Cities, Suburbs and Towns.* San Francisco: Sierra Club Books, 1986.

## On the Rise of Edge Cities Worldwide

Kostin, David J. *Sydney Real Estate Market.* New York: Salomon Brothers, September 1988.

Shulman, David, and David J. Kostin, *London Office Market.* New York: Salomon Brothers, September, 1988.

Shulman, David, David J. Kostin, Danielle Kadeyan, and Alison Howe. *Paris Real Estate Market.* New York: Salomon Brothers, August 1989.

## On Community

Anderson, Sherwood. *Winesburg, Ohio.* New York: Huebsch, 1919.

Bellah, Robert, Richard Madsen, William M. Sullivan, Ann Swidler, and Steven M. Tipton. *Habits of the Heart.* New York: Harper & Row, 1985.

Gans, Herbert. *The Urban Villagers: Group and Class in the Life of Italian-Americans.* New York: Free Press, 1962.

————. *The Levittowners: Ways of Life and Politics in a New Suburban Community.* New York: Pantheon, 1967.

Kahn, Bonnie Menes. *Cosmopolitan Culture.* New York: Atheneum, 1987.

Lemann, Nicholas. "Stressed Out in Suburbia: A Generation After the Postwar Boom, Life in the Suburbs Has Changed, Even if Our Picture of It Hasn't." *Atlantic,* November 1989.

Lewis, Sinclair. *Main Street.* New York: Harcourt, 1920.

————. *Babbitt.* New York: Harcourt, 1924.

Louv, Richard. *Childhood's Future: Listening to the American Family; New Hope for the Next Generation.* Boston: Houghton Mifflin, 1990.

Nisbet, Robert A. *The Quest for Community: A Study in the Ethics of Order and Freedom.* New York: Oxford University Press, 1970.

Rousseau, Jean-Jacques. *The Social Contract.* Chicago: Henry Regnery, 1954.

Sennett, Richard. *The Fall of Public Man: On the Social Psychology of Capitalism.* New York: Knopf, 1977.

————. *The Conscience of the Eye.* New York: Knopf, 1990.

Whyte, William H. *The Organization Man.* New York: Simon & Schuster, 1956.

## On Technology, Progress, and Values

Adams, Henry. *The Education of Henry Adams: An Autobiography.* New York: Modern Library, 1931.
   See especially "The Dynamo and the Virgin," chap. 25.
Beniger, James. *The Control Revolution.* Cambridge: Harvard University Press, 1986.
Giedion, Siegfried. *Mechanization Takes Command.* New York: Oxford University Press, 1948.
Hughes, Thomas P. *American Genesis: A Century of Invention and Technological Enthusiasm, 1870–1970* . New York: Viking, 1989.
Nisbet, Robert. *History of the Idea of Progress.* New York: Basic Books, 1980 .
   All of these volumes make explicit reference to how industrialization split our modes of thinking from our modes of feeling, and offer ideas about how to bridge that gap.

## On How Scientific Thought Is Changing

Gleick, James. *Chaos: Making a New Science.* New York: Viking Penguin, 1987 .
Kuhn, Thomas S. *The Copernican Revolution.* Cambridge: Harvard University Press, 1957.
———. "The Structure of Scientific Revolutions." New York: International Encyclopedia of Unified Science, 1962.
———. *The Structure of Scientific Revolutions.* Chicago: Chicago University Press, 1970.
   Kuhn originated the concept "paradigm" to suggest that any body of research is shaped by the current dominant world views, institutions, and beliefs of the researchers. Hence, these paradigms, or world-view structures, are subject to sharp, discontinuous transformations as new structures are found that describe reality better. These breaks, or "paradigm shifts," are referred to as scientific or societal revolutions.
Mallove, Eugene. *The Quickening Universe: Cosmic Evolution and Human Destiny* New York: St. Martin's Press, 1987.

## On Christopher Alexander

Alexander, Christopher. "A City Is Not a Tree." *Design Magazine,* 1965.
———. "The Nature of Order: An Essay on the Art of Building and the Nature of the Universe." Draft manuscript, 1988.
———, Sara Ishikawa, Murray Silverstein, Max Jacobson, Ingrid Fiks-

dahl-King, and Shlomo Angel. *A Pattern Language: Towns, Buildings, Construction*. New York: Oxford University Press, 1977.

————, Hajo Neis, Artemis Anninou, and Ingrid King. *A New Theory of Urban Design*. New York: Oxford University Press, 1987.

Grabow, Stephen. *Christopher Alexander: The Search for a New Paradigm in Architecture*. Stocksfield: Oriel Press, 1983.

### On Civilization, Soul, and Values

Campbell, Joseph. *The Power of Myth*. Garden City, N.Y.: Doubleday, 1988.

Charles, Prince of Wales. *A Vision of Britain: A Personal View of Architecture*. London: Doubleday, 1989.

Clark, Petula. "Downtown." Words and music by Tony Hatch. Epic Records.
>    The way it is supposed to be.

Hiss, Tony. *The Experience of Place*. New York: Knopf, 1990.

Macdonald, Dwight. *Against the American Grain*. New York: Da Capo Press, 1962.

Morris, James. *Venice*. London: Faber & Faber, 1983.

Moyers, Bill. *A World of Ideas*. Garden City, N.Y.: Doubleday, 1989.

Murray, Charles. *In Pursuit: Of Happiness and Good Government*. New York: Simon & Schuster, 1988.

Oldenburg, Ray. *The Great Good Place*. New York: Paragon House, 1989.

Sale, Kirkpatrick. *Human Scale*. New York: Coward, McCann & Geoghegan, 1980 .

### On Growth

*America's Real Estate: A Review of Real Estate and Its Role in the U.S. Economy*. Washington, D.C.: National Realty Committee, 1989.
>    Lest we forget, the National Realty Committee reminds us we are talking big bucks here. Lavishly illustrated.

Baldassare, Mark. "Suburban Support for No-Growth Policies: Implications for the Growth Revolt." *Journal of Urban Affairs* 12, no. 2 (1990).

"The Future of American Cities: To Grow or Not to Grow?" *Reason* 21, no. 4 (August–September 1989), special issue.

Harvey, Douglas Pegues. "Escape from the Planet of the Modernists: Beyond the Growth Syndrome." *Texas Architect* (October 1988).

Heilbroner, Robert. *Behind the Veil of Economics*. New York: Norton, 1988.

LeGates, Richard T. *Public Opinion Gridlock on California Growth Issues*.

San Francisco: San Francisco State University Foundation and the Public Research Institute, September 1989.

Morris, Charles R. "The Coming Global Boom." *Atlantic*, October 1989.

Postrel, Virginia I. "The Ideology Shuffle: Forget Left and Right—Our Politics Are Breaking Down into Growth vs. Green." *Washington Post*, April 1, 1990, *Outlook* section.

Wagner, Kenneth C. *Economic Development Manual*. Jackson: University Press of Mississippi for the Mississippi Research and Development Center, 1978.

## On the Land

Bramwell, Anna. *Ecology in the 20th Century: A History*. New Haven: Yale University Press, 1989.

Cronon, William. *Changes in the Land: Indians, Colonists, and the Ecology of New England*. New York: Hill & Wang, 1983.

Kostmayer, Peter H. *The American Landscape in the 21st Century*. Opening Remarks, Oversight Hearing, Subcommittee on General Oversight and Investigations, Committee on Interior and Insular Affairs, U.S. House of Representatives, May 18, 1989.

In 1989, Representative Peter Kostmayer, who represents Bucks County, Pennsylvania, a beautiful area facing intense development pressure, convened a series of subcommittee hearings on the future of the American landscape. The result was that rarity—congressional testimony worth reading. It ranged from that of Ian McHarg to John Herbers to Ed McMahon.

Harris, Larry D. "Edge Effects and Conservation of Biotic Diversity." *Conservation Biology* 2, no. 4 (December 1988).

As I researched Edge City, I was intrigued to learn that it has a biological, ecological, natural analogy. The zones of transition between one ecology and another—for example, the wetlands where the water meets the land, or the strip where the woods meet the meadow—are known to professionals as "edge ecologies." They are of tremendous value because a high diversity of plants and animals are associated with them. It would be nice to think that Edge City is a similarly fertile ecology, equally full of possibilities.

Leopold, Aldo. *A Sand County Almanac and Sketches Here and There*. New York: Oxford University Press, 1949.

The twentieth century's *Walden*.

Lopez, Barry. *Arctic Dreams*. New York: Scribner's, 1986.

———. *Crossing Open Ground*. New York: Scribner's, 1988.

———. "Unbounded Wilderness." *Aperture* 120 (Late Summer 1990).

Lyon, Thomas J., ed. *This Incomperable Lande: A Book of American Nature Writing*. Boston: Houghton Mifflin, 1989.
> The selections are stirring and the bibliography—with enlightening commentary—splendid.

MacKaye, Benton. *The New Exploration: A Philosophy of Regional Planning*. Urbana: University of Illinois Press, 1962.

McHarg, Ian. *The Fitness of Man's Environment*. Washington, D.C.: Smithsonian Institution Press, 1968.

——. *Design with Nature*. Garden City, N.Y.: Doubleday, 1969.

McPhee, John. *Encounters with the Archdruid: Narratives About a Conservationist and Three of His Natural Enemies*. New York: Farrar, Straus & Giroux, 1971.

——. *The Control of Nature*. New York: Farrar, Straus & Giroux, 1989.

Sloane, Eric. *Our Vanishing Landscape*. New York: Ballantine, 1974.

Stegner, Wallace. *The Sound of Mountain Water*. Garden City, N.Y.: Doubleday, 1969.

Stokes, Samuel, and A. Elizabeth Watson. *Saving America's Countryside: A Guide to Rural Conservation*. Baltimore: Johns Hopkins University Press, 1989.

Teltsch, Kathleen. "U.S. Gets 100,000 Acres in Largest Gift of Land." *New York Times,* July 1, 1990 , A1.
> Including the Cornfield at Antietam, the site of the bloodiest day of fighting of the Civil War.

Thoreau, Henry David. *Walden*. New York: New American Library, 1960.

Yaro, Robert D., Randall Arendt, Harry L. Dodson, and Elizabeth A. Brabec. *Dealing with Change in the Connecticut River Valley: A Design Manual for Conservation and Development*. Amherst: University of Massachusetts Press, 1988.

Yaro, Robert D., Neil Jorgensen, Mark S. Finnen, and Harry L. Dodson. *Massachusetts Landscape Inventory*. Boston: Massachusetts Department of Environmental Management, 1982.

Whyte, William H. *Conservation Easements*. Washington, D.C.: Urban Land Institute, 1959.

## On the Civil War and Its Enduring Impact

Abell, Sam, and Brian C. Pohanka. *Distant Thunder: A Photographic Essay on the American Civil War*. Charlottesville: Thomasson-Grant, 1988.

Burns, Ken, et al. *The Civil War: A Film Series*. Florentine Films and WETA-TV, 1990.

Catton, Bruce. *The Centennial History of the Civil War*. Vol. 1, *The Coming Fury*. Vol. 2, *Terrible Swift Sword*. Vol. 3, *Never Call Retreat*. Garden City, N.Y.: Doubleday, 1961, 1963, 1965.

Davis, George B., Leslie J. Perry, and Joseph W. Kirkley. *The Official Military Atlas of the Civil War*. New York: Fairfax Press, 1983.

Foote, Shelby. *The Civil War: A Narrative*. Vol. 1, *Fort Sumter to Perryville*. Vol. 2, *Fredericksburg to Meridian*. Vol. 3, *Red River to Appomattox*. New York: Random House, 1958, 1963, 1974.

MacDonald, John. *Great Battles of the Civil War*. New York: Macmillan, 1988 .

McPherson, James. *Battle Cry of Freedom: The Civil War Era*. New York: Oxford University Press, 1988.

> The Pulitzer Prize winner.

Taylor, William. *Cavalier & Yankee: The Old South and American National Character*. Cambridge: Harvard University Press, 1979.

Ward, Geoffrey C., with Ric Burns and Ken Burns. *The Civil War: An Illustrated History*. New York: Knopf, 1990.

> The companion volume to the celebrated PBS television series.

Wicker, Tom. *Unto This Hour*. New York: Viking, 1984.

## On the Shaping of the New York Metropolitan Area, Especially the New Jersey Side

Butterfield, Fox. "Is Life in New York Really Getting Worse?" *New York Times*, March 10, 1989, B1.

> The moment that as loyal a publication as the *New York Times* put this headline on the front page of its local section, and allowed as distinguished a reporter as Butterfield to vividly answer yes, was when I started to really worry about Manhattan.

Byrne, Thérèse E. *The Edge City as a Paradigm: Remodeling the I-78 Corridor*. New York: Salomon Brothers, 1989.

Caro, Robert A. *The Power Broker: Robert Moses and the Fall of New York*. New York: Knopf, 1974.

*Communities of Place: The New Jersey Preliminary State Development and Redevelopment Plan*. Vol. 1, *A Legacy for the Next Generation*. Vol. 2, *Strategies and Policies*. Trenton: New Jersey State Planning Commission, 1988.

Glaberson, William. "The Little Engines That Could . . . and Do: In Allentown and Elsewhere, Small Companies Are Fueling a Big Growth in Jobs." *New York Times*, May 1, 1988.

> Songster Billy Joel had it all wrong when he lamented the decline of heavy industry in places like Bethlehem, Pennsylvania.

Graf, Don. *Convenience for Research: Buildings for the Bell Telephone Laboratory, Inc., Murray Hill, New Jersey*. New York: Voorhees Walker Foley & Smith, Architects and Engineers, 1944.

> An oversized picture book that carefully and proudly details the

design of one of the first Edge City corporate campuses—the Bell Labs facilities built in Murray Hill during World War II. Today, the book seems more impressive than the buildings that it glorifies. Produced by the designers and builders of the complex, it proclaims an esthetic of "character" for a place that looked exactly like what it was—a factory for research.

Hamill, Samuel M., Jr., John C. Keene, David N. Kinsey, and Roger K. Lewis. *The Growth Management Handbook: A Primer for Citizen and Government Planners.* Princeton: Middlesex Somerset Mercer Regional Council, 1989.

*NJ Theatre & You, Perfect Together: New Jersey Theatre Group Presents New Jersey's Professional Theatres 1988–89 Calendar with Transit Information.* Florham Park, N.J.: New Jersey Professional Theatre Foundation, 1988 .

"New Jersey/Manhattan Economic Comparison" and "New Jersey Takes a Smaller Personal Tax Bite." In *New Jersey Facts and Facets.* Trenton: New Jersey Department of Commerce and Economic Development, circa 1989.

Invidious comparisons of New Jersey with New York City and New York State.

Shulman, David, et al. *New York Metropolitan Area Office Market.* New York: Salomon Brothers, 1988.

Sterba, James P. "Even a Real Genius Notes That Bambi Is a Relevant Factor: When Deer Hunting Starts in Princeton, Equations Become Really Complex." *Wall Street Journal,* October 12, 1989.

Sternlieb, George. *Patterns of Development.* Piscataway, N.J.: Center for Urban Policy Research, Rutgers University, 1986.

———, and James W. Hughes, eds. *Revitalizing the Northeast.* New Brunswick, N.J.: Center for Urban Policy Research, Rutgers University, 1978.

———, and Alex Schwartz. *New Jersey Growth Corridors.* New Brunswick, N.J.: Center for Urban Policy Research, Rutgers University, 1986 .

### On the Shaping of the Boston Metropolitan Area

Arnst, Catherine. "MIT: the Engine That Drives Massachusetts' Economy." Reuters, October 25, 1987.

"Boom." *New England Monthly,* February 1987.

The storm before the lull. Ironically and tragically, *New England Monthly* magazine is dead—a victim of the bust.

Byrne, Thérèse E., and David J. Kostin. *The Boston Office Market: Will It*

*Survive the Massachusetts Miracle?* New York: Salomon Brothers, December 1989.

Daly, Christopher B. "Plans for Developing Walden Raise Star-Studded Opposition." *Washington Post,* April 26, 1990.

> Including Don Henley of the Eagles, Bonnie Raitt, and actor Don Johnson in benefit fund-raising stints.

Drier, Peter, David C. Schwartz, and Ann Greiner. "What Every Business Can Do About Housing." *Harvard Business Review,* September-October 1988.

King, John. "Overnight Real Estate Fortunes End As Housing Sales in Boston Sag." *Washington Post,* July 23, 1989.

Stein, Charles. "128: Why It Will Never Be the Same." *Boston Globe,* January 3, 1989.

Stout, Hilary. "Jobless Aren't Migrating to Boom Areas: Great Disparity in Living Cost Is Major Deterrent." *Wall Street Journal,* February 21, 1989, 1.

Tye, Larry. "The Boom Produces a Boomerang." *Boston Globe,* 1 March 1988, 1.

> Not only did housing costs skyrocket. So did the cost of water, electricity, natural gas, car insurance, a plumber, and an electrician.

"U.S. Ranks New England as Wealthiest Region." *Providence Journal,* August 21, 1987.

## On the Shaping of the Detroit Metropolitan Area

Conot, Robert. *American Odyssey.* New York: Morrow, 1974.

Gavrilovich, Peter. "Money Tells Story of Detroit's Rise to Fame." *Detroit Free Press,* Sunday, September 15, 1985, 1G.

Lacey, Robert. *Ford: The Men and the Machine.* New York: Ballantine, 1986.

"Toronto and Detroit: Canadians Do It Better." *The Economist,* May 19, 1990, 17.

## On the Shaping of the Atlanta Metropolitan Area

Dedman, Bill. "The Color of Money." Series in the *Atlanta Journal and Constitution,* May 1-4, 1988, and after.

Hartshorn, Truman A., et al. *Atlanta: Metropolis in Georgia.* Cambridge, Mass.: Ballinger, 1976.

———, and Peter O. Muller. "Suburban Downtowns and the Transformation of Metropolitan Atlanta's Business Landscape." *Urban Geography* 10, no. 4 (1989): 375-95.

*Perimeter Center: The Art of Environment.* Atlanta: Taylor & Mathis, n.d.

A rather more breathtaking than average glossy-stock, lushly photographed paean to an Edge City, it features such lines as "To
have succeeded in creating a masterpiece to the art of environment can only be the beginning." An artifact worth going out of
your way to obtain.

*Scenes of Black Atlanta: A Full Color Pictorial Guide and Location Directory.*
Atlanta: Farris Color Visions, Inc., 1989.

"The Shaping of Atlanta." Series in the *Atlanta Journal and Constitution,*
May 3–7, August 9–16, December 27–31, 1987.

White, Dana F. "The Black Sides of Atlanta: A Geography of Expansion and Containment, 1970–1870." *Atlanta Historical Journal* 26,
nos. 2–3 (Summer-Fall 1982).

————, and Timothy Crimmins. "Celebrating 150 Years of 'Can-do'
Spirit: New Voices Rise to Make Atlanta Sun Belt Capital"; "Recon-
struction Transformed City into Metropolis"; and "As the Suburbs
Spread, the Downtown Grew Higher." *Atlanta Journal and Constitution,* October 4, 1987, 1S.

### On the Shaping of the Phoenix Metropolitan Area

Dragos, Stephen. "Desert-Cities: Look to the Future." *Urban Land*
(November 1989).

Laake, Deborah. "The Pfuture Without Pfister: If the Head of the Salt
River Project Doesn't Keep Phoenix Safe from the Storm, Who
Will?" *New Times,* November 14–20, 1990 .

McKeough, Margaret E. "Phoenix Community Alliance: Leading
Downtown Development." *Arizona Business and Development,* Fall
1990.

Sargent, Charles, ed. *Metro Arizona.* Scottsdale: Biffington Books, 1988.

*A Valley Reborn: The Story of the Salt River Project.* Phoenix: The Salt
River Project, n.d.

### On the Shaping of the Dallas Metropolitan Area

*Big D: Why Did They Put Such a Big City So Far Out in the Country?
(Answer: John Bryan Thought He Had Found the Next Galveston.)* Dallas:
Community Access, 1986.

Cartwright, Gary. "Paradise Lost." *Texas Monthly,* October 1987, 116.

Dillon, David. "Las Colinas Revisited." *American Planning Association,*
December 1989.

Dimeo, Jean. "This Is Exxon: Streamlined Economic Powerhouse
Heads for Las Colinas Home." *Dallas Times Herald,* May 13, 1990.

Ingersoll, Richard. "Las Colinas: The Ultimate Bourgeois Utopia,"
*Texas Architect* (January-February 1989).

"The Swearingen Report." The Swearingen Company, Commercial Real Estate Services, midyear 1990.

## On the Shaping of the Houston Metropolitan Area

Feagin, Joe. *Free Enterprise City*. New Brunswick, N.J.: Rutgers University Press, 1988.

Fox, Stephen. *Houston: Architectural Guide*. Houston: American Institute of Architects/Houston Chapter and Herring Press, 1990.
> More than a guide, and more than just about Houston, this is a critical, lively, and thoughtful analysis that takes seriously—but not too seriously—the ultimate free-enterprise individualist landscape that is at the heart of every Edge City.

Morgan, George T., Jr., and John O. King. *The Woodlands: New Community Development, 1964–1983*. College Station: Texas A&M University Press, 1987.

Shulman, David, and Mari Canton. *Houston Real Estate Market*. New York: Salomon Brothers, June 1986.
> Brutal.

Trow, George W. S. "Our Far-Flung Correspondents: Empty or Nearly So in Houston." *The New Yorker*, January 30, 1989, 84.

West, Richard. "My Home, the Galleria: Under the Glass Roof Is Everything That Makes Life Worthwhile—Food, Drink, Fine Clothes, Sex, Gossip, and Intrigue." *Texas Monthly*, July 1980, 97.

## On the Shaping of the Los Angeles Metropolitan Area

Baldassare, Mark. *Trouble in Paradise*. New York: Columbia University Press, 1986.

Banham, Reyner. *Los Angeles: The Architecture of the Four Ecologies*. Harmondsworth: Penguin Books, 1971.

Brodsly, David. *L.A. Freeway: An Appreciative Essay*. Berkeley: University of California Press, 1981.

*Entering the 21st Century/Portrait for Progress: The Economy of Los Angeles County and the Sixty-Mile Circle Region*. Los Angeles: Security Pacific Bank, July 1988.

Himmelsbach, Eric, Sunni Bloyd, and Eve Belson. "Nixon: Now More Than Ever—The Enduring Influence of Orange County's Favorite Son." *Orange Coast: The Magazine of Orange County*, July 1990, cover story.

Kotkin, Joel. "I Love L.A.: Why Los Angeles Is Fast Replacing New York City as the Economic Capital of America." *Inc.*, March 1989, 96.

————. "Fear and Reality in the Los Angeles Melting Pot." *Los Angeles Times Magazine*, November 5, 1989.

*LA 2000: A City for the Future*. Los Angeles: Los Angeles 2000 Committee, 1988.

Lockwood, Charles, and Christopher B. Leinberger. "Los Angeles Comes of Age." *Atlantic*, January 1988, 31.

McWilliams, Carey. *Southern California: An Island on the Land*. Santa Barbara: Peregrine Smith, 1973.

Manasian, David. "California: A Survey." *The Economist*, October 13, 1990.

Mathews, Jay. "Cities in West Steering away from Growth: More Compact Style Marks California Life." *Washington Post*, June 14, 1987, A3.
  Including the news that Californians now commute about the same distance each day as do average Americans and consume less gasoline per capita.

Morrison, Patt, T. Jefferson Parker, and Steve Harvey. "L.A. vs. O.C.: A Special Report." *Los Angeles Times Magazine*, June 17, 1990.
  Wickedly accurate and funny comparison of Los Angeles and Orange County, confirming and skewering the prejudices of the residents of both.

Rose, Frederick. "California Babel: The City of the Future Is a Troubling Prospect If It's to Be Los Angeles: To Cultural Stew Add Crime, Poverty, Pollution, Traffic, Film Fantasies and Tofu; Economic Base: Cheap Labor." *Wall Street Journal*, June 12, 1989, A1.

Shulman, David, Mari Canton, and David J. Kostin. *Los Angeles Real Estate Market*. New York: Salomon Brothers, January 1987.

Soja, Edward W., "The Orange County Exopolis: A Contemporary Screen-Play."
  A paper with a through-the-looking-glass quality, nonetheless based on fact, written by the UCLA professor in the Graduate School of Architecture and Urban Planning, and scheduled to appear in an as yet untitled book on the "city of the future," edited by Michael Sorkin for Pantheon.

Starr, Kevin. *Inventing the Dream: California Through the Progressive Era*. New York: Oxford University Press, 1985.

Timmons, Tim. *Anyone Anonymous*. Old Tappan, N.J.: Fleming H. Revell Company, 1990.

## On the Shaping of the San Francisco Metropolitan Area

Beers, David. "Tomorrowland: We Have Seen the Future, and It Is Pleasanton." *San Francisco Examiner*, January 18, 1987. *Image* magazine.

Dowall, David E. *The Suburban Squeeze: Land Conversion and Regulation in the San Francisco Bay Area.* Berkeley: University of California Press, 1984.

Jordan, Susan. *San Jose/Silicon Valley Research and Development and Office Parks.* New York: Salomon Brothers, January 1989.

Kroll, Cynthia. *Employment Growth and Office Space Along the 680 Corridor: Booming Supply and Potential Demand in a Suburban Area.* Berkeley: Center for Real Estate and Urban Economics, Institute of Business and Economic Research, Graduate School of Business Administration, University of California at Berkeley, 1984.

————, and Efza Evrengil, *The San Francisco Bay Area Economy: A Profile of the Region as It Approaches the 1990s.* Berkeley: Center for Real Estate and Urban Economics, Institute of Business and Economic Research, Graduate School of Business Administration, University of California at Berkeley, May 1989.

————, and Elizabeth W. Morris. *Economic Conditions and Forces of Change in San Joaquin County.* Berkeley: Center for Real Estate and Urban Economics, Institute of Business and Economic Research, Graduate School of Business Administration, University of California at Berkeley, 1988.

LeGates, Richard T., and Claude Pellerin. *Planning Tomorrowland: The Transformation of Pleasanton, California.* San Francisco: San Francisco State University Foundation and the San Francisco State University Public Research Institute, Working Paper No. 89–12, June 1989.

Rosen, Kenneth T., and Susan Jordan. *San Francisco Real Estate Market: The City, the Peninsula and the East Bay.* San Francisco: Center for Real Estate and Urban Economics, Institute of Business and Economic Research, Graduate School of Business Administration, University of California at Berkeley, November 1988.

Vance, James E., Jr. *Geography and Urban Evolution in the San Francisco Bay Area.* Berkeley: University of California, Institute of Governmental Studies, 1964.

### On the Shaping of the Washington Metropolitan Area, Especially the Virginia Side

Canton, Mari, Adele M. Hayutin, and David J. Kostin. *Washington, D.C. Real Estate Market.* New York: Salomon Brothers, April 1987.

Downey, Kirstin. "Emerging Cities: The Boom Goes On." *Washington Post,* April 3, 1989.

Faux, Patricia L., Michael Hickock, Eric Smart, and Barbara Kaiser. *A Pilot Study of Suburban Activity Centers: Tysons Corner, a Hybrid Downtown.* Washington, D.C.: Urban Land Institute, 1987.

Gardiner, John Rolfe. *In the Heart of the Whole World*. New York: Knopf, 1988.

> If a place is not a place until it has a poet, Tysons Corner is now a place. This is the first engrossing novel of literary merit I am aware of that takes that exotic clime as its stage.

Jefferson, Thomas. *Notes on the State of Virginia*. Edited by William Peden. New York: Norton, 1982.

Kotkin, Joel. "The Future Is Here: The Apple Is History. In the 21st Century, Washington and Los Angeles Will Dominate the American Economy." *Washington Post Magazine*, June 25, 1989, 17.

Mastran, Shelley S. *The Evolution of Suburban Nucleations: Land Investment Activity in Fairfax County, Virginia, 1958–1977*. College Park: University of Maryland Geography Department, 1988.

McDowell, Martha Shea. "The Ungreening of Tysons Corner: Hay One Dollar a Bale?" *Virginia Country*, Spring 1988, 13.

O'Donnell, Frank. "They Came, They Saw, They Built! . . . and Built, and Built, and Built: The Men Who Made—and Made Out in —Tysons Corner." *Regardie's*, September 1988, 167.

*A Policies Plan for the Year 2000: The Nation's Capital*. Washington, D.C.: National Capital Planning Commission, National Capital Regional Planning Council, 1961.

> One plan for an urban area that was pretty much built—with, of course, utterly Unintended Consequences.

"The Power Elite: Our Annual Roster of the 100 Local People Who Have True Clout. If the Establishment Still Exists, This Is It." *Regardie's*, vol. 9, 1989.

> This was the year both Til Hazel and Annie Snyder made it onto the list.

Richardson, Lynda, and Caroline E. Mayer. "Tysons Squared." *Washington Post*, August 28, 1988, A1; August 29, 1988, A1.

Stuntz, Connie Pendleton, and Mayo Sturdevant Stuntz. *This Was Tysons Corner, Virginia*. Marceline, Mo.: Walsworth Publishing, 1990.

### On the Final Battle at Manassas

Save the Battlefield Coalition, P.O. Box 110, Catharpin, Virginia 22018, has an exhaustive library of newspaper, magazine, and video references to its fight. In fact, this huge yet scrupulously indexed and constantly updated and maintained file of information—plus a home copying machine to duplicate it—was its most potent weapon. Would-be activists, take note.

Those who cannot find or even pronounce Catharpin would be well advised to consult a database storing the articles of the *Washington Post* and search appropriately under the byline of John F. Harris, who followed the story fairly and indefatigably.

*Congressional Record*, 100th Cong., 2d sess., October 7, 1988, 134, no. 142, pt. 2:S15149.
  The key battle and vote in the Senate.
*Manassas National Battlefield Park Amendments of 1988, Hearing Before the Subcommittee on Public Lands, National Parks and Forests, of the Committee on Energy and Natural Resources, United States Senate, One Hundredth Congress, Second Session, on H.R. 4526 to Provide for the Addition of Approximately 600 Acres to the Manassas National Battlefield Park, September 8, 1988* (Washington, D.C.: Government Printing Office, 1989)
Rhodes, Karl. "The Third Battle of Manassas." *Virginia Business*, December 1988.
Webb, Robert. "Manassas Tragedy: Paving over the Past." *Washington Post*, March 13, 1988, *Outlook* section.

### Indispensable References

*Historical Statistics of the United States, Colonial Times to 1970.* Washington: U.S. Bureau of the Census, 1975.
Hoffman, Mark S., ed. *The World Almanac and Book of Facts.* Annual. New York: Pharos Books.
King, Glenn W., et al., ed. *Statistical Abstract of the United States: The National Data Book.* Annual. Washington, D.C.: U.S. Bureau of the Census.
  One of the best-kept secrets in Washington. Own this book and you will never be at a loss for instant expertise.
*Rand McNally Road Atlas: United States, Canada, Mexico.* Annual. Chicago: Rand McNally & Company.
  The authentic sound of spring for me is that of this atlas hitting the paperback bestseller list.

# Notes

Chapter 1    The Search for the Future Inside Ourselves:
                Life on the New Frontier

**3**  the majority of metropolitan Americans now work: Residential and job statistics from U.S. Bureau of the Census, *Statistical Abstract of the United States, 1990,* 110 th ed. (Washington, D.C., 1990). Office space statistics from Salomon Brothers, Inc., New York, and the Office Network, Houston. See also Robert Fishman, "Megalopolis Unbound," *Wilson Quarterly* (1990): 24.

**3**  High Mall: *Oxford English Dictionary,* see "mall."

**4**  the best-housed civilization: See, for example, Irving Welfeld, *Where We Live: The American Home and the Social, Political, and Economic Landscape, from Slums to Suburbs* (New York: Simon & Schuster, 1988).

**5**  Already, two thirds of all American office facilities: Peter O. Muller, *Journal of Urban History* 13, no. 3 (May 1987): 352.

**5**  By the mid-1980s, there was far more office space: Existing prime office space inventory, March 1988: midtown Manhattan, 155.6 million square feet; downtown Manhattan (Wall Street), 78.2 million square feet. Existing prime office space inventory in New York suburbs (Edge Cities), December 1987: 183.7 million square feet (21.1 million on Long Island, 33.5 million in Westchester, 40.1 million in Fairfield, and 89.0 million in northeastern New Jersey). Even by the mid-1980s, more than twice as much space was under construction in the Edge Cities of the New York area than in all of Manhattan, a trend that continues into the 1990s. By 1988, 11.6 million square feet were being absorbed in the Edge Cities, but the Manhattan figure actually turned to a negative 800,000 square feet. See David Shulman et al., *New York Metropolitan Area Office Market* (New York: Salomon Brothers, July 1988); Thérèse E. Byrne, *The Edge City as a Paradigm: Remodeling the I-78 Corridor* (New York: Salomon Brothers, September 1989). Also see "The Office Network Office Market Report" (Houston, various dates); Peter O. Muller, "A Review of *Suburban Gridlock* by Robert Cervero," *Geographical Review* 78, no. 4 (October 1988): 447–48.

**5**  Most of the trips metropolitan Americans take: "According to the 1980 U.S. Census, there were twice as many suburbanites commuting to suburban jobs in metropolitan areas as there were to jobs in the central cities. Between 1960 and 1980, intrasuburban commuting accounted for 57 percent of the increase in metropolitan commuting. Less than 8 percent of regional workers —ranging from 3 percent in Los Angeles to 10.9 percent in San Francisco— are employed in the 10 largest urbanized areas. For a typical area, the central business district commuter probably represents less than 10 percent of all highway travelers during the heaviest rush hour." *Myths and Facts About Transportation and Growth* (Washington, D.C.: The Urban Land Institute, 1989). Also see Robert Cervero, *Suburban Gridlock* (New Brunswick, N.J.: Rutgers University, Center for Urban Policy Research, 1986); Cervero, *America's Suburban Centers: A Study of the Land Use/Transportation Link* (Washington, D.C.: U.S. Department of Transportation, January 1988); Alan E. Pisarski, *Commuting in America: A National Report on Commuting Patterns and Trends* (Westport, Conn.: Eno Foundation for Transportation, 1987); U.S. Bureau of the Census, *Statistical Abstract of the United States.*

**5**  a casual glance at most Yellow Pages: In the 1989 Bell Atlantic Yellow Pages for the District of Columbia (not its Maryland or Virginia "suburbs," which are served by separate directories), eighty-five numbers were listed under "Television & Radio—Dealers." Of those, only ten could be construed as being in the area's otherwise large and thriving downtown. Of those ten dealers, more than half were located in neighborhoods that stretched the definition of "downtown"—Georgetown or southwest D.C., for instance.

**5**  urban villages: Christopher B. Leinberger and Charles Lockwood, "How Business Is Reshaping America," *Atlantic,* October 1986.

**5**  technoburbs: Robert Fishman, *Bourgeois Utopias: The Rise and Fall of Suburbia* (New York: Basic Books, 1987).

**5**  suburban downtowns: Truman A. Hartshorn and Peter O. Muller, "Suburban Downtowns and the Transformation of Metropolitan Atlanta's Business Landscape," *Urban Geography* 10, no. 4 (1989).

**5**  suburban activity centers: Urban Land Institute, Washington, D.C.

**5**  major diversified centers: Thomas Baerwald, "Major Diversified Centers in Midwestern Metropolises" (Paper presented to the West Lakes Division of the Association of American Geographers, November 1983).

**5**  urban cores: Robert Charles Lesser & Co., Los Angeles.

**5**  galactic city: Peirce F. Lewis, "The Galactic Metropolis," in *Beyond the Urban Fringe,* ed. Rutherford H. Platt and George Macinko (Minneapolis: University of Minnesota Press, 1983).

**5**  pepperoni-pizza cities: Peter O. Muller, University of Miami.

**5**  a city of realms: James E. Vance, Jr., *This Scene of Man: The Role and Structure of the City in the Geography of Western Civilization* (New York: Harper & Row, 1977), 408–9.

**5**  superburbia: *Philadelphia* magazine.

**5**  disurb: Short for "dense, industrial, and self-contained suburban region." Mark Baldassare, University of California, Irvine.

**6** service cities, perimeter cities, and even peripheral centers. James Timberlake, Kieran, Timberlake & Harris, Philadelphia.

**6** Tomorrowland: David Beers, "Tomorrowland: We Have Seen the Future, and It Is Pleasanton," *San Francisco Examiner*, Sunday, January 18, 1987, *Image* magazine.

**6** majority of Americans: The 1970 Census showed that the U.S. population included more suburbanites than city dwellers or farm residents. The 1980 Census showed that in the fifteen largest U.S. metropolitan areas, the majority of residents lived outside the central city in every one except Houston, which had an aggressive policy of annexing former suburbs.

**6** Ninety-two percent of the people: U.S. Bureau of the Census, 1987 estimate for New York–northern New Jersey–Long Island, NY-NJ-CT CMSA: 18,053,800. New York County, 1989 update: 1,428,285, or 7.91 percent of the total.

**7** Who put Captain Kirk in charge: I am indebted to the *Wall Street Journal* for first addressing this burning question.

**8** "barbaric yawp over the rooftops of the world": Walt Whitman, "Song of Myself," *Leaves of Grass* (1892; reprint, New York: New American Library, 1955).

**8** "hog-stomping Baroque exuberance": Tom Wolfe, *From Bauhaus to Our House* (New York: Farrar, Straus & Giroux, 1981).

**10** "Nonsense is talked by our big skyscraperites": Frank Lloyd Wright, *The Living City* (New York: Horizon Press, 1958), 81. This book incorporates the work published under the title *When Democracy Builds* (1945).

**11** "After all is said and done": Ibid., 81–82.

**12** "regenerative power is located in the natural terrain": Leo Marx, *The Machine in the Garden: Technology and the Pastoral Ideal in America* (London: Oxford University Press, 1964), 228.

**12** Barlowe: Ibid., 36–37.

**13** Shakespeare: Ibid., 41.

**13** Bradford: Ibid., 41–42.

## Chapter 2 New Jersey: Tomorrowland

**17** "For these are not as they might seem to be": John Cheever, "A Miscellany of Characters That Will Not Appear," in *The Stories of John Cheever* (New York: Knopf, 1978), 467.

**24** It is the first state . . . to be more urban: New Jersey, 1027.3 people per square mile; Japan, 844.9 people per square mile. New Jersey, 89 percent urban; Japan, 76.7 percent urban. Mark S. Hoffman, ed., *The World Almanac and Book of Facts* (New York: Pharos Books); U.S. Bureau of the Census, *Statistical Abstract of the United States*, 110th ed. (Washington, D.C., 1990).

**24** It has 127 miles of beaches: Hoffman, *World Almanac*, 634.

**24** Its truck farms supply local supermarket chains: *Communities of Place: The New Jersey Preliminary State Development and Redevelopment Plan*, vol. 1, *A Legacy for the Next Generation* (New Jersey State Planning Commission, November 1988), 7.

**24**  largest such horizon-to-horizon wild area: New Jersey Department of Environmental Protection, Division of Parks and Forestry, Region 1.

**25**  In the late 1980s, New Jersey's Edge Cities grew more rapidly: Michael Barone and Grant Ujifusa, *The Almanac of American Politics 1990* (Washington, D.C.: National Journal, 1990), 742.

**26**  for the last eight thousand years, cities have been shaped by seven purposes: See, for example, Lewis Mumford, *The City in History, Its Origins, Its Transformations, and Its Prospects* (New York: Harcourt Brace Jovanovich, 1961); James E. Vance, Jr., *This Scene of Man: The Role and Structure of the City in the Geography of Western Civilization* (New York: Harper & Row, 1977); Fernand Braudel, *The Mediterranean and the Mediterranean World in the Age of Philip II*, vols. 1 and 2, 2nd rev. ed. (New York: Harper & Row, 1972); Siegfried Giedion, *Mechanization Takes Command* (New York: Oxford University Press, 1948); Jane Jacobs, *The Death and Life of Great American Cities* (New York: Random House, 1961); Edmund N. Bacon, *Design of Cities* (New York: Penguin Books, 1976).

**27**  "High costs of land in Manhattan," "high living costs," and "the urban noise and dirt": "Facilities Planning at the Laboratories, 1925–1942," (Warren, N.J.: AT&T Bell Laboratories, n.d.).

**27**  That is more than exists in downtown Seattle: The Office Network, Houston, February 1990.

**28**  It contains more than sixteen million leasable square feet: Thérèse E. Byrne, *The Edge City as a Paradigm: Remodeling the I-78 Corridor* (New York: Salomon Brothers, 1989).

**28**  That's larger than downtown New Orleans: The Office Network.

**29**  "One lure may lie in the basically unsettled nature of life on the edge": *Inc.*, March 1989, 90.

**30**  In 1850 . . . 85 percent of the U.S. population was rural: Giedion, *Mechanization Takes Command*, 41.

**30**  only 3 percent of all Americans farm: Statistically defined as directly employed in agriculture.

**30**  more than three quarters are metropolitan slickers: As of 1987, 76.9 percent of the U.S. population lived in OMB-defined metropolitan areas. Bureau of the Census, *Statistical Abstract*, 1989, chart 32, p. 29.

**30**  it makes a ton of steel with fewer work hours than any nation on earth: *Business Week*, January 8, 1990, 71.

**30**  sank below 50 percent: Jean Gottmann, *Megalopolis* (New York: Twentieth Century Fund, 1961), 52.

**31**  critical mass at five million square feet of leasable office space: Christopher B. Leinberger was the first to suggest this number. He is the managing partner of Robert Charles Lesser & Co. and co-author of the seminal article "How Business Is Reshaping America," *Atlantic*, October 1986.

**32**  "like today's *autostrada*": Braudel, *The Mediterranean and the Mediterranean World* 1:276.

**37**  For all of its attenuation: see especially John Herber's *The New Heartland: America's Flight Beyond the Suburbs and How It Is Changing Our Future* (New

York Times Books, 1986) and Richard Louv, *America II* (Los Angeles, Jeremy P. Tarcher, Inc., 1988).

**39** Richard Milhous Nixon lives and writes his books in these parts: Nixon put his 1968-built, fifteen-room, 7000-to-8000-square-foot Saddle River home on four acres, thirty minutes from Manhattan, on the market for $3.25 million to move to a "very elegant" Tudor town house in nearby Park Ridge. *Los Angeles Times*, Sunday, June 24, 1990, K1.

**40** Today, the Lehigh Valley is booming: William Glaberson, "The Little Engines That Could . . . and Do: In Allentown and Elsewhere, Small Companies Are Fueling a Big Growth in Jobs," *New York Times*, Sunday, May 1, 1988, sec. 3, 1.

**41** General Electric, the corporation that in the 1990s began to challenge IBM: Measured in market capitalization: stock price times number of shares outstanding. *Wall Street Journal*, July 23, 1990, C1.

**41** Even in Nassau County, which, like Suffolk, is comparable to Manhattan in population: Nassau County, 1.3 million; Suffolk County, 1.3 million; New York County, 1.4 million. U.S. Bureau of the Census, 1989 update of 1980 final count.

**41** 62 percent never leave the Island to go to work: Robert Charles Lesser & Co., Los Angeles.

**42** "the heart of Constantinople": Braudel, *The Mediterranean and the Mediterranean World* 1:312.

**43** Granada and Madrid were primarily governmental: Ibid., 323, 348.

**46** Babylonia was ruled by a Council of the Gods: Mumford, *The City in History*, 19.

**48** "Gilgamesh": Ibid., 220.

**48** Walled cities with gates that closed at night: Braudel, *The Mediterranean and the Mediterranean World* 1:371.

**53** "slurb" . . . "cliché conformity": Ada Louise Huxtable, quoted by Robert Fishman, "Megalopolis Unbound," *Wilson Quarterly* (Winter 1990): 43.

**57** "corporate campuses are designed as refuges for wildlife" and "our homes in new subdivisions are clustered": *Communities of Place* 1:15.

**58** A relationship with nature is seen as a key element: Gallup Organization, "New Jersey Land Use Planning: A Survey of Public Opinion," prepared for the New Jersey State Planning Commission, Technical Reference Document 86–3, December 1986, 13–14.

**58** 76 percent of all Americans consider themselves environmentalists: Harper's Index, *Harper's*, January 1990, 41.

**58** the Institute for Advanced Study had to name a Wildlife Control Officer: James P. Sterba, "Even a Real Genius Notes That Bambi Is a Relevant Factor: When Deer Hunting Starts in Princeton, Equations Become Really Complex," *Wall Street Journal*, October 12, 1989, A1.

**58** the hottest topic among foresters today: Henry H. Webster, "Urban Development in Forests: Sources of American Difficulties and Possible Approaches," *Renewable Resources Journal* 6, no. 3 (Summer 1988): 8. Also see "Forest Resources in the Northeast: Contributing to Economic Development and Social Well Being," prepared by the state foresters of the twenty northeastern states, July 1985 (2nd printing), 37.

**59** Tourism is now the number one industry in New York City . . . It is also the fastest growing: Tony Hiss, *The Experience of Place* (New York: Knopf, 1990), 66, 87.

**60** "Tourists don't like to visit office districts": Ibid., 87.

**61** Only 8 percent of all Americans live in politically defined cities: All percentages by calculation from the 1986 and 1988 U.S. Census estimates. Bureau of the Census, *Statistical Abstract*.

**63** "In these ancient paleolithic sanctuaries": Mumford, *The City in History*, 8.

**64** Cotton Mather wrote of the Massachusetts minister: D. W. Meinig, *The Shaping of America: A Geographical Perspective on 500 Years of History*, vol. 1, *Atlantic America, 1492–1800* (New Haven: Yale University Press, 1986), 108.

**65** A large modern church functions like nothing so much as a spiritual shopping mall: I am indebted to Dan Morgan of the *Washington Post* for this concept.

### Chapter 3    Boston: Edge City Limits

**70** "Form ever follows function": Louis Sullivan, "The Tall Office Building Artistically Considered," *Lippincott's*, March 1886.

**74** Companies that made history clustered around the verdant interstates: The Edge Cities of the Boston area have had more prime office space than its downtown since 1984. Robert Charles Lesser & Co., Los Angeles, 1987.

**74** Massachusetts Miracle of the 1980s: In the 1970s, when per capita income figures were correlated with cost of living figures, New Englanders, state by state, were less well off than Southerners. Figures as of 1986.

**74** In 1988, New Hampshire posted the lowest state unemployment rate: *New England Monthly*, February 1987, special section called "Boom!"

**77** "In almost every category": Larry Tye, "The Boom Produces a Boomerang," *Boston Globe*, March 1, 1988, 1.

**77** "The confidence had been excessive": Frederick Lewis Allen, quoted by Chip Jones, "That Was Some Party," *Virginia Business*, 5, no. 12 (December 1990): 62.

**78** healthier than downtown: Spalding & Slye, Boston.

**78** the Chicago market became so comparatively healthy: Report by Spalding & Slye Colliers, cited by Kirstin Downey, "Office Rents Are Declining Abroad: U.S. Not Alone in Seeing Construction Outpace Demand," *Washington Post*, January 12, 1991, F1.

**78** "Boston State-House is the hub of the solar system": Oliver Wendell Holmes, *The Autocrat of the Breakfast-Table* (1858), chap. 1.

**82** highest mountain range: Christopher B. Leinberger, "Urban Cores: Development Trends and Real Estate Opportunities in the 1990s," *Urban Land* (December 1990): 4.

**84** The typical single-family home in 1987 in the Boston area: Peter Dreier, David C. Schwartz, and Ann Greiner, "Special Report: What Every

Business Can Do About Housing," *Harvard Business Review* (September-October 1988).

**84** "The reasons for the slowdown": Christopher J. Chipello, "Real Estate Market in New England States Hits Slump: Banks Are Feeling the Pinch as Sales Slow and Prices Lose Ground," *Wall Street Journal,* July 11, 1989, A2.

**84** "people simply cannot afford to move to Boston": Dreier, Schwartz, and Greiner, "Special Report."

**85** In Hollis, New Hampshire: Douglas R. Porter, "Deflecting Growth in Exurban New Hampshire," *Urban Land* ( June 1989): 34.

**86** Boston area's four million . . . half the area's land: Boston-Lawrence-Salem, MA-NH Consolidated Metropolitan Statistical Area, U.S. Bureau of the Census, 1988 statistics: population estimate, 4,109,900; land area, 3097.7 square miles; population density, 2.07 per acre, by calculation. Wellesley 1988 population estimate, 27,000; land area, 10.35 square miles; population density, 4.08 per acre, by calculation.

**89** maximum desirable commute has been forty-five minutes: Ronald F. Abler, Geography Department, Pennsylvania State University, interview with the author. Also see James E. Vance, Jr., *This Scene of Man: The Role and Structure of the City in the Geography of Western Civilization* (New York: Harper & Row, 1977).

**89** a city like Istanbul: Fernand Braudel, *The Mediterranean and the Mediterranean World in the Age of Philip II,* vols. 1and 2, 2nd rev. ed. (New York: Harper & Row, 1972), 1:348.

**90** Law of Accessibility: Pamela Manfre, partner, Robert Charles Lesser & Co., Washington, D.C.

**93** a great map: William H. Whyte: *City: Rediscovering the Center* (New York: Doubleday, 1988), 288.

**96** "The mass of men lead lives of quiet desperation": Henry David Thoreau, *Walden* (New York: New American Library, 1960), 10.

**96** "I went to the woods because I wished to live deliberately": Ibid., 66.

**96** "At a certain season of our life": Ibid., 59, 60.

**96** "None can be an impartial or wise observer": 14, 15, 16.

**97** "Love your life": Ibid., 216, 217, 218.

### Chapter 4   Detroit: The Automobile, Individualism, and Time

**99** "Americans are in the habit of never walking": Quoted in Barry Bruce-Briggs, *The War Against the Automobile* (New York: Dutton, 1977).

**104** thirty cents an hour: Robert Conot, *American Odyssey* (New York: Morrow 1974), 6.

**104** Oklahoma land rush: Ibid.

**105** The key ingredient for a high-rise city: Joel Garreau, *The Nine Nations of North America* (Boston: Houghton Mifflin, 1981), 59.

**106** Travel time and freight costs: Conot, *American Odyssey,* 8ff.

**106** In 1848 , a railroad cut the travel time: Ibid., 42.

**108** "the electrical system gave every point in a region": Robert Fishman,

*Bourgeois Utopias: The Rise and Fall of Suburbia* (New York: Basic Books, 1987), 186.

**108**   "Indeed, it is not too much to say": H. G. Wells, "The Probable Diffusion of Great Cities," in *Anticipations and Other Papers,* vol. 4 of *The Works of H. G. Wells* (New York: Scribner's, 192 4), 41.

**108**   "smeared mass of humanity": Richard Sennett, *The Fall of Public Man: On the Social Psychology of Capitalism* (New York: Knopf, 1977 ), 50.

**110**   In 1919, General Motors started building: Conot, *American Odyssey,* 242.

**110**   But it was also close to GM's factories: Ibid., 213.

**110**   River Rouge plant: Ibid., 253.

**112**   from 1970 to 1987, the number of cars in America more than doubled: The increase was 103 percent over seventeen years: 1970, 89.2 million; 1987, 181.0 million.

**113**   Population growth in America: The increase was 19  percent over seventeen years: 1970, 204 million; 1987, 243 million. U.S. Bureau of the Census, *Statistical Abstract of the United States, 1990,* 110th ed. (Washington, D.C., 1990).

**116**   there were basically only two states . . . growth and high crime: Joe Schwartz and Thomas Exter, "Crime Stoppers," *American Demographics* (November 1990): 27.

**117**   "The main point to keep in mind": Quoted in Diane Katz, "Metro Detroit Rated World's 6th Best Spot to Live," *Detroit News,* Sunday, November 19, 1990, A1.

**119**   anyone parking a chariot: Catherine G. Miller,  *Carscape: A Parking Handbook* (Columbus, Ind.: Washington Street Press, 1988 ).

**121**   But that's the highest building density you're going to get: It is actually possible for a clever developer to squeeze an FAR of 0.45 out of a piece of land without having to build structured parking. But explaining how that trick works is too daunting for me to get into.

**123**   "The urbanized portion of Los Angeles County": Robert Cervero, *Suburban Gridlock* (New Brunswick, N.J.: Rutgers University, Center for Urban Policy Research, 1986), 24.

**126**   as much as $4.00  a gallon: Third-quarter 1990 figures, reflecting prices after the Iraq invasion of Kuwait: Milan, $4.73, up $0.62; Stockholm, $4.57, up $0.77; Paris, $4.24, up $0.78; Dublin, $4.15, up $0.70; Tokyo, $3.76, up $0.19. Runzheimer International, cited in *Washington Post Magazine,* November 11, 1990, 16.

**127**   There are already 19 percent more legally registered motor vehicles: In 1988, there were 140.7 million cars, 42.8 million trucks and buses, and 4.7 million motorcycles registered in America, for a total of 188.2million registered motorized ground vehicles. In 1986, there were only 158.5 million licensed drivers. Bureau of the Census, *Statistical Abstract,* table 1029, p. 604, and table 1040, p. 608.

**127**   The Census is expected to find only four states: Interview with Alan Pisarski, author of *Commuting in America: A National Report on Commuting Patterns and Trends* (Westport, Conn.: Eno Foundation for Transportation, 1987).

**127** There are not many more women who can work: The total increase expected to the end of the century is about half a percent per year. Bureau of the Census, *Statistical Abstract,* chart 625, p. 378.

**127** "supercommuters": See, among dozens of others, Rodney Ferguson and Eugene Carlson, "The Boomdocks: Distant Communities Promise Good Homes but Produce Malaise: Census Shows People Moving so Far from Jobs That They Lack Time to Enjoy Life," *Wall Street Journal,* October 25, 1990, A1.

**127** But fewer than 4 percent: Transportation Research Board.

**129** Californians now actually consume less gasoline: An annual rate of 494 gallons per capita, below the national average of 526 gallons per person, according to federal estimates. Jay Mathews, "Cities in West Steering Away from Growth: More Compact Style Marks California Life," *Washington Post,* Sunday, June 14, 1990, A3.

**129** They also require fewer cars: California, 693 per 1000; Florida, 868 per 1000; Texas, 772 per 1000. Ibid.

**131** forecasts for recent light-rail projects: In Buffalo, Pittsburgh, Portland (Oregon), and Sacramento.

**131** A merely huge fifteen million square feet: Interview with C. Kenneth Orski, president of Urban Mobility Corporation, citing the study "Urban Rail Transit Projects: Forecasts Versus Actual Ridership and Costs" by the Urban Mass Transit Association, and "Urban Rail in America" by Boris Pushkarev.

**133** A newspaper published by the *Detroit Free Press* or the *Detroit News:* Interview with Bob Burns, senior vice president for operations.

**134** That detachment is linked: Interviews with Katy Blackwell, public affairs, systems; Jim Trainer, public affairs, Ford Parts and Service.

**135** This was pointed out by Edwin S. Mills: "Sectoral Clustering and Metropolitan Development," in *Sources of Metropolitan Growth and Development* (New Brunswick, N.J.: Center for Urban Policy Research, Rutgers University, 1991).

**135** The Human Interface Lab is regarded by many: Doug Stewart, "Through the Looking Glass into an Artificial World—via Computer," *Smithsonian,* January 1991, 36.

**136** The National Aeronautics and Space Administration now has a virtual reality generator: Ibid., 40.

### Chapter 5    Atlanta: The Color of Money

**144** Almost a third make more money: In 1989, 28.76 percent of all black families in the Atlanta region had combined incomes in excess of $35,000 at a time when the median white family income in America was slightly in excess of $34,000. Claritas, L.P., 1989. Claritas is a national marketing demographic firm.

**144** Throughout this chapter in reference to demographic data, *typical* is used interchangeably with the more technical word *median.* Median income is one for which 50 percent of all families have incomes greater and 50 percent have incomes lower. That is usually not the same as *average* or *mean,* which refers to the total of all incomes divided by the number of families. In demographic analyses such as these, *median* or *typical* is thought to offer a more reliable snapshot of the middle ground than *mean* or *average.*

**144**　Forty percent are suburbanites: Suburbs here are defined as political jurisdictions in the eighteen-county Atlanta region that are outside the city of Atlanta. Claritas, L.P.

**145**　A third live in predominantly white areas: In 1988, 31.83 percent of the nonwhite population of the seven-county Atlanta region lived in the twenty-three Census-tract-based "superdistricts" that were majority white in 1988. Of that black population in majority white neighborhoods, 63.2 percent were on the north side. Atlanta Regional Commission, "Atlanta Region Outlook," rev., August 1989, A-8, A-9.

**145**　Middle-class black families: Census tracts in which the median black family income in 1989 was more than $35,000. Claritas, L.P.

**145**　virtually the same income as their white neighbors: In the Atlanta area Census tracts in which the majority of black families make more money than the typical white family in America, the median income for such black families is $42,194. The median income for their white neighbors in the same Census tracts is $43,983. The difference is 4 percent. Ibid.

**145**　In the Oakland area: All figures are for Metropolitan Statistical Areas and reflect the number of black families that had a median income in excess of $35,000 when the median white family income in America was slightly over $34,000. Ibid.

**146**　One in four young black males in America is in jail: John Leo, *U.S. News & World Report,* October 1, 1990, 23.

**146**　That would compare: *Black Enterprise,* June 1990, p. 113.

**147**　E. Franklin Frazier: *Black Bourgeoisie: The Rise of a New Middle Class in the United States* (New York: Free Press, 1957), 116.

**147**　In 1950, less than 1 percent: Ibid., 49.

**147**　Right after World War II: Roughly comparable to $52,500 in 1990, by calculation, using Frazier's figure of $3232 for the median white family income in 1949. Ibid., 48.

**148**　Perhaps seventy-five thousand black people in the whole country: Frazier reports five in every 1000 with an annual income of $5000. Ibid., 49. The total black population in 1950 was 15,042,000. U.S. Bureau of the Census, *Statistical Abstract of the United States, 1990,* 110th ed. (Washington, D.C., 1990), chart 18.

**148**　system of terrorism: See especially Chapter 27, "Desegregation," in Michael Barone, *Our Country: The Shaping of America from Roosevelt to Reagan* (New York: Free Press, 1990), 272.

**149**　Claritas: Claritas' clients include such national giants as General Motors, Coca-Cola, J. C. Penney, and Chase Manhattan.

**149**　Detroit had the largest proportion of skilled black craftsmen: Frazier, *Black Bourgeoisie,* 44.

**149**　"I grew up in California, and I never knew about Jim Crow": Quoted by Barbara Matusow, "Alone Together," *The Washingtonian,* November 1989, 153.

**149** Today Los Angeles: The black population was 17 percent in the 1980 Census, but it was expected to be 12 percent in the 1990 Census.

**150** the number of black-owned businesses: Judith Waldrop, "Shades of Black," *American Demographics* (September 1990): 33.

**150** Roughly a third: March 1988 Census.

**150** "underclass neighborhoods": *U.S. News & World Report*, December 25, 1989–January 1, 1990, 73.

**150** in 1983 the unemployment rate: Ibid., 76.

**151** Only 38 percent of young adult blacks: Young adult is defined as ages 25 to 29. Bureau of the Census, *Statistical Abstract*, chart 215, p. 133.

**151** Of all black kids who had graduated from high school in 1988: Kids is defined as eighteen to twenty-one. Ibid., chart 249, p. 150.

**151** a higher percentage of young black Americans: Larry Harrison, "Five Ethnic Groups in America," draft, p. 34. Figures are from the World Bank, "World Development Report," 1989 ed. Percentage of post-secondary age population actually enrolled: Switzerland, 23 percent; England, 22 percent.

**152** "increased access to integrated, non-ghetto schools": Quoted in Kenneth J. Cooper, "Assessing Black Students in the '80s," *Washington Post*, April 8, 1990, Education Review, p. 1.

**153** averages are not fully representative: Bill Dedman, when he was with the *Atlanta Journal and Constitution*, won the 1989 Pulitzer Prize for investigative reporting for his series "The Color of Money" (May 1–4, 1988). In it he demonstrated that among stable neighborhoods of the same income, white neighborhoods always received the most bank loans per 1000 single-family homes. Integrated neighborhoods always received fewer. Black neighborhoods—including Cascade Heights, where then–Mayor Andrew Young lived —always received the fewest. This discriminatory effect had pervasive and negative social consequences.

The majority of Atlanta's black population lives in predominantly black neighborhoods. So Dedman, who helped me generously in my work on this chapter, properly examined those neighborhoods. He also wished to be conservative in his judgments. So as not to contaminate his findings by including neighborhoods with wide swings in growth, he eliminated any neighborhood that grew by more than 10 percent in the number of single-family houses from 1980 to 1987. In such fashion he conclusively demonstrated that in the neighborhoods in which the majority of black people live, the banks' lending practices were discriminatory and hurtful.

At the same time, I do not believe his work contradicts, nor is it contradicted by, any findings in this chapter. By definition, he was not looking at the booming areas outside the established center of the Atlanta area where the majority of the black middle class lives.

**154** class has become a more important predictor of behavior: William Julius Wilson, *The Declining Significance of Race: Blacks and Changing American Institutions* (Chicago: University of Chicago Press, 1978).

**154** Throughout the middle of this century: Frazier, *Black Bourgeoisie*, 43.

**154** The total black migration from the South was 1.6 million in the 1940s and 1.5 million in the 1950s: Barone, *Our Country*, 273.

**154**    In 1900 , nine tenths of all blacks: Frazier, *Black Bourgeoisie,* 23.

**154**    Today it is half that: By calculation using figures from U.S. Bureau of the Census, *Statistical Abstract of the United States, 1989* (Washington, D.C., 1989). The share of the total American black population residing in the South, defined as eleven southern states, is 44 percent. In the Census definition of the South—sixteen states plus the District of Columbia—the share of the black population in 1988 was 56 percent.

**155**    tie to the declining old downtowns: Nonetheless, the percentage of all blacks living in the Northeast dropped from 19 to 17 percent from 1980 to 1988, according to the Census.

**155**    "That's a profile of people who migrate for job opportunities": *Time,* January 22, 1990, 27.

**157**    convicted church bomber J. B. Stoner: Durwood McAlister, "Thank the Parole Board for J. B. Stoner's Candidacy," *Atlanta Journal,* June 3, 1990. McAlister is editor of the editorial pages for the *Atlanta Journal.*

**161**    "I say to you today, my friends": *The Words of Martin Luther King, Jr.,* ed. Coretta Scott King (New York: Newmarket Press, 1987), 95.

**166**    seeking the black university experience: From 1985 to 1989, the number of blacks attending black colleges increased 10percent, to 294,427, according to the National Association of Equal Opportunity in Higher Education. That increase occurred as the percentage of black eighteen-to-twenty-four-year-olds enrolled in colleges had declined, according to the U.S. Department of Education.

**167**    "If you are buying a home": Susan Wells, "Middle-class Black Belt Spans Southside," "Shaping of Atlanta," Series in the *Atlanta Journal and Constitution.*

**168**    racial patterns of residence are still very strong: Douglas S. Massey and Nancy A. Denton once performed a study they called "Hypersegregation in U.S. Metropolitan Areas: Black and Hispanic Segregation Along Five Dimensions" *(Demography,* 26, no. 3 [August 1989]). It was fascinating in that it broke out aspects of racial segregation along five dimensions for sixty U.S. urban areas. It argues that the Atlanta area, for example, has a high level of "unevenness," to the degree that the percentage of minority members within residential areas does not equal the citywide minority percentage. But it had a low level of "clustering" because minority neighborhoods were scattered widely in space—they were not ghettoized.

**169**    in Chicago the residential patterns: Sam Bass Warner, Jr., *The Urban Wilderness: A History of the American City* (New York: Harper & Row, 1972), 108.

**174**    clubs, whips, and tear gas: "Fiftieth Birthday Tribute to Congressman John Lewis" program. See also Michael Barone and Grant Ujifusa, *The Almanac of American Politics 1990* (Washington, D.C.: National Journal, 1990), 306.

**177**    "I owe a great deal to my early life, and to the chickens": Taylor Branch, in *Parting the Waters: America in the King Years, 1954–1963* (New York: Simon & Schuster, 1988), explains: "Young Lewis lived in a world of his own. He had no feeling whatsoever for hogs, dogs, or most farm animals, but endless hours of study convinced him that chickens were worthy of adoption as the world's innocent creatures . . . If a small chicken died, Lewis buried it in a lard can and made sure flowers grew on the site. He also baptized the new chicks. Once he got carried away in his prayers and baptized one too long, which became one of his worst childhood . . . nightmares," 262.

### Chapter 6   Phoenix: Shadow Government

**184**   Sun City, Arizona: Martha Moyer, public information, the Del Webb Corporation, developers of Sun City.

**185**   These shadow governments have become the most numerous, ubiquitous, and largest form of local government: There is one federal government; there are fifty state governments, and 83,166 relatively conventional local governments in America, according to the most recent Census of Governments (1987) of the U.S. Bureau of the Census. These local governments are divided into five types: county, 3042; municipal, 19,205; township, 16,691; independent school district, 14,741; and independent special district, 29,487. Many of the independent special districts, in turn, have gained so much power that they are more usefully thought of as public shadow governments. Bruce D. McDowall, U.S. Advisory Commission on Intergovernmental Affairs, Washington, D.C.

**187**   What makes these outfits like governments: I am indebted to Walter A. Scheiber, former executive director of the Metropolitan Washington Council of Governments, for first offering me this three-part formulation.

**190**   Charles Keating buried C C & Rs in the deeds: Interview with Jana Bommersbach of *New Times*.

**192**   These native Americans built a 250-mile canal system: *A Valley Reborn: The Story of the Salt River Project; SRP Canals;* and other histories published by the Salt River Project, Phoenix.

**194**   Moses "had glimpsed in the institution called 'public authority' a potential for power": Robert A. Caro, *The Power Broker: Robert Moses and the Fall of New York* (New York: Knopf, 1974).

**194**   Over the years it has taken on the rights: D. Michael Rappoport, assistant general manager for government affairs, Salt River Project.

**197**   As recently at World War II: Charles Sargent, ed. *Metro Arizona* (Scottsdale: Biffington Books, 1988).

**200**   "Them that has, gits": Edward Noyes Westcott, *David Harum* (1898), chap. 35.

**204**   "Two forms of government—democracy and socialism": James E. Vance, Jr., *This Scene of Man: The Role and Structure of the City in the Geography of Western Civilization* (New York: Harper & Row, 1977), 10–12.

### Chapter 7   Texas: Civilization

**209**   *"What happened to you living in England"*: Philip Roth, interview by Jonathan Brent, *New York Times Book Review*, September 25, 1988, 3.

**217**   "America's boldest testing ground of the 1880s": Siegfried Giedion, *Mechanization Takes Command* (New York: Oxford University Press, 1948), 222.

**217**   "Oh, yeah, Venice was bizarre": Larry Gerkins, interview.

**221** fresh insight and artistic vision: I am indebted to Neil Barsky of the *Wall Street Journal* for this formulation.

**221** more households have a car than have a water heater: Households owning a car: 87.7 percent; households owning a water heater: 84.2 percent. For that matter, 75.1 percent of households are connected to a public sewer. U.S. Bureau of the Census, *Statistical Abstract of the United States, 1990,* 110th ed. (Washington, D.C., 1990). Cars and water heaters: chart 1280, November 1987 data (represents appliances possessed and generally used by a household). Public sewers: Ibid., chart 1272, 1987 data (as a percentage of occupied housing units).

**223** "There is no zoning, only deals": Sam Lefrak, quoted by Robert Fishman, "Megalopolis Unbound," *Wilson Quarterly* (Winter 1990): 36.

**228** "We might hope": Robert Fishman, *Bourgeois Utopias: The Rise and Fall of Suburbia* (New York: Basic Books, Inc., 1987), 204.

**229** The world moved on July 15, 1972: Tom Wolfe, *From Bauhaus to Our House* (New York: Farrar, Straus & Giroux, 1981), 74.

**232** *Costs of Sprawl* report: *The Costs of Sprawl* (Washington, D.C.: Government Printing Office, 1974).

**235** In addition, the Paris area has five Greenfield Edge City sites: David Shulman et al., *Paris Real Estate Market* (New York: Salomon Brothers, August 1989).

**235** Sydney, Australia, even without a beltway: David J. Kostin, *Sydney Real Estate Market* (New York: Salomon Brothers, September 1988).

**236** the greater London area is now more than a hundred miles across: Christopher B. Leinberger, interview with the author.

**236** London's outer Edge Cities: David Shulman and David J. Kostin, *London Office Market* (New York: Salomon Brothers, September 1988 ).

**237** In Amsterdam, in 1989: Leinberger, interview with the author.

**237** Bangkok: David E. Dowall, professor of planning, University of California at Berkeley, interview. Also Djakarta, page 238.

**238** In Mexico, on the west side of Guadalajara: Louis B. Casagrande, Science Museum of Minnesota, interview with the author.

**238** Seoul is trying to force Edge Cities at two locations: Stephen S. Fuller, chair, Department of Urban and Regional Planning, The George Washington University, Washington, D.C., interview with the author.

**240** architects control a mere 30 percent of their market: Andrew Saint, *The Image of the Architect* (New Haven: Yale University Press, 1983), 160.

**242** "the people's architect": *Wall Street Journal,* September 11, 1990, A6.

**242** but not before he was summoned to a high inquisition: Dan Martin, office of John Portman, Atlanta.

**243** Hudson Street: A reference to the street in New York on which Jane Jacobs lived and to which she frequently referred in *The Death and Life of Great American Cities* (New York: Random House, 1961).

**248** "Messy vitality over obvious unity": Robert Venturi, *Complexity and Contradiction in Architecture,* 2nd ed. (New York: Museum of Modern Art, 1977), 16.

## Chapter 8 Southern California: Community

**261** "Man is returning to the descendants": Frank Lloyd Wright, *The Living City* (New York: Horizon Press, 1958), 26.

**267** the Irvine that has been such a market success: Median home prices, second quarter of 1990: Honolulu, $345,000; San Francisco, $263,000; Anaheim–Santa Ana, $248,900; Los Angeles, $216,000; Bergen-Passaic, $193,000. National Association of Realtors.

**267** the outpouring of journalism, fiction, and sociology: I am indebted to Nicholas Lemann, "Stressed Out in Suburbia: A Generation After the Postwar Boom, Life in the Suburbs Has Changed, Even if Our Picture of It Hasn't," *Atlantic*, November 1989, 34, for many of the literary citations here.

**267** pungently described the shots: Herbert J. Gans: *The Levittowners: Ways of Life and Politics in a New Suburban Community* (New York: Pantheon, 1967), xv.

**267** "myth of suburbia": Phrase coined by Bennett Berger. Ibid.

**268** *"For literally nothing down":* John Keats, *The Crack in the Picture Window* (Boston: Houghton Mifflin, 1956).

**268** "If suburban life was as undesirable and unhealthy": Gans, *Levittowners*, xvi.

**269** Here we were, more than thirty years after: *The Lonely Crowd* was published in 1950, *The Organization Man* in 1956.

**270** But the third, the size of downtown Seattle: Downtown Seattle was at 21.9 million square feet (Office Network) when the John Wayne Airport area, including Newport Beach–Fashion Island, was at 25.6 million (Grubb & Ellis, Newport Beach).

**271** *The Californias:* Quoted by Edward W. Soja, "The Orange County Exopolis: A Contemporary Screenplay," unpublished.

**274** It was no less than an attempt to create from scratch: Gans, *Levittowners*, xvii.

**274** In his book *The Urban Villagers:* Herbert J. Gans, *The Urban Villagers: Group and Class in the Life of Italian-Americans* (New York: Free Press, 1962).

**275** "an aggregate of people": Ibid., 104.

**275** "I expected emotional statements about their attachment": Ibid., 104–5.

**279** There's Sinclair Lewis' *Main Street* and Sherwood Anderson's *Winesburg, Ohio: Main Street* (1920), *Winesburg, Ohio* (1919).

**279** *Stadtluft macht frei:* James E. Vance, Jr., *This Scene of Man: The Role and Structure of the City in the Geography of Western Civilization* (New York: Harper & Row, 1977), 12, 150.

**279** Richard Louv: *Childhood's Future: Listening to the American Family; New Hope for the Next Generation* (Boston: Houghton Mifflin, 1990).

**280** Americans think nothing of moving: Between 1987 and 1988, 17.6 percent of the American population (one in every 5.7 Americans) moved to a different house within the United States. In the West, 21.3 percent (one in every 4.7 people) moved in that one year. U.S. Bureau of the Census, *Statistical*

*Abstract of the United States, 1990,* 110th ed. (Washington, D.C., 1990), chart 25, p. 19.

**281** "Avoid eccentricities": Barbara Jane Hall, *101 Easy Ways to Make Your Home Sell Faster* (New York: Ballantine, 1985), 18.

**282** "A community is more than a set of customs": Richard Sennett, *The Fall of Public Man: On the Social Psychology of Capitalism* (New York: Knopf, 1977), 222, 39, and passim.

**282** If you were to draw a circle: Security Pacific Bank has pioneered the metaphor of the Sixty-Mile Circle as a way of looking at the Los Angeles region as one place. It periodically issues invaluable reports based on that image. Many of the numbers in this portion of the chapter are drawn from *Entering the 21st Century/Portrait for Progress: The Economy of Los Angeles County and the Sixty-Mile Circle Region* (Los Angeles: Security Pacific Bank, July 1988).

**283** Greater Los Angeles is served by five major commercial airports: Los Angeles International (LAX), Burbank, Long Beach, Ontario, and John Wayne.

**284** "We are going to be different from anywhere": Marc Wilder, quoted by Joel Kotkin, "Fear and Reality in the Los Angeles Melting Pot," *Los Angeles Times Magazine,* November 5, 1989.

**286** In Los Angeles, white Anglos are down: David Shulman of Salomon Brothers, interview with the author.

**287** when the common good was faced with narrow: Alexis de Tocqueville, *Democracy in America,* 2 vols., ed. J. P. Mayer, trans. George Lawrence (New York: Anchor/Doubleday, 1975).

**287** " 'Individualism' is a word recently coined": Ibid. 2:506–8.

**288** "Americans are forever forming": Ibid., 513–17.

**294** In fact, Timmons is running something of a spiritual shopping mall: I am indebted to Dan Morgan of the *Washington Post* for this idea.

### Chapter 9   The San Francisco Bay Area: Soul

**303** "Until it has had a poet, a place is not a place": Wallace Stegner, *Crossing to Safety* (Garden City, N.Y.: Doubleday, 1969), 137.

**313** in Petaluma, the widening of a freeway: See especially David E. Dowall, *The Suburban Squeeze: Land Conversion and Regulation in the San Francisco Bay Area* (Berkeley: University of California Press, 1984), 29.

**318** "You have to give this much to the Luftwaffe": Prince Charles at the 150th anniversary of the Royal Institute of British Architects, Hampton Court, 1984, cited by Benjamin Forgey, "Prince Charles, Architecture's Royal Pain: Continuing the Great Debate over Modernism," *Washington Post,* February 22, 1990, B1, and Steve Lohr, "Critic Charles Spurs Debate by Londoners," *New York Times,* Sunday, December 6, 1987, sec. 1, 9.

**321** One project, he said, came out "still a bit more funky than I would have liked": Christopher Alexander, quoted in Stephen Grabow, *Christopher Alexander: The Search for a New Paradigm in Architecture* (Stocksfield: Oriel Press, 1983), 170.

**321** Indeed, Reynar Banham . . . succinctly stated what can be described as the Establishment position: *Times Literary Supplement,* January 3, 1986, 15.

**322** "What really irks many people about Alexander": Pilar Viladas, "Harmony and Wholeness," *Progressive Architecture* (June 1986): 92.

**322** "Like Thoreau, Alexander marches to a different drummer": Robert Campbell, *Technology Review* (October 1984): 14.

**323** "The crucial thing": Christopher Alexander, "The Nature of Order: An Essay on the Art of Building and the Nature of the Universe" (Draft manuscript, 1988), 14.

**324** "form ever follows function": Louis Sullivan, "The Tall Office Building Artistically Considered," *Lippincott's,* March 1886.

**324** "a house is a machine for living in": Le Corbusier, *Vers une Architecture,* 1923.

**328** Charles rails against: Charles, Prince of Wales, *A Vision of Britain: A Personal View of Architecture* (London: Doubleday, 1989), 7–10.

**335** "paradigm shift": Thomas Kuhn, *The Structure of Scientific Revolutions* (Chicago: University of Chicago Press, 1970). Also see Kuhn, *The Copernican Revolution* (Cambridge: Harvard University Press, 1957).

**335** "Modern architecture no longer produces buildings that satisfy people's needs": Grabow, *Christopher Alexander,* 3.

**335** "the existing or current paradigm": Ibid., 4.

**336** "Like H. G. Wells, Julian Huxley, or Teilhard de Chardin": Ibid., xvi.

**341** "It was Edmund Burke who wrote that a healthy civilisation": Charles, Prince of Wales, *A Vision of Britain,* 155.

## Chapter 10  Washington: The Land
### Part I  Manassas: Long Ago and Far Away

**343** "The past is never dead": Quoted by Willie Morris, *The National Geographic,* March 1989.

### Part II  Present at Creation

**349** "In the beginning all the world was America": Quoted in Leo Marx, *The Machine in the Garden: Technology and the Pastoral Ideal in America* (London: Oxford University Press, 1964), 120.

**350** a landscape that John Rolfe Gardiner referred to: *In the Heart of the Whole World* (New York: Knopf, 1988).

**350** the largest urban agglomeration between Washington and Atlanta: Also larger than any submarket in the Miami, Kansas City, St. Louis, or New Orleans areas.

**354** Arlington County . . . is more densely populated than Dallas or Denver or Cincinnati: Arlington County 1980 population density, 5,869.2 *(Virginia Statistical Abstract, 1987,* table 16.17, p. 489); 1988 population densities: Dallas, 2,965; Denver, 4,609; Cincinnati, 4,750 (U.S. Bureau of the Census, *Statistical Abstract of the United States, 1990,* table 40, p. 34).

**354** Its airport, Washington National: Bureau of the Census, *Statistical Abstract,* chart 1067, p. 622.

**354**    Urdu: Sharon Cavileer, "Arlington: A World Ahead," *Washington Flyer,* November-December 1990, A-8.

**354**    a motorist caught in the rain: Michael Barone, *Our Country: The Shaping of America from Roosevelt to Reagan* (New York: Free Press, 1990), 3.

**354**    "people feel the ground give way beneath their feet": Joseph A. Schumpeter, *Business Cycles: A Theoretical, Historical, and Statistical Analysis of the Capitalistic Process* (New York: McGraw-Hill, 1939), 2:911.

**354**    By the time Hazel was two: Barone, *Our Country,* 43.

**354**    Birth rates . . . had plummeted: Ibid., 43–44.

**356**    At the time of first founding: Conrad M. Arensberg, "American Communities," *American Anthropologist* 57 (1955): 1151, cited by D. W. Meinig, *The Shaping of America: A Geographical Perspective on 500 Years of History,* vol. 1, *Atlantic America, 1492–1800* (New Haven: Yale University Press, 1986), 155.

**358**    Indeed, almost nobody in America expected this: Barone, *Our Country,* 185, 197. Barone notes that in 1945, when asked by the Gallup Poll to cite a problem facing the country, 42 percent of Americans volunteered "jobs"—a larger percentage than mentioned any other issue.

**358**    The pessimists' worst fears seemed confirmed: Ibid., 186, 197.

**359**    Following 1948, America's gross national product . . . at an average rate of 4.0 percent every year: U.S. Bureau of the Census, *Historical Statistics of the United States, Colonial Times to 1970* (Washington, D.C., 1975), 1:226–27, 229. Cited by Barone, *Our Country,* 197.

**359**    That kind of sustained boom: Barone, *Our Country,* 197.

### Part III   The Machine, the Garden, and Paradise

**362**    "Man aint really evil, he jest aint got any sense": Quoted by Willie Morris, *The National Geographic,* March 1989.

**362**    limestone from Ontario to Indiana, iron ore from northern Michigan: Joel Garreau, *The Nine Nations of North America* (Boston: Houghton Mifflin Company, 1981), 59–60.

**363**    Again and again, our most respected writers: I am indebted for most of these literary references to Leo Marx, *The Machine in the Garden,* especially pages 10 and 16.

**363**    There is in the writings of these Americans a constant yearning: Ibid., 13.

**363**    "The train stands for a more sophisticated, complex style of life": Ibid., 24.

**363**    "regenerative power is located in the natural terrain": Ibid., 228.

**364**    Seventy-six percent of all Americans describe themselves as environmentalists: Harper's Index, *Harper's,* January 1990, 41.

**364**    "freedom from the grip of the external landscape": Sigmund Freud, *General Introduction to Psychoanalysis* (1920), cited by Marx, *Machine in the Garden,* 8, 9.

**364**    "By placing the machine in opposition to the tranquillity and order": Ibid., 18.

**365**    The idea of progress originated in the belief: Robert Nisbet, *History of the Idea of Progress* (New York: Basic Books, 1980), 10.

**365**  The Greeks saw the natural growth . . . They got this idea in part: Ibid., 47–48.

**365**  As early as Augustine's *The City of God:* Ibid., 76.

**365**  By 1750, progress was not simply an important idea among many: Ibid., 171.

**365**  More important, they became seen as the very goal of progress: Ibid., 236.

**365**  By the 1800s, the idea of progress . . . For it was thought that the redemption and salvation: Ibid., 237.

**366**  "I have been over into the future, and it works": On Steffens' return from the Bullitt mission, 1919. Lincoln Steffens, *Autobiography* (1931), chap. 18.

**366**  The Nazis' Final Solution was so called in order that it be viewed as—progress: Nisbet, *History of the Idea of Progress*, 287.

**366**  That is the point . . . from which the technological imperative "If possible, then necessary," rang hollow: Siegfried Giedion, *Mechanization Takes Command* (New York: Oxford University Press, 1948), 714ff.

**367**  But in 1776, James Boswell described the moment of epiphany: James Boswell, *The Life of Samuel Johnson* (1791).

**367**  In Soho he visited a factory: Marx, *Machine in the Garden*, 145.

**367**  During the dawn of the Industrial Age here . . . No other country could match even one of these boasts: James M. McPherson, *Battle Cry of Freedom: The Civil War Era* (New York: Oxford University Press, 1988), 6.

**370**  "We will fight with all our might": Umbro Apocconio, ed., *The Documents of 20th Century Art: Futurist Manifestos* (New York: Viking, 1973), 24–25.

**371**  "What is the future of the idea of progress": Nisbet, *History of the Idea of Progress*, 322, 323.

**372**  "Things fall apart; the centre cannot hold": William Butler Yeats, "The Second Coming," in *The Collected Poems of W. B. Yeats* (New York: Macmillan, 1956), 184.

**372**  "Only, it seems evident from the historical record": Nisbet, *History of the Idea of Progress*, 357.

### Part IV  Pilgrim's Progress: Boom

**373**  "For we must consider that we shall be a city upon a hill": John Winthrop, "A Model of Christian Charity" (1630), a sermon delivered on board the *Arbella.*

**373**  Melpar: The name is formed from the last names of its founders, Thomas Meloy and Joseph Parks.

**377**  atomic bomb: E. M. Risse, Synergy Planning, Fairfax, Virginia.

**378**  the Beltway would become known as Washington's Main Street: Washington demographers George and Eunice Grier coined this formulation.

**378**  In 1954 . . . In 1965, William Levitt: Associated Press, "Great Dates in Suburban History," released January 8, 1990.

**379**  Clarke was charged with being the kingpin of a scheme: The *Washington Post* in a page one story on September 20, 1966, reported:

The indictment charges:
• Checks totaling $27,487 were to go from Clarke to Burrage, paid either directly to him or put into banks on his behalf, in exchange for his favorable recommendation for the rezoning, in four separate payments—of $16,287; $8100; $2700 and $400.
• $10,000 was to be put in a bank for Schumann, in exchange for his support.
• The sum of $15,000 was to be set aside for Clarke, from which he would make "contributions" to the Board of Supervisors.
  Out of the $15,000, according to the indictment, Clarke paid:
• $2000 to a campaign fund for Parrish.
• $3000 to DeBell and $3000 to Leigh.
• $1000 to a campaign fund for Cotten and $1000 to a campaign fund for Moss.
• $2000 to Cotten himself.

The indictment read: "The Grand Jury charges: That from on or about September 13, 1961 to on or about July 1, 1962, in the Eastern District of Virginia and within the jurisdiction of this Court, the defendants Andrew W. Clarke [and] William C. Burrage did travel in interstate commerce, use facilities in interstate commerce, and willfully cause the travel in interstate commerce and the use of facilities in interstate commerce with the intent to promote, manage and carry on and to facilitate the promotion, management and carrying on of an unlawful activity, to wit, bribery . . ." *Northern Virginia Sun,* September 21, 1966.

**379** Next, he got the federal counts dismissed: Maurine McLaughlin, "1 Fairfax Bribe Case May Be Thrown Out, Law Voted Too Late," *Washington Post,* November 16, 1966, B1.

**379** By the time the population of Fairfax had passed half a million: Thomas Grubisich, "Lawyer Alters Fairfax Patterns, Its Population," *Washington Post,* April 27, 1975, B1.

**379** America . . . was changing profoundly: For much in my discussion of the history of the idea of ecology, I am indebted to Anna Bramwell, *Ecology in the 20th Century: A History* (New Haven: Yale University Press, 1989).

**380** man's foremost allegiance had to be to his planet: Bramwell, *Ecology in the 20th Century,* 211.

**380** The answer that deeply penetrated the national consciousness: Ibid., 238.

**381** change specifically did not mean progress: Ibid., 4.

**381** No culture can truly survive . . . It was not progress: Ibid., 241.

**381** "Human beings dwell in the same biological systems that contain the other creatures": Barry Lopez, *Arctic Dreams* (New York: Scribner's, 1986), 38.

**382** "crack open watersheds": Grubisich, "Lawyer Alters Fairfax Patterns."

**382** Meanwhile, the hookups resumed: "Board Allows Fairfax Sewer Hookups," *Washington Post,* June 16, 1970.

**382** an "unlawful, imprudent intrusion into the rights of private business":

Kenneth Bredemeier, "7 Builders Launch Attack on Fairfax's Housing Law," *Washington Post,* October 29, 1971.

**382** Elected on a platform of skepticism toward growth: Grubisich, "Lawyer Alters Fairfax Patterns."

**382** "I think your approach is bankrupt": Joseph D. Whitaker, "Rezoning Ban Held Illegal: Judge Calls Fairfax Move 'Capricious,' " *Washington Post,* March 9, 1972, B1 .

**383** "You'd have thought we were out to rape the county": Bill McAllister, "High Court Bars Va. Zoning Case," *Washington Post,* November 4, 1975.

**383** He described the county's attempts to limit growth as "pie in the sky": Grubisich, "Lawyer Alters Fairfax Patterns."

**383** "We've got a tiger by the tail": Ibid.

**385** becoming one of the larger local jurisdictions in America: John Ward Anderson, "Lambert Tenders Letter of Resignation to Fairfax Board," *Washington Post,* October 31, 1990, B1.

**387** He saw that as a waste: "Tract Zoned for Homes in Fairfax," *Washington Post,* September 12, 1967.

### Part V   But What About the Land?

**389** "was the absence of anything like European society": Marx, *Machine in the Garden* (London: Oxford University Press, 1964), 120.

**389** *"land in which to live":* Benton MacKaye, *The New Exploration: A Philosophy of Regional Planning* (Urbana: University of Illinois Press, 1962), cited in Tony Hiss, *The Experience of Place* (New York: Knopf, 1990), 201.

**390** "The crop they raise is serenity": Jean Gottmann, *Megalopolis: The Urbanized Northeastern Seaboard of the United States* (New York: Twentieth Century Fund, 1961), 265.

**390** 1.22 percent of all the land in the United States: In 1989, there were 92.8 million households in the United States (Bureau of the Census, *Statistical Abstract,* chart 55, p. 45). Housing those households on quarter-acre lots would thus occupy 23.2 million acres, which is 1.22 percent of the 2,962,031 square miles (1.896 billion acres) of land in the lower forty-eight states.

**390** In fact, right now, 70 percent of all Americans: Irving Welfeld, *Where We Live: The American Home and the Social, Political, and Economic Landscape, from Slums to Suburbs* (New York: Simon & Schuster, 1988), 46.

**390** 75 percent of all Americans will live within fifty miles of a coast: *Coast* is defined as that of the Atlantic, the Pacific, the Gulf, and the Great Lakes, but not of other large interior bodies of water, including rivers.

**390** It is easy to demonstrate that it is possible to build every single road: I am indebted to E. M. Risse of Synergy Planning for first demonstrating to me the logic of these calculations.

**391** "All ethics so far evolved rest upon a single premise": Aldo Leopold, *A Sand County Almanac and Sketches Here and There* (New York: Oxford University Press, 1949), 203.

**391** "The places where we spend our time affect the people we are": Hiss, *Experience of Place,* xi, xii.

**392**  Since the 1850s, a "total environment": Hiss reporting on the work of nineteenth-century German educator Friedrich Froebel as well as Frederick Law Olmsted. Ibid., 182.

**392**  Over a nine-year period: Hiss reporting on the 1984 work of Roger S. Ulrich, then a professor of geography at the University of Delaware and at the time of Hiss's writing a professor in the College of Architecture at Texas A&M. Ibid., 183.

**393**  "terrain and vegetation are molded, not dominated": John Stilgoe, cited ibid., 116.

**393**  "fragile equilibrium between natural and human force": Ibid., 117.

**393**  biologist René Dubos wrote about the "charm and elegance": René Dubos, *The Wooing of the Earth* (New York: Scribner's, 1980).

**393**  "an environmental diversity that provides nourishment for the senses": Hiss, *Experience of Place*, 117.

**393**  There are three ways that humans feel connected to the land: Ibid., 126.

**394**  "The first 5 percent of development in a countryside region": Albert F. Appleton, quoted in ibid., 167.

**395**  "Conservation," after all, is merely "a state of harmony between men and land": Leopold, *Sand County Almanac*, 207.

**395**  "One basic weakness in a conservation system": Ibid., 210.

**397**  "The fate of the American landscape, its ponds and hollows": Barry Lopez, "Unbounded Wilderness," *Aperture*, no. 120 (Late Summer 1990), 2.

**399**  "dark Satanic mills" . . . "green and pleasant land": William Blake, *Milton* (1804–1808), prefatory poem.

**399**  "Man takes a positive hand in creation": Frank Lloyd Wright, quoted in mailing by Friends of Taliesin, Scottsdale, Arizona, received by the author March 29, 1990.

**400**  you grow up caring about most: I am indebted for this formulation to Robert D. Yaro, co-author of *Dealing with Change in the Connecticut River Valley: A Design Manual for Conservation and Development* (Amherst: University of Massachusetts, 1988), cited by Hiss in *The Experience of Place*.

### Part VI   The Final Battle

**402**  "Look! There stands Jackson like a stone wall!": McPherson, *Battle Cry of Freedom*, 342. This version of the Bee quotation was used as a slogan by the Save the Battlefield Coalition.

**403**  the testimony of Princeton's James M. McPherson: *Manassas National Battlefield Park Amendments of 1988, Hearing Before the Subcommittee on Public Lands, National Parks and Forests, of the Committee on Energy and Natural Resources, United States Senate, One Hundredth Congress, Second Session, on H.R. 4526 to Provide for the Addition of Approximately 600 Acres to the Manassas National Battlefield Park, September 8, 1988* (Washington, D.C.: Government Printing Office, 1989), 166–69.

**404**  Their reports, day after day, had their impact: Particularly pivotal was the work of Robert A. Webb of the *Washington Post*. Webb, an editor of *Outlook,* the argument and opinion section of the Sunday paper, wrote a piece in that section on March 13, 1988, that profoundly altered the tone of the debate. Entitled "Manassas Tragedy: Paving over the Past," it transformed the issue from a local zoning dispute with a developer who appeared to hold all the aces to one of national policy that had to be taken seriously by anyone who wished to be viewed as a heavy federal player. That it was carried on the *Los Angeles Times–Washington Post* news wire and reprinted worldwide hardly lessened its impact.

**407** "Society is always patriarchal": Joseph Campbell, *The Power of Myth* (Garden City, N.Y.: Doubleday, 1988), 100–102. Lewis Mumford, also looking at the dawn of time, picked up on the same male-female distinction. In *The City in History* he saw the differences between men and women as those of at least two different cultures, if not two different species: "The interplay between the two cultures took place over a longer period. Women's interest in child nurture and plant care had changed the anxious, timorous, apprehensive existence of early man into one of competent foresight, with reasonable assurance of continuity—no longer entirely at the mercy of forces outside human control. But in the end the masculine processes over-rode by sheer dynamism the more passive life-nurturing activities that bore woman's imprint." *The City in History: Its Origins, Its Transformations, and Its Prospects* (New York: Harcourt Brace Jovanovich, 1961), 25–26.

**407** The intense struggles over the use of the land began almost before the Rebel yells: Ken Burns et al. *The Civil War: A Film Series*, Florentine Films and WETA-TV, 1990.

**407** One reporter checking the clips back to 1890: John F. Harris, "How Often Must We Fight Third Battle of Manassas? It's Time to Let This Bull Run Its Course," *Washington Post*, May 13, 1988, B1.

**409** HUGE MALL PLANNED AT MANASSAS: Cornelius F. Foote, Jr., and John F. Harris, *Washington Post*, January 29, 1988, A1.

**409** Edward J. DeBartolo Corporation—the largest shopping center developer: "20th Annual Survey: Top 50 Leaders in Management, Development, Acquisition and New Ownership," *Monitor: The Shopping Center Industry Magazine*, January 1991, 28.

**410** "does not even resemble the good faith agreements": Letter from William Penn Mott, Jr., director of the National Park Service, U.S. Department of the Interior, to Kathleen K. Seefeldt, chair, Prince William County Board of Supervisors, February 5, 1988.

**410** The Charlie Grahams of the 1980s: William R. Taylor, *Cavalier and Yankee: The Old South and American National Character* (Cambridge: Harvard University Press, 1979), 317–18.

**412** Some anthropologists view the shopping bag as the most human of archeological artifacts: I am indebted to Ron Abler of Pennsylvania State University for this formulation.

**415** The first mass meeting in opposition to the William Center mall: Clint Schemmer, "It's War: Park Service Chief, Hundreds Join Fray over Mall Proposal," *Potomac News*, February 8, 1988, A1.

**415** Quartz lights turned the night into death-pallor day: John F. Harris,

"William Center Foes Pin Hopes on Environmental Concerns," *Washington Post,* June 18, 1988, B1.

**416** "challenging" and "the town iconoclast": Michael Barone and Grant Ujifusa, *The Almanac of American Politics 1990* (Washington, D.C.: National Journal, 1990), 55.

**417** "[Longstreet] sent out a couple of brigades": *Congressional Record,* 100th Cong., 2d sess., October 7, 1988, 134, no. 142 , pt. 2:S15149.

**417** "Sixteen thousand men in about forty-eight hours": Ibid., S15150.

**417** "I told you about these hospitals": Ibid., S15151.

**417** "There is not a single battlefield free from development pressures": Ibid., S15153–54.

**419** On Friday, October 14, George Bush, in a speech in La Jolla: David Hoffman, "Optimism Reigns in Bush Camp: Staff Warned to Guard Against Post-Debate Overconfidence," *Washington Post,* October 15, 1988.

**420** Nonetheless, at 1 A.M. on the twenty-second . . . the bill did pass: John F. Harris, "Manassas Preservations Win a Last-Minute Hill Victory," *Washington Post,* October 23, 1988, A1.

**420** " 'We're done,' said Robert Kelly, a spokesman for Hazel/Peterson Cos.": John F. Harris, "Battlefield Fate Settled by President," *Washington Post,* November 12, 1988, B1.

**420** the next morning Annie Snyder led fifty of her resistance fighters into the promised land: Richard Leigh, *Journal Messenger,* November 21, 1988.

**421** It featured a March of the Ghosts: Ed Raus, historian at the battlefield.

**422** Behind that little buzzing plane was this reminder: The precise telegraphese wording of the message was, "FEDERAL TAKING OF PRIVATE LAND— UNAMERICAN." Leigh, *Journal Messenger.*

### Chapter 11   The List: Edge Cities, Coast to Coast

Here are some key sources I drew on to help identify Edge Cities in the following metro areas:

**426** Atlanta: Gregg Logan, Robert Charles Lesser & Co., Atlanta.

**427** Austin: Jerry Lumsden, Coldwell Banker Commercial, Austin.

**427** Baltimore: Pamela Manfre, MPC & Associates, Washington.

**427** Boston: Spalding & Slye, Boston.

**428** Charlotte: Clayton Pritchett, C. P. Pritchett, Inc., Charlotte.

**428** Chicago: Harvey B. Camins, Frain Camins & Swartchild Corporate Real Estate Services, Chicago.

**428** Cleveland: Robert Nosal, Grubb & Ellis, Cleveland.

**428** Dallas –Fort Worth: Patricia L. Dajda, The Swearingen Company, Dallas.

**429** Denver: Hilary Horlock, Frederick Ross Co., Denver.

**429** Detroit: Leo Tosto, Trerice Tosto, Southfield, Michigan.

**429** Fort Lauderdale: Deborah Page, Sunbank South Florida, Fort Lauderdale.

**429** Houston: Katherine Gehbauer, The Office Network, Houston.

**430** Kansas City: Richard Ward, Development Strategies, Inc., St. Louis.

**430** Los Angeles: Robert J. Gardner, Robert Charles Lesser & Co., Los Angeles.

**432** Memphis: John Dudas, Belz Enterprises, Memphis.

**432** Miami: Greg Kessel, CB Commercial, Miami.

**432** Milwaukee: Michael A. Rooney, The Rooney Group, Milwaukee.

**432** Minneapolis: Dennis Panzer, The Shelard Group, Inc., Minneapolis.

**432** New York: Salomon Brothers, New York.

**433** Orlando: Frank Pallini, KPMG Peat Marwick, Tampa.

**434** Philadelphia: Salomon Brothers, New York.

**434** Phoenix: Robert J. Burnand, Jr., CBS Property Services, Inc., Phoenix.

**434** Pittsburgh: Oliver Realty/Grubb & Ellis, Pittsburgh.

**435** Portland, Oregon: David Fansler, Property Counselors, Seattle.

**435** St. Louis: Richard Ward, Development Strategies, Inc., St. Louis.

**435** St. Petersburg: Frank Pallini, KPMG Peat Marwick, Tampa.

**435** San Antonio: Wayne Harwell, Harwell, Hicks Real Estate Research, Inc., San Antonio.

**435** San Diego: Ron Barbieri, KPMG Peat Marwick, San Diego.

**436** San Francisco: Cynthia A. Kroll, Center for Real Estate and Urban Economics, Berkeley.

**436** Seattle: David Fansler, Property Counselors, Seattle.

**437** Tampa: Frank Pallini, KPMG Peat Marwick, Tampa.

**437** Toronto: Hilary Horlock, J. J. Barnicke Ltd., Realtor, Toronto.

**437** Washington: Coldwell Banker Commercial, Washington.

### Chapter 12   The Words: Glossary of a New Frontier

**450** half a football field: A football field is 160 feet wide and 300 feet long— 48,000 square feet. (An acre is 43,560 square feet.)

### Chapter 13   The Laws: How We Live

**464** Whyte's Law of the Number of Blocks an American Will Walk in Most Downtowns: William H. Whyte, *City: Rediscovering the Center* (Garden City, N.Y.: Doubleday, 1988), 65.

**464** The Number of Blocks an American Will Walk in New York City: Ibid.

**464** The Speed an American Man Will Walk in a Big-City Downtown: Ibid.

**464** Strolling Speed Past a Shop Window or Merchandise Display: Ibid., 66.

**465** The Number of Pedestrians Per Hour at Midday Required to Make an Urban Center Work and Be Lively: Ibid., 6.

**465** For every $1.00 of tax revenue that comes in: Loudoun County, Virginia, planning staff, 1984.

**465** The Amount of Growth in an Established Edge City: Pamela Manfre, Robert Charles Lesser & Co., Los Angeles, Cal.

**466** The Rule of Thumb for Calculating How Much Traffic Edge City Will Produce: C. Kenneth Orski, president, Urban Mobility Corporation.

**466** The Average Distance from the Main Office of a Company in Edge City: Whyte, *City,* 288.

**467** The Probable Maximum Number of Riders You Can Hope to Switch Out of Their Cars: C. Kenneth Orski.

**467** The Number of Riders a Heavy-Rail System Needs Per Day: C. Kenneth Orski, citing Boris Pushkarev, *Urban Rail in America,* which Orski considers the bible on the economics of rail transit.

**467** Number of Riders a Light-Rail System Needs per Day: Ibid.

**471** "You name a place for what is no longer there": *Notre Dame Magazine,* February 1989.

**471** The Three Laws of Building: Steven Hayward, director of the Claremont Institute's Golden State Project, *Reason,* August-September 1988, 28.

# Index

ABOUT THE AUTHOR

Joel Garreau, a *Washington Post* staff writer, is the author of the bestselling *The Nine Nations of North America*. He is also a principal in The Edge City Group, an organization dedicated to making better communities out of Edge Cities nationwide.